Gerry Frank's

Where To
Find It
Buy It
Eat It
in
New York

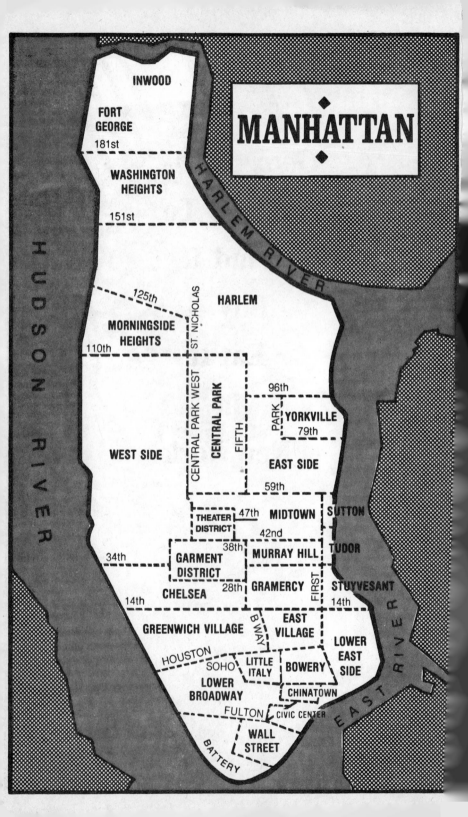

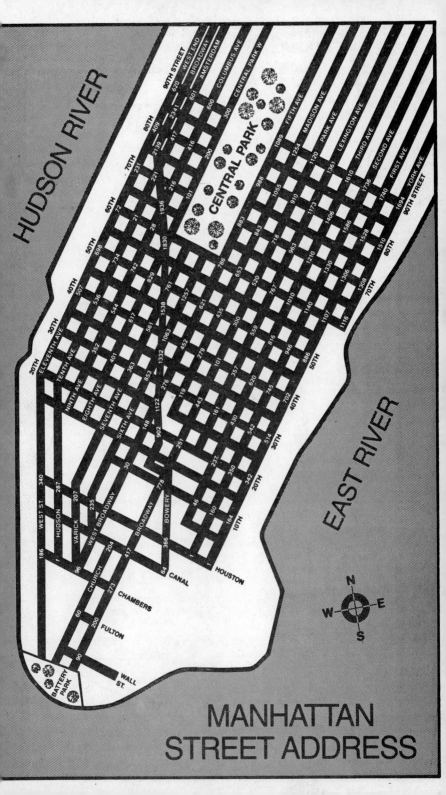

MANHATTAN
STREET ADDRESS

Gerry Frank's
Where To
Find It
Buy It
Eat It
in
New York

Gerry Frank's
Where To Find It, Buy It, Eat It
in New York
Copyright © 1980, 1981, 1983, 1985, 1987, 1989 by Gerald W. Frank
Printed in the United States of America
Library of Congress Catalog Card Number 80-7802
ISBN: 0-9612578-7-3
First Edition 1980
    Second Printing 1980
Second Edition 1981
    Second Printing 1981
    Third Printing 1982
Third Edition 1983
    Second Printing 1984
    Third Printing 1984
Fourth Edition 1985
    Second Printing 1986
    Third Printing 1986
    Fourth Printing 1987
Fifth Edition 1987
    Second Printing 1988
Sixth Edition 1989

Foreword

Since 1980, when the first edition of *Where To Find It, Buy It, Eat It in New York* was published, the story of this book has become something of a legend in the publishing world. It is now in its sixth edition, and more than 350,000 copies have been sold.

The big question, which is still asked over and over again, is how a man who lives in Oregon and works in Washington, D.C., could write a best-selling guide to the Big Apple? Well, it isn't as complicated as it may seem. I was born into a retailing family in Oregon, and during my early years I spent a great deal of time working in our stores and with our buyers in the markets of New York. I fell in love with the city at that early age, and the love affair has continued all my life.

After the family department-store business was sold, I decided to go into public service. I soon became Chief of Staff for United States Senator Mark Hatfield. Of course, the work in Washington is fascinating, but for variety and change of pace, I have spent two weekends a month for the past 22 years in New York.

As a former retailer, I have visited literally thousands of stores, evaluating their services, selections, and the value of their merchandise. As the proprietor of a konditorei, a European-style gourmet food emporium, in Oregon, I feel I've earned my credentials to pass judgment on food shops and restaurants. I've tried over 1,400 eating spots in Manhattan and picked out the best values in every category for you. As a world traveler (I've visited every continent and over 130 countries), I feel qualified to comment on hotels and other travel services for visitors and sightseers.

Probably the biggest difference between this book and other guidebooks to New York (and the thing that I think has made it so popular) is that this is one person's evaluation of the New York scene. Since most guidebooks are written by a group of people, there is little continuity in the assessment of restaurants, stores, services, hotels, sights, and the like. This book reflects how I view the most exciting city in the world, and I hope my thoughts and ideas will help you save time and money. You may not agree with all my opinions, but at least this book can be a starting point for your own adventures in New York.

You will also notice that unlike many other guidebooks, this one is written in a very casual and informal style. Through the years I've learned that readers aren't interested in profound words. They want an easy-to-read and easy-to-use compilation of things to do (and things *not* to do) in what can sometimes be a very intimidating city.

I'm sure you realize that in a city the size of New York things can and do change rapidly. Stores and restaurants—especially restaurants—come and go quickly. New owners, new chefs, new locations, new policies. Because I publish this book myself, I am able to make changes and corrections right up to the last minute before publication. At that time, as far as I know, the information is current and correct.

As I mentioned, *Where To Find It, Buy It, Eat It in New York* is my own publishing venture, and that is one of the things that has made this book the "legend" I spoke of earlier. When I first started collecting information about New York and its shops and restaurants, I had no idea that I would one day write a book. But when New York-bound friends kept asking me where to get this and that, where to go, and what to do, I decided to write it all down. After five years of gathering data, I took my bulging manuscript to a few New York publishers. Someone from Oregon writing a book on how to cope with New York? Absurd, they said. Not being the sort of person who likes to be told "no," I went back to Oregon and found a company to publish the first book. But what do you do with 10,000 copies of a book on New York in Portland, Oregon? I headed to New York, making my way from one store to another and from one distributor to another, selling, displaying, and promoting the book. One success led to another. Today, the book is distributed worldwide. It can be found in every major bookstore in New York. It's available, in part, on diskettes. (The restaurant program is easy to use and costs only $19.95. Call 914/339-2502 for details.) And it is considered by many to be "the book that New York lives by." Now, some of the publishers who once wouldn't give me the time of day are eager to publish this book. How satisfying it is to politely thumb my nose at them: "No, thank you. Where were you when I needed you?"

Where To Find It, Buy It, Eat It in New York is available in a smaller, pocket version ($5.95), which mainly features the restaurant section of the book, but also includes highlights of touring and shopping. Both volumes are available in quantities at very substantial savings; you can contact me directly.

None of this would have been possible without the advice and support from you, my readers. I have heard from thousands of you in person (at autograph parties and book fairs), by phone, and by mail. I appreciate your suggestions, your comments, and your criticisms. I have tried to give them all serious consideration; what you read here reflects that. And I shall continue to solicit your input. Please feel free to contact me at P.O. Box 2225, Salem, Oregon 97308 (503-585-8412). I enjoy hearing from you and helping you with your New York plans. I've had fun helping a bridegroom-to-be pick out the "most romantic" place in New York to propose, helping a Canadian mother plan a New York Christmas holiday for her children, and working with a young couple to find exactly the right fur coat that they could afford.

I am deeply indebted to a number of special people for their help with this book. First, I send my most polished Oregon apple to Esther Benovitz, my right arm throughout all these editions. She is a tremendous provider of ideas and information and helps with the places I can't really evaluate, like beauty shops. Esther knows and loves New York like no one else, and provides the perspective of someone who has lived all her life in the New York area. Reliable Cheryl Johnson has done much of the nitty-gritty administrative work, and done it so efficiently. I have been blessed with the wonderful help of LaVelle Blum, my trusted and efficient secretary for over 30 years. Brant Mewborn is an editor extraordinaire, who has provided superb professional skill in so many ways. And there is Jeryme English; Phyllis McFarland, who has made countless phone calls; and Freda Prock, who assisted with the indexing. Tim Prock did the cover.

With the exception of those places that Esther has evaluated, I have personally visited every establishment listed in this book. It has been a lot of work, a lot of fun, and immensely rewarding. New York and New Yorkers are absolutely unique, but don't let anyone tell you that you can't find the same kind of friendly and wonderful people on Broadway that you can find on Main Street in any city throughout this great country.

Happy reading!

Contents

III. WHERE TO FIND IT: FUN IDEAS AND ACTIVITIES FOR RESIDENTS AND VISITORS

IV. WHERE TO EAT IT: NEW YORK'S BEST FOOD SHOPS

VI. WHERE TO BUY IT: NEW YORK'S BEST STORES

VII. "WHERE TO" EXTRAS

I. The World's Greatest City

Introduction

New York! The very name conjures images of the fast life—and it's faster in New York than in any other spot on the globe. New York is big—it feels bigger than any other city in the world. New York is excitement. Whatever you're seeking, New York is the most likely place to find it. And New York is the ultimate stamp of approval. As the song says, "If I make it there, I can make it anywhere." To millions of people, success in New York means success in life.

But there are other songs and other sides to New York. Virtually anyone can "trip the light fantastic" in this city, if you know enough about it. And that is the purpose of this book. I aim to show you where to find, buy, and experience the very best of New York. I hope that using this book will enable everyone to consider New York their city and help make a visitor nearly indistinguishable from a lifelong resident.

Indeed, in this supposedly cold city, anyone can become a New Yorker. I think that only in New York can this happen. Geographical birth has nothing to do with it. Neither does land ownership. If it did, only the likes of Donald Trump and Harry Helmsley would be New Yorkers. But spend some time here, particularly during a city crisis—a strike, a blackout, or dramatic weather conditions—and you become a bona fide New Yorker.

How you dress won't give you away. From staid to weird, you can wear anything in New York. Carrying a camera won't brand you as a tourist, either. Cameras are standard equipment for legions of professionals in the city. How you speak won't give you away. Everyone in New York has an accent, and for many, English is a second language. There's not even any danger in being seen at the most obvious tourist attractions, because there won't be any

1

New Yorkers there to see you. Natives don't go to those places at all.

There are things, however, that draw the scorn of New Yorkers. Chief among them is ignorance. New Yorkers have no tolerance for people who want to buy the Brooklyn Bridge, or ask where Brooklyn is. Local neophyte newscasters often lose their jobs for not being able to pronounce Kosciusko, as in Kosciusko Bridge. It sets commuters' teeth on edge to hear that name mangled, even though they probably can't pronounce it correctly either. In New York, for instance, the name Andrew Carnegie, of Carnegie Hall fame, is pronounced Car-n-GEE. Everywhere else the philanthropist lived, his name is Car-NAY-gee. And while Houston is in Texas, the street in New York named for Sam Houston is HOWston. That's just the way it is.

If you know something about the city's history and geography, it goes a long way toward understanding the city psyche. New York consists of five boroughs, four of which are on islands. Only the Bronx is part of the United States mainland. This creates a very insular feeling among New Yorkers, for whom the words *New York* never refer to the state or any borough other than Manhattan. In fact, residents of the other boroughs will even say "I'm going into New York" when they are already politically and geographically in New York, New York. This book adheres to the same logic; I cover only Manhattan, but mainly because of space limitations. Steinberg's famous illustration "A New Yorker's View of the World" is so popular because it is so true. Anyone can be a New Yorker, and only a New Yorker could be so arrogantly and lovably myopic.

I don't know how many times I am asked how New York came to be known as the Big Apple. Here's the story: In the early part of this century, many entertainers, especially jazz musicians, used the term to mean that playing in New York was the pinnacle of success in show business—the Big Time, the Main Stem, the Big Apple. In 1971, the president of the New York Convention and Visitors Bureau, Charles Gillett, resurrected the term in his promotional efforts to polish up the city's image, and the name stuck. New York became known as the bright, shiny apple at the top of the tree of success, and it has never fallen from that lofty perch.

Where To and Where Not To

Like any great city, New York not only has a host of wonderful things to do and see, but it has its share of things that make it unpleasant. The following list is certainly not complete, but it will give you an idea of what to expect.

On the plus side, try:

Taking a Staten Island ferry ride for just 25¢.

Shopping Orchard Street on Sunday.

Visiting the United Nations.

Touring St. John the Divine, the world's largest Gothic cathedral (Amsterdam Ave at 112th St).

Feasting your eyes on the marble and glitter of Trump Tower (Fifth Ave at 56th St).

Having an evening meal in the Crystal Room at Tavern on the Green in Central Park.

Taking a ride through Central Park in a hansom cab.

Buying a hot bagel from H&H Bagels (80th St and Broadway or 1551 Second Ave).

Having drinks and conversation in the Rainbow Room atop Rockefeller Center.

Attending the flea market and antiques sale on Sunday at Sixth Avenue and 26th Street.

Having tea or Sunday brunch in the Palm Court at the Plaza Hotel (Fifth Ave and Central Park S).

Enjoying the awe-inspiring view from atop the World Trade Center.

Touring backstage at the Metropolitan Opera.

Sampling Dim Sum in Chinatown.

Having a cup of espresso or cappuccino in Little Italy.

Walking along the promenade at Battery Park and watching the lights on the Statue of Liberty.

Viewing the model furniture rooms at Bloomingdale's (Third Ave and 59th St).

Enjoying the New York skyline from the River Cafe in Brooklyn (1 Water St).

Getting fresh coffee at Zabar's (80th St and Broadway).

Seeing the Knicks and the Rangers at Madison Square Garden (Seventh Ave and W 33rd St).

Getting lost in the downstairs book stacks at the Strand Book Store (12th St and Broadway).

Enjoying the open-air entertainment at the South Street Seaport.

Getting stuffed at the Carnegie Deli (Seventh Ave and 55th St).

Enjoying the Easter flower show at Macy's (Herald Square).

Catching a ballet at Lincoln Center.

Gawking at the dinosaurs at the American Museum of Natural History (79th St and Central Park W).

Watching the Christmas show at Radio City Music Hall (50th St and Sixth Ave).

Taking the overnight AMTRAK Executive Sleeper from New York to Washington, D.C. (where you can visit one of America's finest shopping complexes at the fabulous new $160 million Union Station).

Getting the early Sunday edition of *The New York Times* to read in bed on Saturday night.

Taking a run in Central Park before heading to the office.

Listening to the "Ted Brown show with Nola Worley" on WNEW while driving to work.

Stopping for a box of Rondo ice cream goodies at a street-corner vendor.

Getting a massage at the Lotus Health Studio (N.Y. Penta Hotel, Seventh Ave and 33rd St).

Taking the kids for an after-dinner treat at Peppermint Park (1225 First Ave).

Browsing through the "New York Is Book Country" book fair on Fifth Avenue in September.

Taking advantage of the weekend package at the Vista International.

Spending an afternoon at the Museum of Modern Art (11 W 53rd St).

Getting a loaf of Eli's bread (at almost any gourmet shop) and having it for toast tomorrow morning.

Spending the day getting pampered (and sending the old man the bill) at Elizabeth Ardens (691 Fifth Ave).

Having one of the finest French dinners anywhere at La Reserve (4 W 49th St).

Buying one of the last necktie bargains left in New York at Heritage Neckwear (194 Allen St).

Visiting Theodore Roosevelt's birthplace and George Washington's headquarters (28 E 20th St and 1785 Jumal Terrace, respectively).

Finding a bargain ticket for a Broadway matinee at the TKTS booth in Times Square.

Getting into a political discussion with a cab driver.

Going dancing at the Palladium (126 E 14th St).

Having a hamburger at Jackson Hole Hamburgers (232 E 64th St).

Taking in the Sunday brunch at the Grand Hyatt Hotel (42nd St at Grand Central Station).

Taking home fresh fruit and vegetables from Balducci's (426 Sixth Ave).

Getting a glass of fresh-squeezed orange juice at 1428 Sixth Avenue (just off 58th St).

Buying a new outfit at a real discount price at Ben Farber (462 Seventh Ave).

Reading *Seven Days* magazine and catching up on current New York doings.

Visiting the new Winter Garden shopping area at the World Financial Center.

Feeling healthy eating an oat bran muffin from David's Cookies.

Strolling through the "Place des Antiquaires" (Lexington Ave and 57th St).

Eating until you burst at the Polish Veselka Coffee Shop (Second Ave and Ninth St).

Enjoying the happy hour at Molly Bloom's (150 W 47th St).

Finally, taking advantage of any rest room you come across, especially those in hotels. Others may not be so handy or clean.

Then there are the negatives:

Restaurant maitre d's who seat you in the bar when the dining room is not filled.

Cab drivers who smoke, and then take you on the Triboro Bridge rather than the 59th Street Bridge to La Guardia Airport.

Preprogrammed messages on answering machines.

Upper East Side singles bars.

New York in August.

Buying drinks at the Palladium.

Buying an overpriced pretzel on Fifth Avenue near Central Park.

Trying to find a bargain apartment in the Sunday real-estate section of the *Times*.

Street phones that don't work.

Street addresses, especially on Fifth Avenue and Park Avenue, that don't really exist (entrances are on side streets).

Cabs that take short corner turns, moving the puddle from the gutter to your new suit.

Restaurants including the tax in the check total so the tip will be larger.

The person who knows so much about New York that no one can tell him (or her) anything ("I've lived here all my life").

Department-store clerks who remind the customer, "That isn't my section."

People who need to draw attention to themselves by having the largest and loudest portable radio on the street.

The V.I.P. (in his or her mind only) who instructs their secretary not only to ask who is calling, but also to inquire about the subject matter.

Garbage bags sitting in the hot summer sun.

Dogs whose manners are unacceptable to everyone but their owner.

Trying to get a cab at 5 p.m. on a wet Friday afternoon.

Watching an unsuspecting person buy one of those fake Rolex watches from a street vendor.

Getting ripped off by an electronics store on Fifth Avenue.

Restaurants adding a 15 percent to 20 percent service charge to the check automatically.

"Happy Birthday" being sung off-key by waiters at serious restaurants.

Wearing a gold necklace! You're bound to attract rip-off artists on the street.

Getting Around in the City

The city sprang up in what is now called downtown, the southern tip of Manhattan island. It was originally a Dutch colonial settlement, and areas like Greenwich Village were the suburbs and rural outskirts. As a result, none of the downtown streets have numbers, only names, and they often meander, following the original cow-paths and former waterways. For example, in the Village, Waverly Place crosses itself, and West 4th Street crosses West 10th Street. Wall Street was the northern walled perimeter of the city; Canal Street was in fact a canal; Spring Street still has a spring beneath it. They are decidedly not designed for modern-day vehicles. This is a problem the city is still grappling with, and short of banning on-street parking, the city will not be able to solve it anytime soon.

Eventually, as the city stretched northward, a more logical gridiron pattern was established. (It won't do you much good south of Fourth Street or east of First Avenue, but it's pretty good for midtown and upper Manhattan.) Numbered streets run east-west up Manhattan through the 200s. (A bit of trivia: Spuyten Duyvil creek used to go through 232nd Street, separating Manhattan from the Bronx. The creek was retrenched and moved, and the Marble Hill section of Manhattan became the Bronx. But Bronx residents still vote in Manhattan, and they have Manhattan addresses and the Manhattan telephone area code.) Avenues run north-south, with First Avenue parallel to the East River and 12th Avenue parallel to the Hudson River. Where the city expands in width, there are Avenues A, B, C, and D, and York on the East Side. Fifth Avenue runs through the middle, dividing the island into east and west, so addresses and streets take their names from their proximity to Fifth Avenue. Two West 34th Street, for example, is the first building to the west of Fifth Avenue. It also happens to be the Empire State Building.

Here's a crash course in simplifying New York geography. Think in terms of downtown, midtown, the West Side (that's above 59th Street and below 92nd Street), and the East Side. Although there is an East Village and a Lower East Side, New Yorkers do not use "Upper" when they refer to uptown East. East Side means uptown, and that is the area above midtown.

There are four basic modes of transportation in the city, and the automobile is not one of them. Between parking fees (which can rival hotel-room charges), alternate-side-of-the-street parking regulations (which is peculiar to New York), and heavy traffic, it is almost never worth driving yourself. True New Yorkers very seldom own cars. If they're really affluent, they either have drivers who work as hard at parking as they do at driving, or they subscribe to a parking service. (Yes, really. There are people whose sole job is to move their clients' cars from one side of the street to the other.) So, the main means of transportation are:

Buses—Most buses run straight north-south or east-west routes. Thus, the M101 bus has a route of several miles, while the 42nd Street crosstown bus travels less than a mile. There have been some concessions for the Jacob Javits Convention Center, which has no parking facilities or convenient subway stops. The best way to get there is by bus.

Buses require exact change. They will also accept subway tokens. Passengers are entitled to one free transfer to another line (i.e., not the same route back) upon boarding. You must ask for it at the time you pay your fare. Stops are usually made every two to three blocks, and you are expected to exit through the rear door. Watch your wallet, especially if you are the first person off the bus and have to push the doors open. Bus stops are marked with the route number and map on a pole near the stop. (The same is true for privately operated express buses, which run to communities in the outer boroughs. The fare there is considerably more than a token, but the route is quicker and there are fewer stops.) Bus maps are available at subway token booths in every borough. If you want the map for more than one borough, or want the information before you can reach a subway station, write to the Transit Authority's Information Office at 370 Jay Street, Brooklyn, New York. Enclose a self-addressed envelope with sufficient postage. They can also supply subway maps.

HINT: *Several buses may use the same corner stop. Never board a bus until you confirm that it is the number and route you want. There are dozens of buses with almost the same number yet very different routes.*

Subways—The subway system operates continuously, 24 hours a day, but tokens can only be purchased from manned booths. During late-night hours, look for colored-light balls at the entrance to each station. Green means everything is running and the booths are manned; red means that that particular entrance is closed or the token booth is closed. There are local and express trains; if you are only going a few stops, it really doesn't make much difference which you take. The routes were not designed with the modern commuter in mind, so they often overlap on short distances and then skip long stretches, particularly in Harlem, which was considered the outskirts of civilization when the subways were first mapped out. Most of the lines were designed to bring people into the city from the outer boroughs, so they run north and south, parallel to the avenues above ground. The only crosstown routes are the Flushing and Carnarsie lines and the 42nd Street and 14th Street shuttles. There are a few uptown-downtown stations that allow transfers to those crosstown lines. All of this is spelled out on the free subway maps available at the token booths or from the Transit Authority.

A word about subway safety. During rush hours and evenings, there are manned patrols aboard every train, but a little caution of your own still helps as well. Stand back from the platform at all times, but especially when a train is pulling into the station. Never wear jewelry prominently displayed outside your clothing, and take special care of your wallets and bags. A favorite trick of the petty thief is to yank a pocketbook from a passenger just as the train doors are closing and the train is pulling out of the station. Finally, always stand in the center of the platform, where it is well lit and well populated. If there's no one there, you shouldn't be there either. By the way, the New York Transit Authority operates the subways and the buses. For further information, call the Transit Authority at 718-330-1234.

Walking—At one point, the cover of this book was going to be the picture of a shoe that had been worn out from walking. The city is perfect for shank's mare. There are few hills and plenty of diversions for rest breaks. Walking is my first choice of city transportation, as it is for most New Yorkers. New York consumes more pairs of walking shoes than any other spot in the world. Walkers dress for comfort, so you won't be out of place in a hotel lobby in your sneakers and sweat socks. During snowstorms, people have cross-country-skied to work.

Taxis—The taxi industry is tightly regulated in New York. There is a limited number of legal cabs on the street, and they are subject to many constraints. They are not allowed to refuse fares. Neither are they allowed to refuse a reasonable amount of passengers (usually not more than four), even though the fare is per trip and not per person. And they are not allowed to charge for bags stowed in the taxi. In addition, the passenger has the right to select the music, smoking or nonsmoking conditions, and the route, which may include multiple stops. That's the law.

Now let's talk reality. All the jokes you've heard about not getting a cab in the rain or not getting one to travel outside Manhattan are based on truth. It's almost impossible. You may even have a problem getting one to go to the airport. As for telling a cabbie that reggae is not your style of music—well, *you* try it. Not me. Many of the current cabbies are newcomers to New York *and* the United States, so their knowledge of the city isn't always very good. It never hurts to know the best route yourself, and it helps to tell the cabbie how you'd like to get there. Avoid asking *how* to go—that can hurt! Every cab has a light and a number atop the vehicle. If the number is lit, that cab is required to stop for anyone who hails him. There is a similar number and license displayed inside the cab, which also gives the driver's name. If you have a problem, *do not* bring it to the driver's attention. But do write down his name and taxi number and contact the Taxi and Limousine Commission (221 W 41st St, New York, NY 10036; 212-869-4237 or 382-9301).

HINT: *How To Get a Cab!*

Stand at the entrance to one of the major department stores.

Go to the nearest bus or train terminal.

In the morning rush hours, when most people are headed downtown, look for taxis on uptown avenues. In the evening rush hours, reverse strategies. Always stand at avenues, not at cross streets.

At night, walk to the nearest expensive restaurant or hotel.

After theater—one of the worst times to find a cab—head west away from the center of the theater district to the good hotels in the area. The Marriott Marquis seems to have its own taxi corps at-the-ready.

During rush hours on the East Side, go to First or Second Avenue in the low 60s. Drivers returning from Queens after changing shifts come off the Queensboro Bridge there.

In lower Manhattan, go to 10th or 11th Avenue, where the diners are favorite eating spots for cabbies. Or especially late at night, look for nightclubs.

Near Wall Street, head for the Vista Hotel.

And above all, don't wave. Put your arm straight out and stand slightly in the street.

Key to Manhattan Addresses

To determine the approximate cross street for addresses located on the avenues, try the following formula. Cancel the last figure of the house number. Divide the remainder by two, and add the key number below. The result is approximately the nearest cross street.

Ave A, B, C, D	Add 3
1st and 2nd Ave	Add 3
3rd Ave	Add 9 or 10
4th Ave (Park Ave South)	Add 8

5th Ave
- Up to 200. . . . . Add 13
- Up to 400. . . . . Add 16
- Up to 600. . . . . Add 18
- Up to 775. . . . . Add 20
- From 775-1286
    - Cancel last figure and subtract 18
- Up to 1500. . . . . Add 45
- Above 2000 . . . . Add 24

Ave of the Americas (or 6th Ave). . . . . Subt 12 or 13
7th Ave . . . . Add 12
- Above 110th St . . . . Add 20
8th Ave . . . . Add 9 or 10
9th Ave . . . . Add 13
10th Ave . . . . Add 14
11th Ave . . . . Add 15
Amsterdam Ave. . . . . Add 59 or 60
Audubon Ave . . . . Add 165
Broadway . . . . Up to 750 is
below 8th St
- 756 to 846 . . . . Subt 29
- 847 to 953 . . . . Subt 25
- Above 953 . . . . Subt 31
Columbus Ave. . . . . Add 59 or 60
Convent Ave . . . . Add 127
Ft. Washington Ave . . . . Add 158
Lenox Ave. . . . . Add 110
Lexington Ave. . . . . Add 22
Madison Ave. . . . . Add 26
Manhattan Ave . . . . Add 100
Park Ave. . . . . Add 34 or 35
St. Nicholas Ave . . . . Add 110
West End Ave. . . . . Add 59 or 60
Central Park West
- Divide house number by 10 and add 60
Riverside Drive
- Divide by 10 and add 72

To determine which avenue is nearest to a street address, use the following chart. Example: 356 West 34th Street is located between 8th and 9th Avenues.

East Side
- 1 at 5th Ave
- 101 at Park or 4th Ave
- 201 at 3rd Ave

301 at 2nd Ave
401 at 1st Ave
501 at York Ave or Ave A
601 at Ave B

West Side
  1 at 5th Ave
101 at 6th Ave (Lenox Ave north of 110th St)
201 at 7th Ave
301 at 8th Ave
401 at 9th Ave (Columbus Ave north of 59th St)
501 at 10th Ave (Amsterdam Ave north of 59th St)
601 at 11th Ave (West End Ave north of 59th St)

If the above formula is too confusing, try this chart guide, which roughly covers the area between Union Square and Times Square.

CROSSTOWN GUIDE

5th AVENUE	
6th AVENUE	100W
7th AVENUE	200W
8th AVENUE	300W

STREET GUIDE

Street	Madison Avenue	5th Avenue	6th Avenue	7th Avenue	Broadway
18		130	615	135	875
20		150	655	170	900
22		170	695	210	935
24	20		730	245	1100
26	45	210	770	285	1135
28	80	250	810	320	1180
30	120	275	855	365	1215
32	155	320	885	405	1255
34	185	350		440	1315
36	215	390	980	480	1350
38	250	420	1020	525	1400
40	280	450	1065	560	1430
42	300	500	1100	600	1470

Shopping Districts

Unlike almost any other city, New York's merchants, be they wholesale or retail, clump together in districts. The city has dozens of such areas, and shoppers instinctively flock to them first. The boundaries change, sometimes slowly by expansion or by loss of popularity for the stores' products, and sometimes so rapidly that whole districts, which have existed in the same place for years, up and move in less than six months. The electronics area around the World Trade Center gave way for that edifice in record time. Here are the shopping districts of the city as they exist now.

Antiques: Antiques shopping depends upon your pocketbook and inclination. The historic antiques district was Madison Avenue in the seventies. (What they threw out nurtured the thrift shops which sprung up on Lexington and Third in the same area.) High rents forced them first to the side streets, then to shows and such collective exhibits as the Antiquarium Market. Several no longer have galleries at all. Others, primarily wholesalers, moved down to the antiquarium book area below 14th Street near Union Square. Twelfth, Eleventh, and Tenth Streets, near University Place and Fourth Avenue are thriving with antiques dealers. And the funky "near antique" dealers are in the early twenties, the East Village, and Greenwich Village, where they sell such popular pieces as roll-top desks.

Appliances, Fashions, Housewares: And I could add Sheer Madness to that list. Where else do you find all of them but at that throbbing international bazaar, the Lower East Side. Don't miss it! Thanks to the famous discounts on electronics at 47th Street Photo, we should now list the mid-forties off Fifth Avenue, on the West Side, as another hot spot for these items. As its name implies, the original store was a camera specialty shop, in the diamond district. Because of its great deals, it became phenomenally successful; it expanded its inventory to include computers and other electronics, opened several other stores, and spawned a host of imitator-competitors. Check out the ads in the Sunday *Times* for a good look at what 47th Street Photo offers.

Art: The formal traditional galleries are usually in the neighborhoods near the large art museums (but not the Metropolitan). Look near the Whitney museum, for example, and the Madison Avenue and Park Avenue area in the sixties. These are prime locations with primo prices. Smaller, fringe galleries, with lesser known names and less expensive tags, are found in the Village. But the galleries of Leo Castelli, Mary Boone, and other established contemporary dealers are in trendy SoHo, where they offer pricey uptown deals in a downtown setting.

Books: In the old days, Union Square was book country. Today, the Strand and Barnes and Noble's original store are two vestiges of the old-, used-, and rare-book venue. The rest have moved uptown and became antiquarians (read expensive).

Carpets: Tread lightly here. The really big names in carpets, such as Schumacher, still follow a "to the trade only" policy and operate within the fortress of the D & D (Decoration and Design) Building. (But even that is finally changing. I predict by the next edition of this book that it will not be necessary to hire a decorator to gain access to showrooms. Until recently, storming Buckingham Palace was easier.) Traditionally, dealers of area and oriental rugs have clustered downtown, near the flower district, around 27th and 28th Streets between Madison Avenue and Park Avenue. That neighborhood is experiencing a trendy resurgence and the high rents that go with that, so carpet dealers have moved to the area near West 12th Street and the Hudson River. (The warehouses there were originally built for distributors and wholesalers.)

Diamonds: The diamond district is 47th Street between Fifth Avenue and Sixth Avenue. They don't give out samples. Every year there are exposés about the dangers of buying here. Suffice it to say that you shouldn't take anyone's word for quality here, especially not an "appraiser" that the seller sends you to. They are often in cahoots. Rather, give a deposit or postdated check, and take the jewel to a certified gemologist that you find on your own. Ask to see Gemological Institute of America's report on the stone (GIA). The buyer has every right to see the report. Do not buy without one, no matter what you are told. But there are bargains to be had, and virtually every New Yorker has a "friend on 47th Street," so happy shopping. Just don't go unprepared.

Feathers, Beads, and Trimmings: An auxiliary to the garment district, the area off Sixth Avenue in the upper twenties, offers flowers, bows, and buckles. There are probably more beads and bangles on 28th Street than in all of Ohio.

Fish: The Fulton Fish Market, across from the South Street Seaport, is the source of nearly every fish or seafood item in the metropolitan area, if not the Eastern Seaboard. If you want it fresh, six a.m. is considered a late time to shop, and the fishmongers preparing for the A&P are not about to stop and discuss the virtue of the day's catch with you. But the price is right. They sell to the general public, and there is now a series of tours and lectures, which implies that they are doing *something* to upgrade their image, if not their smell.

Flowers: From 26th Street through 30th Street and from Sixth Avenue to Seventh Avenue, business is blooming. Most of the flower merchants are open for early-morning wholesale only. But the normal business day sees plant accessories, pots, baskets, planters, and artificial flowers sold to all.

Fur: The area around Seventh Avenue, between 27th Street and 30th Street, could pass for an outpost of the Yukon. Manufacturers, wholesalers, distributors, and showrooms burrow into these three blocks, and many of the operations run a retail business that puts Macy's to shame.

Furniture: The fraternal headquarters of the furniture industry (not the manufacturing plants) are on Lexington Avenue between 29th Street and 33rd Street. The buildings in this area house either official dealers and showrooms, or such accessory industries as upholstering, cooperative showrooms, or clearance centers. Note, however, that this is not the interior-design center. The D&D Building is located at 979 Third Avenue, and it is not usually open to the public.

Handbags: The thirties off Fifth Avenue. For some reason, few of these stores are on ground level, but wholesale and retail handbag operations abound on the higher floors.

Hats and Fabrics: These may seem like strange bedfellows, but both of these Garment Center accessories can be found in the upper thirties and lower forties between Sixth Avenue and Seventh Avenue.

Junk: The Canal Street area, which borders the financial district and SoHo, is a bargain hunter's dream. In front of the stores are bins full of everything from rusty nails to used raincoats, but the neighborhood specialty is hardware and household items. The scene resembles nothing so much as last year's rummage sale, but those who do rummage through merchandise can unearth great finds.

Kitchenware, Lighting, and Restaurant Supplies: Starting at the Bowery and Houston Street and walking north to Cooper Square, you'll want to ignore the neighborhood bums and concentrate on professional kitchenware. Everything from Garland stoves to specialized light bulbs can be had here for laughable fractions of the usual retail prices. Most of the "local color" is too busy sleeping it off to bother shoppers, but you might feel more comfortable if you shop with a partner.

Men's Wear (Discount): Walk to Fifth Avenue between 18th, 19th, and 20th Streets. The usual comment overheard at these haberdasheries is, "I got two suits for less than I usually spend on one."

Museums: Museum Row may be known as the longest mile to those who don't love museums. But between 70th Street and 103rd Street on Fifth Avenue stand the Frick Collection, the Guggenheim, the Metropolitan, the Jewish Museum, the Cooper-Hewitt, and the Museum of the City of New York—a culture lover's paradise.

Musical Equipment: Classical sheet music and piano stores are located around Carnegie Hall (57th Street and Seventh Avenue). Other instruments, acoustic and electronic, are found in the shops clustered on the block between Sixth Avenue and Seventh Avenue on West 48th Street.

Photographic Supplies: It may not be a coincidence that the photographic supply sources of the East Coast are located in the lower thirties and forties between Seventh Avenue and Broadway, next to the Garment Center, whose showrooms display fashion photographs of their models and products. Many of the city's professional photographers have studios in this area. Although 47th Street Photo has become much more than a camera store, it still offers its original specialty. Likewise, many of the discount electronics houses, both in midtown and the Lower East Side, also sell cameras and photo supplies.

Theater: Even out-of-towners know the streets of the theater district, because of the plays and songs that have made them famous, like "Give my regards to Broadway," or "Come and meet those dancing feet on the avenue I'm taking you to, 42nd Street." Now that I've got you singing, let me give you a quick update. The real theater district today is a bit further uptown and decidedly on the west side of Broadway—basically 44th Street to 51st Street. And don't forget the TKTS booth (reduced-price tickets) in Duffy Square.

Thrift Shops: Third Avenue in the upper east seventies, all of the east eighties, and part of the east nineties is "resale country." Note the neighborhood. The Salvation Army outposts are elsewhere; the merchandise on Third Avenue is high-class.

Women's Clothing: The Garment Center, Seventh Avenue, Fashion Avenue—each term is synonymous, and each one says it all. From 35th Street to 39th Street and from Broadway to Seventh Avenue, there is only one industry—the wholesale dressing of America's women. There's nothing quite like it.

Manhattan at Night

I was once scheduled to do a late-night talk show. Actually, the producer must have been on Oregon time, because his definition of late night was 3 a.m. New York time. I politely asked if it was worth my loss of sleep; would there really be anyone listening at that hour? He just as politely told me that he had a larger audience than some of the talk shows at midday, when everyone was at work.

And he was right. I stood corrected. Some years ago, Citibank started advertising with the slogan "The Citi never sleeps." They were right, too. There are a number of businesses in New York which use 24-hour shifts. Office cleaning crews, theater personnel, typesetters, and news crews (including late-night talk-show staffs) are just a few that come to mind. And the city provides facilities and support systems for all of them. So, if you're from another time zone or an insomniac, this is the city for you.

AMBULANCE—The city's emergency number is 911. Private ambulance services based in Manhattan include Associated Ambulance Service 409-4357 (HELP) and Medical Transportation Ambulance Corporation (677-8787).

ANIMAL SERVICE—The Animal Medical Center (510 E 62nd St, 838-8100) is the first choice day or night for emergency animal medical care. They are open 24 hours a day.

AUTO SERVICES AND REPAIR—Don't expect to get a new transmission installed at 3:30 a.m., but at least these guys are open 24 hours a day to help you with most automotive emergencies. Beware of places that offer 24-hour towing and nothing else, though. The last thing you need is to have your car towed to a garage where it can be held hostage until they do the repairs that *they* decide you need.

    AAA Road Service (757-3356)

    A&A Service Station (279 10th Ave, 736-9628)

    A&M Auto Repair (556 W 37th St, 465-8250) Their service includes towing.

    Avi's (539 W 47th St bet 10th and 11th Ave, 246-5084)

    Clinton Auto Repair (547 47th St., 307-1266) 24-hour towing and repairs.

    Gasateria (2 W End Ave at 59th St and 11th Ave, 307-1099) The repair franchise is Sammi Transmission, and they have a mechanic on duty 24 hours a day.

    Great Bear (352 Ninth Ave at 30th St, 563-4680, 563-4682) Full service and towing.

    Jimmy's Towing Service (35 W End Ave at 62nd St) Full service and towing.

    Lida Auto Repairs (276 Seventh Ave at 26th St, 580-9857, 242-5811) The tow is free, if they do the repairs.

BANKS—You can call these numbers to find the location of the nearest automatic teller machine.

CIRRUS 800/4-CIRRUS
NYCE 914/899-6777
PLUS 800/843-7587
For information concerning American Express traveler's checks, call 800-CASH NOW.

BOOKSTORES
Doubleday (724 Fifth Ave at 57th St, 397-0550)
  Mon-Sat until midnight
Gryphon (2246 Broadway at 80th St, 362-0706)
  Daily until midnight
St. Marks (13 St Mark's Pl, 260-7853)
  Mon-Thurs: until 11 p.m.; Fri, Sat: until midnight
Shakespeare & Company (2259 Broadway at 81st St, 580-7800)
  Sun-Thurs: until 11:30 p.m.; Fri, Sat: until 12:30 a.m.

CLEANERS
Midnight Express (921-0111)
  Mon-Fri: until midnight
Mr. Dry Clean (92 Eighth Ave, 627-5980; 181 Seventh Ave, 691-4313) You can leave your garment in special built-in machines anytime.

DELIVERY AND MESSENGER SERVICE
Air Couriers (563-8899)

ELECTRICIAN
Michael Altman (80 Fifth Ave, 681-2900) 24-hour service every day.

EMERGENCIES—911 is the citywide emergency number. You can even call it from a phone booth without coins. For dental emergencies, the First Dental Society (679-3966) maintains a rotating list of dentists on call. Medical emergencies can be treated in the nearest hospital emergency room or by dialing O for operator or 911. Most hotels have a doctor on call who will be as good as the privately run services.

FLORIST
Flora Plenty (1135 First Ave at 62nd St, 254-7777)
New York Flower and Plant Exchange (209 W 96th St, 663-4256, 662-4400)
Rialto Florist (707 Lexington Ave bet 57th and 58th St, 688-3234)

FOOD: Eat In (see "Manhattan a la Carte")

Argonaut Coffee Shop (1020 Third Ave at 61st St, 421-0562)
Astor Riviera Restaurant (452 Lafayette St, 677-4461)
Brasserie (100 E 53rd St, 751-4840)
Burger King (106 Liberty St, 732-8381; 1557 Broadway, 391-0890; 1156 Sixth Ave, 302-0473)
Chelsea Square Restaurant (368 W 23rd St, 691-5400)
Chung Shing Tea Parlor (11 Pell St, 349-2635)
Cooper Square Restaurant (87 Second Ave, 420-8050)
Empire Diner (210 10th Ave, 243-2736)
Green Kitchen (1477 First Ave, 988-4163)
Homer Restaurant (121 W 10th St, 741-0438)
Keystone Restaurant II (462 Second Ave, 686-2020)
Kiev Restaurant (117 Second Ave, 674-4040)
Market Diner (256 West St, 925-0856; 572 11th Ave, 244-6033)
Midnight Express Restaurant (1715 Second Ave, 860-2320)
Morning Star Restaurant (401 W 57th St, 246-1593)
Munson Diner (600 W 49th St, 246-0954)
Sheridan Square Restaurant (72 Grove St, 255-8788)
Silver Star Restaurant (1236 Second Ave, 249-4250)
Tiffany II Restaurant (222 W Fourth St, 242-1480)
Tivoli Restaurant (515 Third Ave, 532-3300)
Tramway Coffee Shop (1143 Second Ave, 758-7017)
Village Restaurant Inn (169 Bleecker St, 533-0823)
Washington Square Coffee Shop (150 W Fourth St, 533-9306)
Waverly Restaurant (385 Sixth Ave, 675-3181)
Wo Hop Restaurant (17 Mott St, 267-2536, 962-8617)

FOOD: Take Out—The following supermarkets are open 24 hours a day.

Food Emporium (316½ Greenwich St, 215 Park Ave S, 228 West End Ave, 1498 York Ave, 1052 First Ave, 1331 First Ave, 969 Second Ave, 1172 Third Ave, 1450 Third Ave, 452 W 43rd St)
Grand Union (350 E 86th St, 535-2205, deli department)
Pathmark (227 Cherry St, Pike Slip, 227-8988; 410 W 207th St, 569-0600)

Most of the following smaller establishments are open all night.

Bagels on the Square (7 Carmine St, 691-3041)
Cathedral Market (2853 Broadway, 662-7535)
Delion Grocery (729 Broadway, 260-3759)
Eden Farms (729 Hudson St, 242-3069)
866 Deli (866 Third Ave, 838-6920)
Empire Fruits and Vegetables (200 W 96th St, 866-9337)
Georgetown Deli (596 Ninth Ave, 265-5390)

Green Village Food and Vegetable (468 Ave of the Americas, 255-4728)

H&H Bagels (2239 Broadway, 595-8000)

Sarge's Delicatessen & Restaurant (548 Third Ave bet 36th and 37th St, 679-0442)

Savoy Market (940 Second Ave, 355-5132)

Sim's Deli (235 Lexington Ave, 889-6110; 7 Park Ave, 685-5244)

696 Deli (696 Third Ave, 490-7115)

Smiler's Food Stores (469 Lexington Ave, 986-5120) There are nine Smiler's in Manhattan. This is the only one open 24 hours.

Vinnie's Market (523 Ninth Ave, 563-0545)

West Side Supermarket (2171 Broadway, 595-2536)

GAS STATIONS

Amoco (2276 First Ave at 96th St, 534-4881, 410-6440)

Capitol 640 First Ave at 36th St, 679-7585
1102 First Ave at E 60th St, 838-0785
1124 First Ave at E 62nd St, 759-9334

Gasateria 4566 Broadway, 569-9345
300 Lafayette St, 226-9530
2 West End Ave, 245-9830

Merit Gasoline Station (128 W 145th St, 283-9354)

Mobil (842 11th Ave, 582-9269)

2 M Gulf Service (500 W 23rd St, 924-1260)

HAIR

Larry Matthews Twenty Four Hour Beauty Salon (536 Madison Ave at 54th St, 246-6100) Despite the name, they aren't open 24 hours. But nearly. Last appointment is currently 8:30 p.m.

LIMOUSINE

Sabra (410-7600)

LOCKSMITHS—Locksmiths, it seems, don't mind working round the clock. All of them offer 24-hour emergency service, and those listed here have a good reputation for showing up when summoned and for not charging too exorbitantly. But always ask for an estimate, and if you don't like it, continue down the list. There are certainly plenty of them to choose from. If the list is top-heavy with names starting with *A* it's not because I was lazy. Actually, in addition to claiming to be on call all night, these guys jockey for first positions in the phone book.

A Locksmith (115 E 96th St, 860-2400)

A-Art Locksmiths (187 Second Ave, 674-7650)

A J A Lock & Key Corporation (384 Amsterdam Ave bet 78th and 79th St, 595-1824)

A & M Locksmiths (171 Third Ave bet 16th and 17th St, 242-4733)

A & R Discount Locksmith (134 E 27th St, 685-4677, 777-2555)

A-1 Locksmith (662 Amsterdam Ave bet 92nd and 93rd St, 362-4177)

Abbey Locksmith (1558 Second Ave bet 80th and 81st St, 535-2289)

Aid Locksmiths, Inc. (987 Lexington Ave bet 71st and 72nd St, 288-8463

All City Locksmiths (288 Lexington Ave, 683-4315)

Always Ready Locksmith (1049 First Ave bet 57th and 58th St, 888-0111)

Award New York Locksmith (115 E 96th St, 860-2400)

C B Lock & Gates (102 E 125th St, 534-1654)

Consumer Locksmiths (2711 Broadway bet 103rd and 104th St, 222-3500)

Fischer Locksmiths (300 W 44th St at Eighth Ave, 247-6747)

Manhattan Locksmiths (2449A Broadway, 877-7787)

McGivney Brothers Locksmiths (4789 Broadway, 567-4409)

Metro Lock (630 Ninth Ave, 769-2915)

Trade Center Locksmiths (120 Greenwich St at Albany St, 962-1086)

NEWSSTANDS

First Ave at 65th St., 79th St, and 86th St

Second Ave at St Mark's Pl, 50th St, and 53rd St

Third Ave at St Mark's Pl, 23rd St, 35th St, and 54th St

Lexington Ave at 64th St and 89th St

Park Ave at 45th St (Pan Am Building)

Sixth Ave at 8th St and 48th St

Broadway at 42nd St (for the freshest copies of *The Times*), 72nd St, 79th St, 94th St, 96th St, and 104th St

Seventh Ave S at Sheridan Sq

Eighth Ave at 23rd St, 41st, 42nd St (Port Authority Bus Terminal), and 46th St

PHARMACY

Kaufman Pharmacy (Lexington Ave and 50th St, 755-2266)

PLUMBERS—Plumbers must have a license from the Department of Buildings. Ask to see it. For complaints, call 312-8217.

The following are the most likely to appear rather than merely take a message.

Brennan Plumbing and Heating (123 W 79th St, 873-8626)

Brill & Brill, a division of Consolidated Contracting Company (303 E 111th St, 535-3210, 876-8730)

Effective Plumbing Corporation (147 E 24th St, 299-0700)

Plumbers Unlimited (200 W 72nd St, 724-0339)

R-R Plumbing Service, a Roto Rooter affiliate (687-1661)

Rapid Rooter (1170 Broadway, 675-4171)

Razor Reamer (1133 Broadway, 614-0200)

Sewer Rooter (473-2024)

POST OFFICES—The main post office (33rd St and Eighth Ave, 967-8585) is open 24 hours a day. With the exception of registered mail and limited service for packages, all other postal services are available. The Church Street Station (90 Church St) and Grand Central Station (Lexington Ave at 45th St) have vending machines for stamps available at all times.

RECORDS

    Tower Records 692 Broadway at Fourth St, 505-1500

                                1965 Broadway at 66th St, 799-2500

                                Open until midnight every night.

SPECIAL SERVICES

    F & L Associates (349 E 52nd St, 752-2879)

        Concierge services around the clock.

    Intrepid New Yorker (1230 Park Ave, 534-4922)

        Personal services anytime.

    La Concierge (322 E 86th St, 737-5289

        Clean-up services until midnight daily.

TAXIS

    UTOG (741-2000)

TYPING AND PRINTING

    FACT (221-1565)

Rest Rooms

We used to bury this section in the back of the book. Since I originally wrote the book for my friends, I figured it just wouldn't do for them to think that pit stops were one of my priorities. However, friends that I have made as a result of doing this book have caused me to change my mind.

After all, we're talking about a basic necessity, and respectable rest rooms can be very hard to find in New York. It used to be that you could use the facilities in any subway station, but those days are long gone. So, don't even think about it. By law, public buildings have public facilities. Aside from museums and department stores, they include schools, theaters, libraries, and hospitals. In any other city, I would add hotels and restaurants to that list without reservation, but for the most part it is easier to storm Fort Knox than to get to the rest room in a snooty restaurant. As for hotels, anyone is allowed to enter the lobby. If you act like you belong, you can ask your way to the rest room. The exception to that is any hotel on the Fifth Avenue parade route during an event. On St. Patrick's Day, for example, you may have to walk miles to find a place.

Here's the most exclusive list in town. (To all the folks back home: yes, I've visited these places personally—purely in the name of research, of course!) In midtown, try the following buildings. You'll do best at places that offer other public accommodations; they are accustomed to providing for the public's needs.

Citicorp Center (153 Lexington Ave at 53rd St, lower level) Very friendly and convenient.

Trump Plaza (56th St and Fifth Ave) In our last edition, Trump's pink marble rest rooms, complete with attendant, won our first prize. Some would say that they've since been upstaged by the waterfall-at-the-urinal in the revamped Royalton Hotel. But if you prefer quality to glitz, the vote should still go to Trump.

Royalton Hotel (44 W 44th St) The Royalton has been dramatically redecorated by the people who gave us Studio 54. This time around, the aforementioned waterfall (triggered by a laser), not the clientele, is the talk of the town.

Philip Morris Building (41st St and Park Ave) The public accommodation includes a branch of the Whitney Museum. This is a very pleasant facility with easy access.

Olympic Tower (Fifth Ave at 51st St) If you have the time, go to Trump Tower. But in an emergency, this will do quite well.

Paine Webber Building (51st St and Ave of the Americas, lower level) You have to pass a guard to get in, so act as though you have a right to be there. You do.

30 Rockefeller Center The concourse level is a shopping arcade, and the bathrooms are accessible. Nothing special, but clean.

Park Avenue Plaza (55 E 52nd St) This Plaza has two rest rooms in its public space on the lobby level. They work.

The Waldorf Astoria (50th St and Park Ave) You have to walk through the Waldorf lobby, a treat at any time. The décor is posh art deco, and each area of the rest room has its own sink.

The New York Public Library has rest rooms that are open and well attended during library hours, but finding them can be a chore. The men's room is on the third floor; the women's room is on the first floor (to the right of the 42nd St entrance) as well as on the third.

Rumor has it that both **Grand Central** (E 42nd St and Vanderbilt Ave) and **Port Authority** (W 42nd St and Eighth Ave) facilities are policed, attended, and safe during the day. But don't count on it. These are the kind of rest rooms that contributed to my reputation for having the ability to go hours without using one.

Downtown, the **Forbes Building** (Fifth Ave at 12th St) is a first-rate choice. There are also several schools in the area.

The South Street Seaport must be affected by its proximity to all that water. There are dozens of places with rest rooms there—maybe more per capita than any other area of the city.

The World Trade Center is an office complex, but it is also a depot for the PATH trains, and there are well maintained and attended (ladies only) rooms on the PATH concourse level.

And finally, despite my warning about rest rooms in restaurants, try to visit **Lola's** (30 W 22nd St). How many restaurants equip their powder rooms with VCRs? And the video selection changes daily. Way to go, Lola!

II. Where To Eat It: Manhattan à la Carte

It seems that the most popular and most asked-about section of this book is the one on restaurants. More and more New York residents and visitors are becoming a part of the restaurant scene, and everyone has an opinion on what's good and what isn't. Because it is so much a matter of individual taste—and depends on what you are looking for at a particular time—there are bound to be disagreements.

There are a number of excellent restaurant guides to New York, some of them written by people whose main business is food. Experts like Bryan Miller, the restaurant critic of *The New York Times,* make a full-time job of dining out. Unlike the usual restaurant handbook, the restaurant section of this book is merely meant to be a helpful partner that can save you time and money and help you get the most pleasure from eating out—or taking good food home. I have literally spent years visiting restaurants and food shops of all sizes and kinds, and have made notes on the best items and dishes served in many of them. I don't mind saying that I think my list of the "best of the best" is one of the best available anywhere. I hope you like what you find on this "best seller" list.

There are certain trends and fashions in the restaurant business, just as there are in the clothing world. For a time, the poshest and most expensive restaurants were attracting the most attention, but that trend seems to have abated. Today diners are more interested in value and good food rather than snob appeal. There are so many Italian restaurants, you could try a different one every night for a year and still not cover the choices. But strangely, New York does not have a really good German restaurant or a good Southern barbecue house. Most restaurants have taken note of the healthier, diet-conscious diners, and now you can find "lighter" choices on most menus.

For some folks, it is very important to be seated in just the right spot in a restaurant. Generally, a restaurant likes to showcase their prominent diners at the front of the house. Tables in the back of the room, near the kitchen or rest rooms, or in a drafty spot by the front door are less desirable. The most status conscious, for example, vie to be seated to the right as you enter Le Cirque, at the round table in the right window at Mortimers, or around the pool at Four Seasons. Siberia, in terms of seating, includes upstairs at the Coach House, the far wall at La Grenouille, and upstairs at the Russian Tea Room. If you are going to the River Cafe, the tables by the window are the prime real estate.

I have tried to organize this section into categories that will be of the most interest and help. When you have a particular urge for French food, a midnight snack, a visit to a coffeehouse, or a "cheap eats" dinner, you can simply refer to these pages. To collect all this information, I visited over 1,400 restaurants in Manhattan; nearly 225 are described in detail. These selections represent the best of a particular style of food, perhaps the best food in a certain area of town, or exceptional service or value. You will find restaurants in every price range. Many of the restaurants in the inexpensive and moderate categories serve food that's as good as that in the expensive ones.

Speaking of prices, I categorize restaurants as follows: Inexpensive is less than $15 per person; moderate is $15 to $25 per person; moderately expensive is $25 to $35 per person; and expensive is $35 and above per person. These figures refer to a normal two or three course meal without drinks, tip, or taxes. Remember please that prices do change frequently, and unfortunately they usually change on the up side. An inexpensive place may move quickly into another category overnight. Not only do prices change, but nearly everything about a restaurant in Manhattan is very fluid these days. It seems that chefs play a never-ending game of musical chairs, and places go in and out of business overnight or change their names in the space of one day (like Harry Cipriani). It is very distressing for any author to publish inaccurate information, so I apologize to you right here and now if a restaurant goes out of business or goes downhill because of a change in management, personnel, or location after this edition goes to press.

I like to think that my ratings of restaurants is based on good common sense. I try to put myself in your place. I make no pretense of being a food or wine expert. As a matter of fact, I omit wine evaluation for just that reason. I like a place that is clean and well-lit; where reservations are taken gladly and honestly; where the table is ready when you arrive; where the maitre d' is humble and helpful (boy, is that a rarity); where the kitchens and rest rooms are spotless; where the waiters are knowledgeable and helpful, not part-time actors; where the hot food is served hot and the cold food is served cold; where the presentation makes your saliva run; where the bread is warm and crisp—well, you get the idea. Fancy descriptions of exotic sauces and esoteric presentations are just not my forte. I am writing for the average diner.

Now let's turn to the subject of tipping. A very unattractive and, in my opinion, bad practice has begun in some of the higher priced restaurants in Manhattan (like the Quilted Giraffe). A hefty (18 percent) service charge is added to your bill automatically. Let us go back to the origins of TIP; it's an acronym that means "to insure promptness." We should be able to determine for ourselves if the service we have received is worthy of special consideration, and that is what tipping is all about. I don't want someone telling me how much to leave, and I don't think you do either. If you feel you have received service that is pretty good, then a 15 percent tip would be appropriate. Poorer service should be rewarded with less, superior service with more. And there are times when no tipping is called for—when the service is really bad. As far as the maitre d' is concerned, tip him if you want to establish a continuing rapport with that restaurant, if you want to have a particular table or impress your guests, or if you are asking for some kind of special service. For him, $5 would be a good tip. The bartender should get 15 percent of the bill at the bar; the wine steward should get 10 percent of the price of the bottle; the busboy is taken care of by the waiter; the captain, if he is really helpful, should get 5 percent; and the rest room and coatroom attendants get 50 cents to $1 per visit or per coat.

Smoking in public has become a heated issue, especially in relation to places that serve food. I personally feel that smoking should not be allowed in a fine food shop or restaurant. The smell of smoke can't help permeating the food as well as the air. More and more restaurants are confining smokers to special sections, and some are prohibiting smoking altogether. When making reservations, it's a good idea for nonsmokers to mention that they would like to be seated in a "No Smoking" area.

Reservations are usually a smart move for most good restaurants. Many places will give the diner a hard time for showing up unannounced, even if there are tables available. If you don't have reservations, go before 7:00 or after 9:30 in the evening. Don't be put off by restaurants that claim they have "nothing until a week from Wednesday." Nonsense. Try again, or just show up. To avoid "no shows," some establishments will ask for your phone number. In fairness to the restaurant, call and cancel if you can't keep your reservations. On the other hand, if you have a reservation and you arrive on time, don't allow the restaurant personnel to make you cool your heels at the bar. All too often, it's a gambit for increasing your bar tab.

If you have a complaint, deliver it to the maitre d' or owner or whomever is in charge at the time. You will be doing them a favor, and most of them will be happy to try and do something to ameliorate the circumstances. They realize that your negative comments may lose them too many customers otherwise.

Dress? Overall, it is much more casual in most places now than it used to be. If it is a pricey restaurant and you are unsure, ask at the time you make your reservation if coat and tie are necessary, or if jeans or slacks are permitted. (At the World Trade Center, for example, Windows on the World has a strict dress code.) If you do happen to arrive without a coat and tie when it is required, many places have a "house uniform" they will lend you. You may not look like you stepped out of *Esquire,* but you will be allowed to dine.

Some restaurants do not take credit cards, in order to cut down on their expenses. These are noted in the following reviews. If you are caught short on cash, most places will take a check with proper identification. Of course, it is always smart to bring along a blank check or adequate cash, just in case. Be sure to check your bill carefully. Yes, even the best restaurants make mistakes in arithmetic. Remember also that tips should be figured on the price of the food, not including tax.

A number of restaurants reviewed in previous editions have been eliminated. Some have gone out of business. Others have gone downhill since they were reviewed. And others are no longer "the best" in their particular category or price range or their part of town. You'll notice that I do not use stars or ratings. How can you compare a good hamburger place with a fine French restaurant, a superb seafood choice with a place that serves only vegetarian food? I don't think you can. I list only those that I think are worthy of visiting. If they aren't, I say so in the "Don't Bother" section, or I don't mention them at all. Some of the restaurants featured in the listings are not given a complete review. Because of space limitations, it was not possible to include write-ups of every place mentioned. Neither are addresses always included, again for lack of space.

Eating out is one of the most popular pastimes for both New York residents and visitors. It is easy to understand why: no other city in the world offers such variety and excellence. I hope this book will make your dining experiences more pleasant and more satisfying.

Best Taste Treats (Eat In and Take Out): An Exclusive List

Afghan Bread at 764 Ninth Ave
Hot Antipasti at Pasta Roma (315 W 57th St)
Gourmet Appetizers at Russ & Daughters (179 E Houston St)
Apple Cake at the Cream Puff (1388 Second Ave)
Apple Pie at William Greenberg Jr. Desserts (912 Seventh Ave)
Apple Ring at Lafayette (298 Bleecker St)
Apple Tart at Quatorze (240 W 14th St)
Apple Turnovers at La Boulangère (49 E 21st St)
Cheddar Crust Apple Pie and **Walnut Sour Cream Apple Pie** at
    Little Pie Company of the Big Apple (424 W 43rd St)
Sour Cream Apple Pie at Gindi Desserts (935 Broadway)
Bagels at H&H Bagels (Broadway at 80th St)
Baked Alaska (by order) at G&M Pastries (1006 Madison Ave)
Baklava at Alleva Dairy (188 Grand St) and Anatolia (1422
    Third Ave)
Corporate Baskets at Manhattan Fruitier (210 E Sixth St)
Picnic Baskets at In a Basket (226 E 83rd St)
Striped Bass at Scarlatti (34 E 52nd St)
Beef Bourguignonne at Philippe (1202 Lexington Ave)
Beef Wellington at One If By Land, Two If By Sea (17 Barrow St)
Roast Beef at Adams Rib (1340 First Ave)
Imported Beer (greatest selection) at De Roma's (323 Broadway)
Bialys at Kossar's Bialys (367 Grand Ave)
Bigoli (Venetian pasta) at Remi (323 E 79th St)
Pepper Biscuits at Vesuvio Bakery (160 Prince St)
Black Forest Cake at Eclair (141 72nd St)
Blackout Cake at Gertel's (53 Hester St) and Serendipity 3 (225
    E 60th St)
Homemade blintzes at Mama Leah's (429 Amsterdam Ave) and
    Kiev Restaurant (117 Second Ave)
Bratwurst at Schaller & Weber (1654 Second Ave)
Basil Bread with Mozzarella at Patisserie Encore (141 Second Ave)
Eli's Bread at E.A.T. (1064 Madison Ave) and other gourmet shops
Indian Bread at Akbar (475 Park Ave) and Dawat (210 E 58th
    St)
Raisin-Nut Bread at E.A.T. (1064 Madison Ave) Outrageous
    price!
Swiss Health Bread at Thorough Bread (450 Park Ave)
Whole Wheat French Bread at Dean & Deluca (560 Broadway)
Brioche at Cafe Europa (347 E 54th St)
Oat Bran Brownies at Karen's (187 Columbus Ave)

Butter Cream and Chocolate Cake at Moishe's Bakery (181 E Houston St)

Cajun Rib Steak at the Post House (28 E 63rd St)

Calamari at Extra! Extra! (767 Second Ave)

Calzone at Little Italy Gourmet Pizza (65 Vanderbilt Ave and other locations) and Piatti Pronti (34 W 56th St)

Cannelloni at Piemonte Ravioli Company (190 Grand St)

Cannoli at Caffe Vivaldi (32 Jones St) and De Roberti's Pastry Shop (176 First Ave)

Carrot Cake at Carrot Top Pastries (5025 Broadway at 220th St)

Cassoulet at Cafe 58 (232 E 58th St) and Man Ray (169 Eighth Ave)

Caviar at Petrossian (182 W 58th St)

Beluga Caviar at Iron Gate (424 W 54th St)

Caviar Beggar's Purses at Quilted Giraffe (550 Madison Ave)

Ceviche (marinated seafood) at Albuquerque Eats (First Ave bet 76th and 77th St)

Champagne at Garnet Wines and Liquor (929 Lexington Ave) and Gotham Liquors (1543 Third Ave)

Cheese Selection at Grace's Market Place (1237 Third Ave)

Cheese and Onion Pie at Chalet Suisse (6 E 48th St)

Combination Fruit Cheesecake at Eileen's Cheese Cake (17 Cleveland Pl)

Hazelnut Cheesecake at Miss Grimble (1199 First Ave)

Gourmet Cheese Sticks and **Cheese Rolls** at Cheesestick Factory (410 E 13th St)

Chicken-in-the-Pot at Fine & Schapiro (138 W 72nd St) and Golden's Restaurant (148 W 51st St)

Chicken Liver with Truffle Mousse Paté at Main Course (1608 Third Ave)

Chicken Pot Pie at Cafe at Between the Bread (145 W 55th St) and Jim McMullen's (1341 Third Ave)

Chicken Salad at China Grill (60 W 53rd St)

Chicken Soup at Second Ave Deli (156 Second Ave)

Baked Chicken at Harper (1303 Third Ave)

Cajun Chicken at Susan Simon (32 E Second Ave)

Coriander Chicken Salad at Petak's (1244 Madison Ave)

Dijon Chicken at Zabar's (2245 Broadway)

Fried Chicken at Yellow Rose Cafe (450 Amsterdam Ave)

Grilled Chicken at Rainbow Chicken (2801 Broadway at 108th St) and Les Poulets (27 E 21st St)

Roast Chicken at Chez Louis (1016 Second Ave)

Sesame Chicken Salad at Indiana (80 Second Ave)

Smoked Chicken Salad at Madelines (177 Prince St)

Chili at Home on the Range (135 Third Ave), Manhattan Chili Company (302 Bleecker St), and Exterminator Chili Restaurant (305 Church St)

Texas Chili at As You Like It (120 Hudson St)

Chinese Barbecue Items at Quon Jan Meat Products (79 Christie St)

Chinese Vegetables at Kam Man (200 Canal St)

Chocolate Cake at Hard Rock Cafe (221 W 57th St)

Chocolate Cappuccino Cake with Walnuts at Cafe du Parc (106 E 19th St)

Chocolate Chip Soufflé at Trumpet's (Grand Hyatt Hotel)

Chocolate Chubbie Cookie at Sarabeth's Kitchen (423 Amsterdam Ave at 80th St)

Chocolate Dessert Plate at Quilted Giraffe (550 Madison Ave)

Chocolate Hazelnut Meringue at De Roberti's (176 First St)

Chocolate Meringue Cake with Chocolate Mousse at Bakery Soutine (106 W 70th St)

Chocolate Pecan Pie at Gindi Desserts (935 Broadway)

Chocolate Truffles at Rich Treats (18 W 55th St)

Belgian Chocolate Truffles at Manon (872 Madison Ave)

Hand-Dipped Chocolate Pretzels, Cookies, Etc. at Evelyn's Chocolates (4 John St, 9A Beaver St)

Viennese Chocolate Torte at Peacock Caffe (24 Greenwich Ave)

Cholent at Second Ave Deli (156 Second Ave)

Chorizo (Spanish sausage) at La Ideal (166 Eighth Ave) ·

Cioppino at Coastal (300 Amsterdam Ave)

Tender Baked Clams at Frank's Trattoria (371 First Ave)

Coconut Tarts at Saint Honoré Bakery (28 Bowery)

Fresh Coffee at Porto Rico Importing Company (201 Bleecker St)

Morning Coffee at Caffe Dante (81 MacDougal St)

Cold Cuts at Bremen House (220 E 86th St)

Fortune Cookies (wholesale prices) at Key Lee Fortune Cookies (178 Lafayette St)

Homemade Cookies at La Delice (372 Third Ave)

Corn Bread at Moishe's Bakery (181 E Houston St, 115 Second Ave)

Corned Beef Hash at Broadway Diner (1726 Broadway)

Cornish Hens at Lorenzo and Maria's Kitchen (1418 Third Ave)

Couscous at Provence (38 MacDougal St, on Sunday)

Crab Cakes at Acme Bar and Grill (9 Great Jones St) and the Coach House (110 Waverly Pl)

Crab Meat Salad in Dill Sauce at Fledermaus (1 Seaport Pl)

Cranberry Relish at Artichoke (968 Second Ave)

Creme Brulée at Le Cirque (58 E 65th St)

Creme Caramel at Barbetta (321 W 46th St)

Croissants at Paris Croissant (609 Madison Ave, 1776 Broadway, and other locations)

Cucumber Salad at Neuman and Bogdonoff (1385 Third Ave)

Cheese Danish at Budapest Pastries (206 E 84th St)

Natural Dates at Gillies 1840 (160 Bleecker St)

Italian Deli Items at Lisa's (901 Park Ave)

Delicatessen Assortment at Dean & Deluca (560 Broadway)

Delices Cake at Les Delices Guy Pascal (1231 Madison Ave, 2241 Broadway, and 939 First Ave)

Delizia Torte at Sant Ambroeus (1000 Madison Ave)

Dover Sole at Le Regence (37 E 64th St)

Peking Duck at Peking Duck House Restaurant (22 Mott St)

Chinese Dumplings at Pig Heaven (1540 Second Ave) and Great Shanghai (27 Division St)

Egg Cream at Carnegie Deli (854 Seventh Ave), Dave's Corner Restaurant (Broadway and Canal St), Mill Luncheonette (2895 Broadway at 112th St), and Moisha's Luncheonette (239 Grand St)

Eggplant Salad at Juliana (891 Eighth Ave)

Fresh Jersey Eggs at (72 E Seventh St, only Thurs: 7-5:30)

Scotch Eggs at Myers of Keswick (634 Hudson St)

Empanadas at Ruben's (964 Fulton St)

Enchiladas at Lucy's Restaurant (503 Columbus Ave)

English Trifle at John Clancy's (181 W 10th St, 206 E 63rd St)

Espresso at Caffé Dante (79-81 MacDougal St)

Falafel at Lox Around the Clock (676 Sixth Ave) and Pita Cuisine of SoHo (65 Spring St)

Fettuccine Alfredo at Parioli Romanissimo (24 E 81st St)

Fresh Fish at Citarella (2135 Broadway) and Central Fish Company (527 Ninth Ave)

Smoked Fish at Russ & Daughters (179 E Houston St), Barney Greengrass (541 Amsterdam Ave), and M. Schacht Company (99 Second Ave)

Smoked Fish with Toasted French Bread at Delices de France (289 Madison Ave)

Walnut Apple Flapjacks at West Side Story (700 Columbus Ave)

Swiss Fondue at Auberge Suisse (153 E 53rd St)

Best All-Around Food and Kitchen Extravaganza in the World at Zabar's (2245 Broadway)

French Fries at Tout Va Bien (311 W 51st St)

Frog's Legs at Le Cygne (55 E 54th St)

Fruit Tarts at Bett's Best (203 Eighth Ave) and Laurent (111 E 56th St)

Fresh Fruit and Vegetables at Fairway (2127 Broadway at 74th St)

Fresh Fruit Dessert Plate at Primavera (1578 First Ave)

Milanese Italian Fruit Cake at Bleecker Street Pastry (245 Bleecker St)

Fudge Layer Cake at Caffé Bianco (1486 Second Ave)

Fresh Game at Ottomanelli's Meat Market (285 Bleecker St)

Gateau Charlene Blanche at Lanciani (275 W Fourth St)

Gelati at Kron Chocolatier (37 E 18th St) and Caffe Dante (81 MacDougal St)

Mixed Grill at Delmonico's (56 Beaver St)

Guacamole at Manhattan Chili Company (302 Bleecker St)

Gumbo at Century Cafe (132 W 43rd St)

Hamburgers at Jackson Hole (232 E 64th St and other locations), Corner Bistro (331 W Fourth St), Hamburger Harry's (157 Chambers and 145 W 45th St), and Taste of the Apple (1000 Second Ave)

Apricot Glazed Ham at Word of Mouth (1012 Lexington Ave)

Westphalian Ham and Brie Sandwich at the Food Store (58 Greenwich Ave)

Chinese Herbs at Hang Fung Tai (78 Mulberry St)

Heros at Italian Food Center (186 Grand St) and Hero Boy (492 Ninth Ave)

Hot Dogs at Hotdiggity (140 Eighth Ave)

Hot Dogs with Sauerkraut at Gray's Papaya (Eighth St and Sixth Ave)

Japanese Hotpot at Seryna (11 E 53rd St)

Hungarian Pastries at Budapest Pastries (207 E 84th St)

Hazelnut Praline Ice Cream at Sofi (102 Fifth Ave)

Ice Cream Mud Pie at Ravelled Sleave (1387 Third Ave)

Dove Ice Cream Bars (wherever you can find them)

Coffee Praline Ice Cream Cake at Grossinger's (337 Columbus Ave)

Jambon at Raoul's Boucherie (180 Prince St)

Key Lime Pie at Little Pie Co (424 W 43rd St)

Kielbasa at First Avenue Meat Products (140 First Ave)

Lamb Stew at Pamir (1437 Second Ave)

Baked Lamb Sandwich at Arizona 206 (206 E 60th St)

Rack of Lamb at the Coach House (110 Waverly Pl)

Roast Lamb at Village Green (531 Hudson St)

Lasagna at the Green Noodle (313 Columbus Ave)

Linzer Torte at T.A.S.T.E. Sensations (412 E Ninth St)

Liqueur a la Mode (sundae) at Agora (1550 Third Ave)

Lobster at Shell Lobster & Seafood (412 W 13th St)

Lobster Bisque at Neuman and Bogdonoff (1385 Third Ave)

Poached Lobster at Le Petite Ferme (973 Lexington Ave)

Marzipan at the Cream Puff (1388 Second Ave) and Elk Candy Company (240 E 86th St)

Meat Loaf at Cafe Mortimer (155 E 75th St)

Prime Meats at Jefferson Market (455 Sixth Ave) and City Whole-sale Meats (305 E 85th St)

Mince Pie at As You Like It (120 Hudson St)

Morels at Amazing Foods (807 Washington St)

Moussaka at Periyali (35 W 20th St)

Mozarella at Alleva Dairy (188 Grand Ave) and Melampo (105 Sullivan St)

Homemade Mozzarella and Ricotta at Russo and Son Dairy Products (334 E 11th St)

Muffins at Between the Bread (145 W 55th St) and Petak's (1244 Madison Ave)

Oat Bran Muffins at David's Cookies (all over town)

Wild Mushrooms at Grace's Market Place (1237 Third Ave)

Mutton Chops at Keens (72 W 36th St)

Natural Foods at Whole Foods in SoHo (117 Prince St)

Bittersweet Non Pareils at Sandler's (140 W 55th St)

Chinese Noodles at Yat Gaw Min Company (100 Reade St)

Cold Noodles with Hot Sesame Sauce at Sung Chu Mei (1367 First Ave)

Nuts and Packaged Dried Fruits (great prices) at J. Wolsk and Company (81 and 87 Ludlow St)

Olives at International Grocery Store (529 Ninth Ave)

Omelets at Romaine De Lyon (29 E 61st St)

Onion Rings at the Palm (837 Second Ave)

The Freshest Squeezed Orange Juice at the hole-in-the-wall stand at 1428 Sixth Ave

Oyster Stew at Oyster Bar and Restaurant (Grand Central Station)

Long Island Oysters at Cafe des Artistes (1 W 67th St)

Pancakes at Friend of a Farmer (77 Irving Pl)

Pasta at Todaro Brothers (555 Second Ave)

Angel Hair Pasta at Contrapunto (1009 Third Ave)

Handmade Egg Pasta at Balducci's (424 Sixth Ave)

Inexpensive Pasta at La Marca (282 Third Ave)

Pasticciotto at Siracusa (65 Fourth Ave)

Pastrami at Bernstein-on-Essex (135 Essex St) and Carnegie Delicatessen (854 Seventh Ave)

Old World Pastries at Hungarian Pastry Shop (1030 Amsterdam Ave)

Paté at Les Trois Petits Cochons (453 Greenwich St)

Pecan Pie Cookies at Plumbridge (30 E 67th St)

Pecan Squares at Slice of Orange (987 Lexington Ave)

Penne with Prosciutto at Petak's (1244 Madison Ave)

Stuffed Peppers at Bo Ky (80 Bayard St)

Pickles at Hollander/Guss Pickles (35 Essex St, South St Seaport)

Pig (Pulled Pork) Sandwich at Hard Rock Cafe (221 W 57th St)

Pineapple Cheese Cake at Jimmy Red's (171 Mulberry St)

Pizza at John's Pizzeria (278 Bleecker St), Yellowfingers Di Nuovo (200 E 60th St), and Famous Ray's (465 Sixth Ave)

Deep Dish Pizza at Pizza Piazza (785 Broadway)

Sicilian Pizza at Sal's and Carmine Pizza (2533 Broadway)

Gourmet Popcorn at Nancy's Gourmet Popcorn (700 Third Ave)

Popovers at Popover (551 Amsterdam Ave)

Pork at Faicco's Pork Store (260 Bleecker St)

European-Style Cured Pork at Salumeria Biellese (376 Eighth Ave)

Homemade Potato Chips at Amsterdam's Bar and Rotisserie (454 Broadway)

Home-Fried Potatoes at Ideal Lunch and Bar (238 E 86th St)

Stuffed Potatoes at Gourmet Gazelle (1204 Third Ave)

Potato Pancakes at Ideal Lunch and Bar (238 E 86th St)

Potato Salad Nicoise at Manny Wolf's (145 E 49th St)

Pot Au Feu at La Grenouille (3 E 52nd St)

Pot Pies at Alain's Cheese Please (158 E 39th St)

Pot Roast at Cafe des Artistes (1 W 67th St)

Profiteroles at Chez Ma Tante (189 W 10th St)

Fresh Produce at Balducci's (424 Sixth St)

Rabbit Stew at Le Cafe de la Gare (143 Perry St)

Raspberry Charlotte at Dolci on Park Caffé (12 Park Ave)

Ravioli at Piemonte Homemade Ravioli Company (190 Grand St) and Di Palo Dairy Store (206 Grand St)

Steamed Vietnamese Ravioli at Indochine (430 Lafayette St)

Raw Bar at Citarella Fish Company (2135 Broadway)

Ribs at Tony Roma's (400 E 57th St and other locations) and Wylies (891 First Ave at 53rd St, 59 W 56th St)

Rum Pecan Pie at A Sweet Place (301 E 91st St)

Best Salad Bar at Miss Kim's (270 Park Ave)

Fresh Salads at Courtyard Cafe (130 E 39th St) and the Salad Bowl (566 Seventh Ave)

Homemade Salads and Sandwiches (inexpensive) at Food (127 Prince St)

Salmon Mousse at Silver Palate (274 Columbus Ave)

Marinated Salmon at La Reserve (4 W 49th St)

Smoked Norwegian Salmon Sandwich at Peter Dent (120 Hudson St)

Sandwiches at Donald Sacks SoHo (120 Prince St, 3 World Financial Center)

Sauerkraut at Katz's Delicatessen (205 E Houston St)

Sausages at Kurowycky Meat Products (124 First Ave)

French Sausage at P. Carnevale and Son (631 Ninth Ave)

Hungarian Sausage at Tibor Meat Specialties (1508 Second Ave)
Scones at Mangia (54 W 56th St)
Scnecken at William Greenberg Jr. (1377 Third Ave, 1000 Madison Ave, 912 Seventh Ave)
Seafood Dinners at Wilkinson's (1573 York Ave) and Le Bernardin (155 W 51st St)
Shepherd's Pie at Landmark Tavern (626 11th Ave)
Shrimp Creole at Jezebel (630 Ninth Ave)
Blackened Louisiana Shrimp at Four Seasons (99 E 52nd St)
Frozen Shrimp at Hyfund Company (75 Mulberry St)
Smorgasbord Plate at Aquavit (13 W 54th St)
Snails at Lutece (249 E 50th St)
Sorbet at La Boite En Bois (75 W 68th St)
Soufflés at La Côte Basque (5 E 55th St)
Black Bean Soup at the Coach House (110 Waverly Pl)
Mandalay Fish Soup at Road to Mandalay (380 Broome St)
Minestrone Soup at Il Vagabondo (351 E 62nd St)
Southern-Style Food at Memphis (329 Columbus Ave)
Spices at Aphrodisia (282 Bleecker St)
Greek Spinach Pies at Poseidon Bakery (629 Ninth Ave)
Indian Spices at Mahal (135 Lexington Ave)
Spring Rolls at Indochine (430 Lafayette St)
3 S's (snacks, soups, sandwiches) at Serendipity 3 (225 E 60th St)
Steak at Post House (28 E 63rd St)
Steak and Fries at Le Steak (1089 Second Ave)
Old-Fashioned Strawberry Shortcake at An American Place (2 Park Ave)
Sushi at Hatsuhana (17 E 48th St)
Grilled Swordfish at Chez Ma Tante (189 W 10th St)
Tabbouleh at Benny's (321½ Amsterdam Ave, 37 Seventh Ave)
Tacos at Rosa Mexicano (1063 First Ave)
Spanish Tapas at El Cid (322 W 15th St)
Stuffed Puff Pastry Tarts and Logs at Dufour Pastry Kitchen (808 Washington St)
Tartufo at Erminia (250 E 83rd St)
Tea Sandwiches at Mortimer's (1057 Lexington Ave)
Tempura at Mitsukoshi (461 Park Ave)
Tira Mi Su (Lift Me Up) Dessert at Biricchino (260 W 29th St)
Tomato Soup at Sarabeth's Kitchen (412 Amsterdam Ave, 1295 Madison Ave)
Champagne Truffles at Teuscher (25 E 61st St)
Grand Marnier Truffles at Normandie Chocolat (338 E 116th St)
Truffle Tart at Encore (141 Second Ave)

Tuna Salad at Todaro Bros. (555 Second Ave)
Roasted Tuna at Rakel (231 Varick St)
Veal Cutlet at Trastevere (309 E 83rd St)
Veal Scaloppine at Zinno's (126 W 13th St)
Vegetable Paté (five layers) Sandwich at Lamston's (205 E 42nd St) and Fisher & Levy (1026 Second Ave)
Vegetable Salads at Michelle's Kitchen (1392 Madison Ave)
Vegetable Soup at Country Host (1435 Lexington Ave)
Vegetable Terrine at Montrachet (239 W Broadway)
Chinese Vegetables at Sun Kwong Lee (85 Mulberry St)
Vinegars at Marketplace (54 W 74th St)
Waffles at Berry's (180 Spring St)
Malt Whiskeys at SoHo Wines and Spirits (461 W Broadway)
European Wines at Quality House (2 Park Ave)
Wursts at the Wurst (2832 Broadway)
Lite Bite Yogurt Shake at TCBY (1452 Second Ave)
Zabaglione at Il Monello (1460 Second Ave)

HINT: *Here's a New York recipe for you—egg cream, a unique New York specialty drink. It consists of one quart of milk, a bottle of seltzer water, and two scoops of Fox syrup. You combine these ingredients and shake them up. Actually, you see, there is no egg and no cream in the drink!*

Afternoon Pick-Me-Ups

Where do you go when the strain of the office or afternoon shopping gets to you? You might try some of the places listed in the upcoming section "Shopping and Snacking." If those suggestions are not handy, and you are downtown, **Ferrara** (195 Mulberry) is a good bet for Italian gelati, assorted sweet things, and cappuccino. In the Village, try **Pappa's Place** (510 Sixth Ave), where the calories are secondary to the fun. In midtown, **Serendipity 3** (225 E 60th St) is a favorite for the young-at-heart, and **Rumpelmayer's** (50 Central Park S) appeals to more mature souls. The **Carnegie Deli** (854 Seventh Ave) serves big platters, if you need major revitalization. **Sant Ambroeus** (1000 Madison Ave) is fancy and filling. **Delices de France** (289 Madison Ave) is indeed delicious. **Succes la Cote Basque** (1032 Lexington Ave) is successful in treating hunger pains. **Dolci on Park Caffe** (12 Park Ave) is an undiscovered treasure. **Peppermint Park** (1225 First Ave) has an outrageous offering of sweets, sandwiches, candy, and calories that'll make you think you've gone to heaven. If you are near **Zabar's** (80th and Broadway), their goodies shop on the corner serves great coffee and ice cream—standing room only. Finally, if you're rushing for a train, the **Eclair Pastry shops** (Grand Central Terminal, Herald Square, 54th St and First Ave, and 141 W 72nd St) always have a selection of good things to eat that probably aren't so good for your waistline.

Before Theater

For relaxed pretheater dining, you should consider choosing a restaurant that is as close as possible to your theater and has very efficient service. And it is always a good idea to tell your waiter that you are going to the theater. Many of the following restaurants have special pretheater menus, and some of them are more reasonably priced than their regular dinners. Be especially careful about your timing if the weather is inclement; getting a cab in the rain is a well-known New York hassle.

Andiamo	Edwardian Room (Plaza Hotel)
Antolotti's	Gino
Arqua	Island Grill
Barbetta	Jacqueline's
Cafe de Bruxelles	JW (Marriott Marquis)
Cafe Luxembourg	Le Chantilly
Cafe Un Deux Trois	Marchi's
Cameos	Marie-Michelle
Carolina	Olde Garden and Winery
Chef Chan's	Orso
Chez Jacqueline	Rainbow Room
Dawat	Sam's

Breakfast

Doesn't anyone eat breakfast at home anymore? In Manhattan, the "power breakfast" has become a big thing. Even if you're not consumating a deal to take over General Motors, it's fun to watch the major players (and some minor leaguers who think they are) emptying briefcases and calling from portable telephones. The action these days is centered around the **Plaza Hotel's Edwardian Room** (59th and Fifth Ave), the **Regency Hotel** (540 Park Ave), **"21"** (21 W 52nd St), **Peninsula Hotel** (700 Fifth Ave at 55th St), **Carlyle Hotel** (35 E 76th St), **Cafe Pierre at the Pierre Hotel** (61st and Fifth Ave), the **Helmsley Palace's Trianon Room** (455 Madison Ave), and the **Grand Hyatt Hotel** (at Grand Central Station). If people watching is secondary to good solid fare to start the day, try **Chelsea Square Restaurant** (369 W 23rd St), **Good Enough to Eat** (424 Amsterdam Ave bet 80th and 81st St), **American**

Festival Cafe (20 W 50th St), Courtyard Cafe (130 E 39th St), Empire Diner (210 10th Ave), Sarabeth's Kitchen (1295 Madison Ave bet 92nd and 93rd, or 423 Amsterdam Ave bet 80th and 81st), the Cottonwood Cafe (415 Bleecker St), which features Grandma Bronson's buttermilk biscuits on weekends, Viand Coffee Shop (300 E 86th St), the Cupping Room Cafe (359 Broadway bet Grand and Broome St) for French toast, Pink Tea Cup (42 Grove St), or the Paris Commune (411 Bleecker St near Eighth Ave). You might also try Delmonico's (way downtown at 56 Beaver St), Aggie's in SoHo (146 W Houston St), Carnegie Deli in midtown (854 Seventh Ave at 55th St), or West Side Story (700 Columbus at 95th St) on the Upper West Side. Don't miss the blintzes at B&H Dairy (127 Second Ave at St Mark's Pl) or the freshest orange juice in town at the tiny hole-in-the-wall stand at 1428 Sixth Ave (bet 58th St and Central Park S). If price is no problem, the breads and other temptations at Eli Zabar's E.A.T. (1064 Madison Ave) are as delicious as they are outlandishly priced. The bakery section at Bloomingdale's opens early; it's a great place to go at the start of the day for a large selection of temptations.

Brunch

Personally, I don't care for the usual eggs and sausage brunch. I look for restaurants with broader and more appealing menus. The two classiest Sunday brunches are at the Palm Court at the Plaza Hotel (59th and Fifth Ave) and the Grand Hyatt Hotel (42nd St near Grand Central Station). The entire Palm Court is opened up on Sunday to showcase a dazzling array of hot and cold dishes, seafood, salads, and fresh fruit, along with a dessert selection that can only be equaled at Gerry Frank's Konditeroi in Salem, Oregon! The Grand Hyatt has a superb brunch with just about anything you can think of presented in a most appetizing buffet. Also consider Windows on the World (World Trade Center), where the thrilling view enhances the good food; Cafe des Artistes (1 W 67th St), where both the ambiance and the food are classy; Berry's (180 Spring St) for Nova Scotia salmon; Hurlingham's at the New York Hilton; Mortimer's (1057 Lexington Ave at 75th St) for people watching; Aurora (60 E 49th), where it's fun to choose great desserts from the rolling carts; Voulez-Vous (1462 First Ave at 76th St) for marvelous steak tartare; and Cafe Luxembourg (200 W 70th St) for mouth-watering homemade biscuits. Other possibilities are the Rainbow Room (Rockefeller Center) for nostalgia; Greene Street (101 Greene St) for caviar; Tavern on the Green (Central Park at W 67th) for your guests; Friend of a Farmer (77 Irving Pl); the Russian Tea Room (150 W 57th) which is a lot better than anything in Moscow; and **Julia** (226 W 79th St), where you can enjoy the garden.

Burgers

Everyone has a nominee for the best burgers in town. I vote for **Jackson Hole Wyoming Burgers** (232 E 64th St, Third Ave and 35th St, or Second Ave and 84th St). These burgers are seven juicy ounces of sheer goodness. Runners-up include **Corner Bistro** (331 W Fourth St), **Hamburger Harry's** (157 Chambers St, 145 W 45th St), **Hard Rock Cafe** (221 W 57th St), where the action is as tasty as the burgers, **Penguin Cafe** (581 Hudson St), **Taste of the Apple** (1000 Second Ave), **Diane's** (249 Columbus Ave), and **Billy's** (948 First Ave).

Cheap Eats and Good Values

If you think there are no really good inexpensive places to eat in Manhattan, you're wrong. The following are really worth trying:

Benito I
Bleecker Luncheonette
Bernstein-on-Essex
Cabana Carioca
Cafe Edison (Edison Hotel)
Chumley
Corner Bistro
Cucina di Pesce
Cucina Stagionale
Dallas BBQ
Dining Commons, City
   University of New York
   Graduate Center
Ecco-La
Food
Frank's Trattoria
Gefen's
Genoa
Golden Unicorn
Good Enough To Eat
Hamburger Harry's
Hobeaus
Horn and Hardart Automat
Jeremy's Ale House
John's Pizzeria

Katz's Delicatessen
La Bonne Soupe
Les Poulets
Madras Woodlands
Manganaro's Hero Boy
Mary Ann's
Maryland Crab House
Moondance Diner
New Wave Coffee Shop
Patisserie Lanciani
Pierre Restaurant Francais
Pizza Piazza
Rao's
Ray's Pizza of Greenwich
   Village
Saigon
Sevilla
Shingkee
Spring Street Natural
   Restaurant
Teresa's
Thai Village
Veronica
Veselka
Wong Kee

Then there are places that are not exactly inexpensive, but do give good value for your dining dollar.

Amsterdam's Bar and
  Rotisserie
Cafe 57
Contrapunto
Darbar
Il Vagabondo
La Bohème

La Fondue
La Mirabelle
Pamir
Park Bistro
Quatorze
Tony Roma's
Yellow Rose Cafe

HINT: *One of the best bargains in town is the BBQ menu featured at the Dallas BBQ (27 W 72nd St; 21 University Pl at Eighth St; and Second Ave and St Mark's Pl).*

Coffeehouses

No city in the world has as many colorful and comfortable coffeehouses as New York. You can relax and enjoy good company and good drink at:

Au Petit Beurre (2737 Broadway)
Café Orlin (41 St Marks Pl)
Caffe Dante (79 MacDougal St)
Caffe Lucca (228 Bleecker St)
Caffe Reggio (119 MacDougal St)
Caffé Sha Sha (510 Hudson St)
Caffe Vivaldi (32 Jones St bet Fourth and Bleecker St)
Cupping Room Cafe (359 W Broadway)
La Laterna di Vittorio (129 MacDougal St)
Pane & Cioccolato (10 Waverly Pl)
Sant Ambroeus (1000 Madison Ave bet 77th and 78th St)
Veniero Pasticceria (342 E 11th St)
Veselka Coffee Shop (144 Second Ave)

The espresso at La Laterna is especially good.

Dim Sum

Dim Sum translates as tidbits or snacks, Chinese style. It's what you'd probably eat on a daily basis in Chinatown or Hong Kong. In Southern China, for instance, you eat Dim Sum while having tea. Dim Sum includes all kinds of dumplings, a variety of noodle and rice dishes, and desserts. Some of the best bets are stuffed bean curds, Peking spareribs, shredded chicken rolls, egg custards, sesame shrimp toast, fried wontons, curry beef dumplings, beef balls, braised duck feet, and crab claws. Dim Sum offerings are often wheeled to your table in carts, offering the diner an amazing array of choices. For the most authentic and delicious Dim Sum in New York, I recommend **H.S.F.** (46 Bowery, or 578 Second Ave at 31st St), **Golden Unicorn** (18 E Broadway at Catherine St), **China Royal** (17 Division St), **Sun Hop Shing Tea House** (21 Mott St), **King Fung** (20 Elizabeth St), and **Mandarin Court** (61 Mott St). The Golden Unicorn makes an especially appetizing presentation.

Diners

There are not too many of the classic diners left in Manhattan, but the best survivors are **Empire Diner** (210 10th Ave at 22nd St), **Moondance Diner** (Sixth Ave and Grand St), **Market Diner** (43rd St and 11th Ave), and **Veselka** (144 Second Ave at Ninth St).

Dining Solo

Arizona 206 and Cafe
Aurora
The Ballroom
Brasserie
Cafe de Bruxelles
Cafe des Sports
Carnegie Deli
Chez Napoleon
Corner Bistro
Cotton Cafe
Elephant and Castle
Food
Grand Central Oyster Bar
    and Restaurant
Hamburger Harry's

Indochine
Jackson Hole Wyoming
    Burgers
La Bonne Soupe
Lucy's
Mme. Romaine de Lyon
Market Dining Rooms
Raoul's
Restaurant Florent
Sant Ambroeus
Second Avenue Deli
Stage Deli
Terrace 5, Trump Tower
Union Square Cafe
Viand Coffee Shop

Don't Bothers

With so many great choices in Manhattan, why waste your time and money in poor or mediocre establishments. Many on the following list are quite well-known and popular, but I feel you can get better value elsewhere.

Albero d'Oro: Elegant atmosphere, not so elegant otherwise.
Algonquin Hotel: Old hotels never die, they just . . . .
Angelo of Mulberry St: The portrait of former prez Reagan is their only claim to fame.
Au Grenier Cafe: High hopes as you climb up; great disappointment on the way down.
Bahama Mama: Leave it to the kids.

Bice: Very in, very noisy, very unimpressive.

Black Sheep: Once was fun, but that's history.

Cafe Crocodile: Too bad Andree took her name off.

Cafe de la Paix: Only thing worth watching are the other customers.

Cajun: The Southern accent has faded.

Camelback and Central: The street signs of the décor are the most appealing aspect.

Carlyle: Social climbing can be very expensive.

Charley O's: The Benetton of the food scene.

Columbus: He surely wouldn't have dined here.

David K's Cafe: Not up to David's usual standards.

Devon House: If they would only get their act together . . . .

Due: Noisy and frantic and not worth the stress.

Elaine's: You gotta be kidding.

Ernie's: The pickup scene must be awfully good, though.

Gloucester House: A major setting; a minor presentation.

Healthworks: A good idea gone tired.

Jockey Club: Way behind in the stretch.

Lello: A few smiles would help.

Le Veau d'Or: Heaven help the stranger.

Mama Leone's: Tourissimo!

Manhattan Ocean Club: The tide went out and never came back.

Metro: Humble pie is not on the menu.

Mickey Mantle's: Two strikes and three balls.

Mondrian: Pretty face, but too young for the price.

Mortimer's: For the eyes only.

Mosaico: Is there a jinx on this address?

New York Deli: It was better as an automat.

Nusantara: Indonesia is a long way from here.

Ottomanelli Cafe: Haven't they heard what happens to conglomerates?

Positano: Positively not up to the billing.

Ratner's: Why pay to get insulted?

Rosolio: Plain Jane ambiance and Plain Jane plates.

Sardi's: Pretty sad.

Sfuzzi: What's all the "sfuss" about?

Shun Lee Dynasty: Time for a new emperor.

Sign of the Dove: Beautiful and romantic, period.

Sloppy Louie's: Lives up to its name.

SPQR: An insult to Rome.

Tennessee Mountain: There's not much at the top.

Village Green: A little T.L.C. would help

You might notice that several of New York's most expensive restaurants are not mentioned in this book. Yes, I've visited them, and yes, in some cases, they are quite good. But more and more New York residents and visitors are realizing that high prices do not necessarily translate into high quality. If you read this book carefully, you'll be able to find excellent meals at realistic prices. One day restaurant operators will wake up to the fact that they may be pricing themselves out of business; many of the more expensive restaurants in Manhattan already have more empty tables than they'd care to talk about. Besides, today it's not even fashionable to pay sky-high restaurant checks, and companies are keeping tighter reins on expense accounts. **Aureole, Box Tree, China Grill, Mondrian,** and **Palio** are quality places, but whether they're worth their high tabs is another matter.

Foreign Flavors

Because of the ethnic mix of New York's population, you can find fine foods from just about every corner of the world. Here are some of the best.

Afghan: Khyber Pass
Belgian: Cafe de Bruxelles
Brazilian: Brazilian Coffee Restaurant, Brazilian Pavilion
British: Bull and Bear at the Waldorf-Astoria
Cambodian: Indochine
Chinese: Canton, Chef Chan's, Chin Chin, Fu's, Fortune Garden Pavilion, H.S.F., Lotus Blossom, Oriental Town Seafood, Phoenix Garden, Pig Heaven, Shun Lee Cafe, Tse Yang
Cuban: Sabor
Czech: Vasata
Danish: Old Denmark
French

Bistro Bordeaux
Bouley
Cafe Europa and La Brioche
Cafe Luxembourg
Capsouto Freres
Chanterelle
Chez Jacqueline
Chez Josephine
Chez Louis
Chez Ma Tante
La Boite en Bois

La Bonne Soupe
La Caravelle
La Côte Basque
Lafayette
La Fondue
La Grenouille
La Metairie (Uptown and Village)
La Petite Ferme
La Reserve (the best of the lot)
La Tulipe

Le Bernardin	Montrachet
Le Biarritz	Park Bistro
Le Cirque	Provence
Le Cygne	Rakel
Le Régence	René Pujol
Les Pleiades	Restaurant Florent
Lutèce	Terrace
Marie-Michelle	

German: Ideal's, Kleine Konditeroi
Greek: Periyali
Hungarian: Green Tree Restaurant, Mocca
Indian: Akbar, Darbar, Dawat
Italian

Alo Alo	Palio
Antolotti's	Paola's
Arquà	Parioli Romanissimo
Barbetta	Pietro's
Bravo Gianni	Pinocchio
Chelsea Trattoria Italiana	Primavera
Contrapunto	Rao's
Costa Azzurra	Remi
Dieci	San Domenico
Frank's	Sandro's
Gino	Scarlatti
Giordano	Sistina
Graziella	Time and Again
Il Mulino	Toscana
Il Vagabondo	Trastavere
Il Valletto	Union Square Cafe
Lattanzi	Vivolo
Marchi's	Yellowfingers di Nuevo
Orso	

Irish: Landmark Tavern
Japanese: Hatsuhana, Kitcho, Mitsukoshi, Nishi, Nishi NoHo, Seryna, Seto, Shinwa
Jamaican: Jamaican Hot Pot
Korean: Woo Lae Oak of Seoul
Mediterranean: Eze
Mexican: Albuquerque, Caliente Cab Company, Rosa Mexicano, Zarela
Middle East: Pamir
Polish: Christine's, Veselka Coffee Shop
Russian: The Russian Tea Room
Scandinavian: Aquavit

South American: Cabana Carioca
Spanish: Alcala, The Ballroom
Swiss: Auberge Swisse, Chalet Suisse
Thai: Baan Thai, Thai Express, Thai Royale, Tommy Tang's
Turkish: Anatolia
Vietnamese: Monsoon

Grazing

As part of the continuing interest in lighter fare and healthier eating, grazing has become a popular trend. Grazing-style food is better known to most of us as appetizers, and it appeals to those who like to snack in the kitchen or taste a bit of everything at a buffet. Some of the best grazing pastures in Manhattan are **The Ballroom** (253 W 28th St), **Huberts** (575 Park Ave), **Orso** (322 W 46th St), **Shun Lee Cafe** (43 W 65th St), and **Ménage à Trois** (134 E 48th St). Huberts is expensive; the rest are reasonable.

Healthy Fare

Menu alert from the Mayo Clinic: If you are watching your diet, be cautious about menu items described as *au jus, in broth, in cocktail sauce, in tomato base, pickled,* or *smoked.* The experts also tell you to avoid the words *au gratin, basted, braised, buttered, buttery, casserole, creamed, crispy, fried, hash, hollandaise, in butter sauce, in cheese sauce, in cream sauce, in its own gravy, marinated in oil, pan fried, parmesan, pot pie, prime, sautéed, scalloped,* and *stewed.* My goodness, what's left to enjoy? Quite a lot more than you might think, and you can find it at the following restaurants, some of which have special health menus.

Akbar (475 Park Ave at 57th St) Indian.
Buckwheat and Alfalfa (182 Eighth Ave bet 19th and 20th St)
Four Seasons (99 E 49th St bet Park and Lexington Ave) Expensive.
Fraunces Tavern Restaurant (54 Pearl St) Historic.
42nd Gourmet Health Bazaar (20 E 42nd St)
Great American Health Bar (several locations throughout the city)
Health Pub (371 Second Ave at 21st St)
Lavin's (23 W 39th St bet Fifth and Sixth Ave)
Salad Bowl (717 Lexington Ave bet 57th and 58th St)
Spring Street Natural Restaurant (62 Spring St at Lafayette) Your best bet.
"21" (21 W 52nd St) For the health- and status-conscious.

Hotel Dining

Gone are the days when the thought of dining in a hotel conjured up unpleasant images. Today, some of the finest meals in New York are served in the restaurants of leading hotels. The following are especially recommended.

Courtyard Cafe at the Doral Court
Time and Again at the Doral Tuscany
Cafe Suisse and **Lafayette** at the Drake
Trumpets at the Grand Hyatt
Le Trianon at the Helmsley Palace
Ménage à Trois at the Lexington
The View at the Marriott Marquis
Le Cirque at the Mayfair Regent
Adrienne at the Peninsula
Cafe Pierre at the Pierre
Palm Court and **Edwardian Room** at the Plaza
Le Régence at the Plaza Athénée
540 Park Avenue at the Regency
American Harvest at the Vista International
Bull and Bear at the Waldorf-Astoria
Polo at the Westbury

Kids' Day Out

If you want to treat your kids to something special, here is a selection of places popular with young folks:

America: Big and brassy.
American Festival Center: At the Rockefeller Plaza skating rink.
Arizona 206 and Cafe: A touch of the Southwest.
Carnegie Deli: For growing appetites.
Coastal: Seafood.
Corner Bistro: Burgers.
Food: The best value.
Food Fairs at Pier 17 (South St Seaport) and **A&S Plaza**
Gray's Papaya: Hot dogs.
Hamburger Harry's: The name says it all.
Hard Rock Cafe: The status scene for rock lovers.
Horn and Hardart Automat: Something different and almost historic.
Jackson Hole Wyoming Burgers: The best.
John's Pizzeria: Pizza, pizza, pizza.
Landmark Tavern: For history.
Mickey Mantle's: For the sports enthusiast.

Moondance Diner: Nostalgia.
Pappa's Place: A kid's dream.
Penguin Cafe: Easy on the budget.
Peppermint Park Cafe: Candy and ice cream heaven.
Pig Heaven: Chinese.
Serendipity 3: The meeting place.
Tavern on the Green: For special occasions.
Tony Roma's: The best ribs.
Windows on the World: Great view.

Kosher

There will never be a shortage of pastrami or chicken soup in New York, but nowadays the kosher diner can sample a wider variety of flavors, from Afghan to Indian. Here's a partial list:

Bernstein-on-Essex (135 Essex St) Quintessential kosher deli.
Boychik's (19 W 45th St) Pasta, salads, and quick take-outs.
Cheers (120 W 41st St) The accent is Italian, the menu meaty.
Dairy Planet (182 Broadway) Health food, vegetarian.
Diva (306 E 81st St) Mainly Italian, dairy menu.
Deli Kasbah (251 W 85th St) Grill, deli, and salad house.
Eden Terrace (475 Park Ave S) Elegant deli and restaurant.
Galil (1252 Lexington Ave) Middle Eastern grill.
Gefen's (297 Seventh Ave) The dairy menu is a favorite with the "rag trade."
Goldie's (211 E 46th St) Crowded noontime deli.
Great American Health Bar (all over town) Vegetarian and dairy menu.
Jerusalem II (1375 Broadway) Pizza and falafel.
Kosher Delight (1365 Broadway) Kosher burger joint.
La Kasbah (70 W 71st St) Moroccan.
Levana (141 W 69th St) Outstanding European cuisine.
Lou G. Siegel (209 W 38th St) Businessman's delight.
Maccabeem (147 W 47th St) Chicken soup, etc., cafeteria style.
Madras Place (104 Lexington Ave) Vegetarian South Indian.
Madras Woodlands (308 E 49th St) Indian vegetarian.
Mosha Peking (40 W 37th St) Elegant Chinese.
Naftali's (77 Fulton St) Continental meat and seafood.
Verve Naturelle (157 W 57th St) California-style health food.

HINT: *If you want to be "in," refer to Bernstein's-on-Essex as "Shmulk's."*

Late-Evening Munching
(see also "Manhattan at Night")

America
Amsterdam's Bar and Rotisserie
Arquà
Bouley
Brasserie
Cafe des Artistes
Cafe Luxembourg
Cameos
Carnegie Deli
Chelsea Trattoria Italiana
Chez Jacqueline
Chin Chin
Claire
Dieci
Dock's
Empire Diner
Frank's
Graziella
Great Jones Street Cafe

Indochine
Kiev
La Gauloise
Le Chantilly
L'Ecluse
Le Zinc
Lox Around the Clock
Lucy's
Market Diner
Mezzogiorno
Moondance Diner
103 Second Avenue Restaurant
Orso
Remi
Restaurant Florent
Sam's
Tommy Tang's
Umberto's

Neighborhood Bests

Chelsea
Artie's Warehouse Restaurant
Bistro Bordeaux
Chelsea Central
Chelsea Place
Chelsea Trattoria Italiana
Frank's
Harvey's Chelsea
Olde Garden Cafe and Winery
Quatorze
Sofi

Chinatown
Bo Bo
Canton
H.S.F.
Say Eng Look
Wong Kee

East and West Village
Au Troquet
Cafe de Bruxelles
Cafe Loup
Caffe Dante
Chez Ma Tante
Coach House
Corner Bistro
Cucina Stagionale
Da Silvano
Graziella
Home on the Range
Il Mulino
Indochine
Joe's
John Clancy's
John's Pizzeria
La Bohème

La Metairie
La Ripaille
La Lunchonette
Lavin's
Lou G. Siegel
Maryland Crab House
Periyali
Rakel

Midtown
Akbar
American Festival Cafe
Aquavit
Barbetta
B. Smith's
Cafe des Sports
Cafe Europa and La Brioche
Cafe Suisse
Cafe Un Deux Trois
Carnegie Deli
Chalet Suisse
Chez Josephine
Chez Louis
Chin Chin
Darbar
Dawat
Dock's
Fortune Garden Pavilion
Four Seasons
Grand Central Oyster Bar
    and Restaurant
Guido's
Hard Rock Cafe
Hatsuhana
Kitcho
La Bonne Soupe
La Caravelle
La Côte Basque
Lafayette
La Fondue
La Grenouille
La Reserve
Lattanzi
La Tulipe
Marvlou's

Minetta Tavern
One If By Land,
    Two If By Sea
Paris Commune
Pizza Piazzi
Provence
Ray's Pizza of
    Greenwich Village
Sabor
Scarlet
Second Avenue Kosher Deli
Ye Waverly Inn

Grammercy Park
America
Brandywine
Union Square Cafe

Lower East Side
Katz's Deli
Sammy's Roumanian

Lower Midtown
An American Place
The Ballroom
Cafe Society
Courtyard Cafe
Da Umberto
Eze
Island Grill
Jezebel
Keens Chop House
Landmark Tavern
Laurent
Le Bernardin
Le Biarritz
Le Chantilly
Le Cygne
Les Pyrennes
Lutèce
Kitcho
Marie-Michelle
Mickey Mantle's
Orso
Palm and Palm Too

Palm Court and Edwardian
   Room at the Plaza Hotel
Pietro's
Quilted Giraffe
Rainbow Room
René Pujol
The Russian Tea Room
Sam's
San Domenico
Shinwa
Smith and Wollensky
Sparks
Trumpets at the Grand Hyatt
   Hotel
"21"
The View at the Marriott
   Marquis Hotel
Woods
Woo Lae Oak of Seoul
Wylie's Ribs

Murray Hill
Dolphin
La Colombe d'Or
Marchi's

SoHo and Little Italy
Ballato
Berry's
Ferrara
Food
Greene Street Cafe
I Tre Merli
Mezzagiorno
Moondance Diner
Provence
Raoul's
Spring Street Natural

South Street Seaport
Cafe Mondain
Sweets

TriBeCa
Arqua

Bouley
Capsouto Freres
Chanterelle
Duane Park Cafe
Le Zinc
Lotus Blossom
Montrachet

Upper East Side
Alo Alo
Arizona 206 and Cafe
Azzurro
Boathouse Cafe
Bravo Gianni
Ciaobella
Contrapunto
Dieci
Divino
Erminia
Fu's
Gino
Huberts
Jackson Hole Wyoming
   Burgers
Jim McMullen
Kleine Konditeroi
La Metairie
La Petite Ferme
Le Cirque
Le Refuge
Les Pleiades
Lion's Rock
Nicola's
Old Denmark
Pamir
Paola's
Parioli Romanissimo
Pig Heaven
Pinocchio
Primavera
Rao's (Spanish Harlem)
Ravelled Sleave
Remi
Sarabeth's Kitchen
Sistina

Table d'Hote
Trastevere
Vico
Vivolo
Voulez-Vous
Wilkinson's

Upper West Side
Amsterdam's Bar and
    Rotisserie
Andiamo
Cafe des Artistes
Cafe Luxembourg
Cameos
Coastal
Dock's
Good Enough To Eat
Julia
La Boite en Bois
La Mirabelle
107 West

Sarabeth's Kitchen
Shun Lee Cafe
Sidewalker's
Tavern on the Green
Terrace
West Side Story
Yellow Rose Cafe

Way Downtown
American Harvest
Delmonico's
Donald Sacks
    (World Financial Center)
Fraunces Tavern
Harry's
Harry's at the American
    Exchange
Market Dining Rooms
Restaurant Florent
Tommy Tang's
Windows on the World

Offbeat

The Boathouse Cafe (Central Park) seems to define "off the beaten path," but it's sitting in the middle of Central Park, which is actually the very center of the city. The following places qualify as offbeat for any of a variety of reasons, whether it's location, décor, ambiance, clientele, menu, or all of the above.

Acme Bar and Grill (9 Great Jones St bet Lafayette St and Broadway)
Artie's Warehouse Restaurant (539 W 21st St)
Banana's (29 St Mark's Pl bet First and Second Ave)
Bellevues (496 Ninth Ave)
Canal Bar (511 Greenwich St)
Great Jones St Cafe (54 Great Jones St at Bowery)
Landmark Tavern (626 11th Ave at 46th St)
NoHo Star (330 Lafayette St)
Rao's (455 E 114th St)
Restaurant Florent (69 Gansevoort St at Washington St)
Ruby's River Road Cafe (1754 Second Ave bet 91st and 92nd St)
Sabor (20 Cornelia St at Sixth Ave)
Sammy's Roumanian (157 Chrystie St)
Veselka Coffee Shop (144 Second Ave)

Old-Timers

A lot of history has been made at these spots.

Antolotti's
Barbetta
Cafe des Artistes
Delmonico's
Frank's
Fraunces Tavern Restaurant
Harvey's Chelsea
Keens Chop House
Landmark Tavern
Marchi's
McSorley's Old Ale House
Minetta Tavern

Olde Garden Cafe and
   Winery
Oyster Bar at Grand Central
   Station
Palm
Peter Luger
Pete's Tavern
Ratner's
The Russian Tea Room
Sweets
"21"
Ye Waverly Inn

Outdoor Dining

The following restaurants feature garden, patio, or sidewalk dining.

American Festival Cafe
Aureole
Cafe Bel Canto
Caffe Dante
Chez Ma Tante
Ciaobella
Coastal
Courtyard Cafe
Figaro
Fountain Cafe
Ginger Man
Julia
La Bohème
La Goulue
La Petite Ferme
Le Bilboquet
Le Relais

Lion's Rock
Maruzzella
Mezzogiorno
Mortimer's
Museum Cafe
One If By Land, Two If By
   Sea
Pete's Tavern
Provence
Raphael
The Riviera
The Saloon
Stanhope Hotel
Sumptuary
Tavern on the Green
211 Restaurant
White Horse Tavern

Party Rooms

Barbetta
Bouley
Chin Chin

Coach House
Darbar
Delmonico's

Four Seasons
Frank's
Fraunces Tavern Restaurant
Ginger Man
Jim McMullen
John Clancy's
Keens
Kitcho
La Grenouille
La Reserve
Laurent
Le Bernardin
Le Cirque
Le Cygne
Le Régence
Lutece

Marylou
Montrachet
One If By Land, Two If By
  Sea
Peter Luger
Primavera
Rainbow Room
Sam's
San Domenico
Sign of the Dove
Smith and Wollensky
Sparks
Tavern on the Green
Windows on the World
Most hotels

People Watching

These places offer a good view of the passing parade.

America
Bellini
Bice
Bouley
China Grill
Elaine's
Four Seasons
Jezebel's
Jim McMullen's
La Reserve
Le Cirque

Mickey Mantle's
Mortimer's
Palio
Palm
Palm Court at the Plaza
  Hotel
Rainbow Room
The Russian Tea Room
Tavern on the Green
"21"

Pubs

The pub seems to be an endangered species in Manhattan, but there are still a few of these venerable institutions, where you can go for good brew, good times, and sometimes good food. Here are the heartiest survivors.

Billy's (948 First Ave at 53rd St)
Chelsea Place (147 Eighth Ave bet 17th and 18th St)
Great Jones St Cafe (54 Great Jones St)
Jimmy Day's (186 W Fourth St)
Landmark Tavern (626 11th Ave at 46th St)
McSorley's Old Ale House (15 E Seventh St at Third Ave)

Pete's Tavern (66 Irving Pl) New York's oldest continually operating pub.
P. J. Clark's (915 Third Ave at 55th St)
White Horse Tavern (567 Hudson St)

Romantic

Romance is never out of style at:

Barbetta
Bouley
Cafe des Artistes
Cafe Pierre
Cafe Trevi
Chanterelle
Chez Jacqueline
Chez Josephine
Four Seasons
La Bohème
La Caravelle
La Côte Basque
La Grenouille
La Metairie (uptown)
La Reserve
La Ripaille
Le Train Bleu

One If By Land, Two If By
    Sea
Palm Court and Edwardian
    Room at the Plaza Hotel
Paola's
Pete's Tavern
Rainbow Room
Sign of the Dove
Sofi
Tavern on the Green
    (Crystal Room)
Terrace
Time and Again
Trastevere
Under the Stairs
Windows on the World

Sandwiches

There are thousands (yes, thousands) of places that serve sandwiches in Manhattan, and most of them are pretty ordinary. But the following choices turn out exceptionally good combinations for eating in or taking out.

America (9-13 E 18th St)
Burke and Burke (2 E 23rd St)
Brasserie (100 E 53rd St)
Carnegie Deli (854 Second Ave at 55th St)
Cleaver Company (229 W Broadway)
Delices de France (289 Madison Ave)
Donald Sacks (120 Prince St and World Financial Center)
Food (127 Prince St)
Manganaro's Hero Boy (492 Ninth Ave bet 37th and 38th St)
Peter Dent (120 Hudson St)
Telephone Bar and Grill (149 Second Ave)

Seafood

Coastal
Dock's
Dolphin
Grand Central Oyster Bar
  and Restaurant
Island Grill
John Clancy's
Le Bernardin
Le Cirque

Maryland Crab House
Marylou's
Primola
Remi
Sweets
Trumpet's at the Grand
  Hyatt
Wilkinson's

Shopping and Snacking

In another era, eating in a department-store lunch room was a special treat. Because they were operated as a customer convenience and not necessarily to make a profit, they served excellent food at reasonable prices. Well, you can still eat well, if not so inexpensively, at these stylish restaurants in some of New York's major department stores:

Le Cafe (women's store) at Barney's

Cafe Vienna (7th floor) and **Pasta and Cheese** (5th floor) at Bergdorf's

40 Carrots (lower level), **Le Train Bleu** (6th floor), and **Showtime Cafe** (7th floor) at Bloomingdale's

Intermission (6th floor) and **Soup Bar** (10th floor) at Lord and Taylor

Cafe L'Etoile (balcony), **the Fountain** (5th floor), and the **Patio** (8th floor) at Macy's

Steaks

Ben Benson's
Christ Cella (but not what it
  used to be)
Frank's
Le Steak
Manhattan Cafe
Palm and Palm Too

Peter Luger (in Brooklyn)
Pen and Pencil
Pietro's
Post House
Smith and Wollensky
Sparks

Sunday Dining

Alo Alo
America
American Festival Cafe

Arizona 206 and Cafe
Aurora
B. Smith's

Cafe des Artistes
Cafe Luxembourg
Carnegie Deli
Chelsea Central
Chez Jacqueline
Chez Louis
Chin Chin
Coastal
Coach House
Contrapunto
Corner Bistro
Darbar
Dawat
Dock's
Fu's
Good Enough To Eat
Indochine
John Clancy's
La Bohème
La Boite en Bois
La Bonne Soupe
La Gauloise
La Metairie (Village and
    Uptown)
Landmark Tavern
La Tulipe
Le Chantilly
Little Nell's Tea Room

Manhattan Island
Marie-Michelle
Mezzaluna
Mezzogiorno
Mickey Mantle's
Minetta Tavern
Oriental Town Seafood
    Restaurant
Orso
Pamir
Pig Heaven
Primavera
Provence
Quatorze
Remi
Restaurant Florent
River Cafe
The Russian Tea Room
San Domenico
Sarabeth's Kitchen
Sign of the Dove
Sistina
Tavern on the Green
Trastevere
Wilkinson's
Ye Waverly Inn
Most hotel dining rooms

Take It Home, Eat At Home

With both members of the household working and little time to prepare for guests, taking home already prepared food has become very popular. In the "Food Shops" section of this book's regular edition, you'll find reviews of numerous places that have excellent carry-out food. Prime dishes can be obtained at Balducci's, Dean & Deluca, Grace's Marketplace, and Zabar's.

Dial-a-Dinner (779-1222) is the brainchild of David Blum, who guarantees that within 60 to 90 minutes he will deliver (in a tux and with an orchid from Rhinelander Florist) dinners from a selection of restaurants listed in his catalog (he will send you one upon request). His hours are 3-7 p.m. daily, but he offers noon-time service for businesses. The tab: the restaurant bill plus a 20 percent service charge and optional tip.

The following restaurants offer take-out dishes.

Acme Bar and Grill
Amsterdam's Bar and
  Rotisserie
Arcadia
The Ballroom
Carnegie Deli
Chez Lanu
Chez Louis
Chin Chin
Coastal
Carolina
Darbar
Dawat
Divino
E.A.T.
Ecco-LA
Fraunces Tavern Restaurant
Hamburger Harry's
Hard Rock Cafe
Harper

Jackson Hole Wyoming
  Burgers
John Clancy's
Kitcho
La Colombe d'Or
La Gauloise
Le Bistro
Levana
Lou G. Siegel
Manhattan Island
Mocca Hungarian Restaurant
Mortimer's
Parma
Pig Heaven
Positively 104th St
Quilted Giraffe
Ravelled Sleave
Sarabeth's Kitchen
Sidewalker's
Zarela

Tea

The real heart of the classic British afternoon tea is the scone, a cousin of the biscuit. It is served warm, with preserves and clotted cream. The best teas are Earl Grey (light), Darjeeling (strong, dark Indian), and China Tea (mild and floral). Besides cream and sugar, proper accessories include a pitcher of hot water and a small silver strainer to catch the tea leaves. You can partake of this civilized ritual at a number of New York hotels, restaurants, and department stores.

Atrium at the Berkshire Place (21 E 52nd St)

Barclay Restaurant at Hotel Inter-Continental (111 E 48th St)

Cafe Vienna (754 Fifth Ave)

Cocktail Terrace at the Waldorf-Astoria (301 Park Ave at 49th St)

Gold Room at the Helmsley Palace (455 Madison Ave)

Le Cafe at Barney's (Seventh Ave and 17th St)

Le Salon at the Stanhope (995 Fifth Ave at 81st St)

Le Train Bleu at Bloomingdale's (59th St and Third Ave)

Les Delices Guy Pascal (939 First Ave at 52nd St, 1231 Madison Ave at 89th St)

Little Nell's Tea Room (343 E 85th St bet First and Second Ave)

Lounge at the Mayfair Regent (610 Park Ave at 65th St)
Oak Room at the Algonquin Hotel (59 W 44th St)
Palm Court at the Plaza (Fifth Ave and 59th St)
Peninsula Hotel (700 Fifth Ave at 55th St)
Polo at the Westbury Hotel (Madison Ave at 69th St)
Rotunda at the Pierre (2 E 61st St)
Sant Ambroeus (1000 Madison Ave at 77th St)
Serendipity 3 (225 E 60th St)
Stone Room at the National Academy of Design (1083 Fifth Ave
   at 89th St)
Terrace 5 (Trump Tower, 5th level)
"21" (21 W 52nd St)

Views

Contrary to the axiom that good food does not come with a good view, the food at all of these "rooms with a view" is very good.

American Festival Cafe (Rockefeller Plaza) From the sidelines of the skating rink, the art deco monuments of Rockefeller Plaza tower above you.
Boathouse Cafe (Central Park, East Side entrance) From lakeside, you get a you-are-there view of Central Park, and the city skyline looms above the tree tops.
Rainbow Room (Rockefeller Center) This elegant and romantic perch provides a panoramic midtown view.
River Cafe (1 Water St, Brooklyn) A window seat gives you that famous view of the downtown skyline you've seen on post cards and in movies.
Terrace (400 W 119th St) The windows here show you what the city looks like from uptown.
View (Marriott Marquis Hotel) You're high above Times Square— and revolving.
Windows on the World (World Trade Center, 107th floor) You can't dine and gaze from a higher point, unless you're in a plane.

Western

These places are a good distance from the Wild West, but they do their best to deliver a taste of cattle country. Arizona 206 and Cafe (206 E 60th St), Border Cafe (2637 Broadway at 100th St), Cadillac Bar (15 W 21st St), El Rio Grande (Third Ave bet 37th and 38th St), and Yellow Rose Cafe (450 Amsterdam Ave bet 81st and 82nd St).

Wine Bars

Manhattan's better-known wine bars include **Cafe Europa** and **La Brioche** (347 E 54th St), **Cellar in the Sky** (1 World Trade Center), **I Tre Merli** (463 W Broadway bet Prince and Houston St), **Jacqueline's** (132 E 61st St), **Lavin's** (23 W 39th St), **SoHo Kitchen and Bar** (103 Greene St bet Prince and Spring St), and **Terrace 5** (Trump Tower, level 5). If you are really interested in the world of wine, I suggest you contact Stephen Tanzer, Tanzer Business Communications, P.O. Box 392, Prince Station, NY 10012 (777-1006). His bimonthly publication, *The New York Wine Cellar*, can save you money and provide important information on wine locations.

Alphabetical Restaurant Listing

ADAMS RIB

338 First Ave
535-2112
Lunch, Dinner: Daily
Moderate

There was a good deal of consternation by many, including myself, when word got out that Adams Rib was moving. Would it be as good or as comfortable as it was at its old location in the Volney Hotel? Thank goodness, the answer is affirmative. The atmosphere may not be all that it was before, but the new spot is very cozy, especially the back dining room. There just aren't that many good roast-beef houses in New York, and this one has to be at the top of the list. The showpiece, of course, is Adam's Rib, but they even have Eve's Rib for lighter dining. All this is accompanied by wonderful Yorkshire pudding, a strong horseradish sauce, fresh broiled mushrooms, and a real Idaho baked potato, not the mushy foil-wrapped variety. Non-beef lovers can savor the shrimp scampi, lobster tails, breast of chicken Milanese, or several other seafood dishes. They even bake their own bread here, which leaves the place smelling just like Grandma's kitchen. For lunch there is a roast beef sandwich served on toasted French bread with French fries, along with some great salads. The Garden of Eve salad is full of forbidden vegetables, or so they claim. The apricot torte or Swiss chocolate pie will finish filling you up. For those of my readers who have tried Lawry's Prime Rib in Los Angeles, which I think is terrific, this is the closest equivalent in New York.

AMERICA
9-13 E 18th St
505-2110
Lunch, Dinner: Daily; Brunch: Sat, Sun
Inexpensive to moderate

Only in New York could you find a place like this. It's big, big, big! The building is enormous—it used to be a carpet showroom. The bar is enormous—when it's full, it looks like a yuppie convention. The menu is enormous—not dozens, but hundreds of items. The portions are enormous. And the noise level is enormous when all 350 to 400 seats are filled. But the good news is that the tab is small. Well, where do you start? They have a dozen or so egg dishes and just as many omelets. There are delicious griddle cakes, including sweet-potato pancakes. Excellent side dishes range from "hash-slinger" potatoes to white-corn hush puppies to Boston brown bread and even Cincinnatis (shoestring French fries drenched in gravy). Appetizers run the gamut from New Orleans Cajun popcorn (deep-fried crawfish tails) to buffalo chicken wings (deep-fried and marinated) to New Mexican black-bean cakes to Oregon mushroom cakes—to which, as you'd expect, I am partial. There are several dozen main-course entrees, from American chop suey to New England roast turkey to shrimp jambalaya to South Carolina crab cakes and everything in between. Oh, and add hamburgers, chili, pasta, pizza, and absolutely the best sandwiches you can imagine. Then there are the desserts. Tennessee Black Bottom pie, Tollhouse cookies, Death by Chocolate, Key Lime mousse, New Orleans pralines—you name it, they've got it. Come on down, especially if you're escorting a group of youngsters.

AMERICAN FESTIVAL CAFE
20 W 50th St
246-6699
Lunch: Mon-Fri; Dinner: Daily; Brunch: Sat, Sun
Moderate

The big attraction here is the location. The ice rink at Rockefeller Center is glamorous in summer or winter, and when you add the novelty of various ethnic promotions to the setting, the American Festival Cafe fills the bill as a unique New York attraction. There's always a lot going on at Rockefeller Center: entertainment, shopping, eating, and people watching. I'd say it's a must for any visitor to the city. The regular menu features an excellent fisherman's combo platter of oysters, clams, shrimp, and lump crab meat for appetizers, and there are good salads, sandwiches, and items from the charcoal grill. The Salmagundi salad (greens, veal bacon, corn-cob ham, smoked turkey, peppered beef, and cheese) is delightful, as are the grilled leg of lamb and the skewer of shrimp and scallops with fried rice. For kids, the hamburgers are just right, and the desserts are unusually appetizing. Try the key lime pie, the bread pudding with sour mash whiskey sauce, or the flaming crepe with New York State apples (not as good as Oregon ones, however!). A large selection of domestic and imported beers are also available.

AMERICAN HARVEST

Vista International Hotel
3 World Trade Center
938-9100, 432-9334
Breakfast, Lunch: Mon-Fri; Dinner: Mon-Sat
Moderate to expensive

I usually don't get excited about dining in hotel restaurants, be-cause their convenience is often their best quality. But this one is a bit different. Hilton International has done an excellent job. The décor is Early American; a selection of antiques enhances the ambi-ance. The restaurant is divided into three areas, and the tables are arranged far enough apart to create a very comfortable and plea-sant dining experience. The menu changes, as the name implies, with each month's harvest. For example, Long Island duckling ap-pears on the menu every month, with the preparation varying ac-cording to the seasonal harvest. The vegetable or produce that is featured during a specific month is prepared in a variety of ways. Order from an extensive à la carte menu or select dinner at a fixed price with appetizer or soup, main course, three vegetables, plus dessert and coffee or tea. Actually, the fixed-price dinner is the best value. A typical selection of vegetables includes carrots, spring squash, cauliflower, and buttered herb crumbs, sweet and sour beets, broccoli buds with cashew nuts, and new potatoes with dill— quite an offering! For the main course, the seafood is excellent; sea trout, Florida pompano, and butterflied shrimp are among the best selections. I also recommend the stuffed lamb chops and the steaks. Make way for the dessert trolley! It's magnificent, laden with choc-olate cheesecake, chocolate layer cake, maple-date pecan pie, maple mousse loaf, et cetera—all made in the hotel. The American Harvest is a delightful place to bring guests. It's well worth the trip downtown.

AN AMERICAN PLACE
2 Park Ave (at 32nd St)
684-2122
Lunch: Mon-Fri; Dinner: Mon-Sat
Moderately expensive to expensive

Larry Forgione, the owner-chef of An American Place, hopes that the third time is a charm. His relatively new quarters are in a location that has had two unhappy restaurant experiences. It is obvious that Larry is the expert in the kitchen, for there is no question about the quality and attractiveness of the food here. It's just too bad that he isn't as talented when it comes to the front of the house. His room is big, dull, and unattractively lit. And to add to the dullness, his help are dressed in the drabbest gear imaginable: plain white shirts, ugly neckties, and nondescript trousers. The art deco lighting does nothing for the guests or the ambiance. But enough of the negatives. If I had guests from overseas, and I wanted to give them a quick, all-American taste experience, I'd bring them here. With lunch and dinner dishes featuring the best from across the land, Larry Forgione features such delicacies as Florida's Key West shrimp, Chicago stockyard chowder with white beans, fried New England Ipswich clams, and grilled Maine sea scallops. The dessert selections come wrapped in the old red, white, and blue: banana betty, apple pan dowdy, old-fashioned berry shortcake, domestic farmstead cheeses, and angel food chiffon. Forget about the funereal atmosphere. Let the talented and polite personnel pamper you, and concentrate on some of the best food presentations in Manhattan.

ANDIAMO
1991 Broadway
(at 67th St, in the back of Cafe Bel Canto)
362-3315
Lunch: Mon-Fri; Dinner: Daily
Moderate

The old saying "If you have something good, people will find you" surely applies to Andiamo. Tucked away in the back of the popular Cafe Bel Canto in the Lincoln Center area, Andiamo is one of the most attractive and tasteful rooms in town. The airy bi-level restaurant is decorated with artwork from the personal collection of the owner, Lewis Futterman. The lighting is flattering, and the staff gives you a sincere and pleasant greeting. The selection of hot and cold openers include sautéed shrimp, marinated beef carpaccio, and poached lobster. I'd suggest saving room for a pasta dish; the crab meat tortelli in carrot butter sauce is one of the best. Larger portions of pasta are available as a main course, or you can feast upon grilled rack and loin of lamb, grilled Norwegian salmon, seared sea scallops, or roast squab. The portions are king sized and expertly presented. Sheer artistry is the only way to describe the desserts. There is a layered mousse of chocolate and raspberry, homemade gelato in a choice of flavors and toppings, mascarpone cheese terrine with espresso sauce, and a chocolate ganache torte in vanilla sauce. Andiamo is destined to become a fixture in the neighborhood.

ANTOLOTTI'S
337 E 49th St
223-9609
Lunch: Mon-Fri; Dinner: Daily
Moderate

When you've been successful in the same business for nearly four decades, you must be doing something right. And Antolotti's surely is. You can tell from the moment you enter: the greeting is pleasant, and the seating prompt and efficient. You have no sooner taken your place in the pleasant, compact room, decorated with an eclectic mix of pictures and memorabilia, than one of the crisply professional staff places excellent bread, healthy nibbles, and cole slaw in front of you. Then you're presented with a huge menu of Italian and continental choices. It seems impossible for a kitchen to do a dozen veal dishes so well, but they do. In addition, there are wonderful seafood items, from sole to lobster, chicken any way you want it, pork and lamb chops, steaks, and a wide choice of typical Italian dishes. The homemade manicotti, canelloni, and lasagna can't be beaten. All the dishes that are supposed to be served hot are steaming, and the cold ones taste as though they just came from the refrigerator. Nothing is cooked ahead of time. If you can muster up the appetite for spumoni or rum cake, more power to you. I chose the big iced dish of fresh fruit to finish the meal. Two generations of the Antolotti family are on the job: Dad is seated at a booth, keeping an eye on his success story, while his son tends bar and greets a host of regular customers who have been coming here for years. An attractive party room is also available.

AQUAVIT
13 W 54th St
307-7311
Lunch: Mon-Fri; Dinner: Mon-Sat
Cafe: Moderately expensive; Dining Room: Expensive

Just as you would expect from the organized and hospitable Scandinavians, Aquavit presents an attractive, wholesome background for some very tasty—and expensive—meals. The setting is also a feast for the eyes: you have a choice of eating upstairs in the moderately priced cafe, or in several areas downstairs, including an attractive covered patio with a waterfall. Here the diner looks eight stories skyward at an unusually attractive atrium. The meal starts with a healthy breadbasket, including delicious seven-grain bread. Upstairs, the Cafe offers appetizers heavy on the fish side: a herring plate, Scandinavian shrimp soup, and smoked Swedish salmon. Main course specialties include delicious Swedish meatballs, whole cold poached lobster, a typical smorgasbord plate, and Kaldolmar (Savoy cabbage rolls with ligonberry). Downstairs, hold on to your wallet for the three-course, price-fixed banquet that rose over 30 percent in price in just the first few months of operating. The first course features a choice of some 10 items, including blinis, traditional gravlas, and marinated arctic venison. Then on to such second course entrees as poached halibut, turbot or salmon, filet of veal and sweetbreads, and snow grouse (a real delight!). No ordinary dessert menu here. Choices include Swedish pancakes, Swedish blueberry pie, and a fabulous chocolate cake with burned almond crust. You will be impressed with the very polite and attractive ladies and gentlemen who guide you through this sumptuous banquet. They are as low-key as the prices are high.

ARIZONA 206 AND CAFE
206 E 60th St
838-0440
Lunch, Dinner: Daily
Moderate

This establishment has had several reincarnations, and the last one is certainly, well, different! The best of Southwest cuisine and atmosphere has been transported to Manhattan, cactus and all. The front area—a room for drinks and conversation, complete with a fireplace—is pleasant. There is a good-sized bar in the center of the restaurant, and there are tables for serious dining in the back. They've provided some benches with cushions for those who find the wooden fixtures uncomfortable. Arizona 206 is noisy and slightly disorganized—the help get a bit frantic—but don't let that discourage you. Interesting lunch offerings are the baked lamb sandwich with roast garlic mayonnaise, a Farmer's Market salad with goat's blue cheese, pears and hickory-smoked bacon, and an excellent corn-dough pizza with queso blanco cured ham. The dinner menu is much the same, but with a couple of special offerings, like pounded potato with crab meat and chili-rubbed free-range chicken with sautéed broccoli. You might finish up your meal with sweet potato pie or a very passable black-walnut chocolate cake. Lighter dishes are offered at the adjoining cafe.

ARQUA
281 Church St
334-1888
Lunch: Mon-Fri; Dinner: Mon-Sat
Moderate

There are Italian restaurants of every size, price range, and specialty in almost every neighborhood of Manhattan. I sometimes wonder if there aren't more Italian restaurants in Manhattan than in all of Italy. So, to be outstanding in New York, an Italian restaurant must have something special going for it. Arqua is really special because the staff does things so plainly and simply. This is not a fancy, pricey restaurant of the moment. Arqua (named for a small city near Venice) is situated in an old warehouse with high ceilings, which adds to the noisy atmosphere. The folks who run this place are not fancy either. It shows in the TLC they give all the patrons, and the food is exceptional. There's a wonderful salmon mousse or carciofi ripieni (artichoke) starter that I could make do for an entire meal. You can have your choice of any kind of pasta; the best is a delicious ravioli di zucca with pistachios. There are also a number of excellent veal and game dishes. The flourless espresso chocolate cake is so good that I took some home to the bakers at my cake shop in Oregon.

ARTIE'S WAREHOUSE RESTAURANT
539 W 21st St
989-9500
Dinner: Daily
Moderate

Some folks have told me that they are interested in really out-of-the-way places. Well, this one surely falls into that category. Artie's Warehouse Restaurant is located in a warehouse district, and it's actually part of a working warehouse. For a friendly greeting, prompt and efficient service, and good food at reasonable prices, I haven't found too many that beat it. And it certainly is different! Artie himself is a frustrated piano player, who entertains and table-hops. And he keeps a steady eye on the help; they're right on the job, providing informed, courteous service. Start with fried wontons or steamed fish in a bag. Then go on to one of the daily special entrees of veal, chicken or fish, or an Oriental offering. I can heartily recommend the spareribs or the shrimp scampi. If you're a vegetarian, there is even a special sautéed vegetable plate. All the entrees are served with potato or rice and a fresh vegetable. Be sure to save room for the great homemade desserts. What an offering! Chocolate or orange cheesecake, chocolate mud cake, lemon mousse, chocolate mousse, pecan pie, and even marzipan-apricot cake. What a spot for relaxing and enjoying a leisurely dinner, topped off with such exotic drinks as amaretto coffee, an Irish Float, a Tipsy Monk, or an Angel Cloud. You'll have to go there to find out exactly what they are! There are a dozen different coffees on the menu. Dinner in a warehouse? Sure, but you don't have to wear your overalls.

AU CAFE DE BRUXELLES
118 Greenwich Ave
206-1830
Lunch: Tues-Sat; Dinner: Daily; Brunch: Sun
Moderate

One of the treats at a county fair is the Belgian waffles booth. There always seem to be a queue at that concession, and for good reason. In New York, you don't have to go to the county fair. Just make your way to the Village, where Thierry, the chef, and his wife, Patricia, set an informal table brimming with specialties from Belgium. The waffles are served with whipped cream and chocolate and strawberry sauce; they are a meal in themselves. But here I go talking about desserts before we've even started our meal. Hot chicken liver custard in port wine sauce, homemade country paté, and stuffed mussels with garlic (yes, heavy on the garlic) are some of the house hors d'oeuvres. Entree choices range from medallions of monkfish to dark Belgian beer stew, a house specialty, to several steak dishes. On certain nights, Belgian dishes like chicken water-zooi, Bruxelle bouillabaisse, and a very tasty choucroute (sauer-kraut) dish are offered. They're also available anytime, if you give them adequate enough notice. But back to those desserts. If you don't try the waffles, at least sink your teeth into the tasty apple or apricot tarts made in Thierry's own kitchen.

AU TROQUET
328 W 12th St
924-3413
Dinner: Daily
Moderate

This is one of those difficult-to-find places in the Village. If you're arriving by taxi, allow extra time since most drivers will have trouble delivering you to the front door. And be sure you call for reservations; the place is small, and it is very popular with neighbors as well as knowledgeable people who have previously enjoyed

Au Troquet's dining delights. This is a no-nonsense French country restaurant, where professional people prepare food professionally. Your plate looks like a colorful magazine ad—flamboyant in presentation—and it's especially good in the taste category. Au Troquet deserves special mention for its seasonings alone; they know how it's done. The soups are all delicious, as is the paté de foie de canard. You can go on to filet of sole, grilled salmon, lobster, or a fabulous rabbit dish. There is almost always a fine selection of lamb dishes available. Homemade desserts include a great soufflé, mousse, and sorbets. This is the kind of place you want to go to when you feel like having a relaxed, cozy dinner for two. It will surely help cement that business relationship—or maybe even a more personal one!

AZZURRO
1625 Second Ave (at 84th St)
517-7068
Dinner: Daily
Moderate

I'd give this place an A-plus for their polite and well-informed help. What a joy it is to find a restaurant that has no affectations, no unnecessary waiting, and no maitre d' with permanently outstretched palm. Instead, you find really nice folks who want to make your dining experience a pleasant one. Azzurro is a tiny hole-in-the-wall with a dozen-plus tables, a tile floor, and a wholesome, informal atmosphere. Neither the waiters nor the customers are dressed up, but the food is! An absolutely marvelous fresh minestrone soup is great to start with, as is the mixed eggplant, Sicilian style. The linguini with tuna fish or the maccaruna chi sarde (bucatini with fresh sardines, raisins, pinoli nuts, and wild fennel) are outstanding. For heartier appetites, there are grilled lamb chops, a breaded veal chop, and steak. The boys in the kitchen are evidently as talented as the ones out front. You'll have a great time and a great meal. Be sure to call for reservations; they are very busy.

BARBETTA
321 W 46th St (at Ninth Ave)
246-9171
Lunch, Dinner: Mon-Sat
Moderate to expensive

This is an elegant restaurant with Piemontese cuisine; Piemonte is located in the northern part of Italy, and the cuisine reflects that charming part of the country. You can dine here in European elegance. It is one of New York's oldest restaurants still owned by the family that founded it, and the family has been here for nearly eight decades. One of the special attractions about Barbetta is dining alfresco in the garden during the summer. There is a brunch-type multicourse menu, as well as a before-theater dinner menu, which offers a choice of a fish specialty, baby salmon, calf's brains, and a number of other selections served expeditiously so that you can make the opening curtain. If you have more time and can enjoy a leisurely dinner, think about the minestrone soup, that is almost a meal in itself, the ravioli that is made by hand, or the fabulous mushroom salad. Barbetta specializes in fish and game dishes that vary daily. If you're lucky enough to find squab on the menu, by all means try it. Other selections include veal kidneys, beef braised in red wine with polenta, or a delicious sirloin of beef. Desserts include several chocolate offerings and an assortment of cooked fruits, as well as one of the best creme caramels in the city. To be in business in the highly competitive restaurant field for such a long time, Barbetta's has to be doing something right—and they are.

BETWEEN THE BREAD	**CAFE AT BETWEEN THE BREAD**
141 E 56th St	
888-0449	145 W 55th St
Breakfast, Lunch: Mon-Sat;	581-1189
Dinner: Mon-Fri	Lunch: Mon-Fri;
	Dinner: Mon-Sat

Moderate

These two sister operations serve a variety of healthy and appetizing dishes. They also offer fine packaged foods and a delivery and catering service. Between the Bread is a spotless establishment; you can eat at a counter or at a table. The menu covers a wide assortment of sandwiches and salads, plus a selection of heartier dishes; my favorite is chicken pot pie. A fine selection of desserts is available. One of the highlights of the establishment is the enormous selection of delicious oversized homemade muffins, all baked daily. The variety is tremendous: fresh bran and honey, oat bran, apple cinnamon, apricot, pineapple, carrot, banana, chocolate chip, strawberry, peanut butter, coconut, peach, and on and on. The Cafe is a bit more formal, with a very attractive light and airy garden room. The big winner here is roasted red snapper with rosemary and red wine sauce, served with crisp potatoes. Both are very professional establishments.

BILLY'S

948 First Ave
355-8920, 753-1870
Lunch, Dinner: Daily
Moderate

If you like old-fashioned setups, complete with white tiled floors, checkered tablecloths, and a busy bar right in the center of the dining area, then Billy's is your kind of place. Established in 1870, this bustling pub-restaurant is a First Avenue institution, where the food is just as inviting as the atmosphere. It's been in the same family since opening day! No menus, just a blackboard listing steaks, scallops, chops, hamburgers, and the like. All are well prepared, with large portions accompanied by fair French fries or non-foil-wrapped baked potatoes. Cole slaw is served when you are seated. Oh, yes. The waiters are vintage New York. For example, when a party of four arrives, they'll ask, "Do you wish to sit together?" But they are efficient, pleasant guys. A word about the bread. The ethnic mix of the Big Apple makes for exceptional talent in baking, and you can take advantage of these fine breads at many restaurants like Billy's. Desserts include delicious ice cream, cheesecake, pies, and homemade rice pudding. Try the Irish coffee with real whipped cream to top it all off.

BISTRO-BORDEAUX

407 Eighth Ave
594-6305
Lunch: Mon-Fri; Dinner: Mon-Sat
Moderate

It's not easy to find a pleasant, reliable spot to eat in the Madison Square Garden area, but Bistro-Bordeaux, a delightful French restaurant, is a very satisfactory place for either a pre-Garden or after-Garden meal. Alan and Gerard (one's in the front and one's in the kitchen), who have had lots of experience in various New York restaurants, have put together an unpretentious, homey bistro with tasty and well-prepared food at reasonable prices. I was struck by how eager they and their staff are to provide for their guests. If there are any complaints, it's that the portions are too big. This is one place from which you can be sure you won't go away hungry. Escargots, paté, smoked salmon—all are available for starters, along with fresh artichokes and fresh asparagus, if in season. The filet mignon is done to perfection, the grilled sole and grilled chicken are both delicious, and the escalope de veau is really special. The vegetables have a home-cooked flavor. Desserts seem a bit expensive compared to the rest of the dinner, but they're good. Of all the desserts (and there are nearly a dozen), the creme caramel is the best. Instead of wasting your money on junk-food places in and around Madison Square Garden, I suggest this bistro as a handy, satisfying alternative.

BOATHOUSE CAFE
Central Park
517-CAFE
Lunch, Dinner: Daily
Moderate

Central Park has come back to life, and the Boathouse Cafe is one of its best attractions. It's situated in a charming spot on the east side of the park, between the 72nd Street and 79th Street entrances; a free trolley brings patrons from the 72nd Street and Fifth Avenue park entrance. The dockside has been partially tented, and authentic Venetian gondolas are available (by reservation) for rent, as are rowboats. The view is great, the setting couldn't be more romantic, and the food is tasty and well presented. The menu is Northern Italian, with a variety of pasta and unusual ravioli. There is a great private party area located in a landscaped English garden. What a spot to launch your hot new product!

BOULEY
165 Duane St
608-3852
Lunch: Mon-Fri; Dinner: Mon-Sat
Moderately expensive

A young lady rushed into a New York store to get the latest edition of this book, breathlessly announcing to the clerk that her boyfriend was going to propose within the next few days and she wanted the setting to be a very romantic one. Where else should she look for such a spot, she said, but in this book! Well, if I had had the opportunity to speak personally with the young lady, I would have recommended Bouley in the TriBeCa area. David Bouley of Montrachet Restaurant fame has outdone himself in creating this beautiful dining spot. It's spacious and charming, with very able personnel to complement the outstanding food. There are wonderful decorative touches, like the marvelously ornate doors and the attractive Limoges china. It would be difficult to go wrong with any item from the varied and complete menu; there are a number of salads, seafood dishes (halibut, scallops, lobster, and sea bass), and game in season. Absolutely wonderful bread is served warm and fresh; I couldn't get enough of it. And what a selection of desserts! Each one is an absolute picture. The soufflés are a specialty, as is the chocolate ganache terrine. There's also a refreshing marinated fresh fruit plate. If you're having an engagement party or any kind of special event, consider having it here.

BRAVO GIANNI
230 E 63rd St
752-7272
Lunch: Mon-Fri; Dinner: Mon-Sat
Moderately expensive

Fans of Bravo Gianni—and there are many—may be upset that I'm mentioning it in this book. They want to keep it a secret. It's so nice and comfortable and the food is so good that they don't want it to become overcrowded and spoiled. But it doesn't look like there's any real danger of that happening, as long as Gianni himself is on the job. The room—not too large—is pleasantly appointed, with beautiful plants on every table; the intimate atmosphere makes it seem as though you're in your own private dining room. And what tastes await you there! You can't go wrong with any of the antipasto selections or soups. But do save room for the tortellini alla panna or the fettuccine con ricotta; no one does them better. I can recommend every dish on the menu, with top billing going to the fish dishes and the rack of lamb. Marvelous desserts, many of them made in house, will surely tempt you. Legions of loyal customers come back again and again; it's easy to see why. But please, keep all of this to yourself!

BULL AND BEAR
301 Park Ave (Waldorf-Astoria Hotel)
872-4900
Lunch, Dinner: Daily; Brunch: Sun
Expensive

The Bull and Bear in the Waldorf-Astoria is as close to London as you can get in Manhattan. The bar is very popular; it has a certain dignified charm. The meal is good, the service professional, and the atmosphere appealing. If a huge hunk of roast beef or some lamb chops make your mouth water, this is the place to go. Excellent seafood is also available. The place exudes solid English tradition and a clublike atmosphere, but the "club" is more of an Englishman's club than an American's. No one was ever burned from too much warmth here. And here's a bit of New York trivia. The Waldorf is built over the tracks of Grand Central Station. If you look to where the Waldorf meets the sidewalk, you will see that they do *not*, in fact, meet at all. The hotel does not rest on the ground but upon piles. Special after-theater suppers are served every night.

CABANA CARIOCA II

133 W 45th St (bet Sixth Ave and Broadway)
730-8375
Lunch, Dinner: Daily
Moderate

There are two Cabana Cariocas, located just several doors from each other. Make sure you go to the one at 133 West 45th Street, not the branch at 123 West 45th Street. The latter is unattractive, smelly, and generally unappetizing, while the former features the best Brazilian and Portuguese cuisine in the city. The atmosphere is homey, the waiters eager to explain their native dishes, and the portions huge. Wonderful homemade chicken soup, fried Portuguese sausage, or a Portuguese omelet will get you off to a good start. Feijoada completa, the Brazilian national dish, is a house favorite. Besides a large selection of seafood, steak, pork, veal, chicken, and liver dishes, there are several different specials every day. Of course, the black beans are a must, and they are delicious. The Cabana is a handy, sensibly priced place for lunch in midtown.

CAFE DES ARTISTES

1 W 67th St
TR7-3500
Lunch: Mon-Fri; Dinner: Daily; Brunch: Sat, Sun
Moderate

With Cafe Des Artistes, owner George Lang created an absolute masterpiece on the West Side, just off Central Park. It's truly a landmark. There are several different dining levels and some hidden tables, giving each diner the impression of being in a small, cozy establishment. Beautiful murals by Christy complement the charming décor, the personnel are wonderfully accommodating, and the food is absolutely delicious. Try the unusual Sunday brunch. Some of the mouth-watering selections include smoked salmon benedict, asparagus omelet, spicy Virginia crab cakes, and delicious stuffed French toast. Dinner appetizers include dill-marinated fish, duck or chicken liver, and a number of seafood items, like oysters, clams, and snails. For the main course, there are sea bass, grilled Coho salmon, broiled veal chops, pork, lamb and beef dishes, and a pasta. By all means, don't overlook the desserts: such dandies as mocha dacquoise, key lime pie, toasted almond cake, chestnut cream torte, and a great dessert platter that features a sample of each. This is a lovely, romantic place at any time, but I especially recommend it for an after-theater supper.

CAFE DES SPORTS
329 W 51st St
581-1283, 974-9052
Lunch: Mon-Fri; Dinner: Daily
Inexpensive

This is a cozy spot, with an intensely loyal following developed over many years of serving good, wholesome food in generous amounts at a reasonable price. The selections change daily, depending on what is available from the marketplaces. I have found the homemade sausage and the London broil to be exceptionally good values. Blue jeans and your most comfortable house dress are perfectly acceptable here. You'll smile along with the hospitable personnel, especially when they hand you a very realistic tab for a most satisfying meal. A second generation of management is carrying on the same quality tradition.

CAFE EUROPA and LA BRIOCHE
347 E 54th St
755-0160
Lunch: Mon-Fri; Dinner: Mon-Sat
Moderate

A charming cafe. It gives you the feeling that you're walking in from the streets of Paris or Munich. I recommend it for either lunch or dinner. For lunch, you might be interested in the imperial sandwich (steak tartare with caviar, icy vodka, and beer), but my choice is the chicken brioche with fresh tarragon, celery, carrots, and mushrooms. It's a hefty portion and just right for a delightful lunch. The brioche offerings change from time to time, variously featuring curried beef, veal marengo, or shrimp and mushroom. The dinner menu is also varied, with entree selections ranging from chicken breast to beef stroganoff to filet of beef Wellington. There is a large selection of desserts, from chocolate mousse to lemon Bavarian cream or bananas with rum. Another dessert alternative is the French, English, or Italian cheese selection served with fruit or nuts. There is an interesting combination of European and Oriental personnel in the kitchen and out front. It all adds up to a most pleasant dining experience.

CAFE LUXEMBOURG
200 W 70th St
873-7411
Dinner: Daily; Brunch: Sun
Moderate

If atmosphere doesn't mean too much to you, you might enjoy Cafe Luxembourg. Physically, it is anything but attractive: the dining room is ugly, and the tables are too close together. However, the food is excellent, and the prices are right. It's no wonder the place is so busy. For appetizers, try the poached oysters in champagne sauce, the chicken-liver terrine, or the country salad with chicory, Roquefort cheese, garlic croutons, and bacon. Go on to the cassoulet, a casserole of pork, duck, white beans, garlic sausage, and tomato sauce, or the sliced breast of duckling salad with pickled turnips, lettuce, and raspberry vinegar sauce. The grilled Coho salmon is done to perfection by executive chef Patrick Clark. The selections vary by season. For dessert, try the white and dark chocolate mousse in chocolate sauce. An annoying policy here is that they don't seat you until everyone in your party arrives.

CAFE MONDAIN
32 Cliff St (bet Fulton and John St)
233-7910
Lunch, Dinner: Mon-Fri
Moderate

One of the drawbacks of the South Street Seaport area is the poor quality of most of the eating establishments. The logic of the restaurant owners must be that tourists come only once, so we don't have to worry about repeat trade. Well, there is one exception to this sad state of affairs. Cafe Mondain, located just a block from the center of the seaport, is a delightful place to lunch when visiting this fascinating part of New York's harbor life. The chef is the proprietor, and he makes sure things run right. The flavors are French, with emphasis on seafood, which certainly makes sense in this district. You can dine on shrimp, filet of sole, boneless filet of trout, or snails. Of course, there are also entrees like veal scaloppine, boneless lamb chops, and excellent steaks. Cafe Mondain is a favorite with the local office workers, which is always a good sign. So, don't waste your time or money on some of the glitzier places in the seaport.

CAFE UN DEUX TROIS
123 W 44th St
354-4148
Lunch: Mon-Fri; Dinner: Daily
Moderate

Paper tablecloths and napkins may seem like a stingy way to dress a restaurant table, but at this bustling cafe, there's a reason. Two reasons, in fact. One is that it helps keep the tab down. The other is to provide drawing paper; crayons are furnished on every table. Doodling helps pass the time, and isn't it something you've always wanted to do since you were a kid? The surroundings (an old hotel lobby) are plain, but the location is handy if you're going to the theater. Service is very prompt and friendly, and prices are moderate. Though the menu is limited, each item is handled with obvious attention to quality and taste. Begin with a hearty onion soup, salade nicoise, or paté de canard. Seafood en papillote is an excellent selection. This spot is popular with the big names in the recording industry and with young people. Maybe aspiring singers will be able to make the deal of their lives over a cup of cappuccino.

CAFFE DANTE
81 MacDougal St
982-5275
Inexpensive

If you are in the mood for a light lunch or supper, Mario Flotta will take good care of you at this busy, popular cafe, one of the oldest in the city. The simple menu features delicious, light Italian-style sandwiches, cold platters, and salads. The real treats are the fabulous Italian cake specialties, like Sacher Sant Ambroeus, ambrosia cake, zabaglione cake, and tiramisu. There are also dozens of Italian pastry items, and the homemade rum cake with gelati is heaven-sent. Speaking of gelati, no one does it better. They make their own, and the fresh fruit gelati is sensational. Of course, no session would be complete without espresso or cappuccino. You can have it any way you want, from Caffe Fantasia, an exotic combination of orange and chocolate and whipped cream, to Cappuccino Dante, a cinnamon and cocoa concoction. Through it all, Dante Aligheri, framed on the wall, is looking down upon you.

CAMEOS
169 Columbus Ave
874-2280
Lunch: Mon-Sat; Dinner: Daily; Brunch: Sun
Moderate

It's a good thing that you'll have to use up a few calories to climb the stairs to this art deco room overlooking busy Columbus Avenue on the Upper West Side. You'll need to make room for the special limited number of dishes on the small Cameos menu. Personally, I prefer a restaurant that does a few things well to one that has a huge selection and every one of them mediocre. Cameos offers a number of perfectly light dishes for those watching their belt size. A number of excellent salads (especially the eafood, the lime, and the salmon) are good choices. Among the entrees, my choice would be tortellini with wild mushrooms or grilled chicken with raspberry vinegar. In the evening, to the accompaniment of popular piano music, you can feast upon marvelous crab cakes or quail to start, and then go on to brook trout, pheasant, or medallions of beef. Desserts prepared in-house include country apple spice cake, creamy cheesecakes, and a great flourless bittersweet chocolate torte. Service is pleasant, even if the kitchen is a bit slow when business is booming. This is definitely not one of the come-and-go trendy operations so common on the West Side.

CANTON
45 Division St
226-4441
Lunch, Dinner: Wed-Sun
No credit cards
Moderate

For those in the know, Canton has been a favorite spot for some time. Why? The place is clean, and the personnel are friendly and very polite. But most of all, unlike so many Chinese restaurants, the cooking is done on an individual basis. It's almost like stepping into the kitchen of a Chinese family. Visit with the waiter and tell him the kind of Cantonese delicacies you wish to have. You will be delighted with the results! I would suggest the butterfly shrimp, the diced chicken with Chinese vegetables and mushrooms, or the fried young squab, Chinese style. All the seafood is fresh and tasty. So, gather up a group of friends for a special Chinese treat. You'll be pleased with the quality of your food *and* the moderate bill.

CARNEGIE DELICATESSEN AND RESTAURANT
854 Seventh Ave (at 55th St)
757-2245
Breakfast, Lunch, Dinner: Daily (6:40 a.m.-4 a.m.)
No credit cards
Moderate

There's no city on earth with delis like New York's, and the Carnegie is one of the best. Its location in the middle of the hotel district makes it perfect for midnight snacks. Everything is made on the premises, and Carnegie offers free delivery at any time between 7 a.m. and 3 a.m., if you're within a five-block radius. Where to start? Your favorite Jewish mother didn't make chicken soup better than the Carnegie's homemade variety. It's practically worth getting sick for! It comes with matzo balls, garden noodles, and fresh rice or fresh, homemade kreplach or real homemade kasha.

And there's more: Great blintzes. Open sandwiches, hot and delicious. Ten different deli and egg sandwiches. A very juicy burger with all the trimmings. Lots of fish dishes. A choice of egg dishes unequaled in New York. Salads. Side orders of everything from hot baked potatoes to potato pancakes. Outrageous cheesecake topped with strawberries, blueberries, pineapple, cherries, or just plain. Desserts from A to Z—even Jell-O.

CHALET SUISSE
6 E 48th St
355-0855
Lunch, Dinner: Mon-Fri
Moderate

When a place is packed every day, you know that something good is going on. And indeed, Chalet Suisse has all the right elements: a small but interesting space, pleasant and accommodating help, a handy midtown location, and hearty food at a reasonable price. You'll find such Swiss offerings as cheese and onion pie, bundnerschinken, veal à la Suisse, and bratwurst. For less Alpine taste buds, there's English sole amandine, breaded veal cutlet (very good), or a refreshing shrimp salad. Desserts include chocolate fondue, kirschtorte, and Swiss apple tart. I would come here just for dessert! Chalet Suisse has been a New York institution for many years.

CHANTERELLE
2 Harrison St (at Hudson St)
966-6960
Dinner: Tues-Sat
Expensive

I knew it was only a matter of time before Karen and David Waltuck would have to move from their tiny SoHo restaurant on Grand Street. The place simply wasn't big enough to handle the legion of loyal customers who feel that Chanterelle is one of the top restaurants in New York. Well, the Waltucks have finally moved to a new space with a larger dining room (seats about 60), a bigger kitchen, and a cute after-dinner area. The setting is formal and attractive, with interesting high stamped-tin ceilings in the historic Mercantile Exchange Building in TriBeCa. The menu changes periodically, but that really isn't important since every dish is a masterful creation. With David in the kitchen, making good use of his marine-biologist background and preparing great fish and lobster dishes, and Karen out front pampering her guests, it is a good bet you won't even notice the size of the tab for the *prix fixe* dinner or the tasting menu.

CHEF CHAN'S
845 Second Ave
687-7471
Lunch, Dinner: Daily
Moderate

Chef Chan's presents excellent Hunan cooking in a clean and efficient Chinese restaurant. The joy here is in Chef Chan's specialties, including my favorites, Chef Chan's Royal platter (lobster and jumbo shrimp with mixed vegetables in a white wine sauce) and the Triple Crown (beef, shrimp, and chicken cooked in a delicate brown sauce). For the hearty diner, there is Hunan beef and lamb or bamboo steamer spareribs. Of course, you can also get the usual Chinese appetizers, soups, and meat, poultry and seafood items, but try something different for a change. They will adjust the degree of spiciness according to your specification. The luncheon menu, served everyday until midafternoon at very moderate prices, features shrimp with garlic sauce, fillet of fish, shredded pork with garlic sauce, and eggplant family style, all served with rice and ice cream. Free delivery is offered for those who want a private Chinese feast at home. Chef Chan has been highly honored for his cooking abilities both in Houston and New York.

CHELSEA CENTRAL
227 10th Ave
620-0230
Lunch: Mon-Fri; Dinner: Daily
Moderate

You're in for a real surprise at Chelsea Central. The tile floor, unimposing atmosphere, and paper tablecloths belie an establishment that turns out some of the best and most sophisticated food in Chelsea. Before you order a meal, be sure to get a reading of the many specials offered by the well-trained and highly efficient staff. Cherrystone clams on the half shell, grilled eggplant and fresh mozzarella served warm, or the fried oysters are all delicious starters. A number of salad dishes are also available, and all portions are very large. But save room for some absolutely great entrees, like roasted rare leg of lamb, grilled salmon filet with spinach pasta, or charcoal-grilled sirloin with pan-roasted new potatoes. The dessert presentations are a feast for the eye as well as the stomach; they look as though they came from an artist's pallet, and all are made in house. When you combine professional service and reasonable prices with delicious, eye-pleasing food, you're a winner. There's every reason to predict that this will be the central place for dining in the Chelsea area for some time to come.

CHELSEA PLACE
147 Eighth Ave (bet 17th and 18th St)
924-8413
Lunch: Mon-Fri; Dinner: Daily
Moderate

Chelsea Place is different—very different. I think the exact word is *eclectic*. You won't be impressed by the neighborhood or the rather disheveled antiques shop through which you enter. A door at the rear of the shop takes you into a noisy, crowded, smoke-filled bar, where the biggest challenge is elbowing through without Gertrude spilling her tray of drinks on you, or getting tangled up with the neighborhood's answer to Ginger Rogers and Fred Astaire as they wheel around the tiny dance floor. Down some stairs and through another room, you enter what looks like a maiden aunt's room, circa 1929: hanging plants, a strange collection of pictures, mismatched chairs, water fountains, ceiling fans—you name it, it's here. But you don't come to Chelsea Place for the décor; you come for the Italian food. And it's excellent. The menu includes traditional fare: baked manicotti, scampi alla Romana, and scaloppini francese. But don't look at the menu. Instead, listen to your waiter recite the list of daily specials, which include fish, poultry, and meat served with first-class vegetables. I recommend this eatery as a very unusual dining experience. It may look like it has been put together by the Marx Brothers, but the culinary satisfaction is strictly first-rate.

CHELSEA TRATTORIA ITALIANA
108 Eighth Ave
924-7786
Lunch: Mon-Fri; Dinner: Mon-Sat
Moderate

The Bitici brothers, the owners of the Chelsea Trattoria, are hard-working Italian boys who know how to make a restaurant tick, and the brother who personally takes care of it is a jewel. Working in the kitchen and out front, he runs a good show. The restaurant, complete with a tile floor and brick walls decked out with wine bottles, looks like the local trattoria in an Italian village. The whole place is friendly, unimposing, and bustling; it's definitely not a trendy, pricey Italian novelty. You come here for good, hearty Italian food, beautifully presented by professional waiters who haven't just graduated from high school. The menu runs the gamut from great soups and pasta to veal scaloppine, boneless breast of chicken sautéed in white wine, sausage, mushrooms and garlic, bay scallops, scampi, and many daily specials. The dessert cart is gorgeous; you can't help bumping into it on your way in. It's loaded with goodies made in-house, including an incredible white and dark chocolate cake. Chelsea is sprouting many excellent eating spots, and this is one of the best. The folks here couldn't be more accommodating; they will even do their best for the drop-in diner. But I strongly suggest you make early reservations.

CHEZ JACQUELINE
72 MacDougal St
505-0727
Dinner: Daily
Moderate

If you dislike the frantic, one-upmanship dining so prevalent these days in Manhattan, then try this modest French bistro in the Village. The atmosphere is very relaxed. You can see cozy couples eating at the bar, or serene seniors holding hands at one of the small number of tables in this popular neighborhood restaurant. Fresh, large salads are a specialty, as well as country paté, duck liver mousse, and mussels with garlic. Among the dozen items regularly available as entrees, house favorites are the broiled rack of lamb, chicken casserole, veal kidneys and veal sweetbreads, and a hearty beef stew in a red wine, tomato, and carrot sauce. The portions are very generous, and the young lovers like the fair prices. If you can manage a dessert, the creme brulée or the white and dark chocolate mousse cake will convince you that someone in the kitchen sure knows what they are doing.

CHEZ JOSEPHINE
414 W 42nd St
594-1925
Dinner: Mon-Sat
Moderate

Those of you who fondly remember the late, great entertainer Josephine Baker will be delighted to know that her classy, cosmopolitan spirit is very much alive in this midtown bistro named in her honor. The proprietor is one of her adopted children, Jean Claude, and he has created a first-class room with sexy and attractive décor and delicious food to match. This is a great rendezvous for late-night diners, particularly those who love show business. Warm crispy oysters and the homemade paté are great for starters. Entrees include such interesting dishes as a delicious boudin noir (blood sausage), lobster cassoulet (with shrimps, scallops, and seafood sausage), and of course, frog's legs, French style. For dessert, bombe pralinée or tartufo caps a tasty meal. A private party room is available upstairs. This place is a charmer, and so is Jean Claude.

CHEZ LOUIS
1016 Second Ave (bet 53rd and 54th St)
752-1400
Lunch: Mon-Fri; Dinner: Daily
Moderately expensive

Faithful readers of this book know your author likes "hands on" operations, the color red, warm bread, and good potatoes. Well, I've found a place where all four are present, and boy, is it a winner! I'm talking about Chez Louis, a family-type French bistro in what was once the Manhattan Market. Start by filling yourself up with the delicious warm bread; then go on to have a meal like you won't find anywhere else in New York. David Liederman of David's cookies fame is a food pro in every sense of the word, and sure enough, there he is doing the baking himself in the downstairs kitchen. It's easy to see why everything tastes so great. There are some novel presentations, like the large platters of tender roast vegetables, roast chicken, roast baby lamb, roast prime rib steak, or the grilled fish of the day. All the dishes are a sight to behold, and just as tasty as they are good to look at. But the real winners are the superb potato cakes sautéed with a bit of garlic. And what a selection of desserts: homemade sorbets, David's cookies and ice cream, and a wonderful deep-chocolate cake. A special late-evening menu is also available. This is a great spot to finish a busy day.

CHEZ MA TANTE
189 W 10th St
620-0223
Lunch: Tues-Fri; Dinner: Daily; Brunch: Sat, Sun
Moderate

This Village cafe is small and unassuming, and you've probably never heard of it. Its main claim to fame is that it's next door to La Metairie, one of the Village's better known (and most expensive) dining spots. The difference between the two restaurants is in the price. Chez Ma Tante does an excellent job at a very reasonable tab. Friendly and cozy in the winter, this bistro opens onto the sidewalk in summer. Two partners do the duties out front and in the kitchen, and they obviously do a consistently good job, since the place is filled with regular patrons. Hors d'oeuvres include duck liver paté, fresh fish terrine on a bed of dill sauce, and a different pasta each day. Outstanding entrees are casserole of jumbo shrimp, "French's favorite dish" (steak, French fries, and green salad), and grilled Norwegian salmon in a cucumber sauce. Grilled swordfish is also a specialty of the house. The profiteroles topped with white-and dark-chocolate sauce (and served hot) is a delicious variation on this popular dish. As a matter of fact, all the desserts rate special mention: warm, fresh caramel apple, triple-layered mousse cake of orange, lime, and lemon, sorbet of orange, passion fruit, and honey in creme sauce. The partners' aunt must have been particularly talented in the kitchen, and fortunately for us, they've invited us to have dinner with her in the Village.

CHEZ NAPOLEON
365 W 50th St
265-6980
Lunch: Mon-Fri; Dinner: Mon-Sat
Inexpensive to moderate

With all the problems of daily life, it's fun to go to a place where the atmosphere is cheerful. Chez Napoleon is that kind of place. The lady who owns it greets you like a long lost friend and seats you in a small, clean dining area. It's an old house—warm and cozy and obviously a neighborhood favorite for many years. The cooking is dependable and hearty, and although the portions are small, you'll be satisfied. My top recommendations from the large menu are coquille St. Jacques, bouillabaisse (only served on weekends), rabbit with mustard sauce, broiled sea scallops, and sweetbreads. Many of the desserts are homemade. But the big plus here is the freshness of the dishes and the gracious feeling of "We're glad to have you."

CHIN CHIN
216 E 49th St (bet Second and Third Ave)
888-4555
Lunch: Mon-Fri; Dinner: Mon-Sat
Moderate to moderately expensive

This is a very classy Chinese restaurant, and the ambiance and price reflect the superior style of Chinese cooking. There are two rooms, including a garden in back. The soups and barbecued spare-ribs are wonderful for starters. The Szechuan jumbo prawns are sensational. As a matter of fact, I'd concentrate on the seafood dishes; some of the other presentations are a bit bland. You might try the wonderful Peking duck dinner with your choice of soup, crispy duck skin with pancakes, fried rice, poached spinach, and homemade sorbet or ice cream. The menu is much the same for lunch or dinner. This is an excellent choice for a business lunch with a client who has a hankering for improving East-West relations.

COACH HOUSE
110 Waverly Pl
777-0303, 777-0349
Dinner: Tues-Sun
Expensive

For some perverse reason, when something is highly successful, there is always a chorus of detractors who want to shoot it down. For years the Coach House has been a popular and distinguished room in Manhattan. The quality of the food and service under the ever-watchful eye of the talented owner, Leon Lianides, was always top-notch, but some reviewers took shots at this Village institution. It was very unfair, in my opinion. I have dined here dozens of times, and each experience has been pleasant, satisfying, and a treat for my guests. Yes, there is a dress requirement—men must wear a coat and tie—but what's wrong with that? Believe me, though, you'll have to loosen that tie after a meal of their black bean soup, rack of lamb, and a piece of their famous flourless chocolate cake. I can think of few more attractive places to spend a Sunday evening, savoring a truly first-class dining experience.

COASTAL
300 Amsterdam Ave (at 74th St)
769-3988
Dinner: Daily; Brunch: Sun
Moderate

If you are over 20 and under 40, head for this Coastal spot on Amsterdam Avenue. This is a small, very noisy, and very "in" place. It also has some very tasty food. The plain wooden tables without tablecloths add to the nautical atmosphere, and the waiters are visibly coping with a work environment that must require a daily dose of aspirin to maintain sanity. The confusion is mind-boggling. But come here with all that in mind, and it can be fun. A number of fresh seafood dishes are available every day, and one of the nicer features is the large choice of accompanying sauces. The cioppino conjures up images of Fisherman's Wharf in San Francisco: a great stew with jumbo shrimp, scallops, mussels, clams, and assorted fish served with buttered pasta. Homemade dessert selections change daily, but try to catch the intense dark chocolate cake with white chocolate mousse.

COCONUT GRILL
1481 Second Ave (at 77th St)
772-6262
Lunch, Dinner: Daily; Brunch: Sun
Moderate

A lighthearted staff will serve you a delicious light meal in a light, pleasant atmosphere at this popular Upper East Side cafe. There are several different dining spaces, including an airy glass-enclosed room that looks out on Second Avenue. A huge bar in the center of the cafe is teaming with girl talk and business chat from dusk to the wee hours, and the outside tables are a delight in the nice weather. The menu at lunchtime ranges from fettucine to your choice of several salads to sandwiches or cold salmon. The shrimp salad with avocado and artichokes is a treat. For Sunday brunch, the usual fare is available, but the cinnamon raisin-bread French toast is worthy of special mention, as are the delicious waffles served with your choice of apples and cinnamon, blueberries, strawberries, or maple syrup. At night you can feast upon Cajun fried chicken or steamed seaweed-wrapped mahi-mahi, among other delights. Be sure to ask for the house chutney of tomato, mango, and cilantro, an unusual taste treat. Top all of this off with a dense chocolate and white-mousse cake floating in a raspberry sauce.

CONTRAPUNTO
1009 Third Ave (at 60th St)
751-8616
Lunch: Daily; Dinner: Mon-Sun
Moderate

The thing that struck me first about Contrapunto was the airiness and lightness of the dining room. It's located on the second floor of a busy corner building across the street from Bloomingdale's, with full-length windows allowing a view of the activity on Third Avenue. It's a delightful place for a delicious and different Italian lunch. For appetizers, you might have a salad Di Casa (seasonal greens with Tuscan olive oil) or Pinzimonio Caprese (tomatoes, sweet peppers, fresh fennel, and mozzarella with Tuscan olive oil). The pasta is unique. On the imported side, there is the angel-hair pasta with imported dried red tomato, fresh artichokes, mushrooms, chives, and aged parmesan cheese, or another delicious angel-hair pasta with clams, shallots, leeks, and Japanese basil. Of the fresh pasta, I recommend the pasta squares with crab meat, white wine, fresh mushrooms, or an unusual thin pasta with sweet red pepper, zucchini, eggplant, and tomato. All the portions are a good size, and you will be impressed with the quality. If there is one drawback, it's that service is very slow; don't come here if you have an appointment within the hour. This place advertises itself as a pasta, wine, and gelati house, and it is just that. Be sure to save room for dessert; the chocolate cake is absolutely sinful. I also recommend that you try the chocolate, praline, or strawberry gelati.

CUCINA STAGIONALE
275 Bleecker St
924-2707
Lunch, Dinner: Daily
No credit cards
Inexpensive

When you serve good food at a small price, the word gets around. So it's no wonder there's a line in front of this small Village cafe almost any time of the day. Its name translates as "seasonal kitchen," and the seasonal specialties are real values, indeed. It's a bare-bones setup, with seating for only several dozen hungry folk. Service is impersonal and nonprofessional, but who cares at these prices. Innovative Italian cuisine is served here—tasty, attractive, and filling —and you can do very well on a slim budget. Appetizers include sun-dried beef on a bed of arugula, smoked salmon with endive and radiccio, and sautéed wild mushrooms. For a few pennies more, you can get a large dish of vegetarian lasagna, linguini, or ravioli. I'm constantly asked about inexpensive places that serve quality food; I have no hesitation in recommending this spot. But one word of warning: don't go if it's raining, because you'll probably have to wait to get seated, and the wait is outside.

DARBAR
44 W 56th St
4-DARBAR
Lunch, Dinner: Daily
Moderate

It's a joy to walk into a very appealing and well-designed restaurant, where the tables are separated by partitions and one can really have a private conversation. Darbar is such a spot, and all of the staff wait on you in a quick and respectful manner, at the same time providing informed, efficient service and presenting fresh, attractive Indian dishes. A wonderful start for your meal would be the murgh pakoras, tender pieces of chicken sautéed in yogurt and Indian spices and batter fried. Specialties from the charcoal clay oven are sizable in selection: chicken, prawns, and lamb. My favorite is the tandoori prawns. By all means, try some of the Indian breads. A real taste treat is the vegetarian paratha, unleavened whole wheat bread filled with vegetables and baked in the tandoor with butter. Rice dishes are excellent, and the desserts are exceptionally good. The chocolate cinnamon ice cream is worth the visit in itself. There is a buffet lunch daily.

DAWAT
210 E 58th St
355-7555
Lunch: Mon-Fri; Dinner: Daily
Moderate

Dawat is a quality operation. It serves tasty, reasonably priced Indian food in a refined atmosphere with superior service. There are a number of wonderful seafood choices, including a sensational shrimp entree cooked with herbs and spices. You'll also find chicken and egg dishes, a number of goat and lamb offerings, and such vegetarian selections as homemade cheese cubes with delicious vegetables, eggplant with sweet-and-sour tamarind sauce, and stir-fried cauliflower with ginger and cumin seeds. One of the trademarks of an Indian restaurant is its bread, and Dawat is no exception. They do it to perfection. A number of different varieties are offered, and no meal is complete without trying a couple of them. Forget about the desserts here; they're nothing special.

DELMONICO'S
56 Beaver St
422-4747
Breakfast, Lunch, Dinner: Mon-Fri
Moderate to expensive

Those who are familiar with the Wall Street area already know about Delmonico's. It has been a tradition for decades and is still a class act, resplendent with elegant furnishings and polite service well-honed from years of experience. Whether you're here for a "what's new in the market lunch" or for a social dinner, I heartily recommend this consistent, established institution. It's hard to pick out only a few specialties, but I would suggest: the swordfish; the marvelous filet of sole glazed with white wine, mushrooms, and tomatoes; the boneless breast of chicken in brandy mustard sauce; or the mixed grill Delmonico (lamb chop, filet mignon, liver, and bacon). All of these should be at the top of anybody's list. And bitter chocolate with vanilla sauce is the Delmonico dessert showpiece.

DIECI
1568 First Ave (bet 81st and 82nd St)
628-6565
Dinner: Daily
Moderately expensive

What a jewel this is! Joseph Franco says that the restaurant business is the only thing he knows about, and he knows a lot. It certainly shows in the professional kitchen and dining room, which he operates in the best hands-on manner. The place is small, noisy, and crowded, but don't let that keep you from trying some of the best Northern Italian food in town. Crispy fried zucchini will get you started, as well as such delicious appetizers as baked clams, mozzarella and bread with anchovy sauce, and made-to-order soup. Then on to some fabulous pasta, like the linguini with white clam sauce and caviar. Leave room for one of these main courses: chicken sautéed with white wine and artichokes, any kind of veal chop you could imagine, and a thick grilled swordfish steak. Some low calorie plates are also available, but not in the dessert category. Try the hot zabaione with raspberries or the homemade tartuffo. For those who like an early dinner on Sunday, Dieci opens at 5 p.m.

DINING COMMONS
City University of New York Graduate Center
33 W 42nd St (18th floor)
642-2013
Mon-Fri: 10-8
Inexpensive

This is definitely a find for those who don't mind cafeteria dining. Right in the center of town, on the top floor of City University Graduate Center, is a first-class all-day cafeteria that offers excellent food in nice surroundings at very reasonable prices. Continental breakfasts, featuring muffins, danishes, croissants, bagels, and fruit, are available from 10 a.m. to 11:30 a.m. Lunch and dinner— deli sandwiches, salads, hot entrees with vegetables and potatoes, desserts and beverages—are available until 8 p.m. You can eat heartily for under $10; if a sandwich is all you want, the tab would be half of that. Seating is available, but all items may be taken out. A full-service bar is adjacent to the Commons, which even offers a special catering menu with rock-bottom prices. The cafeteria is open to faculty, students, and the general public, with students getting a special discount upon presentation of CUNY identification cards. This is not your run-of-the-mill fast-food operation. Restaurant Associates does a particularly good job in offering tasty and very adequate portions, without the fancy touches that cost extra bucks. A great midtown spot for groups, young people, singles, and people in a hurry.

DIVA
306 E 81st St
650-1928
Dinner: Sat-Thurs
Moderate

Several years ago, Lou Stuart turned the lower level of his townhouse into an Italian restaurant and named it Diva. Offering excellent Italian food in an elegant setting, complete with an antique Russian player-piano, was certainly a novel twist on a classic theme. But recently Stuart took an even more dramatic step toward distinguishing Diva from the numerous other Italian restaurants in the area. Diva went kosher! Since kosher food does not mix dairy and meat dishes, Diva was faced with giving up either its meat menu or its dessert menu. As one diner said, "Lou's desserts are fabulous, so he gladly sacrificed veal for cream filling." Today the menu is almost vegetarian: heavy on pasta and fish and excelling in desserts. (Diva could have made a go of it as just a dessert house.) The appetizers include an exquisite marinated artichoke as big as a cabbage, fried red peppers, and broccoli salad with anchovies. There are two soups—a minestrone and a vegetable when I was there—and several salads. Portions are enormous, unlike the tab, which is quite reasonable. And you don't have to be kosher to like Diva.

DIVINO
1556 Second Ave (at 80th St)
861-1096
Lunch: Mon-Fri; Dinner: Daily
Moderate

Divino is a professional Northern Italian restaurant—professional service, professional cooking, professional supervision. It's always a thrill to watch a well-trained team in action, and Divino has one of the best in town. The owner is on the job, and the place is orchestrated with the baton of a master. The moment you enter (better make reservations), you notice an attractive and unusual bowl of relishes on the bar. Every sight and sense is a happy one, and there's plenty of good, hot, fresh Italian bread. To start, try the seafood salad or, if it's a cold evening, the tortellini in brodo (meat-filled pasta in broth). What a selection of pasta! Pasta stuffed with meat, spinach, and cheese; Genovese-style pasta in garlic and basil sauce; and pasta and seafood. Steamed clams, Italian-style bouillabaisse, and scampi with tarragon are featured, but my prime choices are the veal chop Primavera or swordfish Divino. All entrees are served with fresh vegetables. Desserts are baked daily on the premises.

DOCKS

2427 Broadway	633 Third Ave
(bet 89th and 90th St)	(at 40th St)
724-5588	986-8080
Lunch: Mon-Sat; Dinner: Daily	Lunch: Mon-Fri;
Moderate	Dinner: Daily

For seafood lovers on the Upper West Side, I do not hesitate recommending that you sail right up Broadway to Docks' Oyster Bar and Seafood Grill. At both lunch and dinner, you can get fresh swordfish, lobster, tuna, Norwegian salmon, red snapper, and other seafood specials of the day. In the evening, you can enjoy a shell bar with four oyster varieties and three different selections of clams. All this comes with Docks' cole slaw and potatoes or vegetables. For a lighter meal, try the steamers in beer broth or the mussels in tomato and garlic. Delicious smoked fish, like lake sturgeon and white fish, is available, along with grilled tuna and your choice of a shrimp salad crab cake sandwich. The lobster, in particular, is delicious and reasonably priced. Nothing fancy about the setting, but the personnel are helpful and accommodating. You can enjoy the same fare at Docks #2 on Third Avenue.

DUANE PARK CAFE

157 Duane St
732-5555
Lunch: Mon-Fri; Dinner: Mon-Sat
Moderate

More and more interesting places to dine are appearing in the TriBeCa area, and many are located on or near Duane Street. Some have revamped already existing operations that couldn't make the grade; Duane Park Cafe is one of them. Housed in the former Tapis Rouge, this nondescript room serves much better food than the décor would suggest. The menu is eclectic, just what you would expect from several Japanese chefs who have had varied cooking backgrounds. There is a touch of Italian, a heavy emphasis on seafood, and a nod to Cajun influences. The dishes sparkle with interest, especially because of the tasty manner in which herbs are used. Even some of the delicious bread has herbal flavors; by the way all the breads are made in-house. A selection of pasta is offered at all times. The desserts are also done on the premises, and show off the vivid imagination of the pastry chef. My top choice has to be the biscotti pudding on an espresso custard sauce

EDWARDIAN ROOM
Plaza Hotel (Fifth Ave and Central Park S)
759-3000
Breakfast, Lunch, Dinner: Daily
Expensive

There are some New York experiences that one never forgets. I remember a magical evening in the Edwardian Room at the Plaza Hotel, overlooking the heart of New York at Fifth Avenue and Central Park. Outside, the streets and sidewalks were being dusted by a snowfall; inside, the tables sparkled with the finest silver, china, and glassware. The candles flickered, and the piano music provided the final romantic ingredient. This was years ago. Alas, the room has undergone many changes over a long period of time by a series of uncaring owners. Now Ivana and Donald Trump have arrived on the scene. The magic is back, and there just isn't another spot like it anywhere in New York. Hansom cabs sit outside your window, soft piano music soothes your nerves, and the kitchen is once again turning out superb cuisine in keeping with the room's history. This is the place to take your guests for that very special New York evening, to celebrate an engagement or important occasion. This is not just another hotel dining room! A special sous-chef at the Plaza takes care of just the Edwardian Room, and it shows. With gorgeous flowers and old-time waiters, along with an extensive dinner menu of continental favorites, who could ask for anything more?

ERMINIA
250 E 83rd St
879-4284
Dinner: Mon-Sat
American Express
Moderate

The Trastevere operation now has five branches, and Erminia, the smallest, is really the jewel in the crown. It has about a dozen tables in a most pleasant, informal, and rather rustic atmosphere—just right for a leisurely, intimate dinner. I found it an absolutely charming spot with helpful personnel and outstanding food. To start, try the artichokes cooked in olive oil. In the pasta category, you can't go wrong with the tender dumplings with potatoes and tomatoes or the large noodles with ricotta cheese. The number of entrees are limited and all are grilled, but they are tasty and served with delicious vegetables. There is grilled chicken, various seafood items on a skewer, a special fish dish, and lamb or veal chops. The dessert selections vary daily.

EZE
254 W 23rd St
691-1140
Dinner: Tues-Sat
Expensive (almost!)

When you pay nearly $40 for a price-fixed dinner, that is expensive. But at this charming Chelsea room, you probably won't mind. Thus the word *almost* in the price classification above. Gina Zarrilli, who spent time in the tiny French village of Eze, between Nice and Monte Carlo, has brought to New York a warm, inviting table of understated elegance. Nothing flashy or abrasive, just wonderful food served in a friendly ambiance. Gina is well suited for this achievement, having served her apprenticeship at Chanterelle, the Quilted Giraffe, and Roxanne's. The room is small, maybe a dozen tables, with a huge flower arrangement providing the only splash of color. The personnel seem almost elated to serve you. Eli's bread, New York's best, is served warm and crusty. There's a wonderful choice of appetizers, like ravioli with Swiss chard and prosciutto, chicken livers with wild rice and pecans, or marinated trout. Loin of venison, whole red snapper with couscous, or rack of lamb are among the stars on the list of entrees. The coffee cake with ice cream and fig sauce or praline ice cream cake with chocolate sauce will make a trip to Body By Jake necessary in the morning. But that isn't the end. A wonderful assortment of pecan goodies, coconut tuiles, and candied grapefruit rind along with truffles is also placed before you. What a way to go!

FOOD
127 Prince St
(no phone)
Mon-Wed: 12-10: Thurs-Sat: 12-11; Sun: 11:30-4:30
No credit cards
Inexpensive

I recommend Food without qualification. For a while, it was a very small "in" spot in the SoHo neighborhood. But it became so popular that it had to expand. Service is cafeteria style, and what a selection: great salads, soups, sandwiches, and desserts—all homemade and many of them vegetarian. The portions are enormous. Substantial entrees are available, as well as outstanding dessert selections. If you're looking for good, hearty food at sensible prices, this is the place.

FORTUNE GARDEN PAVILION
209 E 49th St
753-0101
Lunch, Dinner: Mon-Sat
Moderate

This is a garden delight. Make sure that you are seated upstairs, where the hanging plants and patio add to the charming, sophisticated atmosphere. Don't be in a rush at the Pavilion! All the Chinese food is cooked to order, and it's well worth the extra time. The help know what they're doing; be sure to confer with them so that you get exactly what you want. The appetizer selections are absolutely marvelous: barbecued spareribs, delicious crab meat and vegetables in lettuce leaf, steamed beef dumplings, and the best Shanghai chicken soup I've ever tasted. If you don't find what you want on the menu, check with the maitre d'. He'll be more than happy to have the staff prepare your choice. There are a number of hot spicy items, like seafood sautéed in Hunan chili sauce, crab meat malay (crab meat braised with black and straw mushrooms), and a red snapper topped with a spicy Szechuan sauce. Milder offerings include ginger pineapple beef (marinated fillet of beef sautéed with pineapple, sweet ginger, and other vegetables), velvet chicken (shredded chicken sautéed in light egg-white sauce and served on spinach), and marinated medallions of pork.

FOUR SEASONS
99 E 52nd St
754-9494
Lunch, Dinner: Mon-Sat
Expensive

This is a Manhattan "must try." Nearly everything about this famous restaurant is special. The setting around the pool is spectacular. The tables are far enough apart to allow for private conversations. The huge menu changes with every season. The staff is very professional and well trained. Every dish is a masterpiece of presentation. The dessert selection is almost obscene, and the individual soufflés in coffee cups are something special. The grill room, outside the main dining hall, is the setting for more power lunches than are ever served at the White House. Take along a *Who's Who in New York* for lunch, and you'll be able to identify dozens of the country's top movers and shakers. It is a particular favorite for big names in the publishing world. If you really want to spend some bucks—and almost get your money's worth—you can't do better than Four Seasons.

FRANK'S
431 W 14th St
243-1349
Lunch: Mon-Fri; Dinner: Mon-Sat
Moderate

At lunch, this old-time spot is crowded with nearby butchers, sporting blood on their aprons and large stomachs to fill. If that kind of clientele doesn't bother you, come on down early. But dinner is really the best at Frank's, which is operated by five members of the Molinari family, the third generation in a business started in 1912. Reservations are difficult, especially on weekends (a week in advance is necessary), since they can take care of only 65 people. When cloths come out on the tables for dinner, the family chef (well trained at the now-defunct Brussels Restaurant) will offer you superb prime ribs of beef, fresh fish, great steaks, and pasta. The neighborhood is seamy, the desserts are ho-hum, and the ambiance is Pittsburgh diner, but the food is absolutely top-drawer.

FRANK'S TRATTORIA
371 First Ave (at 22nd St)
677-2991
Lunch, Dinner: Daily
Cash only
Inexpensive

It's true in New York just as it is anywhere else in the country: No one knows the best inexpensive places to eat better than the local boys in blue. Manhattan's finest are some of the best customers of this modest trattoria, and it is easy to see why. The menu runs the gamut of Florentine dishes, each one prepared to order and each served piping hot. And so is the bread, which is always a good sign. There is a large seafood selection, and all the fish are first quality and very fresh. You can choose from over 20 different pizzas, and have them served whole or in individual pieces. Everyone here is very informal and friendly, and Mario, the boss, is delighted that the good word about his place has spread to others beyond the neighborhood regulars.

FRAUNCES TAVERN RESTAURANT
54 Pearl St
269-0144
Breakfast, Lunch, Dinner: Mon-Fri
Moderate

General George Washington is supposed to have said goodbye to his officers at a reception at Fraunces Tavern in 1783. General

George obviously had good taste, if the tavern was as top-notch then as it is now. It's an inviting, historic spot located in a charming part of lower Manhattan. The dining areas are spacious and comfortable, the service is very professional, the prices are reasonable, and the menu is sizable. One of the outstanding appetizers is a seafood sampler, consisting of fresh lump crab and Maine lobster meat, shrimp, oyster, and clams—a feast in itself. A specialty of the house is the baked chicken à la Washington (cubes of tender chicken and mushroom baked en casserole au gratin). Absolutely delicious. Salads and cold platters are full meals! Seafood items, such as steelhead trout, lobster, scallops, and Norwegian salmon, are available in season. For heftier appetites, roast beef, London broil, lamb chops, and chicken schnitzel (boneless breast of chicken sautéed with Parmesian cheese breading) are offered. I'd suggest making a beeline here on Wednesdays for the Yankee pot roast with red cabbage and potato pancakes. And don't overlook dessert! The cheesecake, Georgia pecan pie, and chocolate mousse are well worth investigating. After lunch, go upstairs and visit the Fraunces Tavern Museum, one of the oldest museums in the city and a historic landmark. There you'll find exhibits focusing on 18th- and 19th-century life in America. The "long room" is especially well done. By the way, there's a breakfast menu offering a fine selection of omelets, eggs, fruit, and muffins. It's one of the best buys in New York.

FU'S
1395 Second Ave (bet 72nd and 73rd St)
517-9670
Lunch, Dinner: Daily
Moderate

The guests at this attractive Chinese restaurant look well-fed and well-heeled, and they obviously enjoy the quiet, comfortable, non-ostentatious atmosphere. The menu selection is large. For openers, I recommend the stuffed crab claws or the honey baby spareribs. There are a large number of spicy dishes, and make special note that Fu's will omit MSG, cornstarch, sugar, or salt upon request. A number of interesting specialties are offered; one of the best is the jumbo shrimp FU's style (large prawns sautéed with mushroom, snow peas, water chestnuts, and ginger scallions in rice baked in sealed aluminum foil). Another hot, spicy dish is crispy orange beef (sliced filet of beef fried till crisp and sautéed in sweet-and-hot preserved orange). A good chicken dish is Fu's lemon chicken (a breast of chicken cooked exquisitely in a unique lemon sauce). A special takeout menu features some prices slightly under those charged in

the restaurant itself. Free delivery is available within seven blocks
of the area. The restaurant personnel are exceedingly attentive, the
pinkish lighting is flattering to all, and the food would rate very
highly even in Hong Kong.

GINO
780 Lexington Ave (at 61st St)
758-4466
Lunch, Dinner: Daily
Cash only
Moderate

As you look around the crowded dining room of this famous
New York institution, you can tell immediately that the food is
great. Why? Because this Italian restaurant is filled with native
New Yorkers. You'll see no tourist buses stopping out front. The
menu has been the same for years: a large selection of popular
dishes (over 30 entrees), from antipasto to soup to pasta to fish.
There are daily specials, of course, but you only have to taste such
regulars as the linguini al pesto or the Italian sausages with peppers
or scampis a la Gino, and you are hooked. Gino's staff has been
there forever, taking care of patrons in an informed, fatherly manner. The best part of the whole experience comes when the tab is
presented. East Side rents, as you know, are always climbing, but
Gino has resisted the price bulges by taking cash only and by serving delicious food that keeps the tables full. No reservations, please,
so come early and don't expect your waiter to know where Peoria
is.

GIORDANO
409 W 39th St
947-9811
Lunch, Dinner: Mon-Sat
Moderate

When a restaurant has been in the same family for 30 years, it
should be a fine-tuned establishment. And indeed, the Creglia family runs a first-rate operation at Giordano. An attractive bar greets
you with trays of appetizers during the cocktail hour. There are several pleasant dining areas, including an outdoor patio. The cuisine
is Northern Italian highlighted by such delicious pasta as fettuccine
al fungetto, tortellini alla panna, fettuccine alfredo, or linguini al
sugo. For entrees, I'd suggest the langostine alla mugnaia, an excellent seafood dish, or the calf's liver alla veneziana. A side order of
fried zucchini or eggplant parmigiana tops off a superb meal. Although the food is excellent, I was most impressed with how com-
forting it is to have old-time waiters taking care of you; they sure

know what they're doing. For no-nonsense Italian food at a reasonable price, you can't beat Giordano. A new banquet room has recently been added.

GOLDEN UNICORN
18 E Broadway (at Catherine St)
941-0911
Lunch, Dinner, Dim Sum: Daily
Inexpensive

Spencer P.S. Chan presides over this bustling Hong Kong-style two-floor Chinese restaurant that serves delicious Dim Sum every day of the week. And besides the delicacies from the rolling carts, diners may choose from a wide variety of Cantonese dishes from the regular menu. Pan-fried noodle dishes, rice noodles, and noodles in soup are house specialties. Despite the size of the establishment (they can take care of over 400 diners at one time), you will be amazed at the fast service, the cleanliness, and most of all the price tag. This has to be one of the best values in Chinatown.

GOTHAM BAR AND RESTAURANT
12 E 12th St
620-4020
Lunch: Mon-Fri; Dinner: Daily
Moderately expensive

Yes, there is an after-life! Your author (along with many others) had showered the original Gotham with some very unflattering words. What has happened in the past several years proves that restaurants may indeed go up the ladder as well as the reverse. The Gotham today is well worth the sizable price tag. In a cavernous setting, anything but intimate, the high-ceilinged coldness is broken by direct lighting spots on each table. Beautiful orchid plants give a bit more color, but the real treat is the delicious food. Several wonderful salads, including a seafood presentation of squid, scallops, Japanese octopus, mussel and lobster in lemon and olive oil, will get you off to a good start. The entrees are uniformly appealing: beautifully seasoned, attractively presented, and obviously made from first-quality ingredients. The rack of lamb has to be one of the finest served in the city. A dozen homemade desserts, including such waist-busters as a peanut butter coupe (vanilla and peanut butter ice cream, nut brittle and milk chocolate sauce), raspberry gratin and a chocolate mousse filled with a coffee bean flavor, are expensive and exciting. Low-key personnel combined with the talented chef Alfred Portale make dining here a special experience.

GRAND CENTRAL OYSTER BAR AND RESTAURANT

Grand Central Station (lower level)
490-6650
Mon-Fri: 11:30-9:30
Moderate

If you are a native New Yorker, you know about the half-century institution that is the Old Oyster Bar at Grand Central; it was once popular with commuters and residents. A midtown institution that was neglected for years, it is now restored and doing nicely, thank you. (They serve over 2,000 folks a day!) Located in the caverns of Grand Central, it is attractive, the young help most accommodating, and the drain on the pocketbook minimal. The menu boasts more than 90 seafood items (new, fresh entrees daily), a dozen different kinds of oysters, super oyster stew, clam chowder (Manhattan and New England), oyster pan roast, bouillabaisse, coquille Saint Jacques, Maryland crab cakes, and marvelous homemade desserts.

GRAZIELLA

2 Bank St (at Greenwich Ave)
924-9450
Lunch: Mon-Fri; Dinner: Daily
Moderate

Since there are so many Italian restaurants, new and old, in Manhattan, they must be special to be included in this book. Graziella is very special in terms of value, cleanliness, ambiance, and service. The restaurant is a family affair: Graziella herself is out front, and her brothers are in the kitchen. Graziella is not the usual table-hopping proprietor, who constantly and insincerely asks, "Is everything all right?" Graziella's English has a lovely Spanish tilt to it, and she makes sure that everything is absolutely spotless and that place settings are arranged picture-perfect. The restaurant has less than 20 tables and is always booked with neighborhood regulars, so reservations are decidedly in order. Nonetheless, the atmosphere is casual and unhurried. Try a fabulous appetizer platter to start, then you can have your choice of a number of homemade pasta and veal dishes, boneless shell steak, breast of chicken, or grilled scampis. This is definitely a place for big appetites. Diet-conscious gourmets should head in the opposite direction and leave one of New York's best bargains to the real eaters in the family. By the way, Graziella's Bank Street entrance is just off Greenwich *Avenue,* not Greenwich Street.

GUIDO'S
511 Ninth Ave (at 39th St)
502-4842
Lunch: Mon-Fri; Dinner: Mon-Sat
No credit cards
Inexpensive

You might ask yourself what a nice person like you would be doing in the middle of Ninth Avenue having lunch in the back room of a macaroni factory? Well, this is no usual back room and no usual macaroni factory. Up front, as you walk in, you'll see a display of 23 brands of macaroni. That was the original business, but now it's just a sideline. The real draw is the smallish restaurant in the back, which is as busy as Times Square. Tom Scarola is the third-generation family member who runs this unusual operation. Whether you're coming for lunch or dinner, make sure you have a reservation; you might even rub shoulders with Olivia Newton-John, Robert de Niro, or other celebrities. Even if they're not there in person, their pictures (along with the blue checkered tablecloths and wine bottles on the ceiling) help create a special atmosphere at Guido's. You don't want to miss the shrimp francese, the veal sorrentino, or the house specialty, chicken alla Guido. The pasta is freshly made, authentic, inexpensive, and delicious. Finish with spumoni or rum cake, and you will have had a marvelous meal. Lunch specials include four different chicken, veal, and shrimp entrees, as well as linguini or spaghetti with all the trimmings.

HARD ROCK CAFE
221 W 57th St
489-6565
Lunch, Dinner: Daily (11:30 a.m.-4 a.m.)
Inexpensive

This New York offshoot of the original and very successful Hard Rock, which opened in London in 1971, is a noisy, swinging hangout for the younger generation. Stop at the small counter as you enter and get one of the Hard Rock Cafe sweat shirts for your son or daughter, and your popularity rating at home will go up. The food is really good here. Specialties of the house include the Pig Sandwich (hickory-smoked pulled pork, served with cole slaw and French fries), barbecue chicken and pork ribs, a great BLT sandwich, and marvelous burgers and salads. But the real treats are from the fountain and dessert menu: homemade apple pie, hot-fudge brownies, homemade shortcakes, and absolutely outrageous sundaes and shakes. The multilevel cafe is decorated with artifacts of rock and pop culture (gold records, musical instruments once owned by famous stars, etc.), and the background music is just what you'd expect—loud rock and roll. But come on now, let your hair down and see how the other half has fun.

HARRY'S
The Woolworth Building
233 Broadway
513-0455
Lunch, Dinner: Mon-Fri
Moderate

Never mind that you're not a member of the Harvard or Yale Club, or that you don't have a gold pass to the private dining room of Citicorp or Chase Manhattan. Just head for the Woolworth Building, go down to the lower level, and you'll find a remarkable eating spot called Harry's. You would probably never know about it unless you work in one of the nearby offices—or read this book! What with all the wood and leather (a very masculine atmosphere), good food, and reasonable prices, it's a real find. Although dinner is served until 10:30 at night, this is basically a luncheon spot. Ladies are certainly welcome, but the clientele is predominantly male (the important-looking, three-piece-suit variety). While big deals are being made at the tables around you, you can feast on clams, smoked trout, marinated herring, and smoked sturgeon. Omelets and pasta are available, as well as a number of selections from the cold buffet, including chicken-salad, sliced-turkey, and tuna-salad platters. There are also grilled items, cold sandwiches, seafood, and several specials each day. If you drop by on a Tuesday, try the braised sauerbrauten, and if you visit on Friday, the boiled brisket of beef is outstanding. This is the ideal place to take business associates, who will probably be pleasantly surprised to learn about it. Harry's is open on weekends only for private events.

HARVEY'S CHELSEA RESTAURANT
108 W 18th St (at Sixth Ave)
243-5644
Lunch: Mon-Sat; Dinner: Daily; Brunch: Sun
No credit cards
Moderate

Since 1890, Harvey's has been a New York favorite, and the atmosphere hasn't changed that much in nearly a century. It is still a charming and warm establishment, a place for relaxed eating and convivial conversation. Everything is cooked to order, so your meal may take a bit of time. How about trying an unusual salad? It's called the German Snack Platter, and it consists of sliced knock-wurst, German cheese, cherry tomatoes, and pretzels, and it's almost a meal in itself. A specialty of the house is two bratwurst sausages served with potato salad, pickles, and hot mustard. (The potato salad is definitely not the usual bland variety.) Another great dish is the shepherd's pie: chopped beef and lamb sautéed with herb spices and topped with rosettes of mashed potatoes, peas, and carrots. Along with the English atmosphere goes a fish-and-chips dish served with malt vinegar as well as tartar sauce and a great prime rib. Don't pass up the pecan pie served with fresh whipped cream. Sinful Sunday brunch is fun here, too. Chelsea is becoming a more and more interesting place for browsing, shopping, and dining, and Harvey's is one of the landmarks of the area. Harvey's also has fine, new banquet facilities.

HATSUHANA
17 E 48th St
355-3345
Lunch: Mon-Fri; Dinner: Mon-Sat
Moderate

Hatsuhana has deservedly become known as the best sushi house in Manhattan. One can sit at a table or at the bar and get equal attention from the informed help. There are several dozens choice appetizers, including broiled eel in cucumber wrap, steamed egg custard with shrimp, fish and vegetables, squid mixed with Japanese apricots, and chopped fatty tuna with aged soybeans. Next, try the salmon teriyaki (which is fresh salmon grilled with fresh teriyaki sauce) or any number of tuna or sushi dishes best described by the personnel. Forget about the desserts, and concentrate on the exotic offerings for your meal.

HUBERTS
575 Park Ave (at 63rd St)
826-5911
Lunch: Mon-Fri; Dinner: Daily
Expensive

Faithful readers of this book will remember that Huberts got less-than-glowing reviews in previous editions. Well, things have finally changed for the better. Huberts has not only moved its location uptown, but it has moved up the scale in ambiance and quality. The new digs are in a tonier section of town, and of course, the tab reflects the increased rent. But the luncheon concept here is a priceless delight. The diner is given a choice of the dishes from an extended menu of hot, cold, and dessert choices. The portions are medium-sized, so you don't really have a main course as such. For a bit extra (the tab is fixed-price), you can have a selection of four goodies. Interesting items to choose from include Russian Ice House soup, shrimp and smashed cucumber, tuna sashimi, fettuccine with sweetbreads and oysters, or braised artichokes and chanterelles with blue potatoes—an outstanding dish. Save your third choice for the mint chocolate-chip sandwich, the winner among the desserts. The evening menu reverts back to a more usual fixed-price operation without the snacking opportunities. I recommend the noon-hour fun.

IL MULINO
86 W Third St (bet Sullivan and Thompson St)
673-3783
Lunch: Mon-Fri; Dinner: Mon-Sat
American Express
Moderately expensive

Never mind that you usually have to reserve a table a week or so in advance. Never mind that when you arrive it's always crowded, the noise level intolerable, and the waiters nearly knock you down as you stand waiting to be seated. It's all part of the ambiance of one of New York's best Italian restaurants. Your greeting is usually "Hi, Boss," which gives you the distinct impression that the staff is accustomed to catering to members of the, uh, "family." When your waiter finally comes around, he reels off the lengthy list of evening specials with glazed-over eyes and about as much interest as your kid would have while you recited your favorite Shakespeare sonnet. On the other hand, there is a beautiful, mouth-watering display of the daily specials on a huge table at the entrance. Once you're seated, your waiter delivers one antipasto after another to your table, while he talks you into ordering one of the fabulous veal dishes with portions plentiful enough to feed King Kong. The dover sole is just as delicious and abundant. By the time you finish one of the luscious desserts, you'll know why every seat in the small, simple dining room is kept warm all evening. Il Mulino can become habit forming.

IL VAGABONDO
351 E 62nd St
832-9221
Lunch: Mon-Fri; Dinner: Daily
Inexpensive

One of the major airlines advertises with the phrase "doing what we do best." It could just as well be the motto of this bustling restaurant, which has been a favorite with knowledgeable New Yorkers for more than 20 years. The atmosphere is strictly old-timey, complete with checkered tablecloths, four busy rooms, and an even busier bar. No menus are offered; the pleasant but harried waiters reel off the regular items and the daily specials. Depending on when you go, you may have spaghetti or ravioli, an absolutely marvelous minestrone soup, chicken parmesan, prime rib steak, or sliced beef. I would also heartily recommend the Friday scampi or lobster special. There is no pretense in this place. It is a great spot for office parties and for folks with slim pocketbooks. Be sure to take a look at the way the kitchen is set up, and on the way out, walk past the butcher shop (which Il Vagabondo also owns) just down the street; you can see why the quality of the meat is so high. You won't see Jackie O. or Halston here, but you'll see happy faces, compliments of a delicious meal and the extremely reasonable bill. Save room for the great Bocce Ball dessert (tartufo). Il Vagabondo, you see, is the only restaurant in New York with an indoor bocce court.

IL VALLETTO
133 E 61st St (at Lexington Ave)
838-3939
Lunch: Mon-Fri; Dinner: Mon-Sat
Moderate to expensive

I'd suggest Il Valletto for one special reason: pasta! You can't go wrong—any kind you order will be something special. This multi-level restaurant is not terribly attractive, but it does have a pleasant, friendly atmosphere, and the service is exceptionally good. The menu features a large choice of appetizers, fish, game, fresh vegetables, and several dozen Italian specialties, including scaloppina alla francese, filetto di bue alla griglia, and saltinbocca alla romana. You're not going to leave this place hungry, or with a full wallet, but it's worth visiting a spot where those helping you are obviously eager to please and where they do one thing *very* well.

INDOCHINE
430 Lafayette St
505-5111
Dinner: Daily
Moderate

Indochinese cuisine has become very popular, which is probably due to the number of American military men who have spent time in that part of the world, as well as the number of talented chefs and cooks who have immigrated to our country. Indochine is undoubtedly the best restaurant of its type in New York, and it's located right across the street from Joseph Papp's famous New York Public Theater. The staff is happy to explain the delicious exotic dishes they offer. Soups are a specialty of the house, and the best is the PHO: sliced filet of beef, rice noodles, and bean sprouts in broth. Several salads and appetizers are worth trying. One is called Bi Coun, steamed Vietnamese ravioli. Another delicious dish is Nhom Ban Kann, steamed shrimp served with fresh mint and red snappers in lemon juice. For entrees, I recommend the fresh filleted fish steamed in coconut milk with lemon grass and wrapped in banana leaf; the frog's legs in coconut milk; or Banh Hoi Bo Lui, a brochette of filet of beef with lemon grass and angel hair noodles. Be brave and try one of these delicious dishes combined with sticky rice, Indochinese style. Such desserts as hazelnut mousse cake rate special mention. You'll understand why Phnom Penh was such a gourmet paradise in its heyday.

JACKSON HOLE WYOMING BURGERS

232 E 64th St	Third Ave at 35th St	Second Ave at 84th St
371-7187	679-3264	737-8788
Mon-Sat:	Mon-Sat:	Mon-Thurs:
10:30-1 a.m.;	10:30-1 a.m.;	10:30-1 a.m.;
Sun: 12-12	Sun: 12-12	Fri, Sat: 10:30-4 a.m.;
		Sun: 11-midnight

No credit cards
Inexpensive

You might think that a burger is a burger is a burger. But having done a burger taste test all over the city, I choose Jackson's as the best. Each one weighs in at seven juicy, delicious ounces. All ingredients are fresh, and the taste tells the story. You can get all types of hamburgers, along with great coffee and French fries. You can have a pizza burger, an alpine burger, an English burger, or maybe a Baldouney burger (mushrooms, fried onions, and American cheese)—or omelets, if you prefer. The atmosphere isn't fancy, but once you sink your teeth into a Jackson burger accompanied by great onion rings and one of the homemade desserts, you'll see why I'm so enthusiastic.

JACQUELINE'S
132 E 61st St
838-4559
Lunch: Mon-Fri; Dinner: Mon-Sat
Moderate

Hidden away on East 61st Street is one of the most romantic spots on the East Side. Jacqueline, a charming lady, personally presides, serving not only as hostess but as chef. Jacqueline is also a painter, and her works of art decorate the three cozy rooms of her French bistro; there is an attractive room in the back for private parties that would be ideal for medium-sized groups. Jacqueline is talented and effusively friendly, so it's easy to see why the restaurant has a regular neighborhood clientele. The menu is relatively small, with emphasis on fish dishes. For hors d'oeuvres, there is marinated salmon, sea scallops, escargots, and a selection of salads. Game is well represented with emphasis on crispy Long Island duck, roast local pheasant, or medallions of venison. But the real winner is the Indonesian barbecued lamb with curried saffron rice and pickled cucumber! A very simple dessert tray features an upside-down Indonesian apple tart that's very special. Now if Jacqueline would just spend a little less time loving her customers and a little more time working on the uneven service, this would be a real winner. But it is a great restaurant for hearty food, and the champagne-by-the-glass adds to the romantic atmosphere.

JANE'S BAR AND GRILL
208 E 60th St (at Third Ave)
935-3481
Lunch: Mon-Fri; Dinner: Mon-Sat
Moderate to moderately expensive

Another good retreat for the hungry Bloomies shopper. This slim, classy operation serves non-slimming food, but in a very classy manner. At both lunch and dinner, excellent salads are featured: a seasonal salad, nicoise salad, and a delicious combination of frisee, bacon, roquefort, and roast garlic. Don't miss the sautéed crab cakes with tomatoes and chiles; it's a special appetizer. Also at both lunch and dinner, there is a nice selecton of seafood dishes, including sea scallops, sea bass, and a sautéed paillard of salmon. At noon a grilled lamb or grilled steak sandwich will tide you over until you check out all those bargains across the street. In the evening, the menu includes muscovy duck, rack of lamb, and a veal dish. There's quite an assortment of desserts at all times. Mouth-watering temptations like a napoleon of strawberry and rhubarb, pecan waffle with chocolate sauce and bourbon ice cream, frozen caramel soufflé with oranges and grand marnier, warm chocolate truffle cake with espresso ice cream, and poached peach pistachio ice cream with raspberry sauce are only the highlights of one of the best dessert menus in town.

JIM McMULLEN'S
1341 Third Ave (at 77th St)
861-4700
Lunch, Dinner: Daily
American Express
Moderate

I'm always a bit suspicious of a restaurant where the waiting line moves with irregular motion, and this is one spot where that happens. If the maitre d' or Jim McMullen knows you, or if your name is well-known, the wait is short. Otherwise, it's ridiculous. But people do wait, I guess, not only because it is chic to see and be seen here, but because the food is good and the prices are certainly right. Jim was a model, and the place is a favorite hangout for the famous and near-famous. The menu is unimaginative, with the usual appetizers, ranging from barley soup to clams on the half shell. But I find the chicken pot pie worth the visit in itself. There is a good selection of fish dishes, including poached salmon and several steak offerings. The chocolate brownie pie is an A-1 dessert, and the hot fudge sundae is not the usual ice-cream store variety. An attractive selection for supper served after 11 p.m. includes popular sandwiches and salads at bargain prices. There is also a private dining room (seating 30-50 guests) available for lunch or dinner. Now, a new wine and spirit store at 1381 Third Avenue (288-2211) bears the McMullen name.

JOE'S
79 MacDougal St
473-8834
Lunch, Dinner: Wed-Mon
Moderate

Joe's belongs in the very good Italian category, not only for the quality of the food but also for the value you get from your dining dollar. Joe himself is on the job, as he has been for several decades, imparting Old World charm to this small Village establishment. His staff is also made up of experienced, efficient, no-nonsense old-timers. Spaghetti (in six different ways), baked ziti, linguini, or homemade egg noodles are all excellent starters. I'd stick to the veal scaloppine (fixed five different ways), the veal chops, or the veal cutlets for entrees. Shrimps and clams are featured, and the breast of chicken alla parmigiana is a winner. My favorite meal here is cannelloni served with great Italian bread and a very fresh salad "alla Joe's." A perfect meal at a tiny price. If the name of this place was Valentino's instead of Joe's, you'd pay double!

JOHN CLANCY'S
181 W 10th St	206 E 63rd St (at Second Ave)
242-7350	752-6666
Dinner: Daily	Lunch: Mon-Fri; Dinner: Daily
	Moderate

It's always a bit dangerous when a successful restaurant expands; it's more difficult to maintain the hands-on operation. For years, John Clancy's was one of the better seafood houses in the Village, and now there is a branch uptown. The atmosphere in both is a bit stuffy—the staff is somewhat affected—but so far the same good food is served up in both places. Specialties of the house include a hearty Fisherman's stew, Lobster Americaine, and delicious barbequed jumbo shrimp. The mesquite-grilled items are very tasty, especially the swordfish teriyaki. Desserts always seem to go especially well after a seafood dinner, and all those at John Clancy's are homemade and delicious. There are usually several selections of outrageous chocolate items (like chocolate velvet cake), and the English trifle is first-rate.

JOHN'S PIZZERIA
278 Bleecker St
243-1680
Mon-Thurs: 11:30 a.m.-12 p.m.; Fri, Sat: 11:30 a.m.-
12:30 p.m.; Sun: 12-11:30 p.m.
No credit cards
Inexpensive

Why is it that most pizzerias are called Joe's or John's or Jack's or Jimmy's? Couldn't we have a Priscilla's or Penelope's pizzeria? The boss here isn't even named John—he's Pete Castellotti, a.k.a. the Baron of Bleecker Street. Pete offers 55—count 'em—varieties of pizza, from just cheese and tomatoes to a gourmet extravaganza of cheese, tomatoes, anchovies, sausage, peppers, meatballs, onions, and mushrooms. If spaghetti or cheese ravioli or manicotti (all homemade) are your preference, this is also the place for you. The manicotti filled with ricotta and mozzarella cheese, covered with plain tomato sauce and served with great Italian bread will make even your Uncle Menachem a believer. The surroundings are shabby, the menus are shabby, the plates are shabby, and the neighborhood is shabby, *but* the pizzas are perfection.

JULIA
226 W 79th St
787-1511
Lunch, Brunch, Dinner, Supper: Daily
Moderate

Julia is a charming spot, particularly in nice weather when one can eat in a covered garden with the sun or stars in full view. But even in nasty weather, the setting is pleasant, with the food matching the atmosphere. If you can't eat in the garden, there is a pleasant dining area upstairs. Another nice thing about Julia's is that they are open seven days a week for lunch, brunch, dinner, and supper. Moreover, the service is polite, efficient, and unobtrusive. Grilled items are the house specialties: fresh fish, steak, chicken breast, and game. Of the homemade desserts, the bittersweet chocolate marquise is the best.

KATZ'S DELICATESSEN
205 E Houston St (at Ludlow St)
254-2246
Sun-Thurs: 7 a.m.-11 p.m.; Fri, Sat: 7 a.m.-1 a.m.
No credit cards
Inexpensive

When you are down on the Lower East Side and need an extra big bite, try Katz's Delicatessen. It is a super place with some of the biggest and best sandwiches in town. The atmosphere goes along with the great food, and the prices are reasonable. You can go right up to the counter and order (it is fun watching the no-nonsense operators slicing and fixing), or sit at a table where a seasoned waiter will take excellent care of you. Try the dill pickles and the sauerkraut with your sandwich, and I guarantee even Rolaids will not diminish the memories of one of New York's great institutions. Katz's is a perfect way to sample the unique "charm" of Lower East Side establishments. When you wait at a table for an hour, or discover that the salt, pepper, and napkin containers are empty and the ketchup is missing, you'll know what I mean.

KEENS CHOP HOUSE
72 W 36th St
947-3636
Lunch: Mon-Fri; Dinner: Mon-Sat
Moderate

It seems that some of the best old restaurants in New York get lost in the shuffle. With the openings of glamorous new places every week and people always wanting to know which places are "in," we forget about the dependable restaurants that consistently do a good job. One of them is Keens Chop House, a unique New York institution. I can remember going there decades ago when those in the garment trade made Keens their lunch headquarters. This has not changed. Keens still has the same attractions: the bar reeks with atmosphere, and there are great party facilities and fine food to match. Keens opened in 1885 and has been a fixture in the Herald Square area ever since. For some time, it was a "gentlemen only" place, and although it still has a very masculine atmosphere, ladies now feel comfortable and welcome. Of course, the famous mutton chop with mint is the house specialty, but other delicious dishes include veal, liver, lamb, and fish, and a special omelet of the day. For the light eater, especially at lunch, there are some great salads. My favorite is the sliced breast of chicken with fusini and pesto salad. There's a hearty, robust atmosphere about the place, and the waiters are the no-nonsense type. If you have a meat-and-potatoes lover in your party, this is the place to take him. Make sure you save a little room for the maple pecan or deep-dish apple pie.

KITCHO
22 W 46th St
575-8880
Lunch: Mon-Fri; Dinner: Sun-Fri
Moderate

In Japanese, *kitcho* means good omen, and I'm sure you'll find your dinner to be just that. This is one of the better Oriental restaurants in Manhattan: you can tell by the fact that most of the patrons are Japanese. Like many Chinese and Japanese restaurants, the décor and atmosphere are nothing special—clean and functional, but not much more. The charm lies in the delicious Japanese food. Start with ishi yaki, a hot rock in an attractive container, upon which you cook your own shrimp, squid, or beef. The aroma is tantalizing, the results spectacular. Other delicious appetizers include boiled spinach with sesame, fried bean curd, and red caviar with grated white radish. The usual tempura or teriyaki (beef, pork, chicken or fish) are available; another favorite is yaki-tori, broiled chicken and onions on a skewer. Rice (in many forms) tastes better in this setting than at home, and the sushi is a real winner.

KLEINE KONDITOREI
234 E 86th St
737-7130
Sun-Thurs: 10 a.m.-midnight; Fri, Sat: 10 a.m.-1 a.m.
Moderate

If you're in the mood for sauerbraten and potato dumplings and red cabbage, wiener schnitzel, goose, venison, steak, or an outrageously calorie-laden linzer torte, try Kleine Konditorei. It is one of the very few German restaurants worth visiting in New York; the cakes and pastries would do credit to the fine little pastry shops you find in Munich. East 86th Street is one of New York's most colorful areas, and a walk around the neighborhood (which you'll need after a stop here) is interesting. I recommend Kleine Konditorei for an after-the-show visit, or for a special lunch when a golden-brown German pancake sounds just right. There is also a bakery section for take-out orders.

LA BOHÈME
24 Minetta Lane
473-6447
Dinner: Tues-Sun; Brunch: Sun
Moderate

Pari Dulac likes people and food, and it shows. The part-Iranian, part-French hostess is right on the job in her cozy, informal Bohemian bistro, dispensing delicious edibles at moderate prices.

The setting is on a quiet, charming street in the Village. When the front doors are open in the nice weather, you get the impression you are in a quaint European town. Inside, soothing music puts you in the mood to enjoy some of the best pizza you have ever tasted; it's made with very thin pasta right in front of your eyes. In the back, an open kitchen puts out pasta, salads, and great French dishes done to perfection. On Sundays, you can't beat the Country French brunch or the unique omelet selection. Dessert specialties include tarts made in-house, as well as first-class chocolate mousse cake and lemon soufflé with raspberry sauce. Pari has been wise in using only the best ingredients in her dishes, and has resisted the temptation to raise prices to a point where value is questionable. Pari is part of a restaurant family; her husband runs the reincarnated Le Chantilly on East 57th Street.

LA BOITE EN BOIS
75 W 68th St
874-270⁷
Dinner. Daily
No credit cards
Moderate

The building that once housed Simon's Restaurant has undergone a thorough renovation, and a delightful, busy restaurant is packing them in every evening—for obvious reasons. The owner, an ex-chef, has hit upon that winning combination: delicious food, personal service, and moderate prices. The salads are unusual; the escargots aux champignons des bois is a great beginner. For an entree, I recommend the filet of snapper, fricassee of chicken, or the escalope of veal. The intimate atmosphere allows you to become acquainted with your neighbor, if you so desire, and all the niceties of service are operative from start to finish. All the desserts are made in-house; I suggest choosing one of their sorbets. By all means, call for reservations, since the place is very small and very popular.

LA CARAVELLE
33 W 55th St (at Fifth Ave)
586-4252
Lunch: Mon-Fri; Dinner: Mon-Sat
Expensive

For years I enjoyed La Caravelle because it was a truly classic restaurant, in food, service, and ambiance. For a while, though, I felt it was going downhill, relying on past glory instead of keeping up with the times. True, if they knew you, the attention would be superb. But alas, if you were a stranger, it was another story altogether. Now things seem to have undergone a revival, and even the old décor, beautiful murals, flowers and all, have taken on a new life. The classic menu is still there, but now it de-emphasizes the heavier dishes of the past. As with so many new restaurants, concern for health is evident in a number of the menu selections. There is even a hint of Oriental influence in some of the preparations. If you are looking for an absolutely superb meal, I'd order the duck and finish off with one of La Caravelle's great soufflés. Tell them you just concluded a big deal with Donald Trump, and watch them pour on the special attention!

LA COLOMBE D'OR
134 E 26th St
689-0666
Lunch: Mon-Fri; Dinner: Mon-Sat
Moderate

It's easy to see why La Colombe d'Or is always busy. They provide well-prepared meals at a reasonable price. The place has an intimate French provincial atmosphere, and the service is prompt and efficient. Take note of this spot, since there are not too many good eating establishments in this part of town. I'd suggest the super bouillabaisse maison for a very good lunch dish. I also recommend the pasta. For dinner, you might start with ratatouille (vegetable stew) or the snails in Roquefort sauce. Then go on to the roast chicken with black olives, chopped tomatoes, and garlic. A superb dish. The roasted squab, however, is not done too well. Gateau Victoire, their chocolate cake, is first-rate. One of the nicest features is the number of specialty coffees with cognac, triple sec, calvados or even cafe morello, with kahlua, whipped cream, chocolate shavings, orange rindlets . . . *wow!* Let's start with coffee and dessert for a change!

LA CÔTE BASQUE
5 E 55th St
688-6525
Lunch, Dinner: Mon-Sat
Expensive

My uncle started taking me here 25 years ago. I remember thinking even then that it was a fantastic place to see, to be seen, and to enjoy. It still is. The beautiful people flock to this restaurant for fine French food, and if you're a gourmet, this is a spot you won't want to miss. The food is as tasty as the people watching is enthralling. And the elegant murals and flowers are matched by the elegant guests. Once in a while, we are all tempted to try some spectacular dish that we can't make at home. This is the place to go (with a very full wallet or the company credit card) when you have that desire. Specialties of the house include pepper steak, Dover sole, roast duck, sweetbreads, and quail. The appetizers, especially the smoked salmon, seafood casserole, and seasonal salads are among the best in the city. Save some room for raspberry soufflé or the out-of-this-world hazelnut daquoise. Note: La Côte Basque regulars get distinctly preferential treatment over newcomers.

LA FONDUE
43 W 55th St
581-0820
Lunch, Dinner: Daily
No credit cards
Inexpensive

This business is an outgrowth of a cheese store that was founded in Greenwich Village over 25 years ago. La Fondue is always busy —a great spot for a quick snack, a good lunch, a no-frills dinner, or an after-theater repast. Because of its popularity, they have added more than 100 seats. My favorites for starters include onion soup, cheddar-cheese soup, or Swedish green-pea soup—all very well made and very filling. The specialty of the house for light snacks is a cheese and sausage board, featuring a great variety of imported cheeses and sausages from Denmark, Poland, the Netherlands, Spain, Norway, Austria, Switzerland, Germany, Italy, Hungary, and almost any other place you can think of. This attractive offering includes salad, bread, and relishes. You can also have fun with a prime filet mignon fondue or a genuine imported Swiss cheese fondue. For heartier dining, try the cheeseburgers, the boned breast of chicken, the cheese omelet, a very hefty chef's salad, a variety of superb quiches, or the sirloin steak. There's even a Continental Cheese Tour, in which you get a fine selection of international cheeses, plus bread, fresh fruit, and crackers. I also recommend the Swiss chocolate fondue with fruit and fruit bread for dessert, or perhaps the banana fruit bread, rum raisin ice cream, and chocolate fondue sauce. This is a number-one spot, where your stomach will be satisfied and your pocketbook treated kindly.

LA GAULOISE
502 Sixth Ave (at 13th St)
691-1363
Lunch: Tues-Fri; Dinner: Tues-Sun; Brunch: Sat, Sun
Moderate

This unassuming French bistro could be turn-of-the-century San Francisco or present-day Paris. Simplicity in décor and in presentation is the secret of success at La Gauloise, where Village gourmets

go when they want to get away from the trendy places. The folks
who run the place fit right into the picture. No cutesy stuff here.
The salad selection is especially good; ravioli stuffed with lobster or
shrimp and sole paté are other good starters. The entrees include
just about anything you want, from sweetbreads and duck breast to
grilled seafood items, steaks, and chicken. Each dish comes with its
own special accompaniment. For example, the roast veal tenderloin
with asparagus ratatouille is a marvelous combination. The rice
pudding with fruit for dessert will give you less of a guilt complex in
the morning. So will the tab.

LA GRENOUILLE
3 E 52nd St (at Fifth Ave)
752-1495
Lunch, Dinner: Tues-Sat
Expensive

Giselle Masson and her son, Charles, have set their establishment
apart. La Grenouille is one of those special places that one really
has to see to believe. It's impossible to describe. The beautiful fresh
flowers are but a clue to a unique, not-to-be-forgotten dining experience. The food is just as great as the atmosphere, and although
the prices are high, it's worth every penny. The celebrity watching
adds to the fun. The French menu is complete, the staff professional. Be sure to try their cold hors d'oeuvres; they're a specialty
of the house, as are the clams and the Bayonne ham. Don't miss the
soufflés for dessert—they're superb. The tables are very close together, but what difference does it make when the people at your elbows are so interesting?

LA LUNCHONETTE
130 10th Ave (at 18th St)
675-0342
Lunch, Dinner: Daily
No credit cards
Moderate

I've got news for readers who think that only fancy restaurants
are included in this book. Of course, that is not true at all. Many of
these restaurants are quite plain and inexpensive, but they serve
good food at an attractive price. La Lunchonette definitely falls into the "unfancy" category. It's located in a rather run-down neighborhood of the city, and since it lacks an eye-catching sign out
front, you're likely to pass La Lunchonette without a second look.
But some distinctive and delicious things happen on the inside. In a

space that looks as though it were decorated with objects that didn't sell at last year's church bazaar, Zoe Porte serves up some of the tastiest dishes around. The selection is sophisticated: you could have sweetbreads vinaigrette or lobster bisque to start, and go on to swordfish with capers and lemon butter, or a delicious gratinée of lobster, crab, and scallops. Part of the kitchen area is curtained off, but one can still see that really primitive equipment can turn out some of the best food. The talent lies with the user, and that's the case at this no-pretense bistro.

LA METAIRIE
189 W 10th St (bet W Fourth and Bleecker St)
989-0343
Dinner: Daily
Moderate

La Metairie (it translates as small communal farm) has built its reputation through a succession of individual owners, who have given tender, loving care to this tiny hole-in-the-wall in the Village. The menu changes every three months, so I suggest you call ahead to see if your favorite is being featured that day, be it tripe, rabbit with mustard sauce, or bouillabaisse. The room accommodates only 22 people, the tables are close together, and the atmosphere extremely cozy and friendly. How they can operate in a thimble-size kitchen and produce such tasty morsels is a mystery, but the owners are carrying on a quality tradition.

LA METAIRIE (uptown)
1442 Third Ave (bet 81st and 82nd St)
988-1800
Lunch, Dinner: Daily
Moderately expensive

Gracious greeting at the door. Prompt seating. Inviting food displays. Beautiful table settings with unusual china and fresh flowers. A cozy fireplace. Real birds in a pretty cage. Napkins unfolded and placed in your lap. Spotless wooden floors. Get the picture? Sylvain Fareri "loves the food business," and it shows. This restaurant is the big brother of the original, smaller one in the Village, and it is as pleasant and charming a place as you will find in New York. Best of all, the food matches the superior environment. In a room reminiscent of a French country inn, you dine on such delicacies as sautéed snails, ravioli filled with seafood in a champagne sauce, and a mousse of artichoke hearts. A hearty veal or lamb dish makes a great meal. Each platter is served from under a shining silver cover, the butter is carved in the shape of a tiny bird, and the table water is not just from the tap, it is Evian. An apple tart or homemade sorbet will top off one of the nicest dinners you could imagine.

LA MIRABELLE
333 W 86th St
496-0458
Dinner: Mon-Sat
Moderate

You don't have to be big to be successful, and the petite La Mirabelle has proven that being busy and crowded is appealing to diners. Of course, there has to be a reason, and at La Mirabelle it's the food. This is the dining room off the lobby of a hotel on the Upper West Side, an area where good food too often takes a back seat to trendy presentations. Here you will find wholesome food served in a romantic pink-and-white setting with a French accent. There are always specials, but you can't go wrong with the daily offerings of sole, scallops, duckling, chicken, veal, steak, and lamb chops. La Mirabelle recently expanded their seating capacity.

LANDMARK TAVERN
626 11th Ave (at 46th St)
757-8595
Sun-Thurs: noon-midnight; Fri, Sat: noon-1 a.m.; Sun: Brunch
Inexpensive

What to do and where to go for lunch on Sunday? Many smaller restaurants have look-alike brunches, with the usual selection (omelets, eggs, sausages, etc.) and very little imagination. So, I suggest you get out your strolling shoes and proceed to the Landmark Tavern, a New York institution since 1865. The usual brunch items are indeed available (at very nominal prices), but you also have the options of such house specialties as shepherd's pie (ground lamb sautéed with herbs), lamb steak (delicious!), or English-style fish and chips. To accompany your selection is Landmark's homemade (every hour) soda bread served with imported jams and marmalade. Some of the desserts are also homemade; the chocolate walnut torte, apple pie, and carrot cake are all above average. Of course, Sunday is not the only time to enjoy this three-story historic dining spot. (The top floor is available for banquets.) Drop in for their daily regular dinners, which include sandwich platters, a variety of salads, fresh seafood, steaks, and roast prime ribs of beef. The bar is friendly, the help is harried, the atmosphere reeks of nostalgia, and the food is a bargain. Take it in after church next Sunday.

LA PETITE FERME
973 Lexington Ave (at 70th St)
249-3272
Lunch, Dinner: Mon-Sat
Moderate

La Petite Ferme was a very small spot down in the Village, the first time I visited it. It has since grown to be a larger, fancier place on Lexington Avenue. The atmosphere is still intimate, and the same sort of menu (printed on a blackboard) is available to a large group of faithful customers. As the seating is quite limited, calling for reservations is a good idea. Without them, it is easier to get in during the early part of the dinner hour. The cuisine is French country style, and the three or four featured entree selections are all tastefully prepared, whether it's poached bass, veal, sole, or whatever. I have to give high marks to their vegetables, because they don't overcook them. There is an attractive garden downstairs, and although the service is a little confusing (the kitchen is upstairs), the staff manages to do a very satisfactory job.

LA RESERVE
4 W 49th St
247-2993
Lunch, Dinner: Mon-Sat
Expensive

The question I'm asked most frequently is "What is your favorite restaurant?" It's a difficult question to answer, because there are so many variables involved in choosing a place to eat. But if I am pinned down, my answer is "La Reserve." This beautiful room is perfection personified, as is the ever-present owner, Jean-Louis Missud. His influence is evident in every detail: the professional greeting, the knowledgeable and professional waiters, the magnificent ambiance, and most of all, the absolutely superb food. The lighting makes everyone look healthy and beautiful, and the dishes placed in front of you are attractive and appetizing. It would be impossible to list the best things to order. My suggestion is to let Jean-Louis make the selection for you, then just relax and enjoy as fine a meal as you could have, at any price, anywhere in the world. A pre-theater dinner is available, as well as private party facilities.

LA RIPAILLE
605 Hudson St (at W 12th St)
255-4406
Dinner: Mon-Sat
Moderate

There's a new menu every night at this small and romantic Parisian-style cafe, so call ahead to see what's available. I find it to be a cozy spot for an informal dinner. The tables are rickety, but the chef puts his heart into every dish. It is certainly worth a visit. Most entrees are done to perfection, the seafood is always fresh (seafood in puff pastry is a specialty), and they do an excellent job with sweetbreads and rabbit. White chocolate is a house favorite; at least half of the dessert offerings use chocolate as an ingredient. Proudly displayed at the front of the room are rave notices from a number of New York gourmets. If they want, they can add mine, too.

LATTANZI
361 W 46th St
315-0980
Lunch: Mon-Fri; Dinner: Mon-Sat
American Express
Moderate

There's something about West 46th Street, the so-called "restaurant row" in the Broadway theater district, that is unappealing. Sign after sign, one restaurant after another—one wonders how they all stay in business. Actually, they don't! The comings and goings are rapid, and many really don't deserve to stay around. One of the winners, however, is Lattanzi, owned by the family of the same name. It's warm and cozy, with attractive brick walls. Management and service are disorganized and amateurish, but that doesn't take away from the excellent pretheater Italian dinner. The usual pasta and antipasto are available, but I'd like to call attention to the Capellini Primavera, a very fine spaghetti with vegetables that's truly delicious. Then there's a combination seafood dish (some squid with fresh tomato, garlic, peas, and basil) and some of the best veal scaloppine I've ever tasted. Lamb chops, swordfish, and scampi are also featured. There's nothing special about the desserts here; however, you can't go wrong with the Napoleon or tartufo. Don't waste your time with most of the other places on "restaurant row" (except Orso). Head toward Lattanzi (with advance reservation), and you won't go wrong.

LA TULIPE
104 W 13th St
691-8860
Dinner: Tues-Sun
Expensive

La Tulipe is French cuisine at its best—innovative and light fare, with great sauces, and each plate is a work of art. Let me describe the desserts first! You know by now that I'm a dessert nut. All pastries, sherbets, and ice creams are made on the premises. The best is called La Tulipe Javanaise, a creamy coffee ice cream with chocolate sauce in a flower-shaped pastry shell. Magnificent! And there's an apple tart, a floating island with hazelnuts, an apricot soufflé, a hazelnut meringue, and a layered chocolate cake with chocolate tiles. Enough? Okay, let's get back to the basics. Start with the zucchini fritters or the mussel soup with saffron—they're very special. Then proceed to the red snapper, the sautéed chicken, or the grilled sliced squab. I'm partial to the rack of lamb with garlic crumbs and tomato; however, the steamed lobster on a bed of spaghetti is equally good. The service is slow and the management is condescending, but you can be sure you'll get a professionally prepared meal. Note: the *prix fixe* dinner is fixed pretty high.

LAURENT
111 E 56th St (at Park Ave)
753-2729
Lunch: Mon-Fri; Dinner: Mon-Sat
Expensive

Laurent serves excellent food, beautifully prepared and presented (their fruit tart is a work of art) by waiters in black tie. It's a quiet, elegant restaurant patronized by quiet, elegantly dressed diners—the sort of place to go for an intimate dinner *à deux,* or for discussing business over a lobster. The sort of restaurant, in short, that is favored by executives with company credit cards. The menu changes daily, according to the season's best produce. Thus, in spring, soft-shell crabs are offered, while later on, shad and shad roe are available. Year-round favorites are duckling served with orange sauce, and steak au poivre flambé a l'Armagnac. There are three private dining rooms, and the restaurant's wine cellars stock over 54,000 bottles of wine, including those vintages old and rare enough to satisfy the most discriminating palates. Quite a place!

LAVIN'S
23 W 39th St
921-1288
Lunch, Dinner: Mon-Fri
Moderate

Lavin's started the trend toward New American cuisine, and they have been successful ever since. They combine prompt service and moderate prices with a warm atmosphere and very polite personnel. It is a particularly convenient place for a midtown lunch or a pre-theater dinner. Start with the salad of garden rows, which is made with carrots, tomatoes, broccoli, radishes, green beans, and the like, or perhaps you'd prefer the delicious warm chicken salad. Their mesquite grilled chicken, carpaccio of beef, or grilled veal chop are excellent entrees. All kinds of pasta are available, the best being linguini with shrimp and bay scallops. An added feature is the cruvinet, a wine dispenser that offers wine by the taste or the glass.

LE BERNARDIN
155 W 51st St
489-1515
Lunch, Dinner: Mon-Sat
Very expensive

Le Bernardin is a magnificent restaurant, no *ands, ifs,* or *buts* about it. Well, there is one *but,* which I'll get to later. The room itself is tasteful and classy, with colorful fishing scenes adorning the walls. The service is friendly, unobtrusive, and highly professional, just as you'd expect from Maguy and Gilbert LeCoze. The seafood dishes are marvelously fresh, tasty, and superbly seasoned with just the right sauces. Small snails are offered to all diners before the meal, and other tidbits are available to get the juices flowing. The bass, sea scallops, and warm lobster salad are terrific appetizers. Then you may feast upon sea scallops, halibut, salmon done several different ways, snapper, and at least four different lobster dishes. The dessert selection includes warm mousse of passion fruit with raspberry and caramel (this takes first place) and a number of ice creams and sorbets, my favorite being the bitter-chocolate sorbet. Now for the *but.* And it is a big one. The prices are simply outrageous. The same quality dishes, served perhaps in a less impressive atmosphere, are available in several other Manhattan seafood houses at half the price. But there are always those who equate high prices with "*the* place to go," and as long as that is the case, places like Le Bernardin will prosper.

LE BIARRITZ
325 W 57th St (at Ninth Ave)
757-2390
Lunch, Dinner: Mon-Sat
Moderate

What a pleasure to be treated so pleasantly by everyone at a restaurant! This is the kind of homey place where the busboy "lets" you keep the knife from the first course to reuse with the entree. But then, you don't come here for the professional service or fancy trimmings. New York is full of "neighborhood" restaurants, and Le Biarritz is one of the best in that category. It seems like home every evening as the regulars take most of the seats in this warm, smallish eatery. The place has been in the same location and in the same hands for over 20 years. Gleaming copper makes any eating establishment look inviting, and here you can see a first-rate collection of beautiful French copper cooking and serving pieces. If you're in the mood for escargots to start, the chef knows how to prepare them well. Or maybe some real French onion soup or crepes à la Biarritz (stuffed with crab meat). You can't go wrong with either. Entrees range from frog's legs provencale to boeuf bourguignonne to filet de sole veronique. The menu includes all kinds of chicken, lamb, beef, veal, and fish dishes, each served with fresh vegetables. Although there are no unusual desserts, all of them are homemade and very tasty. The reasonably priced dinner includes soup, salad, and a choice of dessert. I recommend Le Biarritz if you are going to a Broadway show or an event in the Lincoln Center area.

LE BILBOQUET
25 E 63rd St
751-3036
Lunch, Dinner: Daily
No credit cards
Moderate

Philippe presides over this cozy Upper East Side Parisian sidewalk cafe as if it were his own backyard. The place isn't really much bigger than that, but in nice weather you can eat outside on the sidewalk. Philippe seems to know everyone; indeed, most of the loyal clientele live in the neighborhood. Nonetheless, hungry visitors looking for good, informal dining all day long will feel just as welcome. It's amazing that such a tiny kitchen can turn out such good food. The paté and the terrine de saumon are both delicious appetizers. Le Bilboquet is best known for its salads; the nicoise and duck salad with mangoes are the best bets. Any one of the assorted tarts are excellent, but my favorite is the lemon. The chocolate gateau is definitely waist expanding! Philippe is looking harassed and a bit fatigued these days; I hope he can keep his strength. His constant presence is surely the secret of Le Bilboquet's success.

LE CHANTILLY
106 E 57th St
751-2931
Lunch: Mon-Sat; Dinner: Daily
Expensive

Some years back, a meal at Le Chantilly was a special New York treat. But, alas, the restaurant went distinctly downhill until a talented, gracious gentleman by the name of Camille Dulac took the reins. With a superior knowledge of the kitchen and a natural understanding of the importance of the owner being on the job watching the operation, Camille has brought back the charm and distinction of this beautiful room. Today one would be hard-pressed to find a better meal, despite the pricey tab, in a more attractive setting. Complementing the food and ambiance, the professional staff ensure that your dining experience is a special one. There is something very elegant about having the dishes served with those gleaming silver covers, and then having them all lifted simultaneously at the table. It's like the opening of gifts. Under those covers, you'll find such delicious luncheon choices as duck confit with ginger, smoked salmon omelet, casserole of fish, and seafood with fennel. A large choice of hot and cold hors d'oeuvres is offered with the fixed-price luncheon: try the chicken sausage with truffles, cold poached salmon, or the delicious fresh vegetable soup. À la carte offerings are also available. For dinner, you can order à la carte as well, or go with the fixed-price menu. Special dinner treats include breast of squab, roast rack of lamb, and roast muscovy duck. The dessert cart groans with an eye-popping selection of goodies, any one of which will be a fitting end to a magnificent meal.

LE CIRQUE
58 E 65th (at Park Ave)
794-9292
Lunch, Dinner: Mon-Sat
Expensive

Sirio Maccioni is a legend in the restaurant world of New York, and well he should be. While many of the grand, old-time restaurants rest on their laurels, Sirio is innovative and ingenious. Above all, he's a showman. His magnificent restaurant is crowded to the gills with the famous and those who would like to be. Elegant food draws these elegant folk. It is a pleasure to watch as the superbly orchestrated staff makes sure that every person in the room feels that he or she is someone very special. Each dish, whether it's game, fish, or meat, comes with superb sauces, and is served in satisfying portions. The "must try" dishes are the sea scallops fantasy, the fettucine with truffles, and the creme brulée. Take along your goldest credit card, and be prepared for an event that would restore anyone's faith in the concept of the United Nations: a great American restaurant, serving superb French food, and orchestrated by an Italian. Oh, yes, the pastry chef is Austrian!

LE CYGNE
55 E 54th St
759-5941
Lunch: Mon-Fri; Dinner: Mon-Sat
Expensive

A most appealing ambiance combined with a very professional kitchen is really all that needs to be said about Le Cygne. This spot is one that you will not want to miss, but make sure it's saved for a great occasion or when you're dining on an expense account. The whole setting is comfortable, relaxing, and appealing. To begin your meal, how about Maine scallops in a wine and saffron sauce, or perhaps artichoke hearts with sweetbreads, mushrooms, and truffle sauce? And what a selection for the main course: frog's legs sautéed in garlic butter; snails with wild mushrooms; braised squab with olives, mushrooms, and artichokes; breast of duck in honey-vinegar sauce; and absolutely sensational braised sweetbreads with Chanterelle mushrooms. Meals run a hefty *prix fixe* tab, but it's well worth it. There are specialties of the house every day, and private dining facilities are available.

L'ECLUSE
213 Sixth Ave (at King St)
691-5291
Lunch: Mon-Fri; Dinner: Mon-Sat
Moderate

You might be put off a bit when you walk into this French bistro, since the floor, walls, ceiling, and tables look like they've seen better days. But you won't mind if you want to do some serious eating and you're not planning to propose marriage to the light of your life over dinner. The food is the thing, not the service or the atmosphere. The staff is only there to cart the plates out from the kitchen, not to inform you about menu selections or provide any extra amenities. Start with the asparagus and mushroom tart, red pepper soup, or marvelous fresh salads like the Bordelaise with Italian chicory, duck confit, and garlic croutons. Grilled Norwegian salmon, roast herbed chicken, and roasted leg of lamb are great entree choices. Try the cheese platter for dessert; it's varied and delicious. Come hungry! The portions are sizable.

LE REFUGE
166 E 82nd St (bet Second and Third Ave)
861-4505
Lunch, Dinner: Daily
No credit cards
Moderate (overpriced desserts)

In any city other than New York this would be one of the hottest restaurants in town. But aside from the folks in the neighborhood, nobody seems to have heard of Le Refuge, a charming, three-room French country inn that offers excellent food, professional service, and delightful surroundings. The front room (for nonsmokers) is cozy and comfortable, and the back two sections provide nice views and pleasant accommodations. This is another house where the owner is the chef, and as usual, it shows in the professionalism of the presentations. To start, I suggest the excellent salads, carpaccio, or raviolis langonstine. Then you have your choice of three seafood, three poultry, and three meat entrees. The Norwegian salmon with caviar is superb. Desserts are very special in taste and price. Creme brulée, a flourless chocolate gateau, and the poached pear with white and dark chocolate sauce are winners. Seek Le Refuge, and be prepared for a very special evening.

LE RÉGENCE
37 E 64th St
734-9100
Lunch, Dinner: Daily
Expensive

Hotel Plaza Athénée is well-known in Paris; now there is a New York version with a very classy restaurant. Not only is the setting understated and immensely attractive, but the tables are even far enough apart to have a private conversation. The presentation is outstanding, and the food is superb! One of the most impressive points of Le Régence is that the personnel are not impressed with their own importance. The waiters and maitre d' are pleasantly accommodating, hard-working, and well-informed. Other expensive New York restaurants, take note; it can be done. This spot is suitable for either lunch or dinner. You can't go wrong with any of the selections, but a few favorites stand out. Since it's mainly a seafood house, I strongly recommend the Dover sole filets in champagne sauce, the lobster ravioli, and the braised striped bass in a marvelous wine sauce. The luncheon salads are magnificent; a real treat is the sliced chicken breast salad with hazelnuts. It's so inviting to look at, you hate to eat it! Even mundane French-fried potatoes are done to perfection. And don't overlook the meat entrees, like the veal chops and the delicious steaks. The famous French family of restaurateurs, the Rostangs, supervise this fine operation.

LES PLEIADES
20 E 76th St
535-7230
Lunch, Dinner: Mon-Sat
Moderate to expensive

What a well-organized restaurant this is! It's obvious that the folks here know the ins and outs of the business—another case of the management being on the job. I have seldom encountered a restaurant with better trained, more courteous personnel. From the time you call to make a reservation to your farewell at the door, your host, captain, waiter, and busboy—everyone—give the impression that they know what they're doing and that they're pleased to serve you. The clientele are strictly Upper East Side matrons and their husbands, or perhaps their middle-aged sons and daughters taking the "old folks" out to dinner. But what a nice, comfortable place to do so! The food is excellent, the atmosphere is charming, and the entire evening can be a most satisfactory experience. Many of the hors d'oeuvres are displayed at an attractive table near the entrance, and the choices are numerous: coquilles au safran, sardines a l'Huile, le saumon fume, a great lobster salad, and so on. For entrees, try the coquilles St. Jacques with white wine and saffron, or the frog's legs sautéed with garlic. Specialties of the house include sweetbreads, rack of lamb, and broiled Dover sole. If you feel really hungry, tell them at the start that you'd like one of their soufflés for dessert—either the Grand Marnier or the chocolate.

LE TRAIN BLEU
1000 Third Ave (Bloomingdale's, sixth floor)
705-2100
Lunch, Brunch: Mon-Sat; Afternoon snacks: Mon-Fri;
Dinner: Thurs
Moderate

Those who are old enough to remember when eating on a train was elegant and fun can re-live a bit of that experience on the sixth floor of Bloomies, at the end of the "Main Course" housewares area. You are seated in a mock dining car, with authentic atmosphere and accessories. The view through the windows, however, does not change. The menu is unusual and well done. You can dine lightly or with gusto on salads (there's one with goat cheese), pasta, or omelet. An especially tasty dish is the fish soup with croutons, scallops, lobster, white fish, and mussels. Very rich desserts will fortify you for additional use of your plastic card: creme brulée, Irish cream soufflé, and hot crepes are just a few examples. Le Train Bleu is available for private receptions and dinners, and features one of the most extensive wine lists of any department-store restaurant. But what else would you expect from the ever-innovative folks at Bloomingdale's.

LION'S ROCK
316 E 77th St
988-3610
Lunch: Mon-Fri; Dinner: Daily; Brunch: Sat, Sun
Moderate

More than 100 years ago, Jones Wood was a favorite picnic spot for New Yorkers. Part of an estate owned by Bishop Samuel Provost, it was distinguished by its outcroppings of red granite, which made it a popular place for romantic trysts. Today, the Lion's

Rock restaurant operates in the same area, and it even has one of those large slabs of red granite in its backyard. It's a particularly delightful place in nice weather because of its sizable outdoor patio and beer garden, where cool water trickles down the rock. When it snows, the patio becomes a winter wonderland. The restaurant uses natural fresh herbs, no frozen foods, and no artificial flavorings. The menu includes hot and cold hors d'oeuvres, such as sliced raw salmon, bay scallops, and deep-fried clams. Their special creole chowder with fresh crawfish is a popular dish. The lobster with sautéed sea scallops is a real winner. I was particularly impressed with the vegetable selection; my favorites include the couscous (African crushed millet and rice) and the ratatouille (sautéed eggplant, peppers, onions, tomato, garlic, and basil). The Saturday and Sunday brunch menu is an unusual one, with selections ranging from chilled strawberry soup to whole-wheat pancakes, from omelets to a roulade of seasonal vegetables steamed in savoy cabbage. For dessert, try the white chocolate mousse with raspberry topping or the homemade sorbets. The excellent food and the atmospheric setting make Lion's Rock a unique Upper East Side dining experience.

LITTLE NELL'S TEA ROOM
343 E 85th St (bet First and Second Ave)
772-2046
Lunch: Mon-Fri; Dinner: Daily; Tea: Daily;
Brunch: Sat, Sun
Moderate

Little Nell is really Judy Nell Pickens, whose mother is also Nell. So it is only natural that she should be intrigued with Nell of Dickens' Old Curiosity Shop fame. Nell's cozy restaurant features Dickens on the wall, eclectic English memorabilia throughout, and especially friendly people who seem to be having a wonderful time serving you. There are two small rooms, with a kitchen in between. Try and be seated in the room to your left as you enter; it is brighter and more attractive. The food goes along with the surroundings: hearty but not fancy, served with tender loving care, and sure to satisfy. For lunch there are salads, pasta, and light entrees. Afternoon teas are very popular with homemade goodies. Dinners feature grilled Cornish hen and grilled marinated swordfish, along with a wonderful chicken breast sautéed with apple calvados sauce. The brunches are a neighborhood favorite, offering melt-in-your-mouth buttermilk waffles topped with fresh fruit and potato pancakes with scallions and sautéed mushrooms. Nell and her associates seem intent to make Dickens come to life with fond memories of friends, food, and fun.

LOTUS BLOSSOM
319 Greenwich St
219-0005
Lunch, Dinner: Daily
Moderate

In an area of TriBeCa that has come to life recently with several attractive new residential buildings, a new school, and a number of first-class restaurants, Lotus Blossom stands out as the best choice for true Hong Kong-style Chinese food. The room is immaculate and comfortable, the personnel friendly and efficient, and all the food fresh, with no M.S.G. used. Besides the usual selection found in a Chinese restaurant, Lotus Blossom offers superb Hakka specialties such as stuffed eggplant, Hakka scallops, and salt-baked gray sole with hot pepper. Other specialties of the house include Beijing duck (served in two courses) wrapped in homemade pancakes; crispy steak; shredded chicken and beef tenderloin served in a taro nest; and seafood with vegetables also served in a taro basket. The atmosphere is rather elegant for a moderately priced Chinese establishment; there is a noticeable absence of the usual noise and confusion. Free delivery service from the wide-ranging menu is available, and they cater for any event (up to 150 people).

LOU G. SIEGEL
209 W 38th St
921-4433
Sun-Thurs: 11:30-10; Fri: 11:30-3
Moderate

Lou G. Siegel has been around longer than most New Yorkers can remember. It opened its doors in 1917, and customers have been pushing through them ever since. Its reputation—of which it is well aware ("The best-known kosher restaurant in the world," says Siegel's Eddie Share)—is based mostly on their cold cuts, especially the pastrami. Workers in the garment district fill the place during lunch and dinner hours. Remember that, and schedule your visit for an early lunch or a "white tablecloth" dinner.

LUTÈCE
249 E 50th St (bet Second and Third Ave)
752-2225
Lunch: Tues-Fri; Dinner: Mon-Sat
Expensive

The standard by which so many of the restaurants in Manhattan are judged is Lutèce. It's so high-toned that there aren't even prices on the menu. Almost every restaurant guide lists it as number one. I'm not sure it's that, but certainly the chefs are masters, and the service is impeccable. The owner, Andre Soltner, has received many awards, and they're well deserved. Lutèce is housed in a former brownstone that's tastefully decorated with handsome furnishings and shimmering tableware. An indoor garden at the back adds to the charm. The restaurant also features three great *s*'s— soups, snails, and sauces. All of them are about the best in New York. Try the saumon à la mousse de moutarde or the carré d agneau caramelisé. But be prepared for less than great service if they don't know you. Nonetheless, you can't beat Lutèce. Considering their prices, ask if you can take home the beautiful menu as a souvenir!

MANHATTAN CAFE
1161 First Ave (at 64th St)
888-6556
Lunch: Mon-Fri; Dinner: Daily; Brunch: Sat, Sun
Moderate to expensive

New York does not have all that many classy steakhouses, although several have opened in recent years. Manhattan Cafe is one of them, and it is indeed an attractive, pleasant place to dine. Start with the shrimp, the lump of crab meat, or even the overpriced Nova Scotia salmon. The steaks are large and delicious, as are the lamb chops and prime rib. Even the seafood, especially the filet of sole, is worth trying. A number of veal dishes are available, with the veal piccata being particularly good. Accompany your choice with the excellent cottage fried potatoes. For dessert, the tartufo equals any I've tasted in Italy (except for Tre Scalini's in Rome), and the cheesecake absolutely melts in your mouth. This polished establishment is an excellent place for an expense-account outing.

MARCHI'S
251 E 31st St
679-2494
Dinner: Mon-Sat
Moderate

It's amazing that I didn't discover this place earlier. It must be one of the best-kept secrets in New York. Indeed, there's no sign out front, but Marchi's has been a New York fixture since 1930, when it was established by the Marchi family in an attractive brownstone townhouse. The Marchi's, joined by their three sons, are still on hand, giving a homey flavor to the restaurant's three dining rooms and garden patio (a great spot for a private dinner). It's almost like going for dinner at your favorite Italian family's house, especially since there are no menus. Be sure you have a hearty appetite when you arrive, so you can take full advantage of a superb feast. The first course is a platter of antipasto, including radishes, finocchio, and Genoa salami, plus a salad of tuna fish, olives, and red cabbage. The second is an absolutely delicious homemade lasagna. The third is either crispy deep-fried fish or sautéed chicken livers; the side orders of cold beets and string beans are light and tempting. The entree is delicious roast chicken served with fresh mushrooms and a tossed salad. For dessert, there is a healthy bowl of fresh fruit, cheese, a lemon fritter, and sensational Crostoli (crisp fried twists sprinkled with powdered sugar). The price tag is decidedly *under*whelming. Come to Marchi's for a unique, leisurely meal—and an evening you will long remember.

MARYLOU'S
21 W Ninth St
533-0012
Lunch: Mon-Fri; Dinner: Daily; Brunch: Sun
Moderate

Marylou owns a fish store in the Village, so it's only natural that she should want to see her product served in an appealing manner. She has done just that at Marylou's, also in the Village. There are several rooms—some with fireplaces, some with books—all very cozy. Not-too-close tables help set the stage for a very pleasant meal. For starters, there's quite a selection of fish dishes, including cold mussel salad, smoked trout, and great soups. The entree menu is large, including many things other than fish, although they are the specialties. Of particular note are the broiled filet of sole, the seafood brochette, the trout almondine, and mesquite-grilled jumbo shrimp. Inasmuch as Marylou has a number of special fresh fish items in her market, the menu reflects these daily specials. Before you order, make sure you ask about them. For those not wanting fish, the chicken pot pie is scrumptious, and the steak Madagascar is equally good. All the entrees are served with rice or potatoes and a vegetable. All desserts are homemade! After a most satisfying meal, try the lemon or raspberry mousse or the special chocolate plate featuring all sorts of goodies! I was very impressed with the efficient and friendly but not overbearing help, the reasonable prices, and the delicious food. This is definitely one of the Village's better spots.

McSORLEY'S OLD ALE HOUSE
15 E Seventh St (at Third Ave)
473-8800
Mon-Fri: 11-midnight; Sat: noon-midnight;
Sun: 1-midnight
No credit cards
Inexpensive

If it's local color you want, you've got to visit McSorley's Old Ale House. Established in 1854, it's one of the original pubs of

New York. Abe Lincoln, the Roosevelts, and John Kennedy have guzzled here. It's certainly not on the beaten track, but the atmosphere is terrific, and the ale is great. One can conjure up visions of all the good times spent in this old watering hole. It completely lacks the pretentiousness of so many New York eating places. The sawdust on the floor completes the picture of the classic spot to take your drinking buddy. And now, after all these years, women are welcome. The menu is limited and secondary to the ales, but hearty sandwiches, cheese platters, and burgers are available. Put on your jeans, take a stroll down to old New York, and listen while you sip. Everyone in the place is a character—except you, of course.

MEZZOGIORNO
195 Spring St
334-2112
Lunch, Dinner: Daily
Moderate

Florence, Italy, is one of the most charming places to visit, not only for its abundance of great art, but for the wonderful small restaurants you find on every street. Mezzogiorno, a Florence-style trattoria in New York, is located in what used to be the SoHo Charcuterie. It certainly adds a tasty new dimension to the SoHo area. The place is busy and noisy; the tables are so close together that a private conversation is impossible. The décor is best described as "modern Florence"; check out the unusual writing on the ceiling. Better yet, keep your eyes on the food. The salad selection is outstanding, and all of them are delicious and unusual. Fine entrees of linguini, fettuccine, and ravioli are available, as well as some tasty veal and steak dishes. Mezzogiorno is already famous for the pizzas it serves during the noon hour and in the evening. Dessert possibilities include melon mousse with strawberry kiwi and ananas sauce and blinis with raspberry cream and heated chocolate. You'll find all the necessary ingredients here for a wonderful make-believe evening in Florence.

MINETTA TAVERN
113 MacDougal St
475-3850
Lunch, Dinner: Daily
Moderate

Do you want to take your kids or guests to a Village restaurant, where the coat-and-tie, meat-and-potatoes set will feel comfortable? Well, the Minetta Tavern, established in 1937 and serving excellent food to generations of the famous and not so famous, is the place to go. Located on the spot where the Minetta Brook wandered through Manhattan in the very early days, this Tavern was made famous by Eddie "Minetta" Sieveri, a friend of many of the sports and stage stars of yesteryear. Dozens of old pictures adorn the walls of this intimate, scrupulously clean Tavern, where professional personnel serve no-nonsense Italian food at attractive prices. Stuffed mushrooms, baked clams, or the traditional spinach and egg soup are good ways to get the juices flowing. Follow that up with the pasta with red lettuce and shrimps or perhaps Branzino, a great combination of sea bass, onions, vinegar, tomato cubes, and white wine. If you'd like something a bit heftier, grilled Cornish game hen or steaks are also available. The almond cake would be a wonderful cap to a satisfying meal. By the way, if you have to wait, the bar stools at the Minetta have to be the most comfortable in New York.

MME. ROMAINE DE LYON
29 E 61st St (at Madison Ave)
758-2422
Breakfast, Dinner: Mon-Fri; Lunch: Daily
Moderate

The best omelets in New York are at Mme. Romaine's. If you can't find what you want from their 545 varieties, it probably doesn't exist. Don't be put off by the unpleasant attitude of the hostess; she could learn from her brother how to take care of people. But when you're in the mood for a light lunch or dinner, this is the place to go. If omelets are not your bag, you might try the chef salad or the smoked salmon, and at dinnertime, duck, chicken, calf's liver, and veal dishes are available.

MONTRACHET
239 W Broadway
219-2777
Lunch: Fri; Dinner: Mon-Sat
American Express
Moderately expensive

The TriBeCa area is not picturesque, but it is thriving, and exciting places like Montrachet make TriBeCa (the triangle below Canal, get it?) a very appealing place to visit. Once inside Montrachet, the feeling of drabness dissipates. The staff used to wear awful black outfits, but that has changed. Now you can concentrate, undistracted, on a fine array of seafood, game, and meat prepared to perfection by the restaurant's latest super chef, Debra Ponzek. One of her predecessors, David Bouley, was so good that he has gone on to open his own successful restaurant. The menu changes regularly, with exciting new things done with fresh produce. If you are lucky enough to find a bouillabaisse dish on the menu, go for it. Roast pheasant, roast chicken, and roast duck are outstanding choices, and Debra does lobster dishes to perfection. The presentation is half the fun, and the three simply decorated rooms do not detract from the main reason you are there: good eating. The desserts have finally come up to par with the rest of the menu, with soufflés at the top of the list. Having tasted many creme brulée dishes, I can say with authority that Montrachet's version is one of the best.

MOONDANCE DINER
Sixth Ave at Grand St
226-1191
Sun-Thurs: 8:30 a.m.-midnight;
Fri, Sat: 24 hours
No credit cards
Moderate

Remember that old song: "Dinner in the diner, nothing could be finer." Well, of course it *could* be finer than the Moondance, but it would surely cost you a heck of a lot more, and I'm not sure the quality would be any better. Larry Panish, a graduate of the Culinary Institute of America, turned an old greasy-spoon diner into a spotless, efficient operation that serves absolutely first-class "simple" food at a price anyone can afford. There is the usual counter and about a dozen tables; what isn't usual is the great taste of wholesome salads and sandwiches for lunch and the gourmet-style chicken, steak, veal, and what-have-you for dinner. The help is extra polite, the plates are balanced and attractive, and Larry is in the kitchen several nights a week to make sure things are running smoothly. Specialties include great onion rings, outstanding chili, and homemade apple pie. Daily specials are listed on the blackboard, and take-out orders are available. Drop by for breakfast, and you'll be starting the day out right! Larry's Lox Around the Clock (676 Sixth Ave) is equally well operated. Note the extended weekend hours!

NICOLA'S
146 E 84th St
249-9850
Dinner: Daily
No credit cards
Moderate

First, a few basics: (1) Make sure this is the only place you're going to eat today, because the servings are hefty; (2) bring cash, because they don't accept credit cards; (3) you're in luck if you like veal, because they have more than half a dozen veal dishes (all delicious) on the menu. Let's start with the veal: veal scallopine with mushrooms, piccata, emiliana, pizzaiola, veal parmigiana, veal Milanese, paillard of veal, or broiled veal chops. They sure know how to fix 'em. As a matter of fact, the other dishes fade into the background in comparison. Home-fried potatoes or hash browns make a nice addition, and a good selection of vegetables are usually available. If it's strictly Italian fare you're looking for, there is also tortellini, cannelloni, fettuccine, manicotti, or just about anything Italian your heart desires. Backing up just a bit, I'd opt for the clam dishes as starters: clams on the half shell, clams casino, or mussels marinieri. They do them well. The Italian bread is some of the very best. As a matter of fact, I have filled up on just their delicious bread and butter—it's that good.

OLD DENMARK
133 E 65th St (at Lexington Ave)
744-2533
Mon-Sat: 9-5:30
No credit cards
Inexpensive to moderate

Old Denmark is really a gourmet food shop, but it is also a good spot to go for a light, quick, different kind of lunch. And if you are keen on Scandinavian food items, you can stock up here. There is no menu, but you have your choice of a number of assorted salads and appetizers, tasty breads, and cakes. Old Denmark is very handy when you are out shopping and don't want anything too heavy. The personnel are particularly helpful. And with all the emphasis on calories these days, this choice is one that won't make the scales tip in the wrong direction the next morning.

OLDE GARDEN CAFE & WINERY
15 W 29th St
532-8323
Lunch: Mon-Fri; Dinner: Mon-Sat
Inexpensive to moderate

So you're all worn-out after pushing through the crowds at Macy's or shopping the discount photo stores, or maybe you just got off the train at Penn Station. Whatever the case, it's an easy walk to the Olde Garden Cafe & Winery on West 29th Street, an enchanting place established in 1912. It was originally an antiques shop that offered tea and sandwiches to its customers. Folks liked the eats so well that the owners decided to give up the antiques and concentrate on the treats. There was an open garden in the back which has now been covered. The restaurant encompasses several warm and attractive rooms with wooden floors and partial brick walls. A smattering of antiques are still around, and the comfortable captain's chairs and wooden tables add to the inviting ambiance. This is a great place for lunch. All kinds of salads are offered: diced chicken platter, Olde Garden Club salad, or the executive salad bowl with Swiss cheese, ham, shrimp, and anchovy and herb dressing. Entree selections include ocean sole, sea scallops, wiener schnitzel, eggs benedict, and several different kinds of omelets. All entrees are served with potato and garden vegetables. Reasonably priced desserts include a wonderful apple strudel and freshly baked assorted pies. This is a great spot for a leisurely lunch, particularly with friends from out of town.

107 WEST
2787 Broadway (at 107th St)
864-1555
Dinner: Daily; Brunch: Sun
Moderate

107 West is attractive and clean, with a pleasant glassed-in sidewalk area. The menu definitely has a Southern accent. Crispy chicken wings, Louisiana crab cakes, Cajun popcorn, and the like are offered as appetizers for such entrees as hickory-smoked ribs, crispy Southern fried chicken with mashed potatoes, jambalaya, and Mississippi Delta catfish. There are side orders of Southern favorites, like fried bananas and Cajun rice. Pasta is also available. The menu is interesting, the service is prompt and pleasant, and the price is right. Y'all come!

ONE IF BY LAND, TWO IF BY SEA
17 Barrow St (bet Seventh Ave and W Fourth St)
228-0822
Dinner: Daily
Expensive

Finding this place is a bit of a challenge, but what a reward when you do! The building that was once Aaron Burr's old carriage house is truly unique, and the atmosphere is warm and friendly. One If By Land is especially popular with young people, who appreciate the romantic ambiance, as well as the extraordinarily good food. Make reservations before coming down, and allow yourself enough time to find Barrow Street (one of the Village's most charming yet hard-to-find side streets) and the restaurant (there's no sign out front), so that you'll have a few minutes to enjoy a drink at the spacious bar by the fireplace. Try to get a table on the balcony level; it's especially romantic. As for dinner, crab claws, shrimp, snails, beef Wellington, and spinach salad are all excellent. For dessert, there is an ever-changing selection of delicious homemade goodies.

ORSO
322 W 46th St
489-7212
Mon, Tues, Thurs, Fri, Sun: 12-11:45;
Wed, Sat: 11:30 a.m.-11:45 p.m.
Moderate

This restaurant features the same menu all day, which is great for those with unusual dining hours and handy for those going to the theater. Orso is one of the most popular places on midtown's "restaurant row," so if you're thinking about a six o'clock dinner, be sure to make reservations. The smallish room is cozy and comfortable and watched over by a portrait of Orso, a Venetian dog who's the mascot for this no-nonsense Italian bistro. The kitchen is open in the back and visible to the diners; you can see for yourself just how experienced the staff is. The menu includes many good appetizers, like grilled shrimp, cold roast veal, and fried artichokes. A number of pizzas and some excellent pasta dishes are also offered. For an entree, you can't go wrong with the lamb sausage or the veal shank. The truffle gelato, one of many homemade desserts, could finish off a great meal.

PALM
837 Second Ave (at 44th St)
687-2953

PALM TOO
840 Second Ave (at 44th St)
697-5198

Lunch: Mon-Fri; Dinner: Mon-Sat
Expensive

Steak and lobster lovers in Manhattan have a special place in their hearts for the Palm and Palm Too. These two restaurants are located across the street from each other, and both have much the same atmosphere. The waiters will tell you what's available—there is no printed menu. They're noted for huge, delicious steaks, chops, and lobsters, but don't miss the Palm fries—homemade potato chips. They're the best. Or try a combination order of fries and great onion rings. It's an earthy spot, so I wouldn't get too dressed up. There is sawdust on the floor, thick tobacco and grease smoke in the air, and outrageous caricatures on the dirty walls. You are only part of the passing scene to the indolent waiters, but come early (it's usually crowded) and enjoy the good bread, an excellent salad, and the expensive entrees. You won't forget it.

PAMIR

1437 Second Ave (bet 74th and 75th St)
734-3791
Dinner: Tues-Sun
Inexpensive

You probably don't have Afghanistan at the top of your list of places to visit, but this Afghan restaurant definitely should be. The room is small, the personnel refreshingly low-key, modest, and friendly, and the food different enough to make an evening here a novel experience. Turnovers are an Afghan specialty, and Pamir offers several: one stuffed with scallions, herbs, and spices; another stuffed with potato, ground beef, and spices. If you like extra-spicy food (like that served in the native country), they will gladly oblige, but you needn't worry if that is not to your liking. And the Afghan bread! It's great, and you get it with each entree. Lamb is the order of the day: seasoned lamb with rice, almonds, and pistachios; chunks of lamb in an onion- and garlic-flavored spinach sauce; lamb and eggplant cooked with tomatoes, onions, and spices; lamb on a skewer, marinated in spices; lamb chops broiled on a skewer— all worth a try. The best choice, however, is Pamir kabab: four different kinds of kabab on skewers, broiled with vegetables and served with brown rice. Several vegetarian dishes are also available. Eat heartily from the start, because the desserts are zilch. The folks here are so unpretentious, the desire to please so sincere, and the prices so modest that this just has to be one of the best ethnic-restaurant choices.

PAOLA'S

347 E 85th St
794-1890
Dinner: Daily
American Express
Moderate

One of the pleasures of writing a book such as this is getting the opportunity to visit with readers who have a special question or an unusual need. Several times young ladies have called asking me to suggest a place to take their boyfriends for a cozy and romantic evening. One young lady even called the next day to tell me it had worked: the young man proposed! Paola's, a tiny hole-in-the-wall, is a prime spot for such an evening. The only problem might be that you'll have an audience for the proposal, since the room has just 10 tables and it gets crowded and intimate. But no matter. The Italian home cooking is first-class. Paola's brother is in the kitchen taking care of the food, while his sister greets the guests out front. Great homemade pasta, superb veal dishes, and tasty hot vegetables (like grilled radicchio) are house specialties. Take along a Velamint if romance is in the air because they don't use garlic sparingly. The folks here are pleasant and informal, the mirrors reflect the warmth and flicker of the candles, and the lady of the house will charm any guest. To top off the reasonably priced dinner, try a dish of espresso ice cream, so creamy and rich. There are dozens of small Italian restaurants going in and out of business almost weekly on the Upper East Side, but Paola's is here to stay.

PAPPA'S PLACE
510 Sixth Ave (at 13th St)
924-3799
Lunch, Dinner: Daily
Moderate

Pappa has gone wild. Under one roof, he has assembled a treasure house for kids. Appetizers and soups and snacks. Big burgers with all the trimmings. Delicious sandwiches with homemade fillings. Healthy salads and cold plates. Tasty entrees like lasagna and pot pies. Quiches and individual pizzas. Brunch items like blintzes and pancakes and omelets and waffles that are served all day, every day. But the real eye-openers are in the sweets departments. Candy jars line the walls. Next to these temptations are dozens of different kinds of ice creams, including the less caloric Weight Watcher and American Glace varieties. Wash all this down with a selection of international cappuccinos and coffees. How's this for a teaser: the kahlua momma, a magnificent dish of mocha chip and vanilla ice cream with chocolate syrup, kahlua, whipped cream, and ground coffee beans. Let's go!

PARIOLI ROMANISSIMO
24 E 81st St
288-2391
Dinner: Tues-Sat
Expensive

When you pay these prices, you want class and great food. You get both in abundance at Parioli. Outstandingly helpful personnel serve you in a rather intimate room (or garden area) on tables appointed with Tiffany-style china, glassware, and silver. Save your appetite, even if that means passing up the Macadamian nuts at the bar! Instead, feast upon scampis or some delicious pasta, like trevette or fettuccine alfredo. Appetizer selections change with every season. And what a selection of veal dishes. Each one is a treat in itself. Choose from sautéed veal, breaded veal chops, rolled veal scalloppine, filet of veal, or rack of veal. Of course, chicken, beef, and steak dishes are also offered, with superbly done (and very expensive) vegetables as side orders. The zabaglione is marvelous, and the chocolate cake—a bittersweet and brownie delight—is not only sinful, it's downright exciting! The cheese cart is also sensational.

PARIS COMMUNE
411 Bleecker St
929-0509
Dinner: Daily; Brunch: Sat, Sun
Moderate

Mayo and Marcus, a.k.a. M&M, operate this small, charming Greenwich Village bistro. It is a neighborhood gathering place, and each evening the rooms fill up quickly with the regulars. The food is absolutely first-rate, with prices no one could possibly complain about. There are just a dozen tables, each one promptly served by attentive, friendly waiters. Even the owners take orders, bus dishes, and help with all those important little things that make dining a pleasure. At noon on Saturday and Sunday, a super brunch features the best French toast anywhere, along with cereals, eggs, omelets, English muffins, and pomme frits. The delicious omelets include cheddar cheese and bacon, apples and jarlsberg cheese, and marinated artichoke hearts and mozzarella. On the regular dining menu, which changes seasonally, there is always a good selection of soups, salads, and poultry, meat, and fish entrees. The mustard grilled chicken is a house favorite. The dessert course is a must; the M&M boys make their own cheesecakes in a variety of flavors. They manage to make the chocolate chip bundt cake, served with mounds of whipped cream, seem so light that you won't realize how much you've sinned. Join the community at the Paris Commune. It's a real Village find.

PARK BISTRO
414 Park Ave S (bet 28th and 29th St)
689-1360
Lunch: Mon-Fri; Dinner: Mon-Sat
Moderate

This is a bistro you will want to visit over and over again. Some of the folks from the short-lived Maxim's Hotel moved downtown to take over this small, homey dining room, which specializes in cuisine from the Provence region of France. It's a jewel. From the start, when warm and tasty bread is placed before you, to the finishing touches on rich and luscious homemade desserts (like creme brulée, gateau basque, tortes, and a sinful chocolate gateau), you are surrounded by attentive service and magnificent food. Don't miss the shellfish soup at the start. The entrees include fresh codfish or skate fish or lobster, all presented with tasty and attractive side dishes.

PARK SIDE
107-01 Corona Ave (at 51st Ave and 108th St, Queens)
(718) 271-9274
Lunch, Dinner: Daily
Moderate

You want to show that person who "knows everything about New York" something he doesn't know? You want to eat on your way to or from LaGuardia or Kennedy airport? You want a special meal in an unusual setting? Well, any of the above is an excellent reason to visit Park Side, in Queens. Yes, I know this is a book on Manhattan, but this place is worth making an exception. Ed D'Angelo runs a first-class, spotlessly clean restaurant that serves wonderful Italian food at prices that make most New York restaurateurs look like highway robbers. Start with the garlic bread and then choose from two dozen different kinds of pasta and an opulent array of fish, steak, veal, and poultry dishes. The meat is all prime cut—nothing frozen here. You'll also find polite, knowledgeable waiters in an informal atmosphere. Get a table in the garden room, eat until your heart's content, and be amazed when you see the tab. You'll see why Park Side is so exceptional.

PEPPERMINT PARK CAFE AND BAKERY
1225 First Ave (bet 66th and 67th St)
288-5054 (cafe); 288-5415 (candy)
Lunch, Dinner: Daily (open late)
American Express, Diner's Club
Moderate

There are a number of excellent reasons to visit Peppermint Park: if you want a light meal, if you're a dessert lover, if you want to eat after a show, if you've got the kids with you, or if you simply prefer informal restaurants with carnival-like atmospheres. For sustenance, there are fantastic crepes, like the Crepe Train Robbery (creamed spinach with your choice of sharp cheddar or Roquefort cheese) or Crepe Canaveral—they say it blasts your spirits into orbit. Another good combination: fresh mushrooms, sautéed onions, melted Gruyère, and blended herbs. Several dessert crepes are also available, like the one with maple syrup, melted butter, and powdered sugar. There are all kinds of Belgian waffle concoctions and a few quiches. The big news, though, is the fantastic selection of homemade ice creams (from mocha chip—number one for me—to rum raisin and black raspberry), several sherbets and sorbets, big banana splits, really thick shakes, yogurts, a selection of 10 toppings—among them, walnuts in syrup, crushed cherries, and hot butterscotch—and an array of pastries, cakes, and cookies you won't believe, all made with fresh eggs.

PIETRO'S
232 E 43rd St
682-9760
Lunch: Mon-Fri; Dinner: Mon-Sat
Expensive

Pietro's Restaurant is a steakhouse with Northern Italian cuisine; everything is cooked to order. The menu features steaks and chops, seafood, chicken, and an enormous selection of veal. Tell your companion not to bother getting dressed up. Bring your appetite, though, because the portions are huge. Although steaks are the best known of Pietro's dishes, you will also find eight chicken dishes and ten veal selections (marsala, cacciatore, scallopini, piccata, francaise, etc.). And for meat-and-potato lovers, there are eight different potato dishes. Prices border on the expensive, and the service is boisterous, but you'll certainly get your money's worth.

PIG HEAVEN
1540 Second Ave (bet 80th and 81st St)
PIG-4333
Lunch, Dinner: Daily
Moderate

Well, this is a unique one! The look is French country, the food is Chinese delicious, the pigs are everywhere. You'd never know you were in a Chinese restaurant, judging from the wood-covered walls and the fresh flowers. This is one of David Keh's operations; he owns and operates a number of Chinese eating spots in Manhattan. The menu offers many hot/cold pork dishes, the best of which are the spring rolls and steamed little dumplings in a basket. The barbecued spareribs are also super. Other winners include beef with snow peas, and flattened shrimp in shells with hot pepper sauce. A number of dishes are very spicy, so be prepared. You can look in through a glass window at the kitchen and see the various items being prepared for both in-house consumption and orders to go. And hallelujah! Finally, someone got smart about desserts in a Chinese restaurant. Instead of the limited selection offered in most, here you can enjoy American apple pie, Peking snow balls, and a sensational frozen praline mousse. I wonder what Chairman Mao would have said about a banana split in a Chinese restaurant!

PINOCCHIO
170 E 81st St
650-1513, 879-0752
Dinner: Mon-Sat
American Express
Moderate

Pinocchio is off the beaten path: a small and inexpensive restaurant that serves the kind of Italian food Geppetto's grandmother used to make. You won't find the menu limited to spaghetti and pizza. Pinocchio specializes in regional Italian cooking, and if you're puzzled about what to order, the friendly waiters are happy to advise. And, unlike too many restaurants, families are welcome here, perhaps because it's a family-run place. Sal Petrillo and his four children do the honors. Small parties are also treated well. What a difference a little personal attention can make! Some of the classier restaurants downtown could learn a lesson from Pinocchio's.

PIZZA PIAZZA
785 Broadway (at 10th St)
505-0977
Lunch, Dinner: Daily
Inexpensive

Does deep-dish pizza sound good to you? If so, go to Pizza Piazza in a hurry. Their pizza comes in three sizes, all made to order and absolutely chockablock full of cheeses, vegetables, and meats. All are prepared without any preservatives. If you're a crust lover like I am, you'll definitely like these. The pizzas are served piping hot, and they look as good as they taste. There is a choice of over a dozen possibilities, from chicken Mexicana to Piazza pepperoni to Cajun or Hawaiian pizza and the ultimate Piazza special, which includes bacon, sweet sausage, sliced mushrooms, broccoli, pepperoni, onions, artichoke hearts, roasted garlic, tomato sauce, and three cheeses. Get the picture? Forget about the burgers and chili; concentrate on the absolutely super specialty of the house. If you have any room left for dessert, you might ask for the Bailey's Bombe: coffee ice cream with Irish cream liqueur and chocolate coffee beans.

PLAZA HOTEL PALM COURT
59th St at Fifth Ave
759-3000
Breakfast, Lunch: Mon-Sat; Tea, Supper: Daily;
Brunch: Sun
Moderate

If there is just one place in the city that could be singled out as the embodiment of all that folks dream of as the New York of yesteryear—romantic and carefree, delicious and proper—it would have to be the Palm Court at the Plaza Hotel. The great and near-great have laughed and loved here with the likes of Eloise and Auntie and Uncle, creating thousands of memories of special times. You can enjoy breakfasts, luncheon quiches, omelets, salads, wonderful teas with tea sandwiches, and caloric goodies, all to the accompaniment of classic piano and violin music. There are also supper snacks, like cold prime rib of beef, seafood salad, assorted smoked fish, and the usual sandwiches and pastries. The fabulous Sunday buffet is a popular New York tradition; you see many three-generation families showing the young ones where they used to go in the "good old days." A real treat, day or night, and a must for the New York visitor.

POLO
Westbury Hotel (Madison Ave at 69th St)
535-9141
Breakfast, Lunch, Dinner: Daily; Tea: Sat, Sun
Moderately expensive

Ralph Lauren has made the word *polo* synonymous with what's fashionable and in good taste. The Polo Restaurant, located just three blocks down the street from Ralph's magnificent Rhinelander mansion store, captures the caché of its name. In an intimate hotel dining room, with tables far enough apart to make it comfortable and personal, you can enjoy a "power" breakfast, a pricey but delicious lunch, or a dinner in just the right setting for the 40th wedding anniversary of your in-laws. The guests and staff are on their very best behavior, the room is bathed in piano melodies, and the dishes are served in a flurry of polished silver covers. Under them you find such delicacies as poached turbot, sautéed swordfish, breast of duck, or delicious rack of lamb. Before the entrees, how does a salad of string beans with roasted quail breasts sound? The ravioli of shrimp with Parmesan sauce is another appetizing treat. The luncheon menu offers some unusual sandwiches and salads, like club sandwich of shrimp or a salad of lobster on poached vegetables and citrus fruits. Save some appetite for the most creamy and delectable chocolate mousse cake imaginable; it's so light you can't believe it has so many calories. This restaurant, like the stock market, has its ups and downs, but the current outlook is very bullish.

POST HOUSE
28 E 63rd St
935-2888
Lunch: Mon-Fri; Dinner: Daily
Moderate to expensive

The best way to describe the Post House would be as a social and political "in" hangout on East 63rd Street, which serves excellent food in comfortable surroundings. The guest list usually includes many well-known names and easily recognizable faces. They are attracted, of course, by the fact that this spot has been written up favorably in the gossip columns. Hors d'oeuvres like crab-meat cocktail, lobster cocktail, and stone crabs are available in season, but the major draws are the steaks and lobsters. Prices for the latter two entrees are definitely not in the moderate category; ditto for lamb chops. However, the quality is excellent, and the cottage fries, fried zucchini, hashed browns, and onion rings are superb. Save room for the white chocolate mousse with raspberry sauce. If you can walk out of the place under your own steam after all this, you're doing well! The Post House is not as earthy as the Palm or as masculine as Christ Cella, but it is a really fitting spot to take your favorite lady for a hearty dining experience.

PRIMAVERA
1578 First Ave (at 82nd St)
861-8608
Dinner: Daily
Expensive

There are hundreds of Italian restaurants in Manhattan. When I'm asked which is the greatest, my answer is always Primavera. So many times an establishment reflects a proprietor's personality and talents; nowhere is this more apparent than at Primavera. Nicola Civetta, the owner, is the epitome of class. He knows how to greet you, how to make you feel at home, and how to present a superb Italian meal. Don't go if you're in a hurry, though. This place is for relaxed dining. I could wax eloquently with descriptions of the dishes, but enough said: you can't go wrong no matter what you order. Let Nicola choose for you, as there are specials every day.

To top it all off, they have one of the most beautiful desserts any-where: a gorgeous platter of seasonal fruit that looks too beautiful to eat. Primavera is always busy, so reservations are a must. Tell Nicola I sent you. If Primavera is not as good as any place at which you've dined in Italy, I'd be very surprised.

PROVENCE
38 MacDougal St (at Prince St and Sixth Ave)
475-7500
Lunch, Dinner: Tues-Sun
Moderate

Provence, of course, is a region of France, where some of the world's best cuisine originated. A bit of that area has been trans-ported to New York's Greenwich Village. Large windows in the front offer a not terribly exciting view of MacDougal Street, but it is exciting inside, where bustling waiters and a very stressed-out maitre d' are busy coping with large, hungry crowds. To tell you the truth, I was surprised at how good the food was, when I discov-ered the owner was formerly of Régines, a place never known for its professionalism. However, he must have discovered what *not* to do, for Provence serves delicious food in very sizable portions and in a most attractive manner at a reasonable price. I suppose paper tablecloths are economical, but I do object to them. With good food like this, gentlemen, can't you do better? But back to the food. For starters, try the scallops baked in their shell with vege-tables or the rabbit paté in aspic. A tasty fish soup is a treat as well as the onion and anchovy tart, a specialty of the Provence region. On to escalope of rabbit saddle, poached seafood in broth, or roast baby chicken with herbs and roasted garlic. By all means, get a side order of French fries. They're good and not greasy, just like the ones you had in that little French bistro on your last trip to Europe. If you can make it on a Friday, there's a wonderful bouillabaisse, and on Sundays couscous is featured. Leave room for some great sorbets for dessert.

QUATORZE
240 W 14th St
206-7006
Lunch: Mon-Fri; Dinner: Daily
American Express
Moderate

Fourteenth Street seems an unlikely place to find a really special place to eat, but Quatorze fills the bill. Although it's a rather plain-looking restaurant, the big attraction is the quality of the food and the way the chef works wonders with a very limited menu. The por-tions are enormous! At lunchtime, I strongly recommend the sandwich and a cup of soup. The kinds of sandwiches and soups vary daily, so call ahead for the day's offerings. Other great lunch selections are the roast duck, sautéed brook trout, chicken fettuccini, and the house specialty, choucroute garnie (sauerkraut, roast pork, and three different kinds of sausage). The dinner menu is much the same, except assorted cold vegetable salads are offered instead of sandwiches. The chocolate regal dessert (take it from this inveterate chocolaholic!) is absolutely superb. It's not overpowering, but it has a taste you'll never forget. The personnel are obviously proud of their fine reputation, and I'm in complete agreement with them.

QUILTED GIRAFFE
550 Madison Ave (at 55th St)
593-1221
Lunch: Tues-Fri; Dinner: Mon-Sat
Expensive to very expensive

We all have our favorite animals, and I've always been fascinated with the giraffe because it's so haughty and rare. That description also fits this restaurant; it is indeed unusual and rare, and it can certainly be a bit haughty. When a restaurant reaches the four-star category, it has to be good, and the Quilted Giraffe is just that. Susan and Barry Wine have put together a superb dining spot. The fixed-price dinner (believe me, it's not inexpensive) is something you'll long remember. The dishes are unusual, to say the least. Specialties include lobster and truffles in tomato bouillon, caviar beggar's purses, confit of duck with garlic potatoes, and sweetbreads with sesame potato chips. Each one is presented in a kingly manner. There's a fabulous selection of cheeses and such desserts as spice cake with warm pear and caramel sauce, chocolate soufflé with espresso ice cream, apple tarts with cinnamon ice cream (absolutely delicious), and fresh fruit sorbets in cranberry soup. Or you might want to try the "grand dessert," which features samples of many of the offerings. I could make a whole meal of just that. Barry and Susan are to be congratulated. They set out to carve a special niche in Manhattan dining, and they've succeeded in doing it in spades.

RAINBOW ROOM
30 Rockefeller Plaza (65th floor)
632-5100
Dinner: Mon-Sat
Expensive

On October 3rd, 1934, the Rainbow Room opened atop Rockefeller Center, giving New Yorkers and visitors a thrill to be found nowhere else. The lights of the city below were vibrant and visible from the opulent room, where famous chefs and famous bands worked to make the evening a very special event. On December 29th, 1987, that scene was re-created when a spectacular new two-floor facility, redone by the Rockefellers at a cost of $20 million, opened on the same site. Joe Baum has turned the 64th and 65th floors into a magnificent private club during the day and a great dining and dancing spot in the evening. The Rainbow Room, a two-story, glass-enclosed jewel, is the showpiece of the new layout. Smartly uniformed personnel serve gourmet food to the accompaniment of a 12-piece dance band. The Rainbow Promenade is a smaller room, with cozy tables and light meals. Rainbow and Stars is the dining and supper club, which features live cabaret entertainment. One room specializes in food for those who are particularly health conscious; the staff can even keep your diet requisites on file in the Rainbow computer. Views from all rooms are spectacular, but the one facing directly north to Central Park is breathtaking. The views inside the rooms aren't so bad either; a million dollar collection of 40 pieces of American modern art adorn the walls. An evening of being pampered and spoiled by Joe Baum and his professional crew is certain to be quite an occasion for even the most jaded diner. The Rainbow also offers party and banquet facilities.

RAKEL
231 Varick St
929-1630
Lunch: Mon-Fri; Dinner: Mon-Sat
Moderate to moderately expensive

Where Houston and Varick Streets meet may seem an unlikely area for a classy restaurant, but when I say classy, I mean classy food, because the setting leaves a lot to be desired. The room is lofty and cold, with stark and unattractive décor. But if you can keep your eyes focused on the sparkling table settings and the outstanding food, you will come away happy and satisfied. Rakel is an offspring of SoHo's classic French bistro, Raoul's, and the connection is obvious. Every plate is an absolute showpiece; someone in the kitchen is an artist. Whole grain bread rolls are served hot and fresh. Marinated salmon, cappuccino of wild-mushroom consommé, and poached foie gras with sherry-vinegar sauce are unusual appetizers. For entrees, roast saddle of lamb, grilled sweetbreads, rabbit roasted with rosemary, poached lobster, and grilled veal chops are all absolutely superb dishes. For dessert, go for the warm tart with pear coulis or the three-citrus tart with raspberry sauce. Also, there is a nice offering of handmade chocolates for two, which is great if you're with a chocolate lover. Now if they would just float some clouds under that soaring ceiling and get rid of those hideous wall pieces, Rakel would be a winner in every category. By the way, the young personnel go out of their way to be polite and helpful. What they lack in refinement, they make up for in earnestness.

RAO'S
455 E 114th St
534-9625
Dinner: Mon-Fri
No credit cards
Inexpensive

What are you doing for dinner three months from tonight? Sound ridiculous? Not really, if you want to go to Rao's, an intimate, old-time (1896) Italian-type restaurant run by an aunt and an uncle in the kitchen and a nephew (Frank) out front. The regulars know it, and the place is crowded all the time for two very good reasons: the food is great, and the prices are ridiculously low. Don't walk, but don't take your car either. Take a taxi and get out right in front of the restaurant. When you're ready to leave, have Frank call a local taxi service to pick you up and deliver you to your home or hotel. (A sizable tip to the driver will be necessary for this.) Frank is a gregarious and charming host, who makes you feel right at home; he'll even sit with you at your table while you order. Be prepared for leisurely dining; while you're waiting, enjoy the excellent bread and warm atmosphere (what looks like last year's Christmas decorations are still hanging over the bar). Among the offerings that are especially tasty, I enjoyed the pasta and piselli (with peas). The veal marsala and veal piccata are excellent choices, as well as any number of shrimp dishes. Believe it or not, the Southern fried chicken is absolutely superb; it would be my number-one choice. Don't miss this spot in Spanish Harlem. HINT: *Try just appearing unannounced at the door. Tables are often available on the spur of the moment.*

RAOUL'S
180 Prince St
966-3518
Dinner: Daily
Moderate

The dining-out scene in SoHo has certainly changed for the better. Now there are dozens of good places to eat in this colorful area, and Raoul's is one of the best. The long, narrow restaurant used to be an old saloon. There are paper tablecloths and funky walls covered with a mishmash of posters, pictures, and calendars of every description. No menu is presented; you read the day's selections from the blackboard. The bistro atmosphere is neighborly, friendly, and intimate, the prices moderate, and the service attentive. The trendy clientele runs the gamut from jeans to mink. The house specialties are the turbot with wild mushrooms and the rack of lamb. Don't pass up the sensational sweetbreads in vinaigrette sauce as an appetizer.

(THE FAMOUS) RAY'S PIZZA OF GREENWICH VILLAGE
465 Sixth Ave (at 11th St)
243-2253
Sun-Thurs: 11 a.m.-2 a.m.; Fri, Sat: 11 a.m.-3 a.m.
No credit cards
Inexpensive

There are an untold number of pizzerias in New York, and you can smell many of them blocks away! But none of them is really too distinguished, except a special place called Ray's Pizza, located in the Village. It's a busy parlor, serving over 2,000 customers a day. The pizzas are super. Because Ray's is so busy, you don't have to worry about the slice being stale; of course, you can buy a whole pizza. And why not try one of the Sicilian squares or one of the Neapolitan wedges for a change? Unusual toppings are available, and I guarantee this place is the ultimate for the pizza crowd in the Big Apple. They even offer the "Famous Slice," a slice of pizza with *all* the toppings on it. Calzones and baby pizzas are new arrivals. Note: This may be fast food, but there's usually a long, slow waiting line.

REMI
323 E 79th St
744-4272
Lunch: Sat; Dinner: Daily; Brunch: Sun
Moderate to moderately expensive

Venice used to be such a charming place to visit: ornate, historic buildings, wonderful food, nice accommodations, and romantic gondola rides. Nowadays Venice has too many tourists, high prices, and rampant mediocrity. But don't fret. Just head to Remi, a marvelous Venetian-style restaurant on East 79th Street in Manhattan. The only thing missing is your gondolier, but the food makes up for that. One of the owners is the chef, and it shows in the tender care he gives each dish. The bread is warm and delicious. And wonderful pasta, superb grilled salmon, and risotto dishes head the parade of fabulous food. The creme brulée is a great dessert. The room is decorated with attractive Venetian glass fixtures on the walls and oars on the ceiling. The crowd is upscale early in the evening; yuppies show up later. The personnel, particularly the manager, are extremely accommodating. The whole experience will save you the hassle of going for the real thing in Italy.

RENÉ PUJOL
321 W 51st St
246-3023
Lunch: Mon-Fri; Dinner: Mon-Sat
Moderate

This very attractive French restaurant is an ideal spot for a pre-theater dinner. It's always busy, and it's obvious that a large number of the customers are regular patrons, which always speaks well for a restaurant. One of the reasons this is such a successful operation is because it's a family enterprise. The owner is on the job, and his son-in-law is the chef. Housed in an old brownstone, the restaurant has two warmly decorated, cozy, and comfortable dining rooms, complete with a working fireplace in the winter. There are private party rooms upstairs, and they are attractive, too. The menu is vintage French. A nice dish of paté awaits you at the table. Start with the vichyssoise or perhaps quiche Lorraine. For entrees, I suggest the poached salmon, the poached turbot, duck, boeuf bourguignonne, or if there are two of you, maybe a chateaubriand. Every dish is beautifully presented, and to me that's half the fun of dining. I can personally vouch for all the desserts. They're homemade; each one is better than the last. Try the crepe suzette, chocolate mousse, or the peach Melba.

RESTAURANT FLORENT
69 Gansevoort St (bet Washington and Greenwich St)
989-5779
Open 24 hours
No credit cards
Moderate

When you have something good, people will find you no matter where you are. A case in point: Restaurant Florent, a run-of-the-mill diner transformed into a chic, popular restaurant, is located—of all places—in the heart of the seamy meat-packing district on the Lower West Side. This noisy, busy French bistro never closes, and the level of activity seems to increase by the hour in the evening. The menu is simple, and perhaps that is one of the keys to its success. Escargot, paté, sautéed calf's brains, coho salmon, and grilled chicken are all good choices. And it's a great place for people watching, New York style.

RESTAURANT RAPHAEL
33 W 54th St
582-8993
Lunch: Mon-Fri; Dinner: Mon-Sat
Expensive

Expensive, but worth it. This classy, intimate, French restaurant, which does a few things very well, is for the serious diner. Tasty smoked salmon, ravioli de St. Jacques, or duck salad will get you off to a great start. Main courses of pigeon, lamb, veal, and duck are served imaginatively with superb seasonings and sauces. There is no on-the-job training for the servers; they all know what is expected in a first-class operation. Take your time, savor the taste of classic French cooking, and finish with a chocolate mousse that is as rich and delicious as any you have ever tasted.

RIVER CAFE
One Water St (Brooklyn)
(718) 522-5200
Lunch, Dinner: Daily
Moderately expensive

The River Cafe isn't *in* Manhattan. It's in Brooklyn, but it *overlooks* Manhattan. And that's the reason to come here. The view from the window tables (be *sure* to ask for one) is fantastic, awesome, unequaled, romantic—you name it. There's no other skyline like it in the world. And so, just across the East River, in the shadow of the Brooklyn Bridge, the River Cafe remains an extremely popular place. Be sure to call at least a week in advance to make reservations. This is a true, Yankee, flag-waving restaurant that's proud of its American cuisine. But there's no point in describing the dishes in detail, since you'll be looking out the window more than down at your plate. The seafood, lamb, and game entrees are particularly good. And the desserts are uniformly rich and fresh. You won't forget to hold hands at this romantic spot—once you've made the trek across the bridge.

THE RUSSIAN TEA ROOM
150 W 57th St (at Seventh Ave)
265-0947
Lunch, Dinner: Daily; Brunch: Sat, Sun
Moderate

The Russian Tea Room is a popular place with Manhattan social-ites and showbiz people. Warren Beatty has a table here, as do many Broadway and Hollywood producers, directors, writers, and actors (among them Mel Brooks, Woody Allen, Cheryl Ladd, and Neil Simon). Unless you specially request a table in the main room (sort of a Grand Central Station for celebrities), you'll be seated in Siberia, way back from the line of action. Assuming you're coming here to fill your mouth as well as your eyes, note that the specialties on the à la carte menu are eggplant à la Russe, blinchiki with cheese and sour cream, and shashlik Caucasian. Or there's hot and cold borscht, cream of spinach soup, caviar, and meats grilled with a Russian flair. And check out the décor! It's kitsch with class. Any other restaurant looking like this would be laughed out of business, but the Tea Room is an institution. Look for the cute little building that refuses to be gobbled up by all the high-rises springing up around it. A banquet room is also available.

RUSTY'S
1271 Third Ave (at 73rd St)
861-4518
Lunch, Dinner: Daily
Moderate

There is only one way to describe this restaurant: it's all-American. The menu is all-American, the help is all-American, the customers are all-American. It is as red, white, and blue as apple pie. Don't get too dressed up to come here, or you'll feel out of place. A great starter is the Grand Slam Salad, made up of everything you could put in a salad bowl: ham, cheese, tomato, black olives, cucumbers, shrimp, eggs, etc. You name it, it's there. The French onion soup is another winner. The specialty of the house is the rack of ribs: whole baby back ribs marinated and cooked with barbecue sauce. Other winning entrees are the seafood New Orleans, a blend of lobsters, shrimp, clams, mussels, and scallops simmered in red wine, garlic, tomatoes, and a special seafood sauce; and the Louisiana chili topped with onion, mild cheddar cheese, and grilled franks. All entrees are served with bayou rice. The portions are for hearty eaters. (This could be why the place is always filled.) Note to Rusty's: take the foil off your baked potatoes.

SABOR
20 Cornelia St (at Sixth Ave)
243-9579
Dinner: Daily
Moderate

Don't expect anything fancy at Sabor's, and don't come with a sensitive tummy. But if you're out for an adventure and some really good Cuban food, then head down to what has become one of Manhattan's best Cuban restaurants. I'm not well versed in this kind of food, but I found the apervitos—like the chilled cooked pickled fish with vegetables and the Caribbean root vegetable puréed with garlic and parsley—delicious and unusual. In the fish category, the best dish is the Zarzuela de Mariscos (clams, shrimps, mussels, scallops, and calamares in a tomato sauce); it's a whole meal in itself. The most popular meat dishes are Carne Estofada (pot roast stuffed with chorizo, olives, capers, raisins, and prunes) and Ropa Vieja (flank steak seasoned with tomato sauce, cloves, and cinnamon). I'm told that a Cuban dinner wouldn't be complete without key lime pie or Coco Quemado (warm baked coconut with sherry and cinnamon), and both are good here. Delicious frozen drinks are also available.

SAN DOMENICO
240 Central Park S
265-5959
Lunch: Mon-Sat; Dinner: Daily
Expensive

The owners of this Northern Italian charmer on the corner of Central Park have spared no expense in creating a beautiful dining room, from the marble and tile floors to the comfortable and handsome leather chairs. They have also assembled an attractive, competent crew. The result is a first-class restaurant, with food matching the fine ambiance and helpful service. You pay for what you get, so the saying goes, and the tab here is a bit hefty (especially for the desserts). You can choose from a three-course, price-fixed menu, or try the à la carte menu, which doesn't change from lunch to dinner. Antipasti choices include such delicacies as cured tuna roe, steamed sea scallops, medallions of pan-roasted sweetbreads, and smoked breast of goose. Then you can try braised guinea hen, sautéed goose liver, boneless squab, or lobster and artichoke fricassee for your entree. Of course, there are the usual Italian specialties, like spinach and potato gnocchi, seafood ravioli, and if you really want to splurge, handmade quills with Beluga caviar and chives. A large selection of delicious desserts is offered, including the unforgettable mascarpone cream with espresso sauce. The ice creams and sorbets, as well as the other dolci choices, are all made in house.

SANDRO'S
420 E 59th St
355-5150
Dinner: Mon-Sat
Moderate

Don't waste any time in getting over to the far end of East 59th Street to try Sandro's. The dining room is not too large, but it's big enough to feel comfortable. Tile floors and unusually attractive serving pieces give it a clean, crisp look. The big winners, however, are the efficient service and the absolutely delicious food. You'll be impressed at how quick, helpful, and professional the service is, and it's done in a very unobtrusive way. There's nothing like good fresh warm Italian bread, and they serve it here. The homemade ravioli with sea urchin in a sauce of baby scallops and the fried ricotta with tomato sauce are sensational starters. There are a number of fish specialties; I especially enjoyed the striped bass with artichokes. Other worthwhile entrees include the veal scaloppine (any way you want it), tripe, and a very tasty sirloin of beef. A most unusual cart with a large selection of dressings is not only attractive to look at but also helps make a very delicious salad dish. Top off the meal with some of Sandro's own gelati and very rich espresso, and you'll be talking for days about what a pleasant evening you had. Sandro's is a classy operation in every sense of the word.

SARABETH'S KITCHEN

423 Amsterdam Ave (at 80th St)	1295 Madison Ave (at 92nd St)
496-6280	410-7335
Breakfast, Lunch, Dinner:	Breakfast, Lunch, Dinner:
Tues-Sun	Daily

Moderate

Swinging, it is not. Reliable, it is. One is reminded of the better English tearooms when visiting either of Sarabeth's two locations. The East Side location has been considerably expanded; it now has a bar. The big draw is the homemade quality of all the dishes, including the baked items and the excellent desserts. They also make gourmet preserves and sell them nationally. Menu choices include excellent omelets for breakfast, a fine assortment of light items for lunch, and fish, game, or meat dishes for dinner. Service is rapid and courteous. This would be an ideal place to take your mother-in-law. P.S. The chocolate truffle cake, lemon soufflé, and cinnamon apple ice cream with macadamia nuts are outrageous.

SCARLATTI

34 E 52nd St
753-2444
Dinner: Mon-Sat
Moderately expensive

The rave reviews that this house has received are well-deserved. The ambiance is totally top-drawer; one would feel out of place here if one didn't put on the best bib and tucker. Tables are far enough apart to allow for pleasant, private dining. The waiters act as if they're prime candidates for a stress clinic, so service can be hectic. But the food is excellent. Scarlatti reminds me of Sans Souci in Rome, which is a real compliment, indeed. One of the nicest ways to start your meal is to order a selection of antipasto; the house serves each person a small portion of a number of delicious dishes. The outstanding entrees are the striped bass in wine; scampi baked in mozzarella; scallops with mushrooms and wine; broiled calf's liver; and stuffed veal chops. The servings are just right, and the presentation is superb. A low cholesterol menu is also available. But try to order a decent Italian dessert, and they act as if they don't even know what tartufo is!

SCARLET
284 W 12th St (at Eighth Ave)
675-3447
Dinner: Daily; Brunch: Sun
Moderate

As you sit in this two-room, Southern-style restaurant in the Village, you could easily picture Scarlet and Rhett waltzing in at any moment. Spotless wooden floors, lace curtains, and flowers on every table complement the restaurant's *Gone With the Wind* ambiance. The creole cuisine is the work of a Louisiana-trained chef, who is responsible for some of the best Southern cooking in the city. Cajun popcorn (French-fried crawfish tails), barbecued shrimp, or oysters in champagne sauce will get you off to a good start. For hearty diners, I suggest the wonderful seafood gumbo, filled with crab, shrimp, and tomatoes. Entree winners are Louisiana crab cakes, fillet of pompano baked in parchment, and shrimp Creole. The side dishes—jambalaya, candied yams, sautéed collard greens, hushpuppies, and brabant potatoes—are the real things. Save room for pecan pie for dessert. A three-course dinner, with your choice of appetizer, entree, and dessert, is featured at a very reasonable price. As you might expect, you'll be breathing fire after digesting some of the dishes, but an ample assortment of liquid fire extinguishers are also available.

SECOND AVENUE KOSHER DELICATESSEN
156 Second Ave (at 10th St)
677-0606
Daily: 5:30 a.m.-midnight (Fri, Sat until 2 a.m.)
No credit cards
Inexpensive

You've heard of the great New York delicatessens; now you should try one of the really authentic ones located in a historic area of the city, the East Village. From the traditional K's—knishes, Kasha varnishkes (buckwheat groats with pasta), and Kugel—to boiled beef or chicken in the pot (with noodles, carrots, and matzo balls), no one does it quite like the Lebewohl family. The selections are enormous; homemade soups, three-decker sandwiches (the tongue or the hot corned beef is sensational), deli platters, complete dinners—you name it, they've got it. The smell is overwhelmingly appetizing, the atmosphere is "caring Jewish mother," and they don't mind if you want to take your meal with you instead of dining in the colorful back room. Don't leave without trying their chopped liver or the warm apple strudel. Then break out the Alka-Seltzer.

SERENDIPITY 3
225 E 60th St
838-3531
Sun-Thurs: 11:30 a.m.-midnight; Fri: 11:30 a.m.-1 a.m.;
Sat: 11:30 a.m.-2 a.m.
Moderate

For decades, Serendipity 3 has been the "in" place for youngsters and the young at heart, offering the most trendy foods and gifts in an atmosphere of nostalgia. The restaurant is housed in a quaint, two-floor brownstone. While folks wait to grab one of the busy tables, they can browse through the eclectic selection of goodies, gifts, books, clothing, and accessories. The tummy gets satisfied with tasty selections from the light menu of sandwiches, sundaes, salads, and pasta. I can't think of another establishment that has been at the forefront of style for over 30 years. How does Serendipity do it? By constantly changing much of its merchandise while maintaining the charm and décor of an old-fashioned ice cream parlor.

SETO
356 E 51st St
838-8980
Lunch: Mon-Fri; Dinner: Sun-Fri
Inexpensive

There are a number of good fancy Japanese restaurants in New York and a number of very poor ones, but not too many fall in the middle as Seto does. Here is a small, authentic, neighborhood Japanese restaurant serving delicious food at very reasonable prices. The menu is large and varied, with all kinds of appetizers, ranging from stir-fried vegetables to crab and avocado wrapped in vinegared rice and seaweed. Of the salads and soups, the best is the egg-drop soup, a thick concoction of egg and vegetables. The hot entrees and the raw fish entrees are available à la carte or with dinner, which includes soup, salad, fruit, and plum wine. There are any number of fish entrees, such as sashimi (fresh fillets of raw fish), and a wonderful combination called makimono (tuna, crab, avocado, Japanese pickles, sweet gourd, cucumber or spinach wrapped in vinegared rice and seaweed). The hot entrees include cabbage rolls, pork tempura, all kinds of teriyaki (chicken, salmon steak, and shell steak), and a tasty rolled beef (beef rolled around cheese and scallions). Of course, plum wine, saki, and various kinds of beer are also available. You can even try calpis, a Japanese milk-based soft drink.

SHINWA
645 Fifth Ave (at 51st St)
644-7400
Lunch, Dinner: Mon-Sat
Moderate to moderately expensive

If you're looking for a classy, authentic Japanese restaurant, look no further. Shinwa, in the midtown high-rent district, offers a full menu of traditional Japanese dishes, served beautifully in an understated atmosphere that puts the emphasis on food. Each course is brought to your table on a tray; the presentation is a feast of color and flavor. As much as I dislike the typical Japanese "picture menu," it does give you a good idea of what to expect. There are literally dozens of appetizers from sushi and tempura to more exotic dishes like eel and cucumber with vinegared rice or preserved squid. Entrees include tempura zen with seasonal appetizers; sashimi zen, with appetizers, vegetable soup, and ice cream; unagi zen, with a choice of kabayaki and rice; and una jue, with eel. My favorite is Shabu Shabu, sliced prime rib of beef, which you dip and cook to your liking in a boiling broth. There are two kinds of noodle dishes, one made from wheat flour and one from buckwheat flour. If you can find room at the end of the meal, you might try seaweed, codfish, or cooked squid in a dish called Chazuke, which is served with green tea and white rice. The green-tea ice cream is also fabulous. If you want to sample and savor the flavors of Japan, this is one of the best places to do it. You might want to try the 10 or 12 course meal that Shinwa calls the "Japanese celebration."

SHUN LEE CAFE
43 W 65th St
769-3888
Lunch: Sat, Sun; Dinner: Daily
Moderate

This is an unusual addition to the Chinese restaurant scene of Manhattan. Dim Sum and street-food combinations are served in an informal setting, adjoining Shun Lee West, an old, well-respected West Side Chinese restaurant. A large selection of special items are offered by a waiter who comes to your table with a rolling cart and describes the various goodies. The offerings are different from time to time, but don't miss the stuffed crab claws if they are available. Go on to the street-food items: delicious roast pork, barbecued spareribs, a large selection of soups and noodle and rice dishes, and a menu full of both mild and hot, spicy entrees. The sautéed prawns with ginger, the boneless duckling with walnut sauce, or the baby clams cooked in black bean sauce are all great choices. There's even a vegetarian dish of shredded Chinese vegetables cooked with rice noodles and served with a pancake (like Moo Shu pork but without the meat). It's a fun place, where you get the opportunity to try some unusual and delicious Chinese dishes.

SISTINA
1555 Second Ave (at 80th St)
861-7660
Lunch: Mon-Fri; Dinner: Daily
American Express
Moderate

Don't come here expecting beautiful decorations and extravagant surroundings. One comes to Sistina just for the food, and for that it can't be beat. Four brothers run this outstanding Italian restaurant; one is in the kitchen, the others are out front. The only decoration is a picture of its namesake, the Sistine Chapel, on the wall. The specialty of the house is seafood; both the Mediterranean red snapper and the salmon are excellent dishes. There are also the usual choices of veal and chicken as well as a number of daily specials. The philosophy of this family operation is that the joy is in the eating, not the surroundings, and for that they get top marks.

SMITH AND WOLLENSKY
797 Third Avenue (at 49th St)
753-1530
Lunch: Mon-Fri; Dinner: Daily
Moderate to moderately expensive

This is a big place for big appetites. If you have teenagers or some college friends whom you want to treat to a special meal, I can't think of a better place. Fancy and elite, it is not. Hearty, fun, and satisfying, it is. It has two floors of facilities, nicely divided to give it a comfortable and rather masculine atmosphere. There is no shortage of help; lots of bright, young men eager to help you—a bit of a contrast to the older, disinterested waiters at the Palm and Palm Too. The bread is varied, tasty, and warm. The lobster cocktail, though expensive, is the best in New York. The big sellers among the entrees are the steaks, prime ribs of beef, lamb chops, and lobster. On the side, you don't want to miss the cottage fries, onion rings, and fried zucchini. A word about the baked potatoes: they don't use foil—*three cheers!* And a couple of words about the desserts: the pignola nut cake is super, and the hot deep-dish apple pie with vanilla sauce can top off a great dinner.

B. SMITH'S
771 Eighth Ave (at 48th St)
247-2222
Lunch: Mon-Fri; Dinner: Daily; Brunch: Sat, Sun
Moderate

One of the fun parts of doing a book about New York is the opportunity to be a guest on various radio and TV talk shows. On one such show I was very impressed with another guest, a most attractive lady by the name of B. Smith, who talked about the opening of her restaurant. She was such a striking and down-to-earth lady, and she seemed to know so much about her subject that I had to try her establishment. Sure enough, it was just like her—*B* stands for the *beautiful* Barbara Smith as well as for a *bountiful* eating establishment. Conveniently located on the edge of the theater district, the restaurant is crisp, clean, and professional. My only complaint is that it's very noisy, but one can put up with that since everything else is appealing to the eye and the palate. The menu is eclectic. In the meat department, the lamb chops are first-rate. For pasta, consider the linguini with roasted plum tomato sauce or the whole-wheat noodle dish with vegetables and herbs. And, oh, the desserts! Savor these suggestions: sweet-potato pecan pie, coconut tuiles with white chocolate ice cream and macadamia nuts, cranberry nut-bread pudding with a maple bourbon custard, and a triple chocolate torte with fresh fruit and cream anglaise. Enough said? Come early, enjoy a scrumptious dinner, meet the charming hostess, then take off for the theater. There is a private dining room upstairs.

SPARKS
210 E 46th St
687-4855
Lunch: Mon-Fri; Dinner: Mon-Sat
Moderately expensive

You come here to eat, period. Don't expect classy ambiance or service, but this well-seasoned and very popular meat-and-potatoes restaurant does an excellent job of doing what it does best. For years, businessmen have made an evening at Sparks a must, and the house has not let time erode its reputation. In the meat category, you can choose from veal and lamb chops, beef scaloppini, and medallions of beef, as well as a half dozen steak items, like steak fromage (with Roquefort cheese), prime sirloin, sliced steak with sautéed onions and peppers, and top-of-the-line filet mignon. Seafood dishes are another specialty; the rainbow trout, fillet of tuna, and halibut steak are as good as you'll find in most seafood houses. The lobsters are enormous, delicious, and expensive. You might want to skip the appetizers and dessert, and concentrate on your main dish, which comes with great hash browns and spinach.

SPRING STREET NATURAL RESTAURANT
62 Spring St (at Lafayette St)
966-0290
Lunch, Dinner: Daily
Inexpensive

With all the interest these days in healthy eating, I am constantly asked to recommend a good "all-natural" restaurant. Spring Street has been in business since 1973, and it serves only fresh, whole, unprocessed foods cooked to order. No canned items are used, and great emphasis is put on whole foods. Lunch includes sandwiches, eggs, and salads, plus blackboard specials of the day. For dinner, you can dine well on a large selection of salads, pasta, seafood, and chicken. With all the calories that you'll be saving, splurge on a no-sugar apple pie, Manhattan mud cake, or lime cheesecake for dessert.

STEPHANIE'S
994 First Ave
753-0520
Lunch: Mon-Fri; Dinner: Daily; Brunch: Sat, Sun
Moderate

If you are tired of the noisy, trendy restaurants, then I suggest you consider Stephanie's, a simple, spotless neighborhood establishment that turns out excellent food at modest prices. The secret is in the kitchen—a husband-and-wife team, and in this case the lady is the chef and her assistant wears the white trousers. Stephanie's is owned by three partners, including the daughter of Joan Bennett, the actress, so the place has a theatrical clientele. The menu changes daily, but it usually includes such popular dishes as pan-fried rainbow trout, grilled gulf prawns, sautéed soft-shell crabs, and roast duck. Sunday brunch favorites recommended by the regulars are the macadamia-nut pancakes and the chicken and wild-rice burritos. For dessert, the gingerbread with caramel sauce and grand marnier cheesecake are delicious, and they're home-made. An especially large selection of beers is available.

TABLE D'HOTE
44 E 92nd St
348-8125
Lunch: Daily; Dinner: Mon-Sat; Brunch: Sun
No credit cards
Moderate

Here are the rules: (1) You call and leave a message on the Table D'Hote answering machine. You tell them how many are in your party and when you want to dine. (2) They call back and tell you whether they have space. If they do, they then ask that you confirm the day of the booking, and read you the menu. And what do you experience when you finally get there? An absolutely delightful four-course, home-cooked meal at a reasonable price. It's served in an unpretentious storefront cafe at a leisurely pace by the friendly, charming owners. The tables, chairs, and china are definitely mix-and-unmatch, but you won't care a bit. It's part of the charm. The menu changes weekly; each of the four entrees seems like it just came from your mother's kitchen. For a delicious casual meal where substance is more important than style, try this little-known winner. Table d'Hote can only take care of about 25 guests, so you best book your table early. Sunday brunch is a new addition, featuring tasty selections like salmon filet, salt-roasted shrimps, and pan-grilled chicken breast.

TAVERN ON THE GREEN
Central Park (at W 67th St)
873-3200
Lunch, Dinner: Daily
Moderate to moderately expensive

You go to Tavern on the Green mainly for the superlative setting. There is nothing quite as magical as dining in the beautiful Crystal Room in the evening, with the Tavern's dramatic outdoor lighting twinkling in Central Park, which is all around you, just outside the windows. Recently, several million dollars was spent on the décor, and it's quite spectacular. For a first-time visitor to the city, I recommend it as a must. Unfortunately, the continental cuisine can be very mediocre. Dealing with so many diners on such a grand scale can mean less-than-the-best food and hurried service. Still, it is a popular place for kids' birthday parties and all kinds of anniversary celebrations. The menu is particularly appealing to youngsters. And balloons and singing waiters are all part of the festivities.

TERRACE
400 W 119th St
666-9490
Lunch: Tues-Fri; Dinner: Tues-Sat
Moderate

You'll have to go a bit out of your way to visit the Terrace Restaurant, but I assure you it's well worth the time. The Terrace is located on the roof of a Columbia University building, providing a superb view of Manhattan. Try to reserve a table by the window. In the evening, it's absolutely enchanting. You'll be impressed by the classy atmosphere, the beautiful table settings (attractive china, candlelight, and a single red rose), and the soft dinner music. The tables are spaced nicely apart, giving one a chance to talk confidentially. Indeed, if there's one word that describes this operation, it's *style*. The Terrace has it in spades! The food is as good as the atmosphere. The menu is classic French. Special services include free valet parking.

TIME & AGAIN
116 E 39th St
685-8887
Lunch, Dinner: Mon-Sat
Moderate to moderately expensive

Warm, elegant, friendly, and decidedly upscale—that's Time & Again. Located in the Doral Tuscany Hotel, the restaurant features new American cuisine with a European flavor. The chef, Derrick Dikkers—very young, talented, and trained in Europe—brings flair and excitement to his work. When you arrive, you're greeted by exceptionally polite folks and seated in a room where the tables are nicely spaced apart. The menu offers a selection of 8 to 10 starters; I recommend the spicy crab cakes or the sweet potato soup with bacon, scallions, and sour cream. Then try the excellent lobster, tasty roast breast of chicken, fillet of salmon, or seared loin of lamb. Most of the entrees come with fresh veggies and light sauces. The desserts are a bit high priced, but they're delicious. The chocolate terrine with bits of orange is my top choice. This place first gained a good reputation with the locals, but the word is spreading.

TOMMY TANG'S
323 Greenwich St
334-9190
Lunch: Mon-Fri; Dinner: Mon-Sat
Moderate

Because of the reasonable prices and unique flavors of Thai food, Thai restaurants are flourishing all over New York. Tommy

Tang's is one of the very best (there's also a branch in Hollywood, California). At Tommy Tang's, the servings are smaller than usual so that each member of your party can taste a number of specialties served family style. (If you prefer regular individual servings, they are available, of course.) Another nice feature is that the menu indicates whether a dish is spicy, very spicy, or very, very spicy, so that you know what you're in for. You could make a meal just from the appetizers: won tons stuffed with chicken, potatoes, and sweet peas; egg rolls; angel wings (chicken wings stuffed with mushrooms, noodles, and bamboo shoots); or "Nam," a very spicy blend of pork, chili, ginger, onion, and lime juice. A full selection of salads, soups, and meat dishes with veggies are featured as well as a number of noodle, curry, and rice specialties. The best choices are barbecued beef (great!), blackened chili fish, crab and shrimp in the pot with noodles, and "the original Tommy duck," which is only available Thursday through Saturday. Stick to the Thai specialties on the menu; the American dishes are not as good.

TONY ROMA'S

400 E 57th St	450 Sixth Ave	1600 Broadway	565 Third Ave
421-7427	777-7427	956-7427	661-7406

Sun-Thurs: 11:30 a.m.-12 a.m.;
Fri, Sat: 11:30 a.m.-4 a.m.
Inexpensive

The "big wheels" in production in this country could take a lesson from Tony Roma's, "A Place for Ribs." It's a part of a national restaurant chain, with several noisy, bustling spots in Manhattan. They sure know what they're doing; the turnover is so fast that they hardly sweep away the paper menu place mats before the next folks are seated. And what kind of folks come here? You name them, they're here—in high-fashion designer gowns and in blue jeans; young and old; thin and fat. In short, anyone who's attracted to fast, tasty, inexpensive barbecued food. Featured are superb barbecued baby back ribs, a combination barbecued chicken and rib platter, and barbecued chicken by itself. Each of these dishes is served with not-very-good French fries and reasonably good cole slaw. Also available is filet mignon on a skewer, their own hamburger called a Romaburger, and a variety of daily specials, salads, and the like. Really sensational is their loaf of onion rings, and it is indeed a loaf—not the usual greasy lump, but a crisp, filling side dish. Unless you're awfully hungry, a half order should do nicely. Potato skins and chicken fingers are also featured, and there is a special children's menu.

TRASTEVERE
309 E 83rd St
734-6343
Dinner: Daily
American Express
Moderate

This is one of my favorites. The atmosphere reminds me of the Italian countryside. The room is very small (about a dozen tables), and the décor is far from glamorous. But the food preparation is just as professional as the atmosphere is not. The brochette of cheese and prosciutto with anchovy sauce, the mussels in light tomato sauce, the pasta la spaghettini and vegetables, or the fettucine with peas, prosciutto, mushroom, and cream—all are sensational! Also first-rate are sizable offerings of various chicken dishes, the rack of veal breaded with tomato salad on top, and the filet of sole with mushrooms, scallions, and wine. And be sure to save a bit of room for the Napoleon dessert or the chocolate cartufel. You can tell a lot about a restaurant by the little things, and these people obviously know what they are doing. The glassware literally gleams, the bread is warm and delicious, the vegetables are fresh, and their seasonings have just the right amount of garlic to be tasty without being offensive. And the waiters are well-informed and friendly. It's a good idea to call early for reservations, since the place is always busy.

TRUMPET'S
Grand Hyatt Hotel
109 E 42nd St
883-1234
Lunch: Mon-Fri; Dinner: Daily
Moderately expensive to expensive

This superb dining attraction is an absolute must! These may sound like strong words for a hotel restaurant, but I have to admit that the Grand Hyatt has done an outstanding job. A very attractive room outfitted with beautiful appointments and staffed with courteous, well-trained personnel is certainly the right setting for an immensely satisfying dining experience. There are many special offerings, such as the poached salmon in dill sauce and the sea scallops in champagne sauce with caviar. Since Trumpet's prepares seafood dishes particularly well, I recommend any of them. Some of the best are the lobster ragout, poached sea bass, and salmon paupiette in duxelle sauce. There's also a fine selection of chicken, veal, lamb, and beef dishes. It's not too often you can get a superb Grand Marnier or chocolate chip soufflé (order it at the same time you order the rest of your dinner); either of these would top off a sensational evening.

UNION SQUARE CAFE
21 E 16th St
243-4020
Lunch, Dinner: Mon-Sat
Moderate

Maybe restaurant operators really do read this book! In previous editions, I had recommended this interesting cafe, but complained of the noisy downstairs dining room and the "funny food" that seemed a bit too offbeat and pretentious for my taste. Well, lo and behold! The Union Square Cafe has simplified its presentation and even soundproofed the room. Thank you! Now the chef is offering delicious Italian and French dishes that most of us know how to enjoy. Still, I prefer the grilled offerings, like smoked shell steak, marinated filet mignon, and fillet of salmon. The hot garlic potato chips are something extra special.

VERONICA
240 W 38th St
764-4770
Breakfast, Lunch: Mon-Fri
Inexpensive to moderate

A friend who works in the garment district told me about a fantastic Italian restaurant in his area, but he wouldn't give me the exact location or the name (he did hint that it was a woman's name) because he was afraid I'd put it in my book and spoil his secret. He didn't want to battle crowds. As you can imagine, this was enough to pique my interest, so I did some investigating. The restaurant in question turned out to be Veronica, a tiny place in the heart of the garment district, and it's only open for breakfast and lunch. Well-known by neighborhood workers, it is one of the busiest spots in town at lunchtime. This marvelous cafeteria-style restaurant serves sensational home-cooked food, and it's run by three amusing sons. What wonders they serve up! There is a marvelous veal piccata, mouth-watering homemade lasagna, delicious tortellini, and chicken salad. Other favorites are the pasta primavera and the chicken florentina (breast of chicken with creamed spinach, prosciutto, mozzarella, and mushrooms in cream sauce). Fortunately, as you enter the cafeteria line, there are signs with prices and descriptions of the daily specials, because once your eyes focus on the most appetizing dishes this side of Florence, you'll have a hard time making a decision. The clientele is sophisticated, and the atmosphere is informal and homey. Don't forget to try the homemade cheesecakes. Most of the food is available for takeout, for individual orders, or for parties and special occasions.

THE VIEW
Marriott Marquis Hotel
1535 Broadway (Times Square)
398-1900
Dinner: Daily; Brunch: Wed, Sun
Moderate to moderately expensive

Many restaurant reviewers say that you should avoid: (1) hotel restaurants, (2) restaurants on the top floors of buildings, and (3) restaurants that revolve. Well, I found a place that falls into all three categories, but it's a must *not* to avoid! I recommend brunch or dinner at the View, the revolving rooftop dining room in the Marriott Marquis Hotel on Times Square. Be sure to get a table by the window, of course. It's popular with businessmen and theatergoers, so be sure to call for reservations and come early. There's a pretheater *prix fixe* dinner menu with four courses. In the evening, there are several menus: American and some ethnic choices, which change monthly. On the American side are delicious buffalo wings, swordfish steak with Cajun spices, and crab pancakes. The chocolate mousse Marquis or the Bavarian cream will round out a delicious meal. The Marriott is known throughout the country for its flair with restaurants; this one is no exception. It's a good choice from any point of view.

VIVOLO
140 E 74th St
737-3533
Lunch: Mon-Fri; Dinner: Mon-Sat
Moderate

An old townhouse converted into a charming two-story, moderately priced Italian restaurant has become a neighborhood favorite. There are cozy fireplaces on both levels, but the second floor is reserved exclusively for nonsmokers. Consistency is the name of the game here. You know that whatever dish you order will be presented in a professional manner every time you visit. Other restaurants could learn about daily specials from Vivolo! They print the list of specials each day and include it with the regular menu, so that the waiters don't have to stumble through a bad recitation. Menu choices run the gamut of the unusual antipasti: carpuccio, baked clams, cold seafood salad, and mussels in tomato sauce. A complete selection of pasta, from angel hair with fresh vegetables, to spinach with bacon, onion, and tomato, are available daily. The tortellini and linguini are done with true Italian flair. Popular entrees are the broiled shrimp, stuffed veal chops, scaloppine in lemon and butter, and breast of chicken with artichokes and mushrooms. For a different dessert, try the cannoli alla Vivolo, a pastry filled with ricotta cream. And don't be surprised if Paul Newman or Robert Redford are seated next to you.

WEST SIDE STORY
700 Columbus Ave (at 95th St)
749-1900
Daily: 7 a.m.-11 p.m.
No credit cards
Moderate

This is not a fancy place, but if you're looking for a wholesome, delicious, and inexpensive meal, you'll find it here. The breakfast plates include French toast and flapjacks with delicious whipped butter and Vermont maple syrup. In fact, walnut apple flapjacks are the specialty of the house. You also have your choice of Vermont cheddar cheese omelets; country cream cheese and parsley omelets; herb omelets; ham, green pepper, and onion omelets; or nova and cream cheese omelets. All the eggs and omelets are served with home fries and toast; you can also get sweet breakfast pastries. (If you're not an early riser, you'll be happy to note that breakfast is served late.) The salads are equally great. The West Side Chef's Salad is a delicious combination of cold meats, cheese, bean sprouts, cherry tomatoes, seasonal vegetables, herbs, and an artichoke heart—and you won't believe the very moderate price. All the salad bowls are served with fresh bread and whipped butter. And what a selection of sandwiches! You name it, and they'll make it. You also have your choice of breads. Hot dishes include quiche, grilled hamburgers, a fried-chicken basket, chili, hot roast beef, and hot turkey. No one else makes deep-dish Chicago Peaches pizza. And the small fry can dine for pennies (almost!) on frankfurters and beans or spaghetti and meatballs. It's easy to see why this is such a popular spot for quick dining.

WILKINSON'S
1573 York Ave (bet 83rd and 84th St)
535-5454
Dinner: Daily
Moderate to expensive

Everything looks good at Wilkinson's! The people look good because the lighting is very flattering. The pink tones make the diners look as though they've just returned from a holiday in the sun. The food looks good because it really is! This is a delightful, intimate seafood cafe. It does not pretend to be everything to everybody, but does particularly well with a somewhat limited menu. The appetizer dishes are unique. My favorite is the cured Norwegian salmon. For an entree, don't miss the crab imperial with sweet peppers. Other possibilities are the broiled swordfish and the tuna with tomato sauce. As a thoughtful gesture, no cigars or pipes are allowed in the main dining area, so you can enjoy such delicious desserts as chocolate mousse cake or the carmelized apple tart without distraction.

WINDOWS ON THE WORLD
1 World Trade Center
938-1111
Dinner: Daily; Buffet: Sat, Sun; Brunch: Sun
Expensive

Windows on the World, on top of the World Trade Center, features one of the most spectacular views in all the world. It's worth going up just to see the great panorama from the 107th floor. (You can't wear jeans.) You need reservations for the restaurant, but I recommend that you *don't* stay for dinner—the food is not all that great. If you do decide to eat, I suggest the grand buffet table on weekends, which is attractive and reasonably priced. There is a super dessert selection, which includes chocolate Sabayon cake, warm apple tarts, and white chocolate mousse. Or you might have cocktails and some hors d'oeuvres in the Hors d'Oeuvrerie. Music and dancing start at 7:30 p.m. On Sundays, dancing starts at 4 p.m. and continues until 9 p.m. Also available is the Cellar in the Sky, where a preset menu (it changes every two weeks) features a seven-course dinner with five wines at an appropriate sky-high price.

WOO LAE OAK OF SEOUL
77 W 46th St
869-9958
Lunch, Dinner: Daily
Moderate

If you've had the opportunity to visit Korea, you've undoubtedly enjoyed Korean barbecue, certainly one of that country's tastier delights. In New York, there's an outstanding version of the real thing, brought to you by an establishment that's been in business for more than 40 years, Woo Lae Oak. One word of warning: many items are very hot and spicy, so order carefully. Start with the goki jun (egg-roll meatballs). These are very different from any egg roll you've ever tasted. Another delicious appetizer is sewu tuigim (deep-fried shrimp and vegetables). Of course, the big attraction is the authentic Korean barbecue. The meat, broiled right at your table, is marinated in a special sauce and served with rice, soup, and vegetables. Choice of meat includes sliced beef, short rib cubes, sliced chicken, beef tongue, beef liver, beef heart, beef tripe, and sliced pork. Hot pot casserole is also cooked at your table and served with rice and vegetables, as well as your choice of sliced beef, shrimp, fish, or chicken. A large assortment of rice dishes, porridge, and noodles are available. Reservations are a necessity for large groups; be prepared to wait if you arrive with a small party at regular dining hours. Service is rapid, but don't rush through your meal. Take time to savor that barbecue.

WYLIE'S RIBS AND COMPANY   WYLIE'S II
891 First Ave (at 49th St)   59 W 56th St
751-0700   757-7910
Daily: 11:30-1:00 a.m.
Moderate

Finding a convenient, pleasant, not-too-crowded spot that serves great food at a reasonable price is not always easy. But here are a couple of candidates. If you like Texas-style barbecued chicken and ribs, Wylie's is the best in this department, offering ample platters of the tastiest, crispiest back ribs you have ever gotten all over your fingers—and some of the tenderest Northern fried chicken available. I suggest the combination dish served with excellent steak fries and cole slaw. Of course, you can also get half-pound burgers, barbecued beef sandwiches, salads, chili, and a very special brick onion loaf. The dinner menu leans more toward steak and fish, in addition to their famous ribs. The atmosphere is informal, the service efficient. Early evening hours are the least hectic. I heartily recommend dropping in at either of these locations, especially if you have young people in tow.

YELLOWFINGERS DI NUOVO
200 E 60th St
751-8615
Lunch, Dinner: Daily
Moderate

Some of you will remember the old Yellowfingers, a quick hamburger-and-sandwich place. Well, put those memories behind you. The new Yellowfingers is another story altogether. Hostess Patricia Snaric is right on the job, negotiating her way through the busy tables, which look down the street to Bloomingdale's. Yellowfingers was reconceived with a wonderful idea called "fa' vecchia." The name comes from "faccia vecchia," which was used in the past for pizzalike breads baked without a topping. Yellowfingers has put together absolutely delicious fa vecchia combinations, like the one baked with fresh tomato and buffalo mozzarella and the one baked with potatoes, pancetta, and rosemary (my favorite). You can also order them garnished with such items as prosciutto, braised onion, and parsley. They are crusty, but not too filling—just right for a unique lunchtime meal. If this kind of pizza is not to your liking, there are plenty of excellent salads, the best being the rosemary-roasted chicken salad with sweet peppers, pine nuts, and greens. The focaccia farcita sandwich (grilled eggplant, mozzarella, roasted peppers, basil, capers, and gremolata) is worth a try. For more substantial appetites, there's a house-ground hamburger on grilled focaccia. Various homemade desserts are usually available. This place is noisy, fun, handy, and moderately priced—a great addition to New York's Upper East Side lunch scene.

YELLOW ROSE CAFE
450 Amsterdam Ave (at 82nd St)
595-8760
Lunch, Dinner: Daily
Inexpensive

Barbara Clifford of Fort Worth, Texas, has transplanted Texas-style chicken-fried steak, Southern fried chicken, smothered pork chops, and El Paso cheese enchiladas to her 12-table Upper West Side cafe. Accompanied by buttermilk biscuits, red chili, real mashed potatoes, and home-grown vegetables from her father's garden in Texas, Barbara's portions are huge, delicious, and incredibly inexpensive. The cafe is cactus filled, homey, and very busy. Strawberry shortcake, pecan pie, or sweet potato pie will top off a great meal during the week or a hearty country brunch on weekends. Look for the unique Western bar next door.

YE WAVERLY INN
16 Bank St
929-4377
Lunch: Mon-Fri; Dinner: Daily; Brunch: Sun
Moderate

English food is not very fancy, but English pubs do have atmosphere, and they do some things quite well. In the Village there's Ye Waverly Inn, a picturesque pub in confined quarters, which dates from the early part of the century. There are four rooms and an outside eating area with adequate though uncomfortable furnishings, but the atmosphere is truly delightful. One is certain the food is good, because the place is always crowded and there are a number of famous folk who often dine here. If all this is not reason enough to go to the Inn, their chicken pot pie should be. It is absolutely one of the best I have ever eaten. Other possibilities would be the sautéed calf's liver, barbecued rack of ribs, boiled beef and horseradish sauce, or the boneless chicken breast. Before the main course, try the fresh fruit and cheese, French-fried eggplant, or a delicious fresh vegetable marinade. For the light eater, I suggest the smoked brook trout or the quiche and Waldorf salad. The dessert selection is excellent, especially the tasty pecan pie. I can see why legions of Village regulars flock here, and you will, too.

ZARELA
953 Second Ave (bet 50th and 51st St)
644-6740
Lunch: Mon-Fri; Dinner: Daily; Brunch: Sun
Moderate

If you really want the very best Mexican meal in New York, you should get yourself invited to the home of Zarela Martinez. Failing that, the next best thing is to head for her charming and busy restaurant, a two-story building on Second Avenue. Don't let them seat you downstairs, the second-floor dining room, complete with a fireplace, is much more quaint and colorful. You'll understand how Zarela has earned her reputation for the best south-of-the-border cuisine when you taste her antojitos, which include a wonderful poblano chile stuffed with chicken and dried fruit, rolled fried-chicken tacos, and fried calamari in a spicy sauce. And there is so much more: such seafood dishes as shrimps sautéed in a spicy jalapeno sauce and grill-smoked salmon; several chicken dishes, and a grilled duck breast with peanut and pumpkin seed sauce; delicious meat entrees, like the jalisco-style pork and hominy stew; and a great selection of Mexican side dishes, from refried black beans to golden fried cauliflower to fried plantain slices with mole sauce. Even the desserts are special. The chocolate crepes filled with almond pastry cream and served with chocolate and raspberry sauces, and the chocolate pecan mocha layer cake swimming in warm chocolate sauce—both are heaven-sent. But if you're going Mexican all the way, try the Mexican fruit bread pudding with applejack brandy butter sauce or the banana guave black cake with ice cream and guave sauce.

Safety in the City

"But is it safe?" These are the words you often hear when you announce plans for touring around the Big Apple. My answer is always a resounding "yes." The percentages are with you. New York is big. Very big. And any area with millions of people is bound to have its share of crime. But despite its density of population, New York doesn't even make the top ten in the nation's crime statistics. Common sense, of course, is always the best armor. As you take advantage of some of the exciting tours and things to do on the next pages, keep in mind the following advice, and you will be fine.

Be prudent. You are your own best security. Don't leave tempting items on the front seat of the car. Don't flaunt your gold necklace. Leave your flashy diamond ring at home.

Always be alert. Don't trust anyone you don't know. Pickpockets work by nudging or jostling their mark in a few brief seconds. Remember, they work best in crowds. Be particularly alert at sidewalk displays and public transportation, including elevators.

Sticking to the so-called "good" neighborhoods is no guarantee of safety. In all my years of walking around New York, I've "lost" my wallet only twice. But the first time was at Park Avenue and 63rd Street in the most reputable area of town; the second was at Madison Square Garden surrounded by incredibly tight security.

Never ask for trouble. You don't need to be in Alphabetland" (Avenues A, B, C or D in the downtown East Side area), the recesses of Central Park at night, or anywhere "dressed up" clothes look out of place.

Always act as if you know what you are doing. If you must ask for directions, do so inside a hotel or shop and preferably from a telephone. If you must look at a map, take it to a rest room and consult it in privacy.

When you are "giving" directions, always be as specific as possible. A taxi driver probably knows 10 very long ways to get from any one place to another.

One further note: The predominance of crack on the drug scene has changed the nature of crime in the city. There used to be reasonable parameters. No more. All of the city is vulnerable now. You don't have to be so paranoid that you're constantly looking over your shoulder, but you must never sashay through the streets with too obvious a carefree attitude. Subtly and consistently, you must always be on guard.

Have a great time!

III. Where To Find It: Fun Ideas and Activities for Residents and Visitors

Organized Tours

ADVENTURE ON A SHOESTRING
300 W 53rd St
265-2663

Started as a lark by Howard Goldberg over two decades ago, Adventure on a Shoestring has evolved into the perfect city tour. Its title is self-explanatory: it promises and delivers an offbeat view of New York, and the price is easy on the wallet. How do they do it? There's an annual membership fee that entitles members to discount rates on each trip. Advance notice of trips are published in a newsletter, which is also sent to nonmembers who request it. Tourists and nonmembers can join the tours at a higher rate.

ART DECO SOCIETY OF NEW YORK
385-2744

Indulge your love of art deco and your appreciation for city trivia with this walking tour, which usually starts on 42nd Street. You'll learn, for instance, that art deco architects prized corner sites so much that if they couldn't get one, they would work to create the illusion of one. Another tidbit: 500 Fifth Avenue, opposite the 42nd Street Library, is a mirror image (albeit decapitated) of the Empire State Building.

ART HORIZONS INTERNATIONAL
1650 Broadway
246-5750

Art Horizons tours cover art, architecture, performing arts, culinary arts, fashion and design. They can be arranged for individuals or groups, the latter usually for a specific exhibit. The guides are especially well qualified, and if you hook up with a group tour, the rates are very reasonable. Either way, you'll be getting a backstage view of city art not available elsewhere. The Horizons staff will introduce you to artists' lofts, gallery directors, and museum curators. Art Horizons also offers the more typical tour features—yacht trips, tours by helicopter, and the like.

BACKSTAGE ON BROADWAY
228 W 47th St (suite 346)
575-8065

This tour offers a look at a Broadway that regular theater patrons miss. The tour is reasonably priced, with reduced rates for students and senior citizens, and includes an explanation of how a play is technically produced. The lecture is illustrated by taking you backstage. Often, you'll get a chance to meet and chat with theater people; stage managers, actors, and technical designers describe what they do as you're guided among the props and sets. You'll get a full understanding of how a play develops, from script to opening night. Reservations are required; this gives you a chance to learn, in advance, who will be your guide. Individuals can be confirmed only one week prior to the date of the tour. But don't miss it. It's very good!

CARNEGIE HALL
Seventh Ave at 57th St
247-7800

The recently restored Carnegie Hall is proudly shown to visitors on tours each Tuesday and Thursday at 11:30, 2, and 3 (except in summer). The tour does not go backstage, and the practice rooms and apartments at Carnegie Mews are not on the agenda.

CIRCLE LINE SIGHTSEEING YACHTS
Pier 83 (at 43rd St)
563-3200
Daily: Mid-March through Nov

The Circle Line boats cruise Manhattan's waters for three hours. Along the way, sights are pointed out and explained. Unless there's a snowstorm, you can count on having a pleasant trip. Cynics who are too blasé to be moved by the city skyline (and you'd have to be pretty hard-nosed) amuse themselves by listening for mistakes in the guide's pat spiel and loudly correcting him. Keep an ear cocked for a New York-wise skeptic. Groups can avail themselves of the Circle Line package tours, which are all-inclusive tours of the city on land. They include Broadway shows, restaurants, sightseeing, and all the major tourist spots. For those who really love the water, there are day trips up the Hudson, with stops at Bear Mountain and West Point.

COUNTRY CYCLING TOURS
140 W 83rd St (bet Columbus and Amsterdam Ave)
874-5151
Mon-Fri: 9:30-5

Country Cycling offers walking and cycling tours, which range from quiet one-day rides to two-week European tours. They are geared to the participant's ability, be you a neophyte or a professional. Rental equipment is available, and Country Cycling can arrange group tours, customized tours, and specific treks for visitors with special interests. Some of the more tasty possibilities are daytrips to Dutchess County strawberry fields and apple orchards, Connecticut raspberry fields, and New York wine country. A support vehicle is used on all tours to transport luggage or to provide any kind of emergency assistance.

DAILEY-THORP CULTURAL TOURS
Park Tower S
315 W 57th St (bet Eighth and Ninth Ave)
307-1555
Mon-Fri: 9:30-5:30

Dailey-Thorp works with the Metropolitan Opera Guild, organizing cultural tours around the world. At its home base in New York, Dailey-Thorp offers special tour packages to the Met. Most of the tours center around weekends, the exceptions being the opening night and opening week of the opera season. They include hotel accommodations (usually at the Pierre), center orchestra seats at the opera, transportation, meals, an experienced tour escort, and guided tours through cultural sights, such as the Metropolitan Museum of Art and the Museum of Modern Art. There are similar arrangements for the New York City Opera, the New York Philharmonic, and Carnegie Hall. And for New Yorkers who wish to expand their horizons, there are East Coast, North America, and worldwide opera-based tours. You could sing an aria about the smoothness and efficiency of this operation.

DISCOVER NEW YORK
The Municipal Art Society
457 Madison Ave
935-3960

The Municipal Art Society conducts several tours, but the most famous is the tour of Grand Central Station, which departs every Wednesday afternoon at 12:30. Participants meet under the largest freestanding indoor sign in the grand terminal lobby. The hour-long tour is free (yes, free!), and no reservations are needed. On spring and summer weekends, the society sponsors walking tours at nominal fees. They run about three hours each and cover historic buildings and districts.

DOORWAY TO DESIGN
1441 Broadway (suite 338)
221-1111

In special tours organized by Sheila Sperber, you can go behind the scenes in the world of interior design, visit auction galleries and museums, meet artists and craftspeople, discuss the latest styles with fashion makers, and visit antiques dealers. These tours can be arranged for any time of the day, can last for several hours or several days, and can be designed for any size group. In one of the most popular tours, you visit private homes in the colorful Greenwich Village area.

DYED IN THE WOOL
252 W 37th St
563-6669, 800-HAND-DYE

At this factory loft, various wools are dyed for crafts and fashion fabric. While the work is in progress, tourists are given a guided tour of the entire process, learning how yarn is turned into unique fabrics. There is a "Meet the Artist" program as well, and the tour is free.

FEDERAL RESERVE BANK
33 Liberty St
720-6130

Here is your chance to see big bucks being counted. You'll also see an historical coin and currency exhibit and the gold vault that houses the largest collection of gold in the free world. Tours are available four times daily, at 10 a.m., 11 a.m., 1 p.m., and 2 p.m., Monday through Friday. Tours last one hour, and a minimum of one-week advance notice for reservations is required.

FULTON FISH MARKET TOUR
17 Fulton Fish Market
962-1608

Imagine a fish market that has been in existence since 1831! The Fulton Fish Market, the largest of its kind in North America, has about 70 wholesalers who sell 88 million pounds of fish each year. The market opens to buyers at 3 a.m. on Monday and at 4 a.m. Tuesday through Friday. The market starts closing around 8 a.m.

so that the proprietors of Manhattan's best restaurants (they're in this book) can have fresh produce for the day. The tours, which cost about $5 per person for five people or more, cover the history of the Fulton Fish Market and its operation. The tours also allow visitors to become acquainted with the fish (species from all parts of the world) being sold on that particular day.

GRACIE MANSION TOUR
East End Ave at 88th St
570-4751
Wed: 10-4; every hour March-Nov

The tour of the newly renovated mayor's home only began in recent years, and since it's the first time in history that Hizzoner's home has been open to the public, business is brisk. Reservations must be obtained by writing or calling the tour director. Since the tour is only held one day a week, an out-of-towner doesn't have much of a chance to catch one of the hourly tours, but it's worth a try if you're good at planning ahead. Gracie Mansion remains (as it was when the Gracie family owned it) one of the choicest parcels of real estate on the Upper East Side. The view of the East River and the Fire Boat Station is terrific, and the house is magnificent. There is also a special in-depth tour of the mansion and grounds, which is available year round. The half-day tour, including either continental breakfast or colonial tea, is held on Monday or Tuesday (by advance reservation) and concentrates on the mansion's and the city's social and cultural history.

HARLEM RENAISSANCE TOURS
18 E 105th St
722-9534

The Harlem Renaissance Tours personnel know Harlem as only people who live there can. They conduct busloads of visitors through the Harlem Jazz Festival, the Black Theater Festival, and Harlem Week, as well as specialized tours of shows and other cultural events.

HARLEM SPIRITUALS
1457 Broadway (suite 1088)
302-2594

Muriel Samama, the president of this novel operation, offers a wide variety of programs. There are spirituals and gospel on Sunday, gospel on Wednesday, and many other facets of Harlem (with lunch) on Thursdays. A great soul food and jazz tour is offered on Thursday, Friday, and Saturday evenings.

INSIDE NEW YORK
203 E 72nd St
861-0709

New York here means the fashion industry, and the folks at Inside New York aim to show visitors a behind-the scenes look at the fashion and interior design industries in the city. Tours (group or individual) can be formal affairs or especially designed to gain entrance into wholesale lofts for shopping or shows. There are half-day and all-day tours, and the group tours are quite reasonable.

ISLAND HELICOPTER
34th St Heliport at the East River
Business correspondence: 360 Fifth Ave, Suite 3500
683-4575

Daily, from 9 to 9 (9-6 in January, February, and March), Island Helicopter offers a number of different sightseeing tours. The simplest is a short flight over lower and midtown Manhattan. The more complex can go as far as incorporating bus and boat transportation into two-day trips.

LOU SINGER TOURS
130 St Edward's St, Brooklyn
(718) 875-9084

For years, we heard about Lou Singer's tours, but we used to exclude him because he was based in Brooklyn. Now Lou has become synonymous with the "noshing tour" of New York, and no one does it better. (That may have been another reason to leave him out. We harbored notions of doing it ourselves. Now we know better.) Although Singer can arrange the usual behind-the-scenes tours, his specialty is the gastronomic tour, which makes stops in the Lower East Side, Little Ukraine, and Brooklyn.

LOWER EAST SIDE
TENEMENT MUSEUM
97 Orchard St
431-0233

This is the country's first and only museum devoted to the urban immigrant experience. Sundays at noon, there is the "Peddler's Pack," a 90-minute walking tour of the historic Lower East Side. It is led by a costumed guide who points out such sites as Hester Street, the public baths, and other remnants of turn-of-the-century immigrant life. By 2 in the afternoon, you're back at the museum to see a complete dramatization of immigrant life. I just can't imagine a museum in the middle of the city's busiest shopping bazaar, but here it is, folks.

METROPOLITAN OPERA GUILD
1865 Broadway
582-3512

Monday through Saturday, the Opera Guild gives backstage tours at the Met in Lincoln Center for a very nominal fee. In addition, the Group Sales Department of the Opera itself (870-7447) offers several deluxe tours packaged as "A Night on the Town," which include dining in one of Lincoln Center's restaurants and attending a performance at the opera.

NBC STUDIO TOUR
30 Rockefeller Center
664-7174

Since the Rockefeller Center Observatory closed, this is the only tour of the art deco broadcasting complex. Given from 10 to 4, Monday through Saturday, it's another behind-the-scenes tour.

NEW YORK STOCK EXCHANGE
20 Broad St
656-5168
Mon-Fri: 9:20-3

The New York Stock Exchange is the world's largest securities marketplace and a "must see" attraction for New Yorkers and tourists alike. The NYSE visitors center offers an interesting way to learn about securities trading and how the exchange contributes to the economy. Highlights include a multi-image video, a demonstration of how space-age technology supports trading, and a multilingual explanation of the trading process from the gallery overlooking the world-famous trading floor. Reservations are required for groups of 10 or more.

OLD MERCHANT'S HOUSE
29 E Fourth St
777-1089
Sun: 1-4

If you love Victorian homes, don't miss this one. It took 11 years to restore, it's staffed by volunteers, and it's magnificent. Joseph and Caroline Roberto are the volunteer caretakers, and they treat the house (and you) with dignified warmth, as if the owners had just stepped out for a Sunday ride. Group tours (20 or more people) are available if you call between 9:15 and 5.

PARK RANGER TOURS
New York City Department of Parks and Recreation
397-3080, 397-3081

The Urban Park Rangers (for real!) guide free tours every Sunday at 2 p.m., in Central Park and other parks around the city. Some of the tours point out which herbs and plants in the park are edible and offer other information on the local flower and fauna. All of the tours are very interesting. Afterward, you're much more inclined to contribute to the park projects that invite your financial support.

RADIO CITY MUSIC HALL
Rockefeller Center
50th St and Sixth Ave
632-4041

More interesting than the stage show at Radio City is the behind-the-scenes tour, which is conducted every 45 minutes, from 10 a.m. to 4:45 p.m. every Monday through Saturday (Sunday, 11-4:45). The hour-long tour includes a view of the world's largest organ, the "Mighty Wurlitzer," the underground hydraulic system, the costume department, the famous Rockettes' rehearsal room (if not in use), and the world-renowned art-deco bathrooms. Note: Rockefeller Center has a self-guided walking tour of the complex. Maps are available throughout the complex.

SCHAPIRO'S WINERY
126 Rivington St
674-4404

Schapiro's is one of the only two wineries in the city that is open on Sunday. (The other is Kedem, a block away on Ludlow, but they don't give tours.) The reason they're open is that they're kosher wineries and as such are closed on Saturday. In this cavernous space beneath the streets of the Lower East Side, barrels and barrels of kosher wine are aged and produced. (It was here that I learned that Oregon is prized for its blackberries.) The tour is absolutely fascinating—and free. They give samples.

SHORT LINE TOURS
166 W 46th St
354-4740

The conventional bus tour of the city that Short Line offers is anything but conventional. For one thing, there is not one but eight different tour itineraries, and the line utilizes bus, boat, helicopter, and horse and buggy to see it all. Along the way, tourists can visit Harlem, Grant's Tomb, the United Nations, the Empire State Building, Chinatown, the Statue of Liberty, the South Street Seaport, the World Trade Center, and much, much more. Of course, that requires all eight tours (some of which are combinations of single tours already) and probably much more time than the average tourist has, but there is no better way to get a well-documented orientation to the city. All tours leave from the Times Square headquarters and range from two hours in length to the all-day Big Apple Tour. Though they are more frequent in warm weather, they run all year. Incidentally, New Yorkers *never* take these tours. So, one trip could make a visitor more knowledgeable about the city than the residents, and you can do it in the lap of luxury in the glass-roofed, air-conditioned buses.

VIEWPOINT INTERNATIONAL
1414 Sixth Ave (at 58th St)
355-1055

Viewpoint International organizes events, programs, and tours of New York. Its clients include corporations, nonprofit associations, and visiting groups. The company's partners, Margaret Gins and Allyn Simmons, and their crew have done it all, from two presidential events to Grammy Award galas to centennial events for 15,000. On a smaller scale, they do block parties, black tie events, complete city tours (with native-language guides), and anything that will make a New York visit easier on the planners and more fun for the participants. The Viewpoint folks are true professionals, completely reliable. Since they have a working relationship with travel agents all over the world, they're able to map out a special New York experience for anyone.

WALKING TOURS OF CHINATOWN
70 Mulberry St (second floor)
619-4785

This group offers two tours daily, at 10 and 1. Each lasts 90 minutes and shows the development of Chinatown. Highlights include food stores, restaurants, and historic sites, as well as many places that the average tourist never gets to see. Reservations are required for weekend tours.

Children's Fun

Here are some best bets for amusing the kids.

AT&T Infoquest (550 Madison Ave at 56th St, 605-5555) Communication is the theme.
American Museum of Immigration, State of Liberty National Monument (363-3200) Kids love the ferry ride.

Belvedere Castle (Central Park at 79th St, 772-0210) Family-activity center with emphasis on science.

Children's Zoo (Central Park, east side at 64th St, 408-0271) Enchantment with Noah's ark and all the animals.

Empire State Building (34th St and Fifth Ave, 736-3100) This *is* New York—all 102 stories of it.

Hayden Planetarium (Museum of Natural History, Central Park and W 81st St, 769-5921) The sky's the limit.

IBM Gallery (Madison Ave at 56th St, 407-6100) Hands-on science and art education.

Intrepid Sea-Air-Space Museum (Pier 86, at W 46th St, Hudson River, 245-2533) For the young pilots and sailors.

Radio City Music Hall (Sixth Ave at 50th St, 757-3100) The Rockettes and seasonal theme shows are spectacular.

South Street Seaport (East River, foot of Fulton St, 732-7678) Tall ships, street performers, multimedia *Seaport Experience*.

Staten Island Ferry (South Street terminal) The best ride in town.

United Nations (First Ave, 43rd to 49th St, 754-7713) Budding statesmen will like it.

World Trade Center (West, Church, Vesey, and Liberty St, 466-4170) Breathtaking views of what man has built.

Lower East Side

New York has shopping districts for specific goods rather than the general shopping centers and malls of most American cities. You might therefore expect that the city would also have a specific place that would be the quintessential spot for bargain shopping. And it does—the Lower East Side. This area was the first stop after Ellis Island for many immigrants. Those "huddled masses" had little money and high expectations, so the shopping community that developed was highly ethnic and competitive, resulting in low prices for top-quality products. Many of the businesses are over 100 years old, and even the new ones adhere to traditions established before the proprietor's grandfather was born. The Lower East Side is not a tourist stop, but it's a place most New Yorkers have visited at least once. (That makes it more popular than the Empire State Building!) And when I am asked, I always say that it is my number one choice for people who want to experience a genuinely New York style of shopping. There is nothing like it.

Location: There is no official boundary for the Lower East Side. For a while, the Jewish shopping area spilled over Canal Street to the other side of Allen Street and into Chinatown. The "little diamond district" is a remnant of those times. Nowadays the tables have turned, and Chinatown stretches to Essex Street. Roughly, though, the area is Allen Street to the East River and Houston to

Canal. The heart of the shopping can be found on the axis of Grand, Orchard, and Essex streets.

Manners: Take everything you've heard about New York rudeness and exaggerate it, and you'll get an idea of what to expect on the Lower East Side. There is no such thing as anyone waiting his turn. So, sharpen your elbows and learn to ignore the little old lady at the entrance of the store who insists, "Me next!" She's probably better seasoned at aggressive shopping than you are.

Amenities: There are none. No bathrooms, no checks, occasionally credit cards. The latter two are changing somewhat, but it's always better to take cash. Never flaunt it, and watch your wallet at all times. Actual muggings are few, but purse snatchings are popular.

Hours: Jewish time is kept here. That means no Friday evenings or Saturdays. While this rule is being relaxed more these days, the interesting stores stick to the traditional schedule. Sunday is *the* day, and it starts early, by 10 a.m. During the week, things are looser.

Parking: Whew! On Sunday, your only hope is the municipal garage on Essex and Ludlow above Delancey. On-street parking is possible, but if you find a space, there's a good chance you'll get double-parked in. Orchard Street is virtually a pedestrian mall on Sunday.

What You'll Find: Fashion and food are the strong suits of the area. There's every kind of clothing for everybody. The quality and style can be mind-boggling. The area has sources for getting top-quality goods and selling them at steep discounts. Traditionally, this is what is expected, and usually this is what the merchants deliver. There are exceptions. There are many "knock-off" stores, which exploit the area's reputation, so sometimes you might have to look hard to tell a real Polo shirt from a fake. But if you stick to the stores that I recommend, you can amaze your friends with some incredible bargains.

On Orchard Street alone, you'll find:

Leslie's Bootery (65 Orchard St and 319 Grand St) Leslie is the granddaddy of the designer shoe outlets on the Lower East Side. The store carries both men's and ladies' shoes, all of top quality in a variety of prices. The new Grand Street location has become the main store.

Charles Weiss & Son (38 Orchard St, 331 Grand St) For ladies' undergarments and lingerie, Charles Weiss is without peer. I once saw a salesman demonstrate the properties of a good bra here.

Pan Am Menswear (50 and 59 Orchard St) We have a love-hate relationship with Pan Am. We love the bargains that can be found at the two stores (suits at 50 Orchard and sportswear at 59 Orchard). Their quality probably can't be beat in the area. As for hate—well, suffice it to say that they'd win a rudeness contest even with the entire Lower East Side as competition.

Goldman & Cohen (54 Orchard St) Shop at this brisk, efficient store for ladies' undergarments, robes, lingerie, and loungewear. This isn't the place to browse casually or ask for advice. But if you know what you're after, you'll save a minimum of 25 percent, and it could be substantially more.

A. W. Kaufman (73 Orchard St) Undergarments and hosiery for the rest of the family.

Louis Chock (74 Orchard St) Ditto. Kaufman is the newer of the two, but Chock has the crowds who would bet their socks on him.

Forman's (78, 82, and 94 Orchard St) Forman's earns its formidable reputation with three stores of discount fashions for every female member of the family. You'll find designer clothes at 82 Orchard, petite sizes at 94 Orchard, and "plus" sizes at 78 Orchard. The discount is a minimum of 25 percent for top, in-season merchandise. And the "just reduced" department downstairs at each store is a treasure trove. At Forman's, you can even find things at a discount that haven't yet hit the full-price stores uptown.

Klein's of Monticello (105 Orchard St) Many years ago I was shocked to see a pair of size 2 Calvin Klein jeans for sale here, but I should have taken Klein's for the visionary it is. The very top designers are available here for children and women at deep discounts (that still doesn't mean cheap). If you're not shocked or amused by a size 18 months Yves St. Laurent, or if that's your style, then Klein's is for you.

Lace Up (110 Orchard St) A favorite of the *Times* and the fashion crowd, Lace Up is a super source for the trendiest footwear. The prices are a fraction of what they are elsewhere—if they're available elsewhere. This is a discount store that actually sets the trends.

Fine & Klein (119 Orchard St) We've been naming Fine & Klein the country's number one leather goods store for quite some time now, and we haven't received one nomination for a contender. They offer the finest collection of leather goods, handbags, and attaché cases at the most reasonable prices.

Samuel Beckenstein (118 and 125 Orchard St) This emporium specializes in "dry goods," which is what they used to call fabric in the days when this store was founded. Beckenstein's is the source for virtually any kind of fabric. It is often the only hope of interior decorators, home sewers, and couturiers. It started as a pushcart that dispensed woolens for men's suits, and it still has one of the finest departments for that alone.

Breakaway Fashions (125 Orchard St) There are furs downstairs (an outgrowth of a store of another name on 57th St), but ignore them and concentrate on the designer and brand-name sportswear.

You could spend the entire day here if it's very crowded and the salespeople are too harried to deliver the hard-sell.

Shulie's (175 Orchard St) Tahari is a well-known designer who has his own boutique on Madison Avenue. Less well known is that he has two outlets in the metropolitan area. One is in New Jersey, and the other operates under the guise of Shulie's. For Tahari fans this is an unbelievable opportunity. The designs are first-rate, the styles up-to-date, and the prices affordable.

M. Friedlich (196 Orchard St) A first choice for women who wear European sportswear and knits.

After Orchard Street, the next stop on the Lower East Side would be Grand Street. You'll find more stores specializing in household goods.

Harris Levy (278 Grand St) and **Homeworks Design** (281 Grand St) Virtually every kind of linen and domestic item.

Ezra Cohen (307 Grand St) Probably the best source for such domestics as sheets, both current and discontinued, commode covers, matching towels, and bathroom rugs.

Fishkin (314 Grand St) Trendy designer clothing for juniors. A small shoe department. From the outside, the store doesn't look like much, and it's easy to pass it by, but don't.

J. Schachter (85 Ludlow St) The birthplace of the down coverlet, which had another name in another language when the great-grandparents of many local shoppers first brought it to Schachter for repair. You can also coordinate entire bedroom suites at Schachter.

Kaufman Electrical Appliances (365 Grand St) One of the original electronics outlets in the city. It still stocks anything that can be plugged into a socket (and a substantial amount that cannot), and all of it is greatly discounted. Come here for all kinds of appliances, as well as dishes, pens, cameras, and video equipment. Other local old-timers in this business include **Bondy** (40 Canal St) and **Dembitzer Brothers** (5 Essex St).

Eastern Silver (54 Canal St) Climb the stairs of this nondescript building and enter a gleaming world of shiny silver. The store is small, but you can buy anything imaginable in sterling at great savings.

After all the shopping, you'll be ready for a gastronomic treat. Some of the places not to be missed are **Bernstein-on-Essex** (135 Essex St) for deli and kosher Chinese food; **Yonah Schimmel** (137 E Houston St) for historic and political knishes; **Moishe's Bakery** (181 E Houston St) for great Old World breads; **Russ & Daughters** (179 E Houston St), next door, for appetizers to go with Moishe's bread; and **Ratner's** (138 Delancey St) for the ultimate dairy meal, Lower East Side style.

IV. Where To Eat It: New York's Best Food Shops

Bakery Goods

A. ORWASHER BAKERY
308 E 78th St (near Second Ave)
288-6569
Mon-Sat:7-7

This family business has been in existence for over 70 years, and many of their breads are family recipes handed down from father to son. You'll find Old World breads that used to exist in the local immigrant bakeries and have become extremely rare. Over 30 varieties are always available. Hearth-baked in brick ovens and made with natural ingredients, the breads come in a marvelous array of shapes and sizes—triple twists, cornucopias, and hearts, just to name a few. (I've seen their ovens; they're the real thing.) Be sure to sample the onion boards and cinnamon raisin bread and the challah, available on Fridays. It's almost as good as the home-baked variety. Best of all is their raisin pumpernickel, which comes in small rolls or loaves. When warm, it's moist, delicious, and sensational.

A. ZITO AND SON'S BAKERY
259 Bleecker St (bet Sixth and Seventh Ave)
929-6139
Mon-Sat: 6 a.m.-6:30 p.m.; Sun: 6-1

Those in the know, know Zito's. They flock here at sunrise to buy bread straight from the oven. Among Zito's fans are Frank Sinatra and numerous Village residents. They love Zito's because the bread crust is crunchy perfection, a sharp contrast to the soft, delicate inside. Two of the best sellers are the whole wheat loaf and the Sicilian loaf. Anthony John Zito is proudest of the house specialties: Italian, whole wheat, and white breads. The latter two come in sizes of 4, 7, and 13 ounces.

BONTE PATISSERIE
1316 Third Ave (bet 75th and 76th St)
535-2360
Mon-Sat: 9-6:30; closed Aug

Mrs. Bonte serves a delicious line of pastries and cakes. The style is decidedly French, but the taste has earned universal appreciation. The pastry is flaky smooth, the chocolates creamy satin, and the croissants and éclairs—well, they're perfection. Mrs. Bonte personally supervises the operation, and everything sold here bears her hallmark—that of a tremendously accomplished pastry chef. And her husband is just as talented.

BREAD SHOP
3139 Broadway (at La Salle St)
666-4343
Daily: 8-8; closed July 15-Labor Day

This tiny, out-of-the-way bakery, under the tracks at 123rd Street, supplies some of the best handmade, untainted-by-preservatives bread in the city. Their customers are mostly local stores and New York's better food shops (Jefferson Market is one), but if you arrive between 10 a.m. and 3 p.m., one of the house specialties will be available fresh from the oven. (A gastronomic treat unique to New York is walking into the neighborhood bagel shop and sampling "whatever's hot.") Jenny Buchanan and Jim Fitzer, who run the shop, are big on healthy breads and natural ingredients, so the bread here is not only delicious but good for you.

BUDAPEST PASTRY
207 E 84th St (bet Second and Third Ave)
628-0721
Mon-Sat: 7:30-7:30; Sun: 9:30-5:30

In 1985, Al Maghrebi, a Syrian baker, bought Budapest Pastry from its Hungarian owners. The resulting mixture of baking styles was a success. Of course, they had a few things in common. The Hungarians stuff the thin, flakey babka, strudle, and baklava dough with cabbage or apples, while Middle Easterners stuff the same kind of dough with spinach or eggplant. Nowadays, the bakery resounds with the United Nations mix of Syrian bakers, Hungarian pastry lovers, and all kinds of falafel fans come together to form a model of foreign relations the U.N. would envy.

CHELSEA BAKING COMPANY
259 W 19th St (bet Seventh and Eighth Ave)
242-7692
Daily: 7-7

The Chelsea Baking Company is a wholesale source for restaurants and gourmet stores, but it's also open to retail customers. We rate David Talbot's deep-dish apple pie the very best in New York. The food is now divided into three separate lists to accommodate the wholesale customer. The top is the "Signature" line, which, Talbot says, offers the finest ingredients, style, and presentation available. Layer-cake and breakfast lines feature a renowned cheesecake, a Mandarin cream cake, a real key lime pie, and all-butter Danishes and croissants. Chelsea Baking also specializes in custom orders. You can get an absolutely superb wedding cake, and the ice creams and sorbets are homemade.

COLETTE'S FRENCH PASTRY
1136 Third Ave (bet 66th and 67th St)
988-2605
Mon-Fri: 7:30-7; Sat: 7:30-5:30

Some of the best restaurants in the city buy cakes from Colette's, knowing that the French pastry made and sold here is unexcelled. A mail-order following (they ship anywhere within the United States) developed from former New Yorkers and tourists. The star is the Trianon (a dark heavy chocolate), but there are croissants, brioche, mousse cakes, fruit and chocolate charlottes, specialized cakes, petit fours, tarts, and cheesecakes that are just as good. Colette's is not the place to start a diet, but it's the place for a restaurant-quality dessert. Take-out foods are available.

CREATIVE CAKES
400 E 74th St (at First Ave)
794-9811
Tues-Fri: 8-4:30; Sat: 9-11

Being in the "creative cake" business myself, I know about the fun involved in making all kinds of unusual concoctions. Creative Cakes also knows how to have fun, using fine ingredients and ingenious patterns. Famous and not-so-famous cake lovers are fans of the fudgy chocolate with frosted buttercream icing and the sensational designs. Bill Schultz, the boss, has designed Bella Abzug's hat (on a platter, of course) and has even made a copy of the U.S. Customs House (for a Fourth of July celebration). Prices are reasonable, and the results are sure to be the conversation piece at any party.

DUFOUR PASTRY KITCHENS
808 Washington St
929-2800
Mon-Fri: 7-5; call for Sat hours

The location is not the handiest. The air is full of pastry dough, so you shouldn't wear your best black outfit. And all items are frozen, so you'll have to bake them yourself (instructions included). But these are the only drawbacks! You'll find delicious and creative pastry items of high quality at sensible prices at Dufour, who count many fancy uptown restaurants among their regular customers. Chocolate and regular puff pastry dough is available in sheets and in bulk. Wonderful hors d'oeuvres, like puff pastry logs, savory cheddar swirls, spicy gingered almond nuggets, cheese straws, pizzas and tart shells, can be ordered in any quantity. Try their apple and spice turnovers or yummy mini brie en croûte for desserts. Great puff sandwiches—chili with fresh vegetables, tuna melt, smoked salmon, Manhattan clam, broccoli-spinach gratin and more—provide a satisfying and light meal. And all ingredients are natural.

EROTIC BAKER
582 Amsterdam Ave (bet 88th and 89th St)
362-7557
Tues-Thurs: 11-7; Fri, Sat: 11-8

In keeping with the spirit of the times, this shop is not as erotic as it used to be. Yes, they still make and stock X-rated cookies, cakes, and pastries, but now they also make cakes for corporate advertising, like the one shaped as a cereal box for General Foods. Well, as long as they don't mix-up the deliveries, everything should be okay. I'd hate to think what would happen if they sent out the wrong kind of Wheaties cake.

FERRARA PASTRIES
195 Grand St (bet Mott and Mulberry St)
226-6150
Daily: 8 a.m.-midnight

With branches in Milan and Montreal, Ferrara is truly international in scope. This big store in Little Italy is probably one of the largest (geographically speaking) "little grocery stores" in the world. Undoubtedly, the business must deal in wholesale imports and several other business ventures, but it is easy (and nice) to believe that the sheer perfection of their confections and groceries can support the whole business. Certainly, the atmosphere here would never reveal that this is anything but a very efficiently run Italian grocery store. Their Old World caffe (sic) is famous for its 21 varieties of pastry, ice cream, and coffee.

G&M PASTRIES
1006 Madison Ave (bet 77th and 78th St)
288-4424
Mon-Sat: 8-7; Sun: 8-6

In a neighborhood where everything is chic, elegant, and classic, G&M survives on its reputation as a small immigrant bake shop, which turns out pastry best described as homemade in style. (Frank Gattnig, an Austrian immigrant, started G&M in 1958). As in any local apartment building, there are accents of Jewish, Italian, French, and German, in addition to Gattnig's native Austrian, in the shop's doughnuts, tortes, Danish, marzipan, and creamy cakes.

GERTELS
53 Hester St
982-3250
Sun-Thurs: 7-5:30; Fri: 7-2

The customers who come here are almost evenly divided between those who call this place Ger-tells (accent on the last syllable) and those who call it Girtils (as in girdles), but all agree that the cakes and breads at this store are among the best in New York. Locals seem to prefer the traditional babkas, strudels, and kuchens, but I find the chocolate rolls and chiffon blackout cake to be outstanding. For those who want to sample the wares, there are tables where customers can enjoy baked goods, coffee, or a light lunch. From the regulars at these tables, one can glean the choicest shopping tidbits on the Lower East Side. A final tip: every Thursday and Friday, Gertels makes a potato kugel that is unexcelled. People have come all the way from California for a Thursday kugel. During a slow week, you can occasionally find one left over on a Sunday. It's good then, too.

GLASER'S BAKE SHOP
1670 First Ave (bet 87th and 88th St)
289-2562
Tues-Sat: 7-7; Sun: 7-4
Closed July and half of Aug

If it's Sunday, it won't be hard to find Glaser's: the line frequently spills outside as people queue up to buy the Glaser family's fresh cakes and baked goods. And *one* isn't enough of anything here. Customers always walk out with arms full of bulging packages. The Glasers run their shop as a family business, and pride themselves on their breads and cakes, especially the wedding cakes. Come here for great cakes and cookies; try the chocolate chip.

GROSSINGER'S HOME BAKERY
337 Columbus Ave (bet 75th and 76th St)
362-8672, 362-8627
Tues-Sat: 7 a.m.-8 p.m.; Sun: 7-6

GROSSINGER'S UPTOWN
570 Columbus Ave (at 88th St)
874-6996
Mon-Fri: 8-6; Sun: 9-5

Grossinger's was once known as Grossinger's on Columbus Avenue, when that street was plain and drab, a far cry from today's trendy boulevard. Since 1935 Grossinger's has also been known for top quality cheesecakes and ice cream cakes—and a great homey aroma. The uptown operation is the only kosher shop on Columbus Ave.

H&H BAGEL
2239 Broadway (at 80th St)
595-8000
Daily: 24 hours

H&H starts baking fresh bagels at 2 a.m., an hour at which you can get a piping hot bagel without having to wait on H&H's long daytime line. But the biggest plus is that you can satisfy your bagel craving at *any* hour of the day or night at H&H. Another only-in-New-York special. They are the best in Manhattan.

KOSSAR'S BIALYSTOKER
KUCHEN BAKERY
367 Grand St
473-4810, 674-9747
Daily: 24 hours

Tradition has it that the bialy derives its name from Bialystoker, where they were first made. Kossar's brought the recipe over from Europe almost a century ago, but the bialys, bagels, horns, and onion boards are as fresh as the latest batch from the oven. The taste is Old World, and those who have never had one should try these authentic versions first.

LET THEM EAT CAKE
287 Hudson St (at Spring St)
989-4970
Mon-Fri: 8-5

Primarily a wholesale bakery specializing in gourmet desserts, Let Them Eat Cake is not above offering the house quiches, nut loaves, or cakes to the public. All of them are unusually good, which makes it easy for caterers and restaurants to pass them off as their own. The quiches are made to order and—wonder of wonders!—never frozen. Better still, they're interesting and different, aside from the obligatory quiche Lorraine. Perhaps by the 18th edition of this book, the quiche craze will have peaked in New York, but in the meantime, try the four cheese, asparagus, and crab-meat varieties. They are among the very best. The cakes and pies reflect the health-food consciousness of the neighborhood. Chelsea carrot cake (from a shop in SoHo) is but one of the examples of this, but any bakery that offers zucchini, date-nut, and banana-nut loaves as one quarter of the total offerings from the oven is big on health. In any case, the black-velvet chocolate chip fudge cake or the black-satin chocolate cake won't do a thing for the waistline, but they're sure to please the palate. Cakes are available in catering sizes as well as smaller sizes suitable, as they say, for resale. They are also available by the slice for on-the-spot consumption. Perhaps *that's* the best way to pick your favorite.

LITTLE PIE COMPANY
424 W 43rd St (at Ninth Ave)
736-4780
Mon-Fri: 8-7:30; Sat: 10-8; Sun: noon-5

Former actor Arnold Wilkerson started baking apple pastries for restaurants and food stores when he was working in the kitchen of Curtain Up! Now he operates a unique attraction—a shop that makes handmade pies and cakes using different fresh seasonal fruits. Although Wilkerson specializes in apple pie (available every season), he also makes fresh peach, cherry, blueberry and other all-American fruit pie favorites. Stop by for a hot slice of pie à la mode, along with some delicious cider. Yankee Doodle never had it so good!

MOISHE'S BAKERY
181 E Houston St (bet Orchard and Allen St)
475-9624
Sun-Thurs: 7-6; Fri: 7-4

115 Second Ave
505-8555
Sun-Thurs: 7 a.m.-8:30 p.m.; Fri: 7-5

Jewish bakery specials are legendary, and they are done to perfection at Moishe's. The corn bread is prepared exactly as it was in the old country and as it should be now. The pumpernickel is dark and moist, and the ryes are, well, simply scrumptious. The house specialty is the black Russian pumpernickel, which probably cannot be bested in an old-fashioned bakery in Russia. But by no means should you ignore the cakes and pies. Owners Mordechai and Hymie are charming and eager to please, and they have one of the best bakeries in the city. There is the usual complement of bagels, bialys, cakes, and pastries. Most of all, try the challah on Thursday and Friday; Moishe produces the best. The chocolate layer cakes are also superb.

NEW FIRST AVENUE BAKERY
121 First Ave (at Seventh St)
674-5699
Mon-Sat: 6 a.m.-7 p.m.

This is an old-fashioned bakery with one of the best reputations in town. The diverse ethnic makeup of the neighborhood is reflected in the variety of breads made here, and the quality is endorsed by the local natives from Italy, Poland, the Ukraine, and Russia, who claim the bread tastes as good as Grandma's, if not Great Grandma's. I don't know what to recommend most! The pumpernickel is dark and moist. It tastes nothing like the commercial variety. The babka smells irresistible and is. And the Italian breads are authentic enough to include a pizza dough. The Jewish contingent is represented by bagels, bialys, and corn bread, and each group thinks that New First Avenue is *their* bakery. Is there a higher compliment?

PALERMO BAKERY
213 First Ave (bet 12th and 13th St)
254-4139
Mon-Sat: 7-7; Sun: 7-2

A made-in-the-back specialty is featured here each day. One of the best is the pork-bread—huge slices of pork inside a delicate dough, topped with a crackling crust. Palermo Bakery routinely produces bread in the most unusual and contorted shapes you can imagine, and they taste wonderful. Some of the exotic breads include the proscuitto bread, which contains bits of Italian salami, ham, and Lucatelli cheese. Then there's the French-style butter cookies, Friselli and breadsticks, and challah and babka. Don't miss this one. It's a very inexpensive gourmet tour of the Old World.

PARISI BAKERY
198 Mott St (bet Spring and Kenmare St)
226-6378
Mon-Sat: 8-6; Sun: 8-midnight

The bread's always hot here, because this establishment supplies bread to nearly every restaurant in the neighborhood, as well as uptown eateries. The selection is almost completely French and Italian, but there are many variations, including Sicilian bread in the shapes of dog bones, snakes, eyeglasses, and a lard bread peppered with ham, salami, and roast pork. These exotic loaves are sold for reasonable prices. The cost of a two-foot, one-pound loaf of Italian bread beats the price of the commercial stuff sold in supermarkets.

PATISSERIE LANCIANI
271 W Fourth St (bet Perry and W 11th St)
929-0739
Mon: 8 a.m.-9 p.m.; Tues-Thurs: 8-11;
Fri, Sat: 8-midnight; Sun: 8 a.m.-10 p.m.

Patisserie Lanciani isn't terribly impressive; in fact, it seems a bit pretentious, until you get a look at the cakes and pastries. After that sight, even the extensive credentials of Joseph and Madeline Lanciani are superfluous. For those who haven't yet observed the delicacies at Patisserie Lanciani, a quick resumé is in order. For starters, you have certainly seen Joseph's work. While chief pastry chef at the Plaza (enough of a recommendation in itself), he was the creator of Julie Nixon's wedding cake. He is also a certified expert in spun-sugar creations, and is probably the best pastry baker in the city. Results of this experience can now be sampled firsthand in Lanciani's own shop. The cakes, pastries, tortes, mousses, and breads defy description, and for the impatient, there are tables.

POSEIDON GREEK BAKERY
629 Ninth Ave (bet 44th and 45th St)
757-6173
Tues-Sat: 9-7; Sun: 10-4

Poseidon is a family-run bakery that endlessly and effortlessly produces Greek specialties. There's tremendous pride here. When a customer peers over the counter and asks, "What is that?" the response is usually a long description and sometimes an invitation to take a taste. There is homemade baklava, kataif, trigona, tiropita (cheese pie), spanakopita (spinach pie), sargli, and phyllo. Poseidon was founded in 1922 by super Greek baker Demetrios Anagnostou. Today it is still run by his family—his grandsons, John and Anthony Fable—to the same exacting standards. Poseidon's specialty is phyllo pastry, and theirs is world renowned. Any and all Greek specialties using phyllo are turned out here year-round.

RIGO HUNGARIAN VIENNESE PASTRY
318 E 78th St (bet First and Second Ave)
988-0052
Tues-Sat: 8-6; Sun: 9-4; closed Aug

Many European-type pastry shops have products that look great, but when you taste them, it's a different story. Not this one. Delicious homemade strudels, sacher torte, petit fours, linzer tortes, coffee cakes, and cookies of all kinds are first-rate. No preservatives are used. Wedding and birthday cakes are a specialty.

STREIT MATZOTH COMPANY
150 Rivington St
475-7000
Sun-Thurs: 9-5

Matzoth, for the uninitiated, is a thin waferlike square cracker, which, according to tradition, came out of Egypt with Moses and the Children of Israel when they had to flee so swiftly that there was no time to let the bread rise. Through the years, matzoth was restricted to the time around Passover, and even when matzoth production became automated, business shut down for a good deal of the year. But not today and not in New York. In a small building with a Puerto Rican mural stretching the length of one side, Streit's matzoth factory pours forth matzoth throughout the year, pausing only for Saturday, Jewish holidays, and time to clean the machines. The Streit's factory not only allows a peek at the actual production—which is fascinating because it is both mechanized and extremely primitive at the same time—it also sells matzoth to the general public. It is baked in enormous thin sheets that are later broken up. The matzoth is so fresh that if you ask for a batch that happens to be baking at the moment, they will often break it off the production line for you.

SYLVIA WEINSTOCK CAKES
273 Church St (bet Franklin and White St)
925-6698
Mon-Fri: 8-6; Sat: 8 a.m.-10 p.m.

I am a cake expert. No, I'm not bragging, it is just a fact. As the proprietor of a cake shop, I know when they are good and when they are not so good. And I always keep an eye out for the best. I once came across a New York "blackout" cake that was so good I asked the lady in the local shop for the recipe. She was suspicious; she thought I would be setting up business next door. So I bought some, took it back to Oregon, and had the bakers at my konditorei come up with a similar cake. Lo and behold, it came out better than the New York original. Anyway, the cakes at Sylvia Weinstock's, I can attest, are works of art, and she can make them for any special occasion. If you can't come to Oregon, this is the next best thing.

VESUVIO BAKERY
160 Prince St (bet W Broadway and Thompson St)
925-8248
Mon-Sat: 7-7

Tony Dapolito was born, bred (no pun intended), and nurtured in his family's store in SoHo. In all that time, the family's expertise in baking grew along with the bakery's claim to fame as SoHo's common green. When not manning the ovens, Tony serves stints on the community planning board, and if not involved in either of those activities, he's dispersing SoHo lore to a customer. Visitors who are unaware of Dapolito's status (it doesn't remain a secret long) come for the bread, biscuits, and rolls. They all have a reputation that reaches far beyond SoHo. After all, it isn't every commercial bakery that eschews sugar, shortening, and preservatives and still manages to produce the tastiest Italian bread around. Try the biscotti, the pepper biscuits, or the whole wheat brick-oven-baked bread. And if you've *any* questions about the bread or SoHo, ask Tony. He can supply you with a slice of SoHo life, so to speak.

YONAH SCHIMMEL
137 E Houston St	1275 Lexington Ave
477-2858	722-4049
Daily: 8-6	Daily: 8-7

Yonah Schimmel has been selling the perfect knish for so long that his name is legendary, and national magazines have written articles about him. Schimmel started out dispensing knishes among the pushcarts of the Lower East Side, and a Yonah Schimmel knish is still a unique experience. It doesn't, incidentally, look or taste anything like the mass-produced things sold in supermarkets, at lunch stands, or at New York ball games. A Yonah Schimmel knish has a very thin, flaky crust—almost like strudel dough— surrounding a hot, moist filling. The best-selling filling is potato, but there is also kasha (buckwheat), spinach, and a half-dozen others, not including meat. No two knishes come out exactly alike since each is handmade, but if a particular batch is not up to par, the man behind the counter won't sell it.

Beverages

91st STREET BEVERAGE CENTER
1770 Second Ave
427-4972
Mon-Sat: 9-6

The 91st Street Beverage Center, run by Hector Borrero, mainly supplies wholesalers and large retail orders, but he's not adverse to serving retail customers. The only reason most orders aren't small is because once you've shlepped up there, you might as well take advantage of the good discount. He guarantees that his prices are at least as low as any supermarket. Because Borrero's store already offers merchandise at a discount, he doesn't have sales.

SERRANO
351 W 14th St (at Ninth Ave)
243-6559
Mon-Sat: 9-5

Serrano is a wholesale beer and soda distributor, and while they happily deal with retail customers, trust them when they tell you that most of their business is wholesale. For example, there is free delivery. The only hitch is that it's only available to customers who order 25 cases at a time. But that doesn't mean that those who shop on the premises aren't afforded the same excellent prices and service. For those in the neighborhood, Serrano should be a must for all soda and beer needs. Outside the area, unless there's a great love of lugging bottles, Serrano will probably only be a good bet for parties—large, thirsty parties.

British

MYERS OF KESWICK
634 Hudson St (bet Horatio and Jane St)
691-4194
Mon-Fri: 10-7; Sat: 10-6; Sun: noon-5
(except July, Aug)

In case you haven't noticed, the British are coming—again! According to the British Information Services, the number of expatriate Brits in the city has topped 100,000. Two of them, Peter and Irene Myers, are now doing with English food what Burberry, Church, and Laura Ashley have done with English clothing. They've made it possible for you to visit "the village grocer" for imported staples and fresh, home-baked items that you'd swear came from a kitchen in Soho—the London neighborhood, not the one downtown below Houston Street. Among the tins, a shopper can find Heinz treacle sponge pudding, trifle mix, ribena, mushy peas, Smarties, Quality Street toffee, lemon barley water, chutneys, jams and preserves, and all the major English teas. The fresh goods include sausage rolls, kidney pie, Scotch eggs, Aberdeen kippers, and sides of salmon. There are also cheeses (the double Gloucester is outstanding!) and chocolates. For Anglophiles and expatriates alike, Myers of Keswick is a *luverly* treat.

Candy

CHOCOLATE PHOTOS
637 W 27th St
714-1880
Mon-Fri: 9-6

Chocolate Photos was founded on the premise that virtually anything can be created in chocolate and that nothing is as personal as one's own picture. These unique items are ideal for weddings, anniversaries, corporate logos, almost any kind of novelty business use. They are all custom-molded chocolate, with a minimum of 300 units packaged per order. Wouldn't you like to eat yourself up in chocolate? Victor Syrmis, the president, was a natural for starting such a business. He is a successful child psychologist.

CHOCOLATES BY M
61 W 62nd St (bet Columbus Ave and Broadway)
307-0777
Mon-Sat: 10:30-7:30

Maimie Lee (the "M") felt there should be a fine candy store on the West Side. The Lincoln Center crowd must have agreed, because business has been booming ever since Chocolates by M opened. Much of the stock is geared for instant munching, with tidbits sold by the piece and pound as well as gift-boxed. The prices will also munch a hole in your wallet, though Lee insists that a $5 bag should get you through the "Mostly Mozart" concert series. For a casual evening, try the chocolate-covered fortune cookie. It's reasonably priced and delicious. For the knock-their-socks-off gift, though, why not go all out and order a box of truffles packaged in a Limoges gift box?

ECONOMY CANDY
108 Rivington St
254-1531
Sun-Fri: 8-6; Sat: 10-5

The same family of owners, who have been selling everything from penny candies to beautiful gourmet gift baskets since 1937, are still on the job. What a selection of dried fruits, nuts, candies, coffees, teas, jams, spices, cookies, crackers, and chocolates! The best part, of course, is the price. You can get gourmet items like caviars and patés without exceeding your party budget.

ELK CANDY COMPANY
240 E 86th St
650-1177
Mon-Sat: 9-6:45; Sun: 11-6:45

Elk Candy Company is a glorious kingdom of chocolate. There's a royal selection; every conceivable kind of chocolate can be bought in at least two different forms. It's one sure place to find the old-fashioned European chocolate specialties. Elk Candy is known locally as a haven for the marzipan lover. Think of marzipan in all the configurations of your childhood fantasies, and you'll find it here. If you don't favor marzipan, then sink into the Florentines—thin chocolate layered over cream, fruit, nuts, honey, butter, and who knows what else. If that's not a hit, the little "Cats' Tongues" chocolate bars are bound to be. It's hard to select a favorite, but the most commonly heard comment is "Gee, I haven't had that in *years*."

LE CHOCOLATIER MANON
872 Madison Ave (bet 71st and 72nd St)
288-8088
Mon-Sat: 10-6; Sun (bet Thanksgiving and
Christmas): noon-5

Le Chocolatier Manon offers some of the city's latest enticements in the imported chocolate line. The tiny store doesn't really need much space, since nearly everything offered is handmade in its Belgian offices and imported weekly to the New York store. But not to worry—this transatlantic transport does nothing to diminish the taste of some of the best chocolates in town. The chocolates are made of all-natural ingredients and contain no preservatives. And since the personnel are not busily engaged in production, they devote all of their time to the selling of chocolate. If the weather isn't too warm, they will air-ship the Manon specialties to lucky recipients. I suggest that you sample them here, and then ship them home.

LI-LAC CANDY SHOP
120 Christopher St (at Bleecker St)
242-7374
Sun, Mon: 12-7:45; Tues-Sat: 10-7:45

Since 1923, Li-Lac has been *the* source for fine chocolate in the Village. The most delicious creation is Li-Lac's own chocolate fudge, which is made fresh every day. If you tire of the chocolate, there is maple walnut, which is every bit as good. And there is much more: pralines, mousses, French rolls, nuts, dried fruits, hand-dipped chocolates, and so on.

MONDEL CHOCOLATES
2913 Broadway (at W 114th St)
864-2111
Daily: 11-6:30 (summer hours vary)

You can ask virtually anyone about the excellence of Mondel Chocolates, a store that's been part of the Columbia University landscape since it was founded by Florence Mondel's father in 1943. Fans of Mondel include the Columbia community of Nobel laureates, who credit Mondel for some of the world's prize-winning creations; Katharine Hepburn, who loves the dark chocolates with nuts; and the media, who enthusiastically report on the store's seasonal offerings. The chocolates are homemade and proudly sold in family tradition. There is even a dietetic chocolate line, although Florence Mondel admits that there is no connection she has ever seen between dieters and chocolate. The dietetic chocolate, like everything else in the store, is produced via painstaking research and presented as the best of its kind in the world. As for the rest, hold onto your calorie counters! There are rum balls, solid chocolate figures (rabbits, turkeys, or hearts, depending on the season), truffles, and chocolate cups with flavorings of espresso, mint, kirsch, orange, and amaretto. For further testimonials, ask any Columbia student.

NEUCHATEL CHOCOLATES

Plaza Hotel	66 Trinity Pl	Trump Tower
751-7742	227-1712	(Garden level)
Daily: 9-9	Mon-Fri: 10-6	371-6513
		Daily: 9-8

Neuchatel Chocolates is a class act. And you pay for it. Of course, Neuchatel offers a discount for orders of over $1,000. And it's easy to earn that discount. To create the finest Swiss chocolate from family recipes, the chocolates are prepared by hand with natural ingredients. The taste has been likened to velvety silk. There are 70 varieties of chocolate, with the house specialty being handmade truffles (a new chocolate one is superb!). But that shouldn't keep anyone from trying the marzipan and the pralines with fruit or nuts. Neuchatel's origins are Swiss, but perhaps its greatest virtue is that there is no pretension of "flown in daily" routines. Rather, the original recipes are re-created afresh in New York.

NEUHAUS CHOCOLATES
Saks Fifth Avenue
611 Fifth Ave (at 50th St)
753-4000
Mon-Wed, Fri, Sat: 10-6; Thurs: 10-8

The same year (1857) that my great-grandfather started his one-man store on the riverfront in Portland, Jean Neuhaus settled in Belgium and established a pharmacy and confectionery shop. Succeeding generations of his family have produced some of the finest handcrafted, enrobed, and molded-design bittersweet and milk chocolates in the world. They are still imported from Belgium. The showpiece is the Astrid Praline, named after the beloved late Queen of Belgium; it is a sugar-glazed butter delight!

PLUMBRIDGE
30 E 67th St
744-6640
Mon-Fri: 10:30-5

Douglas and Nanette Petrillo operate one of the oldest and finest confectionary shops in the city. Plumbridge was dispensing fine candy before it became the big fad in the Big Apple. Stoke your appetite with a free sample, then stock up on pecans spiced with brown sugar and cinnamon or dragee chocolate (a concoction of every imaginable ingredient buried beneath a dripping layer of semisweet chocolate). The French mocha nuts are similarly draped and just as good. Plumbridge also features chocolates, caramels, chocolate mints, and salted or unsalted Brazilian cashews. And don't miss the house specialty—steamed, stuffed dried fruits. Even a confirmed chocolate lover has to admire that!

ROCKY MOUNTAIN CHOCOLATE FACTORY
11 Fulton St (South St Seaport, Fulton Market)
393-1270
Daily: 10-9; Summer: 10-10

What is a store called "Rocky Mountain" doing in a place like the South Street Seaport? Believe it or not, the answer is simple. The first Rocky Mountain Chocolate Factory was started high in the Rocky Mountains in a town called Durango. Each batch of chocolate was handmade and hand-dipped. They were also made according to generations-old recipes. Word soon spread, and within a very short time, the concept was franchised across the country. But the popularity hasn't had a bad effect on the quality of the chocolate. Forty percent of it is made on the premises, and it still meets the standards established in Durango. What to try? The chocolates should be your top choices, especially the fudge and truffles. But in season don't miss the dipped fresh fruit, the glazed fruit, the blueberry and raspberry clusters, and the candy or caramel apples. Your teeth squeak just thinking about it. And the fudge is available in a slew of exotic flavors, from Irish Cream to coffee crunch.

TEUSCHER CHOCOLATES OF SWITZERLAND
25 E 61st St (at Madison Ave)
751-8482
Mon-Sat: 10-6

620 Fifth Ave (Rockefeller Center)
246-4416
Mon-Sat: 10-6; Thurs: 10-7:30

If there were an award for the most elegant chocolate shop, it would have to go to Teuscher's. Theirs are not just chocolates; they're imported works of art. Bernard Bloom, who owns these Teuscher stores, imports chocolates once a week from Switzerland. The chocolates are packed into handmade boxes so stunning that they add to the décor of many a customer's home. The truffles are almost obscenely good. The champagne truffle has a tiny dot of champagne cream in the center that lifts it to the super class. The same is true of the cocoa, nougat, buttercrunch, muscat, orange, and almond truffles, each of which has its own little surprise. Truffles are the stars here, but Teuscher's marzipan, praline chocolates, and mints (shaped like sea creatures) are of similar quality.

Cheese

ALLEVA DAIRY
188 Grand St (at Mulberry St)
226-7990
Mon-Sat: 8:30-6; Sun: 8:30-3

Alleva, founded in 1892, is the oldest Italian cheese store in America. The Alleva family has operated the business continuously since the start, always maintaining meticulous high standards. Robert Alleva is the current boss, overseeing the production of over 4,000 pounds of fresh cheese a week: parmigiano, fraschi, manteche, scamoize, and provole affumicale. The ricotta is superb, and the mozzarella tastes like it was just made on some little side street in Florence.

BEN'S CHEESE SHOP
181 E Houston St (bet Allen and Orchard St)
254-8290
Sun-Thurs: 8:15-5:30; Fri: 8:15-3:30

About half of the varieties of cheese sold here are made in the back of the shop. The locals swear by the farmer's cheese in any of its forms. Some favorites include the homemade farmer's cheese embedded with such tasty ingredients as strawberries, scallions, raisins, pineapple, and—my personal favorites—almonds and pistachios. Don't miss the baked farmer's cheese.

CHEESE OF ALL NATIONS
153 Chambers St (bet W Broadway and Greenwich St)
732-0752
Mon-Sat: 8-5:30

Cheese of All Nations is a gastronomic United Nations, a cheese-of-the-month clubhouse, a wholesale supplier to stores and restaurants, a gourmet catering service, a custom cheese spread manufacturer, and on and on. In short, cheese is a way of life here. The five floors of the shop are constantly engaged in various aspects of cheese production. The store has a worldwide business, which for more than 40 years has created, packaged, and shipped more than 1,000 varieties of cheese. That statistic gives the store the distinction of having the world's largest selection of cheese, and the sheer magnitude of it all is amazing. For example, there are 66 different kinds of cheese spreads listed in the catalog. Prices for the spreads, as well as everything else, are supposed to be among the city's lowest. Be prepared: this place is *always* crowded!

CONTINENTAL CHEESE
8 Harrison St (bet Hudson and Greenwich St)
966-2740
Mon-Fri: 8-5

Continental is a super source for cheese and patés, but it doesn't sell retail. For a really big order, though, Continental shows its complete line of imported cheeses from all over the world, and the prices are astonishing. There are spreads, cheddars, breads and crackers, and more types and styles of cheese than you can imagine. And then there are the incredible patés. The paté de canard a l'orange is made with duck paté and Grand Marnier, and the ratatouille paté has artichoke hearts, yellow squash, zucchini, and onions among its ingredients. You may encounter some hassles shopping here, but they'll be worth it. The quality, freshness, and price cannot be duplicated in a retail store.

EAST VILLAGE CHEESE
34 Third Ave (bet 9th and 10th St)
477-2601
Mon-Fri: 9-6:30; Sat, Sun: 9-5:30

Value is the name of the game here. For years, this store has prided itself on selling cheeses at just about the lowest prices in town. Now in larger quarters, they claim the same for bean coffee, fresh pasta, extra virgin olive oil, quiche, paté, and a wide selection of fresh bread.

IDEAL CHEESE SHOP
1205 Second Ave (at 63rd St)
688-7579
Mon-Fri: 9-6:30; Sat: 9-6

There are cheese shops, and there are *real* cheese shops. Ideal is the latter. The selection and quality is equal to any in the city. Besides taking care of the daily needs of their individual customers, they also supply many hotels and restaurants. Cheese, like wine, is an area where special advice is helpful, and the folks at Ideal are eager to share their expertise. If you are looking for a special food gift item, let them fix up a basket of unusual cheeses, patés, and gourmet coffees.

Chinese

CHINESE AMERICAN EMPORIUM
19 Pell St
577-8882
Daily: 9:30-8

You can't find a more authentic source for Chinese food than this one, not even in Peking, and the proprietors speak English. What's more, unlike some of their competitors, Bill Ng and his staff are happy to explain what some of the more exotic items are or to give the exact instructions on how to make your favorite take-out dish at home. Located in Chinatown, the store specializes in the ingredients for Szechuan and Hunan food. But there's an ample selection of Korean food, too, and even Japanese and American goods. The latter are mostly ingredients that don't travel well. Nearly everything else in the shop is imported. Ginseng root, for example, comes from China and Korea. It would be difficult to count all the different tastes or catalog all the unfamiliar items found here. In short, this is a great source for really authentic ingredients for Oriental cooking at great prices.

CHINESE AMERICAN
TRADING COMPANY
91 Mulberry St (at Canal St)
267-5224
Daily: 9-8

If an authentic Chinese dinner is on your menu, there may be no better source than this store in Chinatown. Let it be a warning (or a good sign, depending upon your point of view) that Chinese American Trading boasts that 95 percent of its business is conducted with the Chinese community. In any case, there is an open and friendly attitude here, and great care is taken to introduce you to the wide variety of imported Oriental foodstuff.

FUNG WONG BAKERY
30 Mott St
267-4037
Daily: 8:30-8:30

Fung Wong is the real thing, and everyone from the local Chinatown residents to the city's gourmands extol its virtues. The pastries and baked goods are traditional, authentic, and downright delicious; flavor is not compromised to appeal to Western taste. The bakery features a tremendous variety (enough so that Fung Wong sells wholesale all over town), and it has the distinction of being the oldest and largest "real" Chinese bakery. In survey after survey, Fung Wong is rated number one, and a visit is the surest way to see why.

KAM MAN FOOD PRODUCTS
200 Canal St (bet Mott and Mulberry St)
571-0330
Daily: 9-9

A trip to Kam Man is cheaper than one to China, and there's very little available there that Kam Man doesn't have here. It's the largest Oriental grocery store on the East Coast. Even native Chinese will feel at home in this shop, where you can find every possible ingredient for a Chinese meal. Speaking Chinese is not a requirement for shopping at Kam Man—some of the best English in Chinatown is spoken by the people who work here, and the amenities are totally familiar to those who patronize the city's other gourmet delis and supermarkets. The difference is that at Kam Man the shopping carts wheel past produce displays of water chestnuts, bok choy, winter melon, and tofu; grocery displays of pa pao chai (which is really a conglomeration of Chinese vegetables) and 50 other types of delicacies (shark's fin?); and butcher and fish counters offering duck, sausages, pork dumplings, and shrimp. Desserts and teas (and *more* teas) round out the selection, and the prices for all of this—even American tangerines and oranges—are the least expensive anywhere.

LUNG FONG CHINESE BAKERY
41 Mott St
233-7447
Daily: 8 a.m.-9 p.m.

English is definitely a foreign language here, but you can place your order simply by pointing to the authentic Chinese cookies and pastries of your choice. Molded cookies are in abundance, as are rice cakes and pastries covered with sesame or lotus seeds—or perhaps it's something else. The truth is, these are not your everyday fortune cookies; they defy description. Nevertheless, it's all authentic, and none of it is ordinary. Don't bother asking how anything tastes, because Lung Fong's explanation is liable to be: "Is good. Is good." And it is.

QUON JAN MEAT PRODUCTS
79 Chrystie St (bet Hester and Grand St)
925-5175
Daily: 10-7

William Chan, one of Quon Jan's owners, studied Chinese cooking in Hong Kong, and he devoted two years solely to seasoning and cooking barbecued meats. He is just as meticulous with his staff, making sure that his store is the best Chinese barbecue place in the city. And it is. (*The Daily News* concurs.) Although it is just outside of Chinatown, even by the standards of the ever-expanding borders. Oriental is definitely the theme. English is at such a premium that you'd think Chan was still in Hong Kong; most of the business is conducted either in Chinese or sign language. But sign away. Prices are reasonable, and the taste is authentic and delicious. The best seller is the Mandarin duck, but don't overlook the pork, sausages, or roast chicken. They are equally excellent and exotic.

Coffee, Tea

BELL-BATES
107 W Broadway (at Reade St)
267-4300
Mon-Wed: 9:30-6; Thurs, Fri: 9:30-6:30; Sat: 11-5

Bell-Bates is a caffeine emporium, specializing in all matters of teas and coffees for the retail customer. Their selection is extensive, and the prices are competitive. Bell-Bates considers itself a complete food center. It stocks health foods, vitamins, nuts, dried fruits, spices, and gourmet food, along with the freshly ground coffees and teas. Ask for Mrs. Sayage. She's marvelous.

CAFFE ROMA
385 Broome St
226-8413
Sun-Thurs: 8-midnight; Fri, Sat: 8-1 a.m.

Caffe Roma serves some of the best espresso this side of the Atlantic. To accompany the espresso, you can get such traditional Italian dishes as spumone, gelati, cremolate, cannoli, deep-dish Italian cheesecake, and all kinds of super pastries. The atmosphere is Old World, complete with marble tiled floor and colorful oil paintings. The cappucino made from freshly roasted beans is another reason this spot is so popular.

CAFFE REGGIO
119 MacDougal St
475-9557
Sun-Thurs: 11 a.m.-2 a.m.; Fri, Sat: 11 a.m.-4 a.m.

The owner of Caffe Reggio claims that cappuccino was introduced to this country by a former owner of the same Caffe Reggio. Could be, and this place has other ties with times past. Over 80 pieces of Italian art fill the cafe, and some of them date back to the Renaissance. The staff will be happy to identify the more important works for you. And if you're interested, they'll even tell you the history of the neighborhood. (Louisa May Alcott lived across the street, near the spot where Jo meets the professor in *Little Women*.) Nonetheless, this place wouldn't last two minutes unless the food was good, and in the past 60 years, it's only improved. This isn't the place you want to go to for a seven-course meal, but it's great for a snack. Breakfasts and lunches are served until 7 p.m. Hot beverages, teas, and Italian soft drinks are refreshing specialties (the espresso machine is the room's distinctive centerpiece). The management encourages you to eat a pastry with your cappuccino. And nobody minds if you spend hours at the table, nursing one cup.

EMPIRE COFFEE AND TEA COMPANY
592 Ninth Ave
586-1717
Mon-Fri: 8:30-7; Sat: 9-6:30

Midtown java lovers have all wandered in here at one time or another. There is an enormous selection of coffee (75 different beans), decaffeinated coffees, teas, and herbs. Because of the aroma and array of the bins, making solo choices is almost impossible. Empire's personnel are very helpful, but perhaps most helpful of all is a perusal of their free mail-order catalog *before* entering the shop. Dave Mottel pointed out that fresh coffee beans and tea leaves are available in bulk, along with fresh peanut butter and spices. Everything is sold loose and can be freshly ground. Empire also has a small selection of appliances.

McNULTY'S TEA AND COFFEE COMPANY

109 Christopher St (bet Bleecker and Hudson St)
242-5351
Mon-Sat: 11-11; Sun: 1-7:30

McNulty's has been supplying choosey New Yorkers with their coffees and teas since 1895. Over the years, they have developed a complete line that includes spice and herb teas and coffee blends ground to order. They have a reputation for personalized, gourmet coffee blends, and they work hard to maintain it. That reputation is hard on the pocketbook, but a number of their blends are unique, and the personal service is quite valuable. McNulty's maintains an extensive file on their customers' special coffee blends.

M. ROHRS

1692 Second Ave (bet 87th and 88th St)
427-8319
Mon-Fri: 10-6:30; Sat: 9-5

Dennis Smith owned a candy store in Manhattan before he bought M. Rohrs, which was established in 1896. The tradeoff of candy for coffee beans was primarily for better working hours, but Smith is always on the premises long before the store opens and stays long after it closes. Does he use his coffee to keep him awake? He's not telling. But he is willing to expound on the various types of beans and teas that the store stocks. And his guidance is needed. There are hundreds of varieties of tea, coffee, coffee beans, and honey in the store, as well as accessories. While not a coffee shop, it is possible to get a cup of coffee and sample the wares. And incidentally, despite all that coffee, Smith is one of the most relaxed proprietors in the city. So either he doesn't drink coffee or he's right when he says that all the studies on caffeine don't amount to a hill of beans.

PORTO RICO IMPORTING COMPANY

201 Bleecker St
477-5421
Mon-Wed: 9:30-7; Thurs-Sat: 9:30-9; Sun: noon-7

In 1907, Peter Longo's family started a small coffee business in the Village. Primarily importers and wholesalers, they were soon being pressured to serve the local community around them, so they opened a small storefront as well. That storefront gained a reputation for having the best and freshest coffee available and developed a loyal corps of customers. Since much of the surrounding neighborhood consisted of Village Italians, the Longo family reciprocated the neighborhood loyalty by specializing in Italian espressos and cappuccinos as well as "health" and medicinal teas. Dispensed along with such teas are folk remedies and advice to help mend whatever ails you. The store remains true to its tradition, and Peter added a coffee bar. Now it is possible to sit and sip the various coffees while listening to the folklore or while trying to select the best from the bins. HINT: *The inexpensive house blends are every bit as good as some of the more expensive coffees.*

SCHAPIRA COFFEE COMPANY
117 W 10th St
675-3733
Mon-Fri: 9-6:30; Sat: 9-5

Schapira, also known as the Flavor Cup Shop, has been run by the same family since 1903. Joel and Karl Schapira and Ron Bowen, who run the business now, offer advice on tea or coffee selections to any customer who asks. Many coffee shops disdain tea, but Schapira is fair to connoisseurs of both and is equally knowledgeable in either field. So secure are they in both knowledge and reputation that they will happily send you a mail-order price list and tuck in answers to any questions you might have as well. HINT: *Try Flavor Cup's own brand of tea or coffee.* Coffees are roasted every morning on the premises and are available in bulk, in bean form or ground to personal specifications. Tea is sold similarly (in bulk or bags). There are also coffee- and tea-brewing accessories.

Delis, Catering, Foods To Go

AMAZING FOODS
807 Washington St
645-4166
Wed, Fri: 11-5; Sat: 10-3

Put on your walking shoes, double-check the irregular business hours above, and get going to this amazing food operation. In a most unlikely neighborhood of warehouses and trucks, you will find one of the city's best selections of salad-size produce items. Well-known restaurants like Lafayette, China Grill, and Lutèce come here to buy their miniature baby carrots, turnips, corn, artichokes, and the like. Also available are baby salads, mixed, red and green oak, bibb, argula, and many more varieties. Fresh seafood and shellfish like Belon oysters, scallops, tuna, swordfish, Atlantic and Norwegian salmon, and free-range chicken are available at the same prices restaurants pay. This is a find. You cannot find better price, quality, or selection. Ask for Pat Cummings, and tell him I sent you.

AMERICAN PIE
434 Amsterdam Ave (at 81st St)
877-6740

1590 Second Ave (bet 82nd and 83rd St)
861-9190
Mon-Thurs, Sun: 11-11; Fri, Sat: 11 a.m.-12:30 a.m.

Bring the kids here for no other reason than to see how seven Mautone siblings get along well enough to keep this all-American place running smoothly. The main course is deep-dish stuffed pizza in over two dozen configurations, like the artichoke, tomato, and mushroom pie, the chicken and prosciutto pie, the pepperoni, sausage, and onion pie, and the Cajun pie (chicken, shrimp, and hot sausage). In addition, there are Italian soups, salads, and fancy desserts. American pie offers catering and a convenient delivery service.

ANNABEL'S
523 Hudson St
645-8200
Mon-Fri: 6-6

It runs in the family at this friendly establishment! By that, I mean good things to eat and great talent in its preparation. Annabel and her mother, Mrs. Greene, share the front and back duties, respectively. In an area where good eats are not readily available, Annabel's provides an extensive list of home-baked goodies every day. The list includes dozens of different kinds of biscuits and muffins (the banana honey nut muffin is sensational), coffee cakes, sticky buns, cheese toast, two dozen different danishes, cakes, brownies, cupcakes—and that is only the start. There are salads and hot entrees and homemade soups and sandwiches for home and office. Delivery service is available, and the customer who wants sugar-free baked items will be well taken care of at this gourmet kitchen.

BALDUCCI'S
424 Sixth Ave (at Ninth St)
673-2600
Daily: 7 a.m.-8:30 p.m.

No visit to the Village is complete without a stop at Balducci's. This superb food and appetizer store has been an institution in the area for three generations, becoming more popular and crowded every year. The Balducci clan runs a hands-on operation; members of the family take a personal interest in all phases of the operation. The store started as a produce market, and that is still an area in which it shines. You can find the best assortment of fruits and vegetables every season of the year. There are also bakery items, cheeses, marvelous cakes and desserts, tempting take-home dishes, fish, meat, and much more. Their catalog is an adventure in good things for eating, and their private-label items like pasta, salami, sauces, and preserves are fine values. Half the fun of shopping here is the bustling atmosphere; Village residents and many citywide fans vie for space in this jam-packed emporium. A new "table-top store," called Balducci's Piccola Cucina and featuring interesting accessories for the kitchen and dining room, has opened at 334 East 11th Street.

BARNEY GREENGRASS
541 Amsterdam Ave (bet 86th and 87th St)
724-4707
Tues-Sat: 8:30-5:45; Sun: 8:30-5
Closed Passover and first three weeks in Aug

Barney Greengrass's name is synonymous with sturgeon to New Yorkers, which is as it should be for a family business located at the same place since 1929. Barney has been succeeded by his son, Moe, and Moe's son, Gary (daughter-in-law Shirley is there, too), but the same quality of gourmet smoked fish is still sold over the neighborhood counters just as it was in Barney's day. The Greengrasses lay claim to the title of "sturgeon king," and there are few who would dispute it. While sturgeon is king here, Barney Greengrass also has a school of other smoked-fish delicacies. (And he could start a school on preparing and selling them.) There is Nova Scotia salmon, belly lox, white fish, caviar, and pickled herring in the fish lines. The dairy-deli line including vegetable cream cheese, homemade salads and borscht, and a smashing Nova Scotia salmon with scrambled eggs and onions) is world renowned. In fact, because so many customers couldn't wait to get home to unwrap their packages, Greengrass started a restaurant next door. Devotees claim that the Greengrass brunch is the example *par excellence* of what brunch should be. And after all, how could it be otherwise when the kitchen, which is just a step away, has been producing the ideal brunch menu for more than 50 years?

BENNIE'S
321½Amsterdam Ave (at 75th St)
874-3032

37 Seventh Ave
242-5134

First Ave and 68th St (corner)
249-5460

Daily: 8 a.m.-10 p.m.

Bennie's was founded by Dr. Bennie, a Lebanese plastic surgeon, with his partner and compatriot, a pediatrician. The result was so successful that two branches have been added, and the doctors may never go back to medicine. And while a take-out food business wouldn't usually hold a candle to a medical career, here it's a toss-up. And that's a pun. Bennie's, you see, specializes in salads, and they're among the best anywhere. Homage is paid to the Lebanese roots with the best tabbouleh in the city (it may also be the cheapest) and a plate that speaks with a definite Middle Eastern and European accent. The health aspect is not ignored either. Besides three sensational chicken salads, Bennie's boasts the biggest selection of vegetarian foods in the neighborhood. A prime example is the Muda-data (a salad of rice, onions, and lentils), and it, too, is reasonably priced and excellent. If you see Dr. Bennie, don't be surprised if he tells you business is healthy. Don't be surprised if he doesn't say anything, though. English is not spoken fluently here, but with all these goodies, who cares?

BREMEN HOUSE
220 E 86th St (bet Second and Third Ave)
288-5500
Mon-Sat: 9:30-7:30

Bremen House has gotten bigger and better. It used to have the finest in imported foods and German delicatessen; now it has all that and more. There is a fantastic assortment of German merchandise, including the largest selection of German records in America. Also, there are housewares, gifts, cards, books, and German magazines. The balance of the store is still devoted to esoteric and unique foodstuff from Europe. The highlight remains the fresh-food counters. The baked goods are unrivaled. Between the salads, gourmet foods, ready-to-go items, German deli, and the cheeses, you have all the ingredients for an incredible meal, all from one source. That one-stop shopping advantage hasn't escaped Bremen House, which features picnic baskets ready to go, plus a complete menu of prepared foods for parties and a mail-order menu. A final note: the store is squeaky clean. I've walked in at all hours of the day, every day of the week, and there is always someone cleaning, polishing, or buffing.

CANARD AND COMPANY
1292 Madison Ave (at 92nd St)
722-1046
Daily: 7 a.m.-9 p.m.

It seems as though you are in a rural country store when you step inside Canard and Company. The atmosphere is especially homey, and the personnel are eager to show you the fabulous selection of prepared gourmet foods, specialty jams and jellies, fresh produce, rich desserts, custom gift baskets, fine candy, and some of the best sandwiches to be found in Manhattan. No big-time hustle-and-bustle here; it's a truly enjoyable shopping experience.

CAVIARTERIA
29 E 60th St
759-7410, 1-800-4-CAVIAR
Mon-Sat: 9-6

Caviarteria operates out of a small store, which is sufficient since most of the business is done by phone or by mail. Because of the wholesale business, prices are as reasonable as prices for caviar can be, and the quality is top-notch. The staff is very friendly and helpful, and they assure safe delivery (shipping on ice) anywhere. Caviarteria also stocks paté de foie gras and Scotch and Swedish smoked salmon.

CHARLOTTE'S
146 Chambers St (bet Greenwich St and W Broadway)
732-7939
Mon-Fri: 9-5

Charlotte's can be all things to all people—as long as the cuisine is Swedish or French. Its menu can accommodate an impromptu crepe for one or a dinner for 700 at the Hilton. Other food merchants patronize Charlotte's as well: Restaurant Associates, Healthworks, Bloomingdale's, and Le Cirque are just a few of their clients (the list reads like a who's who of gastronomic New York). But none of this celebrity detracts from Charlotte's ability to cater to individual customers. In fact, they delight in tailoring gourmet delights to individual requests. So there are canapés and cookies, as well as main courses and feuilletes (a puff pastry), gourmet fish, fish smoked the Swedish way (in a log house), mousses and sauces for entrees, and more desserts than can be counted. All of it comes fresh, frozen, partially cooked, or ready to eat, and all of it meets Charlotte's exacting standards.

CHELSEA FOODS
198 Eighth Ave (at 20th St)
691-3948
Mon-Fri: 9-9; Sat, Sun: 9-8

The Upper West Side has Zabar's. The Village has Balducci's. The Upper East Side has Grace's Market Place. SoHo has Dean & Deluca. And Chelsea has its own gourmet emporium—Chelsea Foods. The owner is a neighborhood resident, who combines a love of the area with the experience and skill necessary to run a really first-rate establishment. Catering is also available.

CHIRPING CHICKEN
350 Amsterdam Ave (at 77th St)
787-6631

1260 Lexington Ave (at 85th St)
517-9888

Daily: noon-10

Okay, partners, New York would never settle for just the Colonel's brand of chicken. You all know that. So one of the entries in the sweepstakes to make take-out chicken unique is Chirping Chicken. Can't say I care much for the name, but its charcoal-broiled chicken is excellent. Chickens are available either whole or in half, with the standard cole slaw, potato, or corn on the side. The chicken is broiled in Chirping's own homemade sauce and served with pita. That's got to be a New York touch. Downhome chicken with Middle Eastern bread? It's good enough to make you chirp!

DEAN & DELUCA
560 Broadway (at Prince St)
431-1691
Mon-Sat: 10-7; Sun: 10-6

It was only a matter of time until Dean & Deluca would have to move out of their historic location on Prince St. The counters and the aisles were just too filled with tempting items and busy customers. The solution was the opening of a store almost four times as large as the original. And what a place! There are packaged food items, gourmet take-out selections, fish, meat, chicken, pastries, vegetables, bread, coffee, desserts—you name it, and Dean & Deluca have it in quantity. There is a special kitchen for catering, and they can make any occasion something special. A popular espresso and cappucino bar greets you at the door. Professional kitchen equipment and supplies are available to both wholesale and retail customers. And prices are competitive in most cases, although this is not the place to bargain-shop.

DONALD SACKS

120 Prince St	220 Vesey St
(at Wooster St)	(World Financial Center)
226-0165	619-4600
Mon-Fri: 8-6; Sat,	Mon-Fri: 11-10; Sat,
Sun: 10-6	Sun: 11-7

For years Donald Sacks had been famous in SoHo for huge sandwiches, home-style soups, salads, stews, and desserts for take-out. You can munch there if you want, but the quarters are a bit cramped. There is also a delivery service. Now Sacks has gone bigtime with a bistro operation in the World Financial Center. Home-style cooking is featured in a large restaurant with bar, take-out service, catering, plus all the goodies from the original SoHo location. The desserts (especially the tarts) are special, but the rest is pretty ordinary. Bigness is not betterness, Donald.

FAIRWAY

2127 Broadway (at 74th St)
595-1888
Mon-Fri: 8 a.m.-midnight; Sat, Sun: 8 a.m.-10 p.m.

When you take care of over 50,000 customers a week, you must be doing something right. Fairway is a West Side institution originally known for its fresh fruits and vegetables. But now it has so much more: pasta, cheese, bread, and all kinds of deli items. They offer 30 varieties of olive oil, for example. Fairway has carved out its own niche in the food business, leaving the household items to their busy and aggressive neighbor, Zabar's. Fairway operates its own farm on Long Island, and they have developed relationships with the best produce dealers throughout the state, which has enabled them to capitalize on the trend for healthier items on the dinner table. There is no place like Zabar's for prepared foods, but if you want to prepare them yourself, start with the ingredients at Fairway. Prices are right at both places.

FINE & SCHAPIRO
138 W 72nd St
877-2874, 877-2721
Sat-Thurs: 8:30 a.m.-11:30 p.m.; Fri: 8:30-9

Ostensibly a kosher delicatessen and restaurant, Fine & Shapiro offers some of the best dinners for at-home consumption in the city. Perhaps because of their uptown location, or perhaps merely as homage to the quality of their foods, they modestly term themselves "the Rolls-Royce of Delicatessens." That description is cited here only because it is very apt. Fine & Schapiro dispenses a complete line of cold cuts, hot and cold hors d'oeuvres, Chinese delicacies, catering platters, and magnificent sandwiches. Everything that issues from Fine & Schapiro is perfectly cooked and artistically arranged. The sandwiches are masterpieces; it seems a shame to eat them, but the aroma and taste are irresistible. Chicken in the pot and stuffed cabbage are two of their best items.

FISHER & LEVY OFFICE CATERERS
1026 Second Ave (at 54th St)
832-3880
Mon-Fri: call 9-3 for same-day delivery or until 5 for next-day delivery

Chip Fisher and Doug Levy operate what is probably the best office catering service in the city. Excellent salads, great sandwiches, soups, stuffed pastries, assorted meat platters, and wonderful desserts will please any big client at an office power lunch. There are over a dozen sandwich selections, available individually or in platters. Stuffed pastries like vegetable empanada, spinach and brie, fresh mozzarella, or barbecued chicken make great sandwich alternatives. Minimum order is $20. One of their specialties is catering afternoon and evening events in the office; and Fisher & Levy will provide equipment and professional help. A large selection of hot buffet entrees, side dishes, hors d'oeuvres, and sushi is offered.

FRASER MORRIS FINE FOODS
931 Madison Ave (at 74th St)
288-2727
Mon-Sat: 8:30-7; Sun: 10-5 (closed in summer)

1264 Third Ave (at 73rd St)
288-7716
Mon-Fri: 9-6; Sat: 9-5

Fraser Morris was a gourmet-to-go source eons before the neighborhood knew there was such a thing, and certainly long before the Upper East Side became the center of all such operations.

The result was a carriage-trade store offering gourmet delicacies at not inconsiderable prices. With a monopoly on virtually the whole idea, Fraser Morris was the definitive such stop and set the standards for the breed. But the changing neighborhood has wrought changes in Fraser Morris. First, the business moved to a cleaner more modern store, and then, as a sure sign of success, it opened a second branch. These days the gourmet shop still stocks the finest fruit, cheese (500 different kinds), candy, chocolate, delicatessen (imported sliced ham and paté de foie gras—not chopped liver!), quiche, canned gourmet items, ice cream, cheesecake, caviar, and coffee beans. You get the idea. A catering department offers such delicacies as salmon and crown roast of lamb. A bakery department features fruit tarts, Hungarian pastry, scones, and an international variety of goodies. And finally, for the true gourmet-to-go, there's a sandwich department. This is an old spot that has gracefully and successfully entered the modern age.

FRATELLI CANGIANO
100 W Houston St
477-5377
Mon-Fri: 10-10; Sat, Sun: 8 a.m.-10 p.m.

This rather run-down neighborhood seems a very unlikely location for this specialty food store. It sparkles with first-class edibles: seafood, vegetables, cheese, gourmet dishes, homemade pastries, and fine meats. Essentially, it is a smaller version of Zabar's, Dean & Deluca, Balducci's, and Grace's Marketplace, all of which are the best in the business in their respective neighborhoods. Perhaps the folks who live in the renovated factory lofts in SoHo will find this a handy place to pick up supplies for that special Sunday evening dinner at home.

GINDI DESSERTS
935 Broadway (bet 21st and 22nd St)
505-5502
Mon-Fri: 8-7; Sat: 10-6; closed Sat in summer

Always ahead of the pack, Gindi now offers sugar-free foods (like muffins and fruit pies) and salt-free items. Of course, there are still such marvelous desserts as truffle-mousse cake, cheesecake, fruit tart, and pies. *Simple* is the operative word here, and Gindi does it all with a minimum of fuss and price. The new item list also includes vegetable pies and other vegetable combinations, so you can look and feel just as healthy as those athletes you may be planning to watch at nearby Madison Square Garden. Peggy is the charming boss lady, and she will prepare items to go or invite you to enjoy the goodies at the tables in the back of the shop.

GRACE'S MARKET PLACE
1237 Third Ave (at 71st St)
737-0600
Mon-Sat: 7 a.m.-8:30 p.m.; Sun: 8-7

The Upper East Side finally has a first-class food store. You cannot find a better assortment of fine fruits and vegetables, cheese, gourmet take-out dishes, candy, bakery, and everyday items than the one at this enticing and appetizing emporium. The quality is first-rate, and the selection almost overpowering. The displays seduce you into that "I want one of each" frame of mind. Grace and her family have deep roots in the food business in Manhattan, and her contacts and experience show in every phase of this outstanding operation.

GREAT PERFORMANCES CATERERS
125 Crosby St
219-2800 (catering), 925-9090 (personnel)
Daily: 9-5 phone orders only

Liz Neumark, the owner of Great Performances, should know the business from the bottom up. She is a former photographer who supported herself by working as a waitress in a help-for-hire agency. She soon realized that there were quite a number of moonlighting artists in the city, so she decided to organize her own agency, which supplies New Yorkers with party help from the city's artistic community. Her company is a full-service caterer, handling all kinds of affairs, from small dinner parties to gala dinners for thousands of people. The permanent staff includes party planners, an executive chef, and a professional kitchen crew. The party planners will arrange all the details of your event and provide the necessary personnel. (Corporate clients include many top names like AT&T, Coca-Cola, and American Express.) An especially nice touch is that their personnel know the Heimlich maneuver (in case of choking), they study fire-evacuation procedures, and each carries a "survival kit," which includes such tools of the trade as aspirin, Band-aids, a corkscrew, and even a coffee measure. The folks at Great Performances are the kind you want to have around. Good show!

H&H BAGELS EAST
1551 Second Ave (bet 80th and 81st St)
734-7441
Daily: 24 hours

The initials H&H have long been synonymous with the best bagels on New York's Upper West Side. Now East Siders can feast upon this fresh, delicious New York specialty, along with a choice of homemade croissants, super sandwiches, tasty salads, salmon, lox, and sturgeon. Homemade pickled herring is another specialty. Although this is mainly a take-out operation, there are a few tables for those who just can't wait to start noshing.

HORN AND HARDART
200 E 42nd St
599-1665
Mon-Fri: 6:30 a.m.-9 p.m.; Sat, Sun: 6:30 a.m.-10 p.m.

This automat is all that's left of the thriving chain that once boasted 23 automats. It still serves good, nourishing food at the drop of a quarter, dime, or a combination thereof. The kids, of course, shouldn't miss it, and while they're shoveling coins in slots and watching the food *they* selected appear, the adults can put together a good take-out lunch.

INTERNATIONAL GROCERIES AND MEAT MARKET
529 Ninth Ave (bet 39th and 40th St)
279-5514
Mon-Sat: 8-6

Ninth Avenue is one great wholesale market of international cookery, resplendent with exotic spices. So what would an international market on Ninth Avenue be if not a retailer of exotic spices at wholesale prices? The International Groceries and Meat Market is that, but it is also an excellent source for the rudiments on which to sprinkle the spices. The setup complements the whole aspect of the operation. Translated, this means that the neat glass jars that display food in other such places are replaced here by huge, open burlap bags, which may be disconcerting for some. But be willing to sacrifice the frills for some of the best prices in town and the assurance that the turnover is high enough to keep things fresh. The meat market is really something else. It's a gourmet market for aficionados of baby lamb and kid. It comes seasoned, prepared, and even sliced. If you're unsure about what to do with it, ask!

JOSEPH BURKE (BURKE AND BURKE)
Various locations throughout Manhattan
799-7000

Billed as "New York's fanciest food store," Burke is literally on the spot when there is a need for elegant food or snacks. Each store features a line of fine foods (with an accent on English candy and food products), gift baskets, chocolates, desserts, catering, and imported foods. Those on a lunch break can find sandwiches and food platters, the "Ploughman's Lunch" in two varieties, and a choice of hot dishes. There are also dozens of house specialties, most of which match the shop's aim to "bring together the very best of the Old World and the New." There is a delivery service for getting the goodies to the customer with efficiency.

LA FONTANELLA
1304 Second Ave (bet 68th and 69th St)
988-4778
Mon-Sat: 11-7; Sun: 2-7

Nelly de Oppes came from Argentina to open La Fontanella 20 years ago. She is a caterer who can take care of any kind of gathering, but she claims that her specialty is intimate, formal dinners. She also likes to do buffets, cocktail parties, afternoon teas, wedding breakfasts, and corporate or club luncheons. The accent on her menu is decidedly Spanish, but she is equally, if not more, expert with French and Italian cuisine. Casseroles, quiches, soups, and empanadas are all available on 24-hour notice for reheating at home. The menu for more formal dinners is extensive and à la carte. La Fontanella doesn't care if you order for 2 or 2,000 people. With sufficient advance notice, any combination on the incredible menu can be had. There is even delivery service.

MAISON GLASS DELICACIES
111 E 58th St (bet Lexington and Park Ave)
755-3316
Mon-Sat: 9-6; closed Sat in July, Aug

This is *the* source of gourmet supplies for New Yorkers in the know, and it has been since it was founded by Ernest Glass in 1902. Nowadays, the store is run by Marvin Goldsmith, who has only enhanced the mystique. The house specialties are caviar, foie gras, truffles, Virginia ham, smoked salmon, freshly roasted nuts and coffee, fine chocolates and candies, teas, herbs, spices, oils, vinegars, and jams, to name just a few. Goldsmith says that they have the largest selection of imported and domestic delicacies in the country and possibly the world. In addition to catering, there are gift baskets, package deliveries (including "mystery packages"), and a catalog for gourmet subscribers.

MAMA LEAH'S
429 Amsterdam Ave (bet 80th and 81st St)
724-7755
Daily: 11:30-9:30

Upper West Siders can now treat themselves to some wonderful non-kosher Jewish-American home cooking straight from Mama Leah's kitchen. And you don't have to leave home to take advantage of the goodies; Mama delivers from 70th to 90th Streets and from the Park to Riverside Drive on the West Side. In addition, she runs a restaurant and blintzeria at 1400 First Avenue (between 74th and 75th St) on the East Side. You can order adult and children's dinners, or by the pound or the portion. Specialties include chicken in the pot, roast turkey, chicken and meatball fricassee, pot roast and brisket. Platters of gefilte fish, herring in cream sauce, or potato latkes are always available. Mama features cooked and uncooked homemade blintzes in half a dozen flavors and, of course, chicken soup with matzo balls that is out-of-this-world.

MANGIA
54 W 56th St (bet Fifth and Sixth Ave)
582-3061
Mon-Thurs: 7:30-6:30; Fri: 7:30-6; Sat: 9:30-5:30 (closed in summer)

Joanna Cottrell and Sasha Muniak are a husband-and-wife team of artists. Joanna worked with food, and Sasha played the violin. Together, they became Mangia, which just may be the best, most epicurean gourmet take-out place on the island of Manhattan. And that's saying a lot. Joanna suggests using Mangia's wares to stock a picnic in Central Park (fortunately, you won't have to carry the brimming basket too far) or to take a couple of meals aboard an airplane to offset airfare. If it's a transatlantic flight, many of the ingredients in your lunch may be making a return trip. Cheeses are flown in weekly from France, Italy, and England. Baked goods are homemade in English and Colonial styles. There are more scones and Dundee cakes than can be counted, and all sandwiches are made with sourdough breads. The fresh salads, like everything else in the store, are brought in or made in the shop daily. Mangia is a joy. It's a super source for an impromptu picnic, and even if it's the middle of a blizzard, Mangia will deliver.

MISS GRIMBLE
1199 First Ave (at 65th St)
628-5800
Mon-Thurs: 8 a.m.-11 p.m.; Fri: 8 a.m.-1:30 a.m.;
Sat: 9 a.m.-1:30 a.m.; Sun: 9 a.m.-11 p.m.

Miss Grimble sounds like my first-grade teacher, but whoever she is I'd like to invite her over to do some cooking. This is a very special retail bakery, gourmet shop, and restaurant, all in one. For breakfast there are hearty platters of eggs and omelets. For lunch and dinner (and in-between), you can get pasta, quiche, fondue, soups, salads, sandwiches, seafood, poultry, stuffed potatoes, pot pies, burgers, and a fabulous selection of international coffees.

And that is only a start. No one could possibly pass up the cheese-cakes (more than a half dozen kinds), fabulous pies, Grimbletortes (chocolate genoise and cheesecake covered with bittersweet chocolate), other assorted cakes, brownies, and much more.

M. SCHACHT OF SECOND AVENUE GOURMET DELI
99 Second Ave (at Sixth St)
420-8219
Daily: 7 a.m.-12 a.m.

Aggie Markowitz, part owner of Casual Grace Catering, says that if she were ever on the way to an affair and accidentally dropped the food, she would duck into Schacht's for the replacements. That's heady praise for a self-professed "old-time Lower East Side appetizing store," which is almost totally unknown outside the neighborhood or among noncaterers. What merits such praise? Without a doubt, some of the best smoked fish anywhere. But here it is served New York style. The emphasis is on salmon, salads, gourmet deli, and any elegant fish. Schacht's slices it, platters it, smokes it, caters it, and even ships it worldwide. A really unique aspect of the business is a Scotch salmon presented on a board with a knife and instructions for slicing. It makes an impressive gift and a mouth-watering centerpiece. Those lucky enough to be able to drop in at Schacht's can sample all kinds of fish, cheese, caviar, and gourmet delicatessen meat.

NEUMAN AND BOGDONOFF
1385 Third Ave (bet 78th and 79th St)
861-0303
Mon-Sat: 7:30-7

Neuman is Paul Neuman, the son of Rosedale Fish Market's owner, and Bogdonoff is Paul's wife, Stacy Bogdonoff. Together, they have married the showpiece salads that distinguished Rosedale from being just another fish store to other elegant dishes, and they've created a stylish and trendy catering firm. With a fresh wholesale source for seafood, the menu frankly admits a bias to fish and fish dishes. So, there's shrimp mousse and smoked trout and some of the best seafood salads in the city. If you can't get down to Neuman and Bogdonoff, Paul still makes it for the Rosedale store. But where Rosedale is a fish market cum take-out salad spot, Neuman and Bogdonoff is a caterer with a specialty in seafood. So, the lobster can be accompanied by Cornish hens, ribs, or Paul's special citrus chicken. And vegetarians can pick from a half-dozen vegetable salads or a roasted eggplant in a yummy sauce. In fact, the sauces deserve their own mention. Any fish store maintains a good stock recipe, and Rosedale is no exception. At Neuman and Bogdonoff, stocks of both fish and beef can be purchased as a meal.

PETAK'S
1244 Madison Ave (bet 89th and 90th St)
722-7711
Daily: 7:30 a.m.-8 p.m.; Sun: 9-8

58 Pearl St
558-6000
Mon-Fri: 7:30-5

203 W 37th St
302-1888
Mon-Fri: 7:30-5

Richard and Robert Petak, third-generation cousins of a family that has owned appetizing businesses in the South Bronx and later New Jersey, have now made the leap to New York, offering the first "appy shop" the Carnegie Hill neighborhood has had in a long time. (As housing has gotten scarcer, Carnegie Hill has emerged as a prime neighborhood. Ten years ago, it was the out-skirts of Spanish Harlem.) In any event, no neighborhood could be assessed as truly having arrived without a gourmet take-out shop, and now Petak's (both corporately and personally) fills that need. So there are the "appy" standbys, such as salads (60 of them), corned beef, pastrami, smoked fish, and all sorts of take-out foods. The stores offer full catering, quarter-pound containers of potato salad, gift baskets, picnic hampers, and box lunches. And don't forget the sesame snow peas, baked salmon salad, cheeses, vine-gars, oils, preserves, breads, and other staples of gourmet food em-poriums. In short, Petak's prepares food as mother never did, unless mother was a patron of Petak's in the South Bronx or Fair-lawn, New Jersey.

PIATTI PRONTI
34 W 56th St (bet Fifth and Sixth Ave)
315-4800
Mon-Fri: 8-5; Sat: 11-5

If you are staying in a hotel in midtown or live nearby, note this phone number. This is the greatest alternative to room service in the city, and it's cheaper, to boot! At Piatti Pronti, there is an outstanding fresh salad bar, gourmet pizzas, dozens of pasta dishes, and a daily breakfast special. I recommend any of them for a quick wholesome meal at a small price, but since they do cor-porate catering *(on one hour's notice!)* and delivery, they should be first and foremost considered as an alternative to cooking at home.

They are faster, better, and cheaper (even counting the tip!). Incidentally, David Snedden, one of the owners of Piatti Pronti, is also a co-owner of Fairway Fruits and Vegetables, one of the city's best markets. Fairway supplies the ingredients for the shop as well as for the restaurants around town owned by the other Piatti Pronti partners.

PRANZO
1500 Second Ave (at 78th St)
439-7777
Mon-Fri: 7:30 a.m.-10 p.m.; Sat: 8:30 a.m.-9:30 p.m.;
Sun: 10 a.m.-9:30 p.m.

Besides the delicious food, there are two special reasons to shop at Pranzo. The extended operating hours, offering the convenience of fulfilling your needs at almost any hour. And the free delivery service, from East 57th to East 96th, and from the East River to Fifth Avenue. Prices are not inexpensive, but the quality is apparent in the wide selection of appetizers, like roasted sweet peppers and spicy chicken wings, pasta like meatless lasagna and home-made pizzas, salads in a dozen varieties, and tasty side dishes like stuffed potatoes and oven roasted mushrooms. Entrees that will take care of that special dinner include stuffed chicken breasts, filet mignon, and shepherd's pie.

ROBERT DAY DEAN
36 W 44th St
755-8300
Mon-Sat: 9-7

Robert Day Dean can claim credit for pioneering a trend that was to become popular and important many years later. In fact, this firm has been in the catering business since 1839, so they are justifiably called "New York's First Caterer." Weddings are the specialty. Dean takes care of the whole show, not just the food, arranging for the flowers, music, location, entertainment, the food planning, and even the wedding outfits. The firm is also skilled in doing large corporate functions, as well as private dinners at home or in selected locations. For first-cabin treatment, call Mireille Gannat.

RUSS & DAUGHTERS
179 E Houston St
475-4880
Daily: 9-7

A family business for several generations, Russ & Daughters has been a renowned New York shop since it first opened its doors. There are nuts, dried fruits, paté de foie gras, lake sturgeon, pickled herring, Gaspe salmon sliced and replaced on the skin, and a number of fancy fish dishes, including caviar, smoked fish, sable, and herring. Russ & Daughters has a reputation for serving only the very best. Caviar alone comes in five different varieties, all of which are sold at the lowest prices. They sell both wholesale and over the counter, and many a Lower East Side shopping trip ends with a stop at Russ & Daughters. Their chocolates are premium quality. They also ship anywhere. And be sure to say hello to Ann and Mark Federman (she is a Russ Daughter); they are super people. If I were to give a five-star rating, this shop would qualify. It is clean, first-rate, and friendly—what more could you ask?

SALUMERIA BIELLESE
376-378 Eighth Ave (at 29th St)
736-7376
Mon-Sat: 7-6

This Italian-owned grocery store is the best—and the only— French charcuterie in the city. If that isn't contradiction enough, get this: The loyal lunchtime crowd thinks it's dining at a hero shop when it's really enjoying the fruits of a kitchen that serves virtually every great restaurant in the city, including La Caravelle, Le Veau d'Or, Maxim's, the Manhattan Ocean Club, and Sign of the Dove. To understand how all this came about, a lesson in New York City geography is necessary. In 1945 when Ugo Buzzio (his son Marc is one of the four partners who run the business today) and Joseph Nello came to this country from the Piedmontese city of Biella, they opened a shop a block away from the current one in the immigrant neighborhood called Hell's Kitchen. (Today, it's gentrified and known as Clinton.) The two partners almost immediately began producing French charcuterie. Word spread rapidly among the chefs of the city's restaurants that Salumeria Biellese was producing a quality product that could not be duplicated anywhere.

SANDWICH HOUSE
58 Greenwich Ave
675-5211
Daily: 8-6

Sometimes just a sandwich will fill the bill. Maybe it's for lunch at the office. Maybe for a picnic. Whatever. This place offers some of the "best dressed" sandwiches in town. You have your choice of many different kinds of bread, fresh homemade dressings, and delicious ingredients. There's a vegetarian sandwich, several made with prosciutto ham and different kinds of cheeses, and a super noncaloric turkey-breast special. You can get freshly squeezed juices, plus a number of salad and dessert possibilities, all at such a tiny price you will think you've gone to sandwich heaven.

SARGE'S
548 Third Ave (bet 36th and 37th St)
679-0442
Daily: 24 hours

It ain't fancy, but Sarge's could feed an army. The menu leans toward the burping school of delicatessen, but there's much to be said for the taste, quality, and price. Sarge's can cater everything from a hot dog to a hot or cold buffet for almost any number of people. Prices are gauged by the amount of people served and by what is served, but there are several package deals, and all of them are remarkably reasonable. Even one of the more expensive buffets—the deluxe smoked-fish version—only runs to about $15 per person, and that includes the cream cheese and bagels, as well as sturgeon, sable, and stuffed smoked whitefish. Sarge's also caters deli items and has an excellent selection of cold hors d'oeuvres platters, which offer everything from canapes of caviar, sturgeon, and Nova Scotia salmon to shrimp cocktails. And to make the party complete, Sarge's can supply serving pieces, condiments, and serving staff. My favorite is the guy who slices hot pastrami in front of the guests. The carver, cutting board, knife, pastrami, warming oven, and table can all be obtained from Sarge's. The army never had it so good!

SILVER PALATE
274 Columbus Ave (near 73rd St)
799-6340
Mon-Fri: 7 a.m.-9:30 p.m.; Sat, Sun: 10:30-7:30

There are picnic baskets, and then there are *picnic baskets*. The Silver Palate gourmet gift baskets are of a caliber that has prompted stores like Bloomingdale's to feature them in their own gourmet sections. But you can go to the source and have the Silver Palate prepare anything from a light picnic lunch to a full-course meal or even their "Decadent Box." The basket will be filled with such gourmet specialties as mousses, patés, and croissants, and each item is at its peak of perfection. Take a basket from the Silver Palate, and you can picnic with the best of them! Even those elaborate picnics with wine goblets pale beside a picnic basket of salmon mousse or paté de campagne or smoked filet in Roquefort sauce and a chunk of exotic cheese. The Silver Palate prides itself on the reputation of the shop, a reputation built on the unique take-out baskets and gift packages. Moreover, Silver Palate offers superb foodstuff at unusually good prices. They also have a gourmet condiment line.

SUSAN SIMON
32 E Second St
777-0080
Mon-Sat: 11-6:30

Susan Simon knows her way around the catering business. Before opening her own shop in this unlikely location, she worked for a major catering house to learn the trade. This background, plus her worldwide travels, has enabled Susan to offer a distinctive array of unusual dishes for the private or corporate client. Whether it is a simple luncheon or picnic, a fancy sit-down dinner, or a business cocktail party that features the romance of Thailand, Susan can take care of 2 or 200. You would never guess how much talent there is behind the scenes of this crowded and unpretentious shop.

TODARO BROTHERS
555 Second Ave (bet 30th and 31st St)
532-0633
Mon-Sat: 7:30 a.m.-9 p.m.; Sun: 8-8

Don't come here if you're ravenous or on a diet, because Todaro carries the very best in imported and domestic gourmet foods. Just about everything here is irresistible and will wreak havoc with pocketbook and diet alike. There are imported stuffed pasta, paté, jams, cheeses, homemade sausages, and a half-dozen gourmet items, all top quality. Todaro even stocks fresh truffles, a delicacy seldom seen this side of a haughty restaurant. And then there are the chocolates. Lucien Todaro imports the very, very best from Europe. *The Daily News* rated Todaro's tuna fish salad the best in the city, and our own survey gave them a top award for heros. When a gourmet shop is the best in mundane efforts such as heros and tuna salad, that should be a good indication of the quality of its more exotic items.

WORD OF MOUTH
1012 Lexington Ave (bet 72nd and 73rd St)
734-9483
Mon-Fri: 10-7; Sat: 10-6; Sun: 11:30-5:30
Closed Sun in Aug

The history of Word of Mouth is actually the gastronomic history of Manhattan—or at least the Upper East Side of it. When Christi Finch (an Oregonian—they pop up everywhere!) opened her original tiny shop in 1976, she was one of the very first establishments to offer home-style prepared foods for at-home or picnic use. Success was almost instantaneous, and by 1979 the shop had moved around the corner to larger quarters and become incorporated. Today, she enjoys a reputation as one of the finest sources for pasta, soups, vegetable salads, quiches, baked goods, and specialty meat dishes. The aim is still the same, however. Nothing is catered per se (although Word of Mouth does work with caterers or amateur caterers), and everything is geared for at-home consumption. There is no ethnic orientation, though there are worldwide influences, and the style is still home-style cooking that makes use of the very finest ingredients. As Word of Mouth adds staff, they add staff specialties, but the aim is always to make everything look as though it just came from the customer's kitchen—and that kitchen is usually the kitchen of an epicurean.

ZABAR'S
2245 Broadway (at 80th St)
787-2000
Mon-Fri: 8-7:30; Sat: 8 a.m.-midnight; Sun: 9-6
(Mezzanine: 9-6 daily)

Zabar's is not merely a deli and housewares store. It is a way of life. There is nothing in Manhattan, or anywhere in the country, that can match this incredibly busy store, which takes care of 35,000 customers every week and racks up sales of over $35 million a year. Zabar's has rightfully earned a reputation for top quality food and merchandise at sensible prices in an atmosphere that could be best described as frantic and festive. There are over 20 different varieties of some of New York's best coffees; 35,000 pounds of it are sold every week. The bread selection is overwhelming; if you can't find it here, it doesn't exist. They even sell that wonderful Eli's bread for less than Eli sells it himself (and he's from the Zabar family!). Sharp-eyed, bargain-conscious shoppers take home five tons of caviar a year, and are treated to salmon flown in each week from England, Norway, and Ireland. Over 500 different kinds of cheese are available, and almost every weekend customers walk out with over 5,000 pounds of brie alone. Upstairs on the mezzanine is a housewares extravaganza like you've never seen anywhere. All kinds of appliances and kitchen gadgets are on sale at prices that easily beat out the competition, including the "world's largest store" at Herald Center. Zabar's selection of French copper cookware is the best in the city. This success story started in 1934 when the original Zabar leased a fish counter in an Upper West Side grocery store. Now, under the expert eye of partner Murray Klein, a superb merchandiser, Zabar's is *the* place for the best in prepared foods and all that goes with them. A visit to Zabar's is like no other New York experience for residents and visitors alike. Once you shop here, you'll be able to join in one of New York's favorite pastimes: exchanging Zabar's stories.

Fruits, Vegetables

GREENMARKET
Office: 130 E 16th St
477-3220

The city sponsors these open-air markets in various city neighborhoods. Since there's no overhead, their prices are cheaper than a supermarket's, and the produce is sold fresh from the farms by the farmers who grow it. One of Greenmarket's drawbacks, however, is that there are no stockrooms to supplement the farmer's supply. When the truckbeds are empty, the farmers close shop. So you have to get there early. Another problem is that Greenmarket isn't well organized. But for farm-fresh produce at super prices, you have to put up with a little inconvenience. And it's worth it. These markets are A-1. Most are open from early June through December, one or two days a week; call ahead for exact hours.

LA MARQUETA
Park Ave (under the tracks from 110th to 116th St)

Tucked under the train tracks in Harlem, this is one of the most fabulous shopping places in the city. La Marqueta is famous, and the early-morning babble of voices here is proof that its customers are not only the local residents of Spanish Harlem. Although the accent is definitely South American, there is nothing that isn't sold here. Each building contains several individual businesses that hawk whatever is fresh and reasonable that day. Lest you think that means 600 booths of Florida oranges, you should know that each building has a few stalls that provide really exotic produce. Some of the latter include chitlins, collard greens, bread fruit, celery root, plantains, and Jamaican spice bread. If you can surmount the language barrier and show some curiosity, the merchants are eager to share recipes with you. It's a friendly, informal place. Once in a while, a squawking chicken can be seen among the stalls of papayas, mangoes, and peppers.

Gift Baskets

SANDLER'S
140 W 55th St (bet Sixth and Seventh Ave)
245-3112
Mon-Wed: 10-6; Thurs-Fri: 10-8; Sat: 12-6

Sandler's is a key source for scrumptious candies, delicacies, and some of the best chocolate chip cookies in New York. But Sandler's is best known for its gift baskets, which are the perfect thing for any number of occasions. Those who lack strong willpower should order by phone, because the store's goodies are overwhelmingly tempting.

HINT: *Also try Manhattan Fruitier (210 E Sixth St) for fruit and gift baskets.*

Health Foods

COMMODITIES
117 Hudson St (at N Moore St)
334-8330
Daily: 10-9

Commodities is the largest natural-food store within a 100-mile radius, according to the store's staff. In addition, they are considered the best by virtually everyone in the health-food market. Their produce is of excellent quality, and the prices are comparable to those of local supermarkets. They earned that "largest" reputation with a very well-rounded stock of canned and processed health foods, including vegetable and meat substitutes and a full line of health-food products. They are able to serve everyone from macrobiotics to those who are only marginally interested in chemically free foodstuff. The staff is very helpful, without being fanatical, and the store is so large that you might assume it was just another grocery. It isn't. Commodities is the very best.

COUNTRY LIFE
48 Trinity Pl (at Rector St)
480-9142, 480-9135
Mon-Thurs: 7:30-9:15, 11:30-3, 5-8; Fri: 7:30-9:15,
    11:30-2:30

244 E 51st
980-1480
Mon-Thurs: 11-2:30, 6-8; Fri: 11-2:30; Sun: 6-8

Note the hours. Country Life, in the heart of the financial district, is open for a scant five hours a day. But scant only describes the time of operation and certainly not the ample portions, friendly atmosphere, and the excellent quality of the menu. All of it is vegetarian and is available for take-out. The buffet is so extraordinary that many of Country Life's customers are meat eaters who are enamored of one of the best and most efficient eateries in the area. The only caveat is the time. Don't bother coming after two o'clock. And you might want to know that the first moments after the doors open are reminiscent of feeding time at a zoo. No doubt about it—those people are lined up for *something*. By the way, when you telephone the Trinity Place location, you not only get the menu, you get a Bible verse to start the day.

DOWN TO EARTH
33 Seventh Ave (bet 12th and 13th St)
924-2711
Mon-Fri: 9:30-9:30; Sat: 10-8:30; Sun: 11-8:30

This is probably the Village's most complete, best-run, and most appealing health-food store—at a price. Down to Earth's prices are sky-high. If you can pay them, look over the vitamins, packaged health foods, vegetables, frozen meats, cheeses, and sprouts. All are top quality. The take-out sandwiches are quite filling and wholesome.

EARTH'S HARVEST TRADING COMPANY
700 Columbus Ave (bet 94th and 95th St)
864-1379
Mon-Fri: 9:30-7:30; Sat, Sun: 10-6

This is really a natural-foods supermarket. With all the emphasis these days on healthy eating and healthy looks, you can take care of both in the aisles of this fascinating store. There is organic produce, herbs by the hundreds, a vast selection of organic and natural grocery items, color- and preservative-free cheeses, and a juice bar and deli for a quick healthy snack. And to make sure you radiate that natural look, a full supply of natural cosmetics is available.

GOOD EARTH FOODS
1334 First Ave (bet 71st and 72nd St)
472-9055
Mon, Wed, Thurs: 10-7; Tues, Fri: 10-8; Sat: 10-6

182 Amsterdam Ave (at 69th St)
496-1616
Mon-Fri: 9:30-7:30; Sat: 9:30-6:30; Sun: 12-6

The Good Earth has the reputation of being the finest and best-stocked health-food store in New York—and one of the most expensive. The very helpful and knowledgeable sales personnel will vehemently deny that they are overpriced, but a quick comparison of prices will show that they are, just as surely as a quick visit will confirm their reputation for having one of the largest and freshest stocks. In addition to their enormous selection, the Good Earth offers delivery anywhere within the city, which is further proof that they are not in the reasonable class. On the other hand, one-stop shopping is easy to do here.

INTEGRAL YOGA NATURAL FOODS
229 W 13th St (bet Seventh and Eighth Ave)
243-2642
Mon-Fri: 10-9:30; Sat: 10-8:30; Sun: 12-6:30

Selection, quality, and health are the order of the day in this clean, attractive shop, which features a complete assortment of natural foods. Vegetarian items, packaged groceries, organic produce, bulk foods, juice bar, salad bar, deli, and baked items are all available at reasonable prices for the health-conscious shopper. They are located in the same building as a yoga center that offers classes in yoga, meditation, and philosophy.

Hungarian

PAPRIKAS WEISS, IMPORTERS
1546 Second Ave
288-6117, 288-6903
Mon-Sat: 8-6

Paprikas Weiss started out as a poor immigrant who peddled spices to his neighbors. He began importing them, developed a reputation for the best and freshest in Hungarian condiments, and over the years built a large import-export business that deals as much in prepared foods, gourmet utensils, and imported delicacies as it does in the original condiments. The store's free catalog, which is accompanied by glowing testimonials from the city's leading food columnists, makes fascinating reading. There are special pans, preparatory utensils, and ingredients for dishes that I have never heard of! I have only one complaint: the store is too commercial. Paprikas is *big* business, and they make the most of it, both in price and publicity. Some prices are imaginatively high (similar products can be found in local supermarkets for much less), and "authentic" dishes receive publicity that is either unwarranted (the dish is not *that* authentic) or undeserved (even authentically made, it just isn't that good). But Paprikas is worth a visit, if only for picking up their catalog.

Ice Cream

MINTER'S ICE CREAM KITCHEN
Pier 17, South Street Seaport (608-2037)
4 World Financial Center (945-4455)
Open daily during Seaport and Center hours

Minter's Kitchen became famous dispensing ice cream mixes—combinations of any of 16 homemade ice cream flavors sprinkled with any of over 20 assorted candies, cookies, fresh fruits, and nuts. They are kneaded on a marble slab and dispensed as ice cream scoops, sundaes, milk shakes, malts, and ice cream sodas. At the new World Financial Center location, the concept has been expanded. They serve a variety of all-natural treats made on the premises. These include yogurt shakes, smoothies, salads, bakery items, and Belgian waffles. The Belgian waffle sundae is outrageous!

PRAVINIE GOURMET ICE CREAM
27 St Marks Pl (Eighth St, bet Second and Third Ave)
673-5948

193 Bleecker St (bet MacDougal St and Sixth Ave)
475-1968
Mon-Fri: noon-midnight; Sat, Sun: noon-1 a.m.

Pravinie offers "gourmet ice cream" and much, much more, none of which will reduce the waistline. But the calories are well worth it. Ice cream comes in over 30 exotic flavors, both American and Oriental. Pravinie, dedicated to sweet indulgence, also offers tofutti (in unusual-for-tofutti flavors, of course), cookies, Yodolo, frozen yogurt, crepes, and waffles. The locals claim that Pravinie offers the best milk shake in town. Needless to say, their help look like they never eat the goodies. Or maybe this stuff isn't as fattening as it looks.

Indian

ANNAPURNA INDIAN GROCERIES
126 E 28th St
889-7540
Daily: 10-7

Annapurna looks like a large neighborhood grocery store—which it is—but also functions as an Indian information center for non-Indians and as a home-away-from-home for Indians. Thomas Thoppil runs Annapurna like a school. If you even look curious, you may be subjected to a discourse on the many varieties of whatever foodstuff is at hand and how to cook it. Thoppil has a talent for translating Indian foods to American tastes. The store stocks nearly every variety of Indian spice and condiment (with an emphasis on hot, hotter, and hottest) as well as canned goods and fresh vegetables. Most of the utensils, films, records, religious posters, and gift items are Indian, but Annapurna is also the place to find English products, such as Woodward's Celebrated Gripe Water and Brooke Bond Tea, and even gift items from the Caribbean.

KALPANA
2528 Broadway (at 95th St)
663-4190
Mon-Sat: noon-8

Kalpana is a tiny neighborhood store with an excellent reputation among Indians. Owners Urmilla and Tony Maharaj (Indians from Trinidad) supply the Upper West Side with a variety of Caribbean products by way of Trinidad, Jamaica, and England. They even have Indonesian groceries. Urmilla doesn't mind giving recipes and instructions for the unusual products the store sells. Kalpana also has a catering service.

K. KALUSTYAN
123 Lexington Ave (bet 28th and 29th St)
685-3451
Daily: 10-8

In 1944, Kalustyan opened as an Indian spice store at its present location. After all this time, Kalustyan is still a great spot. Everything is sold in bins or bales rather than prepackaged containers, and everything is available in bulk or wholesale sizes for retail customers. The difference in cost, flavor, and freshness compared to that of regular grocery stores is extraordinary, and the best indication of the latter two points is a simple whiff of the store's aroma. Kalustyan is not strictly an Indian store, but rather an "Orient export trading corporation" with a specialty in Middle Eastern as well as Indian items.

Italian

ITALIAN FOOD CENTER
186 Grand St (at Mulberry St)
925-2954
Daily: 8-7

Joseph De Mattia, the Italian Food Center's proprietor, serves a tantalizing array of Italian food that's a credit to his prime location in the heart of Little Italy. The Food Center is truly that: it stocks fresh and cured Italian meats and cheeses, delicious fresh-baked breads, Italian-American cold cuts, Italian salads, delicacies, groceries, and dry goods. If it's Italian, it's here.

MELAMPO
105 Sullivan St (bet Spring and Prince St)
334-9530
Mon-Sat: 11-8

In a tiny store not much bigger than an oversized closet, Melampo manages to display a large variety of the best in Italian food items. The specialty, however, is *the* sandwich. This is the place to go for some super special combinations, like Battigota (salami, provolone), Ruben (prosciutto, provolone), Cristina (mozzarella, artichoke), and Alessandro (tuna, peppers, bel paese). All sandwiches are served on individual-sized white or whole wheat loaves of bread. A treat you'll never forget: the Bombolo Tricolore. It is made of fresh mozzarella, Jersey tomato, basil, a special dressing, and all on Focaccia bread. Yum, yum.

Japanese

KATAGIRI AND COMPANY
224 E 59th St (bet Second and Third Ave)
755-3566
Mon-Sat: 10-7; Sun: 11-6

Planning a Japanese dinner? Do you have some important clients from across the Pacific that you would like to impress with a sushi party? Katagiri features all kinds of Japanese foods, sushi ingredients, and utensils and provides wholesale items for major hotels and restaurants. You can get some great party ideas from the helpful personnel here, and the prices are more reasonable than those in Tokyo.

Kosher

LEIBEL'S KOSHER SPECIALTIES
39 Essex St
AL 4-0335
Sun-Thurs: 9:30-6:30; Fri: 9:30-1

A handy place to buy all of your kosher food items, including cheese, fish, jams, and frozen goods. Almost every kosher specialty is available at this family-operated store, where personal service is still available, even though it's only on the Lower East Side. Prices reflect the neighborhood; translated, that means there are bargains by the dozen.

SIEGEL'S KOSHER DELI AND RESTAURANT
1435 Second Ave
288-2094
Mon-Tues: 12-11; Wed-Sun: 7 a.m.-11 p.m.

If you are looking for a top kosher deli and gourmet appetizing store on the Upper East Side, you can't do better than Siegel's. Not only do they keep long hours (Sundays, too), but they also deliver, from 9-9. Featured here are fresh, decorated turkey dishes; over-

stuffed sandwich platters; BBQ, roasted, and fried chicken platters; hors d'oeuvre selections; smoked fish platters; fresh baked
breads and salad trays; and a large selection of cakes, cookies, and
fresh fruit platters. The number of selections is awesome, with
nearly two dozen sandwiches on the menu, 10 different soups,
dozens of salads, and side dishes ranging from potato and meat
knishes to kugel and kishka.

Liquor, Wine

CROSSROADS WINES AND LIQUORS
55 W 14th St (at Sixth Ave)
924-3060
Mon-Sat: 9-9

This store may have the best selection of wine in the city, featuring a complete selection from all the great wine-producing countries. There are rare, unique, and exotic liquors as well. Spring and
fall catalogs, offset by "insider special" mailings every three to
four weeks, are also available. Crossroads will special-order items,
deliver, and help in party and menu planning. Finally, they are not
in a snobby neighborhood, and their prices are as low as their attitude is low-key.

FAIRFAX LIQUOR
211 E 66th St
734-6871
Mon-Sat: 10-8

Since you can't pick a liqour supplier by price (although Fairfax
promises that their markup is the absolute minimum allowed by
law—12 percent), you might as well pick one by the company it
keeps and the service it offers. You'd be hard-pressed to beat this
store on either of those counts. The selection is vast, there's hardly
a vintage that's not represented, and the price is guaranteed to be
the lowest in town. And Fairfax claims to supply David Rockefeller, Richard Nixon, and Ronald Reagan, among others. This is
the place to go if you want to be able to place a bottle on the table
and say, "Oh, the Rockefellers recommend this label."

GARNET LIQUORS
929 Lexington Ave (bet 68th and 69th St)
772-3211 or 800-USA-VINO (out of state)
Mon-Sat: 9-9

Don't you love that "800" number? You'll love Garnet's prices
even more. This may be the most inexpensive place in the city for

specialty wines. So If you're in the market for champagne, bordeaux, burgundy, or imported wines, check out the prices here first. And they're equally good on other wines and liquors. This is a first choice for choice spirits.

K&D FINE WINES AND SPIRITS
1366 Madison Ave (bet 95th and 96th St)
289-1818
Mon-Sat: 9 a.m.-10 p.m.

On the Upper East Side, K&D is an excellent wine and spirit supermarket. There are hundreds of choices of top brands and top wines, with prices that are more than competitive. Major ads in the local newspapers occasionally highlight K&D's special bargains, but even on a regular basis the values here are outstanding.

MORRELL AND COMPANY
535 Madison Ave (bet 54th and 55th St)
688-9370
Mon-Fri: 9-7; Sat: 9:30-6:30

The charming and well-informed Peter Morrell is the wine adviser at this small jam-packed store, which has every possible type of wine and liquor. The stock is really overwhelming; since there isn't room for everything to be on display, a good portion is kept in the wine cellar. All of it is easily accessible, however, and the Morrell staff is knowledgeable and quite amenable to helping you find just the right thing. The stock consists of all spirits, including brandy liqueurs, and all vintages of wines, from rare and old to young and "pop."

QUALITY HOUSE
2 Park Ave (bet 32nd and 33rd St)
532-2944, 532-2945
Mon-Fri: 9-6:30; Sat: 9-3; closed Sat in July, Aug

This wine and liquor store is very aptly named, since it has the most extensive varieties of French wine in the city, an equally valued assortment of domestic wines, as well as those from Italy, Germany, Spain, and Portugal. Oenologist Willie Gluckstern says that Quality House's owner, Bernie Freyden, and his son Gary have the best wine palates in the city; Gluckstern says that they are also expert with claret. They have wines in all price ranges, but don't look for bargains. The name is Quality, and you pay for it.

SOHO WINES AND SPIRITS
461 W Broadway (bet Prince and Houston St)
777-4332
Mon-Sat: 10 a.m.-9 p.m.

Stephen Masullo's father ran a neighborhood liquor store on Spring Street for over 25 years. When his local neighborhood evolved into the SoHo of today, his sons expanded the business and opened a stylish SoHo establishment for wine. The shop is lofty. In fact, it looks more like an art gallery than a wine shop. The various bottles are "tastefully displayed" (Stephen's words), with classical music playing in the background. Every advantage is made of the enormous floor space, and Stephen boasts that SoHo Wines also has one of the largest selections of single malt Scotch whiskeys in New York. Again, in keeping with the neighborhood, SoHo Wines and Spirits offers several unique services. Among them are party planning, wine-cellar advice, and specialty items of interest to the neighborhood. Note that this is *not* a liquor store (as Mr. Masullo Sr.'s was). *This* is a wine and spirits shop.

WILLIAM SOKOLIN
178 Madison Ave (bet 33rd and 34th St)
684-3827
Mon-Fri: 9:30-6:30; Sat: 10-5:30

This is a unique wine store, featuring a huge inventory of fine wines at attractive prices. They also have a special program for storing wine in climate-controlled conditions in Bordeaux; they offer this service free for four years. (You can also opt to have your wines shipped to the United States.) Many of these wines are tradable, and they offer that service, too. They have been in the wine business since 1934, and they claim to have a $20 million cellar. They will show you the best domestic and imported brands, will evaluate your rare wine cellar, and will arrange for you to attend a tasting.

YORKVILLE WINE AND LIQUOR
1393 Third Ave (at 79th St)
288-6671
Mon-Sat: 9:30 a.m.-10 p.m.

This fair-sized store has carved out a niche for itself as the very best source for kosher wines and liquors. The selection is incredible; they are frequently the first to introduce a new label or variety of wine. They are a good source (with very good prices) for non-kosher wines as well.

Meat, Poultry

ARBERANN MEAT MARKET
1378 Lexington Ave (at 91st St)
876-1140
Mon-Sat: 8:30-6:30

This is the shop for people who prefer their bacon and hot dogs nitrate-free. If that's you—and a little editorializing would tell you that it ought to be—remember the name of this market. It's one of two such sources in the city. They don't cure the meat themselves; it's imported from Connecticut and processed by No-Dime. And Ralph is a great guy to have wait on you.

BASIOR-SCHWARTZ MEAT PRODUCTS
421-423 W 14th St (bet Ninth and Tenth Ave)
929-5368
Mon-Fri: 5 a.m.-10:30 a.m.

The hours are unusual and the neighborhood is not the best, but Basior-Schwartz is the heart of the wholesale meat district, and that alone is enough to recommend a visit. This is a wholesaler who sells retail customers prime meat, cheese, frozen poultry, and gourmet products at the same prices it charges its regular wholesale customers—hotels and restaurants. Although this had been one of the worst-kept secrets among New York hostesses for years, there have been only minor concessions to the retail trade. The hours are more reasonable than they've been in the past, but the big change has been an additional selection of smoked fish, imported and domestic cheese, and gourmet items that are obviously geared to individual customers. They have even added dried fruits and nuts. But the tradition for freshness and quality remains, and the prices are literally fractions of those uptown. Sure, you may have to get up early and lug your purchases home by public transportation (it's difficult to find parking spaces here), but that's a small inconvenience for some big savings. Basior-Schwartz may well be the main source in the city for meats, cheese, gourmet fish, and appetizing prices, and now that they carry eggs, butter, and grocery items, you may not need to go to a supermarket again.

CITY WHOLESALE MEATS
305 E 85th St (bet First and Second Ave)
879-4241
Mon-Fri: 6-3

The name and the hours are indicative of the wholesale aspects of this business. The many services offered belie the fact that this is a briskly professional place, but the result is that the individual retail customer at City Wholesale Meats receives the same quality and price that is available to hotels and restaurants. Personalized services include delivery, freezer wrapping, and cutting to order. This may be the only such place in the neighborhood that precludes a trek down to the more traditionally wholesale areas of the city.

DELANCEY LIVE POULTRY MARKET
205 Delancey St
475-9875
Tues-Fri: 8-5; Sat: 8-4; Sun: 7-3

Delancey's is one of about half a dozen live poultry markets on Manhattan Island. The only complaint customers seem to have is that it takes you a little too close to the live action. Chickens, ducks, geese, and turkeys inhabit crates that are stacked almost everywhere, and occasional stragglers and freedom fighters wander the floor. The actual purchase and dispatch from live animal to food item takes place on that same floor in full view of all assembled. It is not for the weak of stomach, but it is definitely for those who desire the ultimate in fresh poultry.

FAICCO'S PORK STORE
260 Bleecker St (at Sixth Ave)
243-1974
Tues-Sat: 8-6; Fri: 8-7; Sun: 9-2

An Italian institution, Faicco's has delectable dried pepperoni, cuts of pork, and fresh-frying sweet or sour sausage in two varieties. They also sell an equally good cut for barbecue and an oven-ready rolled leg of stuffed pork. The latter, a house specialty, is locally famous. Note Faicco's full name: the shop really specializes in sausage and cold cuts rather than meats. There is no veal or lamb—and no steaks. If you're into Italian-style deli, try Faicco's first. And if you're a lazy cook, take home some ready-to-heat chicken rollettes: breast of chicken rolled around cheese and then dipped in a crunchy coating. It's the perfect introduction to Faicco's specialties. Already prepared hot foods to take home, like eggplant parmesan and veal marsala, are also available.

H. OPPENHEIMER
2606 Broadway (bet 98th and 99th St)
662-0246, 662-0690
Mon-Sat: 8-6:55

Oppenheimer is one of the first names mentioned for prime meat in New York. Harry Oppenheimer has run the same meticulous shop for over 40 years. It's an old-fashioned butcher shop with the kind of service that used to be expected and which supermarkets never had. The supermarket never had this quality, either. There's milk-fed veal, fresh poultry, and game. All of it is sold at prices that are, according to Harry, "competitive." Oppenheimer is so reliable and trustworthy that over half his customers never even bother to visit the shop in person; they leave the choices and the cuts for their dinners in his capable hands.

JEFFERSON MARKET
455 Sixth Ave (at 10th St)
675-2277
Mon-Sat: 8 a.m.-9 p.m.; Sun: 9-8

Originally a meat and poultry market, Jefferson has expanded into an outstanding full-line store. You'll find high-quality meat, poultry, game, and fish. A deli section features homemade salads and a variety of healthy dishes. And there is a complete line of groceries and gourmet items. The staff is never so rushed that they cannot give personalized service, and they deliver, from 86th Street to Battery Park.

KUROWYCKY MEAT PRODUCTS
124 First Ave (bet Seventh and Eighth St)
477-0344
Mon-Sat: 7-6; closed Mon in July, Aug

Erast Kurowycky came to New York from the Ukraine in 1954. He opened this tiny shop in the same year, and almost immediately it became a mecca and bargain spot for the city's Poles, Germans, Hungarians, Russians, Lithuanians, and Ukrainians. Many of these nationalities still harbor centuries-old grudges, but they all come to Kurowycky's, where they agree on at least two things—the meats are the finest, and the prices are the best available. Erast's son, Jaroslaw ("Jerry"), runs the shop he grew up in, and he maintains the same traditions and recipes his father handed down. Come and taste the thick black bread, sausages, and ham (ask Jerry for a sample). Hams, sausages, meat loaves, and breads are sold ready to eat, as well as in various stages of preparation. There are also condiments, including a homemade Polish mustard, honey (imported directly from Poland), sauerkraut, and a half-dozen other Ukrainian specialties imported or reproduced from the area. On any given day, Kurowycky plays host to native sons coming "home," second generations being introduced to the old-country flavor, and foreigners seeking the real stuff. Jerry treats them all courteously and efficiently, and they all come back for more.

M. LOBEL AND SONS
1096 Madison Ave (bet 82nd and 83rd St)
737-1373
Mon-Sat: 9-6; closed Sat in summer

Lobel's has periodic sales on some of the best cuts of meat in town. Because of Lobel's excellent service and reasonable prices, there are few human carnivores in Manhattan who haven't heard of the shop. It has published four meat cookbooks, and the staff is always willing to explain the best use for each cut. It's hard to go wrong here, since the store carries nothing but the best.

OTTOMANELLI'S MEAT MARKET
285 Bleecker St (bet Seventh Ave and Jones St)
675-4217
Mon-Fri: 8-6:30; Sat: 7-6

The standard variety here is rare gourmet fare. Among the regular weekly stock are such meats as boar's head, whole baby lambs, game rabbits, and pheasant. This is *not* a place to act young and naive. Quality is good, but being served by the right person can make the difference between a good cut and an excellent cut. Other family members run similar operations in other sections of town, but this is the original store, and it's noteworthy. They gained their reputation by offering full butcher services and a top-notch selection of prime meats, game, prime-aged steaks, and milk-fed veal. The latter is available as prepared Italian roast, chops, and steaks, and its preparation by the Ottomanelli's makes it unique. Best of all, they will sell it by the piece for a quick meal at home.

PREMIER VEAL
555 West St (off the West Side Hwy, two blocks south
    of 14th St)
243-3170
Mon-Fri: 5 a.m.-1 p.m.

Mark Hirschorn worked in various jobs in the restaurant business from Albany to Aspen before deciding to join the family wholesale veal distribution center. As a result, he is better attuned to the needs of both wholesale and retail customers than most such distributors. Or, as he says, he's been on both sides of the counter. This translates as a wholesaler who has a good eye for what sells in restaurants and institutions and who has a business that is friendlier than most to small, individual orders. Premier Veal offers veal stew, Italian cutlets, shoulder or leg roasts, and veal pockets for stuffing, at wholesale prices with no minimum order. Of course, if you're going to make a trip to West Street, it might be economical to make the order as big as possible. Hirschorn suggests that three or four customers get together to order a few loins. Less than that leaves too much waste and is not profitable for him or the customer. A loin weighing 18 pounds breaks down to 16 or 24 steaks and chops, and the price is a fraction of that at a butcher shop.

SCHALLER & WEBER
1654 Second Ave (bet 85th and 86th St)
879-3047
Mon-Fri: 9-6; Sat: 8:30-6

Once you've been in this store, the image will stay with you for a long time, because of the sheer magnitude of cold cuts on display. The store is simply incredible. It is a Babes in Toyland for delicatessen lovers, and there is not a wall or a nook that is not covered with an assortment of deli meat. Besides a line of delicatessen items so complete it is hard to believe one store could assemble it, Schaller & Weber also occasionally stocks game and poultry, and they foolishly claim that they are a regular butcher shop as well. Who would buy meat when you can have cold cuts like this? However, if you have the willpower, try the sausage and pork. They will bake it, prepare it, smoke it, or roll it for you, and that's just the beginning.

WASHINGTON BEEF COMPANY
573 Ninth Ave (at 41st St)
563-0200
Tues, Wed, Sat: 6:30-5:30; Thurs, Fri: 6:30-6:30

Washington Beef claims to be the nation's largest meat distributor. They regularly feature New York shells, filet mignon, and beef ribs. The retail store is touted as operating on exactly the same rules as the wholesale operation, but they will also cut meat, sell by the pound rather than the side, and individually wrap it all up. Prices are guaranteed to be the city's lowest, and the quality is good. But there are disadvantages. Washington Beef is *huge*. As a result, the service is brusque and professional, offered on a "take it or leave it, there are others behind you" basis. An attempt to find guidance and recipe suggestions would be a joke. They will cut to order, but lines can be staggeringly long. To sum it up: the prices are fantastic, the quality good. If those are your main criteria, join the crowd.

YORKVILLE PACKING HOUSE
1560 Second Ave (at 81st St)
628-5147
Mon-Sat: 7-6

Yorkville used to be a bastion of Eastern European ethnicity and culture before it became the Upper East Side's swinging singles playground. Here and there, remnants of the previous Old World society remain, and within a four-block stretch on Second Avenue, there are three Hungarian butchers, each of whom offers the best in Hungarian provisions. Yorkville Packing House is patronized by Hungarian-speaking little old ladies in black, as well as some of the city's greatest gourmands. And the reason is simple: except for its neighbors, these prepared meats are available nowhere else in the city and possibly nowhere else on the continent. The shop offers almost 40 different kinds of salami. And that's just for starters. Goose is a mainstay of Hungarian cuisine, so there is goose liverwurst, smoked goose, and goose liver. Fried bacon bits and bacon fried with paprika (another Hungarian staple) are other offerings. And ready for on-the-spot consumption are a selection of preserves, jams, jellies, prepared delicacies, and breads. (Hungarian bread, natch! Try the potato or corn breads.) All of it is authentic and unique.

Middle Eastern

TASHJIAN'S
123 Lexington Ave (bet 28th and 29th St)
683-8458, 685-3451
Mon-Sat: 10-8; Sun: 11-7

One of the oldest food stores in the city (founded over a century ago), Tashjian is Armenian in origin, but it's been in the melting pot long enough to encompass all of the Middle East. The shelves are jammed with all kinds of groceries and foodstuff, and the counters display appetizers. There's even a catering service. Tashjian claims to be an importing business as well, and it would have to be to get some of the items it stocks.

Nuts

KADOURI IMPORT
51 Hester St (at Essex St)
677-5441
Sun-Fri: 9-5

Kadouri is a wholesale-retail store, operating out of burlap bags. Everything here is natural and healthful. The main staples are nuts and dried fruits. The almonds and their derivatives are especially good. Kadouri carries spices as well, but only the more popular varieties. Still, they are extremely fresh, and prices are wholesale, no matter how small the purchase.

YES INTERNATIONAL FOOD COMPANY
165 Church St (at Reade St)
227-4695
Daily: 9-7

Yes is a Middle Eastern food shop, but it's the nuts that attracts their clientele. The nuts are freshly roasted and simply sensational. As a staff member said, "We're nuts about nuts." Also check out the dried fruits and confections, though nothing compares with those nuts.

Pasta

RAFFETTO'S CORPORATION
144 W Houston St (bet Sullivan and MacDougal St)
777-1261
Tues-Sat: 8-6

You could go for pasta at a gourmet place or you could go straight to the source. Raffetto's is the source and has been since 1906. Since that time, they have made all kinds of pasta and stuffing. Though most of the business is wholesale, Raffetto's will dispense ravioli, tortellini, manicotti, gnocchi, fettucine, and spinach fettucine to anyone, with no minimum order. Variations on the theme include Genoa-style ravioli with meat and spinach, Naple's style with cheese, and a nongeographic cheese-and-spinach ravioli. Prices also reflect the fact that this is indeed the source.

Pickles

GUSS PICKLES
35 Essex St (bet Grand and Hester St)
254-4477
Daily: 10-10

The legendary rival businesses that started decades ago with Guss and Hollander each dispensing pickles, tomatoes, sauerkraut, pickled peppers, and watermelon rinds from barrels on the sidewalk has since merged into one business that operates at Hollander's store. Pickles still come sour or half sour, with a half-dozen gradations in between, and the business is still conducted out on the street, with the "stock" taking up the interior of the store. Beyond the barrels outside, customers can actually glimpse a semblance of order and even a refrigerator inside. That refrigerator is stocked with such items as watermelon rind (in season), hot peppers, horseradish, sauerkraut, and even whole pickled melons. But what's really important to remember is that this enterprise is still the best place in the world for fresh-from-the-barrel pickles.

Seafood

CATALANO'S FRESH FISH
1652 Second Ave (at 86th St)
628-9608
Mon-Fri: 9-7; Sat: 9-6

Add youth, consumer interest, and healthy eating to the ancient craft of the fishmonger, and you have Catalano's Fresh Fish market. Owner Joe Catalano is a rare blend of concern, knowledge, and youth. His customers—including many local restaurants —rely on him, as often as not, to select the best items for the dinner menu. And this he does with a careful eye toward health, price, and cookery. He feels strongly that a fish store should not be intimidating and that the only way to get new customers is to educate them. Catalano's also has a good selection of poached fish and super fish cakes. On cold, wintry days, don't miss the Manhattan clam chowder. Joe Catalano is too young to have made the recipe, but he deserves credit for the abundance of clam, ham chunks, and vegetables that goes into it.

CENTRAL FISH COMPANY
527 Ninth Ave (bet 39th and 40th St)
279-2317
Mon-Thurs: 7:30-6:30; Fri: 6:30-6:30; Sat: 7:30-5

Central doesn't look like much from the outside, but the stock is so vast that it's easier to list what is *not* available than what is. They have 35 different species in stock at any given time, including fresh imported sardines from Portugal and live carp. Conducting customers through this whale of a selection are some of the friendliest and most knowledgeable salespeople I've encountered anywhere. Louis and Anthony Riccoborno and Calogero Olivri are skillful guides, who also clean and filet fish. They stock fresh and frozen fish and seafood products. There are fish that even the most devoted seafood lover would have trouble identifying, and the prices are among the most reasonable in town.

CITARELLA FISH
2135 Broadway (at 75th St)
874-0383
Mon-Sat: 8:30-7; Sun: 10-6

The raw bar is the big hit here. It features oysters, clams, and prepared foods for lunch or dinner. The way Citarella's fish are artfully displayed in the windows gives a hint of the shop's vast selection and fine quality. Take home the delicious salads and fish dishes for that special nautical-theme dinner.

DISCOUNT FISH
4250 Broadway (at 181st St)
· 923-1600
Mon-Fri: 9-7:30

There has been a fish market on these premises for decades. The only thing that changes is the ownership and the ethnic composition of the neighborhood, which in turn reflects upon the type of fish they sell. The latest regime knows fish and knows the value of money as well. The French ambassador's wife once mentioned this market in an article in *The New York Times,* which probably explains why it is not uncommon to see limos double-parked in front of the store. Just don't expect a lot of conversation; the owners speak very little English.

LEONARD'S FISH MARKET
1241 Third Ave (bet 71st and 72nd St)
744-2600
Mon-Fri: 8-7; Sat: 8-6; Sun: 12-6

Leonard's, a family-owned business since 1905, is owned and operated by three family members with the same exacting standards that the store has maintained throughout the years. It's a neighborhood store that gears its selection to the neighborhood's menus. Thus, the better, smaller portioned seafoods are always in stock. There are sea trout, oysters, crabs, haddock, scampi, striped bass, halibut, salmon, live lobster, and squid. The latter is usually purchased by people who know what they are doing, but if they don't, a Leonard is happy to assist. They also run daily specials on whatever happens to have been a good buy that day at the Fulton Market. This is not to say that Leonard's is a bargain establishment. Decidedly not. Leonard's is class all the way. And their take-out seafood department includes codfish cakes, deviled crabs and lobsters, and a super Manhattan clam chowder. Leonard's also carries a full range of imported appetizers. Yes, there is caviar, and you can also find filet mignon, smoked meats and fish, and canned delicacies. Barbecued poultry, cooked and prepared foods, and prime meats round out Leonard's selection.

MURRAY'S STURGEON SHOP
2429 Broadway (bet 89th and 90th St)
724-2650
Tues-Fri, Sun: 8-7; Sat: 8-8; Sun (July, Aug): 8-2

The answer to why Arthur Cutler is the owner of a place called Murray's Sturgeon Shop is that Cutler bought out Murray several years ago. That is of interest to every appetizer lover in New York, because Murray's was the definitive place to buy fancy and smoked fish. There was some apprehension when Cutler took over, but doubts were assuaged when Craig Claiborne, *The New York Times* gastronomist, declared Murray's "my favorite purveyor of such things" after Cutler had operated the shop for just a year. (Claiborne's article described how he saved $1,290 by bringing his own dinner on a tourist-class round trip to Europe instead of flying first-class. The dinner was catered by Murray's.) When Murray's is not winning accolades from the *Times,* it is dispensing the finest in appetizing products. There is sturgeon, Gaspe salmon, whitefish, kippered salmon, sable butterfish, pickled herring, schmaltz herring, and caviar. Quality is magnificent and prices fair, even if you're not flying across the Atlantic.

ROSEDALE FISH AND OYSTER MARKET
1129 Lexington Ave (at 79th St)
861-4323, 288-5013, 734-3767
Mon-Sat: 8-6

Rosedale has quality seafood in good supply at all times. In addition, there is a selection of take-out fish dishes and salads that are tasty, unusual, and noteworthy. All are individually prepared for each customer. They are not inexpensive; their high quality is accompanied by equally high prices. But according to many of the city's restaurants and caterers, they are the best fish source in New York. (They don't want people to know that, however!)

Spices

ANGELICA'S TRADITIONAL HERBS & FOODS
147 First Ave (at Ninth St)
677-1549
Mon-Sat: 10-7:45; Sun: 11-6:45

Because of its location in the East Village, Angelica's scent is heavily occult, organic, and home-remedy medicinal. The shop caters to the local Ukranians with fresh, high-grade spices, teas, and coffees, but the bulk of the business is the dispensing of medicinal herbs, organic foods, and natural cosmetics to a trendier clientele. They claim to be the largest and best stocked herb retailer in the country, and they even offer courses in herbal therapy. New features include an organic-food department and an organic deli.

APHRODISIA
282 Bleecker St (at Seventh Ave)
989-6440
Mon-Sat: 11-7; Sun: 12-5; closed Sun in summer

Aphrodisia is stocked from floor to ceiling with every herb and spice that exists. All 700 of them are neatly displayed in easily visible glass jars. Some of the teas, potpourri, dried flowers, and oils are really not what one would expect. The general accent is on the occult and folk remedies, but all the ingredients for ethnic cooking can be found here. Prices depend upon the scarcity of the spice. Aphrodisia conducts a large mail-order business via their catalog, which is available for a minimal fee.

MEADOWSWEET HERBAL APOTHECARY
77 E Fourth St (bet Second and Third Ave)
254-2870
Tues-Sat: 12-7; closed two weeks in Aug, Sept

Arcus and Dorothy Flynn believe in the power of herbs and herbal medicine. They offer a complete assortment of their own mixtures, oils, ointments, medicines, and formulas to aid a variety of ailments from alcoholism to tranquilizer addiction. In addition to their herbal remedies, they have expanded their gift department to include potpurri, unusual incenses, incense burners, candles, dream pillows, smudge sticks, hanging stained-glass pieces, musical tapes, massage oils, crystals, and crystal jewelry. The folks here like to share their own experiences, which helps to make any visit particularly interesting.

SAINT REMY
818 Lexington Ave (bet 62nd and 63rd St)
759-8240
Mon-Sat: 10-7

The name is French, and this spice market is evocative of the best in French herb shops. While it has its share of open bins and bags of fresh nuts, herbs, and plants, those on sale here are the kind a gourmet cook would need. (I asked for black poppy seeds and was told, "We have white only—from the opium fields of Turkey, but white.") Notice the sacks of herbs. The stock is not enormous, but what is there is the best. Saint Remy also carries fabrics and cosmetics under the Saint Remy name, and they give advice on skin care and the use of herbs in cooking. Over the years, Saint Remy has evolved into a store selling the products of the Provence. If French is the accent, then country French is the style. Expect to find dried flowers, tapestry pillows and wall hangings, ceramic accessories, lavender, potpourri, and fabrics in the tradition of Flanders, Fobelins, and Aubusson.

V. Where To Find It:
New York's Best Services

Animal Services

ANIMAL MEDICAL CENTER
510 E 62nd St (bet FDR Dr and York Ave)
838-8100
Daily: 24 hours

If your pet should become ill in New York, try the Animal Medical Center first. This nonprofit organization handles all kinds of veterinary work reasonably and competently with board-certified specialists. The care here is far better than it is anywhere else in the city. They suggest you call for an appointment. Emergency care costs more.

CAROLE WILBOURN
299 W 12th St
741-0397
Mon-Sat: 9-6

Carole is an internationally known cat therapist who has the answer to most of your cat problems. She writes a monthly column for *Cat Fancy* magazine, and seems to have a special way with her furry patients. Carole makes house calls from coast-to-coast, and can take care of many cat problems with just one session and a follow-up phone call.

LE CHIEN DOG SALON
1461A First Ave (at 76th St)
861-8100
Mon-Fri: 8:30-7; Sat: 9-7

Dresses. Coats. Sweaters. 14k gold identification tags. Cultured pearls. Mink stoles. Special brand-name perfume. I mean we are talking class here! Lisa Gilford runs this establishment as an elegant spa for small and large breeds (the latter only on request). The place is a sort of finishing school for the canine set. There is a separate business that grooms and trains cats and dogs. Most of the clients are either being cured of bad habits or being brought in for grooming. If you get a whiff of some seductive perfume when you get home, Mom, it may just be the dog and not what you think!

MANHATTAN PET HOTEL
312 E 95th St (bet First and Second Ave)
831-2900
Mon-Fri: 7-7; Sat: 8-5

This place sounds so good you may want to check in yourself! It's the only venture in Manhattan that boards pets as a primary business. They use the best commercial foods available, have separate exercise areas for cats to sun and play (and scratch), and have luxury suites for those cats and dogs that are used to living in Trump Tower. Services include pickup and delivery, air travel arrangements, provision for medications, and dog and cat grooming. There's even a check-out time for their guests.

PET CARE NETWORK
120 E 31st St (bet Park and Lexington Ave)
889-0756
Daily: 7:30 a.m.-10 p.m.

No need to worry if Fido or Linda Louise is going to be left behind while you vacation, or go away for a day or weekend. Whether it's a cat, dog, bird, or Bugs Bunny, Evelyn McCabe and her crew of pet-sitters can take care of your loved one. They are in 32 locations around the city, or they will come to your residence for service. All personnel are bonded, love animals, and have excellent references. No cages, please, and one pet or set of pets at a time per location. These folks will walk your pet, feed him, pick up and deliver, provide veterinarian care, and are available around the clock. Dustin Hoffman swears by them, and so will your lonesome partner.

WE KARE KENNELS
410 220th St (at Broadway)
567-2100
Daily: 8:30-6; Summer: 8:30-6:30

Nat and Jan Kornhauser's motto—"If you care, send your pet to We Kare"—and the *kute* name can be forgiven, since they really do spend as much time as they claim with their animals. Care (not *kare*) here is first-rate. The Kornhausers offer convenient services for tourists, including pickup and drop-off at home, office, hotel, and even airport. This is especially good for transferred or traveling executives. Furthermore, We Kare's policy is to follow the home schedule of feeding, walking, and bed times, rather than forcing pets to adjust to an institutional routine. They feel this practice makes the animals adjust better to their new home, and since We Kare also accepts long-term boarders, that's important. Grooming, training, and cat boarding are also available, and they sell dogs as well. Cats have a brand-new separate boarding facility.

Antiques Repair

MICHAEL J. DOTZEL AND SON
402 E 63rd St (at York Ave)
838-2890
Mon-Fri: 9:30-4:30

Dotzel specializes in the repair and maintenance of antiques, so nothing will be done to your precious heirlooms that will hurt their intrinsic value. Dotzel won't touch modern pieces or inferior antiques, but if your antique is made out of metal and needs repair, he's the man for the job. He spends a lot of time and pays close attention to detail, and will hand-forge or personally hammer metal work, including brass. If an item has lost a part, he can re-create it. One thing is certain: when the job's finished, your piece will be as good as new. Dotzel also does stripping and replating, although he feels it isn't always good for an antique. He'll probably try to talk you out of it.

SANO STUDIO
767 Lexington Ave (at 60th St, room 403)
759-6131
Mon-Fri: 9:30-5; closed Aug

Mrs. J. Baran presides over this fourth-floor antiques repair shop, and she has an eye for excellence. That eye is focused on the quality of the workmanship and the quality of the goods brought here to be repaired. Both must be the best. Sano's area of specialization is limited to repair of porcelain, pottery, ivory, and tortoise-shell works and antiques. While Hess (see Hess Restorations, under "China and Glassware Repair") repairs everything but the kitchen sink (and might repair that, too, if you could convince them it's an antique), Sano concentrates on specific areas. As a result, both stores have their loyal adherents. Some customers like the idea of being able to bring a hodgepodge of broken items to one repair shop. Other customers, particularly those who repair only one item at a time, prefer the feeling of security you get with specialized service. Perhaps it's safer to say that it's a matter of opinion.

Art Services

ELI WILNER & COMPANY
1525 York Ave (bet 80th and 81st St)
744-6521
Mon-Fri: 9:30-5:30; Sat: by appointment

Eli Wilner runs two separate businesses. The first one offers the unique service of positioning, grouping, and hanging artwork—a real art in itself. But his main business is period (or antique) framing, mirror framing, and framing restoration. He keeps in stock some 1500 19th-century and early 20th-century American and European frames, and if the proper one is not available, he can locate any given size or style with advance notice. Wilner is a handy guy to call in, especially when you and your partner are having that inevitable discussion about what to do with the treasure your mother-in-law just gave you.

GUTTMANN PICTURE FRAME ASSOCIATES
180 E 73rd St (bet Lexington and Third Ave)
744-8600
Mon-Thurs: 9-5; Fri: 9-2

Though the Guttmanns have worked on frames for some of the nation's finest museums, including the Metropolitan, they stand apart from other first-class artisans in that they are not snobby or picky about what work they will take. They will restore, regild, or replace any type of picture frame, and while they are masters at working with masterpieces, they are equally at home restoring or framing a Polaroid snapshot. Even better, the Guttmanns are not only willing to work on cheaper pieces, they are among the few experts who don't price themselves out of the market. When you bring a worn-out frame to them, they will graciously *and* gratuitously tell you exactly what it will cost to fix it. That's when their egalitarian attitude really comes to the fore.

JINPRA NEW YORK PICTURE FRAMING
1208 Lexington Ave (at 82nd St)
988-3903
Wed-Sat: 12-7; Sun: 12-5

The proprietor of Jinpra New York Picture Framing has the intriguing name of Wellington Chiang, and his service is as unique as his name. Jinpra handles art services (cleaning, restoration, and gilding) in general, and picture framing in particular. Chiang makes the high quality frames himself, and they often outshine the pictures they frame. Chiang's artistry is evident in every piece he creates. His frames are the perfect complement to great artwork. They will frame lesser works as well, but because of the price and the fine workmanship, it would be a waste.

JOEL AND TERESA ZAKOW
72 Greene St
226-6093
Mon-Sat: 9-6 by appointment

Don't bring the Rembrandt down to Joel and Teresa Zakow without making an appointment and confirming it on the phone. They just might be too busy working on the restoration of a painting belonging to a museum or destined for one of the Madison Avenue auction blocks. As restorers in residence for the Museum of American Folk Art, the Zakows are particularly adept with any folk artwork. But perhaps because they are not used to working exclusively with the old masters, they seem more receptive to taking on works of greater sentimental than artistic value. This is not to say that the work is cheap; in fact, the opposite is usually true. If one owns a masterpiece, one takes care of it. It's the ancestors' portraits that usually hang forever without a cleaning. Zakows charge according to the work involved rather than the value of the artwork. For this reason, they offer free estimates and a frank appraisal of whether or not it's worth undertaking the work. By the way, Joel is an acknowledged authority at detecting marine and American folk-art forgeries and can offer this expertise to customers.

JULIUS LOWY FRAME AND RESTORING COMPANY
28 West End Ave
586-2050
Mon-Fri: 9-5

There are many firms in the city that specialize in art restoration and framing, but this is the definitive place for both services. Julius Lowy's seems to have no space that isn't heaped with frames, and many look as though they've been there since the place opened 80 years ago. It's obvious that any kind of frame could be unearthed somewhere on their two floors. This means there is no framing job that Laurence Shar of Julius Lowy's cannot do, and the shop's clients include the Metropolitan Museum of Art and the White House. As a by-product of having done some really odd jobs, a sideline was developed in art restoration, antique-frame reproduction, and frame rearrangement. (Rearrangement means enlarging or reducing existing frames to match new artwork.) All of this work is done impeccably. Prices are not as high as might be expected, and there are brand-new custom-made frames available.

READY FRAMES
25 W 45th St (in the A.I. Friedman store)
243-9000
Mon-Fri: 8:45-5:45; Sat: 10-3; closed Sat in summer

Ready Frames does custom framing, but those who want to do it themselves can take advantage of one of the largest stocks of ready-made frames in the city. Nearly all are sold at up to 50 percent off. In addition to fully assembled frames, there are frames that can be put together for specific sizes and come equipped with glass and/or mats.

Babysitters

BABYSITTERS GUILD
60 E 42nd St (suite 912)
682-0227
Daily: 9-9

Established in 1940, the Babysitters Guild charges high rates, but their reputation commends them. The Guild's reputation is based upon a thoroughly professional attitude. All of their sitters have passed rigorous scrutiny and only the most capable are sent out on jobs. There is a four-hour minimum here, but as members of the New York Convention and Visitor's Bureau, they will sometimes relax the rule for tourists. Among their sitters, 16 languages are spoken.

BARNARD COLLEGE BABYSITTING SERVICE
606 W 120th St
854-2035
Mon-Fri: 10-5

Barnard College, the undergraduate women's college of Columbia University, has—counting instructors and graduate students—an unusually large number of kids following their parents around campus. To keep them out of their folks' hair, the Barnard Babysitting Service was started by the Office of Career Services. The service is a nonprofit organization, wholly run by the students. Barnard students become mother's helpers (usually, room and board are exchanged for babysitting services) and full-time or one-time babysitters. Most of the young women prefer to have one-time or occasional babysitting arrangements, though.

C.A.S.H./STUDENT EMPLOYMENT OFFICE
21 Washington Pl (at Greene St, third floor)
New York University
998-4433
Mon-Fri: 9-5

New York University has always been known for its free and easy attitude (perhaps because of its Village location). Its babysitting service is no different, and it's certainly refreshing after the list of restrictions imposed elsewhere. At NYU, rates are reasonable, with no minimum fees. Rates are negotiated between parents and students. With such a large student body, there is usually someone willing to sit, even on short notice. No further commitment is necessary. C.A.S.H. combines all the student employment offices, so this is also the place to hire student bartenders, tutors, housesitters, or odd jobbers.

Beauty Care and Consultation

BORJA AND PAUL
805 Madison Ave (at 67th St)
734-0477
Mon: 9-5; Tues, Wed, Fri, Sat: 9-5:30; Thurs: 9-7

Pierre Henri, formerly of Saks, is in residence here on Tuesday, Wednesday, and Thursday, from 9 to 3:30. Though the other operators are good, Pierre is exceptional. He has a long list of clients who follow him wherever he moves. Indeed, this shop relies on steady clients. The service is courteous and old-fashioned, but the styles they cut are stylish and up-to-date—to a point. "Our makeup girl does elegant, chic makeup to complement our hair coloring. *That,* by the way, is natural coloring. We're not into the punk-rock look," said one operator. The salon also does manicures, haircuts, setting, and pedicures—everything you'd expect from a traditional salon.

ESTEEM
201 E 69th St
744-4660
Mon-Fri: 9-6

This is truly a service company. Esteem markets a line of cosmetics used as concealers, including eye shadows, alcohol-free shampoo, allergy-free foundations, color cosmetics, and skin-care products. Their use is primarily for those with facial disfigurements, but they also work on varicose veins, age spots, stretch marks, and even body scars. The products are waterproof and unusually long-lasting, so that a client doesn't have to worry if he or she is caught in a rainstorm. At Esteem, appointments are required, and during the consultation a company representative will give a personalized analysis. Esteem also markets its products through medical offices and gives free consultations to patients at various area hospitals. The makeup is often the most important aspect in a patient's recovery. Cosmetic therapy really does mitigate scars and birthmarks, and helps people live normal lives.

JOSEPH MARTIN
717 Madison Ave (bet 63rd and 64th St)
838-3150
Mon, Tues, Fri, Sat: 9-5; Wed, Thurs: 9-7

Often there is need for beauty care in a home, apartment, or hotel. For older folks, individuals who are ill, or if time is a problem, Joseph Martin will do services on an out-call basis. Hair coloring, nail care, cutting and makeup are available, but of course, you will pay extra away from the premises.

KENNETH
19 E 54th St (at Fifth Ave)
752-1800
Mon, Thurs, Fri: 9-6; Tues, Wed: 9-8:30

You will remember that Kenneth was *the* hairdresser at the White House in the Kennedy years. He is still considered one of the best, and now anyone can make an appointment with Kenneth himself. Although he books three to four weeks in advance, it's possible to get an appointment with one of his associates the same day that you call. Some staff members will make appointments as early as 8 a.m. They do everything from leg waxing to hair dying. Men may take advantage of all the services of the salon in privacy, and a Kenneth for Kids is available.

LESLIE BLANCHARD
19 E 62nd St (at Madison Ave)
421-4564
Tues, Wed, Fri, Sat: 9-5; Thurs: 12-8

The Private World of Leslie Blanchard (that's the shop's official name, not just flowery writing) offers everything for beauty preparation. The Blanchard salon does haircutting, styling, and makeup, and has been known to do complete make-overs. However, they really specialize in simple but perfectly executed, individual treatments including electrolysis, waxing, and European facials. Blanchard is best known for its coloring techniques. Anyone in New York who wants the best uses Blanchard.

LINDA TAM BEAUTY SALON
680 Fifth Ave (second floor)
757-2555
Mon-Wed, Fri, Sat: 8-7; Thurs: 8-8

The specialty here is hair coloring. Linda Tam, a native of China, has been working in this field for over 25 years, and has assembled a staff of experts who give full service to both men and women. Private rooms and the latest in specialized machines are available.

MAKE-UP CENTER
150 W 55th St (bet Sixth and Seventh Ave)
977-9494
Mon-Wed, Fri: 10-6; Thurs: 10-8; Sat: 10-5

The purveyors of Allure cosmetics for over two decades, the Make-Up Center counts everyone from teenage girls to the rock group Kiss among its clientele. What makes that range interesting is the Center's credo that makeup should be natural and easy to apply and not wash away at night. "Well and good for the 13-year-olds," you say. "But Kiss?" The answer is simple. The Center is set up along parallel lines to serve stage stars, formal events (such as weddings), and the everyday folks. All of it is individually geared to customer and lifestyle and packaged with instructions on how to achieve the look at home. Private one-hour sessions that feature the latest makeup techniques are tailored to the customer for around $25. It may well be the best bargain in town, for in addition to the personalized expertise, the lesson is given with the expectation that the client won't be back for quite a while, and there's only minimal pressure for you to buy Allure cosmetics. Lessons can even be videotaped and purchased.

NAILS DESIGN BY RELLY
1107 Lexington Ave (bet 77th and 78th St)
535-5333
Mon-Sat: 9:30-8

Surreptitiously take your malnutritioned nails to Nails Design for present and future transformations. Relly Papadumitru and Consuello Sipsas will create beautiful plastic or paper nail wrapping, all the while making sure you end up with healthy nails in the long run—your own. TLC is regularly administered to help a client maintain healthy nails. While you're there, you may want to try the body-waxing and eyelash-tinting services.

NARDI SALON
143 E 57th St (bet Lexington and Third Ave)
421-4810
Mon-Fri: 9:30-5:30; Sat: 9:30-4:30

Vincent and Fred Nardi wrote a book called *How To Do Your Hair Like a Pro,* and their two salons (only one is in Manhattan) prove they live up to that title. These are full-service salons: they handle the client from head (hair styling, cutting, perming, coloring, etc.) to toe (pedicures), with makeup (classes and demonstrations as well as application), waxing, and accessory products. The aim is a total look, but it is a look less known for its professional gloss than its ability to be *almost* re-created by the client at home. Nardi even has services for men and children as well. All of this is well worth paying for, but those who wish to avoid 57th Street prices can do so by attending the 6 p.m. classes on Tuesday and Wednesday evenings. At that time, free haircuts by students are offered.

For free or bargain cuts, coloring or styling, here are some suggestions. I recommend that you call ahead to find out the special services available.

Bruno le Salon (16 W 57th St, 581-2780) Training session on Tuesdays at 6:30 p.m.

Clairol Consumer Research Forum (345 Park Ave, bet 51st and 52nd St., second floor, 546-2707) Mon-Fri: 9-3 by appointment only.

David Daines Hair Salon (833 Madison Ave, bet 69th and 70th St, 535-1563) Tuesdays at 6 p.m. for bargain time.

La Coupe (694 Madison Ave, at 62nd St, 355-9460) Tuesdays at 5:45 p.m. for training session.

Penta Hair Design (907 Madison Ave, at 73rd St, second floor, 744-4955) Free haircuts start at 5:45 p.m. on Wednesdays.

Pipino-Buccheri (601 Madison Ave, 759-2959) Selected models get free haircuts on Wednesdays at 6:30 p.m.

Richard Stein Haircutting (1018 Lexington Ave, 897-3663) Free sessions for haircuts start at 6 p.m. on Thursdays.

Nominal rates for walk-in customers are available at **Robert Fiance Hair Design Institute** (1627 Broadway, 757-5820, ask for salon), and **Ultissima Beauty Institute** (22 W 34th St, 564-5777, ask for salon).

Bookbinding

CRAFT STUDENTS LEAGUE
Y.W.C.A. of the City of New York
610 Lexington Ave
755-4500

While even a firm believer in do-it-yourself projects would have to admit that there comes a time when the value of a book forces you to have the binding done professionally, it never hurts to understand what an expert is doing to your valuable property. The best way to become a bookbinding expert in this city is to sign up for Natalie Blatt's class at the Craft Students League. The course is offered days or evenings, and the fee is a deal. The student comes away with a working knowledge of bookbinding and some ability to do it personally. The school also offers dozens of other classes, which range from beginner to professional levels. Send for the free catalog, which explains what they've been doing since 1932.

TALAS DIVISION OF TECHNICAL LIBRARY SERVICE
213 W 35th St
736-7744
Mon-Fri: 9-11:30, 1-5

Talas has tools, supplies, equipment, and books for artists, restorers, collectors, bookbinders, museums, archives, libraries, and calligraphers, and offers the same to retail customers. Elaine Haas presides over a wealth of services for bibliophiles. Should a book be in need of repair and you want to attempt it yourself, there is no better place to take it. After all, if Haas can service professional book repairers, she can certainly help amateurs. The attitude here is briskly professional.

WEITZ, WEITZ, & COLEMAN
1377 Lexington Ave (bet 90th and 91st St)
831-2213
Mon-Fri: 10-6; Sat: 12-3

You have to be good (and politic) to do custom bookbinding for both President Reagan and Premier Gorbachev. And Leo and Herbert Weitz are just that professional. They are masters of high-quality bookbinding, which accounts for their firm having been in the business continuously since 1909. The Weitzes, who also buy and sell very rare books, use only the finest leathers and other materials in their work to produce magnificent volumes. Their prices are very fair.

Calligraphy

CALLIGRAPHY STUDIOS
106 Franklin St (bet Church St and W Broadway)
226-4056
By appointment

Nothing quite sets off a card or a letter like calligraphy. There are many who claim to be experts, but if you want some really first-class work, let Linda Stein and her crew customize your order. The nice part of her service is that she is able to do work in any language that you desire.

Camping Equipment Repair

DOWN EAST
75 Spring St
925-2632
Mon-Fri: 11-6; Thurs: 11-7; Sat: 11-2
Closed Sat in July, Aug

The full name of this shop is Leon R. Greenman's Down East Outdoor Service Center, and owner Greenman provides a phenomenal range of services to outdoorsmen. He started Down East as a service center for hiking, camping, and outdoor equipment. He has excellent credentials, having been the proprietor of another camping equipment store and a veteran of years of hiking, camping, and trailblazing. During those years, he came to appreciate the lack of service centers for camping equipment, and when he was ready to run a store again, Down East was the result. This store is a godsend for campers. It offers guidebooks, hiking maps, and USGS Topo maps. Outdoor gear can be modified, repaired, and customized.

Carpentry

WOODSMITH'S STUDIO
525 W 26th St
879-4300
Mon-Fri: 9:30-4:30

Eric Gaathje ran a carpentry business cum woodworking school until he was forced to move when his old location was demolished. Instead of merely relocating, Gaathje reappraised the entire operation, and when he went back into business, he stressed those aspects of the craft that most appealed to him. So, nowadays, Gaathje is spending his time on custom cabinetry, particularly bookcases, wall units, tables, and even turnings and carvings. A popular sideline of the business is his picture-framing class. Small groups of students are walked through every aspect of picture framing and taught how to turn out picture frames by themselves.

Carriages

CHATEAU STABLES/CHATEAU THEATRICAL ANIMALS
608 W 48th St
246-0520
Daily: 9-5

How would you like to arrive at your next dinner party in a horse-drawn carriage? Well, Chateau is the place to call. They have the largest working collection of horse-drawn vehicles in the United States. Although they would like advance notice, they can take care of requests at any time for weddings, group rides and tours, theater connections, or overseas visitors. There is nothing quite as romantic as a ride in an authentic hansom cab—and they're so *handsome,* too.

Cars for Hire

CAREY LIMOUSINE NY
(212) 599-1122 (reservations)
(718) 898-1000 (office)
24 hours

Carey is considered by many to be the grandfather of car-for-hire services. They provide chauffeur-driven limousines and sedans at any time, and they will take you anywhere in almost any kind of weather. They will accept last-minute reservations on an "as available" basis.

COMPANY II LIMOUSINE SERVICE
430-6482
24 hours

Steve Betancourt provides a responsible, efficient, and confidential service at reasonable prices. His reputation for reliability is well-earned.

PEGASUS ONE LIMOUSINE
432-1322 (out of state call 800-544-6942)
Mon-Sat: 9-8; Sun: 10-2

You can treat your group to a truly special ride and "arrival" with the longest stretch limousine around from Pegasus. It is a great service for proms, visits to Atlantic City, or group travel to theaters and airports. Pegasus features a full line of antique cars and limos (some Rolls Royces) with bars, color TVs, and VCRs.

Chair Caning

CHAIRS CANED
133 W 72nd St (seventh floor)
724-4408
Thurs-Sat: 1-5

Please note the hours carefully, for this is the only time Jeffrey Weiss will answer his phone. The rest of the time he's busy keeping alive the dying art of caning. He does very professional work at very competitive prices, and he comes highly recommended.

VETERAN'S CANING SHOP
550 W 35th St
868-3244
Mon-Fri: 7:30-4:30; Sat: 10-2

Veteran's owner John Bausert has written a book about chair caning, and claims his shop is one of the oldest in the world. Certainly, his prices and craftsmanship are among the best in town, and Bausert believes in passing along his knowledge. Customers are encouraged to repair their own chairs: the procedure is outlined in his book, and the necessary materials are sold in the shop. If you don't want to try (or have had disastrous results on your own), the shop will repair the chair. For a slight charge, they'll pick it up from your home. Since chair caning is such a specialized and limited industry, a company often has a monopoly in its neighborhood. So, it's remarkable that Bausert offers such services at such good prices. Equally remarkable are the stacks of cane—I've never seen so much. In addition to caning, Veteran's also stocks materials for chair and furniture repair; you will be encouraged to tackle these jobs, too.

Chimney Sweep

CHIMINEY CRICKET
319 W 11th St
691-0171
Daily: 24 hours by phone only

Even 15 years ago, WBFP's (real-estate ad lingo for woodburning fireplaces) were detriments rather than attractions in an apartment. At about that same time, Allayne Johnson had become a former actress and sometime writer looking for a full-time job. When a neighbor's flue needed cleaning, Johnson tried doing it. She eventually decided that chimney cleaning wasn't really any dirtier than show business, and Chiminey Cricket was born. In a way, Johnson hasn't completely left the theater. For one thing, her occupation is one that lends itself to fantasy. She has a great sense of humor and tells tales about her funny experiences as a chimney sweep. Chiminey Cricket is of the old school. Johnson eschews fancy equipment and vacuums; instead she relies on telescoping rods and brushes. And she can afford to be picky. Most of her work is in the Village, because it is convenient and because downtown fireplaces are less likely to have been covered over. But she will go elsewhere in the city if her safety and transportation are assured.

China and Glassware Repair

CENTER ART STUDIO
250 W 54th St (room 901)
247-3550
Mon-Fri: 10-6; weekends by appointment

"Fine art restoration and display since 1919" is the motto here. The word "fine" should be emphasized, for owners of really good crystal, porcelain, china, or bronze art should make Center the definitive place to go for repairs. The house specialty is restoration of antiques. Center Art will restore or repair porcelain, terra-cotta, shells, and precious stones. They will also restore antique furniture and decorative objects, using original materials whenever possible. They'll even design and install display bases and cases, and will pack and crate articles for shipment. As probably the oldest and most diverse art-restoration studio in the city, Center Art can offer a multitude of special services, like designs and sketches by FAX, and multilingual personnel for overseas shoppers. The owner, Lansing Moore, has a super-talented staff.

EARTHWORKS POTTERY/M. SIMONDS STUDIO
1705 First Ave (bet 88th and 89th St)
534-9711
Fri-Sun: 12-5:30 (Earthworks)
Wed, Thurs: 12-8; Fri, Sat: 12-5:30 (M. Simonds)

Margaret Simonds ran the M. Simonds Studio for more than 15 years. It was the best place in New York for the restoration of fine-art objects. In 1979, she bought Earthworks—then located around the corner—and the merger created a comprehensive shop that caters to stoneware, pottery, and porcelain pieces from the kiln to "beyond hope" stages. The Earthworks section of the business is both a retail shop and a pottery school. The front of the shop has a fine selection of one-of-a-kind porcelain and stoneware pieces made by potters from all over the U.S.A. (Great for gifts!) The shop also conducts ongoing classes in pottery making, taking advantage of the on-site studio equipment. During the later part of the week (note the hours), Ms. Simonds is in residence. Her specialty is the restoration of pottery, glass, porcelain, jade, cloisonné, clay, and fine-art objects.

GEM MONOGRAM
628 Broadway (at Hudson St)
674-8960
Mon-Fri: 9-5

Junior was playing with the prized Steuben crystal apple, thinking it was a baseball? Then it's time to call Martin Noren at Gem who can repair chipped or damaged Steuben and Baccarat pieces. They ask for a photo before they will undertake the job. Remember that they only work with fine crystal objects.

HESS RESTORATIONS
200 Park Ave S (at 17th St)
260-2255, 979-1143
Mon-Fri: 10:30-5; appointments necessary for later times

Hess bills itself as "repairers of the irrepareable" (sic), and it does a fantastic job on anything but furniture, electrical appliances, and mechanical devices. Their specialties include china, glass, handbags, ivory, jade, lamps, *objets d'art,* and virtually the entire run of items in the alphabet. The important thing, however, is that Hess can usually restore an object so that the damage is unnoticeable. (Broken crystal stemware pieces that cannot be restored are reincarnated as crystal dinner bells.) One specialty—the replacement of blue glass liners for antique silver salt dishes—is said to be unique in the city. Hess accepts parcel-post-insured shipments of items to be repaired. Upon receipt, they mail an estimate for restoration. Many of Hess' best customers are museums and antiques dealers.

Clock and Watch Repair

FANELLI ANTIQUE TIME
1131 Madison Ave (bet 84th and 85th St)
517-2300
Mon-Fri; 10-6; Sat: 11-5

In a beautiful new clock gallery, Cindy and Joseph Fanelli specialize in the care of high-quality "investment type" timepieces. They have one of the nation's largest collections of rare and unusual early-American grandfather clocks and vintage wristwatches. They do both sales and restorations, will make house calls, give free estimates, and even rent out timepieces for special assignments. Granddad would be happy to see his prize in the hands of these exceptionally able folks.

FOSSNER TIMEPIECES CLOCK SHOP
1059 Second Ave (at 56th St)
249-2600
Sun-Fri: 10-6; Sat: 11-5

In Europe, fine watch repairing is a family tradition, but this craft is being slowly forgotten in our country. Fortunately, in Manhattan there is a four-generation family, the Fossners, who have passed along this talent from father to son. You can have perfect confidence in their work on any kind of watch. They will guarantee their work for one year, and in most cases, they will have your work done within a week. Besides, it's a treat to meet this outstanding Czechoslovakian family.

GRACE TIME SERVICE
125 Greenwich Ave (at W 13th St)
929-8011
Mon-Fri: 11-7; Sat: 11-4:30; closed Mon in summer

Grace Szuwala services, restores, repairs, and sells antique timepieces. Her European training makes her particularly expert on antique watches and clocks, with a strong sensitivity for pieces that have more sentimental than real value. This amazing Grace can really do wonders with keepsakes that come from a much more graceful period of time.

SUTTON CLOCK SHOP
139 E 61st St (at Lexington Ave)
758-2260, 473-0196
Mon-Fri: 11-5

Sutton Clock Shop takes its name from Kay Sutton, not the nearby neighborhood of Sutton Place, but the service and selection is every bit as classy as that address. While Sutton's forte is the selling—and acquiring—of unusual timepieces, there is at least an equal interest in the maintenance and repair of antique clocks. Some of the timepieces —even the contemporary ones—are truly outstanding, and there's a long list of satisfied customers endorsing their repair work. And now they do barometer repairing as well.

Clothing Repair

MAGIC MENDERS
118 E 59th St
759-6453
Mon-Fri: 9-5

If you have an emergency with any of your clothing while you're in the vicinity of 59th Street, head over to Magic Menders. They will repair almost any type of wearing apparel, from monogrammed A's to zippers, on the spot. Of course, they prefer to be given some time in which to work, but their reputation rests on emergency repairs. Their vast repertoire includes glove and umbrella mending, and handbag and zipper repairs. If you would like to keep Great Aunt Tilda's linens, although the monogram is all wrong, Magic Menders can fix that, too. Their mending really is invisible.

Currency Conversion

FREEPORT CURRENCIES
3 W 46th St
221-2000
Mon-Fri: 9-6; Sat: 10-3

If you want to make sure you have enough French francs for that weekend in Paris, this is the place to go. Usually their rates are better than most banks or hotels, and they will exchange currency for any country. Freeport will also buy and sell traveler's checks, and will sell precious metals at decent prices.

Delivery, Courier, Messenger Services

JIMINY SPLIT DELIVERY SERVICES
147 W 46th St
354-7373
Daily: 7-7

Jiminy Split can hand-deliver a package from New York to Washington, D.C., in less than four hours. That's remarkably fast; the overnight service of Federal Express can't do that, and the U.S. mail is not even in the running. (It once took three weeks for a package of mine to go from New York to Washington, D.C.—it went by way of Washington, North Carolina!) So, if you want a fast, reliable, and personal service, Jiminy Split can deliver anywhere within the continental U.S. as fast as a plane or train can deliver the messenger. (Rates include travel fare, plus delivery expense.) Within the city, rates depend upon distance traveled (the city is divided into zones) and how long delivery takes. There are several Jiminy Split branches around the city.

KANGAROO COURIER
108 Lexington Ave (bet 27th and 28th St)
684-2233
Mon-Fri: 8-6 (scheduled services all the time)

Messenger services range from bicycle couriers to international shipping firms, and some of them are fly-by-night operations. (And I am not referring to the hours that they travel). We have personally run the gamut from rushing galleys between editors to having literally tons of books shipped cross-country. And I wish I could tell you that our experience has been wonderful. Suffice it to say that no previous edition ever recommended an all-around company until we met Michael Cohen of Kangaroo Courier. Part of the problem is that no company really does it all. If you are used to sending envelopes crosstown, then you are at sea on warehouse distribution cross-country. And so are the companies you usually deal with. Kangaroo's idea is that *all* shipping is in-house, and the same company oversees the entire job. Thus, Cohen boasts that he can do everything from a rush letter (delivery completed within an hour) to a 10,000 pound shipment and track the entire job. And to think that a mailed letter can take a week!

NOW VOYAGER
74 Varick St (suite 307)
431-1616
Mon-Fri: 12-5

Now Voyager runs an international courier service—and you can be a part of it. The firm has a schedule of flights to various areas, mostly Europe and South America, and you can go at a fraction of the regular fare if you have only carry-on luggage. Usually the flights are booked some weeks ahead, and it is a good idea to call or write as early as possible to see what might be available for you. Who knows, you might be able to take an exciting trip and save enough money to buy this book for all your relatives at Christmas!

Doll Repair

NEW YORK DOLL HOSPITAL
787 Lexington Ave (bet 61st and 62nd St, second floor)
838-7527
Mon-Sat: 10-6

The New York Doll Hospital has been fixing, mending, and restoring dolls to health since 1900. Owner Irving Chais has been operating in the cramped two-room hospital since 1947, when he took over from his grandfather, who had begun fixing the dolls of his clients' children in his hair salon. Originally, the children wanted the dolls' hair done along with theirs. When the senior Chais obliged by keeping a supply of doll wigs, he discovered that he had a better business with the dolls than with the women. So, he abandoned the ladies and created the "hospital." Irving Chais came into the business one Christmas season when his father was ailing and needed help. Several flipped wigs later, Chais was the latest family member in the business, despite a lack of formal training and medical credentials. So he learned by doing. By now he has replaced antique fingers, reconstructed China heads and German rag dolls, and authentically restored antique dolls. Additional services include appraisals, made-to-order dolls, and the buying or selling of antique dolls.

Dry Cleaners, Laundries

I haven't found a laundry that's open on Sunday, but I'm still looking. In the meantime, I recommend the following cleaners and laundries.

MME. BLANCHEVOYE
75 E 130th St
368-7272
Mon-Fri: 7-4:30
Because of the shop's location, most of Mme. Blanchevoye's customers prefer to use the pickup and delivery service. Mme. Blanchevoye offers hand laundering with exclusive hand finishing (actually, how could it be anything else?), and the specialty is the care and cleaning of fine and antique linens. The prices are on the high side, but at least Miss Evans (see "Laundry of Miss Evans") and Mme. Blanchevoye are competitive with each other—even though they share the same address.

CLEANTEX
2335 12th Ave (at 133rd St)
283-1200
Mon-Fri: 7-4
Cleantex specializes in drapery, slipcover, tapestry, and lampshade cleaning, with a free pickup and delivery service. It's an essential thing to offer, since no one would go to this location laden with heavy draperies and slipcovers. Their reputation is the best, and they count museums and churches among their customers.

HALLAK CLEANERS
1232 Second Ave (at 65th St)
879-4694
Mon-Fri: 7-6:30; Sat: 8-3; closed Sat in July, Aug
Hallak is a four-decade-old family business run by Joe Hallak and his sons, John-Claude and Joseph Jr., which probably accounts for the exceptional pride they take in personal service. Much of their work comes from referrals by designers of delicate fabrics and pat-

terns (like Georgio Armani, Valentino, and Courreges). In addition, they now have a shirt laundry and fine linen service. For those (like your author) who have trouble with salad dressing landing in the middle of a beautiful necktie, Hallak is the place to go for help. Their skilled work takes time, but they will give 24 hour emergency service.

LAUNDRY OF MISS EVANS
75 E 130th St
234-2334
Mon-Fri: 7-5; Sat: 8-4:30

As the name suggests, Miss Evans runs an establishment from a time gone by. Established in 1911, Miss Evans has hand-laundered and hand-ironed fine linens and clothing—with no markings—ever since. There are families whose heirloom linens are handed down from generation to generation, accompanied by Miss Evans' phone number. Since this plant is located in Harlem, Miss Evans picks up and delivers wherever the customers are. Prices are not cheap, but the best never is. I like the idea that *so* patrician is Miss Evans that its unmarked item is a status symbol.

LEATHERCRAFT PROCESS OF AMERICA
212 W 35th St
564-8980
Mon-Fri: 7:30-6:30

Leathercraft is all things to all suedes, sheepskins, and leathers. They will clean, redye, reline, repair, and lengthen or shorten any suede or leather garment brought in. That includes boots, gloves, clothing, and handbags, as well as odd leather items. Because leather is extremely difficult to clean, the process can be painfully expensive. However, Leathercraft has a reputation to maintain (it dates back to 1938), and their prices have remained competitive. It now shares space with Marvel Cleaners.

MIDNIGHT EXPRESS CLEANERS
921-0111
Mon-Sat: 9 a.m.-midnight

A special hint: put this number in a prominent spot near your phone. What a handy place to know about! It is 11 p.m. and you want some dry cleaning picked up? No problem. Midnight does dry cleaning, shirt laundry, luggage repair, leather and suede cleaning and repair, shoe and boot repair, and bulk laundry. Best of all (with a small minimum), they will pick up and deliver. Prompt return is assured.

MR. DRY CLEAN
92 Eighth Ave, 627-5980
181 Seventh Ave, 691-4313
Daily: 24 hours

Do you think you've seen everything in customer convenience? Well, here is another one to add to your list. This establishment has a unique service element built into the front of the building where the customer can place garments (or bedding and draperies) to be cleaned at any time of the day or night. Service is prompt, with items in by 10 in the morning available at 6:30 the same evening. Items put in the Mr. Dry Clean Machine on Sunday will be processed on Mondays. Very handy for the folks who go to work early, or want to leave their cleaning late in the evening.

TIECRAFTERS
116 E 27th St (at Park Ave S)
867-7676
Mon-Fri: 9-5

Old ties never die or even fade away here, although they may be dyed, widened, straightened, or cleaned. Tiecrafters is dedicated to the philosophy that a tie can live forever, and they provide the services to make that possible. In addition to converting tie widths, they will restore soiled or spotted ties and clean and repair all kinds of neckwear. Perhaps most impressive is Andy Tarshis' willingness to discuss tie maintenance so that frequent visits to the shop won't be necessary. Tiecrafters offers several pamphlets on the subject, including one that tells how to de-spot a tie at home. Tiecrafters accepts business via any carrier, and their charge for cleaning a tie is reasonable. They will make custom neckwear. HINT (for the gentlemen): *If you roll your tie at night, wrinkles will be gone in time for that important meeting in the morning.*

Electricians

MICHAEL ALTMAN
80 Fifth Ave
681-2900
Daily: 24 hours

Usually, electrical emergencies happen at the most inconvenient times, as we all know. What do you do if the electrical socket in your living room begins to smoke an hour before six guests are coming for dinner? Fortunately, Michael Altman's licensed crew will respond immediately with emergency service. They are available around the clock, every day of the year. This outfit will take care of everything from the smallest problem to the biggest wiring job, give free estimates, and are very reliable, having been in business for over half a century.

Exterminators

ACME EXTERMINATING
460 Ninth Ave (bet 35th and 36th St)
594-9230
Mon-Fri: 7-5

Are you bugged? I'm referring to the type that crawls and causes all those screams when you open the kitchen closet. Well, Acme is expert at debugging a private home, office, store, museum, hospital, whatever. Acme is state-of-the-art in pest control.

Eyeglasses Repair

DELL AND DELL
19 W 44th St (at Fifth Ave)
575-1686
Mon-Fri: 9-6; Sat: 9-1
July, Aug: Mon-Fri: 9-5:30; closed Sat

If you desperately need Dell and Dell, you probably can't read this. But no need to worry. Their big advantage is that they do on-the-spot emergency repair on glasses even if they were purchased in Peoria. There are some exceptions (if the frames were trampled by an elephant, there might be a longer wait), but this is the place to go for eyeglasses emergencies in the city. They also repair binoculars. Of course, Dell and Dell won't mind if you stop by for regular optical needs.

Fashion Schools

FASHION INSTITUTE OF TECHNOLOGY
Seventh Ave at 27th St
760-7654 (placement), 760-7675 (admission)

F.I.T. has assumed the position as the world's premier institute serving the fashion industry. The school was founded more than 40 years ago, and includes a graduate roster that reads like "who's who" in the fashion world (Jhane Barnes, Calvin Klein, Norma Kamali are just a few). The school offers a multitude of majors like accessories, advertising, display and exhibit, fur, toy, jewelry, interior, textile and fashion design, illustration, photography, fine arts, fashion buying and merchandising, apparel production management, pattern making and marketing. F.I.T. maintains a student placement service, which will match students' majors in the above fields with people looking for their talents. All students are of top caliber, as they accept only about one-quarter of the applicants. The Edward C. Blum Design Laboratory is the world's largest repository of the history of fashion with over one million articles of clothing. It is open to the public as are the galleries at F.I.T. Call 760-7848 for information about current exhibits and shows.

TOBÉ-COBURN SCHOOL FOR FASHION CAREERS
686 Broadway (bet Fourth and Great Jones St)
460-9600
Mon-Fri: 8:30-5:30; Sat: 10-3

Tobé Coller Davis and Julia Coburn were two of the top names in the fashion industry when they jointly founded the Tobé-Coburn school in 1937 as a training ground for careers in fashion marketing and management. Tobé was a personal friend of mine, and I had the privilege of attending many of her spectacular fashion clinics when I was in the retail business. And what a treat it was to visit with her at her brownstone apartment. She was an incredible person! Today, Ann Wareham and her crew are keeping up the outstanding professional reputation of the great lady. Tobé-Coburn students receive an intensive two-year course in all aspects of the garment industry. Even the liberal-arts courses are oriented to industry application. Universal business-skills courses stress advertising and public-relations writing, and the history courses deal with the history of retailing and merchandising, as well as fashion trends. Over the years, the school has established a better than 95 percent placement record and a reputation as one of the best schools for training in the merchandising, marketing, and management aspects of fashion. The school has co-op programs and internships with the top names in the business, and when the students graduate, they know the city as well as they know the inside of Seventh Avenue. When these people talk fashion, they mean business!

Formal Wear Rental and Sales

A. T. HARRIS
47 E 44th St (bet Madison and Vanderbilt Ave,
second floor)
682-6325
Mon, Tues, Wed, Fri: 8:30-6; Thurs: 8:30-7;
Sat: 10-4 by appointment

A. T. Harris has been in the business of outfitting gentlemen correctly since 1892. This store sells and rents only current formal wear "of the better kind." You will find proper cutaways, tails, and tuxedos rather than iridescent disco wedding outfits. Shoes and accessories run in the same categories and are also readily available. The cut is decidedly English. In addition to imported shirts, Chesterfield top coats, stud and cuff-link sets, and kid and suede gloves, Harris completes the outfit by owning and renting their own Rolls Royce Silver Spur. They not only dress you in style, they make sure you get there in style. A class act!

BALDWIN FORMALS
52 W 56th St (bet Fifth and Sixth Ave)
245-8190, 246-1782
Mon, Thurs: 8:30-7; Tues, Wed, Fri: 8:30-6; Sat: 10-4

If you are suddenly called to a state dinner at the White House, one call to Baldwin will take care of all the dressing details. These folks rent and sell all types of formal attire, suits, overcoats, top hats, shoes, and everything in between. There is free pickup and delivery to many midtown addresses, and a slight charge for other addresses. Same-day service is guaranteed for orders received by early afternoon.

Fur Rental

ABET RENT-A-FUR
231 W 29th St (#304) (bet Seventh and Eighth Ave)
268-6225
Mon-Fri: 9:30-5:30; Sat: 11-3; closed Sat in summer

Abet is one of the few places in the country that operates a fur rental business on a full-time basis. Beautiful fur coats, capes, jackets and stoles are all available for your grand entrance or for that special occasion. Many of the furs that you see on television commercials have come from this shop, which numbers its satisfied customers in legions. Irving Shavelson, the man behind Abet, is taking life a bit easier now, but is still available from time-to-time for his old friends and customers.

Furniture Rental

APARTMENT FURNITURE RENTALS
711 Third Ave (bet 44th and 45th St)
867-2800
Mon-Sat: 9-5:45

Apartment Furniture Rentals can provide furnishings for a single room, apartment, or office. They have recently expanded, so they can show accessories as well, including housewares and bed and bath packages for rent or purchase. An apartment locator service is available. Delivery and setup can be done within 48 hours, and a free professional decorator service is available. Their purchase plan offers the customer the opportunity to make payments toward buying while renting.

CHURCHILL-WINCHESTER FURNITURE RENTALS
44 E 32nd St (at Park Ave)
686-0444
Mon-Thurs: 10:30-7; Fri: 10:30-5; Sun: 11-5

Say Churchill, and you think of staid old England, right? Well, *this* Churchill is starkly contemporary. It can fill any size order for business or residence, and offers free interior-decorating advice and a lease-purchase plan. Churchill has several floors of furniture, so a customer can simply select whatever is needed from stock or borrow from the loaner program until special orders are processed. Churchill can also offer a comprehensive package, including housewares and appliances if needed, and it specializes in executive locations (again, both corporately and personally). They will rent out anything from a single chair to entire homes and have done so for sports-team managers, executives on temporary assignment, and actors on short-term contracts. If modern is the look, Churchill should be the choice.

INTERNATIONAL FURNITURE RENTALS
345 Park Ave (at 51st St)
421-0340
Mon-Fri: 9-5:30; Sat: 10-2

International Furniture Rentals has a small showroom, but claims to be the largest home and office furniture rental firm in the metropolitan area. The quality is very good—the kind of furniture you might actually buy yourself. There's no decorating service, but that's not a great loss since rental agencies seldom excel in the decorating area, anyway.

Furniture Repair and Restoration

ANTIQUE FURNITURE WORKROOM
225 E 24th St (at Third Ave)
683-0551
Mon-Fri: 8-4

William Olsen took over what may have been the definitive antiques-restoration firm in the city and made it even better. Antique Furniture Workroom was the traditional place of choice for French polishing, chair repair, and the restoration of woodwork. Olsen added services that were decidedly lacking, including antique-furniture restoration (with a specialty in American, English, Continental, and Oriental originals), fine French polishing, gold leafing, and caning. The cost of an antiques-restoration project is steep.

However, Olsen's company has two big advantages. One is that they are reliable. Many an antique has lost all value after "help" from a restorer who didn't know what he was doing. The other plus is that estimates are given in the home.

MAX SCHNEIDER AND SON ANTIQUES
225 E 24th St
684-0980
Mon-Fri: 8-noon, 1-4 by appointment

Max Schneider is a family-run business that has restored New York's finest furniture for almost six decades. Certain trades seem to have family traits, and being selective about whom they will accept for customers appears to be the trait of quality furniture restorers. At Schneider, too, an appointment to view the furniture must be made and kept before they will deign to think about doing the actual work. But chances are better that the work will be accepted here because they are not restricted by period, time, or even original quality. In fact, they are not even restricted to wood; they do upholstery, wicker work, and even chair caning. If the dining room chair needs a face-lift to fit your latest decorating motif, this is the place that can do it.

SACK CONSERVATION COMPANY
15 E 57th St (at Madison Ave)
753-6562
Mon-Fri: 9:30-5; Sat: 10-3; closed Sat in July, Aug

This is a class act, and Sack is the proprietor's name rather than the kind of furniture he handles. Rumor has it that among those clients whose furniture has been deemed worthy of Sack's attention have been the White House and countless museums. So, if your favorite sofa is valuable enough for such exclusive attention, this is the place. The firm deals only in 17th and 18th century American Colonial furniture. The work is first-rate, and not inexpensive.

Haircuts

Children

KENNETH FOR KIDS
Macy's (at 34th St and Broadway, fifth floor)
594-1717
Sun: 10-5

Kenneth did Jackie O's hair when she was Jackie K., and for a reasonable fee (by New York standards), this salon inside Macy's will give your child's hair the Kenneth touch, too. Actually, the salon is the showpiece of the Macy's children floor, and you can bet your pogo stick it is well done.

MICHAELS' CHILDREN'S HAIRCUTTING SALON
1263 Madison Ave (at 90th St)
289-9612
Mon-Sat: 9-5; closed Sat in July, Aug

A longtime New York tradition, Michael's drawing card has always been their rapport with children and the consistency of their personnel and style. Nick Di Sisto, the salon's owner, is living proof of this. He worked for Michael for years, and when Michael retired, Sisto bought him out. Many of the hairstylists have worked under both owners. Appointments are unheard of, and lollipops, seats shaped like toy cars, and comic books are *de rigueur*. This place is totally dedicated to children, but there is a sprinkling of mothers who get their hair cut at children's prices.

SHOOTING STAR AT F.A.O. SCHWARZ
767 Fifth Ave (at 58th St)
644-9400
Mon-Sat: 10-6; Sun: 12-5

Reflecting its location, this is a children's hair salon, not a barber shop. Coming to F.A.O. Schwarz for something as ordinary as a barber shop? Never. This is a full-service salon that will make Junior and his sister even more irresistible, with treatments, professional advice, and the latest cuts. And please, don't refer to their personnel as barbers! They suggest waiting until a child is 15 months old for his first cut (Dad will probably do it sooner), and a good cut should last 6-8 weeks.

Family

ASTOR PLACE HAIR STYLISTS
2 Astor Pl (at Broadway)
475-9854
Mon-Sat: 8-8; Sun: 9-6

Astor Place doesn't need its address listed here. Just follow the mob to the spot in Manhattan where getting a haircut is an *event* not unlike being admitted to the hallowed halls of the latest "in" nightspot. The personnel inside what was once a modest neighborhood barbershop don't even have to actually *do* anything to generate the crowds. But they do give the trendiest, wildest, and most unusual haircuts on the scene. The real reason to stand on the sidewalk is to see and be seen. How did this all get started? Well, it seems that the

Vezza brothers inherited a barbershop from their father in the East Village at a time "when not even cops were getting haircuts." Enrico took note of the newly gentrified neighborhood's young trendies and their sleek haircuts and changed the name of the shop to "Hair Stylists." Now, the shop is staffed with a resident manager, doorman (how many barbershops need a doorman?), a loft, and an ever-increasing number of barbers. A haircut at this unique barbershop may also be one of the cheapest, most fun-filled souvenirs the city has to offer.

ATLAS BARBER SCHOOL
32 Third Ave
475-1360
Mon-Fri: 9-9; Sat: 9-6

Atlas is the only barber school in the city. Haircuts here are as cheap as they come, and senior students, under close supervision, work on customers. Custom grooming it's not, but for the price it's excellent.

PAUL MOLE FAMILY BARBERSHOP
144 E 74th St (at Lexington Ave)
535-8461
Mon-Sat: 8-7

Paul Mole is a find. This barbershop does a super job on kids' haircuts without super price tags. During holidays, Saturdays, and after school, the place is jammed, so appointments are suggested. If you want to wait even longer, pass the word along!

Men

FEATURE TRIM
1108 Lexington Ave (bet 77th and 78th St)
650-9746
Tues-Fri: 10:30-7; Sat: 9-7

Salvatore Andenocci started cutting hair when he was 12 years old. For 24 years, he cut hair in a shop in the East Sixties, but some years ago, escalating rent forced him to move further uptown. His clientele followed him, and for the last decade, he has operated a seven-chair shop at the Lexington Avenue location. All those years have given Andenocci expertise aplenty. He specializes in simple haircuts that need nothing more than a combing until the next trim. And despite a clientele that includes scores of prominent businessmen, politicians, and "that sportscaster, what's his name?", Feature Trim is still reasonably priced and fairly unknown. Andenocci and his assistants offer five basic cuts. All follow the natural no-mess-no-fuss edict.

Feature Trim was once named the top haircutting shop in the country by the now defunct *New York Herald Tribune*. As the hair-care ad says, "He's not getting older—he's getting better."

JOHN ALLAN'S MEN'S CLUB
54 Stone St (at Pearl St)
422-3686
Mon-Fri: 8-7

If you have an important interview, or just feel that it's time to be pampered a bit, John Allan's is the place to visit. In comfortable, clean, and spacious surroundings you can have your hair cut, get a manicure, have your shoes polished, enjoy valet service, and even play a game of billiards. There is a bar to help pass the time of day, and the operators indicate that massage service will be available also. This is a classy operation, but prices are very reasonable.

PEPPE AND BILL
Plaza Hotel (Fifth Ave and 59th St)
751-8380
Mon-Sat: 9-6

Fine hair styling for men is available at Peppe and Bills, with prices that would make your hometown barber gasp. But you get the very best treatment—with skilled personnel—whether you come for a haircut, manicure, pedicure, or facial. Marie, who has been at the shop forever, will set up an appointment for you with Peppe or Bill themselves, or with a very talented stylist by the name of Jacques, who just happens to be her husband!

Health Clubs

Health clubs open and close in Manhattan almost as rapidly as Broadway shows. With the great interest in fitness, there are all kinds of clubs, gyms, fitness trainers, and classes available throughout the city. Prices and facilities vary, and for those who live in the city the best plan is to watch for special introductory offers. For the visitor, many of the places listed below will honor reciprocal memberships, while others will charge a reasonable fee for a day or a week's use of their facilities. A few of the major hotels (**Peninsula, Vista International, United Nations Plaza, Parker Meridien**) have excellent facilities. The **New York Health and Racquet Club** locations scattered throughout the city provide probably the most complete equipment and programs for the money. For private fitness training, call Ron Filippi at 753-9700, extension 24. No one is better qualified to help you build that new physique.

Downtown

New York Health and Racquet Club (39 Whitehall St, 269-9800; and 24 E 13th St, 924-4600)

Executive Fitness Center, Vista International Hotel (466-9266)

Apple Health and Sports Club (88 Fulton St, 227-7450; and 211 Thompson St, 777-4890)

Broadway Fitness Center (626 Broadway, 475-5030)

Midtown

Apple Health and Sports Club (321 E 22nd St, 673-3730)

Park Avenue Fitness Center (3 Park Ave, 686-1085)

Madison Avenue Muscle (244 Madison Ave, 687-8196)

Manhattan Sports Club (335 Madison Ave, 983-5320; and 50th St and Eighth Ave, 265-9400)

Vanderbilt YMCA (224 E 47th St, 755-2410) and **YWCA** (610 Lexington Ave, 735-9755)

New York Health and Racquet Club (132 E 45th St, 986-3100; 20 E 50th St, 593-1500; and 110 W 56th St, 541-7200)

Club La Raquette, Parker Meridien Hotel (119 W 56th St, 245-1144)

Upper East Side

The Vertical Club (330 E 61st St, 355-5100) Very classy.

New York Health and Racquet Club (1433 York Ave, 737-6666)

Apple Health and Sports Club (1438 Third Ave, 879-5400)

92nd Street Y (1395 Lexington Ave, 427-6000)

Upper West Side

Lincoln Racquet and Fitness Club (61 W 62nd St, 265-0995)

West Side YMCA (5 W 63rd St, 787-4400)

Paris Health Club (752 West End Ave, 749-3500)

Help for Hire

ACCURATE HOUSE AND WINDOW CLEANING
230 E 93rd St
876-1000
Mon-Fri: 8:30-4:30

Lou Marchesi, Accurate's guiding spirit, is a stickler for "complete house cleaning" and operates a spic-and-span operation. No request surprises him, and his staff will tackle almost any cleaning problem, including the all-time New York impossibility—windows. What is best about Accurate is their attitude. They don't come on as if they are doing you the biggest favor in the world by handling your dirt. Marchesi offers a free advisory service that covers not only what services are needed, but the proper way to do them. Moreover, Accurate is capable of repairing the cleaning errors of others, be they amateur or professional, as well as handling the big cleaning jobs that should be done several times a year. All workers are bonded and insured, and Marchesi vouches for their work.

COLUMBIA BARTENDING AGENCY
280-4535
Mon-Fri: 9-5

The Columbia Bartending Agency uses students so apt at bartending that one wonders what profession they could possibly do as well after college. The service has been around a long time, and there is none better. Columbia also supplies waiters, waitresses, and hat checkers.

DIRTBUSTERS OF CLOSETS AND SPACES
111 W 16th St (bet Sixth and Seventh Ave)
242-2071
Mon-Sat: anytime

Many a New York mother has probably had the thought at one time or another that the quickest way to strike it rich in New York would be to go into the procurement business, particularly the procurement of house-cleaning and child-care help. David Eason is not a New York mother, but he is a New York businessman who, while running a closet- and apartment-design shop called Closets and Spaces, reached the same conclusion. And so, Dirtbusters was born. Eason organized a corps of workers who clean apartments and residences for flat rates, usually two people working in three-hour sessions. But his staff, hours, and rates are flexible. Dirtbusters are bonded, and the service entitles clients to Eason's newsletters, which are models of his strict guidelines. Taking his cue from customer feedback and staff meetings, Eason now offers dog walking, servicemen recommendations, an advertising directory, floor waxing, party servers and cleaners, painters, floor sanders, a homemakers service for new mothers and invalids, and singing telegrams. But no, they don't do windows. What did you expect? Perfection?

EASY HOUSEKEEPING SERVICE
4898 Broadway
569-9200
Mon-Fri: 8-5:30

One day, John and Eleanor Ford of Ford Piano Supply were offered the Easy Housekeeping business previously owned by one of their neighbors. They barely knew the proper way to dust a piano, but when they realized that a dozen or so people relied upon Easy Housekeeping for steady employment, they decided to give it a try rather than leave their neighbor's employees stranded. That happened so long ago that John Ford can't give an exact date. The business has remained a small, friendly organization, where people come before profits, particularly since the Fords have never had much interest in Easy Housekeeping other than to keep the people who depend on it happy. The entire staff numbers less than 20, and the Fords know all of them personally. Most of the staff does day work and housekeeping, but party help can be obtained with a day's notice and a four-hour minimum.

LYNN AGENCY
2067 Broadway (bet 71st and 72nd St)
874-6130
Mon-Fri: 9-5

The great part of Lynn is that they are keeping up with current needs. They have just developed a new division called "child-care system" which is on-site customized child-care programs for conventions, corporate facilities, meetings, and hotels. They are a full-service agency, and can supply baby nurses, bartenders, butlers, chauffeurs, cooks, companions, couples, governesses, maids, nursing aides, and housekeepers. There is also a party-planning service: the agency can supply help for any kind of function, from a small dinner party to a formal corporate affair. The owners claim that Lynn's biggest virtue is its ability to mold its service to clients' needs. They will serve outside Manhattan, their rates are reasonable, and their personnel are reliable.

McMAID AT THE SAVOY
200 E 61st St
371-5555
Daily: 24 hours

McMaid's biggest virtue is that they are on call any time. Of course, a call for a housekeeper at three a.m. Thanksgiving morning may not be greeted with an instant (or even polite) response, but McMaid can produce help in a remarkably short time. But they prefer to be known as a source for other than last-minute clean-ups. Indeed, they provide the standard maids, waiters, and bartenders and are thoroughly insured and bonded. But still, it's hard to ignore that initial virtue, despite McMaid's policy of payment by cash. And even that, given enough notice and patronage, can be waived.

PAVILLION AGENCY
15 E 40th St
889-6609
Mon-Fri: 9-5

This is the agency that the rich and famous in the city turn to for domestic help. Their client roster reads like the financial and society pages of the newspapers. Pavillion supplies cooks, butlers, major-domos, nannies, and domestics to the elite. What's amazing is that the business, which has placed help with Bob Guccione, Bette Davis, Richard Nixon, Harry Helmsley, Carl Icahn, Doris Duke, and Steven Ross, among others, is run by three brothers under the age of 30 who bought out their father's business less than 10 years ago. Each brother specializes in one area: Cliff Greenhouse, for example, specializes in placing nannies (about a third of the business), while older brothers Glenn and Keith Greenhouse provide the butlers and domestic help. The most amazing thing is that they have become the definitive upscale agency in so short a period of time.

SABER'S HARDWARE ARNESTO
15 Avenue A (bet First and Second St)
473-6050, 473-6977
Mon-Fri: 9-6; Sat: 9-5

Marian Burros of *The New York Times* (and a good friend as well) recommends Saber's for general handiwork, bathroom fixtures, and particularly the installation of things like shower doors. She claims they are capable, efficient, and reasonable. Saber's, in turn, claims that Marian's is but one of the many uptown households and stores that use its services. The store is a general housewares emporium with an emphasis on kitchen and bathroom fixtures. Ceramic tile, medicine cabinets, shower doors, kitchen cabinets, and hardware are house specialties. And they can install all of these items. It also has a good display of gates and locks. But where Saber's really shines is in service; as their motto says: "We hang the impossible." Mirrors and shower doors are a matter of course, locksmith emergencies are answered routinely, and they even stock and hang drapery hardware. Regular customers (and it isn't hard to become one) can get Saber's to do almost any kind of handiwork. And in this city—or perhaps this century—that's rare indeed. Think of Saber's, despite its location, as the city's general store and all-around handyman. Tell them Marian Burros sent you.

Hotels

A Few Hotel Hints

1. The message-taking service at many hotels leaves much to be desired. You can be transferred from one person to another indefi-

nitely. In the commercial hotels, it is best to check to be sure your message has been left. Also, check carefully to make sure there isn't a message waiting for you at the desk; the room telephone lights don't always work.

2. Be sure to check on the telephone charges at your hotel. In some cases, there are highly inflated fees for both local and long distance calls. It is too late to complain when your bill is presented.

3. When making reservations, check the rates offered from several different sources. Travel agents, in most cases, provide the lowest prices and the best service. Direct booking to a hotel is the next best option. There can be substantial savings if you ask about special deals or packages for certain days or dates.

4. Important things to look for in a hotel: in-room adjustable thermostat, good reading light, quality towels, comfortable in-room sitting area, on-site coffee shop/snack bar, on-site self-parking (a rarity in Manhattan), comprehensive visitor information, convenient ice machine, rooms for non-smokers, baggage storage after check-out, and alarm clock or clock radio.

5. It is a good idea for you to *keep* your key with you during your stay.

6. Check the price lists on laundry and pressing before you order the service.

ALGONQUIN
59 W 44th St (bet Fifth and Sixth Ave)
840-6800
Moderate

The Algonquin is truly a legend in the city. But years of neglect have not been helpful to this grand old lady, and things have become a bit shabby. Now this home of the famous Round Table, where Dorothy Parker, Harold Ross, Robert Benchley, and others sparred, is getting a much-needed refurbishing, bringing back the 1900 décor. There are only 165 rooms, so the atmosphere is intimate and friendly. The lobby and the lounge, complete with a cabaret, are good places for people watching.

BEVERLY
Lexington Ave at 50th St
753-2700
Moderate

You can tell in a minute that this is a family-owned and family-operated residence. Tastefully furnished and well-kept, the Beverly has the atmosphere of a small European hotel. It has a number of very attractive suites with fully equipped kitchenettes. They're ideal for entertaining, and a businessman can easily use his room as an office during his stay. The location is also convenient.

DORAL COURT
130 E 39th St (bet Park and Lexington Ave)
685-1100, 800-624-0607
Moderate

For those having business in the garment district or visiting the United Nations, the Doral Court's location in Murray Hill is excellent. For weekend visitors, free parking is a decided advantage. 24-hour room service, dressing alcoves, and 25" color TVs are special amenities. A fitness center is close at hand, and an all-day dining facility—the Courtyard Cafe—is a pleasant spot for relaxation. A young and enthusiastic staff is rightfully proud of the better-than-average-sized rooms and the well-done suites, some with balconies. All suites have walk-in kitchens and completely stocked pantries.

DORAL TUSCANY
120 E 39th St
686-1600
Moderate

The Tuscany has a fine reputation for service, with the personal attention only a small hotel can offer. Large rooms, personal exercycles, free overnight shoe-shine service, and refrigerators stocked with complimentary beverages add to the attractiveness of this well-located midtown hotel. The in-house "Time and Again" restaurant provides excellent meals. Kids under 12 stay free in their parents' room. Guests here can enjoy newly renovated rooms at a sensible price in comfortable and safe surroundings.

ESSEX HOUSE
160 Central Park S
247-0300
Moderate to expensive

The view of Central Park is first-rate, and so is the treatment you get at this nicely appointed and well-run hotel. A two-year, $58 million modernization program is now under way. When finished, the hotel will boast a new lobby, completely redone rooms and baths (all with marble), and new restaurant facilities. The business center on the second floor offers special services for the business traveler. A weekday complimentary limo service to Wall Street is also provided.

The luxurious Essex Towers, on the upper floors, have accommodations for permanent guests. An outstanding training program is a feature of this hotel, with all personnel going out of their way to make the guest feel at home.

GRAND BAY
Equitable Center, 152 W 51st St
765-1900
Expensive

Another new upscale resting place for those with expense accounts. A multilingual staff, concierges on every floor, and an electronic paging system are just a few of the special features. For those who don't want to worry about unpacking those wrinkled clothes, or packing up the dirty laundry later on, there is even a personalized valet service. The lobby radiates big bucks with imported marble, oriental carpets, and fine art work. Beautifully appointed executive board rooms are available for meetings, and marble bathrooms and two multi-line telephones are available in the guest rooms and 52 suites.

GRAND HYATT
42nd St at the Grand Central Terminal
883-1234, 800-228-9000
Moderate to expensive

The gleaming glass-and-aluminum exterior of the Grand Hyatt is as cheerfully extravagant as the set of a Broadway musical, and the spacious lobby carries out the theme. A waterfall greets you as you enter. This kind of glossy grandeur isn't for those who like hotels with thick Persian rugs and antique furniture, but if you prefer space to ambiance, it's for you. The least expensive room is larger than those in comparably priced hotels. For a few dollars more, you can also get a sitting room that gives you enough space to host a small cocktail party. The top-of-the-line deal is the Regency Club. Amenities include complimentary continental breakfast, wall-mounted hair dryers, and terrycloth robes. The Grand Hyatt provides a babysitting service. There are also 32 rooms for handicapped guests. The security is top-notch. Guards are everywhere, keeping an unobtrusive eye on things, and an employee told me that every applicant for a Grand Hyatt job is carefully screened and given a polygraph test. Their Sunday brunch is one of the best in the city, and a hot buffet breakfast is available on weekdays. Many of the employees are part-time theatrical personnel. The hotel's Trumpets Restaurant is a superb place to dine in truly "grand" style.

HELMSLEY PALACE
455 Madison Ave (at 51st St)
888-7000
Expensive

You've probably heard of the Helmsley Palace Hotel, located close to Saks Fifth Avenue, one block off of Fifth Avenue itself. It's enchanting in the evening! The public rooms are exceptionally attractive, encompassing the 100-year-old Villard Mansion, one of New York's legendary landmarks. The Villard House used to be the chancery office of the archdiocese of New York. There are no convention facilities here, although there are meeting rooms available. The Helmsley Palace has several hundred apartments and suites, and even some triplex apartments. The glamorous ads for this hotel boast that they "don't hire people who have to be told to be nice," but it takes more than expensive promotion to have a truly friendly establishment. Leona, take note!

HERALD SQUARE HOTEL
19 W 31st St
279-4017
Inexpensive to moderate

The Herald Square Hotel was built in 1893 as the home of the original *Life* magazine. It has undergone numerous renovations through the years, culminating in its rebirth today as a limited-service, budget hotel. Some original covers of *Life* magazine have been reproduced and are displayed in various parts of the hotel. Rooms with shared bathrooms are a real bargain, and large double rooms that will take care of up to four people, rent for less than most midtown single accommodations. All rooms have color TV and air conditioning, plus a good dose of nostalgia that will make up for the lack of chocolates on the pillow and almond cream shampoo in the bathroom.

LEO HOUSE
332 W 23rd St
929-1010
Inexpensive
Cash only

This is the answer to one of the major questions people ask when visiting New York: Where can I find a really inexpensive, safe, and clean place to stay in the city? You should have no qualms about the Leo House. This residence is a Catholic hospice; a secure, refined, quiet place still run by some Sisters of St. Agnes. Reservations are taken no more than one month ahead of the date required. All guests are expected to follow very reasonable house rules. A small non-refundable deposit is required, and the maximum length of stay is two weeks. No smoking is allowed in guest and meeting rooms, and although the outside doors are locked at midnight, registered guests may still get in after that hour. Breakfast, featuring homemade bread, is available at a moderate price. A great place for the single student!

LOWELL
28 E 63rd St
838-1400
Moderate to expensive

With a convenient Upper East Side location and the added attraction of a good restaurant inside (Post House), this small dignified hotel is a charmer. Although its art deco entrance might give another impression, the accommodations are comfortable and homey. Most of the rooms have private serving pantries, wood-burning fireplaces, built-in bookshelves, and even terraces. The Pembroke Room is wonderful for tea. For the shopping enthusiast, this is a perfect place to use as a base for your expeditions.

MANHATTAN EAST SUITES

Beekman Tower
3 Mitchell Pl (at 49th and
    First Ave)
355-7300

Plaza Fifty
155 E 50th St
751-5710

Eastgate Tower
222 E 39th St
687-8000

Shelburne Murray Hill
    (at 37th and 38th St)
303 Lexington Ave
689-5200

Lyden Gardens
215 E 64th St
355-1230

Southgate Tower
371 Seventh Ave (at 31st St)
563-1800

Lyden House
320 E 53rd St
888-6070

Surrey Hotel
20 E 76th St
288-3700

Dumont Plaza
150 E 34th St
481-7600

Moderate

These all-suite hotels are among the nicest, most reasonably priced and conveniently located in New York. Each hotel features 24-hour attendants, and there are modern kitchens in every apartment. Suites of one, two, and three bedrooms are available at very attractive monthly rates. There are nearly 2,000 suites in all. These are particularly convenient accommodations for long-term corporate visitors and traveling families. Families can economize by putting kids on the pull-out couches and by using the fully equipped kitchens. Women like these accommodations when they must travel and dine alone. A great buy!

MARRIOTT MARQUIS
1535 Broadway
398-1900
Moderate to moderately expensive

The opening of this magnificent showplace in the center of Times Square in the summer of 1985 represented a major step in the rejuvenation of the area. Along with over 1800 rooms, huge meeting-and-convention facilities, and the largest hotel atrium in the world, guests can enjoy a 700-seat, three-story revolving restaurant and lounge at the top of the 50-story hotel, a revolving lounge overlooking Broadway on the eighth floor, a legitimate Broadway theater on the premises, a fully equipped health club, suites with walk-in wet bars and refrigerators, oversized rooms, and a sky lounge. There are nine restaurants and lounges in all. A concierge level offers special amenities, including 24-hour room service. All rooms overlook Manhattan on the exterior and open directly to the atrium on the interior. One word describes this hotel: spectacular.

MILFORD PLAZA
270 W 45th St (bet Seventh and Eighth Ave)
869-3600, 800-221-2690
Inexpensive to moderate

Value is the key word here. The Milford Plaza, a Best Western operation that's located at the edge of the theater district in midtown Manhattan, offers extraordinarily reasonable rates that are partially offset by its location. But the hotel has extremely tight security, which lessens the need to be concerned. Rooms are small yet very clean, late-night dining is available, and very attractive rates are available on weekends and for groups.

MORGANS
237 Madison Ave (at 37th St)
686-0300, 800-334-3408
Moderate

If a downtown location and a "boutique" atmosphere are what you're looking for, this new hotel is it. Formerly the Executive Hotel,

Morgans has been completely redone by a French designer, and the result is calm, comfort, and convenience. Twenty-four-hour room service is available, and room rates include breakfast. There is a stereo cassette system in all rooms.

PARKER MERIDIEN
119 W 56th St (at Sixth Ave)
245-5000
Expensive

This is a classic French beauty in midtown, complete with an in-house movie system and a health club with courts, track, and rooftop swimming pool. The rooms are very attractive, the service has a European flair, and the lobby and restaurants are elegant.

PENINSULA
700 Fifth Ave (at 55th St)
247-2220
Expensive

In Hong Kong, the name Peninsula is synonymous with quality. Now this respected hotel group has established a flagship on Fifth Avenue in New York. The recently remodeled rooms are done in Art Nouveau style and feature king-sized marble bathrooms. The hotel has several excellent eating places, and the lounge serves afternoon tea and goodies. But the big plus here is the tri-level, glass-enclosed fitness center with a superb view and swimming pool (a rarity in Manhattan). For physical fitness buffs, this would surely be a best bet.

PICKWICK ARMS
230 E 51st St
355-0300
Inexpensive to moderate

If a good midtown location with low rates and clean—not fancy—accommodations is what you're looking for, this is a good spot. The rooms are small, but perfectly adequate. Groups and large families will save some money here.

PIERRE
2 E 61st St (at Fifth Ave)
838-8000
Expensive

As a Four Seasons operation, you would expect top quality and that is exactly what you get. The Pierre is quiet, modest, luxurious, and expensive. There are a number of beautiful suites, excellent meeting and banquet facilities, and a three to one staff/guest ratio. A number of the rooms and suites are part of a residential co-op building. Even if you don't stay here, a meal in the elegant Cafe Pierre or tea in the Rotunda is a special experience.

PLAZA
Fifth Ave and Central Park S
759-3000
Expensive

If there is one hotel in New York that captures the charm and grace of this great city, it is the Plaza. Now a historic landmark, this gracious old lady has been through decades of glamour, excitement, and, unfortunately, neglect. In recent years, over $100 million was spent in bringing the fabulous building back to top shape, with new furnishings, modern heating and plumbing, and restoration of the public facilities. Then, the magic of the new owners, Ivana and Donald Trump, began to permeate every nook and cranny of this most strategically located building in Manhattan (right on the corner of Fifth Avenue and Central Park). The result is a gorgeous matron with a world-class face-lift. Spectacular flowers greet guests in the lobbies, chandeliers from the "good old days" glisten in the legendary Palm Court, supercourteous bellmen handle bags and guests alike with white glove attention, rooms have king-sized fluffy towels and other guest-pampering amenities, operators call you by name as you take advantage of 24-hour room service, horse-drawn carriages await you at the front door, and the Plaza's most famous inhabitant (Eloise, of course) looks over every hallway to ensure that there isn't a spot of dust or a dirty tray in sight. It's not inexpensive to luxuriate in this grand dame of hotels, but a night or a week being spoiled and pampered by the famous Trump class and attention to detail is surely worth it! And don't miss the Sunday buffet in the expanded area of the Palm Court and Terrace Room; this is a meal memories are made of.

PLAZA ATHÉNÉE
37 E 64th St
734-9100
Expensive

For some, the Plaza Athénée is *the* place to stay in Paris. Now those folks can try its New York sister hotel, a reconstruction job of an older hotel done with considerable good taste. The lobby is intimate and attractive. The rooms are nicely furnished with pantry, individual wet bar, and two lines on each phone. The suites on higher floors provide solariums and roof terraces. Le Régence restaurant is first-class. If price is no object, but service is very important, then you should consider this hotel for your next stay.

ROGER WILLIAMS
28 E 31st St
684-7500
Inexpensive

This may well be one of the better buys in Manhattan. Located in the respectable Murray Hill district at 31st and Madison, the Roger Williams offers kitchenettes—with a small refrigerator, a gas stove, and cabinets—in every room. There is full phone service, adequate security, good eating facilities, and a family plan for kids. At the prices here, don't expect luxury. But this old-time building has been well maintained, and for those staying a week or more the savings will allow you to splurge at some of those great New York restaurants.

ROYALTON
44 W 44th St
869-4400
Moderate to moderately expensive

Run by the same people as Morgans, the Royalton is an 80-year-old hotel that's been reborn (after three years of renovation) into a high-tech facility. It's sure to appeal to some modern travelers. A French designer has created stark rooms, furnished with low beds, VCRs, and finished with mahogany accents. Many of the rooms have working fireplaces, and the bathrooms are king-sized and very attractive. China Grill operates a lobby restaurant, and an attractive "private bar" is available near the hotel entrance. Ugly, black uniforms don't seem to deter the helpful staff, who offer 24-hour room service and will gladly change pieces of art in each of the bedrooms.

SALISBURY
123 E 57th St
246-1300
Moderate

The Salisbury is clean and intimate, with just over 300 rooms. Most of them have been newly redecorated, and many are outfitted with butler's pantries and refrigerators. Suites are large, comfortable, and reasonably priced. This is a favorite place for lady travelers. Bill Dadukian, the president, is one of the most accommodating guys in New York; he and his courteous staff will make you feel right at home. If you want to be in the vicinity of Carnegie Hall and other midtown attractions, this hotel is for you. For those who wait until the last minute for reservations, this is a good place to call as the Salisbury is not too well-known to out-of-towners, and rooms are usually available. There is a cafe just off the lobby, and rooms are available for meetings and banquets.

SHERATON CENTRE
811 Seventh Ave (at 52nd St)
581-1000
Moderate to moderately expensive

A great location, a nationwide referral service, newly appointed guest rooms, and a wide selection of restaurants and lounges (with entertainment) add up to a very convenient and pleasant place to stay. The Sheraton Towers—the more expensive top floors—offer exclusive digs for the business or pleasure traveler. Amenities include terrycloth robes and butler service. The Centre also has a wide selection of package deals, and the price is right. While there, be sure to visit the newsstand. Tell the folks I sent you, and you'll get one of New York's biggest smiles.

SHERATON PARK AVENUE
45 Park Ave (at 37th St)
685-7676
Moderate

Historic Murray Hill is the home of this charming, completely renovated hotel, which is reminiscent of a Parisian hotel on the Left Bank or an exclusive London club. Many of the rooms have their original mantles and period antiques. A popular restaurant and the Judge's Chamber, a new jazz club—both on the premises—have been recently spruced up. The service is personal and low-key, and a concierge is available for special needs. There are floors set aside for nonsmokers, complimentary shoeshines, in-room hair dryers, 24-hour room service, bathrobes, and even telephones and TV speakers in the bathrooms.

UNITED NATIONS PLAZA
1 United Nations Plaza (bet First and Second Ave,
   at 44th St)
355-3400
Moderate to expensive

This is a very fashionable facility in the United Nations area, a gathering spot for the international set. The hotel is very modern, but done in good taste. It has a health club and a restaurant, and it features nicely appointed rooms and international-style service. The suites are particularly attractive. The 288 rooms and suites offer spectacular views, since they begin on the 28th floor.

VISTA INTERNATIONAL
3 World Trade Center
938-9100
Moderate to expensive

If business or other needs bring you to the lower end of Manhattan, I'd suggest you try the Vista International, located right in the World Trade Center. As a matter of fact, you can go directly from the hotel into the shopping and office complex. This is the first major new hotel in Lower Manhattan in nearly 150 years, and it has a lot going for it: first-class restaurants, parking in an underground garage, and a club on the 20th and 21st floors with special accommodations, including a concierge. There's also a well-equipped fitness center and rooftop swimming pool. The fitness center includes racquetball courts, a jogging track, sauna and steam bath, plus a fully equipped exercise facility. The hotel is operated by Hilton International, which does a consistently good job. Excellent weekend rates.

WALDORF-ASTORIA
301 Park Ave (at 50th St)
355-3000
Moderately expensive

For many years the Waldorf stood as the class symbol in Manhattan. Then, sadly, over a period of years the place rested on its laurels. Now Hilton has put in more than $180 million to restore their flagship—and the work shows! The lobby, with magnificent mahogany wall panels and handwoven carpets, is rich and impressive. In response to complaints about the size of some of the guest rooms, renovations were made, creating larger spaces by reducing the number of rooms. All-marble bathrooms and butler pantries were installed in some suites. An event at the Waldorf is sure to be something special, as their banquet service (and facilities) are top cabin. Special low-price packages are available on certain days and at certain times of the year.

WALDORF TOWERS
100 E 50th St
355-3100
Expensive

The Waldorf Towers—home to many celebrities and dignitaries (I once visited Herbert Hoover in his suite there)—is completely separate from the hotel. Guests have their own entrance, elevator, registration desk, bell captain, and concierge. All rooms and suites, ranging from very comfortable to very deluxe, are above the 28th floor, with commanding views. This is A-1 for security and comfort.

WESTBURY
69th St and Madison Ave
535-2000
Moderate to expensive

Completely modernized from stem to stern, with closet safes and exceptionally tasteful décor in all rooms and suites, the Westbury is particularly suitable for the woman traveling alone or the businessman who wants quiet and comfort rather than big-city excitement. There is 24-hour room service, the outstanding Polo Restaurant on the ground floor, and refurbished bathrooms. The top-of-the-line suites are some of the nicest in the city; they are of a manageable size, done in superb taste with every comfort, yet not ostentatious.

WYNDHAM
42 W 58th St (at Fifth Ave)
753-3500
Moderate

This charming hotel is more like a large home where the owners rent out rooms. Many of the guests are folks who regularly make the Wyndham their Manhattan headquarters. The advantages are many: great location, uniquely decorated rooms and suites, complete privacy, individual attention, and no business conventions. On the other hand, the hotel is always busy, and reservations for the newcomer could be difficult. No room service is available; however, there is a small restaurant, and the suites have refrigerators. John Mados has created a winner!

Alternative Housing

ABODE BED & BREAKFAST
P.O. Box 20022, New York 10028
472-2000
Mon-Fri: 9-5; Sat: 10-2

Have your heart set on staying in one of those delightful old brownstone apartments? Or how about a contemporary luxury apartment in the heart of Manhattan? Abode selects their hosts with great care, and all homes are personally inspected to ensure the highest standards of cleanliness, attractiveness, and hospitality. Shelli Leifer, the director, can provide clients with maid or limousine service, conference or meeting space, or whatever else is necessary for a perfect stay. Hosted accommodations with complimentary breakfast begin at $50 for singles, $60 for doubles; unhosted accommodations (minimum stay of 2 nights) start as low as $80 per night.

CHELSEA INN
46 W 17th St
645-8989
Inexpensive to moderate

The Chelsea Inn could well be at the forefront of a new trend in New York, similar to what has happened in downtown San Francisco. 19th century townhouses have been renovated and now provide clean and rather comfortable accommodations for those who don't need a fancy uptown address, or who don't mind sharing a bathroom. There are several very adequate suites at attractive prices, and a great studio room that is a true bargain. Both of these accommodations have private bathrooms. The single rooms that share a bathroom are satisfactory for those on a tight budget. All rooms are equipped with kitchenettes.

INTERNATIONAL HOUSE
500 Riverside Dr
316-8434
Inexpensive

To qualify to use these facilities, you have to pay a yearly membership fee, and be a full-time graduate-level student, researcher, trainee, or intern over 21 years of age. There are all sorts of special features: a low-budget cafeteria, a clothing bank, a dark room, a TV room, a pub with dancing, public rooms, and even a gymnasium. Note the uptown address.

NEW WORLD BED AND BREAKFAST
150 Fifth Ave (suite 711)
675-5600, 800-443-3800

New World specializes in serving both vacationers and business travelers. They offer accommodations in over 120 locations, and Laura Tilden will give you that extra-special personalized service.

92ND ST Y De HIRSCH RESIDENCE
1395 Lexington Ave
415-5650
Inexpensive

This facility offers convenient, inexpensive, and secure housing for men and women between the ages of 18 and 26. The minimum stay in the summer is three weeks; the rest of the year it's three months. There are special discounts for Y health-club memberships, and both single and double rooms are available. Admission is by application, and it is nontransient.

SHORT TERM HOUSING
849 Lexington Ave (at E 64th St)
570-2288
Mon-Fri: 10-6; Sun: 1-5
Summer: Mon-Fri: 10-8; Sat, Sun: noon-5

Recently I read about Short Term Housing as an alternative to finding or buying an apartment. Since then, I've heard it mentioned dozens of times as the solution to all sorts of problems, such as marital separation, roommate problems, and extended visits of relatives or business executives. This agency serves as the go-between between those looking for an apartment and those who will not be using one for an extended length of time. Most of the clients are from North America, Europe, or the Orient, and all are individually matched to their needs. Terms are usually between one month and one year, and almost always involve sublets. One interesting wrinkle is that the fee is paid by the tenant taking occupancy, which means that Short Term works for the renter, not the owner, as most agents do. Even if that were not the case, the fact that these people offer apartments on reasonable Manhattan terms earns them an entry in my book.

URBAN VENTURES
P.O. Box 426, New York, NY 10024
594-5650
Mon-Fri: 9-5; Sat: 9-3

Mary McAulay founded this service, modeled after Britain's famous bed-and-breakfast rooms, because she felt something needed to be done about Manhattan's lack of reasonably priced lodging. After being carefully screened, 650 hosts, who live either in apartments, townhouses, brownstones, or lofts, signed up with Urban Ventures. Hosts range from older people living in big apartments to young artists; both groups need a little help with the rent, and are also friendly and interested in their guests. The spare bedrooms are on the Upper West Side and in the Village, with many in midtown, on the East Side, in SoHo, TriBeCa, and even Brooklyn. Security is good—after all, this is someone's home— and the B&B's, as they are known, are concentrated in areas heavily populated by sons and daughters trying their wings in Manhattan. Hence, these rooms are convenient for visiting parents, since their child's apartment is rarely big enough to accommodate a visitor. Some apartments are even available for two nights to two months without hosts. The price is right, and this is a first-rate chance to get a sense of what it's really like to live in Manhattan.

Interior Decorators

DECORATOR PREVIEWS
777-2966

Having problems finding just the right decorator? Here is a great solution. Decorator Previews has information on over 100 of Manhattan's most trustworthy and talented designers, and will present information about them to you by way of slides and photographs. They will also discuss the designers' fees. Karen Fisher, the genius behind this handy service, was the decorating editor at *Cosmopolitan* magazine and the style editor at *Esquire*. She charges $100 for her services.

NEW YORK CHAPTER OF THE AMERICAN SOCIETY OF INTERIOR DESIGNERS
685-3480
Mon-Fri: 9:30-5:30

This is not a decorating service; it's the credential-granting agency to which most ethical (and qualified) interior designers belong. After an interview—during which you must specify your needs, taste, and budget—A.S.I.D. will recommend up to three members who would be suitable and available for the job. They are not snobbish and treat a $200 job just as seriously as a $5,000 one. Even if you don't go this route, be sure the decorator you *do* choose is A.S.I.D. affiliated.

PARSONS SCHOOL OF DESIGN
66 Fifth Ave (at 13th St)
741-8940
Mon-Fri: 9-5

Parsons, a division of the New School for Social Research, is one of the two top schools in the city for interior design. Folks who call will get their request posted on the school's board, and every effort is made to try and match client and prospective decorator. Individual negotiations determine price and length of the job, but it is incredibly cheaper than what a not-so-recent student charges. The disadvantage is that most of these students don't have a decorator card. (One can always be borrowed.) A good place if you just want a consultation.

Jewelry Services

B. HARRIS AND SONS
25 E 61st St (at Madison Ave)
755-6455
Mon-Sat: 10-5
Closed Sat in summer and last two weeks in Aug

William J. Harris' family started B. Harris and Sons in 1898, and since then, generations of customers have relied upon the family to repair their jewelry. The competence and courtesy displayed here hail from another era, and the classic jewelry available for sale and the ancient heirlooms awaiting repair show that this is a shop of the old school. The jewelry counter is limited to antique and fine contemporary jewelry. East Side godparents have made visits there before a christening almost *de rigueur,* and the selection in baby and young children's jewelry reflects this unusual interest. Others use B. Harris as a prime source for repairs of all jewelry and timepieces. Harris himself (William J., that is) is particularly proud of the restoration they do on watches and clocks, be they antique, modern, or grandfather.

GEM APPRAISERS LABORATORY
608 Fifth Ave
333-3122
Mon-Fri: 8:30-5; closed first two weeks of July

Leopold Woolf, who owns Gem Appraisers Laboratory, is a graduate gemologist. He is also an officer and director of the Appraisers Association of America. As such, he is entrusted with the appraisals for major insurance companies, auction houses, banks, and the New York City Department of Consumer Affairs. In an area where it can't hurt to be too careful, this is a very safe bet. In addition to doing appraisals and consultations for estate, bank, insurance, and tax purposes, Woolf also runs Gem Appraisers Laboratory Designs, which manufactures and designs jewelry. A better man would be hard to find.

GOLDFIELD'S
229 E 53rd St (at Second Ave)
753-3750, 752-3892
Mon-Fri: 8:30-5:30; Sat: 11-2

Goldfield's forte is the repair of jewelry, as well as lighters, electric shavers, watches, and clocks. Gino Signora, the manager, usually lends a personal hand to the shop repairs. He is extremely competent.

RISSIN'S JEWELRY CLINIC
4 W 47th St
575-1098
Mon, Tues, Thurs: 9:30-4:15
Closed first two weeks of July and Christmas week

Joe Rissin is one of the best craftsmen around. He is a jack-of-all-trades in the jewelry business. His chief virtue, however, is that he never turns down a customer, no matter how small or how ludicrous the request. He takes care of eyeglass repair, antique restorations and repairs, and uses quality rating charts so customers can see exactly what they are getting. His prices are very reasonable. On Wednesdays and Fridays he works just by himself, as he says "otherwise nothing would get done." He is just that popular.

SALON METRO
551 Fifth Ave (at 45th St)
983-3636
Mon-Wed: 10-7; Thurs: 10-8; Fri: 10-2; Sun: 11-5

You've heard of short-term housing and clothing operations. Well, now you can add an outlet for "leasing" top-quality jewelry. Salon Metro is a new concept where you can work out a lease-option plan for spectacular pearls, diamonds, rings, necklaces, bracelets, etc. for one, two, or three year terms. They will even let you exchange your original purchase up to two months later for another item of equal value. This is not costume jewelry; this is the real thing. Hmmm, wonder if Nancy Reagan heard about this place?

ZOHRAB DAVID KRIKORIAN
48 W 48th St (room 1409)
575-1262
By appointment only

Most of his work has been the creation of rare and original pieces for neighbors in the diamond district, but in his free time Zohrab David Krikorian will do the work he does wholesale for professionals for you, too. In addition to making jewelry, Krikorian will mend and fix broken jewelry, as only a professional craftsman who is also an artist can. He makes complicated repairs look easy, and has yet to encounter a job he can't handle. If he can't exactly match the stones in an antique earring, he'll redo the whole piece so it looks even better than before. That, too, is unusual for a craftsman who has a healthy respect for old things. He loves creating the latest, newest designs with traditional materials, and his prices are quite reasonable.

Locksmiths

AAA LOCKSMITHS
44 W 46th St (at Sixth Ave)
840-3939
Mon-Fri: 8:30-5:30

You can learn a lot from trying to find a locksmith in New York. For one thing, it's the profession that probably has the most full-page ads in the Manhattan Yellow Pages. For another, a company that answers "AAA" is *not* the place to call about a dead battery. And finally, the phone company and other advertising media list companies alphabetically. So in an industry that has little company loyalty or recommendations, three *A*'s is an important edge. AAA Locksmiths has been in the business for nearly 50 years, and that says a lot right there.

NIGHT AND DAY LOCKSMITH
1335 Lexington Ave (at 89th St)
722-1017
Mon-Sat: 9-6:30 (24 hours for emergencies)

To be safe—just in case you're ever locked out—Night and Day is a number you should be carrying close to your heart. New Yorkers, even those who are in residence for a short time, become experts on locks and cylinders. Cocktail party conversation is frequently peppered with references to dead bolts, Medeco, and Segal, and if you haven't the vaguest idea what all the talk is about, you obviously don't live in the city. On the other hand, a city locksmith is about as professional an expert as there can be. He's got to be ahead of the cocktail circuit fads (as well as the local burglar's latest expertise) and be able to offer fast, on-the-spot service for a variety of devices (no apartment has *one* lock) designed to keep people out. Mena Sofat, Night and Day's owner, fulfills these rigid requirements. They also answer their phone 24 hours a day. Posted hours are for the sale of their own locks, window gates, and keys. If you buy your lock here, you can be sure they'll be willing to help you out (or *in,* as the case may be) when the time comes.

Leather Repair

ARTBAG CREATIONS
735 Madison Ave (at 64th St)
744-2720
Mon-Fri: 9-5:45; Sat: 9-4; closed Sat in summer

Artbag will make, sell, or repair any type of handbag, and they will do it well. The range goes from mounting needlepoint bags to relining heirloom bridal bags, as well as leather, reptile (including some of the best lizard skins in the city), and beaded evening bags. Mssrs. Moore and Price are European craftsmen who modestly advertise themselves as "understanding, genteel, and good listeners. They know their business." Any of their customers could have been quoted as having said the same thing. Artbag is also known for its sense of style. It carries the latest and the best designs, and frequently refashions old handbags into chic trendsetters. It isn't every day that you come across men who know more about handbags than most women do, but these gentlemen certainly know, and they keep up with the latest styles.

CARNEGIE LUGGAGE
1388 Sixth Ave (bet 57th and 58th St)
586-8210
Mon-Fri: 8:30-5:45; Sat: 9-5

Carnegie is handy to most major midtown and Central Park hotels. Service can be fast, if you let them know you're in a hurry.

JOHN R. GERARDO
30 W 31st St (bet Broadway and Fifth Ave)
695-6955
Mon-Fri: 9-5; Sat: 10-2; closed Sat in July, Aug

Minus the glamour, Dan Gerardo manages to dispense luggage and luggage repairs at John R. Gerardo that rival Crouch and Fitzgerald's. Gerardo's stock is a complete one. He carries all the standard brands in almost all kinds of luggage. There are sample cases, over-nighters, two suiters, and drawers with seemingly endless types and amounts of spare parts. There are zippers, handles, locks, and patches of fiber and material for emergency patching. Gerardo does quick, professional repairs. They also have a pickup and delivery service for a nominal fee.

MODERN LEATHER GOODS REPAIR SHOP
2 W 32nd St (bet Fifth Ave and Broadway)
279-3263
Mon-Fri: 8:30-5:30; Sat: 9-2

Sometimes folks get attached to particular items. I, for one, have become sentimentally attached to my forty-year-old Hartmann leather suitcases; I hate to think of giving them up. Well, if you feel the same way about a handbag, piece of luggage, or almost any kind of leather item, this is the place to go for repairs. They also do needlepoint mounting, will clean leather and suede clothing, and will make bags to order.

SUPERIOR REPAIR CENTER
133 Lexington Ave
889-7211
Mon-Fri: 9-6; Thurs: 9-8; Sat: 10-3; closed Sat in summer

Leather repair is the highlight of the service at Superior. Many of the major stores in the city use them for luggage and handbag work. They are experts in the repair or replacement of zippers on leather items. They will work on sporting equipment and fix tents, backpacks, and almost anything the bear you encountered on your last trip ripped apart! If there is a leather problem, Superior has the answer.

Marble Works

NEW YORK MARBLE WORKS
1399 Park Ave (at 104th St)
534-2242
Mon-Fri: 8-4:30; closed July 1-10

Same location, same family since 1900. That's quite a record! Three generations of Louis Gleicher's family have run this business, and it's no surprise to learn that they know the marble business cold (sorry for the pun!). Gleicher will create and custom-design marble pieces and furniture for bathrooms, fireplaces, tables, and mantels. They also repair broken marble, do repolishing, plus craft consoles, pedestals, and tabletops. All of this can be done using the largest selection of floor and wall marble, granite, onyx, and slate tiles in the country. They will ship anywhere in the world.

PUCCIO EUROPEAN MARBLE AND ONYX
232 E 59th St (showroom on sixth floor; factory
    warehouse showroom at 661 Driggs Ave, Brooklyn)
688-1351

Puccio's factory and warehouse are in Brooklyn, but they qualify for a listing since they do have a showroom in Manhattan, which is open only by appointment. Paul Puccio runs both as a showcase for his sculpture and furniture designs, which range from traditional to sleekly modern. It is almost incongruous to see an angular, free-flowing sculpture made of formal marble, when Roman busts on pedestals are what comes to mind. But John Puccio boasts that his tables are found in décors that are strictly modern and very chic. "We strive for plain but luxurious," he says. He succeeds, and the results are startling as well as elegant. A project takes from 6 to 16 weeks for delivery, since it is custom-manufactured, but a commission is not even accepted (even though there is a ready-made line) if it is not received through a decorator or designer. Puccio is just not equipped to deal with retail orders, but a visit to the factory will enable you to see the line for yourself.

Massage

LEWIS HARRISON
40 W 72nd St
724-8782

Lewis Harrison has been an instructor at the respected Swedish Massage Institute in New York, and is recognized as an expert in the field. He has written several books on massage, and is absolutely reliable. He works on both men and women, and will take appointments at his place of business, plus do home and hotel calls.

Matchmaking

FIELD'S EXCLUSIVE SERVICE
41 E 42nd St
391-2233

"New York lives by this book!" That's a pretty big challenge for one book. But I can't let anyone down, so this edition even includes a hint on matchmaking. Dan Field's company has been playing Dan Cupid for three quarters of a century. If Dan is successful for you, how about a testimonial for *Where To Find It, Buy It, Eat It in New York*—the Romance Edition, of course!

Medical Services

DOCTORS ON CALL
718-238-2100

This service answers a real need in the city. In the past, hotels always had staff doctors on call. Medical and dental associations arranged for doctors to cover the city during off hours, and, of course, hospital emergency rooms were open 24 hours a day. But private doctors have stopped making house calls, even to regular patients. Doctors on Call was created to take care of that problem. Though most calls are to people who don't have regular city doctors—patients are usually visitors—many calls are made on residents. The fee in Manhattan is about $65 (accurate at publication date), which covers the cost of parking and transportation, and most calls are completed within two hours of your phone call. All members of Doctors on Call are licensed, and if further tests or treatments are necessary, that can be arranged as well.

PORTNOW SURGICAL SUPPLIES
53 Delancey St (at Eldridge St)
226-1311
Sun-Fri: 9:30-6

People in this neighborhood would say, "You shouldn't know from it," but for any kind of medical, surgical, or home nursing supplies, Portnow should be a first choice. Not only is the equipment modern and vast in selection, the prices are discounted, just as if there were many similar businesses on the block, which there aren't. In fact, for the price, there probably isn't a better source in the city for surgical supplies, convalescent aids, wheelchairs, canes, crutches, walkers, trusses, belts, supporters, or surgical stockings. Portnow's own brand of therapeutic pantyhose comes in every size. The array of blood-pressure machines, ostoscopes, blood-sugar testers, and respiratory aids would make a hypochondriac happy. The healthy come for Portnow's exercise machines and bikes, as well as the best maternity pantyhose around. Most of all, these people know their stuff, just as you'd expect from a business established in 1898. Their immediate concern is the immediate relief of pain. Portnow aims to handle any medical situation with the best, most economical treatment. To your health, Portnow!

QUALITY CARE
25 W 43rd St
730-7077
Mon-Fri: 9-5 (office); on call 24 hours daily

Quality Care is a nationwide organization dedicated to providing temporary health-care personnel on all levels. It was created to meet the changing needs of medical care: formerly, the sick were treated at home, but today they are sent to institutions, and that isn't always what patients want. So, there was a need for professionals who would work at a patient's home. Quality Care supplies registered and licensed practical nurses, home health aides, homemakers, companions (there's a term you don't see often outside 19th-century novels), physical occupation and speech therapists, and just about every other kind of home-care specialist imaginable. These professionals will adapt their program to special needs, such as kosher cooking, small rooming accommodations, or anything else, as well as providing health screening tests and guidance to clients. Here's hoping you won't need them, but it's nice to know that Quality Care is there and that a national organization is behind it.

UNION SQUARE DRUGS
859 Broadway (bet 17th and 18th St)
242-2725
Mon-Fri: 7:30-6; Sat: 9-3.

This store consistently offers the best prices on prescription drugs, industrial first-aid supplies, and vitamins, and is equally well-known for its reliability. The service is so conscientious that the pharmacist will call, long-distance if necessary, to verify prescriptions. (And you know how most salespeople react to the very *thought* of making a long-distance call.) Union Square, which is owned by Alypan Corp., will fill union prescriptions and honor other medical plans.

UPJOHN HEALTH CARE SERVICES
1 Penn Plaza (suite 1618)
465-8400
24 hours

Upjohn is a nationwide service that provides fully screened, bonded, supervised, and trained home health aides. The type of person sent and the subsequent bill depend upon the level of care needed, but they are capable of supplying registered nurses, licensed practical nurses, home health aides, and companions. The general idea is that they will supply complete home-nursing service as well as hospital support.

Metal Work

AMEROM
54 W 22nd St (bet Fifth and Sixth Ave)
675-4828
Mon-Fri: 7:30-5

Florin Carmocanu is a Romanian artisan, whose metal workshop mainly focused on welding and cutting metal to size. Not terribly exciting or demanding of Carmocanu's considerable talent. But then word of his handiwork got out to loft dwellers, co-op remodelers, and interior decorators, and suddenly Amerom is one of the hottest places in town. And no wonder. Carmocanu is a genius with decorative metal, structural steel, and wrought-iron furniture and gates. His spiral staircases are awesome. Amerom can even replace original artwork and wrought-iron designs of old brownstones. As for the name, which doesn't exactly come tripping off the tongue, could it be a combination of the words *American* and *Romanian?*

MICHAEL DOTZEL AND SON
402 E 63rd St (bet First Ave and York Ave)
838-2890
Mon-Fri: 8-4:30

If there is a brass, copper, iron, lead, or pewter object around your home that is in need of attention, look no farther. Michael Dotzel will repair antiques, do refinishing work, duplicate missing or broken parts, polish, do wiring, repair metal shades, reproduce old antique pieces, and take care of just about any need you have in the metal repair field. They specialize in pewter cleaning and repair, as well as quality work on silver pieces.

RETINNING AND COPPER REPAIR
525 W 26th St (at 10th Ave)
244-4896
Mon-Fri: 9-6; closed Christmas to New Year's

Only in New York would a 75-year-old Italian retinning business be headed by a female woodworker in her thirties. Her name is Mary Ann Miles, and hers may be the only business of its kind in the city. The original business was founded on the same spot in 1916. When the second owner went bankrupt, Miles, who owned the woodworking business next door, bought it. Changing chisel for vat was not as easy as she supposed, but employees who had toiled through the two prior owners taught the current owner the business, and *voilà,* Miles became a retinning and copper expert. And expert she is. In addition to the retinning (which is basically what copper repair amounts to), Miles restores brass and copper antiques, designs and creates new copperware (almost all copper pots in use today are heirlooms), and sells restored copper pieces.

Movers

GRADUATE N.Y. MOVERS
558 Broome St
925-5995

Though Graduate Movers started in the Columbia University area, they have matriculated to SoHo and are moving in the adult world. This address also houses a small moving supply store to help with moving needs. These are the same people who supply bartenders, party personnel, and general help for hire. They have expanded the business to include insured moving. The same impeccable service characterizes this endeavor, and their rates are competitive.

IKE BANKS
718-527-7505

Ike Banks probably breaks every rule for inclusion in this book. He's not bonded or licensed, nor is he a resident of Manhattan (he lives in Queens), but he never breaks anything, and I trust him more than anyone else listed here. He was first recommended to me by an appliance store, when a delicate and temperamental washing machine needed to be delivered. Since then, he has moved pianos, households, and dining rooms for friends. Several years ago, estimates for moving a nine-piece dining room ran from $100 to $300. Banks did it perfectly for $25. He will travel anywhere in the city, sometimes further, and will work odd hours (unless he's taking his nephew to a ball game). He's a super guy. The only complaint I have is that he's so careful that he can be very slow. It's a good thing he doesn't charge by the hour.

MOISHE'S MOVING AND STORAGE
1627 Second Ave (at 84th St)
439-9191

Moishe learned the business from the bottom up, packing boxes and handling them personally to make sure the customers were satisfied. He learned well and quickly, and soon parlayed his experiences into organizing one of the largest and most successful moving and storage companies in the area. He now has dozens of bright red trucks, and several hundred bright red-clad employees. Moishe Mana, a Tel Aviv University Law School dropout, is still in his twenties, but can claim he did it the hard way—from nothing to a business that now grosses over 13 million dollars a year. Document storage in modern facilities is just one feature of the storage side of his operation. Boxes and packing materials in all sizes are available for purchase.

MOVING STORE
644 Amsterdam Ave
874-3800
Mon-Fri: 8:30-6; Sat: 9-3

Steve Fiore started West Side Movers in the kitchen of his studio apartment more than 15 years ago. Business was so good that he soon moved into a storefront. He was happy there until he realized the magnitude of requests he was getting from people who wanted to borrow or rent moving pads, ramps, dollies, and, most particularly, boxes of all sizes. A man who knows a good business opportunity when he sees one, Fiore moved into a brownstone storefront on Amsterdam Avenue to sell nothing but moving aids and paraphernalia. Fiore's business is unique in New York and, most probably, in the world. Most of his customers today are either box seekers or descendants of box seekers, so the main stock in trade is still boxes. They come in more sizes than it seems possible, including three different sizes just for mirrors. And since all of the items are built to the specifications of professional movers, they are *very* durable.

WEST SIDE MOVERS
644 Amsterdam Ave
874-3800
Mon-Fri: 8-6; Sat: 9-3; closed Sat in July, Aug

We came to West Side Movers via their Moving Store. But such ecumenical and diverse groups as the Union Theological Seminary and Tiffany & Company came to West Side Movers by recommendation and have added their accolades to the file. A company with a subdivision that specializes in helping people move themselves has to be top-notch. West Side Movers pays particular attention to efficiency, promptness, care, and courtesy. Customer after customer has called their staff the most courteous they've dealt with. If you've ever had to move in the city you can understand why that consideration comes *before* concern over dents on the furniture to New Yorkers. *But* they don't dent the furniture, either!

Newspaper Delivery

LENOX HILL NEWSPAPER DELIVERY
502 E 74th St
879-1822

Lenox Hill Newspaper Delivery is an excellent door-to-door service. For a slight charge, they will deliver the New York papers, the *Christian Science Monitor,* the *Washington Post, Women's Wear Daily,* or the *Sunday Observer* to your door. They will also deliver any foreign publication available in New York. All of these, Lenox Hill claims, can be delivered "earlier than subscriptions reach your mailbox." For many people, that's worth the service charge.

Office Services

AMAL PRINTING AND PUBLISHING
630 Fifth Ave (at 51st St, International Building)
247-3270
Mon-Fri: 9-5:30 (evenings and weekends by appointment)

Run out of business cards on the day you have an appointment for a big deal? Well, don't worry, you can get them done in a day (for a bit extra) at Amal. They do all kinds of printing, from flyers to business forms to invitations, and if the order is large enough, they'll work on weekends. Overnight and while-you-wait service is available, as well as pickup and delivery. This is a good spot to remember for just about any kind of printing need.

PETERS & PETERS
2 Tudor City Pl
883-9119

In 1981, Barbara Peters started her company to offer New Yorkers the proverbial "extra pair of hands." To her surprise, the business was an instant success, and 90 percent of it was spent organizing—that is, organizing everything from desk drawers to checkbooks to entire offices. Peters did it with aplomb, and business soon expanded (often for some of the same customers) into billing, administrative services, typing, writing, editing, transcribing, word processing, insurance claims, and shopping. A disproportionate amount of business is done with people who work at home; and most are inexpensive part-time, or even one-time, assignments. Rates are reasonable, with no job exceeding $40 an hour and straight typing going for $25 an hour, which may be the best rate in town. Short of sprouting another pair of arms, Peters & Peters is probably the best hope for harried, unorganized people. They also specialize in working with conferences, seminars, and lectures.

"WE TYPE IT!" CENTER KBM
60 W 39th St (at Sixth Ave)
354-6890
Mon-Fri: 8:30-7; Sat: 10-4

Trust the folks at KBM to be in touch with the typing needs of New Yorkers. For years they ran a center where people could rent typewriters on a daily basis. But when more and more clients began offering to pay KBM to do the typing for them, in came professionals who can type anything from a letter in Yiddish at three in the morning (that's their line not mine) to a lengthy manuscript. KBM boasts the ability to do any job in record time, at record prices, in a record number of languages. When one checks out the competition, that seems to be true. "We Type It!" is especially geared to the needs of travelers and businessmen who may be far from a home office and in need of a fast, efficient typist. The center offers video rentals, also. "We Type It!" knows how to strike just the right keys.

WORLD-WIDE BUSINESS CENTRES
605-0200, 1-800-847-4276
Mon-Fri: 9-5:30; Sat, Sun: 10-4

Alan Bain, a transplanted English lawyer, has created a highly profitable business, which caters to business executives who need more than a hotel room to work from when visiting New York. The need for the business grew out of Bain's own frustrations in trying to put together a makeshift office, write and get out reports, answer telephones, and still attend to the matters that brought him to the city in the first place. Services by on-premises word processors, typists, etc., are available. Desk space, private offices, and conference rooms may be rented on a daily, weekly, monthly, or quarterly basis. The daily rate includes telephone answering, receptionists, and a private office. The company also operates a full-service travel agency that specializes in corporate travel and travel management service to small and medium-sized companies.

Party Services

BALOOMS
147 Sullivan St
673-4007
Mon-Fri: 10-6; Sat: 12-6; Sun: available for parties

Balooms differs from most balloon services in that customers are not only invited, but requested to visit the office. That is because the Balooms office is a legitimate, albeit small, store that encourages browsing and spur-of-the-moment sales. While there are still skeptics who feel *no one* impulsively buys a balloon, Balooms' sales prove otherwise. In addition to the standard balloon bouquet, there is party decorating and custom-designed or personalized bouquets with either names, logos, or even portraits on each balloon. Balooms will deliver in Manhattan and the boroughs, but they will ship anywhere. The store also has helium rental. As befits this lighthearted business, owners Marlyne Berger and Raymond Baglietto are delightful.

EASTERN ONION/LOONEY BALLOONS
39 W 14th St (room 301)
741-0006

Eastern Onion is in the New York messenger business in a new incarnation. Owner Stan Wilcox offers almost everything except the conventional telegram. Indeed, singing telegrams are as conventional as they get, but even they get pretty far-out when the singer is a professional dressed as a gorilla, Fairy Onion, or Mr. Macho (wonder if they use the same person for both characters?). There are also bellygrams and, of course, Looney Balloons. The latter is a bouquet of 24 multicolored balloons and one mylar balloon, delivered by a suitably dressed messenger.

LINDA KAYE'S BIRTHDAYBAKERS, PARTYMAKERS
195 E 76th St (bet Lexington and Third Ave)
288-7112
Parties seven days a week

Linda Kaye got started in this business shortly after she hired a baker for her daughter's birthday party and it turned out to be a big success. Linda soon realized that there was a big market for well-organized kids' parties. Linda's successful concept is based on showcasing artist bakers who will teach partygoers how to bake a cake as part of the entertainment. Linda's staff takes care of everything; there is even a "party room" outfitted with a fireplace, a kitchen, and a sound system. They will do "grown-up" parties, too. I can well remember a party I had once, where a scantily-clad lady jumped out of a birthday cake. This was in Oregon, but perhaps Linda could arrange something like this in the Big Apple! There is a great catalog for birthdays from age one to one hundred plus, with specific ideas, nationwide gifts, and creative services for that "special someone's birthday."

NEW YORK PARTIES
22 E 13th St
777-3565
Daily: 10-6

When you are thinking big, Jean-Michel Savoca's New York Parties is a great name to remember. These folks take complete charge of everything, including food, liquor, equipment rentals, tents, flowers, lighting, music, and trained personnel. When people like Frank Sinatra, Paine Webber, and Chase Manhattan use a service, you know it has to be first-rate. They can offer prime locations such as grand ballrooms or spacious yachts, if that is what you have in mind.

PRINCE STREET CLUB
177 Prince St (bet Thompson and Sullivan St)
353-0707

If you, your business, or your organization is looking for an unusual place to hold a gathering for a group of 30 to 130, this is a good location to check-out. The club can provide all food, flowers, staff, and anything else for a birthday, anniversary, meeting, press conference, or what-have-you. You could also just rent the club and make all arrangements yourself. The place features hand-painted walls, granite floors, and even gold fixtures in the bathroom.

PROPS FOR TODAY
121 W 19th St (bet Sixth and Seventh Ave)
206-0330
Mon-Fri: 9-5

This is the handiest place in town when you are preparing for a party. Props for Today has the largest rental inventory of home decorations in New York. Whether you want everyday china and silver or unique antiques going back as far as 100 years, they have the goods in stock. There are platters and vases and tablecloths, and everything in-between. There is a Christmas section, children's items, books, fireplace equipment, artwork, garden furniture, foreign items, and ordinary kitchenware. Over 15,000 items are available—that should give you an idea of the selection. Phone orders are taken, but it is a good idea to call for an appointment and see for yourself. Ask for Dyann Klein, the proprietor.

Pen and Lighter Repair

AUTHORIZED REPAIR SERVICE
30 W 57th St
586-0947
Mon-Sat: 9-5

If a business' specialty is the repair of fountain pens and cigarette lighters in this day of disposable ball point pens and no-smoking campaigns, you wouldn't think it could be a viable concern. But you would think wrong. Morton Winston first started the business two decades ago, and it is still incredibly busy—perhaps because it is almost without competition. Those who use fountain pens are devoted customers. Authorized Repair sells and services nearly every brand, and the shop can refill lighters as well as all kinds of pens. (This means ball point and cartridges as well as fountain pens.) Authorized also sells, repairs, and services electric shavers. Tourists can even pick up 220 V appliances or adapter plugs, and the extremely polite and helpful staff is well versed in the fine points of each brand.

FOUNTAIN PEN HOSPITAL
10 Warren St (across from City Hall)
964-0580
Mon-Fri: 8-6

This establishment is one of the only places in town that repairs fountain pens. The Fountain Pen Hospital sells and repairs pens of all types—and other writing implements as well. They are probably the most experienced shop around.

Personal Services

CATHERINE VAN ORMER
(Image Wardrobe Fashion Consultant)
238 Madison Ave
532-4446

Catherine Van Ormer not only associates with diplomats, socialites, executives, and show-business personalities, she dresses them. In fact, she was named the fashion consultant to WCBS-TV's news reporters when she owned a boutique. As more and more people began demanding her fashion-shopping expertise, she closed the store and went into personal shopping full time. She is quite simply the best in the business. Most of her clients are people who have neither the time nor talent to put together a top-notch wardrobe, and they benefit from her close association with the city's top clothing designers. She scouts all of the lines and then shows the best to the client. Clothes can be purchased at Catherine's wholesale cost, which is roughly 50 percent less than retail, and the fashions reflect her eye for couture lines and natural fibers. The fee for all this is a mere pittance for those who simply must have this service. (There *are* those who simply can't keep all those cocktail parties straight.) Van Ormer has a similar service for custom-made bridal gowns and accessories. The gowns are magnificent, and the prices do not reflect the superb quality of the work. Her one-hour consultation fee is included in the price of a wedding gown. There is also a full range of bridal planning.

CREATIVE RESOURCES
305 E 63rd St
974-1185
Mon-Fri: 9-5:30

This is the age of corporate gift giving. It seems that every business venture, from corporate mergers to Christmas bonuses, is marked by a tie pin or a money clip. If you have more of those than ties or money, Janey Holzman Klein's Creative Resources is the place you should recommend to your company. Holzman Klein's aim is to offer unique gifts to the corporate client for all occasions, and she succeeds admirably. A corporate logo can be etched in gold, silver, brass, glass, or chocolate, stitched into needlepoint, or custom-designed. Those who don't need a logo can choose from one-of-a-kind antiques or contemporary designs in china, silver, paintings, watercolors, or bric-a-brac. The list is almost endless, but I am partial to the picture frames, desk sets, and attaché cases. Actually, anything would be better than another tie clip, right?

F & L ASSOCIATES
349 E 52nd St (bet First and Second Ave)
752-2879
Daily: 24 hours

How about having your own concierge? Well, that is possible if you take advantage of the services that Fran Jennings and Pauline Fong provide. They will run errands. They will clean your house or apartment. They will stand in line for you. They will wash your car. They will provide beauty service in your home or office. They will work out travel plans. You get the idea. What handy folks to have around to uncomplicate your life!

THE INTREPID NEW YORKER
1230 Park Ave (bet 95th and 96th St)
534-4922
Daily: 24 hours

Kathy Braddock, founder and owner of this service, is indeed "the Intrepid New Yorker." She was born, bred, and educated in the Big Apple. Like your author, she delights in trying to help folks unravel the hassels and confusion of this great city. She provides one of the most complete personal-service businesses in the area, and is available at any time. Kathy can take you on private guided tours, shopping expeditions, help you find a place to live and take care of your decorating or refurbishing needs. She also offers a membership that will give clients a number of referrals and 10 percent off regular hourly rates when her services are needed. This is handy for those who need quick and complete information or help, but choose to do the work themselves. Of course, you could first look in *Where To...*, but calling Kathy would be the second-best alternative.

IT'S EASY
10 Rockefeller Center
586-8880
Mon-Fri: 9-5:30

Some time ago, David Alwadish found himself trying to remain cool amid an angry crowd of people at the passport office in Rockefeller Center. When someone in line told him that they would pay anything to get off that line, Alwadish took him literally and a new business was born. Over the next decade, Alwadish did so well as a stand-in and gofer that he went national and branched out into doing research for attorneys and businesses, auto leasing, and even motor-vehicle inspecting. Indeed, if there is any occupation or line or work where someone else can do the waiting for a client, then It's Easy will do it. Incidentally, they haven't lost the personal touch, even though Alwadish has gone on to own and manage a Mexican restaurant, North of the Border. Now the company is owned by Alwadish's sister, Leslie Shapiro, who guarantees that no one will wait on line for reservations at It's Easy.

LA CONCIERGE SERVICES
322 E 86th St (bet First and Second Ave)
737-5289
Daily: 7:30 a.m.-midnight

Handy folks to have on call! They will do cleanup work after renovation or construction, or come to a home, store, or office to put things back in shape after a party or big sale. In addition, Jessica Crosby will take care of shopping or catering needs, and provide almost any kind of service personnel.

LET MILLIE DO IT!
532-8775
Daily: 10-whenever!

Millie Emory has been in business for over a decade saving folks time, stress, and money. She especially likes to work with seniors, but will help anyone with a broad variety of tasks. She will do organizing work in home or office, make household inventories for insurance purposes, supervise remodeling jobs while you take it easy in Florida, bid at auctions so you can remain anonymous, entertain out-of-town guests, take care of the checkbook (you'll have to provide the cash), do your Christmas shopping, and even take care of all the many details when tragedy or loss of a loved one strikes your family. Millie charges by the hour, and has had a world of experience being an all-purpose gofer.

MANHATTAN PASSPORT
507 E 80th St (bet York and East End Ave)
744-0203
Mon-Fri: 7-3

Ina Lee Selden, a former teacher, is the brains behind Manhattan Passport—a concierge service dedicated to arranging everything for the New York visitor. They will go way beyond what a travel agent would do, booking everything from breakfast in bed to a night on the town—all tailored to the individual's needs. They will arrange for guided tours and/or leave the client with a customized do-it-yourself itinerary. A very handy touch is their destination management service: for large or small groups, they will make sure that the group's baggage makes it safely from the airport to the hotel, and they will select places for special events. If you have ever tried to arrange group activities (especially from out-of-town), you can appreciate how helpful these folks can be.

PASSPORT PLUS
677 Fifth Avenue (fifth floor)
759-5540; 800-367-1818
Daily: 9:30-5:30

Elise Gans was another person struck by inspiration while waiting in that infamous line at the passport office at Rockefeller Center. Her passport-fetching was one of the first such services and though she has expanded nationwide, she has remained a purist concentrating on the procurement of travel documents. With the expansion, Passport Plus now offers very personalized service with a complete document service. This is a step beyond a regular travel agency in that they will take care of visa, birth, death and marriage certificates, international licenses, passport photos while you wait (they don't send someone for that), and airline ticket pickups, among other things. If you've ever waited months for an errant passport or crucial certificate, you'll understand how invaluable Passport Plus is. Imagine not having to deal with a passport office ever again!

PROJECTS INTERNATIONAL
201 E 69th St (suite 4F)
861-9500
Daily: by appointment

Audrey Speers is an energetic and charming lady who wanted to put her many talents to work in a field that she knows well: helping the newcomer in this vast and confusing city. Her method of operation is working with corporations in helping them relocate personnel to New York. (She can also assist individuals.) This help is given on a very personal basis, trying to take the stress and strain out of a difficult time in anyone's life—a move to the big city. She starts before the family arrives, making hotel reservations, arranging transportation, and providing a headquarters for the newcomer. Then she works with the client in helping select schools (for both young folks and adults), providing advice and assistance in housing (how to find apartments that are not listed or advertised), recommending everything from dentists, housekeepers, lawyers, and barbers to restaurants, clubs, tours, and banking. Really, she is a sort of walking *Where To Find It, Buy It, Eat It in New York.*

SAVED BY THE BELL CORP
11 Riverside Dr
874-5457
Mon-Sat: 9-7

Susan Bell (get it?) is the genius behind this organization. Her goal is to take the worry out of planning virtually any type of job for people who are too busy or too disorganized to do it themselves. Bell says "doing the impossible is our specialty," and you can believe her. They can supervise corporate relocations and vacation trips—from making reservations right down to stocking the refrigerator or putting a great guidebook on the coffee table! They also do weddings, party planning, tag sales, shopping, delivery arrangements, and service referrals.

ULTIMATE SHOPPING SYSTEM
724-2300
Irregular hours (call for appointment)

Susan Guth and Nancy Missett have organized a service for those who are too busy or don't want to take care of their personal shopping needs. They help complete wardrobes, decorate apartments and homes, work with businesses for client gifts, take care of party arrangements, and generally save both men and women hours of work. Guth had retail experience at Bloomingdales, creating and developing the men's shopping service. A major drawback is the fact that the ladies are "out-on-the-town" a majority of the time, and their telephone answering system is less than helpful. Their fee is 10 percent of the retail purchase price of the merchandise selected.

Photographic Services

A.A. IDENTIFICATION SERVICE
698 Third Ave (bet 43rd and 44th St)
682-5045
Mon-Fri: 8-6

A.A.'s main virtue is their ability to do passport and identification photos competently and quickly. This is no small matter, as some photo shops near passport offices can be very unreliable. A.A. has a good reputation for laminating, doing one-day business portraits, and providing one-hour photo lab services.

BACHRACH
48 E 50th St (bet Park and Madison Ave)
755-6233
Mon-Fri: 9-4:45; Sat: 10-4; closed Sat from May
    to Labor Day

If you have never heard of Bachrach, a quick glance at the society page of *The New York Times* will establish its credentials. Bachrach is *the* eminent society photographer in New York, the United States, and possibly the world. For over a century, Bachrach has photographed the social events in its patrons' lives. Most visible are the bridal portraits that appear week after week in the newspapers, but there are also executive portraits, candids, and portraits of debutantes, families, children, and bridal parties. There is also an oil-painting department. Bachrach does magnificent work, but the prices are magnificent, too. And some of the personnel act as though they're doing *you* a favor—which doesn't really fit into today's ultracompetitive world. A little humility, please.

DAN DEMETRIAD
200 W 57th St (at Seventh Ave, suite 200)
245-1720
Mon-Fri: 10-6:30

Dan and Iris Demetriad are European-trained artisans with offices adjacent to Carnegie Hall, but the fine tuning they do is to photographs and prints rather than to musical instruments! Because they were trained as commercial photographers, they are well skilled in their restoration work. Prices are reasonable, considering the difficulty of the work.

GALOWITZ
511 Sixth Ave (at 13th St)
242-8115
Mon-Fri: 8:15-5:30; Sat: 10-4

In a city that has two button shops, two seashell shops, and a dozen pet groomers you would think that there would be a number of photographic restoration establishments. No, sir. This very exacting art is a rare bird, and I am happy to recommend Galowitz as a fine practitioner whose specialty is making old photos look presentable and worth more than sentimental value. One of the specialties here is large blow-ups that can be used for parties or business events. Galowitz is a quality, full-service photo lab.

GENE BARRY PRO PHOTO LAB
130 E 57th St (at Lexington Ave)
838-8316
Mon-Fri: 8-7; Sat: 10-6; Sun: 10-6

1282 Broadway (at 34th St)
695-1519
Mon-Fri: 7:30-7; Sat, Sun: 10-6

Speed is the name of the game here. The folks at Gene Barry not only develop most photographs within the hour, they also do enlargements with the same speed. The work is of excellent quality.

PHOTOGRAPHICS UNLIMITED/ DIAL-A-DARKROOM
17 W 17th St (bet Fifth and Sixth Ave, fourth floor)
255-9678
Mon-Fri: 9 a.m.-11 p.m.; Sat: 10-7; Sun: noon-7

Here's another only-in-New York idea. Photographics Unlimited offers photographers of limited physical means a full range of photographic equipment and a place to work on a rental basis. The shop has everything from the simplest equipment to an 8x10 Saltzman printer, including all manner of printing paper and film supplies, as well as a lab for on-the-spot developing of black and white and color. Ed Lee claims his center is a complete one for the most amateur or most advanced professional photographer, and he aims to prove it. Both studios and darkrooms can be rented, and both come with advice and suggestions from the darkroom's owner. It would be hard to describe all of the resources here. Whatever could be desired in a personally owned studio can be rented. A technical hot-line is available to answer questions.

PROFESSIONAL CAMERA REPAIR SERVICE
37 W 47th St (bet Fifth and Sixth Ave)
382-0511
Mon-Fri: 8:30-5

Rush jobs are the specialty here, so there's no need to spoil your vacation because your camera is on the blink. Professionals will work on still cameras from 35mm and up, and will also repair any kind of movie camera. Designing and building special camera equipment is an important part of their business.

STAT STORE
148 Fifth Ave (bet 19th and 20th St)
929-0566
Mon-Fri: 9-6:30; Sat, Sun: 12-4; closed Sun in summer

In medical parlance, stat means "fast." In photo jargon, stat is short for photostat, and it has come to mean virtually any copy. The Stat Store specializes in both meanings of the word: rapid copying and photo duplication, and it offers Xerox copying, Kodaliths, color stats, cibaprints, custom transfers, photo posters, and photo murals as well as photostats. A new electronic publishing division offers high-resolution computer output and design services. They also assist clients in design, illustration, technical support, and production management of special projects.

Plant Consultation

COUNCIL ON THE ENVIRONMENT OF NEW YORK CITY
51 Chambers St (room 228)
566-0990
Mon-Fri: 9-5

A little-known fact is that the city will loan tools free of charge to groups involved in community sponsored open-space greening projects. Loans are limited to one week, but the waiting period is not long, and for the "price," the wait is worth it. You can borrow the same tools several times a season, as long as there is no one ahead of you on the list. A group can be as few as four people. The Council will also design and install paper recycling programs for hospitals, nonprofit and commercial businesses. They will do tree labeling service for a fee, and have a number of interesting *free* publications

Plumbers

KAPNAG HEATING AND PLUMBING
326 E 91st St
289-8847

As an out-of-towner, I'm not often in need of a Manhattan plumber, so there's a story behind how I learned that Kapnag is a really first-rate operation. A while ago, I was visiting a friend who was having a plumbing problem. She called Kapnag, but got no response. When she called a second time, Kapnag apologized profusely and came out immediately to fix it. There was even a follow-up call to make sure the problem had been completely corrected. Ask any New Yorker, and you'll learn what a rare virtue this story illustrates. Brett Neuhauser, Kapnag's president, has got to be the reason for all this kindness. When we first published this story, Neuhauser wrote to tell us that the sudden surge in sales was due to his mother "supplying the northeast region." May they both continue to thrive!

Postal Services

MAIL BOXES ETC. USA
629-6200 (information on nearest facility)
Mon-Thurs: 9-8; Fri: 9-6; Sat: 10-5

Mail Boxes Etc. have over 800 locations in all major cities, and can provide convenient FAX and TELEX service in all time zones. They also represent all major carriers, and will do professional packaging and shipping. You may "rent an office" with all services at a very inexpensive price at prestigious addresses. Other handy services include stamps and envelopes, mail forwarding, packing supplies, business cards, office stationery, notary and secretarial services, passport photos, laminating, key duplication, and computer letters. In other words, you really don't need a secretary; Mail Boxes Etc. can serve in his/her place. But who's going to bring in the morning coffee? Ask Dolores at the above number; she is so obliging, that might be possible, too!

Quilting Instruction

CRAFT STUDENTS LEAGUE
YWCA of the City of New York
610 Lexington Ave
755-2700

Because not many tools are needed to make a quilt, few stores are devoted solely to quilt-making. The best instruction is to be found in such schools as the Craft Students League. There are limited classes with an average of eight meetings. During the course, each student works on a project and, depending upon proficiency, either starts or completes at least one quilt. The Craft Students League also has any number of other excellent courses. All of them, while "crafty," are immensely practical as well. The bookbinding course is known for its professionalism (see "Bookbinding"). Send for a catalog to get a better idea of what they offer. You won't be disappointed.

Reweaving

FRENCH-AMERICAN REWEAVING COMPANY
37 W 57th St (at Fifth Ave, room 409)
753-1672
Mon-Fri: 10-6; Sat: 11-2

For more than 59 years, this company has been repairing and mending knit, lace, linen, silk, and wool fabrics with an almost invisible mending process that makes the new threads indiscernible from the originals. Even when an item is badly—and seemingly irreparably—damaged, the people at French-American claim that if they can't weave the wound, they can at least repair it so that their work is the next best thing to invisible. Needless to say, one doesn't submit a $3 tie to these costly procedures. But if an item is worth saving, it's almost a sure thing that these people can pull it off.

Rug Cleaning

A. BESHAR AND COMPANY
611 Broadway (Cable Building)
529-7300 (gallery), 292-3301 (rug cleaning)
Mon-Sat: 9-5; closed Sat in summer

Lee Howard Beshar's family has run this carpet and Oriental rug business for three generations. Consequently, there is little he doesn't know or hasn't seen in the carpet business. He can handle any kind of request competently. His expertise and experience are the basis of the Besharizing Cleaning Process, which all floor coverings submitted for correction receive. Naturally, if a rug only needs cleaning, you're ahead of the game. Beshar does not make house calls; all carpets must be cleaned at the company's offices. This can be expensive, so if your carpet isn't very valuable, you might be better off buying a new one. Here, too, Beshar can come to the rescue with a large range of Oriental and antique rugs. All are of good quality and value, and Beshar stands behind—and sometimes *on*—them all.

Scissors and Knife Sharpening

HENRY WESTPFAL AND COMPANY
4 E 32nd St
684-4687
Mon-Fri: 9-6

A Japanese gentleman once brought in his prized Samurai sword for repair at Henry Westpfal's, so you know this place has to be pretty expert at what it does. And they should be. They've been in business since 1874, and the same family has been in charge all of that time. They do all kinds of sharpening and repair, from barber scissors and pruning shears to cuticle scissors, plus all kinds of work on light tools. And for you left-handers, they also sell those hard to find left-handed scissors.

Sewing Machine Repair

MILTON KESSLER
718-763-7897

More elusive than a needle in a haystack is an honest repairman, particularly one who makes house calls. Milton Kessler is one who is polite, thorough, and completely reliable. He is never home when you call, but he does get messages and can usually schedule an appointment within a week. In addition, he has a wealth of information on the care and maintenance of sewing machines in general, and he tells you how yours got into the shape that necessitated his visit in particular. On top of his honesty, promptness, and reliability, Kessler has rates that are dirt cheap. He's also one of New York's nicest people.

Shoe Repair

B. NELSON SHOE CORPORATION
1221 Sixth Ave (bet 48th and 49th St, McGraw-Hill
    Building, C-2 level)

Main Concourse, RCA Building
630 Fifth Ave (International Building)
869-3552
Mon-Fri: 7:30-5:15

While researching this book, I asked several luggage dealers if they knew of a good shoe repair store. I have worn out dozens of pairs of shoes while walking the city, and all of our shoe repair listings have been places that I've personally used. So, I was beginning to fear that there might be an even better spot that I had missed simply because my shoes happened to be intact when I walked by it. And I figured, who better to ask than luggage dealers? Still, I was surprised when three in a row recommended B. Nelson. I was so impressed that I dropped my planned itinerary and headed for B. Nelson. I was armed with "Rockefeller Center" as an address, and that isn't remotely sufficient. Eventually, I found it by asking dozens of people for "a good shoe repair store." I was told over and over again that B. Nelson was it. When I finally got there, Nick Valenti, the owner, was out. But there on the wall of the shop was a laudatory review of his establishment, from the fourth edition of this book! I was glad that Valenti wasn't there to see my embarrassment. It turns out that the branch stores go under the name General Shoe Repair. But under any name at any address, this is a first choice.

JIM'S SHOE REPAIR
50 E 59th St (bet Madison and Park Ave)
355-8259
Mon-Fri: 8-6; Sat: 8-4; closed Sat in summer

This operation offers first-rate shoe repair, shoeshine, and shoe supplies. Shoe repair is a field that is rapidly losing its craftsmen, and Jim is one of the few who upholds the tradition. Jim's owner is Joseph A. Rocco, who specializes in orthopedic work and boot alteration. But people still call him Jim.

MANHATTAN SHOE REPAIR
6 E 39th St	42 E 41 St

683-4210
Mon-Fri: 7:30-5:45

Manhattan Shoe Repair offers a large range of orthopedic and fashion repairs. In addition to the regular resoling and heel repairs, Manhattan does rebinding and redyeing. Their motto is "Work that lasts." That pun is theirs, not mine, but after 35 years in the business, Mr. Lucas is entitled to make jokes about his work.

Silver Repair

BRANDT & OPIS
46 W 46th St (fifth floor)
245-9237
Mon-Fri: 8-3:30

Charles Opis can handle just about anything to do with silversmithing. For nearly 40 years, this shop has been replacing silver, doing gold and silver plating, repairing silver and brass, refinishing silver flatware, and taking monograms off of silver. They are trustworthy and experienced, and are able to handle mail orders.

THOME SILVERSMITHS
49 W 37th St (bet Fifth and Sixth Ave, room 605)
764-5426
Mon-Fri: 8:30-5:30

Thome cleans, repairs, and replates silver in addition to dealing in the buying and selling of some magnificent pieces. They have a real appreciation for the material, and it shows in everything they do. They will repair and polish brass and copper, and they also do restorations, silver and gold plating, pewter repair and cleaning, lacquering, and refining. Incidentally, *don't* attempt pewter repair yourself. Pewter is an alloy and must be handled delicately. Thome also specializes in brass. This company is one of the very few still in that business.

Stained-Glass Work

CUSHEN STUDIO
110 W 17th St (bet Sixth and Seventh Ave)
675-6674
Mon-Sat: 8-5; Sun by appointment only

Jack Cushen moved to New York from Ohio to take advantage of the demand for stained-glass windows in New York churches. He is one of the few people left in the city (or perhaps in the nation) with this expertise. One of Cushen's most recent projects was the restoration of seven 22-foot-high windows from St. Michael's Episcopal Church on Amsterdam Avenue and 99th Street. The windows are the work of Louis Comfort Tiffany (and others), and presented enormous challenges. Cushen not only rose to the occasion, but had been predicting for years (as readers of our previous editions know) that a major renaissance of stained-glass art was about to begin. These days there are more restorations than new work, and it is more than the qualified studios can handle. Cushen is at the leading edge of the art.

GREENLAND STUDIO
147 W 22nd St (bet Sixth and Seventh Ave)
255-2551
Mon-Thurs: 8-5; Fri: 8-2

Melville Greenland is a master conservator. He is also the director of the stained-glass conservation studio that is located in the midst of the restoration work at the 142-year-old Episcopal Church of St. Ann and the Holy Trinity in Brooklyn Heights. In his free time, Greenland runs this studio which also takes on much smaller projects. He does fabrication work, and designs new pieces for stained-glass windows.

Tailors

CLAUDIA BRUCE
140 E 28th St (bet Lexington and Third Ave)
685-2810
By appointment

You just can't part with that beautiful—but outdated—dress you got 10 years ago on your honeymoon in Paris? You don't want to send that special gown you wore to your daughter's wedding to your dry cleaner's tailor to get that tear on the sleeve repaired? Don't worry. Just call Claudia Bruce, a very talented lady who has been taking care of these problems with finesse for over a decade. Not only will Claudia take care of repairs and the rejuvenation of garments, she also will do made-to-order clothing. There are home-fitting appointments—for an extra charge, of course.

MARSAN TAILORS
897 Broadway (at 20th St, second floor)
475-2727
Mon-Wed, Fri: 9:30-5:30; Thurs: 9:30-7; Sat: 9:30-5;
   Sun: 12-4

Before Saint Laurie, one of the biggest emporiums of men's clothing in Manhattan, established its own tailor shop, all its alterations were done by Marsan. Any tailor who survives in the middle of the men's wholesale garment area must be good, and Marsan is among the best. All work is done by hand.

SEBASTIAN TAILORS
767 Lexington Ave (at 60th St, room 404)
688-1244
Mon-Fri: 8:30-5:30; Sat 9-4:30

Tailors are a peculiar breed in New York. In a city that is the home of the garment industry, most garment repairmen build their trade as either custom alteration and design specialists or dry cleaners who incidentally mend whatever bedraggled outfit has been brought in for cleaning. Sebastian Tailors is one of the few shops in the city that is exactly what it says it is—a tailor shop. The custom alterations for men and women are quick, neat, and, wonder of wonders, reasonable. Sebastian also does reweaving. But, best of all, everything is accomplished without the normal ballyhoo most such New York establishments seem to regard as their due. Incidentally, Sebastian was recommended to me by another tailor who particularly praised their alterations. Praise from someone within the trade is the highest praise of all. And when the praise includes the less common skill of ladies' tailoring, it marks a place worth trying. I use him, and I think he's great.

SILLS OF CAMBRIDGE
18 E 53rd St (bet Madison and Fifth Ave)
355-2360
Mon-Sat: 9:30-5:30; closed Sat in July, Aug

Self-styled as a custom English tailor, Sills creates impeccable suits and jackets. With a wide selection of fabrics, styling, and design, no two suits are the same; all are custom-made. Sills is noted for excellent service and craftsmanship, and while there is no comparison to the off-the-rack variety, Sills' prices are not that much higher. For the ultimate luxury experience, try Sills.

Television Rental

TELEVISION RENTAL COMPANY
13 E 31st St (second floor)
683-2850
Mon-Fri: 9-6; Sat: 9-4

Ted Pappas runs a rental service that is fast, good, and efficient. He will rent televisions for long- or short-term periods, and will happily deliver the sets and pick them up. He also rents VCRs, camcorders, and other audiovisual aids. The prices are among the best in the city, and in a business like this, his solid reputation is a formidable recommendation in itself. Tell him I sent you.

Tickets for Events

You must be prepared for hassle and confusion when you try to get tickets for events in New York. I have tried to get the latest facts for you, but things do change very quickly. And besides, the folks in this business are among the rudest in New York. Remember that it *is* possible to get tickets at the last minute for most shows and performances. You just need to know how to go about doing it, and you have to be prepared to pay a premium in some cases.

Broadway Shows: You must first decide which show (or shows) you would like to see. Naturally, getting tickets for the hits will be more difficult and costlier. To find out what is playing, consult the theater section of *The New York Times* or the theater pages of *New York* magazine or *The New Yorker*. You may also get this information from **NYC/On Stage**, a project of the Theater Development Fund and American Express. At the touch of a telephone button, at any hour of the day or night, you can get information on ticket availability, cost, seat location, how to get the tickets, similar plays in production, and information on the subject of the show and its stars. In Manhattan, call 587-1111; outside New York, call 800-782-4369.

To secure tickets ahead of time, you have several choices. You may go directly to the theater's box office. If the show is a hit, be prepared to stand on line. You may order by phone; different organizations sell tickets for different shows. (The newspaper ads or the telephone information service will tell you which organization sells the tickets for the show you want.) **Tele-Charge**, a service of the Shubert organization, sells tickets for the Shubert shows and for several other theaters. They give good phone service, and may be reached at 239-6200 in Manhattan and at 800-233-3123 outside the city. Remember that *all* phone agencies add a service charge. You may use most major credit cards, and tickets will be mailed, if there is adequate time; otherwise, they may be picked up at the box office. Be sure to take your credit card with you, if you are picking up the tickets at the box office. **Ticketron** (947-5850) is practically impossible to reach, with busy lines and recorded messages. Their operators are rude and unhelpful in the extreme. Ticketron information may be obtained at 399-4444. They have outlets in various places around the city, including Grand Central Station and Penn Station. If you are really in a bind for tickets, and price is not important, check with **Florence Read** at the Pierre Hotel, Monday through Saturday, from 11 a.m.-7 p.m.; her phone number is 757-5210. She can sometimes work marvels. Other possibilities include checking with ticket offices scattered throughout the theater area or in major hotels, or taking a chance on finding someone outside the theater of your choice who wants to get rid of their tickets (at a price, of course).

For off-price tickets for Broadway shows, the best place to go is **TKTS**. It was started as a way to fill empty seats in Broadway houses. Empty seats are lost revenue, and a half-empty house is bad for the morale of the actors as well as that of the audience. TKTS (at Broadway and 47th St, 354-5800), is open Mon-Sat: 3-8 (evening tickets); Wed, Sat: 10-2 (matinee tickets); Sun: noon to closing (matinee and evening tickets). The **Lower Manhattan Theater Center** (2 World Trade Center, mezzanine floor) is open Mon-Fri: 11-5:30; Sat: 11-3:30. Go early in the day for the best seats, and keep in mind that their half-price tickets may not be available for the show of your choice. Note also that only tickets for that day's performances are offered.

Off Broadway and Off-Off Broadway: The best bet here is to go to the theater box office or call the theater directly by phone. For information on off-Broadway and off-off Broadway shows, call **Ticket Central**, 1-8 daily, at 279-4200.

Music and Dance Events: Again, the newspaper and magazine listings will help you find out what is available. The **Bryant Park Music and Dance Booth** (42nd St bet Fifth and Sixth Ave) sells full-price tickets for these events, and on the day of the performance it *only* sells half-price tickets. The phone number is 382-2323, and the hours are Tues, Thurs, Fri: 12-2, 3-7; Wed, Sat: 11-2, 3-7; Sun: 12-6. Tickets for these events may also be purchased at the respective theater box offices.

New York Yankees, Nassau Coliseum, Radio City Music Hall, Madison Square Garden, Giant Stadium, Meadowlands, Lincoln Center: Tickets for all of these may, of course, be purchased directly on site. However, **Ticket Master** is a one-stop ticket center for all these attractions, plus certain smaller arenas and clubs. Their phone number for tickets is 307-7171, and they are very polite and helpful (for a change!). Their office number—*not* for tickets—is 713-6300. They will mail you tickets if there is time, or you may pick them up at the box office the day of the performance. All major credit cards are accepted. Ticket Master locations in Manhattan include 17 E Eighth St, 955 Third Ave (at 57th St), 1302 Second Ave (at 69th St), 383 Lafayette St, 120 W 72nd St (at Columbus Ave), 32 Mott St, 40 Union Square E (at 17th St), 1595 Second Ave (at 83rd St), 1977 Broadway (at 67th St), 38 Park Row, 186 W Fourth St (at Sixth Ave), and the Port Authority Bus Terminal (second floor). Hours vary at each location. Tickets for Radio City Music Hall may be obtained at their box office. It is a good idea to call, write, or phone early for their special attractions, especially the spectacular Christmas show.

Television Shows: Tickets for television shows are not always easy to come by. Popular shows fill months early (most are taped), and the taping is not done on a regular schedule. At times, tickets are handed out to passers-by on the corner of Fifth Avenue at 50th Street. If you want to plan ahead, contact the networks as follows: **ABC** (36 W 66th St, 456-7777), **CBS** (524 W 57th St, 975-2476), **NBC** (30 Rockefeller Center Guest Relations, 664-3055). It is also possible to get tickets at the network headquarters on the day of the show. Try to be there by 9 a.m. because tickets are handed out on a first-come, first-serve basis.

Special Ideas for Less Expensive Tickets: Hit Shows (630 Ninth Ave, at 44th St, suite 808) issues discount coupons for shows, but does *not* sell tickets. They offer a club membership; information may be obtained by calling 581-4211. The **School Theater Ticket Program** also offers coupons. They have no location or phone; word-of-mouth will lead you to distribution centers and times. Standing room for sold-out plays is often available on the day of the performance at the individual box offices. The Metropolitan Opera Guild has 24 tickets available for each performance at the **Score Desk**, 1865 Broadway at 61st St, 582-7500, ext. 517). Standing-room tickets for the week's performances are sold at the box office beginning at 10 a.m. Saturday. The New York City Ballet, at the **New York State Theater,** sells day-of-performance standing-room tickets, starting at 10 a.m. (67th St and Broadway, 870-5570). A percentage of the seats at the **New York Shakespeare Festival's Public Theater** are sold at half price two hours before curtain (425 Lafayette St, 598-7150). Many times shows in preview offer tickets at reduced prices. The **Theater Development Fund**'s voucher plan (1501 Broadway, 221-0013) and the **Lincoln Center Theater** subscription program offer good values. Seats for the **New York Philharmonic**'s open rehearsals are sold for almost peanuts on Thursday mornings.

Translations

EURAMERICA
257 Park Ave S
777-7878

Euramerica can provide written translations in technical, advertising, legal, and commercial documents, as well as simultaneous oral translations. These people are truly masters who cannot be adequately described in writing. Suffice it to say that if the U.S. State Department can have a translator mistakenly tell another country that our president desires them obscenely, accurate translating is not an easy thing. Euramerica has had no such accidents.

Typewriter Repair

LINCOLN TYPEWRITERS AND COPY CENTER
100 W 67th St (at Broadway)
787-9397, 874-9113
Mon-Fri: 9-6; Sat: 11-4

When Abdul Majid, Lincoln's owner, branched out on his own, he took with him the skills he had learned at Francis Typewriter (a renowned repair shop in the Village). Lincoln's prices are as low as its basement-level location. There is free pickup and delivery and a tradition of service that even includes free ribbon changing. Now they service word processors and calculators as well.

Upholstering

RAY MURRAY INCORPORATED
121 E 24th St (bet Park and Lexington Ave, second floor)
838-3752
Daily: 8:30-5

Here's the good news: Ray Murray Incorporated is a reliable, capable, talented re-upholstering company. Now, the bad news: it costs just as much to re-upholster your furniture as it does to replace it. Murray's specialty is creating custom-made furniture. Cheap it isn't, but the quality is superb. They can copy any design you want (including heirloom pieces or furniture from museum exhibits), but they specialize in classic, contemporary, and modern furniture. Big, overstuffed sofas are their forte. A seven-foot custom job runs under $1,500, which isn't bad, compared to the cost of ready-made furniture. The reasonable prices disappear when they talk about re-upholstering. Even if the customer supplies the material, a recovered sofa won't be much less than $500. However, if you're redecorating and your furniture is generally in good condition, Murray can coordinate all the work, fabric, and patterns. They can make drapery and accessory pieces to match the recovered furniture, and the total cost will be substantially less than it would be to throw everything out and start from scratch. Joe Sinis, a very talented craftsman, has taken over the Ray Murray business and carries on the tradition of excellence.

VI. Where To Buy It: New York's Best Stores

A Few Helpful Shopping Hints

1. If you shop carefully, you need not pay full retail price for most merchandise. Discount and off-price outlets abound. The Lower East Side is an especially good area for bargain shopping.

2. Be careful in stores that do not mark their goods carefully. Some of them will charge whatever the traffic will bear.

3. Study the section at the front of this book that describes shopping districts. In these areas you will be able to do comparison shopping for selection and value.

4. Credit cards are accepted practically everywhere in the city. You can sometimes get a better price, however, by paying cash.

5. Avoid the electronics stores on Fifth Avenue. Many of them are unreliable when it comes to prices or merchandise.

6. Shop carefully for shoes, neckties, cosmetics, perfume, and floor coverings. Many of these goods are overpriced.

7. Boutiques owned by designers often do not have the best price on their own merchandise. Shop around. Also, some manufacturers have periodic special sales in their showrooms.

8. The smart shopper can save money by waiting for certain times of the year to buy sales items:

January: White goods, cosmetics, stationery, women's clothing
February: Hosiery, housewares, men's clothing, coats, toys
March: Garden supplies, ski equipment, china and glassware
April: Air conditioners, fabrics, spring shoes
May: Boys' and men's clothing, white goods, housewares
June: Summer sportswear, furniture, floor coverings
July: Air conditioners, bathing suits, summer sports items
August: Fans, school clothing, white goods, coats
September: Bicycles, fabrics, paints, floor coverings
October: Camping equipment, school supplies, sporting goods
November: Furs, blankets, shoes
December: Greeting cards, toys, party items

The Best (And Some Not So Good) Places To Shop in New York: An Exclusive List

Things for the Person (Men, Women, Children)

Great discount accessories: Bernard Krieger & Son (316 Grand St)

Best values in women's apparel: Ben Farber (462 Seventh Ave)

Albert Nippon apparel at discount: Lea's (81 Rivington St)

Best aprons: Apron and Bag Supply Company (47 Second Ave)

Attitude adjustment needed: Polo-Ralph Lauren (867 Madison Ave)

Insulting attitude: Gucci (683 Fifth Ave)

Mail-order baby gift service: Life's Little Treasures (516/937-0511)

Best antique bags: Sylvia Pines Uniquities (1102 Lexington Ave)

Overpriced bags: Coach Store (754 Madison Ave)

Excellent selection of inexpensive imported beads: Cesar's (1214B Broadway) and Glori Bead Shoppe (172 W Fourth St)

Best selection of ladies' belts: Accessorie Club (10 E 36th St)

Best for Western boots: Lord John Bootery (428 Third Ave)

Best handmade boots and shoes for men: E. Vogel Boots and Shoes (19 Howard St)

Best briefcases: Carry On Luggage (150 W 26th St)

Best for hair brushes: William Radoff (806 Lexington Ave)

Best button selection: Tender Buttons (143 E 62nd St)

Children's wear at discount: Cici Bebe (39 W 32nd St)

Best antique clothes: Antique Boutique (712-714 Broadway)

Best bet for tall-gal clothes: Shelly's Tall Girl Shop (13 E 41st St)

Best evening clothes: Lucille Chayt (484 Broome St)

Best small-sized clothes: Minishop (14 W 55th St)

Classic men's and women's clothes: Peter Elliot (1383 Third Ave)

Exciting kids' clothes: Glad Rags (1007 Madison Ave)

Italian men's clothes: Manitalia (24 W 55th St)

Beautiful custom-made men's clothing, shirts, and ties: Ascot Chang (7 W 57th St)

Be careful on prices of women's clothing: S&W (165 W 26th St)

Best brand-name men's clothing at discount: L.S. Men's Clothing (18 W 45th St)

Best men's clothing department (department store): Saks Fifth Avenue (611 Fifth Ave)

Best selection of women's small-sized clothing: Piaffe (841 Madison Ave)

Best selection of men's clothing at attractive prices: Saint Laurie (897 Broadway) and Gorsart (9 Murray St)

Best selection of unusual clothing: The Gallery of Wearable Art (480 W Broadway)

Best women's trendy clothing: Betsey Johnson (several locations)

British vintage clothing: Duke's (57 Grand St)

Cartoon clothing, jewelry, and accessories: The Mouse Dynasty (503 Columbus Ave)

Classic clothing for women: Vermont Classics (284 Columbus Ave)

Classy custom-made men's clothing: Alan Flusser (16 E 52nd St)

Classy men's clothing: Oliver Grant (222 Columbus Ave)

French kids' clothing: Jacadi (1281 Madison Ave)

Great selection of children's clothing: Little Bits (1186 Madison Ave) and Wicker Garden's Children (1327 Madison Ave)

Imported designer clothing: India Cottage (1150 Broadway)

Ladies' clothing at great discounts: Simply Samples (150 W 36th St, third floor)

Ridiculous prices for men's clothing: Bijan (699 Fifth Ave)

Women's clothing at good prices: Miriam Rigler (62 W 56th St)

Best prices for women's coats: Rubin's Fashions (242 W 38th St)

Best selection of Loden coats: Loden and Leather Fashions (155 W 72nd St)

Petite, junior, and half-sized coats, suits, and jackets: Rain Barrel (101 Orchard St)

Designer (Calvin, Polo, Yves St. Laurent) cosmetics at discount: Almaya Cosmetics (38 W 30th St)

Discount cosmetics: Apple Cosmetics (135 Canal St)

Most honest diamond merchant: Rennie Ellen (15 W 47th St)

Custom-designed earrings: Sheri Miller (58 W 47th St)

Best imported fabrics: Far Eastern Fabrics (171 Madison Ave)

Best Oriental fabrics: Oriental Dress Company (38 Mott St)

Pricey antique hand fans: Lune (Place des Antiquaires, 57th St and Lexington Ave)

Women's small-sized footwear: Giordano's (1118 First Ave)

Fine selection of brand-name discount fragrances: Kris Cosmetics (1170 Broadway at 28th St)

Great fragrances: Scentsitivity (870½ Lexington Ave)

Fur scarves and hats: Aaron Weining (348 Seventh Ave)

Best furs and salespeople you can trust: G. Michael Hennessy (333 Seventh Ave) and H.B.A. Fur (333 Seventh Ave)

Good selection of hair accessories: Head Master (366 W Broadway)

Best handbag store: Fine and Klein (119 Orchard St)

Best stock of men's hats: Young's Hats (139 Nassau St)

Custom-made hats: Victoria DiNardo (68 Thompson St)

Great custom fur hats: Lenore Marshall (333 Seventh Ave)

Best herbs: Meadowsweet Herbal Apothecary (77 E Fourth St)

Best hosiery values for determined shoppers: Jacob Young and Son (329 Grand St)

Jackets (men and women): Bailey, Browning and Downs (72 Thompson St)

Best jeans prices: Alaska Fashions (41 Orchard St)

Savviest jewelers: Fortunoff (681 Fifth Ave)

Once-great jewelry house sinking (tired, haughty salespeople, poor service): Van Cleef and Arpels (744 Fifth Ave)

Best fashion jewelry: Back in Black (123 Prince St)

Best buys in gold and diamond jewelry: M. Boner and Son (114 Fifth Ave)

Best jewelry in SoHo: Richard Erker (132 Thompson St)

Discount better jewelry: Tiana (389 Fifth Ave, suite 202)

Fabulous American Indian jewelry: Saity (Trump Tower, 725 Fifth Ave)

Great jewelry: Hidden Treasures (Grace Garfinkel, 450 E 63rd St)

Best selection of kimonos: Kimono (120 Thompson St) and East East (230 E 80th St)

Beautiful knitwear: Knit Couture (800 Madison Ave)

Fine leather goods and accessories: Fomo (61 Orchard St)

Best lingerie values: Goldman and Cohen (54 Orchard St)

Sexiest lingerie: Samantha Jones (1391 Second Ave) and Victoria's Secret (34 E 57th St)

When you want custom-blended massage oils: The Fragrance Shoppe (21 E Seventh St)

Best custom-made millinery: Don Marshall (465 Park Ave)

Best outdoor wear: EMS—The Outdoor Specialist (20 W 61st St)

Most overexposed: Benetton (Are they competing with McDonald's?)

Best perfume selection: Warwick Chemists (1348 Sixth Ave)

Perfume copies: Essential Products Company (90 Water St)

Best discount perfumes: Round House Fashions (256 W 36th St) and La Femme (110 W 40th St)

Best piece-goods store: Samuel Beckenstein (125 Orchard St)

High-fashion rainwear: Norman Lawrence (417 Fifth Ave)

High-pressure shirt salespeople: Custom Shops (many locations)

Discount tuxedo shirts and accessories: Ted's (83 Orchard St)

Excellent selection of men's shirts at great prices: Acorn (601 Fifth Ave)

Shoes for millionaires: Susan Bennis/Warren Edwards (440 Park Ave)

Best discounts on designer shoes: Designer Shoes (317 Grand St)

Big and wide shoes: Tall Size Shoes (3 W 35th St)

Bridal shoes: Peter Fox (105 Thompson St)

Custom-made shoes for women: Mathia (20 E 69th St)

Good prices on athletic shoes: Athlete's Choice (2 W 31st St)

Great discount shoes: Aly's Hut (85 Hester St) and Stapleton Shoe Company (68 Trinity Pl)

Upscale kids' shoes: Shoofly (506 Amsterdam Ave)

Silk blouses and dresses at wholesale prices: Omanti Designs (530 Seventh Ave, ninth floor)

Discount sneakers for men and women: Shoe City (133 Nassau St)

Best selection of soaps: Soap Opera (51 Grove St)

Best unisex sportswear: Taverniti (460 W Broadway)

Best women's sportswear prices: M. Friedlich (196 Orchard St) and Giselle (143 Orchard St)

Mod sportswear for men and women: Poco Loco (106 Wooster St)

Name-brand sportswear at discount: Athlete's Choice (2 W 31st St)

Swedish-designed sportswear: Marc O'Polo (214 Columbus Ave)

Women's better sportswear sizes 2 to 12 at discount: Joseph Vincent (382-1780)

Sunglasses: Shades of the Village (167 Seventh Ave S)

Austrian sweaters: Geiger (505 Park Ave)

Beautiful men's and women's cashmere sweaters: Berk (781 Madison Ave)

Italian handmade sweaters: Christina Bomba (59 Morton St)

Made-to-order sweaters (men's and women's): Gwen Byrne (23 Eighth Ave)

Best selection of swimsuits: New York Body Shop (49 W 57th St, 1195 Third Ave)

Best tie prices: Heritage Neckwear Company (194 Allen St)

Made-to-order ties: De Casi (37 W 57th St)

Great discount T-shirts: Eisner Bros. (76 Orchard St)

Best umbrella shop: Uncle Sam (161 W 57th St, 7 E 46th St)

Best for uniforms: Dornan (653 11th Ave)

Natural vitamins: New York Apothecary (11 E 17th St)

Best antique watch selection: Aaron Faber (666 Fifth Ave) and Time Will Tell (962 Madison Ave)

Great for watches: M.A.G. Time (60 W 22nd St)

Best wigs: Jacques Darcel (50 W 57th St)

Great prices on woolens: Raleigh Textiles (294 Eighth Ave)

Best zipper selection: A Feibusch (109 Hester St)

Things for the Home

Decorative antiques: Karen Warshaw (167 E 74th St)

Great antiques: French Country Store (35 E 10th St)

Great Victorian antiques: Somethin' Else (182 Ninth Ave)

Best kitchen-appliance shopping: Zabar's (2245 Broadway)

Discount appliances: Dembitzer Bros. (5 Essex St), Kaufman Electrical Appliances (365 Grand St), and Sam Diamond (94 Fulton St)

Ancient, European, Oriental, and Pre-Columbian works of art: Royal-Athena Galleries (153 E 57th St)

Primitive art: Eastern Arts (365 Bleecker St)

Western, 19th-century art: J. N. Bartfield Galleries (30 W 57th St)

Best for artifacts: Jacques Carcanagues (114 Spring St)

Best for dried-flower baskets: Galerie Felix (968 Lexington Ave)

Best selection of bathroom accessories: Elegant John (812 Lexington Ave)

Korean embroidered bedding: Seoul Handicraft (284 Fifth Ave)

Best for brassware: Ben Karpen (212 E 51st St)

Bustamonte pieces from Mexico: Pavo Real (Pier 17, South St Seaport)

Butcher-block counter, tables, chairs: Alexanders (176 Bowery)

Bird cages: Lexington Gardens (1008 Lexington Ave)

Best candles: The Candle Shop (118 Christopher St)

Best Oriental chests: Min-Yea (79 Madison Ave)

Best Amari china: Bardith (901 Madison Ave)

Best china and glassware department: B. Altman (Fifth Ave at 34th St)

Best discount china and glass: Lanac Sales (73 Canal St)

Great china odds-and-ends bargains: Fishs Eddy (551 Hudson St)

Hand-painted French china: Solanee (138 E 74th St)

Beautiful English antique clocks: Hymore Hodson Antiques (903 Madison Ave)

Best selection of Fiesta dinnerware: Mood Indigo (181 Prince St)

Best selection and best prices on domestics: Ezra Cohen (307 Grand St)

Best electronics selection: Vicmarv Stereo and TV (88 Delancey St)

Electronics values: The Wiz (12 W 45th St and other locations)

Great discounts on electronics: Annex Outlet (43 Warren St) and J&M Electronics (150 W 28th St)

Irish engravings: Irish Books and Graphics (90 W Broadway)

Best ceiling fans: Modern Supply (19 Murray St)

Doulton figurines: Pascoe and Company (18 W 55th St)

Best floor-covering store: ABC Carpets (881 Broadway)

Ikebana floral designs: Frank Luisi (864 Lexington Ave)

Finest selection of silk flowers: United States Flower Co (131 W 28th St)

Best picture frames: Ready Frames (14 W 45th St)

Hand-carved picture frames: D. Matt (223 E 80th St)

Hand-carved traditional furnishings: Devon Shops (111 E 27th St)

Best custom furniture: Navedo Woodcraft (179 E 119th St)

Best furniture department: Bloomingdale's (Third Ave at 59th St)

Best pine furniture: Better Times Antiques (500 Amsterdam Ave)

Formica furniture: Room Service (1123 Broadway)

Good selection of leather furniture: Leather Center (44 E 32nd St)

Modular furniture: Room Plus (1555 Third Ave)

Great gadgets: Brookstone (18 Fulton St, 1 Herald Center)

Fine glass and tableware: Avventura (463 Amsterdam Ave)

Best source for used Steuben glassware: Lillian Nassau (220 E 57th St)

Old globes and maps: E Forbes Smiley (Place des Antiquaires, 57th St and Lexington Ave)

Best home-accessory store: Carole Stupell (29 E 22nd St)

Unusual housewares: D. F. Sanders and Company (386 W Broadway, 952 Madison Ave, 57th St and Lexington Ave)

Icons: Manic (125 E 57th St)

Great custom kitchens: Regba Diran New York (105 Madison Ave)

Best Judaica: Hecker Corporation (605 Fifth Ave)

Best lampshades: Just Shades (21 Spring St)

Best for light bulbs: Just Bulbs (938 Broadway)

Best selection of lighting fixtures: New York Gas Lighting Company (145 Bowery)

Antique linens: Jean Hoffman-Jana Starr (236 E 80th St)

Best locks: Lacka (214 W 48th St)

Lucite bargains: Acrylium (964 Third Ave)

Best selection of Greek marble: SG Marble (900 First Ave)

Great prices on mattresses: Town Bedding (205 Eighth Ave)

Best medical supplies and equipment: Portnow Surgical Supplies (53 Delancey St)

Best movie star photos: Movie Star News (134 W 18th St)

Great prices on movie and TV pictures and posters: Movie Material (242 W 14th St)

Great plant selection: Farm and Garden Nursery (2 Sixth Ave)

Best cactus plants: The Grass Roots Garden (131 Spring St)

Best orchid plants: Robert Lester (280 W Fourth St)

Poster originals from 1880-1940: Philip Williams (phone 226-7830)

Best international theater posters: Triton Gallery (323 W 45th St)

Best posters: PosterAmerica (138 W 18th St)

Botanical prints: W Graham Arader (29 E 72nd St)

Contemporary wildlife and sporting prints: Sportsman's Edge (136 E 74th St)

Best quilts: Kelter/Malce (361 Bleecker St) and Quilts of America (431 E 73rd St)

Antique quilts: Susan Parrish (390 Bleecker St)

Best selection of Oriental rugs: Momeni (36 E 31st St)

Best shoji screens: Katsura Studio (389 Broome St) and Tonee Crafts (108 Wooster St)

Security devices: REM Security (11 E 20th St)

Best silver and wedding gift prices: Rogers and Rosenthal (105 Canal St)

Unusual silver: Jean's Silversmiths (16 W 45th St)

Best values in silverware/holloware: Eastern Silver (54 Canal St)

Office and home stationery items at discount: Tunnel (301 Canal St)

Superb tapestries: Lovelia Enterprises (356 E 41st St) and Saint-Remy (818 Lexington Ave)

Antique silk and satin tassels: Cobweb (116 W Houston St)

One-of-a-kind antique textiles: Pillow Salon (238 E 60th St)

Best selection of ceramic tiles, marble, and wall coverings: The Quarry (114 E 32nd St)

Best garden tools: Zona (97 Greene St)

Best topiary trees: Green Thumb Flowers (22 E 65th St)

Best discount wallpaper: Pintchik (278 Third Ave)

Best selection of weather vanes: Le Fanion (299 W Fourth St)

Things for Leisure Time

Best values in art supplies: Pearl Paint Company (308 Canal St)

Outstanding prices on athletic gear: Modell's (109 E 42nd St)

Best find for autographs: Gallery of History (World Financial Center)

Best selection of baseball cards: Card Collectors (105 W 77th St)

Best selection of bibles in every language: International Bible Society (172 Lexington Ave)

Best bicycle values: Gene's Bike Shop (242 E 79th St)

Best art book selection: Jaap Reitman (134 Spring St) and Hacker (54 W 57th St)

Best for mystical and religious books: Quest Bookshop (240 E 53rd St)

Best military books: Soldier Shop (1222 Madison Ave)

Tribal art books: Oan-Oceanie-Afrique Noire (9 E 38th St, fourth floor)

Best mystery books: Foul Play (10 Eighth Ave)

Best prices on books: Barnes and Noble (many locations)

Best prices on used and reviewers' books: Strand Book Store (Broadway and 12th St)

Best selection of exam study books and science fiction: Civil Service Books (89 Worth St)

Full selection of astrology and artificial intelligence books: New York Astrology Center (545 Eighth Ave)

Great for theater books: Theatre Arts Bookshop (405 W 42nd St)

Largest collection of books and magazines on aviation, military, naval, and uniforms: Sky Books International (48 E 50th St)

Rail and motor books: Albion Scott (48 E 50th St)

Sports books: James Cummings (859 Lexington Ave)

Best camera store: Grand Central Camera (420 Lexington Ave)

Professional movie cameras: Cine 60 (630 Ninth Ave)

Great cinema items: Cinemabilia (611 Broadway)

Contemporary crafts: Civilisation (78 Second Ave)

Rock and Roll discs: Smash Compact Discs (17 St Mark's Pl)

Diving equipment: Pan Aqua Diving (166 W 75th St)

Doll Houses: Charles Miniatures (246 Lafayette St)

Magnificent porcelain dolls: Bon Jour France (155 Spring St)

Best drums: Drummer's World (133 W 45th St)

Best embroidery: Selected Things (226 Front St)

Fly fishing equipment: Hunting World (16 E 53rd St)

Great fishing tackle: Orvis (355 Madison Ave)

Best war games: Compleat Strategist (11 E 33rd St, 320 W 57th St)

Golf equipment at reasonable prices: New York Golf Center (29 W 36th St)

Best block to shop for horseback-riding equipment: Miller's (123 E 24th St) and H. Kauffman and Sons (139 E 24th St)

Best jukeboxes: Back Pages Antiques (125 Greene St)

Kaleidoscopes: After the Rain (149 Mercer St)

Great kayaks: Hans Klepper (35 Union Sq W)

Colorful kites: Big City Kite Company (1201 Lexington Ave)

Great soft luggage: The Bag House (58 E Eighth St)

Best magazine selection: Eastern Newsstand (Pan Am Building) and Magazine Store (30 Lincoln Plaza)

Best back issues of magazines: A & S Books (274 W 43rd St)

Best maps: Hammond Map Store (57 W 43rd St)

Best marine supplies: Goldberg's Marine (12 W 37th St)

Best selection of music from all publishers: Music Store at Carl Fischer (62 Cooper Sq)

Best musical instruments: Sam Ash Music Store (160 W 48th St)

State-of-the-art musical items: Yamaha (142 W 57th St)

Great needlepoint: 2 Needles (1266 Madison Ave)

Out-of-town newspapers: Hotalings (142 W 42nd St)

Elegant papers for correspondence: Il Papiro (1021 Lexington Ave and W.F.C.)

Good prices on Cross and Mont Blanc pens: Amber Palette (436 Madison Ave)

Great photo supplies: Ben Ness (114 University Pl)

Best pipes: Connoisseur Pipe Shop (51 W 46th St)

Best record selection: Tower Records (692 Broadway, 1961 Broadway)

Best used-records store: St Mark's Sounds (20 St Mark's Pl)

Best for out-of-print records: Dayton's (824 Broadway)

Best opera records: Music Masters (25 W 43rd St)

Best selection of Broadway show records: Footlight Records (90 Third Ave)

Sad, sadder, saddest: Hammacher Schlemmer (147 E 57th St)

Best science fiction: Forbidden Planet (821 Broadway)

Best sci-fi gifts: Star Magic (743 Broadway)

When you want ship models: San Francisco Gallery (1089 Madison Ave)

Complete soccer supplies: Soccer Sport Supply (1745 First Ave)

Good selection of lead soldiers: Second Childhood (283 Bleecker St)

Best selection of stamps: Subway Stamp Shop (111 Nassau St)

Best fashion stationery: Ffolio 72 (33 E 68th St)

Best tobacco store: J.R. Tobacco (11 E 45th St)

Best handmade toys: Dinosaur Hill (302 E Ninth St)

Discount toys: Park Row Novelty (248 Grand Ave)

Museum quality toys (1900-1940): Bizarre Bazaar (Place Des Antiquaires, 57th St and Lexington Ave)

Lionel electric trains: Madison Hardware (105 E 23rd St)

Videotapes: RKO Video (1608 Broadway, 168 W 96th St, 1309 Lexington Ave, 507 Third Ave, 93 Greenwich Ave) and New Video (44 Greenwich Ave, 90 University Pl)

Hard-to-find videotapes (buy or rent): Evergreen Video (213 W 35th St, second floor)

Great wine-making supplies: Milan Home Wine and Beers (57 Spring St)

Things from Abroad

Best Afghan imports: Nusraty Afghan Imports (215 W 10th St)

Products of Brazil: Coisa Nossa (57 W 46th St, second floor)

Trendy British imports: 99X (210 E Sixth St)

Caribbean clothing: Island Trading Co (15 E Fourth St)

Best Chinese goods: Chinese American Trading Company (91 Mulberry St)

Guatemala gift items: Artesania (274 Columbus Ave)

Himalayan craft items: Himalayan Crafts and Tours (1219 Lexington Ave)

Best Japanese books, records, art: New York Kinokuniya Bookstore (10 W 49th St)

Unusual Japanese gift items: Five Eggs (436 W Broadway)

Mexican furnishings and crafts: Amigo Country (19 Greenwich Ave)

Scottish kilts and tartans: Scottish Products (133 E 55th St)

Best Spanish antiques: Cobweb (116 W Houston St)

Treasurers from Tibet: Do Kham (51 Prince St) and Tibetan Handicrafts (144 Sullivan St)

Other Things

Astrology items: New York Astrology Center (63 W 39th St)

Real bargains of all kinds: Unredeemed Pledge Sales (64 Third Ave)

Good selection of bird and kennel merchandise: Belmont (30 Rockefeller Plaza)

All kinds of birds: Bird Jungle (401 Bleecker St)

If you like butterflies: Mariposa (128 Thompson St and Pier 17, South St Seaport)

Great canvas goods: Matera Canvas (5 Lispenard St)

Beautiful antique Christmas ornaments: Christmas Inn New York (141 E 62nd St)

Covert equipment: Counter Spy Shop (630 Third Ave, fifth floor)

Rare old duck hunting decoys: Grove Decoys (49 Grove St)

Tropical fish: American Aquarium (810 Lexington Ave)

Most fun shopping: Orchard Street on Sunday

Great prices on gifts: Jompole (330 Seventh Ave)

Interesting hologram watches, pendants, and pyramids: Baggy Pants Express (159 W Fourth St)

Holographs: Holographic Studio (240 E 26th St)

"Ladies of the evening": Sixth Ave at 58th St (Be careful!)

New York memorabilia to take back home: Welcome to N.Y.C. (26 Carmine St)

Best office supplies: Menash (2305 Broadway)

Great discount office furniture: Frank Eastern Company (599 Broadway)

Discount pet supplies: Petland (132 Nassau St)

Best West Side pharmacy: Windsor Pharmacy (1419 Sixth Ave)

Fabulous postcards: French Kisses (144 Bleecker St)

Good taste: Macy's street floor

Poor taste: Lord & Taylor's street floor

Thrift-store find: Everybody's Thrift Shop (261 Park Ave S)

Anatomical Supplies

MAXILLA & MANDIBLE LTD.
453 Columbus Ave (bet 81st and 82nd St)
724-6173
Mon-Sat: 11-7

Henry Galiano grew up in Spanish Harlem, and on the days that his parents weren't running their beauty parlor, the family often went to the Museum of Natural History. His interest in things skeletal increased when Galiano got a job at the museum as a curator's assistant. He soon started his own collection of skeletons and bones. That in turn led to his opening Maxilla & Mandible (the names for the upper and lower jaw respectively), the first and only such store in the world. That's understandable. How many people need complete skeletons (or even a single maxilla)? Apparently many more than you would think. The shop started by supplying museum-quality preparations of skulls, skeletons, bones, teeth, horns, skins, butterflies, beetles, seashells, fossils, taxidermy mounts, anatomical charts and models to artists, sculptors, painters, interior decorators, jewelry manufacturers, prop masters, medical personnel, scientists, and educators. The real business is in the basement storerooms and laboratory. It seems only natural that an anatomical supply company and bone shop should have catacombs beneath Columbus Avenue. It seems to stretch on forever, and each door yields another boney site. This place is a scientific Halloween!

Animals, Fish, and Accessories

BEASTY FEAST
605 Hudson St
140 Ninth Ave (bet 18th and 19th St)
237 Bleecker St
243-3261
Mon-Fri: 12-7; Sat: 10-7

If the name intrigues you, the stock will intrigue you even more. Beasty Feast carries pet food and supplies at good discount prices, and the salespeople are thoughtful, friendly, and cooperative.

BIDE-A-WEE HOME ASSOCIATION
410 E 38th St
532-4455, 532-5884 (clinic)
Mon-Sat: 10-7; Sun: 10-5 (adoption)
Mon-Sat: 9:30-6; 9:30-3 (clinic)

Bide-A-Wee is the only shelter I know of in Manhattan that does not kill animals it can't place for adoption. For this alone, it deserves special mention. Dogs, cats, puppies, and kittens are available for adoption at nominal fees. Bide-A-Wee also has a veterinary clinic open to the public, and provides a pet bereavement program.

CANINE STYLES
830 Lexington Ave (bet 63rd and 64th St)
751-4549
Mon-Thurs: 8:30-7; Fri, Sat: 9-7

Ursula Lehnhardt has been in the doghouse for over 30 years! She specializes in fine dog grooming and bathing, cat and dog grooming aids, dog collars, leads, coats, sweaters, chains, beds, and carriers. You can also find some beautiful Danish china plates of various dog breeds that will make spectacular gifts for your doggy friends.

KAREN'S FOR PEOPLE AND PETS
1220 Lexington Ave (bet 82nd and 83rd St)
472-9440
Mon-Fri: 8-6; Sat: 9-6

Outfitting your pet can be very difficult, and finding a store that understands that there is more to a pet than dog biscuits is also difficult. Not to worry. For over a decade, Karen Thompson has been dressing dog and owner in matching outfits: "Upscale accessories for people and pets," says Karen. Many of the items, trimmed with matching furs or sequins, are her own exclusive designs. Karen is famous for her 100 percent wool hand-knit pet sweaters. When not dressing upscale pets, Karen's offers upscale grooming. After Karen's you'll never want to buy a flea collar in the supermarket again.

PETLAND DISCOUNTS

132 Nassau St	7 E 14th St
964-1821	675-4102
1443 St. Nicholas Ave	2675 Broadway
795-5783	222-8851
304 E 86th St	
472-1655	

Mon-Fri: 9-8; Sat: 10-6:30; Sun: 11-5

The folks at the New York Aquarium recommend this chain of stores for fish and accessories. Petland also carries birds and discount food and accessories for all pets, including dogs and cats.

Antiques

ANTIQUARIUM, FINE ANCIENT ARTS GALLERY
948 Madison Ave (at 75th St)
734-9776
Tues-Fri: 10-6; Sat: 10-5; closed Sat in summer

Antiquarium is a magnificent gallery for those who appreciate museum-quality antiquities and can afford to own them. This gallery specializes in Middle Eastern and classical items, with a particular emphasis on ancient glass, ancient jewelry, marble, and stone statuary and reliefs, bronzes, pottery, and coins. Virtually every ancient civilization is represented. This is definitely not the place to take your three-year-old or the Merrill Lynch bull. On the other hand, you may need Merrill Lynch's help to send a piece home!

BACK PAGES ANTIQUES
125 Greene St
460-5998
Tues-Sat: 11-6; Sun: 12-6

Fixing up a party room? Outfitting your vacation retreat? Looking for a special gift for that guy who has everything? Back Pages Antiques has the answer to all these. Alan Luchnick has assembled a great collection of classic Wurlitzer jukeboxes, slot machines that really work, pool tables, old Coca-Cola vending machines, and old player pianos. You provide the guests, Alan provides the entertainment. He will even rent his SoHo gallery for photo shoots and parties.

COBWEB
116 W Houston St (bet Thompson and Sullivan St)
505-1558
Mon-Fri: 12-7; Sat: 12-5
Closed bet Christmas and New Year's Day and last week of Aug

Cobweb (what a great name for an antiques shop!) is the only store in the New York area which imports country furniture and formal antiques directly from Spain and Portugal. The stunning selection of merchandise includes armoires, brass beds, tables, chairs, benches, trunks, chests, wooden bowls, earthen olive-oil urns and water jugs. All of these pieces are distinctive, original, and authentic. In addition, Cobweb offers customized refinishing of its own furniture. And it's obvious the stock doesn't stay around long enough to house spiders, let alone cobwebs.

DARROW'S FUN ANTIQUES
309 E 61st St (bet First and Second Ave)
838-0730
Mon-Fri: 11-7; Sat: 11-4; Sun: by appointment

There are antiques, and then there are antiques. Darrow's specializes in whimsical antiques for all ages. So expect to find toys (the valuable and collectible as well as the merely nostalgic), slot machines, original animation art, jukeboxes, old pay phones, Mickey Mouse watches, cast-iron banks (remember them?), and toy soldiers. Gary Darrow, the proprietor, says that at any given time there are more than 5,000 items in stock, and he has customers all over the world who swear that he's the best. The store was founded by Gary's father in 1964, and they've since earned a reputation as the prime source for the buying and renting of props and "fun" antiques. Darrow's also sells carefully labeled reproductions that would fool most people. They don't fool Gary, though, and he won't fool you.

DEPRESSION MODERN
150 Sullivan St (at Houston St)
982-5699
Wed-Sun: 12-7

Michael Smith, the owner, stocks nothing made prior to 1929. Much of the merchandise is even more current. Though he handles art deco, he specializes in a style he himself named: Depression modern. He says his stuff was never meant to end up in a museum. Ten years ago, his shop wouldn't have found a market, but today the pieces are valued for their sleek, functional lines. And Smith is a real showman. You'd have to be, if a number of your customers looked at your prized items and said, "Hey, I threw *that* out years ago." There are two floors of streamlined furnishings, lighting, and accessories. There's even a garden courtyard full of casual summer furniture.

HYDE PARK ANTIQUES
836 Broadway (bet 12th and 13th St)
477-0033
Mon-Fri: 9-5; Sat: 10-3; closed Sat in summer

No, ducky. Hyde Park is not the ancestral home of FDR up the Hudson River. Well, maybe it is, but that's not the Hyde Park that Bernard Karr is referring to. His Hyde Park is in merry old England, with the emphasis on old (the 18th-century period, to be exact), and those coming to find pictures of Fala will be vastly disappointed by the floor upon floor of fine English furniture crammed into the showroom. But they are the only people who could possibly be disappointed. Managing director Craig Williams boasts that his gallery has the largest inventory in the world of genuine period English furniture. And who's to argue? William and Mary, Regency, and other Old English periods are represented. To accompany the furniture, there are accents, mirrors, paintings, and porcelains. And if all this isn't enough to make a Roundhead's head turn, Hyde Park maintains a fine workroom for restoring the furniture. It's enough to brag about from a soapbox in Hyde Park!

JAMES ROBINSON
15 E 57th St
752-6166
Mon-Sat: 10-5: closed Sat in summer

Collectors and specialists in antiques (particularly silver from the 17th and 18th centuries) are familiar with James Robinson, and many of them have dealt with the store, if only by mail. James Robinson is the best at what it does, but be warned that what it does *not* do is run an establishment where tourists can pick up knickknacks. Even the Victorian period, which is best-known for its knickknack style of decorating, is represented with only its finest, most silvery, and expensive pieces. James Robinson specializes in antique silver, jewelry, porcelains, and glass. What is not available in the store but existent, personnel will comb the world for. What is no longer in existence will be perfectly reproduced in handmade silver. Nonsilver antiques in which the store specializes include 17th- through 19th-century English bone china and porcelain (many in complete services), jewelry, and glass—and none of it is inexpensive.

LITTLE ANTIQUE SHOP
44 E 11th St (at Broadway)
673-5173
Mon-Fri: 10-5

In a neighborhood that is borderline Village and often referred to as Strand territory, the Little Antique Shop stands out as a gem. This small store specializes in Oriental and European antiques, large and small. There are fine delicate antiques, and the prices are equally fine. There are small accent pieces as well as large screens. All of them are quality pieces, and you'll never believe you found them on East 11th Street.

PLACE DES ANTIQUAIRES
125 E 57th St (at Lexington Ave)
758-2900
Mon-Sat: 11-6

You'll gasp at the beauty—and the price tags—at this new antique center. Located on several levels at the bottom of a 32-story office tower, it houses about 50 different dealers. The small spaces display different antique specialties, with an emphasis on furniture and accessories, many serving as showrooms for larger collections housed elsewhere. Some dealers have come from France, and some have moved here from other New York locations or maintain several showrooms in the city. Several outstanding dealers to visit include E. Forbes Smiley, who has a fascinating collection of antique globes and maps; Bizarre Bazaar, specializing in art deco toys of vintage caliber; Manic, featuring one of the finest icon collections in the country; Kenneth Rendell, the autograph dealer; Lune, which has probably the best display of antique fans in the world; and Ronald Huffman, who offers a fabulous collection of American silver dating from the mid-19th century. After feasting the eyes, hungry shoppers can stop by the cafe on the lower level.

PLACE FOR ANTIQUES
246 E 53rd St
308-4066
Mon-Fri: 10-5; Sat, Sun: by appointment

The word for the Place for Antiques is *eclectic*. Owner Sheila Cole Nilva has set up a mecca for all sorts of odd antiques, with a vast collection of small, serious collectibles, including match safes, snuff boxes, corkscrews, and jewelry. Entertainment production companies come here to find props for their projects.

R. BROOKE
960 Lexington Ave (at 70th St)
535-0707
Mon-Fri: 10-6

Eureka! I've found a well organized antiques shop! If for no other reason, you should stop by and see this delightful shop, where you can find a wonderful selection of antiques arranged for easy shopping. But you should also shop here when you want to indulge, spoil, celebrate, remember, delight, pamper, amuse, inspire, serenade, thank, or enchant.

A ROSE TREE
725 Fifth Ave (Trump Tower, level D5)
421-3879
Mon-Sat: 10-6

This small and intriguing boutique calls itself "an antique gift store." Norman Crider has assembled a fascinating collection of figurines, plates, toy soldiers, jewelry, boxes, autographs—well, you get the picture. The prices are as special as the items (note the location). My favorite piece was an extravagant dresser set.

URBAN ARCHAEOLOGY
285 Lafayette St (bet Houston and Prince St)
431-6969
Mon-Fri: 9-6; Sat: 106

Nowadays people are collecting almost anything and calling it antique. Urban Archaeology offers the best trims and pieces of New York architecture from the 1880s to the 1920s. While the business specializes in house artifacts, owners Leonard Schechter, Gil Shapiro, and Allen Reiven display entire "mood" settings as well. You might find furnishings from barbershops, ice cream parlors, saloons, and who knows what else!

Art Supplies

CHARRETTE
215 Lexington Ave
683-8822
Mon-Fri: 8:30-7; Sat: 10-5; Sun: 12-5; closed Sun in
    summer

This branch of a Massachusetts company is for serious architects, engineers, draftsmen, graphic designers and artists. The stock includes more than 36,000 different items, which means that a practitioner in any of these fields would be hard-put not to find what he or she wanted. Charrette offers quality supplies and good advice; professionals will be pleased to find anything they need, while amateurs had best study the catalog first.

EASTERN ARTISTS
5 W 22nd St (bet Fifth and Sixth Ave)
645-5555
Mon-Fri: 8:30-7; Sat: 11-6; closed Sat in July, Aug

Both amateurs and professionals are served well here. Ad agencies, poster companies, and artists buy their supplies from Eastern, as much for the personalized service tailored to an artist's temperament as for the 20 to 50 percent discount on all supplies. Store manager Ilene Kischel claims that there are more than 20,000 different items in stock, and all of it should please the fussiest of artists.

LEE'S ART SHOP

220 W 57th St (near Broadway)
247-0110
Mon-Fri: 9-7; Sat: 9:30-6

Ricky of Lee's Art Shop claims that her store is the city's most complete art supply store. Indeed, the shop is loaded with all the materials for both the professional and amateur artist. There is even a separate section for architectural and drafting supplies. The staff is among the city's friendliest and is extremely knowledgeable. Their help is needed to guide the uneducated through the wealth of transfer types, lamps, silkscreens, art brushes, and chart types. All are available here in various qualities. A related specialty is same-day framing; they will frame amateur or professional art for home or office within the same business day. I was also impressed by the range of auxiliary services Lee's offers—mail order, catalogs, and free delivery.

NEW YORK CENTRAL ART SUPPLY

62 Third Ave (at 11th St)
473-7705
Mon-Sat: 8:30-6:15

For many years artists have looked to this firm for fine art materials, especially unique and custom-made items. There are two floors of fine art papers: one-of-a-kind decorative papers in various designs and colors and over 100 special Oriental papers from Bhutan, China, India, Japan, Thailand, Taiwan, and Nepal. Amateur and skilled artisans can find a full range of decorative paints and painting materials.

PEARL PAINT COMPANY

308 Canal St (at Broadway)
431-7932
Mon-Sat: 9-5:30; Thurs: 9-7; Sun: 11-4:45

With 10 floors and more than 100 clerks on duty at all times, Pearl claims to be the world's largest art and graphics discount center. Who can disagree? Besides these 10 floors of fine-arts discounts, Pearl has another building at 42 Lispenard Street (226-3520), which is an art-furniture showroom. Pearl's new first-floor entrance opens onto a jam-packed store divided into specialty sections of all kinds. Pearl is the kind of place where house painters shop next to batik craftsmen, and moldings and castings are sold beside materials for etchings and silk screenings. Pearl's personnel are also very friendly, which is quite rare for a professional supply house.

SAM FLAX

425 Park Ave   747 Third Ave
752-5893   620-3050

25 E 28th St   233 Spring St
620-3040   675-8571

12 W 20th St
620-3038

Mon-Fri: 9-6; Sat: 10-5 (Spring and 20th St stores,
    Sun: 12-5)

Superlatives are as common as canvas in the art supply business, and Sam Flax is yet another who claims to be the biggest and the best in the field. Since no one is going to sit and count the paint brushes in stock, the question is moot, but Sam Flax does carry the full range of art and drafting supplies, drawing-studio furniture, and photographic products. There are also framing services at each store. The Sam Flax store at 12 West 20th Street is primarily devoted to furniture. The Flax brothers, Leonard and David, see this neighborhood as the up-and-coming creative district of the city, and they think artists, artisans, and professionals will be living as well as working in the neighborhood. So they stocked this store with basic functional furniture for that lifestyle. The store is so large, though, that it can sport all that furniture and still stock all of the art supplies and paraphernalia of a traditional Flax store. The 19th Street addition houses the furniture, while the 20th Street side offers products, photographic supplies, and pens.

UTRECHT ART AND
DRAFTING SUPPLIES

111 Fourth Ave (at 11th St)
777-5353
Mon-Sat: 9:30-6

We once mused about the name of this art supply outlet, and we received a letter from a reader who pointed out that Utrecht is a large city in Holland, with a long tradition of arts and crafts. Great, but we raised the question because this shop used to be called Utrecht *Linens*. In any case, Utrecht is a major manufacturer of paint and art and drafting supplies, with a large factory in Brooklyn. At this retail store, factory-fresh supplies are sold at factory discounts, and the Utrecht name stands behind every purchase. Quality is superb, as are the discounts. Utrecht also carries the lines of other manufacturers, and they're sold at impressive discounts as well.

Autographs

GALLERY OF HISTORY
Winter Garden at the World Financial Center
225 Liberty St
945-1000
Mon-Fri: 10-7; Sat: 10-6; Sun: 12-5

This exciting store in the fabulous new Winter Garden is a place to browse as well as to shop. The Gallery is one of five in this country (the only one in New York) owned by the American Museum of Historical Documents. It was founded by a former Wall Street broker, Todd Axelrod, who has become one of the nation's foremost experts on historical documents, especially those of presidential material. His charming partner, Pamela Axelrod, is on the job to give expert advice and counsel. On the walls are dozens of historic documents, beautifully framed, scientifically preserved, all authenticated, and many with great pictures as a part of the presentation. Axelrod claims he has over 75,000 documents and nearly 15,000 different historical personalities to choose from.

JAMES LOWE AUTOGRAPHS
30 E 60th St (bet Madison and Park Ave, suite 907)
759-0775
Mon-Fri: 9-5

James Lowe is one of the most established autograph houses in the country. Catalogs, published several times a year, make a visit to the gallery unnecessary, but in-person inspections are fascinating and invariably whet the appetite of most autograph collectors. There is no one specialty; the gallery seems to show whatever superior item is in stock, though there is a particular interest in historic, literary, and musical autographs, manuscripts, documents, and 19th-century photographs. The offerings range from autographed pictures of Buffalo Bill to three bars of an operatic score of Puccini's. Of course, there's much more in between. It all depends on what the buyer finds intriguing. Perhaps that explains why James Lowe prefers that you drop by.

KENNETH W RENDELL
125 E 57th St (at Lexington Ave)
935-6767
Mon-Sat: 11-6

Kenneth Rendell, from Newton, Massachusetts, has been in the business for over 30 years and offers a fine collection of pieces from famous personages in literature, arts, politics, and science. In the new Place des Antiquaires, Rendell shows autographed letters, manuscripts, documents, and signed photographs. All are authenticated, attractively presented, and priced according to the rarity of the item. Rendell evaluates collections for tax purposes, and arranges the purchase or sale of items on a consulting basis.

TOLLET AND HARMAN
175 W 76th St
877-1566
By appointment only

Autographs used to be big business in New York, perhaps because of the number of celebrities in the city. Lately, however, there are less than a handful of reliable dealers. Tollet and Harman is one of the best. They deal almost entirely by catalog and by request rather than through formal retailing. They carry (or will obtain) original autographs, manuscripts, signed books, maps, and vintage photographs. Collectors of specific items (I collect presidents of the U.S. and presidents of the Continental Congresses) can leave requests with them. When they come across the item, they will notify you. Each item is carefully authenticated, and they will also do business by mail or phone.

Baskets

A TISKET A TASKET
246 E 53rd St
308-4066
Mon-Fri: 10-5; Sat, Sun: by appointment

Sheila Nilva started A Tisket A Tasket as a sideline to her main shop, Place for Antiques. Being an energetic person, she saw to it that her new shop took off in high gear. Customers can order from a choice of over 100 baskets, and the list of recipients could fill any society page: Liza Minnelli, Ed Asner, Jimmy Buffet, Tom Cruise, Michael Feinstein, and many more. The baskets contain no perishables unless requested. They're clever, whimsical, and elegant, and they're perfect for births, birthdays, anniversaries, promotions, get-well gifts, and all holidays. There is even a "New York! New York!" basket with a book (shouldn't it be this one?), a New York mug with imported coffee, a linen napkin in a Big Apple ring, and apple cookies.

BE SEATED
66 Greenwich Ave (bet 11th St and Seventh Ave)
924-8444
Mon-Fri: 11-7; Sat: 11-6

In the beginning, Be Seated sold all kinds of chairs out of its tiny store in the Village. As time went by, the small store remained, but the chairs gave way to baskets of all shapes and sizes. Today, the store size is *still* unchanged, but now the baskets have been joined by Oriental rugs and printed materials from India, while the chairs have been crowded out. This explains why a store named Be Seated is a number-one spot for baskets. And there are baskets aplenty. They range from ancient antiques to modern palm-tree containers. All are elegant, and nothing would please Be Seated more than to have every household in the city own a half-dozen different baskets. To achieve that objective, the store specializes in unique baskets for unique uses. (When you have overloaded your space, you can't afford to fill it with trivia.) They recommend using baskets as decoration, containers (in kids' rooms, believe it or not), and for just about anything else you can imagine.

LEE'S GIFT BASKETS
340 Amsterdam Ave (at 76th St, upstairs)
496-2075
Daily: 10-8

When you're looking for an alternative to the standard fruit-and-cheese or candy gift basket, Lee's is just the place to put together a different and interesting basket, nicely wrapped and carefully delivered. Unusual packages, like the "What the doctor ordered" basket (joke book, preserves, crossword puzzles, stationery, stuffed bear, get-well banner) and the "Beautiful Baby" basket (crib toys, flowers for Mommy, and bow tie for Daddy, sparkling cider), are available all during the year. Kosher baskets are a specialty.

Bathroom Accessories

A. F. SUPPLY CORPORATION
22 W 21st St (bet Fifth and Sixth Ave)
243-5400
Mon-Fri: 8-5 and by appointment

As far as I am concerned, the bathroom is the most important room in the house, and the folks at A. F. Supply agree. They offer a great selection of luxury bath fixtures, whirlpools, faucets, bath accessories, door and cabinet hardware, saunas, steam showers, shower doors, medicine cabinets, and even spas from top domestic and European suppliers.

ELEGANT JOHN
812 Lexington Ave (bet 62nd and 63rd St)
935-5800
Mon-Wed, Fri, Sat: 10-6; Thurs: 10-7

After getting over the initial awkwardness of entering a store that displays prominently labeled "john seats" on its walls, you'll be amazed at the array of custom-made shower curtains, dressing tables, coordinated accessories, soap dishes, and, of course, seats, all sold with the aim of creating a bathroom that is every bit as comfortable and striking as the rest of the house. Don't miss the Elegant John's attractive, unusually decorated rolls of toilet tissue.

SHERLE WAGNER INTERNATIONAL
60 E 57th St (at Park Ave)
758-3300
Mon-Fri: 9-5

If you thought the Elegant John was the definitive word on bathroom accessories, you ain't seen nothin' yet. Sherle Wagner takes a topic that even the Elegant John skirted, and places it in the most elegant location in the city, where it rubs elbows with silversmiths, art galleries, and exclusive antiques shops. However, the luxurious bathroom fixtures are almost works of art and are deserving of their 57th Street location. Fixtures come in every possible material, and some are so striking that they make a glass display case seem like their natural setting. Prices are high, as might be expected. One warning! The displays are in the basement, and the world's slowest (almost) elevator gives you a good case of claustrophobia.

Books

American Indian

BOB FEIN BOOKS
150 Fifth Ave (at 20th St, room 623)
807-0489
Mon-Sat: 11-5; closed Sat in summer

Bob Fein claims that his shop is the only one that's devoted to the literature of American Indians. Within this boundary, he also includes pre-Columbian art and Eskimos as subjects, and he has on hand more than 4,000 books and journals on those topics. Many of his items are out-of-print or one-of-a-kind, and Fein is considered the primary source for such material. There is also a good percentage of what Fein terms "scholarly material," along with Smithsonian publications and reports. Most of the stock is unique and rare, and if any new literature is published about Fein's specialties, there's a very good chance that he'll have it first.

Architecture

URBAN CENTER BOOKS
457 Madison Ave (at 51st St)
935-3595
Mon-Wed, Fri, Sat: 10-6; Thurs: 10-8; Sun: 12-5

Urban Center Books, the retail arm of the Municipal Art Society, practices what it preaches. The society was founded in 1892 to preserve the best of New York's historical architectural facades. That the society should be located in the north wing of the Villard Houses—historic homes that make up the base of the Helmsley Palace Hotel—is only fitting. And since most of the rooms in those buildings have been refurbished to resemble drawing rooms and libraries, it is equally appropriate that the society decided to retail publications on its interests in a suite that is a real library. If nothing else, a visit to Urban Center Books gives a visitor a chance to do some further exploration of the public rooms of the houses. Although only the physical amenities are left (wide doorways, parquet floors, painted ceilings), it is still a stunning look back into times gone by. The store specializes in city architecture, history, and the city's physical plan. Publications on the topics of urban planning, design, and historic preservation are available.

Art

E. WEYHE
794 Lexington Ave (at 62nd St)
838-5466
Mon-Sat: 9:30-5; closed Sat in summer

This bookstore dedicated to the subject of art has evolved from a small shop to a specialty store with an upstairs art gallery. Actually, it was only natural since Mr. Weyhe filled the small area with artists and art books (as well as their art) almost from its start in 1923. Over the years, Weyhe gave encouragement to scores of artists, and they reciprocated by giving him some of their paintings, tiles (note Rockwell Kent's offering on the brownstone), and sketches. Eventually, Weyhe was compelled to open the gallery to display the works of his patrons (and those he was patron to) and to prove that art literature is to be lived. Today, under the aegis of Weyhe's daughter, the store and the gallery continue the work Weyhe started. The bookstore carries everything related to art, architecture, or photography. A good part of the business also involves the purchase and resale of private art-book collections.

PRINTED MATTER
77 Wooster St
925-0325
Tues-Sat: 10-6

Printed Matter is almost a misnomer since the store is the only one in the world devoted exclusively to artists' books. That's not books belonging to artists, or even art books, but rather a trade term for a portfolio of artwork in book form. The result is inexpensive, accessible art, which can span an entire artist's career, or a particular period or theme. The idea is carried further by Printed Matter's selection of periodicals and audiowork in a similar vein. Nearly all of the featured artists are contemporary, so just browsing through the store would bring you up-to-date on what is going on right now in the art world.

URSUS BOOKS AND PRINTS
981 Madison Ave (bet 76th and 77th St)
772-8787
Mon-Fri: 10-6; Sat: 11-5

Art lovers can find reference books in all fields and periods, including many out-of-print titles. Browsers will enjoy the fine selection of rare books and appreciate the invitation to sit down and relax, a rarity in bookstores today. A large selection of decorative prints and watercolors is available, as well as custom framing.

WITTENBORN ART BOOKS
1018 Madison Ave (bet 78th and 79th St)
288-1558
Mon-Sat: 10-5; closed Sat in summer

Possibly the ultimate art bookstore in the city, Wittenborn specializes in the arts, architecture, prints, archaeology, and fashion, and whenever fine-quality books on these topics are published, Wittenborn adds them to the stock. The staff makes a point of having it all—and having it all neatly cataloged as well. Besides contemporary tomes, Wittenborn carries out-of-print, rare, and antiquarian volumes and foreign printings. If the topic and pictures meet Wittenborn's standards, it will carry the book, no matter what language it has been published in. Artfully done!

Biography

BIOGRAPHY BOOKSHOP
400 Bleecker St (at 11th St)
807-8655
Tues-Fri: 1-9; Sat: 12-10; Sun: 12-5:30; closed one week
     in Feb, one week in Aug

Here's a New York specialty shop that deals only with books of a biographical nature. If you are researching a particular person, or you have an interest in someone's life story or even a way of life, this is the place to find it. There are biographies, books of letters, autobiographies, diaries, journals, and even biographies for children.

Children's

BOOKS OF WONDER
132 Seventh Ave (at 18th St)
989-3270
Mon-Sat: 11-9; Sun: 12-6

464 Hudson St (at Barrow St)
645-8006
Mon-Sat: 11-7; Sun: 12-6

Books of Wonder established its reputation as a prime source for rare, collectible, and out-of-print children's books, at its store on Hudson Street. Owners Peter Glassman and James Carey stocked the store with their own favorites and established the largest collection of Oz books in the world. When Books of Wonder opened a second and much larger store across the street from Barney's, the second store became the main store. Together they have the largest number of children's book titles in the city. Would you believe that there is an Oz gift wrap and an Oz flag? At Books of Wonder they know all about it. Antique books are now available at the Seventh Avenue location.

EEYORE'S BOOKS FOR CHILDREN
2212 Broadway (at 79th St)
362-0634
Mon-Sat: 10-6; Sun: 10:30-5

25 E 83rd St (at Madison Ave)
988-3404
Mon-Sat: 10-6; Sun: 12-5

Joel Fram, Eeyore's proprietor, runs the shop as if it were a child's haven. There are books for children of every age and interest, and there is even a corner where kids can sit or browse. The majority of the books are within the price range of a good allowance, and if it's an adult who is doing the purchasing, the unobtrusive staff offers guidance and suggestions. Eeyore's will order, at no additional charge, any book not in their extensive stock. The shop's highlight is its Sunday story sessions. These sessions are attended by standing-room-only crowds, and refreshments are served after story hour. Currently, the story sessions are held for kids aged 3 to 6 at 11 a.m. on the West Side and at 12:30 on the East Side.

STORYLAND
1369 Third Ave (at 78th St)
517-6951
Mon-Sat: 10-6; Sun: 11-6

Storyland is the ultimate bookstore for children. Genial owner Jeff Bergman and manager Nerissa Bardfeld have created an atmosphere that children will love and parents will enjoy while shopping for children's books, videos, and casette tapes. Every Sunday (except during the summer) a writer or illustrator is on hand for story hour (1:30 p.m.). A carnival atmosphere reigns at this first-class bookstore.

Comic

ACTION COMICS
318 E 84th St (bet First and Second Ave)
249-7344
Mon-Wed: 11:30-7; Thurs-Sat: 11:30-7:30; Sun: 12-6

Comic book lovers need look no farther than this establishment. You'll find new comics from all publishers, collector's comics from the 1930s through the 1980s, new and collector's baseball cards, and original comic art.

SUPERSNIPE COMIC BOOK EUPHORIUM
P.O. Box 1102, Gracie Station, NYC 10028
879-9628
By appointment only (call Saturdays)

The ultimate comic book emporium. Supersnipe now deals only by phone and mail order. It is well worth your time, however, because their stock is unequaled.

Food

KITCHEN ARTS & LETTERS
1435 Lexington Ave (at 94th St)
876-5550
Mon: 1-6; Tues-Fri: 10-6:30; Sat: 11-6;
       closed Aug and Sat in July

Cookbooks traditionally top the best-seller lists in bookstores, and with the renewed interest in health, fitness, and natural foods, that rule of thumb is more operative than ever. So it should come as no surprise that Nachum Waxman's Kitchen Arts & Letters should be an immediate success as a store specializing in books, literature, photography, and original art about food and its preparation. Waxman claims that his store is the only one like it in the city and one of less than 10 in the country. Waxman is a former editor at Harper & Row and Crown publishing companies, where he supervised several cookbook projects. Bitten with the urge to start a specialty bookshop, he discovered almost immediately that there was a huge demand for out-of-print and original cookbooks. So while the tiny shop stocks almost 3,000 titles as well as a gallery of photography and original art, much of the business is in finding out-of-print and "want listed" books.

Foreign

CHINA BOOKS AND PERIODICALS
136 W 18th St (bet Sixth and Seventh Ave)
627-4044
Mon-Sat: 10-6

This fascinating store carries a large selection of folk art from China, including weaving, embroidery, toys, jewelry, clothing, and toys. They specialize in Chinese medicine books on herbs and acupuncture. This is *the* place to find the best selection of written material about and from China.

LIBRAIRIE DE FRANCE
and
LIBRERIA HISPANICA
610 Fifth Ave (bet 49th and 50th St)
581-8810
Mon-Fri: 9:30-6:15; Sat: 10-6:15

115 Fifth Ave (at 19th St)
673-7400
Mon-Fri: 9:30-6; Sat: 10-6

A short stroll through the Rockefeller Center promenade takes you by the Librairie de France and Libreria Hispanica. Inside, you will find an interesting collection of French and Spanish newspapers, magazines, tourist guides, and light reading. There are more than 1 million French and Spanish books and records in stock. If this isn't overwhelming enough, *all* of them are neatly cataloged and easily found. There isn't a topic on which at least several books in French or Spanish are not available, including a collection of books in Spanish about French literature and vice versa. A partial list of the available categories includes textbooks, dictionaries and encyclopedias, children's books and records, bilingual and bicultural educational records and tapes, games, posters, audiovisual aids, newspapers, magazines, French popular music on CDs and LPs, and Haitian and African literature in French. A new division stocks dictionaries in over 100 languages.

NEW YORK KINOKUNIYA BOOKSTORE
10 W 49th St (at Fifth Ave)
765-1461
Daily: 10-7

Kinokuniya is Japan's largest and most esteemed bookstore chain, and this is its first branch in New York. Located in Rockefeller Plaza, the store has two floors of books about Japan. The atmosphere is the closest thing New York has to Tokyo. On the first floor there are 20,000 English-language books, which leave no part of Japanese culture neglected. Art, cooking, travel, language, literature, history, business, economics, management techniques, martial arts—they're all here. The rest of the floor is rounded out with books on the same subjects in Japanese, and there are paperbacks on the second floor. Kinokuniya definitely has the largest collection of Japanese books in the city and possibly outside of Japan.

PARAGON BOOK GALLERY
2130 Broadway
496-2378
Mon-Fri: 10-6; Sat: 11-5

Roberta Huber has collected more than 60,000 book titles from all over the Orient. Besides the latest art books, Huber has a fine selection of rare and old books. If you have an interest in Asian countries, you'll find nearly everything written about Asian history, culture, literature, and linguistics in stock. A very efficient mail-order service is also available.

UNIVERSITY PLACE BOOK SHOP
821 Broadway (ninth floor)
254-5998
Mon-Fri: 10-5

In this out-of-the-way, dust-covered loft may be the largest collection of books on Africa and the West Indies in the world. After climbing up to its ninth-floor location, it's disconcerting to find piles and piles of books that seem to be arranged by chance. But there are some great finds here, and the salespeople are friendly and very knowledgeable. The selection includes literature in more than 35 African dialects. Compensating for the fact that many African dialects have never been written down, University stocks 200 to 300 books about them; almost any subject or group is covered. University also carries many old, rare, and out-of-print books on Africa and the West Indies. The newer books are those involved with current black America. William French, owner and manager, seems to know every book in the store—an amazing feat. The books he personally values the most are the early printed books (15th to 17th century) and the rare and out-of-print books on Africa, the West Indies, and Afro-Americans.

General

BARNES AND NOBLE
206-8800
Branches throughout city
Hours vary from store to store

Barnes and Noble is a mecca for college students, and many of the universities in the metropolitan area have branches of Barnes and Noble on campus. Generations of New York students have gone through the ritual of buying books from Barnes and Noble at the start of a semester and selling them back after finals. The textbook division continues, but all types of other books are stocked as well, and all are discounted. Its particular specialty is one of the best discounts in town on any book on *The New York Times* best-seller list. As soon as a title makes the list, Barnes and Noble drastically discounts it and advertises that discount in the *Times*. There is an excellent assortment of all types of books, since Barnes and Noble has sources not available to smaller stores.

B. DALTON BOOKSELLER
247-1740
Branches throughout city
Hours vary from store to store

The B. Dalton shop on Fifth Avenue, one of the largest bookstores in the city, is the flagship for one of the largest and best bookselling operations in the nation. Books aren't just sold here—they are theatrically produced. Dalton has access to huge lots of remainders and reprints (due to its nationwide buying power). There are sections for children, technical subjects, special interests, and the arts. Dalton doesn't excel in any one particular area, but it should get an "A" for presentation. Their window displays are always must-sees for the latest in the publishing world.

BURLINGTON BOOK SHOP
1082 Madison Ave (bet 81st and 82nd St)
288-7420
Mon-Fri: 9:30-6; Sat: 10-6; Sun: 12-6

Burlington functions as a small-town bookstore in the big city. Their business card still lists their phone number as "Butterfield 8"! John O'Hara would love it. The store specializes in art books and literature, and offers friendly, neighborly service. How can it be otherwise when you have the name of a book in your phone number? Two specialties of this unique operation: downstairs is a fabulous collection of Burlington antique toys, and on the mezzanine a shop called "Compulsive Collector" features an out-of-print book department.

DOUBLEDAY BOOK SHOPS
397-0550 (main store)
Branches throughout city
Hours vary from store to store

Doubleday, the granddaddy of the Fifth Avenue bookstores, has it all. There probably isn't a topic or title in the world that they don't stock; they are particularly proud of their back list. The two Fifth Avenue stores are the prototype of what a bookstore should be—particularly a bookstore in the city. The first floor of the 57th

Street store is known for its selection of current and best-selling books and for a great travel department. If a title is newly released, Doubleday's main section has it, often before publication date. Other floors in the 57th Street store concentrate on art books, cookbooks, political issues, and back-listed publications, and that is only a partial list. But the quintessential bookstore relies heavily on its personnel, and it is in this area that Doubleday really excels. It still gives service with a capital *S*. Manager Jill Tardiff and her staff are true professionals. All stores reflect their neighborhoods. The other Fifth Avenue store, while smaller, carries a similarly extensive title list, with a selection on New York that must be the envy of the Visitors Convention Bureau. The Third Avenue store is less for tourists than for homebodies, while the Citicorp branch blends perfectly with its locale. Philosophical works are basically nonexistent there, but gift books, coffee-table art books, and light fiction are runaway favorites. All Doubleday stores have a large selection of light reading: fiction, mysteries, self-improvement books, and cookbooks.

GOTHAM BOOK MART
41 W 47th St
719-4448
Mon-Fri: 9:30-6:30; Sat: 9:30-6

The Gotham is a New York institution founded by the late Frances Steloff, a legend herself. Steloff founded the store nearly 70 years ago as a very small, very personal, theatrically inclined bookstore. In the early days, there was a heavy emphasis on poetry and the arts because those were Steloff's passionate interests. Steloff, who could never understand how a book could be banned (imagine what she would be saying about *The Satanic Verses*), once smuggled 25 first editions of Miller's *Tropic of Cancer* into the country from Paris via Mexico. She developed a deep and personal interest in authors and clients alike, and even as she grew older she would always make one daily visit downstairs to the shop around 2 p.m. Steloff lived to reach the century mark; her influence on this charming store will probably live on for another century.

McGRAW-HILL BOOKSTORE
1221 Sixth Ave (bet 48th and 49th St)
512-4100
Mon-Sat: 10-5:45

This huge shop, located downstairs in the McGraw-Hill building at Rockefeller Center, is limited in fiction and general titles, but for anything published by McGraw-Hill or written with a business, technical, or scientific bent, it is excellent. They're all sold at list price, and the wide selection of books would make any engineer happy. They now deal in IBM and Apple computers, and one-third of their books are about computers. A fine, well-run, professional store.

RIZZOLI
31 W 57th St (at Fifth Ave)
759-2424
Mon-Sat: 9-8; Sun: 12-8

Rizzoli has been a fixture on the fine-books scene in the city for years. Rizzoli has managed to retain the elegant atmosphere that makes a patron feel he is browsing in a European library rather than shopping in midtown Manhattan, thanks to the hand-carved marble doorway, chandeliers, and wood paneling. As for the books, titles lean heavily toward art, literature, photography, music, dance (particularly ballet), and foreign language. Additional space on the third and fourth floors house paperbacks, Italian books, and an extended gallery with art objects for sale. The store sells culture, albeit at full retail, but could you expect less from such an elegant place? Rizzoli also operates the books department at Bloomingdale's.

STRAND BOOK STORE
828 Broadway (at 12th St)
473-1452
Mon-Sat: 9:30-6:30; Sun: 11-5

159 John St (South St Seaport)
809-0875
Daily: 10-10

The Strand is a treasure trove for book lovers. Like the best treasure hunts, you may have to search through the nearly eight miles of books to find the prize that you want. There are carts full of books outside, with bargains going for peanuts. Inside the largest secondhand bookstore in the country, you will find almost 2 million books of every kind and description. Book collectors have a field day here. The high ceilings, narrow aisles, and jammed basement house secondhand, scarce, rare, and out-of-print books at reduced prices. The Strand also sells tens of thousands of reviewer's copies at half the publisher's list price. It is just an elevator ride to the rare book room, where you can pick up a signed first edition of Joyce's *Ulysses* for only $30,000. In three rooms scented with old leather, the biggest market is in 20th-century first editions and limited signed editions. In addition to its retail activities, the Strand imports English remainders, sells to libraries, and does a mail-order business that accounts for about half its business. Owner Fred Bass is always on the job at this fantastic emporium; he is an absolutely charming and superbly informed proprietor. The Strand is truly all things to all people who like books.

WALDENBOOKS
57 Broadway (at Exchange Pl)
269-1139
Mon-Fri: 8-6
Branches throughout city

While the other major bookstores have their flagship outlets on Fifth Avenue, Walden chooses the downtown Wall Street area for their major operation. And what an operation it is! The store literally overflows with selections in almost every category, with an emphasis on finance and business, as is only proper for that location. But no matter what you are looking for, Waldenbooks can probably satisfy your need. One of the advantages of a nationwide chain is their immense buying power and reorder system, so the customer is assured that most titles are in stock most of the time. The selection in this store is so vast that the fiction browsers in one area may not realize that nearby is housed one of the largest selections of science, technical, and reference books in the city. In keeping with their reputation as a full-service bookstore, they will special-order titles for you, gift-wrap, send merchandise anywhere, and provide expert answers to a multitude of readers' questions.

WOMRATH
1158 Madison Ave (at 86th St)
737-9330, 737-9379
Mon-Sat: 9:30-6; Sun: 11-6; closed Sun in July, Aug

Walter and Jeffrey Bergman run one of the last independent bookstores in Manhattan, a store that has been at the same location since it was founded 45 years ago. As independents, they aim to please no one but their customers, and they carry a selection that appeals to all of them. There is a heavy emphasis on new releases; you can attend autograph parties for virtually every author on the best-seller list. These gentlemen are also very nice people with a great sense of humor.

Military

MILITARY BOOKMAN
29 E 93rd St
348-1280
Tues-Sat: 10:30-5:30

The inventory here is limited to books of military nature. The specialty is out-of-print and rare books on military, naval, and aviation history. At any given time, there are about 10,000 such titles in stock. Topics run the gamut from Attila the Hun to atomic warfare. The Military Bookman also has a large mail-order business and maintains a subscription mail-order catalog. Its proprietor is the charming Harris Colt.

SOLDIER SHOP
1222 Madison Ave (bet 88th and 89th St)
535-6788
Mon-Fri: 10-6; Sat: 10-5; Sat: 10-3 in July, Aug

The military is a deadly serious business here. This is *not* for the little boy who likes to play soldier, since many of the books are extremely rare and valuable. The general specialty, however, is military in all of its ramifications, and as a result, the Soldier Shop stocks current as well as rare military books concerning history, battles, theory, and biography. A catalog that lists 166 pages of military history books, antique soldiers, arms, and armor is also available.

Mystery

FOUL PLAY
10 Eighth Ave (at W 12th St)
675-5115
Daily: 12-10

1465B Second Ave (at 76th St)
517-3222
Mon-Fri: 12-10; Sat: 11-11; Sun: 12-7

If the urge to curl up with a good mystery grabs you some Sunday afternoon, Foul Play is the only place to satisfy it "between here and Philadelphia," says manager John Douglas. Indeed, Foul Play is the only bookstore devoted totally to mystery and suspense novels that's open on Sunday. It also has a remarkable black and red neon interior design and simply super salespeople. Neither of these distinctions should be taken lightly.

MURDER INK®
271 W 87th St
362-8905
Wed, Fri, Sat: 1-7; Thurs: 1-10

Murder Ink was the first mystery bookstore in the city. When Dilys Winn founded Murder Ink, she started not so much a bookstore as a way of life. Today, Carol Brener runs the store along the same lines as Winn did, although she has added feminist accents. The store still claims to stock every murder or mystery book in print and several thousand selections no longer in print. You'll find some rare books and other artifacts, but the emphasis is on good, entertaining books.

MYSTERIOUS BOOK SHOP
129 W 56th St
756-0900
Mon-Sat: 11-7

Otto Penzler is president of the Mysterious Press, a Baker Street Irregular, a Sherlock Holmes fan extraordinaire (an elementary deduction!), and the Mysterious Book Shop's owner. As a result, the shop is run as a friendly business, and spontaneous conversations among customers are the norm. On the ground floor (actually, a few steps below street level), Mysterious stocks new hardcover and paperback books that deal with any genre of mystery. ("But *not* science fiction. Science fiction is not mystery," says the store's manager, Michael Krugman.) Upstairs, via a winding circular staircase, the store branches out to the width of two buildings, and is stocked floor to ceiling with out-of-print, used, and rare books. Amazingly, they seem to know exactly what is in stock, and if it is not on the shelves, they will order it. (Assume that a book not in stock *has* to be old or rare. This store has everything else.) There is as much conversation as business conducted here, and you can continue the conversation at the store's next autograph party.

New York

CITYBOOKS
61 Chambers St (bet Broadway and Centre St)
669-8245
Mon-Fri: 9:30-4:30

2223 Municipal Building, 1 Centre St
669-8245
Mon-Fri: 8:30-5

These two outlets, both government agencies, have access to more than 120 different official publications, all of which are dedicated to helping New Yorkers cope with their complex lives. The Green Book is the official directory of the City of New York,

and lists phone numbers and addresses of more than 900 government agencies and 6,000 officials. It includes state, federal, and
international listings, the courts, and a license section. It's a very
handy reference guide. There is also a unique collection of New
York memorabilia: city-seal ties and scarves, old New York scenes,
rare New York photographs reproduced in calendars, posters, and
much more.

NEW YORK BOUND BOOKSHOP
50 Rockefeller Plaza (lobby)
245-8503
Mon-Fri: 10-6; Sat: 12-5

Barbara Cohen and Judith Stonehill have assembled a printed
ode to New York. The older and more esoteric a view of New York
a publication has, the more these ladies covet it and try to acquire it
for their shop. The specialty is old, rare, out-of-print, and unusual
ephemera (their word) relating to New York. History buffs will
have a field day with the eyewitness accounts of early life in the Big
Apple. Check out the photographs or browse through the current
catalog, but definitely visit. Old New York is alive and well at New
York Bound.

Occult

SAMUEL WEISER
132 E 24th St (near Lexington Ave)
777-6363
Mon-Wed, Fri: 9-6; Thurs: 10-7; Sat: 9:30-5; Sun: 11-5

For stocking all kinds of publications on metaphysics, religion,
and the occult, Samuel Weiser has a worldwide reputation that is
well deserved. The shop is clean, modern, and so well equipped that
many of its customers have no idea that its selection includes the
eeriest titles found anywhere. The specialties cover almost any topic
that is otherworldly: witchcraft, astrology, alchemy, magic, mys-
ticism, E.S.P., flying saucers, Zen, and herb medicine. These are
explored in books, magazines, periodicals, and foreign publications. (Some of the best in the field seem to be printed in foreign
languages. Many are translated and sold here in both versions.)
Finally, Samuel Weiser is one of the most obliging shops in town.
They maintain a waiting list for out-of-print titles, and when the
title arrives (by whatever mystical means), they will ship it anywhere in the world. It arrives in plain mailing wrappers, but, no, it
is not delivered by broomstick or magic carpet! The shop also rents
topical videos and sells incense and music tapes.

Out-of-Print

CHARLOTTE F SAFIR
1349 Lexington Ave, Apt 9B, New York, NY 10128
534-7933
Phone any time

Looking for a particular book? Well, here is a lady who can save you a lot of time and effort. Charlotte Safir provides a search service for out-of-print books by mail or phone only. She has a fantastic network of contacts, and can locate any kind of book, although she does specialize in hard-to-find cookbooks and children's books. If you want to add to a collection or find out about that special author you enjoy so much, this is the lady to call. Charlotte is efficient, persistent, and a pleasure to deal with.

Paperback

CLASSIC BOOK SHOP
1212 Sixth Ave (at 48th St)
221-2252
Mon-Fri: 8-7; Sat: 10-6; Sun: 12-6

Classic Book Shop pursues the unusual, rare, and esoteric in paperbacks, and its selection is among the best. Although paperback at one time meant inexpensive, this is no longer always true. The 25-cent pocketbook is a thing of the past. Classic has books that cost upward of $10. Classic's forte is paperback "backstock," and it claims to have the best collection in the midtown area. Classic also carries hard-cover books.

Photography

PHOTOGRAPHER'S PLACE
133 Mercer St (at Prince St)
431-9358
Mon-Sat: 11-6; Sun: 12-5; mail order address:
P.O. Box 274, Prince St Station, New York, NY 10012

There is no doubt that photography is an art form to Harvey Zucker and the people who run A Photographer's Place. The shop is a temple to photographers, both past and present. It is *not,* however, a supply shop. Rather, it pays homage to great pictures of various eras and the people who took them. The owners claim to be "the only *all* photographic book shop in the city and perhaps the country." Their interest isn't so much in competing as in being the best they can be. It's a credo they feel is shared by every photographer, and the shop excels at offering inspiration, history, advice, and the latest in technological advances. There is a super catalog.

Rare

J.N. BARTFIELD GALLERIES
30 W 57th St (bet Fifth and Sixth Ave, third floor)
245-8890
Mon-Fri: 10-5; Sat: 10-3

J.N. Bartfield is a legend in the field of old and rare books. His antiquarian book shop has what may be the country's largest and best collection of quality old books. The store is over 50 years old, and manager George Murray has been there for the majority of those years. There are sets of books distinguished by fine leather bindings, many of which were custom bound for family libraries. The books themselves are often in mint condition. Today it is impossible to find editions newly bound in leather, but the antique editions are no more expensive than when they were first issued. Bartfield claims that many of these prized editions are actually less expensive than contemporary volumes of lesser quality. Bartfield's also has a strong reputation for old maps and Western art and prints. There is an array of atlases, color-plate books, fore-edge paintings, bronzes, and watercolors.

PAGEANT PRINT AND BOOK SHOP
109 E Ninth St (bet Third and Fourth Ave)
674-5296
Mon-Sat: 10-6:30

This shop could be as old and rare as the stock it carries. A holdover from the days when this area was the rare and old-book capital of the world, it displays and sometimes sells antiquarian books, maps, prints, and first editions from the 15th to the 19th centuries. I would doubt that anyone inside the shop could readily tell me what year it is today, let alone the date, but then again the shop is as timeless as its attitude. Pageant carries virtually any kind of printed matter. There are etchings and early printed items, and it would require several days just to admire the prints. But remember this is a book and print shop, and the emphasis is on the former. In the old days, this would have been one of a dozen shops. Today, it may be one of the very few places left for an authentic rare-book-buying experience.

XIMENES RARE BOOKS
19 E 69th St
744-0226
Mon-Fri: 9-5 (appointment advisable)

In a profession whose proprietorship immediately calls to mind a stooped Dickensian character peering through a pince-nez in a paneled library, Stephen Weissman of Ximenes stands alone. Though young, he has an understanding and knowledge of rare books that would seemingly come only after years of burial under dusty volumes. Furthermore, Ximenes' collection is among the more affordable (prices start at about $50), and Weissman will happily discourse on his trade, if asked. Listen carefully, because he knows his stuff. Weissman's specialties are English-language first editions printed between 1500 and 1890. In that field, he is a primary source.

Religious

CALVARY BOOK SHOP
139 W 57th St
315-0230
Mon-Fri: 10-6; Wed: 10-7; Sat: 11-4

Down the block from the Calvary Baptist Church, the Calvary Book Shop stocks a wide variety of nondenominational religious books, references, gift items, and articles.

CHRISTIAN PUBLICATIONS BOOK AND SUPPLY CENTER
315 W 43rd St (bet Eighth and Ninth Ave)
582-4311
Mon-Fri: 9:30-5:45; Thurs: 9:30-6:45; Sat: 9:30-3:30

This is the largest Christian bookstore in the metropolitan area. It has over 10,000 titles in stock, along with religious records, tapes, videos, and church and school supplies. There are also a substantial number of these items available in Spanish, as befits the store's Latino neighborhood.

J. LEVINE
5 W 30th St
695-6888
Mon-Wed: 9-6; Thurs: 9-7; Fri: 9-2; Sun: 10-5

The history of the Lower East Side is reflected in this store. Started back in 1902 on Eldridge Street, it was a fixture in the area for many years. Now things have changed, and J. Levine has moved uptown, just off Fifth Avenue. Being one of the oldest Jewish bookstores in the city, they are a leader in the Jewish book marketplace. There are also many gift items, tapes, coffee-table books, and hundreds of items in Judaica, though the emphasis is still on the written word.

NEW YORK BIBLE SOCIETY
172 Lexington Ave (bet 30th and 31st St)
213-5454
Mon, Tues, Thurs: 11-4; Wed, Fri: 11-6

The New York Bible Society sells the world's most popular book in over 30 languages and in all kinds of editions. They can fill large church orders or take care of special gifts. They have the greatest variety of low-cost New International Version Scriptures in the city. In addition, there are all kinds of bibles, from pocket-sized to giant print, NIV on audio and videotapes, and even a children's bible storybook.

STAVSKY HEBREW BOOKSTORE
147 Essex St
674-1289
Sun-Thurs: 9:30-5:30; Fri: 9:30-2; closed Sun in summer

This store supplies synagogues and schools with religious books and objects. While they will fill an order for 10 coloring books, they are more accustomed to outfitting complete congregations, and they do it well. Their prices are fair, and service is excellent. Stavsky has the best collection of Jewish books, cassettes, CDs, Jewish videos, and everyday religious objects of any store in the city.

Science Fiction

FORBIDDEN PLANET
821 Broadway (at 12th St)   227 E 59th St (near
473-1576   Third Ave)
Mon-Sat: 10-7; Sun: 12-6   751-4386
                                                    Mon-Fri: 11-9; Sat: 10-9;
                                                    Sun: 12-7

When Mike Luckman started a science-fiction book cum toy shop in his native London, he quickly discovered that a good percentage of his customers were Americans clamoring for a similar shop at home. So, Luckman obliged and opened a satellite store at 12th Street and Broadway, directly across the street from the Strand. With a location so close to a book giant like the Strand and in an area known as the black hole of New York merchandising, the shop had to be out of this world to succeed. And Forbidden Planet is. In fact, pilgrimages have even been made to this shrine of science-fiction literature and artifacts. While most of the store is devoted to comic books and science-fiction publications, Luckman discovered in London that sci-fi devotees are not catholic in taste. First-edition collectors love Chewbacca face masks and bookends, and Darth Vadar fans browse through the vintage comic books and fantasy art. In between, there are enough toys and games to entertain the crew of *Star Trek*'s *Enterprise* during a trip to Saturn, and there is probably at least one copy of every science-fiction title ever written.

SCIENCE FICTION SHOP
56 Eighth Ave (at Horatio St)
741-0270
Mon-Fri: 11:30-6:45; Sat: 11-6; Sun: 12-6

While there are other sci-fi stores, this is the only one devoted totally to science-fiction literature. There are past and current (but not future) books and magazines in the field, and that includes rare and want-listed literature. This is a very special place for very special people interested in a very special subject.

Theater

ACTOR'S HERITAGE
262 W 44th St (bet Eighth Ave and Broadway)
944-7490
Mon-Sat: 9:30 a.m.-11:30 p.m.; Sun: 11-6:30

Actor's Heritage has an enormous stock of books, T-shirts, cards, records, scripts, and vocal selections relating to the theater. They claim to surpass every other store in the city in those areas. It certainly is worth browsing in, and Actor's Heritage also deserves a nod for being part of the effort to spruce up the Times Square area with interesting legitimate businesses.

APPLAUSE THEATER BOOKS
211 W 71st St (at Broadway)
496-7511
Mon-Sat: 10-8; Sun: 12-6

APPLAUSE CINEMA BOOKS
100 W 67th St (bet Broadway and Columbus Ave)
787-8858
Mon-Sat: 10:30-7; Sun: 12-6

These two stores, under the same management, offer the best selection of theater and cinema books in the world. There is great interest these days in anything having to do with theater literature, and these folks are on the cutting edge of the movement. They specialize in British plays and claim to have the playscripts for all British productions. They're planning to open a shop in London.

DRAMA BOOK SHOP
723 Seventh Ave (bet 48th and 49th St, second floor)
944-0595
Mon, Tues, Thurs, Fri: 9:30-7; Wed: 9:30-8;
     Sat: 10:30-5:30; Sun: 12-5

Talk about drama! When we called to validate information for this current edition, there was a real drama going on at this bookstore! The place was being robbed! I am happy to report that there were no casualties, but the bums got away with $200 in books. Of course, things aren't always quite that exciting in this shop, which probably has the largest selection of drama books assembled outside of the Library of Performing Arts at Lincoln Center. Nearly everything in the shop is confined to the written word. There are works on theater (both American and foreign), performers, scenery, props, makeup, lighting, staging, puppetry, magic, and all aspects of music and dance. One of the more scholarly undertakings are catalogs for each area of entertainment. The shop is best known for having the most complete selection of scores, accent tapes, libretti, arrangements, scripts, and plays in the world. While it is not always the least expensive, it is the biggest and one of the oldest (established in 1923).

RICHARD STODDARD—PERFORMING ARTS BOOKS
18 E 16th St (bet Fifth Ave and Union Sq, room 202)
645-9576
Mon, Tues, Thurs-Sat: 11-6

Richard Stoddard runs a one-man operation dedicated to rare, out-of-print, and used books and to memorabilia relating to the performing arts. Despite a Ph.D. from Yale in theater history and more than 10 years of experience as a performing-arts-materials dealer and appraiser, Stoddard is determined to offer a broad range of items, not just expensive rarities. So, while there is an extensive collection of scarce books, playbills, souvenir programs, original scenic and costume designs, and back issues of performing-arts magazines, Stoddard also stocks a case of paperback plays, which are within the financial reach of the most impoverished actor. There is a similar table of bargain books. Stoddard's pride, though, is his collection of scenic and costume designs. The sole agent for the estate of the late Jo Mielziner, the Broadway designer, Stoddard also has the drawings of a half-dozen other set designers. In fact, this is the only shop in the country that regularly sells such designs.

THEATREBOOKS
1600 Broadway (bet 48th and 49th St, room 1009)
757-2834
Mon-Fri: 10:30-6; Sat: 12-5

Another example of the demand for theater literature, Theatrebooks is just what its name implies. One of the only stores in the city with a selection of out-of-print and used books on the performing arts, it is also the only store with a search service for books not in stock. But the staff is proudest of being, in their own words, "the most trivia-laden staff of any theater bookstore in town." And that proves the real love of theater here. Twofer theater tickets are available at the counter, and the staff couldn't be more helpful in discussing the current status of the Broadway theater. With their location and stock, the folks at Theatrebooks have an eye on it all.

Travel

COMPLETE TRAVELLER BOOKSTORE
199 Madison Ave (at 35th St)
685-9007
Mon-Fri: 9-7; Sat: 10-6; Sun: 12-5

An African safari? How about the Seychelles? How do I get around in China? The Complete Traveller specializes in new travel guides, books, travel literature, maps, and other travel accessories. They also have a fine collection of rare travel books. The store is very intimate, and they encourage browsing. There is an excellent catalog (only $2), which lists many travel series, travel books, maps and accessories. You can obtain it in the store or by mail.

TRAVELLER'S BOOKSTORE
22 W 52nd St (75 Rockefeller Plaza, bet Fifth and
    Sixth Ave, lobby of Warner Communications Building)
664-0995
Mon-Fri: 9-6; Sat: 12-5

When Candace Olmsted and Jane Grossman opened their Traveller's Bookstore in Rockefeller Plaza, they practiced what they sold. Theirs may be the only bookstore in the city with two distinct addresses for one location, and what could be more fitting for a bookstore for people on the move? They've developed a catalog for those who can't travel to their address (addresses?) and who like to do their armchair shopping (and possibly traveling) at home. As in the store, the catalog arranges books geographically, and each area is represented with a selection of maps, guides, dictionaries, fiction and nonfiction both in and about the native tongue. The ladies have a very comprehensive selection, and there is hardly a travel area that they haven't covered in depth. Perhaps they've gained experience from trying to guide visitors to their single shop with double addresses!

Butterflies

MARIPOSA
South St Seaport, Pier 17
233-3221
Daily: 10-9

Butterflies are free, but not at Mariposa, the Butterfly Gallery, where they are regarded as art. Butterflies are unique, and Mariposa (Spanish for butterfly) displays them separately, in panels, and as parts of groups. There are even butterfly farms, which breed and raise butterflies for their brief one-month life span under ideal conditions for creating this art. I admit that sounds a little cold-hearted, but Mariposa has to be seen to be appreciated. Besides, it would be impossible to appreciate so many beautiful specimens during their extremely fleeting lifetimes.

Buttons

GORDON BUTTON COMPANY
142 W 38th St
921-1684
Mon-Fri: 9-5:30; closed first week of July

Peter Gordon's collection of old, unusual, and antique buttons is extensive. I would go to Gordon, however, for its new buttons, since the enormous stock is used by all of the neighboring garment manufacturers. Gordon's quality, selection, and variety are that good. Belt buckles, components, chains, and brass rings are also sold here and at the same excellent discount that comes to the retail customer courtesy of the company's wholesale operation. Courtesy is the "buyword" here. Most Garment Center manufacturers cannot be bothered with small retail customers, and it seems that their courtesy varies in direct proportion to the size of your order. But at Gordon, which also accepts mail orders, the size of the order seems to be irrelevant.

TENDER BUTTONS
143 E 62nd St
758-7004
Mon-Fri: 11-6; Sat: 11-5:30; closed Sat in July, Aug

Retail button stores can only *hope* to match the selection available here. Owners Diana Epstein and Millicent Safro have assembled one that is complete in variety as well as size. One antique wooden display cabinet shows off Tender Buttons' selection of natural, original buttons, many of them imported or made exclusively for them. Here are buttons of pearl, wood, horn, Navajo silver, leather, ceramics, bone, ivory, pewter, and precious stones. The New England scrimshaw buttons are valuable today as artwork, and a good sample can cost as much as a painting. Many unique pieces can be made (by Tender Buttons) into special cuff links—real conversation pieces for the lucky owner. They also have a fine collection of antique and period cuff links. As a cuff-link buff, I have purchased some of my best pieces from this shop.

Candles

CANDLE SHOP
118 Christopher St (bet Bleecker and Hudson St)
989-0148
Sun, Tues-Thurs: 12-8; Fri, Sat: 12-7

Thomas Alva Edison's inventions haven't made a flicker of an imprint on the folks at the Candle Shop. Rob Kilgallen has assembled a collection of beeswax, paraffin, and stearin candles in an assortment of sizes and colors for every possible need. In fact, it's positively illuminating to learn that candles are available in so many configurations.

Canvas

MATERA CANVAS PRODUCTS
5 Lispenard St (one block south of Canal St,
    off W Broadway)
966-9783
Mon-Fri: 10:30-5:30; closed Christmas week

John Matera is an expert with canvas. His store covers the canvas scene, from the raw product to the very elaborate finished items. And since he manufactures as well as sells all of the items, he has a firm hand on the quality of everything that the shop handles. There are custom-made tarps, boat covers, navy tops, automobile covers, artists' canvases, tarpaulins, and even pool covers. Matera also turns out custom-made products for items that require canvas and nylon materials. (One customer used it to repair the top of a rolltop desk. It works fine!) If you need canvas, particularly large pieces, this place should be your first choice.

China, Glassware

Superb showrooms of the best china, glass, silver, and crystal available anywhere:
Daum (694 Madison Ave at 62nd St)
Lalique (680 Madison Ave at 61st St)
Puiforcat (811 Madison Ave at 68th St)
Villeroy & Boch (972 Madison Ave at 76th St)
Although you may be able to find some items from these collections in other stores, no one has as complete a showing as these top-of-the-line houses. Madison Avenue has really become a showcase for the best in designer merchandise, both for the individual and for the home, and these relatively new stores are a part of the trend. But don't expect to find any bargains, unless you happen to drop in at sale time.

EASTSIDE GIFTS & DINNERWARE
351 Grand St (bet Essex and Ludlow St)
982-7200
Sun-Thurs: 10-6; Fri: 10-1:30

If you have been drooling over the beautiful china in the department stores but hesitating because of the price, head down to the Lower East Side to Eastside Gifts. Here you will find Mikasa, Fitz and Floyd, Royal Doulton, Wedgewood, Haviland, Hutchenreuther, Lalique, and many others at great savings. In addition to dinnerware and crystal, they also carry a wide selection of stemware and flatware. This is an excellent house to replace those broken pieces of your best set.

LANAC SALES
73 Canal St (at Allen St)
226-8925, 925-6422
Mon-Thurs: 10-6; Fri: 10-2; Sun: 9-5

Across Allen Street from the old store, Lanac is still a source for chinaware, cut glass, silverware, and gifts at discount prices. Lanac has a reputation for having excellent discounts on everything in stock, and that stock includes some of the finest domestic and imported tableware and crystal in the city. *Lanac,* incidentally, is *Canal* spelled backward—that's in case you get lost!

LOUIS KAPLAN RESTAURANT EQUIPMENT
250 Lafayette St (bet Prince and Spring St)
431-7300
Mon-Fri: 9-5

If you are looking for restaurant quality, heavy-duty merchandise, this is the place! You can find Lenox and Buffalo china, Libbey and imported French and German glassware, and Oneida silver, among many other well-known names. Copper, stainless steel, and heavy aluminum cookware is available at excellent prices, as are commercial-quality appliances. Don't come here expecting to find discounted prices on odd lots. The real bargains are available when you buy in quantity.

ROBIN IMPORTERS
510 Madison Ave (bet 52nd and 53rd St)
752-5605
Mon-Fri: 9:30-5:30; Sat: 10-5; closed Sat in July, Aug

If you don't want to travel way downtown to take advantage of household discount bargains in silverware, crystal, china, cutlery, dinner cloths, and giftware, this is a good place to shop. Prices are not as low as the Lower East Side stores, but the selection and quality are very adequate. Be sure to ask how long it will take for delivery of your purchase, as some of the suppliers in this field are notorious for lengthy waiting periods.

Christmas Decorations

CHRISTMAS EVE
200 Fifth Ave (bet 23rd and 24th St)
929-5500
Mon-Sat: 10-6

Some folk like to get ready for next Christmas the minute this year's event is over. If you are one of those, and you want to beat Santa to the package-wrapping fun, then this is your store. Even on the warmest day, you can cool off among a large selection of all kinds of Christmas decorations and accessories, and prices are a lot lower than they are during the holiday season, especially in the Christmas sections of the department stores. Be sure you take a look behind the scenes at some of the novel items they have in the back room. Merry Christmas!

Clothing and Accessories

Antique

ANTIQUE BOUTIQUE
712-714 Broadway (at Washington Pl)
227 E 59th St (bet Second and Third Ave)
460-8830
Mon-Fri: 10:30-9; Sat: 10:30-10; Sun: 12-8

Despite the name, nothing at Antique Boutique is as antique as it is vintage. Translated, that means that this is the place to find recently recycled clothing, as opposed to a Victorian wedding gown. Prices reflect the fact that these clothes are not one-of-a-kind antiques. The selection is excellent; they carry everything from argyle socks to suede jackets and incredible sweaters in alpaca, mohair, and moth-free wools. There is rack after rack of clothing designed, as they say, to make their customers legends in any time.

HARRIET LOVE
412 W Broadway (at Spring St)
966-2280
Mon-Sat: 12-7; Sun: 12-6; closed Mon in Jan, Feb

Harriet Love is at the front of the parade in vintage apparel and accessories. Her shop is overflowing with beautiful alligator purses, jackets, and Fifties Victoria jewelry. Harriet also buys from vendors who copy old pieces to create new treasures that have an old feeling.

JEAN HOFFMAN
236 E 80th St
535-6930
Mon-Sat: 12-6 or by appointment

In a tiny space, Jean Hoffman offers one of the best selections of quality vintage items in the city. She has laces and trims, linens, jewelry, and all kinds of old clothing. For the bride-to-be who wants something really special, the stock of vintage wedding gowns is without equal in the country.

PATRICIA FIELD
10 E Eighth St
254-1699
Mon-Sat: 12-8; Sun: 12-6

A description of Patricia Field is a little bit like the proverbial blind man's view of the elephant. One patron will launch into a long-winded history of how Patricia Field started as a pants source during the jeans craze (before designer jeans, if you can remember that far back) and ended up as a chic downtown source of uptown fashions. Perhaps the most apt description was offered by one of Field's salespeople, who said, "We have a lot of old, a lot of new. You have to come down and see us to understand." Yes, go see, but even then I won't guarantee you'll understand. The lifestyle Field designs for seems to favor classy sportswear separates. But that doesn't preclude the very dressiest evening wear from both former and ultracurrent eras. For the most part, Patricia Field's line is modern—so modern, in fact, that it is often years ahead of what is seen uptown. Her lines are often copied and seen several seasons later elsewhere.

REMINISCENCE
74 Fifth Ave (near 13th St)
243-2292
Mon-Sat: 11:30-8; Sun: 1-6

It's fun to go back to the Fifties and Sixties at this "cool" emporium, which Stewart Richer created on lower Fifth Avenue. Although he is a child of this era, most of Richer's customers are between the ages of 13 and 30. The finds here are unusual and wearable, with large selections of colorful vintage clothing and attractive displays of jewelry, hats, shoes, and all kinds of accessories. Richer's goods, although vintage in style, are mostly new, and he has become a manufacturer who sells to outlets all over the world. Because of his large distribution, Richer is able to produce huge quantities and sell at low prices. Old or young, this is a store worth reminiscing about. Reminiscence Garage (175 MacDougal St, 979-9440) has better prices and more casual clothes.

SCEAMING MIMI'S
495 Columbus Ave (at 84th St)
362-3158
Mon-Fri: 11-8; Sat: 11-7; Sun: 1-7

Owners Biff Chandler and Laura Wills, two former fashion co-ordinators, outfit their shop and customers with whatever appeals to their personal sense of style. The selection includes styles from the Thirties, Forties, Fifties, Sixties and even the Seventies, as well as currently popular trends. An expanded assortment of men's and women's accessories, a new "Sale Cell" (for budget buyers), and new shoes in addition to vintage styles are now featured. There is also a party-dress and tuxedo rental service.

SECOND COMING
72 Greene St (bet Spring and Broome St)
431-4424
Mon-Sat: 12-7; Sun 1-6

The Second Coming calls itself a "vintage department store" and that's an apt description. Note that it's not an *antique* shop; what's sold here is *vintage*. What's the difference? Well, vintage is valued because it is trendy, but it's not necessarily valuable. There's jewelry to accentuate the clothing, linens and lace to accentuate the furniture (check out the reproduction brass and iron beds), period wallpaper to complete the wall décor, lace objects, never-worn period shoes, and a Western boutique. The Second Coming is one of the few vintage clothing shops to have lasted through the decade, because it has a keen eye for changing trends.

TRASH AND VAUDEVILLE
4 St Mark's Pl (bet Second and Third Ave)
982-3590, 777-1727
Mon-Thurs: 12-8; Fri: 11:30-8; Sat: 11-8:30; Sun: 1-7:30

This place is hard to describe, since the stock changes almost constantly. What stock there is seems to have no boundaries. The store describes its stock as new and antique clothing, accessories, and original designs. Antique clothing here seems to mean 1950s to 1980s rock and roll styles, including some outrageous footwear, although there are some older—much older—things. There are some real finds here, but perhaps because this is a wholesale as well as retail business, you get the feeling that someone else has already escaped with the best values. More recently, the store has concentrated on new "new" clothing from Europe.

UNIQUE CLOTHING WAREHOUSE
718 and 726 Broadway (at Eighth St)
674-1767
Mon-Sat: 10-9; Sun: 12-8

Harvey Russack opened his Unique Clothing Warehouse in 1973 in NoHo, and his beyond-the-fringe clothing consisted of embroidered denims, military-surplus items, and other bygone fads that are merely memories on the fashion scene. Russack started with "antique," and he has successfully worked through all of the latest trends. So the store has seen vintage men's wear à la *The Sting* (Unique was one of the only sources for that style in the early days), military surplus, the Annie Hall look, surgeon's garb (remember that one?), high-tech, and clothes dyed in fluorescent hues. Shopping Unique is, well, a unique experience; the store itself is as much an experience as the clothes. One of the biggest mysteries in town is how Russack and his buyers seem to be able to predict the latest trends. There are those who have a clue. They claim Unique *makes* the trends, and that may be the answer. In any event, Unique is a bona fide success.

Bridal

I. KLEINFELD AND SON

8202 Fifth Ave	8209 Third Ave
Brooklyn, NY	Brooklyn, NY
(718) 833-1100	(718) 238-1500

Tues, Thurs: 11-9; Wed, Fri: 11-6; Sat: 10-6

The bridal business has changed a good deal. Today there are very limited collections at some specialty stores (like Bergdorfs and Saks), but there is only one true bridal complex. I use the word *complex* because it involves two separate buildings. The 47-year-old operation is called I. Kleinfeld and Son. The bridal gown collection (800 to 1,000 models in stock at all times) is located at 8202 Fifth Avenue, Brooklyn. Yes, I know, this is a book on Manhattan, but there is no store anywhere that can match Kleinfeld. The mother-of-the-bride can find a special section called Kleinfeld's P.M., which specializes in evening wear. (Wedding guests will find this selection helpful, also). Kleinfeld carries every major name in bridal wear, including Priscilla of Boston, Carolina Herara, and Scassi. Twenty percent of the collection is of international origin. A separate store for bridesmaids' gowns is located several blocks away at 8209 Third Avenue. The store prefers to operate by appointment; they can handle over 100 a day with their specialized personnel. This is *the* place to come when wedding bells will soon be ringing.

Children's — General

BOY OH BOY
18 E 17th St (off Fifth Ave)
463-8250
Mon-Fri: 11-6:30; Sat: 11-5

For young men, sizes 2 to 20, you can't do better than this, if you're looking for stylish, classic clothing and furnishings. There is a large selection of domestic and imported merchandise, with most of the top designers for boys' clothes represented. Prices are not discounted, but the well-selected stock makes up for it. And while you are buying the necessities, Junior will be able to pick out some toys that he just can't live without!

KINDERSPORT OF ASPEN
1260 Madison Ave (at 90th St)
534-5600
Mon-Sat: 10-6; summer: Mon-Thurs: 10-5; limited hours
    in July, Aug

How New York! How chic! How typical! Where else but Madison Avenue would one find a shop founded in Aspen, Colorado, specializing in exclusive top lines of European clothing, sports, and ski wear for children? Did New York need such an outfitter exclusively for children? Apparently. KinderSport has made a big splash. Stylish tots aged 2 to 16 snap up KinderSport's sweaters, ski suits, and sportswear. If not all of them end up on the ski slopes for which they are intended, at least they make knockout fashion statements. And if Junior really is off for a trip to Aspen or the Alps, have no fear that KinderSport can outfit even a size 2 at a moment's notice. Price? The dearest. But then, what is it worth to have your two-year-old slide down the slopes in the finest togs?

LA PETITE ETOILE
725 Fifth Ave (Trump Tower, level 4)
371-0388
Mon-Sat: 10-6

This is the ultimate children's designer boutique, with a collection of the most unusual and attractive infants-through-preteen clothing for both boys and girls. At this store your kid can get an outfit that no other kid in the neighborhood will have, for sure. Although the name is French, most of the merchandise is made in this country. If you look carefully, there are some items that could be called "reasonably" priced, but don't come here for bargains.

M KREINEN SALES
301 Grand St (at Allen St)
925-0239
Sun-Thurs: 9-5; Fri: 9-4

No sense in spending extra dollars to keep your kids in the most fashionable clothes. This Lower East Side establishment carries only brand-name goods, girls' sizes 7 to 14, and boys' sizes infant to 20. Discounts average about 25 percent, and you can count on the quality being as good as those at higher priced specialty and department stores.

PUSHBOTTOM FOR KIDS
252 E 62nd St (bet Second and Third Ave)
888-3336
Mon-Sat: 11-7

With a name and reputation like A Peter Pushbottom's the goods have to be special. And indeed they are. If your kid is something special (and whose isn't?), get the young ones outfitted here. Pushbottom specializes in sweaters, but can outfit your child from newborn to toddler age. All designs are originals, so your kid can have fun telling his friends that Peter Towtop, or whatever his name is, made this outfit just for him.

RICE AND BRESKIN
323 Grand St (at Orchard St)
925-5515
Sun-Fri: 9-5

If the Lower East Side has a quality shop for children's clothing, Rice and Breskin is probably it. Wrapped in plastic, the merchandise includes good brand names at a 20 percent discount or more. They specialize in infant clothing and baby gifts. Despite its Lower East Side location, the saleshelp are charming, even motherly.

TYKE-OONS
858 Lexington Ave (bet 64th and 65th St)
517-2011
Mon-Fri: 10:30-6:30; Sat: 11-5

Great name, eh? This is a children's retail store, but that isn't our reason for listing it. The unusual service offered here is especially for the mom and dad who are too busy to shop for their kids.

(What fun they are missing!) The folks at Tyke-oons have parents fill out a special form about their offspring, and then they put together a standard or deluxe package of clothing and accessories (not necessarily inexpensive) so that Junior will look just as classy as the old man and the old lady. Who says American ingenuity is dead?

Children's — Used

ONCE UPON A TIME
171 E 92nd St (bet Lexington and Third Ave)
831-7619
Mon-Sat: 10-6

This children's resale shop on the Upper East Side has clothing from infants to sizes 10-12 for boys and girls. Some of the items have never been worn, and all of it is in almost new condition and attractively priced. At the end of each season, the previous season's clothing goes for a fraction of what it would sell for in department stores. In addition, the seasons are a bit more realistically timed. You can buy a bathing suit in July here.

SECOND ACT CHILDREN'S WEAR
1046 Madison Ave (bet 79th and 80th St, upstairs)
988-2440
Tues-Sat: 10-5; summer: Mon-Fri: 10-4:30

The best buys here are the clothes that were bought and used for only one or two occasions, such as communion dresses, Easter outfits, and flower-girl gowns. Some of the other items don't seem worth the one-third-of-the-original-cost price tag, but everything is kept in A-1 condition. All clothing is washed and ironed or cleaned before it is put up for sale, and it is, indeed, in "like new" condition. Clothing is consigned to separate rooms according to sex, and within these rooms everything is sized in order. Sizes go from girls' infant to 14 and boys' infant to 20. In addition to clothing, there are ice skates, riding apparel, ski boots, books, and toys.

Costumes

M.I.S. RETAIL
736 Seventh Ave (at 49th St, second floor)
765-8342
Mon-Sat: 10:30-7:30

Are you going to appear at your office party dressed like Groucho Marx? Is your son going to play Superman at the school benefit? M.I.S. are the specialists for both amateurs and professionals when it comes to stage makeup, wigs, beards, and all kinds of theatrical accessories.

UNIVERSAL COSTUME COMPANY
535 Eighth Ave (bet 36th and 37th St, 21st floor)
239-3222
Mon-Fri: 9:30-5:30

It's quite the thing these days to dress up as an animal of one kind or another. If you'd like to do the same, you should proceed directly to the Universal Costume Company. Of course, animal outfits are not the only thing they stock; indeed, they have one of the largest selections of masquerade, Halloween, show business, period, and industrial costumes in the city. Elaborate headpieces are one of their specialties, and they have worked with many celebrities. Made-to-order costumes, designed by in-house personnel, are also available. Oh, yes, did you get invited to that Louis XIV bash? If so, Louis and most of his friends probably got their outfits at Universal.

Dance Wear

CAPEZIO'S
755 Seventh Ave (at 50th St)
245-2130
Mon-Wed, Fri, Sat: 9:30-5:45; Thurs: 9:30-7

CAPEZIO EAST
136 E 61st St (at Lexington Ave)
758-8833
Mon-Wed, Fri, Sat: 10-6:30; Thurs: 10-7; Sun: 12-5

177 MacDougal St
477-5634
Mon-Sat: 12-8

CAPEZIO'S AT STEPS
2121 Broadway (at 74th St)
799-7774
Mon-Sat: 12-8:30; Sun: 12-5

Capezio's is the definitive store for dance paraphernalia, and if first-timers display any sense of wonder about the shop, they are amazed not because New York can easily support several such fully equipped professional shops, but because Capezio is a name that's known worldwide. The Seventh Avenue store boasts that it is the largest dance-theater retail store in the world. It carries only dance wear and dance-related materials. Each store reflects the style of its neighborhood. The most professionally oriented is Capezio's Seventh Avenue, but the most interesting is the Village shop. It even has a men's wear department. In response to the wave of physical fitness, Capezio has come up with its own athletic wear. Theirs reflects Capezio's years of experience with outfitting dancers and performers. Footwear ranges from aerobic shoes to fashion shoes.

FREED OF LONDON
922 Seventh Ave (at 58th St)
489-1055
Mon-Wed, Fri, Sat: 10-5:45; Thurs: 10-6:45

Freed of London has landed on its toes in New York, and the venerable English establishment has brought along its tradition of supplying the best and finest in dance supplies. The style is definitely traditional, but there is virtually no piece of dance gear that Freed does not carry or cannot order. The store keeps leg warmers, leotards, ballet shoes, skirts, and tutus in stock. A list of the shop's clientele reads like a who's who of stars who've danced in London (the store carries, as a matter of course, the complete line of regulation wear for the Royal Academy of Dancing). For those who can't stop in, there's a measuring chart and mail-order catalog available. Apparently, Freed was getting so many orders from New York that it was cheaper to open a store here than service them from abroad. For dancers, this store is a must. If you're simply a dance fan, this is where you'd be likely to spot your favorite dancer.

Furs

BALENCIA-DAVELLIN
208 W 29th St (ground floor)
244-0005, 244-7601
Mon-Fri: 9-5; Sat: 9-4

The real drawing card in this factory and showroom, which merchandises furs in all shapes and forms, is that each customer is greeted as if she was the most important person in the world. In a city whose wholesale houses are notorious for shutting out the retail customer, this is a great tribute. The showroom is beautifully decorated (primarily to impress out-of-town wholesale buyers), and a personal tour of the factory and vaults is offered. Along the way, the customer is invited to point out anything that is particularly appealing, and once back in the showroom, those selections are brought out for a second look. The stock includes everything furry, even leather with fur, in hats, long and elegant stoles, jackets, and coats. The furs range from frankly fun to unrivaled ranch mink and sable. Balencia's designs are unique, and they will happily make a garment to suit your individual taste.

BREAKAWAY
125 Orchard St (at Delancey St)
475-6660
Daily: 9-6

If price is your only objective in buying a fur coat, this is a place you'll want to visit. They offer designer furs at considerable discounts, but personal advice and attention are in short supply.

FURS BY DIMITRIOS
130 W 30th St (bet Sixth and Seventh Ave)
695-8469
Mon-Fri: 9-6; Sat: 10-4; Sun: 10-4

The thoroughly professional atmosphere and showroomlike inventory belie the fact that this store is what it tries so hard to appear to be: the best source for a man's fur coat at wholesale prices. The racks are shaggy with furs of all descriptions and in all sizes for both genders. Prices are wholesale but go up slightly if the garment has to be specially ordered. This shouldn't be necessary, though, since the off-the-rack selection is probably the most extensive and of the best quality in the city.

G. MICHAEL HENNESSY FURS
333 Seventh Ave (bet 28th and 29th St, 10th floor)
695-7991
Mon-Fri: 9:30-5; by appointment on Sat

Michael Hennessy started as an international fur trader, then switched sides of the counter by running a fur salon in Beverly Hills, and later served as the fur director of Bonwit Teller and the president of Maximilian Furs. In 1982, Hennessy, his wife, Rubye, and another partner (who was later bought out) established this cozy den in the fur business. (Incidentally, Rubye Graham Hennessy is a former editor of *Seventeen Magazine* and *The Philadelphia Inquirer.* Her sense of style is as valuable as Michael's expertise in business.) Hennessy Furs manufactures high-quality designer furs for women, which are sold to top stores in this country as well as in Japan and Europe. New Yorkers benefit because Hennessy also sells retail (with no covert razzmatazz), and the entire collection is available to the public. This means that prices are about wholesale for the same garments that appear in better fur salons around the world. At the annual sales in August and late winter, those prices are even better. The best prices are for the in-stock furs, particularly the house specialty, which is mink. Wonderful values are available for the ladies who want a mink coat made to order. Most are highly styled or made of unusual furs: Tibetan lamb, tanuki, fox, fitch, sheared and longhaired beavers, sables, and several varieties of raccoon. Sizes for the ready-made garments come in a greater range than would be expected.

HARRY KIRSHNER AND SON
307 Seventh Ave (bet 27th and 28th St)
243-4847
Mon-Fri: 9-6; Sat: 10-5

Kirshner should be one of your first stops for any kind of fur product, from throw pillows to full-length mink coats. They reline, clean, alter, or store any fur at rock-bottom prices. What's even better is that they are neither pushy nor snobbish, which may make them the only place to repair Aunt Minnie's tattered but beloved lamb stole. Harry Kirshner offers tours of its factory, and if nothing available appeals to the customer, a staff member will sit down and try to draw a coat to specifications. Many times, however, the factory offers a collection of secondhand furs that the company has restored to perfect and fashionable condition. And many customers come in for a *new* fur and walk out with a slightly worn one, for a fraction of what they were prepared to spend. Harry Kirshner is the only place in New York that offers such a wide choice.

H.B.A. FUR
333 Seventh Ave (bet 28th and 29th St)
564-1080
Mon-Fri: 8:30-5; Sat (Oct-Jan): 9-1

H.B.A. was one of the first of the fur-industry garment lofts to open to the public. As a result, they are more experienced and better attuned to customer requests than some of their neighbors. The stock includes all kinds of furs, but there is a tendency to avoid trends and stick to more classic styles. As a result, this year's fads, while available, are not singled out as *the* only thing to wear. (Please note that Bob Mackie designs for H.B.A.) Rather, there's a good selection of timeless furs, which can be taken off the racks or made to order. Prices are wholesale. Harold Frishman (the *H* of the name) is a knowledgeable and absolutely honest man. Ask for him, and he'll show you one of New York's top fur collections at unbeatable prices. Tell him I sent you.

NEW YORKER FUR SHOP
822 Third Ave (bet 50th and 51st St)
355-5090
Mon-Fri: 10-5:30, Sat: 10-5; closed Sat in July, Aug

The New Yorker Fur Shop, like the Ritz, deals in new and used furs, and will sell, store, repair, and clean them. Because of the number of people who must wear current fur styles, New York is an excellent market for used furs, and both the New Yorker and the Ritz do a brisk business. The Ritz is the better-known shop, partly because of an extensive advertising campaign, which is just fine with the New Yorker, since people who can't afford to be seen selling back a fur prefer to go to the New Yorker. Bernard Glassman, the store's owner, says that half of his stock is new, and since the New Yorker isn't quite as well-known as a recycling center, both sellers and buyers of furs feel more comfortable here. The New Yorker also does alterations, and they encourage browsing. Some of their best sales are made that way.

RITZ THRIFT SHOP
107 W 57th St
265-4559
Mon-Sat: 9-6

Down the block and across the street from Carnegie Hall, the Ritz Thrift Shop is as much an institution as its neighbor. And its clientele is just as loyal. The Ritz Thrift Shop seems to have been in business forever, buying and selling used furs to smart shoppers. And all those years of experience have made the management as knowledgeable and fashion-conscious as the finest retail operations. The Ritz buys used furs outright. Fifty percent of the stock is bought from individual customers, and the rest comes from furriers who took them as trade-ins. Because they are not a consignment operation (and perhaps because they offer free repairs and storage for as long as their client owns the coat), they are very picky about what they will buy. So, if your coat is passé, damaged, or not very good to begin with, the Ritz won't be interested—unless your coat is so outdated it's "in." (1940s jackets and long-haired and silver-fox furs fall in this category. The Ritz can't get enough of them.) So, customers are offered an incredible array of modern, stylish furs at prices roughly one-third of what the fur cost originally. It's understandable why a good portion of their business is with people who trade in their furs every two years or so. The Ritz is also contemporary enough to sell 1980s men's furs.

VEETAL FASHION FURS
86 Rivington St (at Orchard St)
677-1010
Mon-Sat: 8-6; Sun: 9-6

Note Veetal's official name because they dabble in a little bit of everything. But that little bit is only of the very best, and the store resembles the very best hometown ladies' specialty shop with a very eye-catching exterior. But everything is discounted, and some (though not all) prices are sensational. Sensational also describes Veetal's image. The goal seems to be outfitting a woman for a classy formal social occasion from head to toe. So while there is some sportswear, the emphasis is on shoes, bags, jewelry, fine leathers, and dressy evening clothing. The leather and suede coordinates can't be overlooked, except perhaps amidst the glitter of the cocktail dresses. And the fur salon has its own separate section since there is so much available. Virtually every type of fur can be had in jacket or coat length. It's not easy to leave this place empty-handed, and the discount policy makes it less painful.

Hosiery

FOGAL
680 Madison Ave (bet 61st and 62nd St)
759-9782

510 Madison Ave (at 53rd St)
355-3254
Mon-Sat: 10-6

Before Fogal came to New York from Switzerland, the thought of a Madison Avenue boutique devoted to hosiery was, well, foreign. But since its opening in 1982, it's hard to imagine Manhattan without it. If it's new, fashionable, and different leg wear, Fogal has it. Plain hosiery comes in nearly 100 hues, at last count; the designs and patterns of the colors make the number of choices almost incalculable. You might say that Fogal's has a leg up on the competition, but there have never been any serious contenders.

JACOB YOUNG AND SON
329 Grand St (at Orchard St)
925-9232
Sun-Fri: 9-5

Jacob Young has hosiery for men and children, and pantyhose for women, at unbelievably low prices. Hanes underwear for men is also a real find. Don't look for big smiles and pleasant greetings, just grab the bargains.

LOUIS CHOCK
74 Orchard St
473-1929
Sun-Thurs: 9-5; Fri: 9-1

It's hard to find a classification for this store. It seems to stock a little of everything, but perhaps the old-fashioned term "dry goods" sums up the stock sold here. Louis Chock sells dry goods for the home, school, and the entire family. There appears to be a subspecialty in hosiery and family underwear. Children's nightwear —which is only peripherally related to the underwear category—is available in a large choice of colors and sizes, and there is something in the hosiery section for every member of the family. Furthermore, everything in the store is sold at a discount that begins at 25 percent. Another plus: there is a larger discount on items bought in quantity. Louis Chock also has a mail-order department, offering a 25 to 30 percent discount on everything in stock. There is a catalog for $1.

M. STEUER HOSIERY COMPANY
31 W 32nd St (near Fifth Ave)
563-0052
Mon-Fri: 7:45-5:20; Sat: 10-4

By walking one block from Herald Square, hosiery wearers can save a bundle. Steuer is a wholesale operation that treats each retail customer as a wholesaler, no matter how small the order. They even speak a half-dozen languages—the better to welcome visitors to New York. There is a huge selection and large inventory of name-brand hosiery, socks, pantyhose, and dance wear. Steuer has been known to fill unusual requests with aplomb.

WINGDALE HOSIERY
16 W 30th St (at Fifth Ave)
684-4291
Mon-Fri: 7-4

No need to pay regular prices for hosiery for men or women. Wingdale offers top quality and irregulars in men's hosiery, Interwoven support hose, ladies' famous national brands, pantyhose, and socks. The selection is great, and the store personnel couldn't be nicer. Suggestion: buy in quantity, and use for gift items for the whole family. It's a good deal.

Jeans and Casual Wear

ARNIE'S PLACE
37 Orchard St (at Hester St)
925-0513
Sun-Fri: 8:30-5:30

For those who want to be clothed in jeans, the great American uniform, Arnie's has a top-drawer collection of jeans and denims for men, women, and children in more than 20 different brands. Sizes range from toddler to embarrassingly large, and there are also shirts, skirts, and overalls. If you shop carefully, you should be able to save about one-half of what you would pay for the same designer jeans in uptown stores.

CANAL JEANS
504 Broadway (off Spring St)
226-1130, 226-0737
Sun-Thurs: 10-8; Fri, Sat: 10-9

From the moment you walk by the bins full of sweaters, you know Canal Jeans is not your ordinary store. And it's not. Canal Jeans buys, sells, and wholesales the latest SoHo looks and has made itself a popular place. The look is certainly casual. Even their best *new* clothing stretches the meaning of sportswear, but if it's bomber jackets, brightly colored pants, tops, and outfits you want, this is the place to shop. A large percentage of the customers are Europeans who stock up on as many pairs of jeans as they can hoard in their suitcases and backpacks. (If they buy enough, they can sell them back home and make enough profit to pay for their trip.) Other clothing items include punk outfits, bins of junk clothes (don't bother—they're just that), and closeouts.

Judicial, Educational, and Religious Robes

BENTLEY AND SIMON
450 Seventh Ave
695-0554
Mon, Wed, Fri: 8:30-4 by appointment

Bentley and Simon is one of those "only in New York" institutions. In business since 1912, it supplies only one product—robes for judicial, educational, and religious use. They are probably *the* outfitter for judges across the country, up to and including the Supreme Court. But despite a long and unique reputation, ownership by the Oak Hall Cap and Gown Company of Roanoke, Virginia, and a Seventh Avenue address, Bentley and Simon is still run like a small, personal business. As for styles and selection, well, a robe is simply a black thing with pleats in the back, right? Well, sort of. While Bentley and Simon don't make robes in styles per se, they are quite convinced that their judicial robes' design is the ultimate one, and they make it in different sizes. Although clergymen (and women) have more of a choice, Bentley and Simon are convinced that *they* know the proper garment, so most clergymen usually end up relying upon their judgment. And as might be expected in a profession that has such a stodgy image, Bentley and Simon's reaction to the increasing number of women in the judiciary and clergy was barely perceptible. They simply made up smaller and shorter robes.

Leather

BARBARA SHAUM
69 E Fourth St
254-4250
Wed-Fri: 1-7; Sat: 1-6

Barbara Shaum does magical things with leather. The main stock is custom-made sandals, although there are some ready-made pairs available for emergencies. In addition, there are bags, belts (with handmade brass, nickel-silver, inlaid wood, and copper buckles), attaché cases, and briefcases. Everything is designed in the shop, and Barbara Shaum meticulously crafts each item, using only the finest materials. She's a wonder.

NORTH BEACH LEATHER
772 Madison Ave (at 66th St)
772-0707
Mon-Fri: 10-7; Sat: 10-6; Sun: 1-6

If leather wear connotes home on the range or some motorcycle bar on the Village waterfront, then you are obviously unaware that leather is the flip side of fur and can be just as elegant. North Beach Leather's locations are proof enough of that (with stores in Houston, Los Angeles, and San Francisco, to name but a few), and the fashions are further evidence. Madison Avenue isn't the place to look for an outfit to wear when cleaning the barn, and North Beach couldn't oblige, even if it wanted to. But if you need a leather ensemble for an outing in the Mercedes, then North Beach is the place to look. There is, of course, an emphasis on jackets, coats, and outerwear, but there are also suits and even skirts and dresses for women. Their leather jackets for men are just the thing to round out an outfit. But they aren't cheap.

SAN MICHEL LEATHER
379 Fifth Ave (bet 35th and 36th St)
481-4110
Mon-Wed, Sat: 10-6; Thurs, Fri: 10-7; Sun: 12-5

In the heart of Manhattan, less than one block from Altman's department store, San Michel manufactures the finest in leather and suede apparel for both men and women. Designer names are also available, as well as men's and women's shoes. They claim that every piece of merchandise is sold at a price that is 40 to 60 percent lower than elsewhere.

Men's Custom-Made Clothing and Shirts

With off-the-rack suits today selling for big bucks, more and more men are opting for true custom clothing. Depending on whom you go to and the fabric you select, prices for suits can start as low as $400 per suit and go as high as $3,000 plus. For the man who has a tough time being fitted with regular sizes, this may be the best solution to his problem. Be prepared for one to three fittings and for waiting at least several months for your finished garment. The best tailors in the city are rapidly graying; most were trained in Europe or learned their trade from immigrant fathers. Here are some of the top craftsmen in New York: **John Reyle** (20 E 46th St), **Scali** (119 W 57th St), **Piero Dimitri** (110 Greene St), **Alan Flusser** (16 E 52nd St), **Epaulet** (515 Madison Ave at 53rd St), and **Garrick Anderson** (108-110 W 18th St, fifth floor).

True custom-made shirts are made from scratch, whereas semi-custom shirts are made from existing short-body patterns. Semi-custom shirts may be found at Barneys, Bergdorf Goodman, Custom Shop, Paul Stuart, and Saks. For real made-to-order shirts, try **Alan Flusser** (16 E 52nd St), **Arthur Gluck** (37 W 57th St), **Brooks Brothers** (346 Madison Ave), **Mark Christopher of Wall Street** (87 Nassau St), **Seewaldt & Bauman** (17 E 45th St), or **A Sulka & Company** (430 Park Ave). Be prepared to pay from $100 up per shirt; waiting time is an average of six weeks.

Men's — General

CAMOUFLAGE
141 Eighth Ave (at 17th St)
741-9118
Mon-Fri: 12-7; Sat: 11-6; Sun: 1-5 (Sun hours in
    April, May, Nov, Dec only)

In the heart of Chelsea, Camouflage looks like it would be better suited to the Village, while its fashions would be at home on Madison Avenue. It sells American designer clothing for men during hours more in keeping with the Village than with that of its straight-laced nine-to-five neighborhood. It outfitted the new "gentrifiers" of the neighborhood long before it was a fashionable neighborhood. In short, Camouflage has never been just another store, and more often than not, it has managed to shine out of all proportion to its small size. If you've got patriotic tastes, this may be the store for you. It is one of the few shops that eschews foreign designers, selling only American clothing. Names such as Susan Horton, Perry Ellis, J.G. White, Alexander Julian, Garrick Anderson, and Jeffrey Banks are crammed into a tight space. Prices range from very reasonable (their chinos may be one of the best buys in the city) to good, considering those pricey designer names. But one of Camouflage's best virtues is the ability to dress its customer with a dignified but special appearance. There's nothing at Camouflage that would blend into the wallpaper.

EISENBERG AND EISENBERG
85 Fifth Ave (sixth floor)
627-1290
Mon-Wed, Fri: 9-6; Thurs: 9-7; Sat: 9-5:30; Sun: 10-4

The Eisenberg and Eisenberg style is a classic one that dates from 1898, the year they opened. Although Eisenberg and Eisenberg has a loft in the men's wear garment district, it consistently offers top quality and good prices on suits, coats, and sportswear. E & E also stocks outerwear, slacks, name-brand raincoats, women's suits, pure cashmere sports jackets, and 100 percent silk jackets. All are sold at considerable discounts, and alterations are available. London Fog coats are featured here, and no label is better known for wet weather needs.

GILCREST CLOTHES COMPANY
900 Broadway (at 20th St)
254-8933
Mon-Fri: 8-5; Sat: 8:30-5; Sun: 9:30-3:30

No fancy fixtures in this upstairs loft, just very good buys on many top names in quality men's clothing. If you are looking for suits by Ralph Lauren, Alexander Julian, Lanvin, Perry Ellis, or Adolfo, and if the prices uptown make you go back to wearing that same old suit in your closet, then take an hour off to see the Gilcrest operation. The folks here are helpful and knowledgeable, and they are not pushy. While you are looking, ask to see their own line of suits—excellent tailoring at sensible prices. There is no charge for alterations.

GORSART
9 Murray St
962-0024
Mon-Fri: 9-6; Sat: 9-5:30

Gentlemen! If you are the natural-shoulder type, read on. And if you find the style and quality of Brooks Brothers or Paul Stuart appealing but the prices appalling, head downtown to this little known jewel. In 1921, two brothers started catering to the financial community with a new twist at that time: quality merchandise at a discount. The policy has never changed, and today one great guy, Neil Roberts, carries on as store manager in a loft that offers classy suits made by H. Freeman and Arthur Freedberg (among others) at prices that will make you smile. These are not seconds or markdowns. In addition to suits, there is a nice selection of sportswear and furnishings, all discounted. The reason for the great prices? Simple: low overhead. You can pick up a tux for about half the uptown price, and you don't pay for tailoring on anything, unless of course it's a complete restructuring. They have 35 tailors in house on the job all the time. This is special store, fellows, and you will enjoy shopping here. No high-pressure selling, no gimmicks, just value and service.

IRVING BARON CLOTHES
343 Grand St (at Orchard St)
475-1718
Sat-Tues, Thurs: 9-6; Wed: 9-8;
    summer: Sun-Fri: 9:30-6

Once inside, a customer at Irving Baron might think he's in a posh Fifth Avenue store. Such brand names as Groshire, Marzotto, Corneliani, Yves St. Laurent, Halston, Le Baron, Louis Roth, London Fog, Mondo, Torras, Countess Mara, Damon, and Calvin Klein are part of the stock, which, the staff says, can dress a man from top to bottom. (Shoes are an exception.) It is only when the bill is presented that the customer realizes that this is, indeed, a Lower East Side store, for the discount starts at 25 percent. Suits, sport jackets, pants, overcoats, raincoats, outerwear, shirts, sweaters, and ties are carried to suit men sized from 36 short to 50 long. The salespeople are excellent.

JODAMO INTERNATIONAL
321 Grand St (at Orchard St)
219-0552, 219-1039
Sun-Fri: 9-6; Thurs: 9-8

Don't overlook this Lower East Side shop, which sells high-fashion men's clothing from top European designers on a wholesale and retail basis. Most of the designers are Italian. The discount is a minimum of 20 to 30 percent on advance season clothing upstairs, while reduced clothing on the main level can go for 50 percent off. Alterations are free.

J. PRESS
16 E 44th St (bet Fifth and Madison Ave)
687-7642
Mon-Sat: 9:15-5:30

As one of New York's classic, conservative men's stores, J. Press prides itself on its sense of timelessness. Its salespeople, customers, and attitude have changed little from the time of J. Press to that of Richard Press today. Styles are impeccable and distinguished, if not distinguishable. Blazers are blue, and shirts are button-down and straight. Even in the days when button-down collars were out, Press was such a bastion of support for them that it went so far as to make them available in colors other than blue.

LESH CLOTHING
115 Fifth Ave (at 19th St, sixth floor)
255-6893
Mon-Fri: 9-6; Sat: 9-4; Sun: 10-3

Irving Lesh claims that his family business was one of the first, if not *the* first, wholesale men's clothing lofts. He has a certain pride in the bare-piped surroundings, and the quality of the suits, sports jackets, slacks, and outerwear seems designed to prove that here the dollar goes to the merchandise rather than the décor. Lesh manufactures its own suits, and when the overhead (i.e., rent) gets to be too much, they move to another (read cheaper) loft. Consequently, it always pays to call before paying Lesh a visit. Speaking of overhead, that's where you'll find the merchandise. It literally hangs from the rafters and the pipe racks. The selection and quality of suits, tuxedos, and sports coats are great. Since Lesh has been manufacturing them since 1935, they adhere to the fine nuances of tailoring. All of Lesh's suits are made in the same factory as those for the most famous international designer sold in the United States. You won't even need a hint when you see the workmanship. And all of this for one low price. Everything in the warehouse goes for the same price, and that price is almost laughably cheap. The average customer invariably walks out with twice what he intended to buy—and for no more than he'd originally planned to spend.

LOUIS BARALL AND SON
58 Lispenard St (bet Canal St and Broadway)
226-6195
Mon-Fri: 9:30-6; Sat: 9:30-5; closed Sat in July, Aug

Although it has been in existence for almost 75 years and Louis Barall has been succeeded by Irving Barall, this store is one of the best-kept secrets in town. The only possible reason is that the savvy Wall Street types who shop here have no desire to share the market with anyone else. Styles are conservative and traditional at best. But that doesn't mean old-fashioned or even out of season; it simply bypasses the ultratrendy. If your style runs to the tried and true, try Barall. Prices *begin* at one-third off list price and go down from there. Garments—all with recognizable names—come in first-quality or clearly marked irregulars, with the latter going for about 50 percent off list price and more.

L. S. MEN'S CLOTHING
18 W 45th St (bet Fifth and Sixth Ave, room 403)
575-0933
Mon-Thurs: 9-7; Fri: 9-4 (Sun: 10-4 at 19 W 44th St)

L. S. bills itself as the "Executive Discount Shop," but I would go further and call them a must for the fashion-minded businessman. For one thing, their midtown location precludes a trip downtown to the Fifth Avenue-in-the-teens area that is the usual spot for finding men's discount clothing. Better still, as owner Israel Zuber puts it, "There are many stores selling $200 suits discounted, but we are one of the few that discount the $400 to $600 suits *and* are located in mid-Manhattan." The main attraction, though, is the tremendous selection of styles in stock. Style is primarily executive class, and within that category a man could almost outfit himself entirely at L. S. The natural and soft-shoulder designer suits are available in all sizes. This is one of the top spots for top names. I would make it number one on the midtown shopping itinerary.

MANO A MANO
580 Broadway (bet Houston and Prince St)
219-9602
Mon-Thurs: 12-7:45; Fri: 12-8:45; Sat: 11-7:45;
    Sun: 12-6:45

There are monkeys in cages, very hip salespeople, and a general carnival atmosphere here, but don't let all of that keep you from investigating the huge selection of stylish sportswear, leather items, suits, and accessories for men. If you have seen it in one of the men's fashion magazines, you no doubt will find it here at less than uptown prices. Although there is a selection of women's items available, this is definitely the store for the modern man.

NAPOLEON-JOSEPHINE
Trump Tower (Fifth Ave at 57th St)
759-1110
Mon-Sat: 10-6

Trump Plaza
1048 Third Ave (at 62nd St)
308-3000
Mon-Sat: 10-7

This is one of the number-one men's boutiques in the city—or anywhere, for that matter. The customer is emperor here, and what an empire he has! Napoleon has only the finest in haberdashery. The style is set by modern Italian designers; there's an extensive (and exclusive) line by Ermenegildo Zegna. Its superb quality and style are matched only by an incredibly personalized service that makes each person who enters the shop feel that he or she is someone special. Prices are in the if-you-have-to-ask-you-can't-afford-it class, but the merchandise and ambiance make them worthwhile. Napoleon-Josephine really does carry clothes fit for a king and his consort. Tell Denny I sent you.

PAN AM SPORTSWEAR AND MENSWEAR
50 Orchard St (bet Grand and Hester St)
925-7032
Sun-Wed: 9-6; Thurs: 9-8; Fri: 9:30-3 (winter);
    9-5 (summer)

With more stores like this, the Lower East Side could become synonymous with class as well as bargains. From the shiny glass windows (as opposed to the clutter of hangers that usually denotes an entrance) to the extremely fine stock, Pan Am is distinctive enough to be on Madison Ave, except for its prices. They are nothing short of super! Perry Ellis, Mani by Georgio Armani, Polo by Ralph Lauren, and Colours by Alexander Julian are but a few of the names that adorn the racks in all their glory, but sans the excessive price tag (at least a third of the uptown price). What's more, styles are *au courant;* they often preview here first, and they're in classic good taste. There are no screaming purple parachute suits and no 1940s (or even last year's) lapels. Finally, the saleshelp are a major exception to the Lower East Side norm. They are prompt and courteous, although they may be a little too quick to pounce on any customer who walks through the door. But at these prices, that's a minor annoyance. Besides, who ever heard of complaining of too much service on the Lower East Side?

PARKWAY NEW YORK
2056 Broadway (bet 70th and 71st St)
496-8571
Mon-Fri: 10-8; Sat: 10-7; Sun: 12-6

12 Gold St
809-6636
Mon-Fri: 10-6; Sat: 10-5; Sun: 11-5

Parkway is where the best-dressed New Yorkers dress themselves. It carries every major brand, including Manhattan, Botany, Polo, Chaps, Perry Ellis, Bill Blass, and London Fog at excellent prices, which already include sales tax. Quality is magnificent, and the styles are sometimes ahead of the department stores. Parkway is particularly noted for outerwear, but also stocks brand-name sportswear, dress shirts, and ties. The back of the store carries ladies' raincoats, primarily Misty Harbor. The discount there is about 30 percent.

PAUL SMITH
108 Fifth Ave (at 16th St)
627-9770
Mon-Sat: 11-7: Sun: 12-6

The atmosphere here is like the stores on Bond Street in London. Paul Smith has brought to a less-than-classy neighborhood a jewel of a store that offers beautifully designed English men's wear. His collection of suits, coats, slacks, shirts, and sweaters is for the well-dressed, conservative gentleman who spends his weekdays on Wall Street and his weekends in the Hamptons.

PAUL STUART
Madison Ave at 45th St
682-0320
Mon-Wed, Fri: 8-6; Thurs: 8-7; Sat: 9-6

Paul Stuart is to quality what Ralph Lauren is to style. The atmosphere at this laid-back store is gentlemanly, the service unobtrusive, the merchandise conservative and well-made. But there is little to excite the adventurous in men's or women's wear. Natural-shoulder merchandise is featured, with extensive selections of quality suits and sportswear. Shirts, ties, shoes, and all accessories are prim and proper, and the price tags of the goods reflect the upscale surroundings. If you are insecure about your ability to select the right outfit, if you want a suit or jacket that will outlast any style trend, and if price is no object, then this is your kind of store.

ROTHMAN'S
200 Park Ave S (at Union Sq)
777-7400
Mon-Wed, Fri: 10-7; Thurs: 10-8; Sat: 9-6; Sun: 12-5;
    closed Sun in summer

Forget your mental picture of the old Harry Rothman store. Harry's grandson, Ken Gidden, runs this classy new men's store, which offers a huge selection of quality clothes at discount prices (up to 40 percent) in a contemporary and comfortable atmosphere. He is not afraid to mention that he carries top-of-the-industry names, like Hickey-Freeman, Norman Hilton, Perry Ellis, Ralph Lauren (Polo), and Alexander Julian, all at off prices. Gentlemen, be sure to check out the Alexander Julian clothes in particular; no one has more interesting fabric and color combinations. Sizes at Rothman range from 36 to 56 in regular, short, long, extra long, extra short, portly short, and portly. Raincoats, slacks, sports jackets, and accessories are stocked in-depth at the same attractive prices. It's great to see the third generation just as eager and as capable as Grandpa himself!

SAINT LAURIE
897 Broadway (at 20th St)
473-0100
Mon-Wed, Fri, Sat: 9:30-6; Thurs: 9:30-7:30; Sun: 12-5

If you want selection, quality, and value, this is the place to go first. Saint Laurie is a manufacturer, who does not sell its retail line anywhere else in the city; it distributes entirely outside Manhattan. Consequently, the customer can take advantage of the missing middle man. So here you have thousands and thousands of garments in sizes 35 to 48, regular, short, long, and extra long. All are arranged for easy looking and selection. The professional salespeople are informed but not pushy. Saint Laurie also manufactures women's classic business suits made of 100 percent worsted wool. They are outstanding. The relatively new building has a "living museum," demonstrating Saint Laurie's production of its clothing as well as a tour of the workrooms and an exhibit showing various suit styles over the years. Custom-made clothing, at truly reasonable prices, is a new service offered. In addition, a mail-order swatch brochure program is available for the out-of-town shopper. If you are looking for extremely high-fashion goods, this is not the place. If you want the best in comfortable, practical, and stylish clothing at a very attractive tab, start marching with the saints right down to 20th and Broadway.

TOBALDI
83 Rivington St (at Orchard St)
260-4330
Sun-Fri: 9-6

At opposite corners from Veetal, Tobaldi does for the male what the latter does for the female. Here, too, the image is sleek, expensive, and elegant, at a Lower East Side discount. (Be warned: prices are still high.) Virtually all of the items are Italian imports. The store is not large, but the clientele they aim for expects a small, intimate setting, and they get it. The stock includes magnificent shirts (check out the linen ones, but don't overlook the silk; both are made for Tobaldi's own label), leather jackets (as in suede leather, *not* motorcycle chic), and magnificent Italian suits, slacks, and sports jackets. There probably isn't a more elegant store on Madison Avenue (or in Milan), and while the prices will set your budget back, they are the best for the best merchandise. While this clothing is sometimes obtainable uptown in the best stores, it is not available at a discount.

Men's Formal Wear

JACK AND COMPANY FORMAL WEAR
128 E 86th St
722-4609, 722-4455
Mon-Fri: 10-7; Sat: 10-4; closed Sat in July, Aug

Jack's will rent and sell men's ready-to-wear formal wear. They carry an excellent selection of sizes (nearly all) and names (After Six, Lord West, and Palm Beach), and they have a good reputation for service since 1925. In sales or rentals, Jack's can supply head-to-toe formal wear. The people here are excellent at matching outfits to customers, as well as knowing exactly what is socially required for any occasion.

ZELLER TUXEDOS
1010 Third Ave (at 60th St)
688-0100
Mon-Fri: 9-8; Sat: 10-6; Sun: 10-5

You won't have to borrow your rich uncle's moth-eaten tux if you have this address handy. Zeller is tops in sales or rentals for tuxedos, formal shirts, capes, overcoats with fur collars, and all the accessories necessary for making a great entrance at a party. You can even get suited up as an entertainer or a restaurant waiter. Zeller also provides made-to-order service for those who require special attention.

Men's Hats

VAN DYCK HATTERS
127 Greenwich Ave
929-5696
Mon-Fri: 7:30-6; Sat: 9-4

The quintessential hatter, Van Dyck is the first choice for anything that has to do with men's hats in New York. Since 1940, Van Dyck has been known for the quality of its own brand, which it manufactures and sells. Prices and quality can't be beat, but should you not trust its brand (New Yorkers do), Van Dyck also discounts Stetson and Borsalino hats at a minimum of 25 percent. No matter what the brand, Van Dyck can also clean, block, restyle, reband, or renovate any hat brought in.

Men's Large Sizes

IMPERIAL WEAR
48 W 48th St
719-2590
Mon-Wed, Fri, Sat: 9-6; Thurs: 9-8

Among New York's specialty shops, several are devoted exclusively to clothing in extra-large and extra-tall sizes. The salespeople at this one are well trained in the problems that large men usually encounter, and quality is not sacrificed in garments that require more material. It is this, perhaps, that has guaranteed Imperial its clientele *and* kept them returning. Many stores cater to big men, but having a captive audience causes some stores to relax in their standards. The many regular customers who return to Imperial again and again prove that this is not the case here. The new line of designer fashions for big men is also a major attraction.

Men's Neckwear

COUNTESS MARA
445 Park Ave (at 57th St)
751-5322
Mon-Fri: 10-6; Sat: 10-5

Those who remember the former Countess Mara store on East 57th Street will be delighted to visit the attractive and larger new digs just around the corner. At last the famous Countess ties are displayed so you can see them all; choose from the selection of hundreds. In addition, there is a full line of furnishings and shoes and a small but classy line of suits and sport coats made especially for "that one man in a million."

HERITAGE NECKWEAR
194 Allen St (at Houston St)
673-2570
Sun-Fri: 10-4

Richard Guerreiro took over what was one of my favorite stores in the city and made it even better. In the old days, the shop was dark, dank, and dirty. Nowadays, it positively gleams, and it is a joy to shop here. What enhances this joy is that Guerreiro considers himself a consumer and a comparison-shopper. So he frequently scouts the department stores and specialty shops to make sure that his prices are at least 50 percent less. How does he do it? For starters, Heritage imports and/or manufactures the ties that are exclusively silk; many are even handmade. It also helps that the overhead is low and that Guerreiro wholesales his items to the very stores he comparison-shops. The prices for pure silk ties at Heritage are at least half of those elsewhere. And they are magnificent.

Men's Shirts

PENN GARDEN GRAND SHIRT CORPORATION
58 Orchard St (at Grand St)
431-8464
Sun-Wed, Fri: 9-6; Thurs: 9-8

BASSIN MENSWEAR
450 Seventh Ave (at 34th St)
244-7976
Sun-Wed, Fri: 9-6; Thurs: 9-8

G&G INTERNATIONAL
62 Orchard St (bet Grand and Hester St)
431-4530
Sun-Wed: 9-6; Thurs: 9-8; Fri: 9-6 (summer),
    9-4 (winter)

And you thought the Lower East Side pickle business was inbred! It's got nothing on the local men's haberdashery dynasties, and these stores are probably the most typical of the breed. Penn Garden isn't that extensive yet, but give them time. Currently, there are three stores (there may be more masquerading under yet other names) devoted to men's wear. Each considers itself a distinct entity, to the point that the people at Penn Garden will not tell you to go across the street to G&G if you can't find what you want with them. (Tell you? Ha! They won't even give out the others' phone numbers!) Taken separately, however, each store is a gem, and the saleshelp can sometimes be charming. Bassin's, at the edge of the Garment Center, is where the men in the ladies' fashion industry go for their shirts. These men know clothing, fashion, and styling, and if they shop here, everyone can safely follow suit.

SHIRT PLAZA
36 W 40th St (at Fifth Ave)
221-1959
Mon-Fri: 9-6; Sat: 10:30-5

Men's shirt stores are in ample supply in New York, but finding a shirt for an ample man is not so easy. Shirt Plaza specializes in solving this large problem. All of the shirts are ready to wear, but as a specialty store Shirt Plaza is able to garner the best of the field. Add to that the selection in large and tall sizes, and it's an excellent bet for men who haven't much choice elsewhere. The diversity of the selection in big sizes filters down to regular sizes as well.

SHIRT STORE
51 E 44th St (bet Vanderbilt and Madison Ave)
557-8040
Mon-Fri: 8-6:30; Sat: 10-5

The attraction here is that you buy directly from the manufacturer, no middle man to increase the price. The Shirt Store offers 100 percent cotton shirts for men and women, from the smallest (14x32) to the largest (18½ x37) for men and from 6-16 for women. Although the ready-made stock is great, they will also do custom work, and even come to your office with swatches. You excuse yourself from the rest of the office crew to have your shirt maker do some measuring! How's that for status? Even better than those cuff initials! Additional special services include home-order visits, alterations, and monogramming.

VICTORY SHIRT COMPANY
10 Maiden Lane (bet Broadway and Nassau St)
349-7111
Mon-Fri: 9-6

96 Orchard St (bet Delancey and Broome St)
677-2020
Sun-Thurs: 9-5; Fri: 9-4

Victory operates two shops in different parts of town with one goal in mind: selling shirts—their own—that are guaranteed to be equal to, but less expensive than, national brands. And if their ads (which show two seemingly identical shirts side by side) don't convince you, a personal visit for a more substantial comparison probably will. So, for off-the-rack men's shirts, Victory should be a first choice if labels don't mean much to you. Victory manufactures as well as retails shirts for men and women. They have the facilities to taper, shorten, lengthen, alter, or monogram any shirt to individual specifications. They will also special-order unusual sizes, but a shop whose stock includes sizes 14 x 32 and 18½ x 36 doesn't have much call for that service. They also carry 100 percent cotton shirts and silk ties, as well as some men's accessories. But their own shirts are the big drawing card, and periodic sales make their prices even better.

Men's Underwear

UNDER WARES
1098 Third Ave (bet 64th and 65th St)
535-6006, 800-237-8641
Mon-Fri: 10-7; Sat: 10-6; Sun: 12-5

It used to be that the average fellow not only couldn't tell you what kind of underwear he wore, he probably didn't even buy it himself. All that changed with the ads featuring Jim Palmer and other celebrity jocks. These days a man's underwear can make a fashion statement. Ron Lee was on top of the new trend and opened a fashionable shop that sells fashionable underwear in over 70 styles of briefs and boxer shorts—the largest selection of men's undergarments in the whole world. There are also T-shirts and hosiery and gift items. If you are shy about browsing through all the sexy styles, you can call for one of their free catalogs.

Men's Western Wear

BILLY MARTIN'S
812 Madison Ave (at 68th St)
861-3100
Mon-Fri: 10-7; Sat: 10:30-6; Sun: 12-5

Although Billy Martin is not personally connected with this store, his name provides the umbrella for a shop crowded with all kinds of authentic Western wear. The walls are lined with buckskin and leather jackets. Bandanas drape the chairs, and cowboy hats are stacked on the floor. They must be made for well-paid cowboys, though, because these duds are well-tooled, beautifully designed, and expensive. There are also such contemporary items as leather jackets, fur coats and hats, coyote parkas, and one of the best collections of boots (for men and women) in the city. And don't overlook the jewelry, including earrings, silver and exotic gemstone buckles, and belt straps. As a source of Western wear, Billy Martin's is a must.

Men's and Women's—General

BARNEY'S
111 Seventh Ave (at 17th St)
929-9000
Mon-Fri: 10-9; Sat: 10-8; Sun: 12-5

2 World Financial Center
945-1600
Mon-Wed, Fri: 10-7; Thurs: 10-9; Sat: 10-6; Sun: 12-6

What used to be known as the "World's Largest Men's Store" is not only that but also a full-scale (and up-scale) women's store that gives the ladies the same sort of selection (almost) that the men have had for years. Barney's has been added to and changed dozens of times in the men's area, and although you can find everything for men somewhere, trying to locate it in this emporium is not easy. Every major designer and manufacturer is represented, with very adequate selections in the hard-to-find sizes. Prices are competitive, tailoring is free (and so is parking), and their periodic sales are very special. Boystown, on the lower level, offers an excellent selection for every size youngster: thin, medium, or chubby. The new women's store, artfully carved out of limited space, is arranged in dozens of boutiques featuring very stylish fashions (gifts and accessories included) by the world's top names. The junior contemporary section is especially well merchandised. A hint for the ladies: start at the top, walk down and see everything before you begin to shop, and fortify yourself at Le Cafe on the bottom level. As a start on becoming a nationwide chain, a condensed up-scale version is a part of the new World Financial Center.

BURBERRY'S
9 E 57th St
371-5010
Mon-Wed, Fri, Sat: 9:30-6; Thurs: 9:30-7

Visit Burberry's four-storied shop on 57th Street, and you'd swear you were in the original London store. The mood is, in part, created by $600,000 worth of imported furnishings that Burberry's shipped from London. And the clothing styles are strictly British, to boot. The first two floors are dedicated exclusively to men's wear. The sizes range from extra short to extra long, and the store carries almost anything. There are overcoats, topcoats, trenchcoats, raincoats, slacks, knitwear, sweaters, ties, scarves (a famous trademark in the Burberry plaid), and luggage. Women's wear, on the fourth floor, carries a parallel line to the men's wear. There are overcoats, trenchcoats, shirts, blouses, suits, and sportswear, all with the British look. There's also a children's line, featuring clothing, outerwear, rainwear, and accessories.

CASHMERE-CASHMERE
840 Madison Ave (bet 69th and 70th St)
988-5252
Mon-Fri: 10-6; Sat: 10-5:30; Sun: 12-5

595 Madison Ave
935-2522
Mon-Fri: 10-6; Sat: 10-5:30

Silk, thanks in part to the growth of Silk Surplus, is no longer a luxury fabric in this city. Not so cashmere! At this shop, every possible type of clothing from all over the world is available. The weights vary, so that it is possible to wear cashmere year round. The styles vary as well, to reflect different lifestyles. There's clothing for men, women, and children as well as cashmere accessories for the home. A visit here makes cashmere in one's life a necessity!

CHARIVARI
(locations and phones noted within review)
All stores open daily, late Thurs nights, and Sun

The Upper West Side was a fashion desert until Selma Weiser arrived on the scene with her first Charivari. With a smart merchant's sense of location and fashion, Selma and her family have guided the growth of this organization into a six-store chain. Mother Selma still has a major hand in most of the operation, while daughter Barbara and son Jon do most of the buying. The men's store (2339 Broadway at 85th, 873-7242) is the place for the more conservative businessman to find his office clothes. Charivari for women (2315 Broadway, bet 83rd and 84th, 873-1424) has the same image for women. The sports store (201 W 79th, at Amsterdam, 799-8650) is brimming with fun play clothes at reasonable prices. The Workshop (441 Columbus at 81st, 496-8700) features avant-garde Japanese-designed merchandise for both men and women. Charivari 72 (257 Columbus at 72nd St, 787-7272) and Charivari 57 (18 W 57th, 333-4040) feature high-fashion designer clothing for men and women. The 72nd Street store is more intimate; the 57th Street store is cold and uninviting. Running an operation as spread out as this one is difficult at best. The Weisers, who possess a unique flair for the dramatic in merchandise presentation, might well concentrate on passing on that same expertise to their struggling salespeople.

COCKPIT
595 Broadway (bet Houston and Prince St)
925-5455
Mon-Sat: 12:30-7; Sun: 12:30-6

This is a fascinating store for anyone interested in flying. A fabulous collection of flight jackets (the best in the city), Flying Tiger shirts, China-Burma baggies, athletic jerseys, T-shirts, coveralls, trenchcoats, flight boots, sweaters, insignias, books, watches, bags, flight suits, and dozens of gift items are displayed to create an attractive, aviational atmosphere. Royal Air Force jackets, sweaters, boots, and insignia are also available. One of the more interesting specialty items is a collection of pilot's manuals from World War II. I was fascinated by the Army Air Force pilot's cloth charts printed by the Army Map Service in May 1945 for the Allied invasion of the Japanese mainland. They are great gifts for the World War II military buff.

DAFFY'S
111 Fifth Ave (at 18th St)
529-4477
Mon-Sat: 10-9; Sun: 11-6

Daffy's describes themselves as a bargain clothing outlet for millionaires. Well, I guess a lot of folks got to be millionaires by saving money, so perhaps they have something going for them. But millionaire or not, you can find great bargains here in better clothing for men, women, and children. Fine leather items are a specialty, and a jewelry department has been added. This is not your usual "off-price" store; they have done things with a bit of flair.

DEALS
81 Worth St (bet Broadway and Church St)
966-0214
Mon-Wed, Fri, Sat: 9-6; Thurs: 9-8

The frugal Brooks Brothers man or woman should check out the deal at Deals. While the emphasis is on traditional styles, the prices are anything but traditional. The shop manages to stock shirts, pants, skirts, dresses, sweaters, sportswear, accessories, and shoes for men and women, and all of it is sold at 50 percent off regular price. And if that isn't enough, traditional doesn't mean staid here. Deals leans toward natural fibers and exalts designer, or if need be, brand names. Deals is also very patriotic; each holiday brings a sale with even bigger reductions. All of which makes Deals a real find, and one of the few places where both men and women can do well.

EMPORIO ARMANI
110 Fifth Ave
727-3240
Mon-Sat: 10-7

In the lower canyons of Fifth Avenue, where lofts feature off-priced men's clothing, you can now walk into one of the classiest designer showrooms in the city. Armani clothes for both men and women are shown with style and taste, befitting the hefty price tags. There is sportswear and dress-up wear, accessories and jeans, all with the distinct Armani look. It well could be that this boutique will be the forerunner of a move from spendy Madison Avenue for some of the better-known names in the ready-to-wear business. Don't miss this one, especially if you're "just looking"!

HOUSE OF LODEN
155 W 72nd St (bet Broadway and Columbus Ave,
    fifth floor)
362-7443
Mon-Fri: 11-6 (may be closed in summer)

If you can figure out when they are open and snag an "appointment," you will be treated to a room full of the finest Austrian Lodenwool coats, car coats, wools, and capes for men and women. This outlet will custom-order exact sizes, fabrics, and designs. Better still, there is an incredible in-stock selection in sizes and designs. In a city where the top department and specialty stores have a very limited selection of the Loden coat, this is amazing.

LOUIS, BOSTON
131 E 57th St (at Lexington Ave)
308-6100
Mon-Fri: 10-7; Sat: 9:30-5:30

Louis of Boston, a highly respected name in conservative clothing and furnishings in the Boston area, is not widely known in New York. The store is deceiving; the first floor looks like a display area rather than a salesroom. But upstairs there are two floors of women's and men's clothing and accessories that spell *class* and *big bucks*. The fabrics are beautiful, the emphasis is on the Louis name (not designers), and the prices are astronomical in some cases. If you just won the lottery, take a look at the Luciano Barbera suits for men. The personnel are very knowledgeable and intensely protective of the Louis image. When asked why they didn't arrange the ground floor so that it looked more like a sales room, one of them replied, "We believe in featuring the fixtures and displays." Hmm. When I was in the business, the name of the game was selling goods.

MATSUDA NICOLE TOKYO

461 Park Ave
935-6969
Mon-Sat: 11-7

156 Fifth Ave
772-2140
Mon-Sat: 11-7; Sun: 12-5

Mitsuhiro Matsuda is one of Japan's most successful fashion designers. For both men and women he designs lines of business wear, casual and sportswear, and active sportswear. There is also a new line of apparel and accessory basics, including bedding, bath items, nightwear, hats, glasses, jewelry, ties, gloves, belts, socks, and shoes. Madonna and Cher are customers here, so you know the place is at the forefront of fashion.

OTTO PERL
HOUSE OF MAURIZIO

18 E 53rd St
838-8519
By appointment only

Otto and Susanne Perl cater to women who like the functional, fashionable tailored look that suits create. Although they can copy almost any kind of garment, the Perls are known for their coats, two-, three-, or four-piece suits, and mix-and-match combinations. Usually, this look is favored by busy executives, artists, or journalists who have to look very well-dressed but don't have hours to spend dressing. Perl creates blazers (or suits) in a range of 2,000 different fabrics, but those in silk, linen, cotton, or a solid virgin wool are sensational. In addition to the women's garments, the Perls can design and create coats and suits for men in the same broad range of fabrics. They promise fast service, expert tailoring, and moderate prices on everything they do, but no alterations.

POLO-RALPH LAUREN

867 Madison Ave (at 72nd St)
606-2100
Mon-Sat: 10-6; Thurs: 10-8

Without question, this is one of the most attractive specialty shops in the world. Of course, Ralph Lauren has come to embody the American classic look, in the goods that bear his name and his own personal image. As for his shop, it's housed in the magnificently redone Rhinelander mansion. Four floors of merchandise for men, women, and the home is displayed among beautiful antiques and clothing that have been accessorized to perfection. You probably wouldn't mind moving into the home-furnishing rooms just as they are. The clothes all look stylish, classy, and very comfortable. Most of the sales personnel are very impressed with where they work, which is understandable but not very appealing to the customers. If you're thinking of becoming a customer, I suggest you look around and enjoy the surroundings, but be careful: the prices are sky-high, and better-quality merchandise is available at other places, even if it may not have the little horse on it.

Rainwear

NORMAN J LAWRENCE
417 Fifth Ave (at 38th St, suite 1116)
889-3119
Mon, Wed, Fri: 10-3

I have known Norman for more years than either of us would like to admit. Every year he would come to the family department store to show his line of coats, always very special, always high style and high quality. The tradition has endured, and now he has probably the finest selection of daytime and after-five raincoats in the country. He designs the coats himself, and if you're not able to fit into any of the stock items, he will make one just for you in any of the water-repellent materials available: cashmere, velvet, silk faille, or ultrasuede. All of the coats may be buttoned-in or buttoned-out fur-lined, with your own fur or in one of the real furs Norman features. Men can also find some spectacular silk raincoats here. Norman is an engaging guy, a wonderful salesman, and a superior storyteller.

Shoes—Children's

RICHIE'S DISCOUNT CHILDREN'S SHOES
183 Avenue B (bet 11th and 12th St)
228-5442
Mon, Tues, Thurs-Sat: 10-5; Sun: 10-3

There is no sign on the building, and it's difficult to distinguish anything amid the dirty and boarded-up windows on the block, but if you can spot a window displaying shoes next to a movie marquee, Richie's will offer an experience your children's feet will never duplicate. Inside, the décor is probably as old as the surrounding environment outside, but the stock includes the very latest shoes, at a fraction of the prices anywhere else. Brands include Stride Rite, Buster Brown, Blue Star, Jumping Jacks, and Keds sneakers, and the clincher is that the fit will be extraordinary. An inordinate amount of time is spent on each customer, and for each time a pair of shoes has been sold here, a pair has also *not* been sold. Reasons for the latter include the customer's being told that the child's old ones are still good. (Has that ever happened elsewhere?) Salesmen have even admitted that the quality desired just wasn't in stock or that Richie's would not sell a lesser quality to a customer. So, the drawback? The neighborhood. Gentrification hasn't quite reached this block of the East Village.

SHOOFLY
506 Amsterdam Ave (bet 84th and 85th St)
580-4390
Mon-Sat: 11-7; Sun: 12-6

This store is included for two special groups! Shoofly (isn't that a great name?) carries attractive and reasonably priced shoes mainly for the younger set, infants to 14-year-olds. But there are lots of women with tiny feet who have a difficult time finding an adequate selection of footwear. As a matter of fact, this is one of the most common questions I am asked on the call-in radio talk shows. Look no farther, my petite friends. Shoofly takes care of your needs with styles and sizes that will be a surprise and a delight.

Shoes—Family

THE CITY ATHLETE
131, 132A, 132B, 135, and 163 Orchard St (five stores)
475-4875
Daily: 9-6

What used to be separate stores has now been combined into five outlets with the same name, offering good prices on brand-name sneakers, casual and rugged footwear, and children's shoes. Brands featured include Bally, Zodiac, Timberland, Adidas, Nike, Puma, Reebok, and New Balance, among many others. These stores are usually so crowded that you'll probably need a new pair of shoes after all the bargain-hunting customers step on your toes. Family management ensures a hands-on operation.

KENNETH COLE
353 Columbus Ave (bet 76th and 77th St)
873-2061
Mon-Sat: 11-9; Sun: 12-7

This is not a run-of-the-mill shoe store. For one thing, the walls are adorned with clever, irreverant posters poking fun at well-known personalities. ("Imelda Marcos bought 2,700 pairs of shoes and not one pair from us!") But the real treats are the fashionable and trendy shoes for men and women at sensible prices. Cole is a master of public relations, and has developed a deserved reputation for a quality product. I suggest you browse at the high-style shops like Susan Bennis-Warren Edwards, where prices are absurd, and then come here to buy.

LEACH-KALE
1261 Broadway (at 31st St, suite 815-816)
683-0571
Mon-Fri: 9-5

While some custom shoe craftsmen are determined to prove that their product can (and should be) owned by every man, Andre S. Feuerman of the Leach-Kale Company is not among them. Perhaps he has been burned too many times by the bargain hunter who thought that the gap between a high-class shoe salon's product and Leach-Kale's couldn't be as great as it is, or by customers who, prepared to shell out money, think at that price the shoe should cure all their orthopedic problems for life. Feuerman is careful to point out that this is not the case. The business has customers who have been loyal patrons for 25 to 30 years (Joan Crawford was one), and these are the people Feuerman would rather court. They have neither unrealistic expectations nor impossible dreams, but appreciate the quality item that Leach-Kale produces. Leach-Kale specializes in orthopedic work, which is probably why many of their customers come here and pay the price without batting an eye. They have no choice. Shoes start at about $700 for the first pair, but some first orders, and all subsequent orders, can be substantially less.

LESLIE'S BOOTERY
319 Grand St
431-9196

65 Orchard St
966-6877
Sun-Fri: 9:30-5:30

Looking for Bally, Cole-Haan, Timberland, Reebok? Well, Leslie's is the place to find designer footwear for men or women. Prices are right, and it is easy to shop here, since the shoes are displayed by brand name. On the Lower East Side, where service is hardly the "buy-word," this place will save you a lot of aggravation.

LORD JOHN BOOTERY
428 Third Ave (bet 29th and 30th St)
532-2579
Mon-Fri: 10-7; Sat: 10-6; closed Sat in July, Aug

Now here's a real "shoe dog" store. John Kyriannis and three generations of his family have been happily working together for seven decades, and this happiness spills over to their customers. They carry Dan Post and Justin Western boots, discounted by 20 to 30 percent, as well as discounted Timberland shoes and boots and Dexter boots and shoes. There are also imported brands like Evan Picone, Nickels, Joan and David, and many more. It's refreshing to be helped by people who really know the business.

MANUFACTURERS SHOE OUTLET
537 Broadway (bet Spring and Prince St)
966-4070
Mon-Fri: 8-6; Sat: 9-5; Sun: 10-5:30

The hours and phone number are nebulous, and the attitude is "go help yourself, don't bother me." But if a lack of amenities doesn't bother you, then run, don't walk, to this dirty store in SoHo. It carries a wide variety of shoes, slippers, hosiery, and socks, and the sizes range from infants' to large men's. And if that isn't inducement enough, there are such top brand names as Nunn Bush and Freeman sold at a discount. Finally, note the hours. If your son breaks a buckle at 8 a.m., or the heel falls off your shoes an hour before *the* business meeting, this is the place to go for a quick replacement at discount prices. They claim to keep these hours because "everyone else here does." Now you know another difference between SoHo and the Village!

PARADISE BOOTERY
1586 Broadway (bet 47th and 48th St)
974-9855
Mon-Sat: 10:30-7:30

Alex Kaufman supplies the shoes for almost every Broadway show, and that's probably how Elizabeth Taylor heard of him and why she ordered 12 pairs of the same shoe in different colors to augment her wardrobe. And she could have done the same thing for the current man in her life, because Kaufman custom-makes men's shoes as well. The prices are fabulous, and the workmanship is first quality. Paradise has custom-made shoes for less than $100, which is less than the department stores charge for some of their ready-made ones. There is also a large in-house stock that sells for less than half the custom-made rate. If you have difficulty with arithmetic, Kaufman's quality boots in stock sell for $30 a pair and up. The next time you leaf through a *Playbill,* check the wardrobe credits. Odds are you'll find Kaufman's or Paradise's name. Or you could just ask Liz!

SHOE CITY/SNEAKER CITY
133 Nassau St (at Beekman St)
732-3889
Mon-Fri: 8:30-6; Sat: 10-3

Shoe City (don't you like the name?) started as a place to get cut-rate, brand-name shoes for men. With a good selection of such names as Bostonian, Dexter, Herman, Massagic, Hush Puppies, and Timberland at excellent prices, it was no surprise that business was very good. So, Shoe City spawned Sneaker City, in the same building, with sneakers for the entire family. It's easy to do one-stop shopping here.

T.O. DEY
9 E 38th St
683-6300
Mon-Fri: 9-5; Sat: 9-1

T.O. Dey is a fancy jack-of-all-trades operation. Though their specialty is custom-made shoes, they will also undertake any kind of repair on any kind of shoe. In fact, if you ask a New Yorker for the first name that comes to mind in custom-made shoes, odds are that the name will be T.O. Dey. They will create both men's and ladies' shoes, based on a plaster mold taken of the customer, and their styles are limited only by the customer's imagination. Probably because of the size of the operation, T.O. Dey's prices are slightly less than other custom bootmakers. They also do shoe repair, including difficult jobs that few others would undertake. But they are not cheap, and service here is not what it used to be.

VOGEL BOOTS AND SHOES
19 Howard St (bet Broadway and Lafayette St)
925-2460
Mon-Fri: 8-4:30; Sat: 8-2
Closed Sat in summer and first two weeks of July

The Vogels—John, Hank, and Dean (who are the third and fourth generations to join this 110-year-old-business)—happily fit and supply made-to-measure boots and shoes for any adult who can find the store. Howard is one of those streets that even native New Yorkers don't know exists. The many who *have* found it beat a path to the door for top-quality shoes and boots, personal advice, excellent fittings, and prices which, while not inexpensive, are reasonable for the service involved. The fit is not to be taken lightly, for made-to-measure shoes do *not* always fit properly. At Vogel, they do. Once you have a shoe pattern on record at Vogel, they will make up new shoes without a personal visit and ship anywhere. For top craftsmanship, this spot is top-drawer. There are more than 600 Vogel dealers throughout the world, but this is the grandfather store, and the people here are super.

Shoes—Men's

ADLER SHOE SHOPS
141 W 42nd St (bet Sixth Ave and Broadway)
382-0844
Mon-Sat: 9-6

Adler's is a chain of men's shoe stores in New York, featuring Weyenberg and Nunn-Bush brands. At this store, all of the rejects, over-runs, unsalables (for whatever reason), and odd lots are sold at big reductions. Incidentally, after having checked out over 100 shoe stores, I still remember the staff here as having been exceptionally friendly.

CHURCH ENGLISH SHOES
428 Madison Ave (at 49th St)
755-4313
Mon-Fri: 9-6; Sat: 9-5:30

Anglophiles have a ball here, not only because of the *veddy* English atmosphere, but for the pure artistry and Englishness of the shoes. Church has been selling English shoes for men since 1873, and since that date, it has been known for classic styles, superior workmanship, and fine leathers. The styles basically remain unchanged year after year, although one or two new designs are occasionally added as a concession to fashion. All are custom-fitted by shoe salesmen. If a style or size does not feel right, Church's will make up a customized special order at approximately $87 more than the regular price. The salesmen are superprofessional. Foot problems? This is the place for competent advice.

CIPRIANO SHOES
148 Orchard St
477-5858
Wed-Sun: 7:30-5:30

If your work or recreation is the type where boots are a necessity, then come to Cipriano to stock up on some real buys. The shoes are hefty and tough, but the prices are small and sweet.

J. SHERMAN SHOES
121 Division St (bet Orchard and Ludlow St)
233-7898
Sun-Thurs: 9-5; Fri: 9-3:30

Upholding the Lower East Side tradition, J. Sherman has excellent prices on its merchandise. But its shoes are nothing less than top-of-the-line quality. So here's the place to pick up Bally, Bruno Magli, Sandro, Moscoloni, French Shriner, Freeman, Paolo, Ferracini, Dexter, Bass, Zodiac, Timberland, Frye, Giorgio, Brutini, and other brand-name shoes for 20 to 60 percent off list price. J. Sherman boasts the best buys on brand-name shoes in the city. They may be right.

STAPLETON SHOE COMPANY
68 Trinity Pl (at Rector St)
964-6329
Mon-Thurs: 8-6; Fri: 8-5

Their motto is "better shoes for less," but that doesn't begin to cover the superlatives that Stapleton deserves. Gather around, gentlemen, because here is the place to get Bally, Reeboks, Keds, and a slew of other top shoe names at a discount. Stapleton is located on the same block as the Amex (American Stock Exchange). With the money saved here, there should be enough left over to take a flyer in the stock market. There probably isn't a better source for quality shoes anywhere. And that's a free tip on the market!

TO BOOT
520 Madison Ave (bet 53rd and 54th St)
644-5661
Mon-Sat: 10-6:30

256 Columbus Ave (at 72nd St)
724-8249
Mon-Fri: 12-8; Sat: 11-7; Sun: 1-6

Bergdorf-Goodman
Fifth Ave at 57th St
872-8883
Mon-Wed, Fri, Sat: 10-6; Thurs: 10-8

To Boot is one of the most interesting and exciting men's footwear stores in the city. They design and manufacture all their own shoes, with most coming from Italy but also some from England and France. Italian shoes are the best there are, in my opinion, and To Boot shows a collection that ranges from sporty casuals to Wall Street tycoon models. Be sure to take a look at the A. Testoni (Italian) line, with sky-high prices and high-fashion looks. Other designers featured include Cesare Paciotti, Gaultier, and Montana. I'm glad they have given up their Western store image, and are concentrating on their best points: relaxed, easy service and elegant shoes for the non-price-conscious man.

Shoes—Women's

ANBAR SHOES
93 Reade St (bet Church St and W Broadway)
227-0253
Mon-Fri: 8-5:30; Sat: 11-5; closed Sat in July, Aug

You can't judge a shoe store by its décor! As long as you walk out wearing the best shoes for your money, who cares what the store's windows look like? Certainly not the people at Anbar, who just may offer the best shoes in town for the best prices Names like Charles Jourdan, Julianelli, Lamarea, Garolini Mr. Seymour, and Andrew Geller are always discounted, often as much as 50 percent. Overlook the grubby setting. Anbar is a gold mine!

GIORDANO'S SHOES
1118 First Ave (at 61st St)
688-7195
Mon-Fri: 11-7; Sat: 11-6

Susan Giordano has a very special clientele. In fact, if you're a woman whose shoe size is larger than 6½, you can't imagine how important this store is. And if you're a woman with a shoe size in the 4 to 6 medium or 5½ to 6½ AA range, learning about Giordano's will make the purchase of this book more than worthwhile. Giordano stocks a fine selection in a tiny range of tiny sizes of women's shoes. While there are women with smaller sizes still, Giordano's range is nonexistent in regular shoe stores. (Occasionally 5Bs, a sample size, can be found in closeout shops.) Most women in this category shop in the children's shoe departments or have shoes custom-made, either of which can cramp your style. For these women, Giordano's is a godsend.

LACE UP SHOE SHOP
110 Orchard St (at Delancey St)
475-8040
Sun-Fri: 9-5:30

For years, Lace Up was an upstairs appendage to Fine and Klein. Today, however, the demand is such that Lace Up has come into its own. It has moved to the corner of Orchard and Delancey Streets; if you can't find *that* address just look for a crowd of well-dressed women. Lace Up's stock features the best designer styles at the very best prices: Joan and David, Anne Klein, Bandolino, Charles Jourdan, Alberto D. Molina, and Yves St. Laurent, among others. It is the only spot to get Mephisto shoes and boots. All shoes are discounted, and ultrafashionable pairs unavailable anywhere else can be found at Lace Up, often in season. Discounts start at 15 percent. They now carry sizes up to 11½ and C width.

MAUD FRIZON
49 E 57th St (near Park Ave)
980-1460
Mon-Sat: 10-6

This tiny shop is not for the faint of heart—or wallet. But if you have what it takes, you shouldn't miss it. Maud Frizon (who is a real person, alive and well and living in Paris) believes in quality and fashion. Her shoes, handmade in Venice, are personally designed for style and comfort. Her shops are located in places like Cannes, Paris, Milano—you get the idea. Almost anything Maud Frizon designs can be custom-made. Styles include both day and evening wear for men and women. This is not a store for mere window shopping, but if you want to own a truly beautiful shoe, Maud Frizon is the place to find it. You'll appreciate the unusual shoes and boots for men, as well. Maud Frizon shoes can also be found at several major specialty and department stores, such as Bergdorf's and Barney's.

PETER FOX SHOES
105 Thompson St (bet Prince and Spring St)
431-6359

378 Amsterdam Ave (at 78th St)
874-6399

Mon-Sat: 12-8; Sun: 12-7

Peter Fox was the downtown trailblazer for women's shoes. Everything sold in the shop is exclusive, limited-edition designer footwear. Perhaps because of the store's original location, Fox designs seem more adventurous than its uptown competitors, but then, no one ever accused Maud Frizon or Susan Bennis/Warren Edwards of being staid. However, the look seems younger and more casual here than it does with other designers. For those looking for shoes to be seen in, Michael (uptown) and Jacques (downtown) are the people to see. Bridal shoes are also available here.

SOLE OF ITALY
119 Orchard St (at Delancey St)
674-2662
Sun-Fri: 9:30-6

Sole of Italy is the soul mate to Fine and Klein, and it is fittingly located above the latter store. Fine and Klein carries classy handbags and attaché cases, and Sole of Italy offers the perfect complement in footwear. The selection is limited to those labels sold in the finest boutiques; the collection of so many brands and sizes in one spot is awesome. The Fine and Klein (or Lower East Side) discount policy also applies here, which makes Sole of Italy a contender as the sole source for fashionable footwear. Some name dropping is in order: Adige, Pierre Balmain, Jacques Cohen, Collette, Courreges, Caiman Mode, Xavier Danand, Delman, Charles Jourdan, Ted Lapidus, Bally, Walter Steiger, Madame Gres, Vitto Latvada, Menin, and J. B. Martin are just a few of the labels Sole of Italy carries. There are few places to find them all under one roof and virtually none that discounts them all.

TALL SIZE SHOES
3 W 35th St (at Fifth Ave)
736-2060
Mon-Wed, Fri, Sat: 9:30-6; Thurs: 9:30-7

The tall gals do not have an easy time finding a good selection of shoes. But walk easily, ladies. Tall Size Shoes has come to your rescue, with super service, polite saleshelp, and an outstanding selection. They only sell women's shoes in sizes 10 to 15, from narrow to wide widths, and feature their own brand as well as shoes from designers like Bandolino, Amalfi, Evan Picone, and Zodiac. They will take phone orders and ship anywhere in the country.

Sportswear

FINALS
487 Broadway (at Broome St)
431-1414, 800-431-9111
Mon-Fri: 10-7; Sat: 10-6; Sun: 12-6

This is the case of a catalog having a store rather than the other way around. For the last eight years, Finals has published a catalog offering competition swim and running wear to schools, clubs, and YMCAs across the country. In that time, they have garnered 75 percent of the market, in part because no one could match their "factory direct" prices and in part because a majority of the customers were located far from other sources for that equipment. After all, there aren't usually many variations in a lycra competition bathing suit. Yet Finals offers it in pinstripe, solid, and accented colors, when it would be hard to find one at all elsewhere—not to mention coming up with enough to outfit an entire team. The business operated out of New York, and it finally decided to open an outlet store in SoHo. Prices are the same as those in the catalog, but they are so sensational that visitors should not feel that the only savings are the cost of postage and handling. An added fillip is the chance to comb through whatever outdated, discarded, or non-catalog merchandise might be around. But it's really not necessary, when you can get the finest apparel at true factory prices.

GERRY COSBY AND COMPANY
Madison Sq Garden
3 Pennsylvania Plaza (at 32nd St and Seventh Ave)
563-6464
Mon-Fri: 9:30-6:30; Sat: 9:30-6; Sun: 12-5

There's a lot to like about this company. For one thing, they know how to spell my first name correctly! Although it will be difficult for an out-of-towner to find them, they are a briskly professional business, which has actually located itself at the most appropriate spot for its wares. And those wares are sportswear—as in what people active in sports *wear,* not as in people wearing two-piece sweater outfits. In particular, Gerry Cosby designs and markets protective equipment and covers. The covers cover both bodies and equipment, and the protective equipment and bags are designed exclusively for professional use but are available to the general public as well. Much of it is designed for football. Gerry Cosby's designs are coveted and frequently copied, but why not get the original? They accept mail and phone orders for all of their equipment, including personalized (with either team or name) jerseys and jackets. And even if your name isn't Gerry, the staff seems quite competent enough to spell any name right.

PLAYING FIELD
955 Third Ave (at 57th St)
421-0003, 421-0005
Mon-Wed, Fri, Sat: 10-6; Thurs: 10-8; Sun: 12-6

The Playing Field offers sports enthusiasts and fans the chance to dress up and play in the real thing. Their jerseys, uniforms, and professional sports apparel are indistinguishable from that of the pro teams because they are the exact garments that the players wear on the field. The official brand names of the major league teams are sold in a variety of sizes and colors. Since the professional stuff has been tested on the hard turf, amateur players are assured of the best selection of gear with an eye toward durability. Tennis, anyone? Not here. The only sports gear the Playing Field does not carry is tennis and soccer equipment.

WOMEN'S WORKOUT GEAR
121 Seventh Ave (at 17th St)
627-1117
Mon-Fri: 11-7; Sat: 11-6; Sun: 1:30-5:30

Here is a store that specializes in clothes for today's health-conscious woman. Paula Shirk, an avid runner herself, has put together a great collection of women's aerobic and running wear; walking, running, and aerobic shoes; bathing suits and goggles; sports bras; and weights and exercise mats. Paula and her crew give professional advice to their customers, along with brand merchandise from Capezio, Dance France, Brooks, New Balance, Avia, Speedo, and Triangle. Almost everything is specially designed for women, and careful shoppers can find outstanding bargains on off-season merchandise.

Sweaters

BEST OF SCOTLAND
581 Fifth Ave (bet 47th and 48th St, penthouse)
644-0403
Mon-Fri: by appointment; Sat: 10-6

If you've been to London recently, you must have noticed that the price of cashmere sweaters has skyrocketed. Some of the British companies, like N Peal, have opened up branches in Manhattan, offering beautiful sweaters at beautiful prices. But if you walk about 10 blocks from Peal (at 118 E 57th St) to Best of Scotland, you'll find attractive, well-made Bryant cashmere sweaters for men and women being sold at half the price. Best shopping is in the fall when the showroom is open all the time; in the spring, it is advisable to call for an appointment. This is a real find!

GRANNY-MADE
381 Amsterdam Ave (bet 78th and 79th St)
496-1222
Mon-Fri: 11-7:30; Sat: 10-6; Sun: 12-5

Michael Rosenberg did what many others have often wanted to do. He turned his grandmother's handiwork into a business. Michael's grandmother, Bert Levy, who is in her nineties, hand-knitted sweater designs that are now made on knitting machines (handloomed). Like all good grandmothers, Granny-made looks after the little ones. The store carries an extensive collection of newborn, infant, toddler, and children's sweaters up to size 14. Woven skirts and pants to work with the sweater collection for women, mittens, scarves, hats, cotton sweaters, classic cable knits, and 100 percent alpaca sweaters are all of first quality and attractive design. I sure wish I had been fortunate enough to have a grandmother like Michael's. When you shop here, you can still say "Granny made this for me!"

Surplus

59th STREET ARMY AND NAVY
221 E 59th St (bet Second and Third Ave)
755-1855
Mon, Thurs: 10-7:45; Tues, Wed, Fri: 10-6:45;
   Sat: 10-5:45; Sun: 1-5:45

328 Bleecker St (at Christopher St)
242-6665
Mon-Thurs: 10-7:45; Fri, Sat: 10-8:45; Sun: 1-6:45

110 Eighth Ave (bet 15th and 16th St)
645-7420
Mon-Fri: 9-6:45; Sat: 10-6:45; Sun: 1-5:45

   I have long sung the praises of so-called army-navy stores, although the genuine outlets for surplus military supplies have been gone for years. These shops are the best sources for camping supplies as well as durable and practical clothes and equipment. Instead of navy dress pants and sailor uniforms, this chain of stores specializes in rugged outdoor wear, including the largest inventory of 501 Levi's on the East Coast. There are sweats outfits, sneakers (the top brands at excellent prices), Timberland shoes, Schott leather jackets, Ocean Pacific, Gotcha, and Jams. Can you imagine Jams in the army-navy store? And the prices are better than Macy's.

KAUFMAN SURPLUS
319 W 42nd St (bet Eighth and Ninth Ave)
757-5670
Mon-Wed, Fri: 10-6; Thurs: 10-7; Sat: 11-6

   One of the last surviving surplus stores in the city, Kaufman's has long been a favorite among New Yorkers and visitors alike for its extensive selection of genuine military surplus from around the world. Kaufman's is not your average army-navy store! Over the last half century, Kaufman's has outfitted dozens of Broadway and TV shows and has supplied a number of major motion pictures with military garb. The store is a treasure trove of military collectibles, hats, helmets, dummy grenades, uniforms, and insignia. Over a thousand military pins, patches, and medals from armies the world over are on display. Kaufman's is the building painted red, white, and blue, with two U.S. Army cannons outside. You can't miss it!

Thrift Shops

ARTHRITIS FOUNDATION THRIFT SHOP
121 E 77th St (bet Lexington and Park Ave)
772-8816
Mon, Tues, Thurs, Fri: 10:30-5:30; Wed, Sat: 10:30-5

This very friendly store carries donated clothing, furniture, bric-a-brac, and oddities that will appeal to bargain hunters. Their donors include people whose family members have suffered from arthritis.

CALL AGAIN
1735 Second Ave (at 89th St)
831-0845
Mon-Sat: 10-4:30; closed Sat in July, Aug

This one benefits Brandeis University, the Hemophilia Foundation and Women's American ORT. They are very selective, and browsers can find top-notch merchandise.

CANCER CARE
1480 Third Ave (at 83rd St)
879-9868
Mon-Sat: 10-4:45

On thrift-shop row, Cancer Care stands out as being friendly, open, and a good source for furnishings as well as clothing.

COUNCIL THRIFT SHOP
842 Ninth Ave (at 55th St)
757-6132
Mon-Fri: 9:30-4:30; Sun: 12-4; closed Sun from
    June through Aug

The Council runs thrift shops throughout the metropolitan area as a means of fund raising as well as actually supplying some of the people they help. This Manhattan outlet benefits from the lack of competition in the neighborhood. They carry everything from designer gowns to lamps.

ENCORE
1132 Madison Ave (bet 84th and 85th St, upstairs)
879-2850
Mon-Wed, Fri, Sat: 10:30-6; Thurs: 10:30-7;
　　Sun: 12:30-6; closed Sun from July to mid-Aug

There are thrift shops, and then there are thrift shops. Encore is so chic and select that it prefers to be billed as a "resale shop of gently worn clothing," and when one sees the merchandise and the caliber of the clientele, Encore can be forgiven its conceit. For one thing, Encore is a consignment boutique, not a charity thrift shop. Its donors receive a portion of the sales price, and according to owner Carole Selig (who bought the store upon the death of Florence Barry, who founded the business more than three decades ago), many of the donors are socialites and other luminaries who can't afford to be seen in the same outfit twice. So Selig can afford to be picky, and so can you. The fashions are up-to-date, and if Jackie O doesn't mind dropping off her better items here, why should a customer mind grabbing these top fashions at 50 to 70 percent off original retail prices? At any time, there are over 6,000 items in stock, and all of it sells. Prices range from reasonable to astronomical, but just think how much more they sold for originally! Encore may be the only way to go if you're going to appear on the pages of *W* four times in a week and want to look fresh each time. If the sheer savings don't appeal to you, then maybe you should be an Encore donor.

EVERYBODY'S THRIFT SHOP
261 Park Ave S
355-9263
Mon-Fri: 10-5; Sat: 10-4; closed Sat in summer

This shop was founded in 1921 to support the "Bundles for Britain" program, one of the recovery efforts after World War I. Today it serves as the umbrella organization for six charities and has an impressive list of supporters. Knowing who they are and when they donate (the list includes many manufacturers and retail stores) is the reason a queue forms outside the store on some mornings. Everybody's features designer clothing, bric-a-brac, jewelry, furniture, and donations from large corporations.

FOUR CHARITIES THRIFT SHOP
380 Second Ave (bet 21st and 22nd St)
674-1444
Mon-Sat: 10:30-5:30

The Four Charities are the Legal Aid Society, Goddard-Riverside Community Center, Visiting Nurse Service of New York, and the

University Settlement Housing. These are noteworthy organizations. A top New York department store donates new merchandise several times a year when the store clears its racks. The shop stocks new and nearly new merchandise, with an emphasis on furniture and bric-a-brac in addition to clothing.

I, MICHAEL, RESALES
1041 Madison Ave (bet 79th and 80th St)
737-7273
Tues-Sat: 9:30-6; summer: Mon-Fri: 9:30-6

It's not too common to find bargain prices on designer clothes on trendy, expensive Madison Avenue. I, Michael, is an exception. Here you can find an excellent selection of quality merchandise in sizes 4-12 at very substantial discounts.

MEMORIAL SLOAN-KETTERING CANCER CENTER THRIFT SHOP
1440 Third Ave (at 82nd St)
535-1250
Mon-Sat: 10-4:45

Because of its location on the affluent Upper East Side, Memorial benefits from its big-name donors. Try this shop for accessories, and don't miss its designer room, which is better stocked than the ones in some retail stores.

REPEAT PERFORMANCE
220 E 23rd St (bet Second and Third Ave)
684-5344
Mon-Wed, Fri, Sat: 10-5; Thurs: 10-7

Repeat Performance is run for the benefit of the New York City Opera, a cause near and dear to the hearts of wealthy donors and major department and specialty stores. So, while there are the usual thrift-shop furniture, jewelry, bric-a-brac, and occasional paintings, the strong suit here is brand-new, designer-name, often store-labeled clothing at ridiculously inexpensive prices.

RETURN ENGAGEMENT
900 First Ave (at 51st St)
752-2679
Mon-Sat: 10:30-6

This is an animal-welfare organization, which gathers merchandise from donors throughout the city. The clothing features current styles only, and the rest of the stock includes jewelry, home furnishings, and even pet materials. How appropriate.

THRIFT SHOP EAST
336 E 86th St (bet First and Second Ave)
772-6868
Mon-Sat: 10-5:45

Thrift Shop East is run for the benefit of WNET (New York's educational TV station) and the United Jewish Appeal/Federation of Jewish Philanthropies. Its donors are highbrows, whose tastes are reflected in the merchandise. In fact, the management takes great offense at the thought that this could be mistaken for a junk shop. They describe their clothing as "slightly used," the furniture as "antique" rather than secondhand, and the bric-a-brac as *objets d'art* and accessories rather than odds and ends. And that's no pretentious joke. They're absolutely right. This is the place to find slightly worn designer clothing in excellent condition and freshly cleaned. Some of it is even new; it came as donations from regular retail stores. The décor lives up to the shop's self-image and is virtually indistinguishable from that of a small posh retail store. Prices are *not* in the Salvation Army store category, but then neither is the merchandise.

TRISHOP QUALITY THRIFT SHOP
1689 First Ave (bet 87th and 88th St)
369-2410
Tues-Sat: 9:30-4:15; closed mid-July to mid-Aug

Trishop's proceeds benefit the Mental Health Association of New York and Bronx Counties. I mention this, because somehow this charitable organization has struck a particularly responsive chord with major department stores in the city. As a result, the shop's manager, Rose London, is able to boast that the shop's basic stock consists of mainly brand-new (some are a bit shopworn) ladies' dresses, coats, sportswear (including an extensive selection of sweaters), children's and men's wear, costume jewelry, and some household goods. There are frequent shipments of new merchandise. This is a thrift shop that also offers a double benefit. Besides contributing to the sponsoring agency, the shop provides a training and work-experience program. So, in addition to aiding a worthy cause and finding fantastic bargains, a purchase here helps support a unique program for aiding a segment of the population that is too often neglected.

T-Shirts

EISNER BROS.

76 Orchard St (bet Grand and Delancey St)
431-8800
Mon-Thurs: 9-6:30; Fri: 9-3; Sun: 9-5

Except for its tiny, cramped quarters and its adherence to the local practice of hanging merchandise from every available space on walls and ceilings, Eisner Bros. does not fit the usual Lower East Side shopkeeper's mold. Whereas its neighbors sell everything from handbags to shoes to designer clothes, Eisner Bros. specializes in T-shirts. They claim to have the biggest assortment of colors and sizes in the world, and about half of their business is custom orders. So although every neighborhood seems to have at least one T-shirt store, this is the granddaddy of them all. Eisner Bros. also carries jogging suits, sport shirts (that's sports as in baseball, football, soccer, etc., *not* dress shirts with an open collar), nightshirts, and baseball caps and jackets. Sweatshirts have become popular, and this is the place to get them. There's a tremendous selection, and the magnificent discount doesn't hurt, either. Eisner Bros. is constantly upgrading its line.

Umbrellas

UNCLE SAM

161 W 57th St (bet Sixth and Seventh Ave)
247-7163, 582-1976
Mon-Fri: 9-5:45; Sat: 9-5

This is a New York specialty store at its very best. Uncle Sam sells, canes, services, recovers, and customizes umbrellas. There are umbrellas for children, golfers, fashion models, travelers, chauffeurs, doormen—and for the beach. All are hand-carved, hand-sewn, and hand-assembled. Uncle Sam also sells umbrella accessories. I like the double umbrella; you can re-create a scene from *Singing in the Rain* right on Broadway!

Uniforms

DORNAN

653 11th Ave (bet 47th and 48th St)
247-0937 (800-223-0363 outside New York State)
Mon-Wed, Fri: 8:30-4; Thurs: 8:30-6

In 1925, Gabriel Piro began working at Dornan Inc., selling all types of uniforms. By 1949, Piro had bought the company and become the president and expert-in-residence on all manner of uniforms, but particularly those for chauffeurs. In 1976, Piro retired, and his son, Gabriel E. Piro, took over, and he too offers the best service and advice on uniform wear. Dornan can outfit—just to name a few—butlers, maids, beauticians, hospital workers, hotel doormen, bellboys and maids, bartenders, chefs, waiters and waitresses, housemen, ground crews, stewards, stewardesses, airline pilots, police, firemen, postal employees, doctors, nurses, technicians, patients, and even the clergy. But Piro's pride and joy are the chauffeurs' uniforms. Dornan is the oldest and largest continuing supplier of garb for uniformed drivers.

I BUSS UNIFORM COMPANY
112 E 23rd St (bet Park Ave S and Lexington Ave)
529-4655
Mon-Fri: 9-5

I Buss used to be in the military uniform business, but all that has changed. Now they are specialists in uniforms for doormen, police officers, security guards, and the like. They also do custom-made uniforms, and costumes and uniforms are available for rent.

Women's—General

ATELIER/55
101 W 55th St (at Sixth Ave)
245-3650
Mon-Wed, Fri: 10-7; Sat: 11-6; Thurs: 10-7:30

ATELIER/86
144 E 86th St
427-2211
Mon-Fri: 10:30-8; Sat: 10:30-7; Sun: 12-6:30

When a store down the street from ABC and Burlington calls itself a "small family kind of place," it may be a little hard to believe. But Atelier, an Italian store with great fashions from American designers, does just that. Indeed, Atelier even claims that the 86th Street store attracts browsers and tourist clientele, while the 55th Street shop has loyal and devoted customers who, with all of the midtown Manhattan stores to choose from, pick their wardrobes from Atelier, season after season. The reason is simple. Atelier's prices on any quality garment are excellent.

BEN FARBER
462 Seventh Ave (at 35th St, third floor)
736-0557, 800-223-6101
Mon-Fri: 9-5; Sat: 9-4; Sun: 10-4

I'll put my reputation on the line for this one: it's the best women's fashion discount house in New York. Thousands of satisfied customers must agree, because Ben Farber (located just catty-corner from Macy's) has expanded into a bright, attractive new space that gives them nearly three times the area they previously had. This pipe-rack, two-level, fully stocked house offers the finest labels in the fashion industry, at savings you'll find hard to beat. Ben Farber carries coats, suits, dresses, outerwear, sportswear, and rainwear in all sizes, even for the hard-to-fit half-size lady. All the merchandise is fresh and seasonal, and there are no irregulars passed off as first quality. Ben's son, Don Farber, and his always-on-the-job sidekick, Joe Halperin, go out of their way to satisfy the individual customer. When you go in, be sure to mention this book, and you'll get even more attentive service. And for you gentlemen who get bored waiting for the ladies to make up their minds, there are chairs in a comfortable waiting area.

BETSEY JOHNSON
248 Columbus Ave (bet 71st and 72nd St)
362-3364

130 Thompson St (bet Prince and Houston St)
420-0169

251 E 60th St (at Second Ave)
319-7699

Mon-Sat: 12-7; Sun: 1-6

In the 1960s and 1970s, Betsey Johnson was *the* fashion designer. Her designs appeared everywhere, as did Betsey and her personal life. As an outlet for those designs not sold to exclusive boutiques, Betsey helped found Betsey Bunky Nini, but her own pursuits led to more designing and ultimately a store in SoHo. The SoHo store proved so successful that Betsey moved first to larger quarters and then up and across town, as well as into Betsey Johnson Boutiques in such department stores as Bloomingdale's. While her style has always managed to be avant-garde, it has never been way-out. Johnson believes in making her own statement, and each store seems unique despite the fact that over 500 outlets carry her line. Prices, particularly at the SoHo store, which started as an outlet, are bearable and wearable. Incidentally, it's hard to overlook the shop—it's pink, with pink neon accents, and what she simply refers to as "great windows."

BRIDGEHAMPTON CLOTHES HORSE
1033 Lexington Ave (at 74th St)
988-6757
Mon, Fri, Sat: 10-6; Tues-Thurs: 11-7; closed Sat in
   July, Aug

The Hamptons on Long Island is quite simply the summer address for fashionable Manhattanites. Joan Zimmerman's Manhattan shop reflects the classy atmosphere of the Hamptons and features merchandise for the career woman, the traveler, and the weekender. Antiques, background music, silk-flower arrangements, and accessories complement the fashions. The store features after-five clothes in sizes from 4 to 16, and a specialty is customwork for the hard-to-fit woman. A nice selection of gift items, including hand-painted pillows, is available for shipment anywhere in the country.

FORMAN'S
82 Orchard St (bet Grand and Broome St)

FORMAN'S PETITE
94 Orchard St

FORMAN'S PLUS SIZES
78 Orchard St

228-2500
Sun-Wed: 9-6; Thurs: 9-8; Fri: 9-3

Forman's bills itself as "the fashion oasis of the Lower East Side." While you can determine for yourself if that overstates the case just a bit, it is true that they have enjoyed a good reputation for years and years. By Lower East Side standards, the store is enormous. It is laid out in such a way that a teenage daughter, mother, and grandmother can all head for sections designed for their needs and not meet for hours. Even then, it might be at one of the dozen (do you believe it?) dressing rooms or the cash register. The teens are attracted by the top floor—I guess they can best climb the stairs. Denim reigns here, but so does casual sportswear, separates, and trendy outerwear. The main floor dazzles the customer with designer sportswear (Calvin Klein must have a direct line here) and such better-made separates as Jones of New York and Adrienne Victtatini. The basement—excuse me, the lower level!—is dedicated to young suburban-type separates and sportswear. Forman's made its reputation outfitting these images. Prices are the obligatory Lower East Side discount. Read that to mean *very* good.

HARRIS FURS
330 Seventh Ave (at 29th St)
563-0079
Mon-Thurs: 9-5:30; Sat: 9-4:30; Sun: 9-3:30; closed July
This is not just a fur store, although they do carry a large selection in this category, including man-made furs. Women's suits and outerwear, wool jackets, and storm, leather, and wool coats are priced right. This is a factory-showroom operation that has been in business since 1904; they're trustworthy people to do business with.

HONEYBEE
7 E 53rd St (bet Fifth and Madison Ave)
688-3660
Mon-Wed, Fri: 10-6:30; Thurs: 10-8; Sat: 10-6

7 Hanover Sq (at Water St)
269-8110
Mon-Fri: 8-6
HoneyBee is a different shop to different people. To many of the city's fashion models, it is a small, intimate shop with a good collection of desirable clothing easily accessible on a quick visit. To out-of-towners, particularly those from Missouri, this is the flagship of a catalog and local branch store, with modern but not far-out sportswear. To the rising class of executive women, it is a shop where you may call to have a few things set aside appropriate for a trip to Pittsburgh, and know that they will be both appropriate and ready whenever you get there. Primarily, though, HoneyBee relies on its ability to be "totally service oriented." Salespeople carry books that record likes, needs, and previous purchases of customers. Shopping via the catalog is encouraged, and long waits for either service or checkout are taboo. With all this service, prices could be unreasonable. They aren't. In fact, prices in the catalog designed to appeal to Middle America do not differ at all from what is offered in the heart of Manhattan. And styles that appear across the country are au courant enough for fashion models.

LA RUE DES REVES
139 Spring St
226-6736
Mon-Wed, Sat: 12-6:45; Thurs, Fri: 12-8:45; Sun: 1-5:45
Although most SoHo residents live in large lofts, neighborhood shops tend to be small. Not La Rue des Reves. It's big enough to

house a grand piano—the better for music to shop by. And the emphasis is on a woman's complete wardrobe. The businesswoman can find a stylish suit for the office and a strapless, backless evening pants set on opposite racks in the same store. What it all has in common is a sleek elegance that women dream about. And hence the store's French name.

LAURA ASHLEY
21 E 57th St (bet Fifth and Madison Ave)
752-7300
Mon-Fri: 10-7; Sat: 10-6

398 Columbus Ave (at 79th St)
496-5110
Mon-Wed, Fri, Sat: 11-7; Thurs: 11-8; Sun: 12-6

4 Fulton St (at South St Seaport)
809-3555
Mon-Sat: 10-8:45; Sun: 11-7

714 Madison Ave
735-5000
Mon-Fri: 10-7; Sat: 10-6

For Laura Ashley, time and space have stopped in an Edwardian English countryside. Twenty-odd years ago, in response to the growing blue-jean trend and because she was always enamored with the romantic turn-of-the-century dress styles, Ashley and her husband, Bernard, turned out their first dress on their kitchen table. In the years since, the style and fabric have come to be known as Laura Ashley classic, distinguishable in over 130 exclusive shops. And Ashley's death didn't change a thing. There are now three Laura Ashley stores that specialize in clothing in Manhattan. A fourth store on Madison Avenue carries only home furnishings. The dresses are always in a small print fabric, which seems to emerge from the mills looking well worn. (Laura Ashley Ltd. designs and produces its own fabric.) The fabric is then used in a few classic, simple designs that vary only slightly from year to year. It always follows a romantic Victorian-Edwardian theme. In summer, the fabrics are 100 percent cotton; in winter, a light woolen tweed. Except for the seasonal fabric switch, the clothing is timeless, in terms of style and wearability. In recent years, Laura Ashley expanded to include fabrics for home furnishings as well. There are wallpapers, curtains, and even loose fabric available, as well as Laura Ashley dresses for infants and children.

LILLIE RUBIN
22 W 57th St (at Fifth Ave)
757-0370
Mon-Sat: 9:30-6

On classy 57th Street, Lillie Rubin is an institution. However, since institutions age along with their clientele, economic necessity has made Lillie Rubin look for a place in a more modern world. The result is a cautious blending of the two, which does not always work. The older crowd, who patronized the shop for the couture and evening clothing, is put off by the bolts of fabric (original designer though it may be) heaped along one wall. The younger crowd is put off by the salespeople, who are at their side before the front door is closed, and the matronly look of what is on the racks. At its best, however, Lillie Rubin is a gem. The store's trademark is knockoffs of designer clothing—in the original fabric—for a fraction of the original's cost. Prices for the original fashions vary widely, depending upon the designer's line, fabric, and quality, and the copies reflect a similar diversity. So, some of the outfits are easily affordable by people who would otherwise have to settle for off-the-rack wardrobes.

LUCILLE'S
33 W 55th St (Hotel Shoreham, suite 2B)
245-7066
Mon-Sat: 11-5:30; closed July 1-Aug 15

Women who wear sizes 6 to 20 can save substantial sums on designer fashions at Lucille's, a shop that specializes in classic designer clothing at good discount prices. The best part of all—as if that were not enough—is Lucille herself, who presides over her beautifully organized emporium with incredible taste and style. Exactly where Lucille gets her merchandise is uncertain, but somehow she gets fantastic designer clothing in striking colors, patterns, and ensembles. And the labels are intact, unlike nearly every other designer outlet I can think of. Lucille also has an instinct for the needs of her customers. Most are middle-age, very well-dressed, and classically fashionable rather than fad conscious. So Lucille's styles show a prejudice for the larger sizes. They start at 6, and the higher you go (including a very unusual designer 20), the more varied the selection is. Lucille's concern is shown in her selection of summer outfits with coordinating sweaters (to wear when there's air conditioning), jerseys that pack easily, and three-piece ensembles in striking patterns that can be interchanged for various occasions. Finally, don't miss Lucille's formal wear; her dressy outfits are really special. And did I mention that all of these fashions are sold at a 20 to 40 percent discount?

M. FRIEDLICH
196 Orchard St (bet Stanton and Houston St)
254-8899
Wed-Mon: 9:30-5:30

Another typical Lower East Side boutique, Friedlich has the usual fabulous finds in both quality and price as well as the usual abrasive service people. Starting with the good points, Friedlich stocks women's fine imported sportswear in sizes 3 to 14, a range that includes misses and juniors sizes and is somewhat limited on the larger sizes. M. Friedlich seems to favor imports from France and Italy—perhaps because they are the best—but there is a healthy assortment of better-quality American sportswear as well. Another plus is Friedlich's selection of coats and outerwear, which consists of great designer coats and better-brand offerings from both Europe and America. The only problem with a visit here is what one would facetiously call ambiance. Perhaps the saleshelp are always too swamped with customers, or perhaps handling all these good-looking things while wearing a smock gets to them. In any event, *surly* is a polite way to describe their behavior. Never, never ask a question, unless being yelled at in the midst of a horde of tightly packed people turns you on. And that is the final point. The fantastic buys at Friedlich's are not a secret, so the store is always crowded. Would anyone whose pet peeve is standing in line and begging people to take his money come here? You betcha! It's that good!

MIRIAM RIGLER
62 W 56th St (bet Fifth and Sixth Ave)
581-5519
Mon-Sat: 10-6

Miriam Rigler is the quintessential ladies' dress shop. It seems to have it all—personal attention, expert alterations, wardrobe coordination, custom designing, and a large selection in everything from sportswear to knits to evening gowns, in sizes from 4 to 20. Despite the location, all items are discounted, including specially ordered outfits that are not in stock. I don't think there is much more to say. This store meets all of my criteria for being one of the very best.

S&W

Coats:	*Bags, Shoes, Accessories:*
287 Seventh Ave (at 26th St)	165 W 26th St
Dresses, Sportswear:	*Furs:*
165 W 26th St	167 W 26th St
(at Seventh Ave)	

924-6656

Mon-Wed: 10-6:30; Thurs: 10-8; Fri: 10-4; Sun: 10-6

Each location of S&W features a specialty, as indicated above. While it is unclear exactly what the source of supply is, it is a well-known fact that S&W is one of the best places in the city for ladies' designer clothing. Clothing orders include elegant—the suedes and leathers in the coats and suits are magnificent—and top-of-the-line garments only. Unlike so many of the other discount boutiques, S&W maintains a consistent level of quality. It is *not* the place to uncover the buy of the year. Prices, incidentally, are not incidental. The discount is a minimum of 40 percent, but 40 percent off a $300 suede suit still takes a lot out of a working girl's budget. Two serious drawbacks: prices are not marked for the customer to read, and rudeness seems to be a way of life at S&W.

SHULIE'S

175 Orchard St (bet Stanton and Houston St)
473-2480
Sun-Fri: 9:30-5:30

You probably wouldn't think that Orchard Street is the place to come for designer clothes, but think again. Look around uptown in some of the fancier shops for top-label clothing and accessories, then phone or come down to Shulie's. The merchandise will be the same as what you saw uptown, but the shopping bag, the ambiance, and most importantly, the price, will be very different. Special orders are taken here, and service is above the norm for this area.

SPITZER'S CORNER STORE

101 Rivington St	156 Orchard St
477-4088	473-1515

Mon-Fri: 9:30-5:30; Sun: 8:30-6

Spitzer on Rivington is a Lower East Side landmark. There is just one good reason for shopping at these stores: excellent selection at the best prices. You have to put up with less than helpful salespeople, unmarked merchandise, and, at the Rivington store, three rooms jammed with goods. Be especially careful in any store that does not mark its merchandise; make sure you're getting the best price possible. A bit of "bargaining" may be necessary. Now that you know the up side and the down side of shopping here, you'll be able to get some great bargains and some memorable shopping experiences. Good luck.

TERRE GRAFF
248 W 88th St (The Montana)
724-8800
By appointment only
Cash and checks only

Are you one of those shoppers who is very label conscious until you look at the price tag? Well, I have the solution for you. Terre Graff has one of the best collections in the country of Armani, Valentino, Chanel, Yves St. Laurent, Adolfo, Givenchy, and Ungaro dresses, coats and suits, gowns, jackets, sweaters, and blouses. She normally sells these items at 75 to 85 percent off the Madison Avenue boutique retail prices. Terre is a great gal to work with, and she will keep you informed about special sales and events through a monthly newsletter sent to her clients.

22 STEPS
746 Madison Ave (at 65th St)
288-2240
Mon-Sat: 10-6

This is discount shopping for women's apparel, including furs, New York style. Sometimes the discount can climb to 70 percent off, and it's advertised at a minimum of 50 percent off at all times. And we're talking real designer names. Some of them are Alaia, Byblos, Chloe, Chanel, Gaultier, Gianfranco Ferre, Krizia, Karl Lagerfeld, Laura Biagiotti, Lamatta, Les Copain, Mario Valentino, Sonia Rykiel, and Ungaro. At any given time, at least 25 designers are represented, and the prices are half-off on all of them.

Women's Accessories

ACCESSORIE CLUB
10 E 36th St
213-3336
Mon-Fri: 9-6

If you are one of those gals whose waist size changes each season, you should head down to the Accessorie Club, where they feature the largest selection of ladies belts in the city. You can choose from many different styles and colors, all at very reasonable prices. In addition, there are scarves, hats, and hair accessories. With a moderate-size purchase, they will make you a member of the club, which entitles you to a special discount on all the merchandise.

APRON AND BAG SUPPLY COMPANY
47 Second Ave (bet Second and Third St)
673-0835
Mon-Fri: 8-3:30

Stanley Grodzki and his staff are not just standing around waiting for the customer who wants to buy one apron to match the kitchen wallpaper. The majority of their orders are for institutions, kitchen supply stores, linen services, or restaurants. If they are busy filling orders, they are not overly receptive to single orders. On the other hand, why should you pay department store—or even kitchen-supply store—prices, when you can buy the best aprons and bags around for wholesale prices? The aprons come in different colors and materials, but most are in the sturdy, professional line rather than hostess style. Laundry bags, too, are sturdy, mostly canvas or denim bags, sewn up in the familiar contours of laundry bags, school bags, or duffel bags. They are made to last.

BERNARD KRIEGER & SON
316 Grand St
CA6-1929
Mon-Thurs, Sun: 8-4:30; Fri: 8-3; Sun hours may
    vary in summer

The assortment of items here is limited, but they do have one of the best selections anywhere of handkerchiefs, scarves, accessories, and gloves. If this is the Christmas you're giving your grandfather that most exciting of all gifts (a dozen hankies), this is the place to go, because everything is discounted. It also looks as though they have more berets than any store in Paris, and the price tags are certainly a lot more reasonable.

FINE AND KLEIN
119 Orchard St (at Delancey St)
674-6720
Sun-Fri: 9-5:30

No, the finest handbag store for value and selection is not located in Rome or Paris or London. It is not even located on Fifth

Avenue in New York. It is on the Lower East Side, and the name is Fine and Klein. What a selection! There is a bag for every purpose, for any time of day, and in any fabric. If top labels are what you're looking for, they sell them for a fraction of the price you would pay at Bergdorfs. Besides, shopping at Fine and Klein is fun. The crowds, especially on Sundays and during the holidays, are so great that the number of persons allowed to enter is controlled! One Saudi princess bought $9,600 worth of bags here. My good friends Julius Fine and Murray Klein are the epitome of the old-time merchants. Tell them I sent you, and you will be delighted with the service.

HYUK BAGS
39 W 29th St
685-5226, 685-5399
Mon-Fri: 8-5; Sat: 8-1

Hyuk K. Kim runs an importing company exclusively dedicated to handbags. Importing and wholesaling companies are common in this area. What is uncommon is the courtesy and selection the company gives individual retail customers. Kim has a knack for making everyone seem a valued customer, and she does not take offense when a finicky lady picks through the entire stock in search of the right handbag—and it shouldn't be too hard to find, within certain guidelines. *Imported* here usually refers to origins from points west rather than east. So rather than an "LV," expect to see a "Made in Hong Kong." Hyuk seems to import every type of handbag—leather, vinyl, canvas, and nylon. Most of this is your average, serviceable stuff. But there are a few stars in the line, and prices border on magnificent. Spoken English is at a premium here.

J. S. SUAREZ
26 W 54th St (bet Fifth and Sixth Ave)
315-5614
Mon-Fri: 9:30-6; Sat: 10-5:30

J. S. Suarez has been in business for over 42 years, and in that time, he has made his reputation by selling name-brand bags at a 30 to 50 percent discount, and copies of name-brand bags (and *big* names at that) at even better prices. For years, Suarez was the source for unlabeled Gucci bags that were identical to the real thing (naturally, since they came from the same factory), for less than half the price. And, unlike Gucci, Suarez doesn't have the most obnoxious clerks this side of Italy. In fact, Suarez' people, and Suarez himself, are downright pleasant. He discounts name brands as well as "fake" (read "unlabeled") Bottega Veneta, Celine of Paris,

Chanel, Fendi, and Hermes items. There is also a great selection of exotic skins. Suarez takes it as a matter of course that you are *supposed* to deliver top quality, great service, good selection, and excellent prices to all customers. Gucci could learn a few things from J. S. Suarez.

MICHAEL KLEIN'S FOMO
61 Orchard St
925-6363
Mon-Fri, Sun: 9:15-5:30

The name Klein is world-famous on Orchard Street because of Fine and Klein. A second-generation Klein wanted to continue the family tradition of being in the handbag business, but he wanted to flap his own wings. Thus Michael Klein's FOMO. And what does FOMO stand for? *Finally on my own!* Michael offers an outstanding collection of bags, including such top names as Courreges of Paris and Carlos Falchi and Cosci of Italy. Prices reflect a 25 to 50 percent discount, and the imported merchandise includes belts and wallets as well as handbags.

ST. REGIS DESIGNS
58 E Seventh St (bet First and Second Ave)
533-7313
Mon-Sat: 10-7:30; Sun: 12-6:30

From this unlikely spot in the East Village, Andrew Pelensky who used to work for a top handbag designer, turns out handmade, original custom-designed handbags and belts from the finest leathers, including snake and alligator skins. The workmanship is both unique and magnificent, and items can be custom-ordered. For the quality, prices are outright cheap. George Pelensky is listed as being in charge of "sales." I hope this doesn't mean they are going into mass production. Right now, it's the personal touch, like a final fitting before a belt leaves the premises, that makes St. Regis so special.

SYLVIA PINES—UNIQUITIES
1102 Lexington Ave (at 77th St)
744-5141
Mon-Sat: 10-6; closed Sat in summer

Sylvia Pines presides over an emporium of what she calls "uniquities," and that's not an inappropriate name. For years, she has amassed antique, art deco, and art nouveau purses, *objets d'art,* and jewelry. One never knows what can be unearthed here, but with the largest collection of antique purses in the country, Sylvia

Pines has it in the bag. And if it is not the perfect bag, the shop's repair and restoration services can make it so. Those who don't come to view the purse uniquities come for the collection of jewelry of similar vintage, though the best selection is of the Victorian era.

Women's—Business

ALCOTT & ANDREWS

335 Madison Ave (at 44th St)   1301 Sixth Ave
818-0606   315-2796

Mon-Wed, Fri: 10-8; Thurs: 10-9; Sat: 10-6; Sun: 12-5

Now the female Madison Avenue executive can shop for a business suit on Madison Avenue. Alcott & Andrews has opened shop on the premise that these busy women will pay to have good quality clothing that is stylish and flattering. The A & A shopper can buy everything for her personal and professional life under one roof. Shopping by appointment is also available.

Women's Evening Wear

KHANITHA

1034A Lexington Ave (at 74th St)
570-0015
Mon-Sat: 10-7

There are few human beings more graceful than the hostesses on Thai Airways. They are always clad in magnificent Thai silk clothes, beautifully made in spectacular colors. Now one can find this same quality in evening wear at Khanitha, the only one of its kind in this country, although they have five sister operations in Thailand. The designer is Thai, as is the charming store manager, Annette Akaranithikul.

ONE NIGHT STAND

905 Madison Ave (bet 72nd and 73rd St)
772-7720
Mon-Fri: 10-6 by appointment; Sat: 10-3 by
    appointment; closed Sat in July, Aug

Now here's a great idea. You are invited to a gala, and you "don't have a thing to wear." Don't buy. Rent. One Night Stand (a great name, eh?) has over 500 pieces of ladies' evening wear for rent in sizes 4 to 16. Jewelry, evening bags, and cloaks are also available for hire. You can even select your outfit and pick it up the very same day. Sure beats shelling out big bucks for a dress you may not need for another two years, if ever.

Women's Knitwear

JOAN AND LILO KNIT COUTURE
1258 Third Ave (bet 72nd and 73rd St)
861-8190
Mon-Sat: 10-4:30

If you think *knit* when someone says *couture,* then Joan and Lilo are your kind of people. Their store specializes in designer (domestic and imported) knit dresses, sportswear, and suits for women, in sizes 6 to 20. The look is understated sophistication, much the way Joan and Lilo dress themselves. One unique service Joan and Lilo offers is a personal tour of the store, which begins with meeting clients at their hotels. From there, a discreet inquiry into the customer's lifestyle and wardrobe needs will produce exactly the right style for each individual. Of course, it helps if that style is best expressed in designer knits, but with the "unsurpassed quality and elegance" that is the store's motto, it would be hard not to find something to suit you here.

SCALERA KNITS
796 Madison Ave (at 67th St)
988-3344
Mon-Sat: 10-6

In this store devoted entirely to knitwear, women can pick up outfits in silk, wool, cashmere, cotton, or blends of those materials in sizes from 8 to 20. And if that isn't impressive enough, Scalera is the only direct importer of Italian silk knits in the country.

Women's Large Sizes

ASHANTI
872 Lexington Ave (bet 65th and 66th St)
535-0740
Mon-Wed, Fri, Sat: 10-6; Thurs: 10-8

Its name is a throwback to the days when ethnic boutiques were popular in Manhattan, but Ashanti's current image couldn't be more in vogue. Today, Ashanti carries better dresses, clothing, and accessories solely for the "larger woman." What they can't buy, they have made to order. In fact, says Bill Michael, 75 percent of his merchandise is of Ashanti's own design and manufacturing. And, adds Sandra Michael, the craftsmen who work exclusively for Ashanti are often supplied with patterns as well as designs, since the field is so new. There is more to large sizes than letting out seams or sewing up caftans in polka-dot polyester. Now, for the first time, there are boutiques that operate on the belief that big ladies deserve a positive, stylish fashion image. Ashanti will do alterations and ship anywhere. It may be the only place that carries classic, quality clothing up to size 24.

FORGOTTEN WOMAN

888 Lexington Ave   60 W 49th St
   (bet 65th and 66th St)   247-8888
535-8848

Mon-Wed, Fri, Sat: 10-6; Thurs: 10-7:30

Nancye Radmin, a former partner in the Farmer's Daughter Boutique, was so appalled by the dearth of size 20 clothes that she opened her own boutique. The Forgotten Woman thus became the first store in New York devoted exclusively to the larger-size woman and, in the process, became a trailblazer for Seventh Avenue manufacturers as well. The selection was so small in the beginning that Nancye designed much of her own merchandise. (She still creates about 25 percent of what is sold.) Eventually, manufacturers followed her lead, and the Forgotten Woman now stocks everything from Diane von Furstenberg's wrap dress to bathing suits with coordinated skirts for cocktail wear. Better still, as a "forgotten woman" herself, Nancye knows what looks good, and what styles have become almost a uniform for large women. Banished, therefore, are polka dots, polyesters in general, and three-piece polyester pant suits in particular. Nicest of all, sizes at the Forgotten Woman range from 0-8. Even if she is really a 48, the Forgotten Woman is one place where the well-endowed woman can feel wanted—and definitely *not* forgotten.

LANE BRYANT

450 Fifth Ave (at 39th St)
764-3550
Mon-Wed, Fri, Sat: 10-6; Thurs: 10-8; Sun: 12-5

In days of yore, Lane Bryant was the store of choice for women who were either overweight or pregnant. But the store was heavy-handed as well, and over the years it failed to pick up on the popularity of outlets for both of those markets. The Limited purchased Lane Bryant and almost immediately applied its much vaulted marketing technique to the faded lady. The results have been startling. This store is now the prototype of a chain of Lane Bryants stretching across the country. The image is still large, but it is now high fashion as well. Clothing is displayed much like it is at the Limited, with highlighted top fashions and mini-departments for different lifestyles.

Women's—Maternity

LADY MADONNA
793 Madison Ave (at 67th St)
988-7173
Mon-Wed, Fri, Sat: 10-6; Thurs: 10-7

I'd like to reaffirm that I personally visited nearly every one of the stores listed in this book—even the maternity shops. I wasn't exactly a regular customer, but my visits were pleasant and informative and not half as embarrassing as one might think. Okay, back to business. Lady Madonna started with the premise that most pregnant women were adults who would like to dress as adults rather than as Raggedy Ann or Pollyanna. The idea took off beyond anyone's imagination. It was helped along by the rising number of women who combined careers with families and who, therefore, needed good clothing that was stylish even in the advanced stages of pregnancy. Old-fashioned ideas fell by the wayside. One such idea was that a pregnant woman should be hidden, either by staying home or by being swathed in voluminous clothing. Another was that maternity clothes should be inexpensive, since no one wants to pay a lot of money for an outfit worn a maximum of five months. Lady Madonna banished these concepts once and for all with fashionable, functional maternity clothing.

MANOLA MATERNITY
1040 Lexington Ave (bet 74th and 75th St)
861-1227
Mon-Sat: 11-7

Manola is for the classy expectant mother, who wants to look good more than she wants to look pregnant. They carry sportswear, career and office clothes, and evening garments in the same quality and style that the client would normally wear. If a style or size is not in stock, Manola can make or order it, and alterations can be done rather quickly.

PARENT PENDING
1178 Lexington Ave (bet 80th and 81st St)
988-3996

2007 Broadway (bet 68th and 69th St)
769-2232

Mon-Wed, Fri: 11-7; Thurs: 11-8; Sat: 10-6; Sun: 12-5; closed Sun on East Side from Memorial Day to Labor Day

As with most maternity shops today, Parent Pending aims to dress women who just happen to be pregnant. Expect to find stylish, contemporary clothing for business and evening wear, which Parent Pending claims will still be stylish and wearable even after the baby is delivered. In addition to the clothing, there are nursing accessories, maternity and nursing lingerie, and swimwear. But as for continuing to wear the clothing after delivery? The mothers on my staff tell me that that should be the last reason you'd want to buy maternity clothes.

Women's Millinery

DON MARSHALL
465 Park Ave (suite 305)
758-1686
Mon-Sat: 10:30-5; closed Sat from April to Sept

Even in fashion-conscious New York, personal milliners are a rare breed. In fact, Don Marshall, who's been in business over 40 years, says his is a dying art, and he can see the writing on the wall. "It's too bad," he says. "This is a beautiful profession. Years from now, people will look at these hats and be amazed at the care that was taken to make each piece." And he's right, although it shouldn't take years for Marshall's work to be appreciated; Princess Di has already given hats a new lease on life. All of Marshall's hats and clothing (often in matching ensembles) are custom-made. Marshall says that while custom-made hats are rare, couture work is all but dead. A visit here is in order just for the experience. And bear in mind that while an order is a good thing in its own right, Marshall's work may very well be the last of its kind anywhere. So your purchase could well be an instant heirloom, while its quality and style will always keep it fashionable. Marshall, who could be a crabby old craftsman or even a fashion snob, is neither. He is one of the friendliest guys you'll ever meet.

HATS IN THE BELFRY
Pier 17 Pavilion, South St Seaport
406-2574
Mon-Sat: 10-10; Sun; 10-8; closes earlier in fall and winter

The Pier 17 Pavilion, an addition to the South Street Seaport, is a popular gathering place for the young financial-district crowd as well as tourists. Many of the shops have sister stores in Rousse-inspired redevelopment projects in other cities, and Hats in the Belfry is among them. So if you're from Washington, Baltimore, Philadelphia, Annapolis, St. Louis, or New Orleans, you may already be familiar with the shop, which has a stock as cute as its name and a reputation that's unusual for such a location. Novelty hats for children and adults (the Statue of Liberty was big in 1986; animals are more popular now) and theatrical-style hats are lined up alongside ladies' designer hats and some of the sharpest men's hats found anywhere. They're also one of the few places that will still steam, brush, or stretch hats. What about that! First-rate service and selection, and all at the charming Seaport.

MANNY'S MILLINERY SUPPLY COMPANY
63 W 38th St
840-2235
Mon-Fri: 9-5:30; Sat: 9-3:30

Manny's is another New York institution. It carries millinery supplies, and that's an understatement. There are drawers, row after row, built up against the walls, and each is dedicated to a particular aspect of head adornment. The section for ladies' hatbands alone takes up almost 100 boxes and runs the gamut from thin pearl lines to wide leather belts, Western style. The center of the store is lined with tables that display accumulated odds and ends, as well as several bins of larger items that don't fit in the wall drawers. Hat forms can be found here, but they are available on hat-tree stands in the front, too. The front, incidentally, displays sample hats in no particular order. Manny's will help fix up any hat and play with interchangeable decorations for it. Manny's also sells completed hats, closeouts, and samples, and will even re-create an old hat.

MAX MILLINERY CENTER
13 W 38th St (at Fifth Ave)
221-8896
Mon-Fri: 9:30-5:30; Sat: 10-4:30

Max Millinery Center is typical of the shops specializing in bridal millinery. Every conceivable type of headgear for the bride is available, and some that are not so conceivable as well. Mention should be made of the fact that the entire area considers itself a "wholesale only" trading center; therefore, few, if any, of the items on display are meant to be sold. The designer (whether a professional or a one-time customer) gathers the necessary materials, and the whole thing is put together elsewhere. Some of the companies really are wholesale suppliers, and will not tarry with single retail customers. Some begrudgingly do, and a handful—such as Max—conduct wholesale and retail (albeit at wholesale prices) business simultaneously. There are enough of the latter companies to satisfy the bride-to-be without having to face the humiliation of being thrown out of a place where she is not wanted. Prices, however, are slightly higher in wholesale-retail operations, particularly if the premises are a street-level walk-in location. In addition to millinery supplies, Max also carries notions, bridal accessories, and related materials, and will make up hats to order. Max carries bridal veils and hats for the mother of the bride and the bridesmaid, as well as some ordinary hats. They also stock dress trimmings, feather bags, artificial flowers, and bridal favors. If you bring in a picture of what you want, Max's personnel can duplicate it exactly.

PAUL'S VEIL AND NET
66 W 38th St (near Fifth Ave)
391-3822
Mon-Fri: 8:30-4:30; Sat: 8-2:30

It is inconceivable that the mob scene here is being repeated up and down the block, and that even *that* is a mere fraction of the bridal business nationwide. Despite the competition of its neighbors (or perhaps because of it), Paul's would be a first-choice recommendation for any bride-to-be who wants to put together her own bridal headpiece. Although they deal in illusion (lace, that is), they are one of the few stores on the block that does not maintain the illusion that they are a wholesale-only outfit, doing the lowly retail customer a big favor by unbarring the doors to her. The staff at Paul's seems genuinely glad to see you—glad to share your joy and overjoyed to help you create a truly unique bridal veil or crown. The store stocks all the equipment needed for the rest of the bridal party, as well as unusual accessories, bridal supplies, and a great collection of imported headpieces created from flowers. The lucky bride will find the savings—and the outfit—extraordinary.

Women's Small Sizes

PETITE PLEASURES
1192 Madison Ave (at 87th St)
369-3437
Mon-Fri: 10:30-6:30; Sat: 10:30-6; Sun: 12-5 (Sept-Dec, March-May)

Just because you are small doesn't mean that you have to accept less than the most stylish clothes. No more do you have to shop in the young people's departments. Petite Pleasures caters exclusively to the high-fashion woman who happens to be under 5'4". They carry dresses, suits, coats, blouses, sweaters, and pants in petite sizes 0-8 from such well-known designers as St. Gillian, Carole Little, Andrienne Vittadini, and Lloyd Williams. There is also an outstanding private-label collection.

PIAFFE
841 Madison Ave (at 70th St)
744-9911
Mon, Fri, Sat: 10-6; Tues-Thurs: 10-7; Sun: 12-5

Piaffe has built a large business by catering to small women. The store was one of the first to take advantage of the market in high fashion for dainty women. Anne Klein II and Albert Nipon are but two of the top labels available in dresses, coats, suits, accessories, business attire, furs, leathers, and evening wear. They even have their own designer, who will gladly take care of ladies size 6 to 0!

Women's Tall Sizes

SHELLY'S TALL GIRLS SHOP
13 E 41st St (near Fifth Ave)
697-1115, 697-8433
Mon-Wed, Fri, Sat: 9:30-6; Thurs: 9:30-7

Tall ladies don't have much of a choice when shopping for clothing, even in New York. So, it's a bonus when a store specializing in fashions for tall women offers current name-brand fashions at reasonable prices. And Shelly's does. Shelly stands for Sheldon, not Rochelle, and that's the name for the designer line of tall fashions carried exclusively in the shop. Actually, that line is the only such line carried anywhere in the country. And while those fashions are particularly exciting for women who have heretofore been letting hems down no matter what the fashion experts decree, there's more. The store offers a complete wardrobe in sizes 8 to 22: there are sweaters, dresses, tops, skirts, pants, and even coats. That's *complete*. Filling all those requirements is a tall order. Since they are virtually unique, Shelly's also maintains an extensive mail-order business. They will ship anywhere in the country.

Women's Undergarments

A. W. KAUFMAN
73 Orchard St (bet Broome and Grand St)
226-1629
Sun-Thurs: 10-5; Fri: 10-2:30

Kaufman handles only the finest in ladies' lingerie and lounge wear, at prices that are substantially less than what uptown stores charge. In fact, Kaufman's discounts are so good that top quality merchandise here is competitively priced with lesser quality available elsewhere. Kaufman's line includes good, quality practical wear, such as lounge wear, hostess gowns, pajamas, slips, bikini briefs, terry robes, quilted velour robes, and flannel gowns, plus some items, such as the pure silk underwear and hand-embroidered accessories, that are both luxurious and downright frivolous. However, frivolity here is not as expensive as elsewhere, and if you're going to indulge yourself, it's nice to know you can do it at a bargain price. And quality is so good at Kaufman's that everything could last forever.

BRIEF ESSENTIALS
1407 Broadway (bet 38th and 39th St)
921-8344
Mon-Fri: 8:30-5:30

You should shop here, if for no other reason than to be able to brag that you got your sensational lingerie at 1407 Broadway—that veritable bastion of inaccessibility in the wholesale Garment Center. No matter that the store is off the lobby and is a legitimate store (or even that 1407 is known for junior sportswear and the only thing junior about Brief Essentials' stock is the sizes); if you can buy anything in this building, you've arrived! Not incidentally, the selection is great, if only slightly risqué. "Sensuous lingerie for the sensual woman" is their boast, and you'd better believe that a women's lingerie store doing business in a building full of men who wholesale women's fashions has got to offer the best items in terms of quality, fashion, and price. The ladies' lingerie business has really taken off in the New York area. Brief Essentials is just one of the many lingerie specialty stores with cute names that have sprung up all over. No longer are undergarments limited to bras and girdles purchased in a department store. These intimate boutiques consider such items as camisoles, corsets, and nightwear essential. And all of it is made up in such luxury fibers as silk and satin and the more plebian, yet highly popular, 100 percent cotton.

D&A MERCHANDISE COMPANY
22 Orchard St (bet Canal and Hester St)
925-4766
Sun-Thurs: 9-5; Fri: 9-3

Elliott Kivell claims that a good reason to shop at D&A is "my sweet adorable smile," but even he concedes that his mother is probably the only person who would make that the first reason to come here. Most people come because it is a one-stop place to get underwear for the entire family at a minimum 25 percent discount, while ladies are impressed by the large selection of bras, gowns, lingerie, and underwear. (There is also a bit of sportswear.) But really smart shoppers come to D&A for the labels they carry. Dior robes, designer tennis wear, nightwear, and top-of-the-line lingerie at these discount prices would convince anyone to shop here, whether Elliott smiles or not. Besides, who ever heard of an Orchard Street merchant boasting that he smiles? Or that he even knows how to smile? Finally, for those who can't see that smile in person, D&A will order any merchandise not in stock and ship it anywhere in the country. The same discounts apply. They're enough to make *you* smile at Elliott.

GOLDMAN AND COHEN
55 Orchard St
966-0737
Sun-Fri: 9-5:30

Goldman and Cohen specializes in name-brand underwear and lingerie for women at a great discount—up to 70 percent! The lines include almost anything that falls within those two categories. This is one of the best.

IMKAR COMPANY
(M. KARFIOL AND SON)
294 Grand St (bet Allen and Eldridge St)
925-2459
Sun-Thurs: 10-5; Fri: 9:30-2; Sun (summer): 10-3

Inkar carries pajamas, underwear, and shifts for both men and women at about one-third off retail prices. A full line of Carter's infants' and children's wear is also available at good prices. The store has a fine line of women's lingerie, including dusters, gowns, and layettes. Featured names include Model's Coat, Barbizon, Vanity Fair, Arrow shirts, Jockey, Lollipop, and Munsingwear.

JOOVAY
436 W Broadway (south of Prince St)
431-6386
Daily: 12-7

This is a sensitively run lingerie shop, with a sensitivity both for its customers and its stock. Prices range from reasonable for basic lingerie items to expensive for one-of-a-kind luxury items. While everything is made of natural fibers (sensitivity again), the focus is on design, quality, and fit. With a limited display area, they make the most of what they have by not stocking lesser quality. The prizes of the shop are the special pieces made exclusively for Joovay; many are one-of-a-kind. The emphasis on smallness is reflected in virtually everything in the business, except clothing size. There the range is quite generous.

MENDEL WEISS
91 Orchard St (at Broome St)
925-6815
Sun-Thurs: 9:30-5:30; Fri: 9:30-4

Mendel Weiss is one of the stalwarts in the Lower East Side tradition of selling ladies' undergarments and lounge wear at sizable discounts. Depending on the dates of the merchandise, prices can range from wholesale at 10 percent above cost to other items marked down as much as 75 percent. Weiss includes T-shirts and bathing suits in his collection. Trained specialists are available to aid mastectomy fittings. This is not a glamorous shopping environment, but lingerie styles don't change that much from season to season and you can save money here.

SAMANTHA JONES
1074 Third Ave (bet 63rd and 64th St)
308-6680
Mon-Sat: 11-7; Sun: 1-5

Samantha Jones, the owner and operator of her own namesake boutique, specializes in contemporary and glamorous lingerie. Her collection consists of art deco styling in robes, gowns, teddies, and camisoles, and an interesting collection of undergarments and Samantha Jones fragrances. When you're in trouble at home, fellas, this is the place to come for that special little thing for that special little lady.

VICTORIA'S SECRET
34 E 57th St (bet Park and Madison Ave)
758-5592
Mon-Wed, Fri: 10-7; Thurs: 10-8; Sat: 10-6; Sun: 12-5

This has to be one of the sexiest stores in the world. I mean in ambiance, dear reader. The beautiful lingerie and bedroom garb, bridal peignoirs, exclusive silks, and accessories are displayed against the most alluring backdrops. Combine all of this with absolutely charming personnel and, gentlemen, this is *the* place to buy the most personal gifts for your lady.

Coins, Stamps

HARMER ROOKE NUMISMATISTS
3 E 57th St (sixth floor)
751-1900
Mon-Fri: 9:30-5; Sat: 10-2:30

Harmer Rooke is a virtual cornucopia of coins, antique items, and fine collectibles, all stocked to abundance and available in hundreds of different styles and price ranges. Howard Rose, one of the managers, says: "In antiquities alone, we have thousands of items on display, priced from a few dollars to $10,000. We feature Greek, Roman, Judaic, Pre-Columbian, Egyptian, and Middle Eastern coins and artifacts." There are also collections of American antiques, paper money, and tribal arts among others. Each collection can stand among its peers throughout the country. Taken together, under one roof, it's positively staggering. The personnel behind the counters are knowledgeable and helpful, even if you don't make a purchase. They are besieged these days by people seeking estimates on their prized possessions.

STACKS RARE COINS
123 W 57th St (near Sixth Ave)
582-2580
Mon-Fri: 10-5

Stacks, established in 1858, is the country's oldest and largest rare coin dealer. With a specialty in rare coins, medals, and paper money of interest to collectors, Stacks has a solid reputation for individual service, integrity, and knowledge of the field. In addition to specific sales of rare coins and the walk-in business, Stacks runs 10 public auctions a year. Both neophyte and experienced numismatists will do well at Stacks.

SUBWAY STAMP SHOP
111 Nassau St (bet Ann and Beekman St)
227-8637, 800-221-9960
Mon-Fri: 9:30-5:30

Subway has operated a stamp shop for over half a century, offering discounts to collectors and bearing one of the most intriguing store names in the city. In that time, they have become the largest mail-order stamp and coin supply company in the world. A look at their 50-page catalog ($1 postage) will explain why they are so successful. The prices are right for all their merchandise, including reference books, stamps and stamp products, and a new-issue service. Don't you want to know where the name comes from?

Cosmetics, Drugs

BOYD CHEMISTS
655 Madison Ave (at 60th St)
838-6558, 838-5524
Mon-Fri: 8:30-7; Sat: 9:30-6; closed Sat in July, Aug

Boyd is a drugstore in a city full of drugstores, so it has to have something special to be worthy of mention. Naturally, it does. In addition to a complete drug and prescription service, Boyd carries a complete line of cosmetics, soaps, jewelry, and brushes. The latter range from the common to the esoteric: i.e., nail brushes and mustache combs in a variety of sizes and shapes. I started my retailing career in the drug department of the family store, and I do not hesitate to say that Boyd has one of the largest and most complete selections I have ever seen of drugs, cosmetics, and sundries. But shopping in this store is not always a pleasant experience.

CASWELL-MASSEY PHARMACY
518 Lexington Ave (at 48th St)
   (branches at South St Seaport, Herald Center, and
   World Financial Center)
755-2254
Mon-Fri: 9-7; Sat: 10-6

George Washington's favorite cologne is just one of the hundreds of apothecary and toiletry articles sold at the Caswell-Massey Pharmacy, which was established in 1752. The store smells like the garden of specialties it is. In addition to regular pharmaceutical items, Caswell-Massey has a full range of perfumes, colognes, and the ingredients for making them. The apothecary catalog lists articles that have been sold since it was first founded, plus new items designed for the "natural look." It is the latter, in fact, that has brought a resurgence of interest in the shop. Caswell-Massey is one of the few places that sells unadulterated liniments, oils, waxes, soaps, and folk remedies; it may well be the only store in New York to have them all under one roof. Caswell-Massey's mail-order catalog cannot do justice to the rare and unusual items. George Washington's number six cologne isn't for everyone, but if you want to smell like the father of our country, it's available in soap, talc, and after-shave balm.

COSMETIC WORLD AND GIFT CENTER
431 Fifth Ave (bet 38th and 39th St, second floor)
213-4047
Mon-Sat: 10-6:30

Right in the heart of the city you can find cosmetics, crystal pieces, figures, handbags, jewelry, ties, and men's and women's fragrances at discounts that range from 15 to 50 percent. You will not find every major brand in stock at all times, but there are excellent buys in such well-known (read expensive) names as Chanel, Opium, Estee Lauder, Calvin Klein, Krizia, and Albert Nipon.

Cosmetic World has a multilingual staff, a corporate gift program, and telephone and mail-order facilities.

ESSENTIAL PRODUCTS
90 Water St (bet Wall St and Hanover Sq)
344-4288
Mon-Fri: 9-6

Essential Products has been manufacturing flavors and fragrances for nearly 100 years. They know that an enormous percentage of the price of colognes and perfumes pays for advertising and packaging. So they set out to see how closely they could duplicate expensive scents at cheaper prices. They describe their fragrances as "elegant interpretations" of designer names sold at a small fraction of the original's price. Essential features 66 sensual perfumes and men's colognes, and offers a money-back guarantee. If you send them a self-addressed stamped envelope, they will send you 5 scented cards and all ordering information.

KAUFMAN PHARMACY
557 Lexington Ave (at 50th St)
755-2266
Daily: 24 hours

I hope Kaufman's is one phone number in New York you will never need, but it's wonderful to know it's there. In addition to the usual drugstore operation—soda fountain, sundries, cigarettes, electrical goods, and traveling needs—Kaufman's has a prescription department that's always open. Should the nightmare of being ill in a New York City hotel room actually happen to you, it's nice to know a pharmacy is open and ready to deliver your prescription by cab. Bless them! Incidentally, should you need a doctor to write that prescription, check this book's 24-hour numbers.

KIEHL'S
109 Third Ave (bet 13th and 14th St)
677-3171
Mon-Fri: 10-6; Sat: 10-4:30

Kiehl's has been a New York institution since 1851. It is a fourth-generation, family-owned company unlike any you have ever visited. Their special treatments and preparations are made by hand and distributed internationally. Only natural ingredients are used in the full lines of cleansers, scrubs, toners, moisturizers, eye-area preparations, men's creams, masques, body moisturizers, bath and shower products, sports items, ladies' leg-grooming formulations, and hair shampoos, conditioners, and treatments. Customers can also enjoy an unusual collection of memorabilia related to aviation, a great interest of the Aaron Morse family who run this famous shop.

PARISIAN PERFUMES AND COSMETICS
123 Fifth Ave (bet 19th and 20th St, second floor)
254-5300
Mon-Fri: 9-5; Sat: 9-4

This perfume source carries everything from Aramis to Zizanie, all of it discounted. That pretty much covers the perfume market, and the price is right. In addition, there are colognes, cosmetics, and gift items. All are name brands. A great place for gifts!

SOAP OPERA
30 Rockefeller Plaza
245-5090
Mon-Fri: 10-6

The Soap Opera calls itself a "bath boutique," but its specialty is soaps and soap products rather than bathroom furnishings. There is a full range of over 400 natural and herbal soaps, as well as soap powders, bath oils, and bath additives. Some, in fact, are packaged so that they make great gifts. The scents are long-lasting without being sickly sweet, and add a pleasing aroma to any room. There is a good selection of oatmeal soaps, which are supposed to be excellent for the complexion. The store carries a line of decorative bathroom sinks and accessories, and such gift items as potpourri and lace- and flower-adorned baskets.

WILLIAM PAHL
232 W 58th St (bet Broadway and Seventh Ave)
265-6083
Mon-Fri: 9-5:15

The myriad number of artists, models, actresses, and theatrical people whose professions depend upon beauty supplies and cosmetics all seem to name William Pahl as their primary source. And for good reason: not only does the store stock every conceivable type of cosmetic, appliance, and beauty aid, they're all sold at a discount, and most of it is professional quality. L'Oreal, for example, makes a hair mousse in two varieties, one for public consumption and the other for use by hairdressers and salons. The latter is not obtainable by the general public, but Pahl has it, and at a price less than that of the regular product elsewhere. They also know their products. When customers' livelihoods depend upon it, they'd better!

Crafts

A&S GEM AND MINERAL COMPANY
611 Broadway (room 721)
777-6080, 777-6081
Mon-Fri: 9-4; Sat: 10-1

A&S has both precious and semiprecious gems, as well as minerals of all sizes and types. The showroom has five full counters of cut stones, and the wallcases display minerals that weigh from a fraction of an ounce to over 200 pounds. Various stones are on display, and the few spots that are stone-free are stocked with lapidary materials. A&S claims that it carries at least a sampling of every possible type of stone. There are pearls, cabochon and faceted stones, and stone beads. All of these can be cut, ground, or otherwise processed to order for jewelry makers or mineral collectors. In addition, note the antique jade collection (including some super pendants), the stone and ivory carvings, stone boxes, and agate clocks. A word must be said about the attitude here. Perhaps because they are far off the beaten track (at least as far as crafts or jewelry making goes), each customer is treated as an honored guest. When owner Serg Del'Fava died, his wife Anna took over and maintains the tradition.

ALLCRAFT TOOL AND SUPPLY COMPANY
45 W 46th St (third floor)
840-1860
Mon-Fri: 9-4:45

If there is a definitive jewelry-making supply store, Allcraft is it. Its reputation is so old and solid that even the name of its manager, Catherine Grant, is legendary. Allcraft's catalog (write: 60 South MacQuesten Parkway, Mt. Vernon, New York 10550) is so all-inclusive that it's impossible to describe. There is a complete (and it *is* complete) line of tools and supplies for jewelry making, silversmithing, metal smithing, enameling on metal, lost wax casting, and much, much more. Out-of-towners usually deal with the mail-order catalog, but New Yorkers don't miss the opportunity to visit this gleaming cornucopia.

CERAMIC SUPPLY OF N.Y. & N.J.
534 LaGuardia Pl (bet Bleecker and Third St)
475-7236
Mon-Fri: 9-6; Sat: 10-1; closed Sat in summer

Ceramic Supply runs the whole wheel of pottery. They have a school, they sell supplies and equipment, and they hand-make pottery, all from the same location. These people eat and breathe pottery, and their enthusiasm shows through in all of their projects. There are even special programs for the handicapped. If classes aren't convenient, Ceramic Supply has books and materials available for the self-starter. In short, one can do everything at this location from buying an ashtray to casting a mold.

CLAYWORKS
332 E Ninth St (bet First and Second Ave)
677-8311
Fri: 4:30-8:30; Sat: 12:30-8; Sun: 2:15-7;
    call for hours on other days

The most unique feature of Clayworks is that it is a working pottery shop right in the city. You can watch the artist, Helaine Sorgen, at work and ask questions about what is going on. Sorgen is always experimenting with new glazes and clays, as well as new shapes and forms, so you will be able to find some interesting new pieces of decorative and functional handcrafted stoneware and porcelain. You won't see your piece duplicated anywhere, because the majority of the items are one-of-a-kind.

COMMON GROUND
50 Greenwich Ave
989-4178
Mon, Tues, Thurs, Fri: 11:30-7:30; Wed, Sat: 11-6:30;
    Sun: 1-6

Please note that the address is Greenwich *Avenue,* not Greenwich *Street.* Greenwich Avenue is a crosstown street in the Village, and Greenwich Street runs north-south from the Village down into TriBeCa. Coming from Oregon where a multitude of artifacts and crafts are made and sold by the native Indians, I am familiar enough with this kind of merchandise to know that the Common Ground has an excellent selection of American Indian jewelry, rugs, baskets, and the like. The folks in the shop are very proud of their stock, and will take time to explain the origin of each item.

ELDER CRAFTSMEN
846 Lexington Ave (bet 64th and 65th St)
535-8030
Mon: 11-5:30; Tues-Fri: 10-5:30; Sat: 10-4; closed Sat in
    July, Aug

The Elder Craftsmen is a shop that epitomizes all that is great about New York. It is strictly a nonprofit organization. Everything sold here is certifiably handmade by a senior citizen who's at least 60 years old. Often in desperate need of both money and something to do, these talented people are able to satisfy both needs, keeping 60 percent of the purchase price for everything they make (the remaining money goes to operating expenses for the shop). Most of the work is of a higher quality than that of comparable machine-made items.

ERICA WILSON
717 Madison Ave (at 63rd St, second floor)
832-7290
Mon-Wed, Fri, Sat: 10-6; Thurs: 10-7

Erica Wilson is a lady of many talents. This British emigré not only writes books and newspaper columns about needlework, but also finds time to do TV shows and run a store that supplies almost anything a needlework enthusiast would require. There is a huge stock of knitting yarns, ranging from alpaca to cashmere, and the city's finest selection of hand-painted needlepoint patterns from London and elsewhere. You can select hand-knitted sweaters or beautiful accessories from Erica's stock. Her chintz bags are very special. Blocking, padding, mounting, finishing—and classes in these skills—are available at prices that are, well, not inexpensive.

HIRED HAND
1324 Lexington Ave (bet 88th and 89th St)
722-1355
Mon-Fri: 10-6:30; Sat: 10-6; Sun: 11:30-5;
    closed in summer

Hired hand is a busy hand! Fran Stein is busy creating pillows, picture frames, toys, children's clothing, potholders, place mats, quilts, and just about anything that's covered in fabric. Much of the fabric is calico, but there are paisleys and patchworks as well. The Hired Hand would be overjoyed if the hand you hired was your own, and to this end they supply all quilting materials, fabric by the yard, and free instructions.

LESLIE EISENBERG FOLK ART GALLERY
1187 Lexington Ave (bet 80th and 81st St)
628-5454
Mon-Sat: 11-5; closed Sat in summer

Now that quilts have their place beside 18th-century Limoges as items that are venerated as antiques, it shouldn't be surprising to find anything that Leslie Eisenberg stocks being termed as either art or very valuable. Still, it's a bit unsettling to find weather vanes, wood widdles, figureheads, and ship models treated as genuine art. But perhaps the Folk Art Gallery is trying to tell us something, while it is performing the valuable service of preserving it all. All these items—plus the prison art, whirligigs, black folk art, sailor's handiwork, and more—are indeed worthy of being called art; they're the country's heritage in 19th- and 20th-century crafts. Most of it is sculptural, and there are no reproductions. Most of its ilk was thrown out, but that is exactly what makes it so valuable today. Eisenberg treats these items with the respect and veneration their age and workmanship deserves. And much of it is available nowhere else.

LIGHTHOUSE CRAFT SHOP
111 E 59th St
355-2200
Mon-Fri: 10-5

Maria Rodin runs this shop in the Lighthouse Building, which exhibits and sells the work of blind craftsmen. The setup and arrangements are similar to the Elder Craftsmen; the blind craftsman benefits directly from each purchase, and all of the merchandise is strictly professional. The Lighthouse used to be known for its collection of brushes and its chair-caning and reweaving service. It still is. (Chair caning is done by appointment.) But among New Yorkers, the Lighthouse is best known for its twice-a-year celebrity sale.

LOVELIA ENTERPRISES
356 E 41st St (in Tudor City)
490-0930
Mon-Fri: 9:30-5 by appointment only

Lovelia F. Albright and her establishment are one of New York's great finds. From a shop in Tudor City, overlooking the United Nations, she dispenses the finest European Gobelin and Aubusson machine-woven tapestries at a price that is often one-third that of any other place. The tapestries are exquisite. Some of the designs depict the ubiquitous unicorns cavorting in a medieval scene; others are more modern. They come in all sizes. The latest additions include tapestries for upholstery, wool-pile miniature rugs for use as mats under *objets d'art,* and an extensive line of tapestry-woven borders. They're designed by Albright and made exclusively for her in Austria. There is also a very impressive catalog for mail orders.

MUSEUM OF AMERICAN FOLK ART GIFT SHOP
2 Lincoln Sq (Columbus Ave and 66th St)
496-2966
Mon, Tues, Sat: 11-6; Wed, Thurs, Fri: 11-7:30; Sun: 12-6

Some of the best examples of American folk art are for sale in this small museum outlet. Wood carvings, paintings, books, jewelry, glassware, and a wide assortment of gifts will delight the collector. Prices are reasonable, and you won't be seeing the same item in every nifty-gifty store around.

NEW YORK YARN CENTER
29 W 35th St
594-9770
Mon-Wed, Fri: 10-6; Thurs: 10-7; Sat: 10-5

The New York Yarn Center has been turned into a discount establishment, which concentrates heavily on needlecraft items and accessories. They manufacture their own needlepoint and latch hook kits, and they have one of the largest selections of all D.M.C. yarns in the area. You'll find Persian and tapestry yarns, cross-stitch books, kits for cross-stitch, embroidery and crewel, and a tremendous assortment of wools for knitting and crocheting.

PERFORMERS OUTLET
222 E 85th St
249-8435
Tues, Wed, Fri: 12-7; Thurs: 3-8; Sat: 11-5:30

Performers Outlet was started as a cooperative venture to market the non-show-business talents of show-business people who have lots of time and very little money on their hands. The concept worked so well that several would-be performers gave up the lively arts to develop full-time crafts careers. Today, very little of the crafts are of amateur quality, and the standards are so high that very few performers are even represented. Most of the items are made by professional craftsmen from this country and France, and the evolution has been such that the gallery now goes by the name of Francophilia Americana Gallery, as well as Performers Outlet. There is a search service, and craftsmen can be commissioned for specific projects. There is also color coordinating of glass, pottery, rag rugs, picture frames, candles, flowers, and other decorating accessories. The atmosphere is still homey.

SCHOOL PRODUCTS COMPANY
1201 Broadway (bet 28th and 29th St, third floor)
679-3516
Mon-Fri: 9-5; Sat: 10-3

You'll like this one. Despite its name, this company has nothing to do with schools. What it does do is weaving and bookbinding, and it sells all the paraphernalia associated with these occupations. This is the only place in the city that sells spinning wheels for use rather than as conversation pieces. One can even be made from a kit. They also sell knitting machines and instructional videos. School Products has a quarterly sale on yarn, for which mail-order customers will be notified. Orders will be mailed anywhere in the country, so a customer can take advantage of this sale without ever leaving home. Ask to be placed on the mailing list.

SCULPTURE HOUSE
30 E 30th St (near Madison Ave)
679-7474
Mon-Fri: 10-4

In 1918, Bruner F. Barrie's family established a small sculpture and pottery workshop in Manhattan. The business grew and grew, and today, after a move farther downtown, it offers everything necessary for the serious sculptor. Note the *serious,* because Sculpture House, while pleasant and informative, hasn't the time or the space to initiate neophyte sculptors. It's assumed that the customer knows exactly what he wants. Sculpture House offers 16 different types of clay bodies, 12 types of wood suitable for carving, tools for ceramics and pottery, and more than 1,000 wood-carving tools that the Barrie business manufactures itself. While sculpture normally implies ceramics and clay, Claire Brush says that 40 percent of the business is related to wood-carving. Sculpture House offers a wide variety of services as well. There are no formal classes, but every conceivable related book can be found here.

SUNRAY YARN
349 Grand St (bet Essex and Ludlow St)
475-9655
Sun-Fri: 9:30-5; closed one week in July and Dec

Sunray is another of the Lower East Side needlework shops with all of the stock and discounts characteristic of the area. Fortunately, though, it lacks the nasty personnel that's also typical of the area. In addition to the best prices on DMC and precut rug yarns,

Sunray also has yarns for knitting (hand and machine), needlepoint kits and components, stitchery, latch-hook and punch rugs, and crocheting. There is also a brisk business in custom pillow design and needlework framing. Instructors write out knitting and crocheting pattern instructions for customers and help them with any difficulties.

SWEET NELLIE
1262 Madison Ave (at 90th St)
876-5775
Mon-Sat: 10-6

Sweet Nellie is a country place in the heart of the city. In a cozy atmosphere one can find a profusion of vintage fabrics made into pillows, hat boxes, picture frames, and many unusual accessories. There are quilts and antique hooked rugs to go with the one-of-a-kind handcrafts, and tabletops and shelves are chock-full of painted frames, botanical prints, mohair throws, and baskets and painted pottery from talented American artisans. It's like taking a drive through New England!

WOMEN'S EXCHANGE
660 Madison Ave (bet 60th and 61st St)
753-2330
Mon-Fri: 9:30-5:15; Sat: 10-5

The Women's Exchange was started over 100 years ago to provide a marketplace for the crafts of women widowed by the Civil War. Over the years it evolved into a source of income for retired governesses, housekeepers, and down-at-the-heels gentlewomen. In recent years it has regrouped and moved, but the tradition as a showcase for women's crafts continues. They are particularly known for their hand-smocking on children's clothing and their embroidery and needlework on linens and tablecloths. Every item is one-of-a-kind. There are dolls, shawls, mittens, fabrics, pillows, and model furniture for sale. While prices are not cheap, they are certainly competitive. The women receive 75 percent of the sale, so you are helping to support them while dressing your children.

Dance Items

BALLET SHOP
1887 Broadway (bet 62nd and 63rd St)
581-7990
Mon-Sat: 11-8

This shop is a mecca for ballet fans. While the name presupposes that one would be inundated with tutus and leotards, the store has

only a few decorating the walls. The entire display area of the store
is devoted to books, records, and other memorabilia. Available are
new books, gift and novelty items, rare and out-of-print books,
limited editions, albums, programs, posters, art, collector's items,
ballet and opera videotapes, and autographs of stars. I list it all only
to show that truly there are no ballet supplies. But now you know
where to get a Nureyev T-shirt—your choice of several poses.

Department and Major Specialty Stores, Malls

If there is one word to describe the New York department store
scene today it is *change*. What used to be a stable and predictable
operation is no longer so predictable. Some of the old and revered
names in the business—Alexander's, Gimbel's, Korvette—have
either vanished or are about to. The upheaval is in ownership, management, market direction, promotion, and just about every other
phase of the business. At the root of the turmoil has been the real-
ization that many department store chains have some very valuable
real estate; now the store operations seem somewhat secondary. Of
course, all this augurs well for the real-estate tycoons, but what
does it mean for the customers?

The ownership of nearly all the major stores in New York has
changed in the past several years. Some of the new owners are unfamiliar with the New York retail scene, but they are certainly making waves in this fiercely competitive business. They have installed
a new breed of manager (younger, more upwardly mobile, and
more oriented to soft-goods) in the top positions. It used to be that
a major store was a reflection of the owner or manager, like Dorothy Shaver at Lord and Taylor. No longer. About the only established figure still directing things at his store is the legendary Marvin
Traub of Bloomingdale's, but even he has a new boss to report to.

Many of the stores—Saks Fifth Avenue, B. Altman, Lord and
Taylor—are doing major remodeling jobs. Henri Bendel will move
into completely new quarters on Fifth Avenue. Macy's and Bloomingdale's are continually redoing areas on their older floors.

Another almost universal change is in the direction of the merchandising appeal. Practically every store manager I have spoken
to in recent months has said that they are "upgrading" their merchandise and going after the "better customer." How many "better customers" are there? Is there going to be enough of this business to go around for everyone? Where is the not-so-affluent customer going? Is the department store giving up that customer to the
smaller stores, discount houses, and mall chains?

There is also intense competition for the better names in designer
apparel. Again, nearly every one of the major department and spe-

cialty stores is making a play to say, "We have more of the top names." Take a look around and see how many Ralph Lauren boutiques have been installed in the major stores.

For all the emphasis on looking better and attracting upscale customers, the major failing still exists: poorly trained sales personnel. Most store managers give lip service to the need for a massive retraining program for their sales personnel. But in fact, staffs have been cut back nearly everywhere, and as long as store hours remain long (evenings and Sundays), part-time help is essential. Training these workers is extremely difficult. So their knowledge of merchandise is often scanty. Until the major stores find a way to get their clerks to drop their "that isn't my section" attitude and do something about rewarding good salespeople with commission incentives, the problems will remain.

What else are we going to see? Higher prices in most areas. An emphasis on products with higher profit potential, like cosmetics and sportswear. Less and less space devoted to hard goods, like furniture and appliances. And fewer of the conveniences we used to take for granted: free gift wrapping, post offices, waiting rooms, etc. But one thing is certain: you and I are still the real bosses in this business. Rest assured that if we are not happy with the direction taken by the stores, they will change. They must. In the meantime, it pays to shop around. No city in the world has the options and bargains you can find in New York.

One facet of Manhattan life that's surely not the best is the selection of shopping malls. Primarily because of the expensive real-estate costs, most are vertical malls, with all kinds of gimmicks enticing shoppers to explore their upper reaches.

The classiest mall is Trump Tower. Located at the busy corner of Fifth Avenue and 56th Street, it has become one of the major tourist attractions in the city. Many of the expensive boutiques are actually extravagant advertising displays for some of the top names in retailing: Asprey (gifts), Buccellati (silver), Boehm (birds), Harry Winston (jewelry), and Charles Jourdan (shoes). There are also several eating spots, a men's Bonwit Teller store (with direct entrance from the mall to their main store), Abercrombie's (sportswear and accessories), Napoleon (fine clothing for men), and much more. All are ensconced in a dramatic, opulent setting, complete with a huge cascading waterfall.

The most ambitious new project is at the World Financial Center, at Battery Park. In a confusing mélange of buildings, one can visit some of the best-known names in retailing, along with some interesting new faces. The Winter Garden is huge and cold, but there is a wonderful area outside where you can stroll by the river. There are a number of eateries, casual and otherwise, such as

Donald Sacks, Cinco de Mayo, Ecco and Minters. Barney's has a classy entry. Gallery of History sells some of the best historic documents in the country. Il Papiro specializes in beautiful paper goods. And Mark Cross has overpriced leather items and such. If you can find your way around, the place is worth visiting just to marvel at the architecture.

There are just two words to describe Herald Center (at Herald Square, just across from Macy's): *Forget it*. Several floors of dull shops and many empty storefronts make one wonder how Stanley Marcus (of Neiman Marcus fame) ever got involved in this venture. Next door, there's another mall in the old Gimbel's location. A&S operates a store there along with satellite tenants, eating places, and offices. I hope it will turn out to be more appealing than its neighbor.

Pier 17 at the South Street Seaport started off with a bang, but soon began to fizzle. A number of stores and eating places have closed in the Fulton Fish Market building, leaving Pier 17 with a somewhat dull collection of shops. Among the more interesting survivors are Sharper Image (gadgets and gifts), Mariposa (a butterfly gallery), Pavo Real (handicrafts from Peru and Bolivia and Bustamonte figures from Mexico), the Last Wound-up (toys), Rue Britannia (knitwear) and the Weather Store (raingear). Don't bother with the restaurants here, but there are booths in a food-circus promenade that the kids will like.

B. ALTMAN
Fifth Ave at 34th St
679-7800
Mon-Wed, Fri, Sat: 10-7; Thurs: 10-8; Sun: 11-5

If one was to describe the family tree of New York department stores, Bloomies would be the swinging bride, Macy's the family entrepreneur, and B. Altman the kindly, gracious grandmother. Once considered *the* place for upscale New Yorkers to buy quality clothing and home furnishings, Altman's was left behind in the years when fashion excitement became the major focus of Manhattan department stores. However, the store never lost its flair in the home furnishings area. The glassware, china, crystal, and housewares departments have always been tops in the city. Practically every major brand name is represented with depth of stock, and periodic sales of these goods offer some of the year's best bargains. New owners are sprucing up the grand old lady, and perhaps she will come back to reign with class. Let's hope so. You will never go wrong, however, with goods purchased here. They may not always be in the forefront of fashion, but their quality cannot be questioned.

BERGDORF GOODMAN
754 Fifth Ave (at 58th St)
753-7300
Mon-Wed, Fri, Sat: 10-6; Thurs: 10-8

The race for "top of the line" in Manhattan specialty stores has narrowed to Bergdorf's and Saks, with Barney's coming up a strong third. Ira Neimark and Dawn Mello, who orchestrate every phase of this upscale operation, know exactly who their customer is, and they are doing a great job catering to the affluent man and woman. Offering a superb location on Fifth Avenue near Central Park, Bergdorf's has been completely redone, with attractive boutiques on every floor and a convenient vertical transportation system. Just about every top fashion name (many are theirs exclusively) is prominently displayed with a stunning selection of merchandise. Furs and evening wear are specialties. The top floor presents a series of home-accessory rooms, where the taste level is so high you will want to walk out with one of each in linens, gifts, china, glassware, silver, and antiques. Two intimate eating places entice the well-heeled lady to spend the day at this emporium of style. The sales-help are well-trained, snooty, and have little time for the less-spendy customer. A new Bergdorf's for men in the former F.A.O. Schwarz location directly across Fifth Avenue presents a superb collection of nearly every famous name in men's wear. Bergdorf's will now be a major factor in the better men's business, giving Saks and Barney's a run for their money.

BLOOMINGDALE'S
1000 Third Ave
355-5900
Mon, Thurs: 10-9; Tues, Wed, Fri, Sat: 10-6:30;
       Sun: 12-6

Bloomingdale's has become a "way of life" in New York. And rightfully so. A superb eye for the newest and the most exciting merchandise for men, women, children, and the home, combined with a flair for the dramatic unequalled today by any other retailing institution, has put Bloomies (along with Harrod's of London) on the cutting edge of department stores worldwide. Women can find department after dazzling department of top fashion names. New and vastly improved men's departments offer a similarly extensive selection for the gentleman shopper. In home furnishings, no one in the city can equal Bloomingdale's. "The Main Course" floor offers shop after shop of trendy, attractive goods for the home; the fabulous model rooms change several times a year. Visiting them is a special experience in itself. Then there are numerous places to nibble and dine around the store, with Le Train Bleu (fine dining in a simulated railroad car) at the top of the line. A great food selection, with adjacent candy and bakery sections, also attract the hungry shopper. There are even areas with merchandise made especially for Bloomies. Of course, there are shortcomings: service can be maddening, furniture delivery takes much too long, and finding just the item you want when the selection is so vast and scattered can be difficult. But this is *it,* ladies and gentlemen. Marvin Traub and Les Gribetz have a clear and consistent vision of what Bloomingdale's is and what it isn't, and their talents are very apparent to any observer of the current New York retail scene.

BONWIT TELLER
4 E 57th St (bet Fifth and Madison Ave)
593-3333
Mon-Wed, Fri: 10-7; Thurs: 10-8; Sat: 10-6; Sun: 12-5

With a great location on busy 57th Street and connected directly to Trump Tower, you would expect big things from this once-famous name in retailing. Unfortunately, Bonwit's has been another victim of the all-too-prevalent retail affliction of not knowing who your customer is. In cramped, claustrophobic quarters with uncomfortably low ceilings and a poor vertical transportation system, Bonwit's today is just another store. Shoppers will find an appealing enough selection of quality goods, but there is no excitement and no special reason to shop here. Of course, one of the real advantages is the access to the facilities of Trump Tower, and that does make up for some of the shortcomings. There is a separate and rather well-done men's store on the lower level of the Trump building.

HENRI BENDEL
10 W 57th St
247-1100
Mon-Wed, Fri, Sat: 10-6; Thurs: 10-8; Sun: 12-5

The svelte, social movers and shakers used to make this specialty emporium their headquarters. Under Geraldine Stultz, Bendel's symbolized a lifestyle, and there was intense customer loyalty. Alas, the times changed, the competition grew, and Bendel's fell on hard times. Then Leslie Waxman (of the Limited fame) came to rescue the fading lady. He has indeed altered the exclusivity of the store, and you'd have a hard time explaining the difference between Bendel's and the Limited today. The merchandise is trendier, down a tad price-wise, and more keyed to the working girl. She still shops in a boutique atmosphere, with a good deal of personal service offered. But the focus is fuzzy. Perhaps when the new quarters on Fifth Avenue opens there will be a blood transfusion. Those who remember the classic Bendel's are crossing their fingers.

LORD & TAYLOR
424 Fifth Ave (at 39th St)
391-3344
Mon, Thurs: 10-8:30; Tues, Wed, Fri, Sat: 10-6:45;
   Sun: 12-6

Old-time New Yorkers affectionately remember the days when Dorothy Shaver ran Lord and Taylor. She was one of the first female managers of a major department store, and she showed them all how it should be done. Her store was upfront in the fashion world, focusing on the young career woman and young housewife. Upon her retirement, it was downhill all the way. New management didn't have the taste and flair, and the merchandise and physical appearance of the store showed it. The modernization of the street floor several years ago is one of the most unattractive face-lifts ever. With the new owners, May Company, you can expect middle-of-the-road merchandise. Some of the ready-to-wear sections are worth shopping, especially the sportswear, but forget the men's sections. A real attraction each year are the Christmas windows, some of the best in New York.

MACY'S
151 W 34th St (at Herald Sq)
695-4400
Mon, Thurs, Fri: 9:45-8:30; Tues, Wed: 9:45-6:45;
   Sat: 10-6:45; Sun: 10-6

"The World's Largest Department Store" sits in the hub of Manhattan, at Herald Square, with access by car, bus, and subway in every direction. You may remember the old days when it was Macy's versus Gimbels, but Gimbels has bitten the dust and the merchandising giant has little competition from its current neighbor, the dull and unappealing Herald Center. However, new life may be pumped into this busy area with the opening of the A&S Center, a new collection of retail outlets. The major competitor for

Macy's these days is Bloomies, and the battle has really heated up. Section after section of Macy's is constantly undergoing a face-lift, and the results are highly successful. Personnel training has not been as successful. No longer does one equate dowdy styles with this store; their ready-to-wear departments carry a broad range of goods for every pocketbook, including top fashion names. Other special areas include a huge men's furnishings section, a great "Cellar" featuring fine foodstuffs, home appliances and accessories, and other tantalizing boutiques. The cosmetic section is dazzling, as are a number of the home furnishings departments. In today's New York, the two giants offer the shopping public a selection like no other city in the United States. Bloomies still has the edge with glamour and excitement, but they are keeping one eye peeled on the rejuvenated behemoth in midtown!

SAKS FIFTH AVENUE
611 Fifth Ave (at 50th St)
753-4000
Mon-Wed, Fri, Sat: 10-6:30; Thurs: 10-8

For years, Saks has been a reliable source for quality merchandise for every member of the family, from the newborn to the retired gentleman of the house. But this is a store that keeps up with the times; there is nothing stodgy about Saks. Several years ago a magnificent escalator system was installed, and an adjacent space next to the building will house expanded merchandise lines in every classification. The fashion-savvy businesswoman will find an appealing array; the society matron will enjoy shopping among the top designer names of the world; the budget-conscious shopper will be rewarded with excellent values during periodic sales. Children's clothes, furs, designer clothes, cosmetics, and men's suits are outstanding. For the latter, ask for Dennis Weiner. He is one of those special salesmen who really takes an interest in his customers. By the way, gentlemen, any lady in your life will utter a special "aaah" when presented with a gift box from Saks Fifth Avenue.

Display Accessories

NIEDERMAIER DISPLAY
435 Hudson St
675-1106
Mon-Fri: 9—5

The main business here is conducted in trade shows. Niedermaier designs and creates all kinds of displays, and they are considered tops in the business. They usually discourage retail customers looking for just "the right thing" for some special need at home or the office, but if you talk nicely (and mention this book) they probably will take care of you. Think of the fun you can have with all kinds of model pieces of human anatomy at that next birthday party!

Domestics

AD HOC SOFTWARES
410 W Broadway (at Spring St)
925-2652
Mon-Sat: 11:30-7; Sun: 11:30-6

This store is perfectly named, since it supplies exactly that—soft textures for the computer age. There are sleek sheets and chic exercise equipment, alongside hot-tub bath towels and bathroom and small table accessories. This is one soft spot, and I have a real soft spot for a bathroom that is cozy, comfortable, and convenient. Ad Hoc can help make yours that way!

CACHE-CACHE
888 Madison Ave (bet 71st and 72nd St)
744-6886, 744-7060
Mon-Sat: 10-6

The real attraction here are accessories for the home, and a great selection of antique, wedding, and English Victorian gift items. If you are invited out to dinner or for a weekend visit, this is the place to shop for that very special gift. There are linens, neck pillows, sterling-silver photo frames, candle shades, picture bows, and fabulous beaded and embroidered antique pillows. Cache-Cache is the Tiffany of New York's domestic shops. As for the prices, well, there is a reason why the name is pronounced "cash-cash"!

D. PORTHAULT
18 E 69th St
688-1660
Mon-Fri: 10-6; Sat: 10-5

Porthault, the French queen of linens, needs no introduction. Custom-made linens are available in a range of 600 designs (or more, if you count custom designs), several scores of colors, and weaves of super luxurious density. Wherever the name Porthault appears (some fancy hotels), you know they run a top-notch operation. The folks here are definitely top-notch. Their printed sheets seem to last forever; they're passed along from one generation to another. Porthault can handle custom work of an intricate nature for odd-sized beds, baths, and showers. Specialties include signature prints; printed terry towels; decorative accessories like trays, wastebaskets, tissue box covers, drawer liners, and room sprays; and a large selection of other unusual gift items.

EZRA COHEN
307 Grand St (at Allen St)
925-7800
Sun-Fri: 9-5

Ezra Cohen is the first of the Lower East Side linen and dry-goods stores you encounter when coming from Allen Street. While the entire street—on both sides—is lined with them, Ezra Cohen is the only one you really need to know. Its floors are stocked with the finest linens, bedspreads, quilts, and draperies at prices that, at the very least, match the department stores' sale prices. Quality is always top-notch, and at a time when bed linens have styles and fashions like clothing, Ezra Cohen not only has what's current, but what will become current. The first floor is dedicated primarily to linens, and most customers never go any farther, since the vast selection can make up complete trousseaus. The second floor is dedicated to bed coverings, and note the use of the word. It used to display bedspreads by Nettlecreek and custom-made designs, but as the "unmade" bed motif has spread, it has adapted as well. Today, it has coverlet, comforter, and sheet ensembles and such hard-to-find items as sheets for water beds and throws and comforters for platform beds. Ezra Cohen features Croscill products in the bedspread department. There is also a great selection of pillows. There are custom-made comforters, dust ruffles, pillow shams, and custom-sized sheets and blanket covers, as well as vertical blinds and all types of custom draperies. Lighter drapery is on the first floor, along with the Fieldcrest and Martex towel lines. Ezra Cohen has been a family business for as many generations as it has floors. The current generation—Bob, Jerry, Marvin, and Dave Cohen—are great people, who are as well versed as their ancestors in selling the best for the least.

J. SCHACHTER
85 Ludlow St (near Delancey St)
533-1150
Mon-Thurs: 9-5; Fri: 9-2; Sun: 9-4

J. Schachter's is the foremost purveyor of quilts in the New York area and perhaps the entire continent. If your grandparents had a quilt, at one time in its life it probably had some connection with

Schachter's. It was either purchased, restuffed, mended, or sewn anew there, but somewhere, at some point, almost all but those quilts in museums have been to Schachter's. In the days before the home-crafts and conmforter craze in home decorating, Schachter's managed to do a good business. Today, when everyone owns not only quilted coverlets but down-filled jackets and hoods, Schachter's business is booming. This is the oldest quilting firm in New York, and Schachter's knows everything there is to know about quilts and their making. The talents of the staff are almost infinite. They can make a quilt in any size and in one of 20 quilting patterns from any fabric given to them. Schachter's has a complete line of linens as well as quilts. Custom sleeping pillows can be made while you wait. When both lines are combined, entire bedrooms or bathrooms, from rugs to ceiling and wall covering, can be completely coordinated.

PILLOW SALON
238 E 60th St
755-6154
Mon-Thurs: 10-6; Fri: 10-5

Pillows are king here. Pillow Salon's complete line changes constantly, but always involves unique designs. There are decorative pillows, custom-made pillows, and antique textile pillows, all of which are available to the trade and general public.

PRATESI LINENS
839 Madison Ave (at 69th St)
288-2315
Mon-Sat: 10-6

Pratesi says it carries the best linens the world has to offer, and they're probably right. Families hand them down for generations. In fact, the new customers are probably people who didn't have affluent ancestors and/or those who wish to avail themselves of the two new collections, which come out in the spring and fall. The only other reason to buy new Pratesi linens (since they don't wear out) can be redecorating needs. The Pratesi staff is unexcelled in coordinating linens to décor or creating the custom look. Nearly all of the linens are of natural fiber cloth (the upstairs maid can always do the ironing!), although there are some easy-care versions of late. The three-story store boasts a winter garden, which sets the mood for the luxurious linens. Towels are made in Italy exclusively for Pratesi and are of a quality and thickness that has to be felt to be believed. Bath robes are magnificent—again in natural fibers, again plush, and again quietly understated. So are the price tags. The baby boutique has been expanded.

TIGER'S EYE
157 W 72nd St (bet Broadway and Columbus Ave)
496-8488
Mon-Wed, Fri, Sat: 10-7; Thurs: 10-8; Sun: 1-6;
    closed Sun in summer

Tiger's Eye offers the Upper West Side one of the largest selections of bath towels, shower curtains, bathroom rugs and accessories, shower heads, robes, toilet seats, sheets and bedding in the city. This is truly a bedroom and bathroom specialty store. Pillows, rugs, and window treatments can be custom-ordered to match other accessories in your home. This is a "must visit" for those who are planning to remodel or for those who have just moved into new digs.

Electronics, Appliances

AST SOUND
250 W Broadway (bet Walker and White St)
226-7781
Mon-Fri: 9-5:30; Sat: 10-4

This is a city of professional audio people, whose knowledge ranges from expert to genius. Audio Speaker Techtronics is the largest speaker repair house in the area and, in fact, in the entire East. The large showroom displays as much of their merchandise as they can cram into the space. There are loud speakers, speaker systems, mixers, headphones, microphones, signal processors and effects, dividing networks, power amplifiers, and equipment cases. The specialties are pro sound, commercial and high-end hi-fi. Audio Speaker Techtronics also repairs everything it sells, though it wasn't dubbed the "largest repair house" because of repairs on their own models. (Let's hope not.)

BERNIE'S DISCOUNT CENTER
821 Sixth Ave (bet 28th and 29th St)
564-8582, 564-8758
Mon-Fri: 9-5:30; Sat: 11-3:30; closed in July, Aug

Bernie is nowhere to be seen, but the *discount* in the store's name is certainly apt. If you want to get first-class treatment, ask for

George Vargas. Bernie's was the first appliance dealer in the country to discount the 1000 RCA Selectavision video recorder *before* the machine officially came out and at a time when it was the most popular item in town. Among the things that Bernie's stocks are electrical appliances, TVs, videogames, phone machines, radios, tape recorders, and air conditioners. The discount on these items is better at some of the other stores mentioned here, but Bernie's is more conveniently located. Bernie's also services what it sells.

BONDY EXPORT
40 Canal St
925-7785, 925-7786
Sun-Thurs: 10-6; Fri: 10-3

Bondy is typical of the Lower East Side appliances stores. It's also one of my favorites. It is newer, cleaner, and better stocked than many of the others, and the wait never seems to be interminable. Bondy is family-run by the Feigelsteins, all of whom are very friendly (I have never heard a cross word), and they really do try to help. When I wanted a set of Corelle, they asked how old the recipient was. I couldn't understand why they needed that information until they told me which pattern was most popular with people of that specific group. The stock includes all electrical appliances—major and small, many of which are available in 220 volts—cameras, components, dishes, telephones, luggage, watches, sunglasses, and tableware—all brand names and all discounted. Bondy's prices are consistently low, and it is one place where I do not bother to comparison-shop.

GREATER NEW YORK TRADING
81 Canal St (bet Eldridge and Allen St)
226-2808, 226-2809, 226-8850
Mon-Thurs: 10-6; Fri: 10-3; Sun: 9:30-6

Perhaps influenced by its proximity to the Jewelry Exchange on the Lower East Side, the Greater New York Trading Corporation dabbles in fine housewares while selling appliances. In addition to the toasters, VCRs, TVs, stereos, and refrigerators that almost everyone else carries, Greater New York stocks all types of china, silverware (even discontinued silver patterns), and gifts. All are sold at good discounts. Despite the location and the fact that it carries brands and products not readily available elsewhere, prices are said to be wholesale. Even more than the prices, I liked the personnel's boast, "Every one of our staff smiles and is helpful." It matters to them, and that certainly matters to me. In this messy store, one can unearth great buys on brand-name crystal, china, and flatware unavailable elsewhere on the Lower East Side.

HARVEY ELECTRONICS
2 W 45th St (near Fifth Ave)
575-0527
Mon-Fri: 9:30-6; Sat: 10-6

Not everyone understands all the fine points of the new technology flooding the markets these days. For those who need advice and individual attention, Harvey's is the place to shop for consumer electronics. They offer top-of-the-line audio and video components and fully integrated audio and video systems. It's a good idea to avoid shopping here during the noon hour, when the personnel seem to be too busy to give their usual standard of service.

J&R MUSIC WORLD
23 Park Row (one block south of City Hall)
732-8600
Mon-Sat: 9-6:30

These folks bill themselves as New York's most complete home entertainment department store, and I believe them. You can find shelf after shelf of cameras, radios, televisions, speaker systems, VCRs, cassette and CD players, personal electronics, records and tapes and discs, computer systems, telephone answering machines, telephones, typewriters, microwave ovens, and even bread makers. The place is well organized but gets rather hectic at times. The prices are very competitive, and they guarantee all their merchandise.

SHARPER IMAGE
4 W 57th St (at Fifth Ave)
265-2550
Mon-Wed, Fri: 10-7; Thurs: 10-8; Sat: 10-6; Sun: 12-5

If you are a gadget freak like me, you'll go wild at the Sharper Image. This is truly a man's toy store! The very latest in electronic gadgets, household helpers, sports items, games and novelties makes browsing in this fascinating emporium a unique experience. Vinnie Trinkwald, the able manager, and his well-trained crew seem to delight in demonstrating things you'll think you just can't live without. Like the spray that allows you to see through an envelope without opening it and then dries without a trace! While the little lady looks at the jewels across the street at Tiffany's, you can take a look at the more esoteric jewels at this establishment. There's also a branch on Pier 17 at the South Street Seaport.

SPECTRA RESEARCH GROUP
762 Madison Ave (bet 65th and 66th St)
744-2255
Mon-Sat: 9-6

Spectra promotes itself as offering electronic solutions to contemporary problems. If that problem includes being overheard on the telephone, not being able to find and work a pocket-sized computer, or having difficulty spelling *deceive* (is it *ei* or *ie*?), then Spectra can be of great help. While the unreliable Fifth Avenue electronics stores major in customer deception and price rip-off, these people have a one-price policy and offer only state-of-the-art items. After years of being cramped in quarters so small that customers had to vie for space with saleshelp who were eating from odiferous platters atop the adjoining counter, Spectra has moved into larger and more convenient quarters that allows them to show a wider variety of the latest in electronic gear. And they are reliable.

THOR EXPORT SALES COMPANY
1225 Broadway (room 608)
679-0077
Mon-Fri: 10-5:30

Visitors from abroad most often view the New York market as a place to pick up quality appliances at favorable rates. For many, though, their native lands operate on 220 volt/50 cycle electricity, so the American products are of no use in their homes. While some of the Lower East Side stores carry dual-voltage and 220 appliances, Thor is the only store in the area (and possibly the continent) that deals exclusively with those appliances. Thor's name, in fact, is probably better known among the United Nations staff, airline crews, and visitors than it is among natives of the city. That's because the company has been catering to those people for over 40 years, while very few natives have a need for that type of wiring. (In fact, I had never heard of them. Enzo Borges, Thor's president, bought this book at the South Street Seaport and informed me that he thought his company should be included. He was right.) In any event, years of experience have made Thor the expert in the field. They help relocating executives, stateside folks sending gifts abroad, and of course tourists. For the latter, there are dual-voltage appliances, which can be used both before and after the trip.

UNCLE STEVE

343 Canal St (at Church St)
226-4010
Mon-Sat: 9:30-6:30;
　Sun: 11-5:30

216 W 72nd (bet Broadway
　and W End Ave)
874-3317
Mon-Fri: 11-8; Sat: 10-7;
　Sun: 11-5:30

So you're convinced that no one with any regard for his wallet would buy appliances, dishes, televisions, or cameras at retail? Good. But what if the Lower East Side mob scene turns you off? Well, you can try "appliances by phone" brokers, but those who have reliable businessmen behind their phone voices are few and far between. Perhaps the only store in the business that is both price competitive on the phone *and* in the store is Uncle Steve. Uncle Steve will quote prices over the phone (which few other discount appliance stores will do), but you should visit him at least once. Your *real* Uncle Steve probably couldn't give you a better price if he were in the business. In addition to top-notch service, he has great contacts who supply the store with almost any electrical item, along with super service. In survey after survey of discount appliance dealers in the city, Uncle Steve is consistently on top of the list. He almost always manages to deliver the best prices. If you have but one stop to make before you buy an appliance, make it Uncle Steve's.

VICMARR STEREO AND TV

88 Delancey St
505-0380
Sun-Fri: 9-6

In the middle of famed Delancey Street on the Lower East Side, Mal Cohen presides over a treasure house of electronics, including microwave ovens, stereo and hi-fi equipment, telephones, and camcorders, as well as such items as organs, sunglasses, fans, and answering machines. Unlike many electronics outfits, this place has all the items on display, well organized and marked, with none of the high-pressure selling you often encounter. Best of all, the prices are right, and you can be assured you are not getting secondhand merchandise. Vicmarr is one of the largest JVC outlets in the area. You can save yourself some time by calling and getting an idea of prices by telephone.

WAVES

32 E 13th St (bet University Pl and Fifth Ave)
989-9284
Tues-Fri: 12-6; Sat: 12-5

The past lives on at Waves, and Bruce and Charlotte Mager try to make it last forever with their collection of vintage record players, radios, receivers, and televisions. They have scorned the electronic age in favor of the age of radio; their shop is a virtual shrine to the 1930s and before. Here you'll find the earliest radios (still operative) and their artifacts. There are even radio promotion pieces, such as a radio-shaped cigarette lighter and recording discs (as in crank-handled phonographs, not video recorders). Gramophones and anything dealing with the radio age are available, and Waves is capable of repairing privately owned instruments. Waves also rents its phonographs, telephones, neon clocks, and photographica (sic) for media shoots. They also make appraisals, and will help with any questions on repair, sale, or rental.

Fabrics, Trimmings

A.A. FEATHER COMPANY (GETTINGER FEATHER CORPORATION)
16 W 36th St (bet Fifth and Sixth Ave, eighth floor)
695-9470
Mon-Thurs: 9-5; Fri: 9-2; closed July 1-10

What if you've made a quilt and want to stuff it with feathers? What if your latest outfit just has to have an ostrich plume, feather fan, or feather boa? Well, in New York, you're in luck with A.A. Feather, a.k.a. Gettinger Feather Corporation. The Gettingers have been in the business since 1915 and have passed the trade down from grandfather to father to Dan Gettinger, who is the first Gettinger's grandson. There aren't many such family businesses around now, and there are even fewer sources for really fine quality feathers. This is a find!

A. FEIBUSCH—ZIPPERS & THREADS
33 Allen St
226-3964
Mon-Fri: 9-5; Sun: 9-4; closed Sun in summer

Would you believe a large store dedicated entirely to zippers? Well, in New York, nothing is impossible. One of the many amusing aspects of my visit here was hearing the boast, "We have one of the biggest selections of zippers in the U.S.A." *One* of the biggest selections? It's as if they really think there are zipper stores throughout the country! Anyway, Feibusch has zippers in every size, style, and color, and if it's not in stock, they will make it to order. There isn't too much of a demand for that service, however, since there are 200 colors in stock, in an almost infinite selection of sizes and styles. Should you need the matching thread to sew in a zipper, Feibusch carries that as well. A selection of threads rivaling the amazing number of zippers is available in all varieties. Eddie Feibusch assured me that no purchase is too small or too large. When I saw one woman purchase tiny zippers for doll clothes, I wasn't sure if that meant physical or financial size. In both senses, he was right. And he gives each customer prompt, personal service.

ART MAX FABRICS
250 W 40th St
398-0755, 398-0754, 398-0756
Mon-Fri: 8:30-6; Sat: 9-5

The fabric wholesale district is conveniently adjacent to the garment district, and the usual retail-shopper traditions of that area apply here. Some stores welcome the retail customer, some don't, and some fluctuate with the market. Art Max is dedicated to the retail customer. Its three floors are filled to overflowing with outstanding fabrics for clothing. Notice that I didn't mention the person who sews at home, for while there are hundreds of fabrics for home stitchers, the really striking brocades, metallics, and laces require an experienced touch. It would be a shame for a novice to ruin such beautiful fabrics. The real specialty here, however, is bridal fabrics. When the fabrics mentioned above are made into gowns, the wedding party could rival a *Vogue* layout. There are even a dozen different types of nets for bridal veils and infinite combinations of heavier materials. Try to get a look at the fabrics in the basement, not so much for the fabrics as for the basement. It looks like the catacombs!

CINDERELLA FLOWER AND FEATHER COMPANY
60 W 38th St
840-0644
Mon-Fri: 8-5:15; Sat: 9-4:15

A few years back, in the midst of a particularly cold and dreary winter, Seventh Avenue fashions began to blossom with artificial flowers in every possible spot as the "in" look for spring. The department stores quickly got the message, and in just a few weeks, people were removing their fur-lined gloves to hand $10 over the counter for a single flower for their lapel. Many of these transactions were made along 34th Street or Fifth Avenue, and only a few wise New Yorkers walked an extra two blocks to the "trimmings district," where they could have bought the identical flower for 35 cents. There were even buyers of the $10 *variety* who *knew* of the district and assumed that they couldn't get in. Cinderella Flower and Feather Company is for them. Jonathan Wolff, Cinderella's president, brags that they have the country's largest selection of feather trimmings, decorations, craft supplies, and conversation pieces, as well as silk and other artificial flowers. "And," he adds, "since we're the importer, our prices are unbeatable."

FABRIC WAREHOUSE
406 Broadway (bet Canal and Walker St)
431-9510
Mon-Wed, Fri: 9-6; Thurs: 9-7:30; Sat, Sun: 10-5

Fabric Warehouse is a store that has three very full floors of every imaginable kind of fabric and trimming, and since all of it is sold at discount prices, it's one of the best places to buy fabrics. Some of the attractions include an extensive wool collection and such dressy fabrics as chiffon, crepe, silks, and satin. There's enough to equip a wedding *and* all the guests. But most amazing are the bargain spots, where remnant and odd pieces go for so little it's laughable. Since the Fabric Warehouse isn't exactly in the heart of the city, they sell patterns, notions, and trimmings at the same low prices, with the same excellent selection, so that customers don't have to make several stops.

FAR EASTERN FABRICS
171 Madison Ave (at 33rd St)
683-2623
Mon-Fri: 9-5

Far Eastern Fabrics is a small company that imports and retails some of the world's lushest fabrics from some of the world's most exotic places. From India, there are cotton prints, madras cottons, brocades, and silks. There are even silk saris and stoles. From China, there are more brocades and silks, but China also offers damasks and woven and Jacquard tussah silk. Indonesia is represented by batiks, weavings, and cotton sarongs. Japanese silk pongee is among the cheapest silk Far Eastern offers, while Thailand is represented with a selection of cotton prints and silk scarves and stoles. And to show that Far Eastern is really global in its intent to pick the finest and the best, there are striking wax and java print cottons from the Netherlands. Prices for these often unique fabrics are excellent, and there are discounts offered for trade orders.

GAMPEL SUPPLY
39 W 37th St (bet Fifth and Sixth Ave)
398-9222
Mon-Fri: 8:30-4

This is the kind of business New York does best—esoteric. The sole stock in trade here is beads, and they know more about them than you will ever need to know. Just make a request, and you'll find that they have it—cheap. While single beads go for a dollar each at a department store one block away, Gampel sells them by bulk for a fraction of that price. Though they prefer to deal in bulk and at wholesale, individual customers are treated as courteously as if they were institutions, and the wholesale prices remain the same for all. As for the stock, well, a visit to Gampel is an education. Pearlized beads alone come in over 20 different guises, and they are used for everything from bathroom curtains to earrings and flowers. Since many of its customers are craftspeople, Gampel diverges slightly from its specialty to sell a few craft supplies—for bead-related crafts only. They stock needles, cartwheels, cord and chains (in enough different styles to match each bead), threads, poly bags, jewelry tools, and jewelry findings.

HANDLOOM BATIK
214 Mulberry St (at Spring St)
925-9542
Wed-Sat: 11-7; Sun: 1-6; Mon, Tues by appointment

Note the hours here since the limited time can be a problem for anyone who wants to see one of the best collections of batiks outside a crafts museum. Carol Berlin runs Handloom Batik with near reverence for her merchandise. All of the fabrics are handmade, and she is quick to show how each can be set off to its best advantage. Imported hand-woven and hand-batiked fabrics (primarily from India and Indonesia) are sold by the yard as fabric, or made up as clothing, napkins, tablecloths, or handiwork. Handloom Batik will also use its own fabrics for custom-made shirts and other garments. In addition, there is a gift selection featuring handicrafts of wood, stone, brass, and paper from the aforementioned countries. Pillows, bed covers, curtains, and napkins can be custom-made from the store's 100 percent cotton ikat and cotton batik. Incidentally, Carol Berlin says that collection is the largest in the country.

HARRY ZARIN FABRIC WAREHOUSE
72 Allen St (at Grand St)
925-6112
Sun-Fri: 9-5:30

This is a square city block containing all kinds of decorative upholstery and drapery fabrics, as well as window treatments, vertical blinds, mini blinds, draperies, and cornices. Custom-made window treatments are a specialty, and prices are discounted. A complementary supply business at 105 Eldridge Street features rods, trimmings, and other necessary accessories.

HOME TEXTILES

132A Spring St (bet Greene and Wooster St)
431-0411
Mon-Fri: 11-7; Sat, Sun: 12-5:30

SoHo used to be an industrial area, where there were several wholesale fabric and upholstery firms that we recommended. But that was before SoHo became residential. Now the neighborhood has come full circle. The people living in the former factory workrooms need home-decorating textiles and craftsmen, and now SoHo has its first local retail fabric store. What makes it interesting is that in a neighborhood that is distinctly "artsy," Home Textile specializes in exactly that: domestic and international textiles for the home. In addition to claiming title to the largest collection of fabrics for upholstery, window treatments, bed linens, slipcovers and cushions, they also maintain an in-house workroom. A customer can have an entire home-decorating job done at one location. Out-of-towners can ask for the "swatch on file" system, which allows them to take home dozens of samples and then complete the entire transaction by mail. Another bonus is that by having one shop do everything, there is accountability.

HYMAN HENDLER AND SONS

67 W 38th St (at Fifth Ave)
840-8393
Mon-Fri: 9-5:30

Although Hyman Hendler has passed away, the store that proudly features his name is in the capable hands of his sons and niece. In the middle of what may be the trimmings center of the world, Hyman Hendler is one of the oldest businesses (established in 1900) and probably the crown head of the ribbon field. This organization manufactures, wholesales, imports, and acts as a jobber for every kind of ribbon imaginable. It's really hard to believe there really exists as many variations as are jammed into this store.

INTERCOASTAL TEXTILE CORPORATION

480 Broadway (at Broome St)
925-9235
Mon-Thurs: 9-6; Fri: 9-5; closed first two weeks in July;
    Sun: 10-4 (Oct to Dec)

Intercoastal is an eight-story shop that carries decorator fabrics at wholesale prices. You must buy ample amounts of a particular item and know what you want when you come. The employees are accustomed to dealing with large department stores and decorators.

Bloomcraft, Scalamandre, and Schumacker are some of the name brands that can be found here.

LEATHER FACTS
262 W 38th St (bet Seventh and Eighth Ave)
382-2788
Mon-Fri: 9:30-6; Sat: 11-30-3:30

Francois George dispenses all matter of leather, suede, and exotic skins. Not clothing—just skins. The clothing showroom at 247 West 38th Street is where many of the skins turned into garments are sold, but there is no longer a connection between the two showrooms. Nowadays George concentrates upon actual skins and nothing else.

LEW NOVIK
45 W 38th St (at Fifth Ave)
354-5046, 221-8960
Mon-Fri: 9-5; Sat: 9:30-2:30

Lew Novik takes advantage of its location at the intersection of the wholesale millinery and fabric districts and dispenses both products. The millinery is primarily bridal in nature, and there is an enormous selection of lace, veils, flowers, light flower hair sprays, and bridesmaid hats. The bridal mantillas and illusion veils are particularly noteworthy. Accompanying the bridal millinery is a good collection of bridal accessories and favors and good-looking fabrics for made-to-order gowns. The fabric department excels in bridal fabrics, and the lace collection is extensive. There is also a selection of metallic fabrics that shimmer even on the bolt. As gowns, they must be magnificent.

PARON FABRICS
60 W 57th St (bet Fifth and Sixth Ave)
247-6451
Mon-Sat: 9-6; Sun: 11-3 (closed Sun: Dec-Feb, July,
    Aug)

Amazingly, you can find an excellent selection of designer fabrics uptown at discount prices! Paron carries the very latest, and many of their goods are available only in their store. At their outlet (Paron II, 56 W 57th St, fourth floor) you can find a large selection of quality goods priced up to 50 percent off. This is a family operation, so personal attention is assured. Hard-to-find Vogue and Burda patterns are also available.

PIERRE DEUX FABRICS AND ACCESSORIES

870 Madison Ave (at 71st St)   369 Bleecker St
570-9343   243-7740
Mon-Sat: 10-6

Pierre Deux used to be an antiques shop that specialized in French provincial furniture. As such, it was one of the best. A few years ago, this store branched out into fabrics and fabric accessories. Today, Pierre Deux is synonymous with imported fabrics, tapestries, bags, tablecloths, and the like, all sold with the same attitude that characterized the antiques shop. The extraordinary cotton fabrics and the various accessories made from them are the store's highlights. Business is so good that Pierre Deux is gaining a nationwide reputation. The bags here are as much, if not more, of a status symbol as those of French designers. They are selectively distributed to better stores around the country. Antiques can be found at the Bleecker Street store.

SAMUEL BECKENSTEIN

125 Orchard St
130 Orchard St
475-4525
Sun-Fri: 9-5:30

Samuel Beckenstein began business as a pushcart peddler in 1918. When he prospered, he opened a store selling wools for men's garments. Over the years, he became the definitive source for good wools, especially imported ones. Today, three men of the third generation preside over the empire born on that pushcart, and the reputation is meticulously maintained. The main branch is still devoted to woolen fabrics for men's wear, but there are gabardines, polyesters, and others as well. Customers include large stores, private tailors, and individuals who want fabric for custom-made suits. The branch at 130 Orchard Street is now a full trimmings and appliqué supply shop. At the main store, there are couture fabrics, Shetland woolens, home-decorating and upholstery fabrics, as well as some of the most fantastic brocades this side of Damascus. Beckenstein's has a section for home sewers, as well as a home-decorating department that will make up custom slipcovers and matching draperies. The quality fabric sold wholesale at Beckenstein's is not readily available elsewhere at any price. It's worth a trip to the Lower East Side just to see the selection.

SHERU ENTERPRISES
49 W 38th St (near Fifth Ave)
730-0766
Mon-Fri: 9-6; Sat: 9:30-5

Sheru is almost impossible to describe. If you're into hobbies, crafts, or do-it-yourself decorating, Sheru has what you need. If you are an incurable bargain hunter, Sheru will satisfy your wildest dreams. And if you are none of these things, Sheru will guide, teach, and instruct you. Officially, Sheru is a wholesaler of beads and trimmings. Its stockpile includes bases for clips, shoe clips, ear posts, trimmings, artificial flowers, cords, ribbons, notions, buttons, and stringing supplies. You will need help from the friendly personnel, because these treasures are thrown about. Without a guide, many may well be overlooked. Antiquated and unwanted things are stored in the basement in probably the most haphazard order in the entire city. Amazingly, Mr. I. Sherwin seems to know what's down there.

SILK SURPLUS
223 E 58th St (near Second Ave)
753-6511

1147 Madison Ave (at 85th St)
794-9373

Mon-Fri: 10-5:30; Sat: 11-4; closed Sat in July, Aug

Silk Surplus is the exclusive outlet for Scalamandre closeouts of fine fabrics, trimmings, and wallpaper, as well as its own line of imported and domestic fabrics and trimmings. At each store, Scalamandre is sold for a minimum of one-third less than retail prices, and there is a choice selection of other equally luxurious fabrics at similar savings. There are periodic sales even on fabrics already discounted. Lest it appear that Silk Surplus is a run-of-the-mill fabric store, we hasten to add that everything is elegantly run. Each store has a personal manager, and each manager strives to maintain an establishment more like an exclusive boutique than a fabric store. It is felt that the fabrics merit this kind of attention, and they do. Silk Surplus has the qualities I most like to see in a shop: quality, service, *and* a good discount price.

TINSEL TRADING
47 W 38th St
730-1030
Mon-Fri: 10:30-5; Sat: 1-5; closed Sat in July, Aug

Time at Tinsel Trading stopped around 1933, and anyone who spends any time here could believe that (a) all the traffic outside is caused by Model T cars and (b) a couple of hundreds yards of various trims are absolutely mandatory. A comment from the personnel at Tinsel Trading: "We're the only firm in the United States specializing in antique gold and silver metallics, and we have everything from a gold thread to lamé fabric." Tinsel Trading offers an array of tinsel threads, braids, fringes, cords, tassels, gimps, medallions, edging, banding, gauze lamés, bullions, tinsel fabrics, ribbons, soutache, trims, and galloons. All of these trimmings are genuine antiques, but aside from the intrinsic antique value, many of the customers buy them for the accent they lend to modern clothing. The collection of military gold braids, sword knots, and epaulets are unexcelled anywhere in the city.

Fans

MODERN SUPPLY COMPANY
19 Murray St (bet Broadway and Church St)
267-0100
Mon-Fri: 10-5; Sat: 12-5

The name was not an anachronism when Modern Supply conducted business for 42 years at a site now usurped by the World Trade Center. Today, however, it's hard to reconcile *modern* with a store that sells fans and only fans. But Leo Herschman is not about to change his habits of over 50 years, so he still maintains the business name and a firm conviction that fans are the best way to keep things cool and comfortable. From un-air-conditioned offices on the third floor, Herschman dispenses all kinds of fans. The floors are overcrowded with fans, and they hang from the ceiling in abundant formations that resemble a *Casablanca* jungle. Incidentally, did you know that Casablanca is a fan brand name? Herschman says that if you want the movie version, don't order a Casablanca fan, because the brand-name model is nothing like the one in the classic Bogart movie. Instead, ask for "the kind in the movie."

Fireplace Accessories

EDWIN JACKSON
307 E 60th St (Alessandro Building)
759-8210
Mon-Fri: 10-1, 2-6

New Yorkers have a thing for fireplaces, and Edwin Jackson caters to that infatuation. Just as New York fireplaces run the gamut from brownstone antique to ultramodern blackstone, Edwin

Jackson's fireplaces and accessories range from antique bed warmers to a shiny, new set of tools that look like plexiglass and silver. (They're really chrome. Do you know what would happen to silver in front of a fireplace?) The expanded two-store shop also stocks salvaged marble and sandstone mantelpieces, antique andirons, and an incredible display of screens and tool kits. In the Victorian era, paper fans and screens were popular for blocking fireplaces when not in use. Jackson's collection of surviving pieces is great for modern decorating. Along one wall is a group of bed warmers. If New York winters get any colder and fuel any more expensive, there may well be a run on these! Edwin Jackson will also do custom orders on mantels, mantelpieces, and accessories. This is primarily a fireplace *accessory* source, however; neither advice nor information is given on how to put a fireplace in working order. Edwin Jackson has been in business over 100 years, and he assumes every New Yorker who has a fireplace knows how to run it.

WILLIAM H. JACKSON
3 E 47th St (at Fifth Ave)
753-9400
Mon-Fri: 9-4:30

"WBFP" in the real-estate ads stands for "wood-burning fireplace," and they are the rage in New York. William H. Jackson is reaping the harvest of this resurgence in fireplace usage. In business since 1827, the company is familiar with all the various types of fireplaces in the city. In fact, many of the fireplaces were originally installed by the company. William H. Jackson has hundreds of mantels on display in its showroom. The variety ranges from antique and antique reproductions (in wood or marble combinations) to stark modern. There are also andirons, fire sets, screens, and excellent advice on enjoying your own fireplace. Jackson does some repair work (removing and installing mantels is a specialty), but it is better known for fireplace paraphernalia. A handy item: a "Damper is open"/"Damper is closed" reversible hanging sign.

Flags

ACE BANNER AND FLAG COMPANY
107 W 27th St
620-9111
Mon-Fri: 9-5

Rally 'round the flag, boys, and if you need a flag, bumper sticker, or I.D. patch, Ace is the place to go. Established in 1916, Ace prides itself on having the flag of every country in the world readily available; other flags can be ordered. They range from lapel pins to George Washington Bridge banner size. (For those who don't know, the largest flown flag in the world is the Stars and Stripes, which hangs from the New Jersey side of the bridge every holiday.) For those who are not flag-waving types, Ace also sells banners, buttons, pins, patches, balloons, and pennants. If you're running for office (school or national), all of the campaign paraphernalia can be ordered with a promise of quick delivery. Carl Calo, Ace's owner, does not exist on flags and campaigns alone, however. A large part of his business consists of outfitting grand openings and personalizing equipment, such as boat flags. If your boat already has a flag and you're not planning to run for office (as a lot of my friends do), you can always try the T-shirts here. There's a full line, and all are custom-printed.

Floor Coverings

ABC CARPET COMPANY
881 Broadway (at 19th St)
ABC INTERNATIONAL DESIGN RUGS
888 Broadway (at 19th St)

473-3000
Mon, Thurs: 10-8; Tues, Wed, Fri: 10-7; Sat: 10-6;
   Sun: 11-6

ABC has been in business for over 100 years, and has supplied the carpets for such famous places as Madison Square Garden and William Paley's private suite. Starting as a pushcart business, it expanded into a wholesale source for decorators. Then it became a retail store. Now it's a major home-furnishings center. Along the way, it made a reputation as the best carpet place in town, when price is a consideration. ABC claims to have the largest readily available floor-covering inventory in the world. Oriental rugs are available, as well as a major antique furniture department and a bed-and-bath shop.

COUNTRY FLOORS
15 E 16th St
627-8300
Mon-Wed, Fri: 9-6; Thurs: 9-8; Sat: 9-5; closed Sat
   in summer

Country Floors is one of New York's biggest success stories, probably because they are offering a magnificent product. Begun in 1964 in the tiny cramped basement under the owner's photography studio, Country Floors has grown to today's size, which includes huge stores in New York, Philadelphia, Miami, Los Angeles, Sydney and Melbourne, Australia, as well as spacious New York headquarters and 35 affiliated representative stores nationwide. Customers from across the country have learned that Country Floors carries the finest in floor and wall tile, and have sought them out. Their sources include a wide variety of styles and artisans from all over the world. All are unique, and a visit—or at least a look at their catalog—is really necessary to appreciate the fineness and intricacy of each design. Some of the more complex patterns are hard to imagine as a whole when one concentrates on the individual tiles. The only common denominator is that even the simplest solid-color tiles are beautiful.

DESIGNED WOOD FLOORING CENTER
281 Lafayette St (bet Prince and Houston St)
925-6633
Mon-Fri: 9-5; Sat by appointment

A couple of decades ago, the epitome of good decorating was wall-to-wall carpeting. Even 10 years ago, industrial carpeting covered floors, walls, and even seating in the most modern homes. But nowadays, bare floors are in, and people who can provide those floors and care for them are as successful as the "in" can be. So it's no wonder that Designed Wood Flooring Center is in demand. Conventional homes are installing, finishing, or refinishing wood floors, while D.W.F.'s neighbors in former lofts have to deal with industrial flooring totally unacceptable for residential use. With the latter customer, the store can lay subfloor preparations as well as some magnificent wooden floors. These people are experts, and the floors come in almost as many varieties and patterns as that old-time wall-to-wall carpeting. And don't worry about their expertise. Despite the fact that they will accept the smallest private job, they are the choice of several of the city's major museums and department stores as well as major showrooms and building lobbies. From now on, I guess I'll think twice before I walk over a wood floor without noticing it.

DILDARIAN
595 Madison Ave (at 57th St)
288-4948
Mon-Fri: 10-5

Floor covering is almost a misnomer here. These are works of art, and Dildarian treats each antique rug as such. Most of the business is dedicated to the sale of antique Oriental and European rugs, sold by experts who can tell a rug's pedigree by what seems like a mere glance. (It is, in reality, *much* more involved than that!)

Dildarian operates in association with Vigo-Sternberg Galleries of London, and together they cover a significant portion of the antique floor-covering market. (They also handle tapestries.) As a sideline, which is by no means insignificant, Dildarian hand-cleans and repairs carpets of the same quality they sell. (Forget your home-hooked rug!) All restorations must first be cleaned, and both operations are carefully executed by hand.

ELIZABETH EAKINS
1053 Lexington Ave (bet 74th and 75th St)
628-1950
Mon-Fri: 11-6; Sat by appointment

Collectors would certainly choose Elizabeth Eakins' shop as a first-class source for handwoven rugs. Here they custom-design and make their handwoven rugs in standard and hand-dyed colors. To complete the look, they offer coordinated upholstery fabric and such accessories as pillows and throws. There are porcelain bowls, mugs, and pitchers to complete the "collector" look. And finally, they offer white porcelain and stoneware tile hand-painted for kitchen and bath. Though not recommended for hallways or other heavy traffic areas, the tiles are as up-to-date as can be for current decorating styles.

HASTINGS TILE

201 E 57th St	230 Park Ave S (showroom)
(at Third Ave)	674-9700
755-2710	Mon-Wed, Fri, Sat: 10-6;
Mon-Fri: 9-5	Thurs: 10-8

Tile will never seem the same after a visit to the Hastings Tile showroom. They bill themselves as "one-stop shopping for bath and kitchen design," but they are really an entry card for stylish and magnificent decorating ideas. The I. Balacchi collection of bathroom fittings offers towel racks, mirrors, and glass holders that look like red cathode-ray rods. The Principe collection of the same items comes in gleaming high-tech brass or coated satin-chrome brass. The pieces look more like executive desk sets than bathtub fixtures. And the tiles are not just for floors. Hastings' tiles cover walls, cabinets, ceilings, and even windows. There are polka dots, stripes, patterns, and even murals, all made of tile. (The Pannelli collection features hand-painted patterns that are ceramic works of art. Believe it!) The showroom itself is so distinctive that it was cited by *Interior Design* for its complex of circles and polygons, which create a "controlled maze" that is also a vast open display space. A customer couldn't help being inspired by the designs and displays, and with Hastings' products it would be hard not to find sleek and distinctive tiling.

IDEAL TILE
405 E 51st St
759-2339
Mon-Fri: 8:30-5:30; Sat: 10-5

Ideal Tile is an elegant store dedicated to custom tile and tiling. Neatly displayed in the showroom are the finest in imported and domestic floor and wall tiles. Some are so fine that the thought of walking upon them seems absurd. Indeed, the showroom director mentioned that some people have spent thousands of dollars buying these tiles, only to cover them with rugs. All of the tiles sold here are ceramic, and Ideal will do custom installation of any creamic tiles purchased in the store. Much of the best work is destined for framing fireplaces or the backboards of sinks. Even single tiles have become hot plates and trivets in homes where the owner could not resist the sheer beauty of what is available here. Ideal Tile imports Italian tile and distributes Mexican, Japanese, and domestic floor and wall tiles. The tiles are then custom-installed by the store's own craftsmen.

MOMENI INTERNATIONAL
36 E 31st St (second floor)
532-9577
Mon-Fri: 9-5

The people here will tell you that they are wholesale only, and they will do everything short of saying "don't come," but try it anyway. Those who do will be rewarded by what may be the single best source for Oriental rugs in the city, because Momeni is a direct importer. Since they don't suffer individual retail customers officially, their prices reflect the wholesale rather than retail business. That doesn't make it cheap (good Oriental rugs never are), but it does assure the very best quality and the best price. So, don't let the wholesale-only policy scare you. They're really pussycats. But don't tell them I said so.

PASARGAD CARPETS
95 Madison Ave (bet 28th and 29th St)
684-4477
Mon-Wed, Fri, Sat: 9-6; Thurs: 9-7; Sun: 11-5

Pasargad is a fifth-generation family business, established in 1904. They know what they are talking about when it comes to antique, semi-antique, and new Persian and Oriental rugs. They have one of the largest collections in the country, and provide decorating advice, repair and cleaning, and a pickup and delivery service. Pasargad will also buy quality antique rugs.

PILLOWRY
19 E 69th St (at Madison Ave, third floor)
628-3844
Mon-Fri: 11:30-5:30; Sat by chance or appointment;
    closed Aug

Sandwiched between two generations of New York guidebook writers (her mother wrote one for the 1964 World's Fair, and her son, Peter, wrote *A Kid's New York*), Marjorie Lawrence specializes in Oriental rugs and kilims at her latest shop. How she came to sell kilims while her relatives sold books is another story, but Lawrence has been doing so since 1971, and she is the best in the business. The name of the shop comes from the pillows that are made of tapestries, old rugs, and old textiles on the premises. Customers can select fabric from the kilims, knotted rugs, and Oriental carpets lying around the shop, or they can have them made to order. Her fabrics are old and authentic from all parts of the world, and the Pillowry does expert rug restoration as well as pillow creations from old textiles, needlepoints, and rugs. You might say Lawrence has the subject covered. Thank goodness she didn't join the family in the guidebook business. She'd be tough competition!

SAFAVIEH CARPETS
153 Madison Ave (at 32nd St)
683-8399
Mon-Wed, Fri: 9-6; Thurs: 9-8; Sat: 10-6; Sun: 12-5

Time was when it was possible to visit the teaming markets of Teheran and find some real bargains in rugs. No more. But one is still able to see a vast selection of these beautiful works of art, even if the setting is a little less glamorous. Safavieh has one of the finest collections of Iranian, Indian, Pakastani, and Chinese rugs in this country. They're displayed in a showroom spacious enough for you to see the prize pieces spread out so that you can visualize how they would look in your own home or place of business. These rugs are truly heirlooms, and you will want to spend time with the folks here while they tell you the differences in their exotic products. Prices, although certainly not inexpensive, are competitive for the superior quality represented. It doesn't hurt to do a little haggling, even if it isn't in that foreign bazaar.

Flowers, Plants, Planters

BONSAI DESIGNS
855 Lexington Ave (bet 64th and 65th St)
570-9160
Mon-Sat: 10-7; Sun: 12-5

Bonsai was big in New York a few years back, and it's no wonder. A natural art that miniaturizes large things of beauty into small, tight spaces is a natural for this city. The wonder is that it really never took off or developed many professional practitioners. Bonsai Designs is the largest producer and retailer of Bonsai in the East. As such, they maintain a full service shop in Manhattan and a nursery and garden on Long Island. Bonsai Designs also offers design, maintenance, trimming, and repotting services, as well as consultation on "sick" bonsai.

FARM AND GARDEN NURSERY
2 Sixth Ave (bet White and Walker St)
431-3577
Daily: 9-6; Jan, Feb: Tues-Sat: 10-5

Don't miss this—it's one of New York's most unusual enterprises. First, a little background. The towering buildings in this neighborhood are the two spires of the World Trade Center. However, a decade or so ago, the surrounding area was made up of 50-year-old buildings housing government offices, while the site of the future WTC housed tiny and dirty electronics, job-lot, and gardening shops. When construction began on the World Trade Center, all of the small businesses were dislocated. Some retired. Many vanished. A few historic buildings were relocated to the new Independence Plaza several blocks away, and an even smaller handful reestablished their businesses in proximity to the old neighborhood. Those that relocated have done remarkably well. Of the garden centers, Farm and Garden Nursery was the only one to remain in the area. Thus, it is part of a long and honored tradition, and it has done its best to maintain it. Farm and Garden operates like a suburban nursery, dispensing grass seed, fruit trees, vegetables, and sprays, and yet its nursery is, in its own terms, an "outdoor lot," while its customers' lawns are usually six-foot terraces. Oblivious of this fact, the nursery blissfully sells all manner of garden plants, indoor tropical plants, and trees under the assumption that they will grow anywhere. Usually, they do. In addition, one holdover from the old days is the prices. They are cheaper than uptown.

GRASS ROOTS GARDEN

131 Spring St (bet Wooster and Greene St)
226-2662
Tues-Sat: 9-6; Sun: 12-6

Larry Nathanson's grass-roots movement began some years ago, when he turned his hobby into a full-time vocation. The possessor of a genuine green thumb, Nathanson couldn't understand why city pavement had to be an inhibiting factor for would-be urban farmers. So, he blithely set up his Grass Roots Garden, paying no mind to the boutique atmosphere or cutesy merchandising that marked the shops of his peers. Nathanson's shop could be said to be spartan, except that there is no space not crammed with a sprouting green plant. The cityscape is still irrelevant to him. The business is evenly divided between indoor and outdoor plants, and no one here blinks an eye at the sale of a six-foot orange tree or a quarter-inch tall cactus. Somewhere in this city, it will make someone happy. And if having to prune and water plants infringes on your happiness, Grass Roots can handle that, too. In addition to soil, plants, lighting units, insecticides, fertilizers, gardening tools and equipment, and a consulting business to select the best plant for your purposes, Grass Roots makes house calls ''all over town'' and runs a plant maintenance service. They also have a large selection of terra cotta clay pots.

POTTERY WORLD

807 Sixth Ave (at 28th St)
242-2903
Mon-Fri: 7-4:30; Sat: 10-5

Pottery World claims to have the largest selection of planters, fiberglass display pieces, baskets, and pottery for plants in the city, and with a location in the wholesale flower market, they operate on a wholesale-retail basis as well. (This is supposed to mean wholesale prices for retail customers.) Owner Robert Lapidus claims that his years in the business have made him an expert in supplying the best planter and vase for any plant. With such a selection and such a location (he knows what is available to place both *in* the planter and *as* a planter), he really does have an excellent vantage point. If on the off chance that Pottery World does not have *the* piece, Lapidus will search for it, and he can usually locate most any type of planter. What is nice is that the customer usually hasn't the faintest idea that Lapidus' stock will not suffice. But Lapidus is secure and honest enough to know this at a glance, and if necessary, he'll send out for it. Any plant that needs a new home can find one here.

PRESTON BAILEY
88 Lexington Ave (16C)
683-0036
By appointment

Bailey has established himself as one of the most sought-after freelance florists in the city. He is known for his creative talents and his overly abundant floral arrangements for such top clients as *Architectural Digest, House and Garden,* the *New York Times Magazine,* and Oscar de la Renta. Best be on an expense account when you call on this master. But you'll get top quality, and no green leaves for fillers!

PUBLIC FLOWERS OF NEW YORK
479 Second Ave (at 27th St)
684-2850
Daily: 9-6

The Public Flower Market is not *the* flower market, but it is open to the public. It specializes in supplying flowers to retail florists, as well as creating lavish floral decorations for its own retail sale. Most of the latter are destined for weddings or funerals which, while occupying opposite ends of the emotional spectrum, are pretty much the same thing to florists. Ordering in advance assures top quality, and Public Flowers guarantees wholesale prices to retail customers at all times.

RENNY
159 E 64th St
288-7000
Mon-Sat: 9-6

Renny's new headquarters is a brownstone with an enclosed courtyard, complete with an antique fountain filled with a spectacular array of orchid and other exotic plants. Although primarily a florist, Renny really specializes in party pieces. Renny also runs a plant maintenance and landscaping service, and carries materials for centerpieces, bouquets, sprigs, and plain flower decorations.

RIALTO FLORISTS
707 Lexington Ave (bet 57th and 58th St)
688-3234
Daily: 24 hours

A good place to know. Rialto is one of the few florists in New York that is always open and will make deliveries until midnight. Great for patching up late-night quarrels.

ROBERT LESTER ASSOCIATES
280 W Fourth St
675-3029
Tues-Thurs: 8-9 a.m. by appointment only; closed Aug

Robert Lester sells bamboo plants from the greenhouse on the roof of his townhouse. He has at least 150 different plants available at any time. The catch is that you have to phone for an appointment (hours are limited) and see for yourself. Lester will overwhelm you with information about plants that range in size from 8 inches to 25 feet in height.

SIMPSON & COMPANY
1318 Second Ave (bet 69th and 70th St)
772-6670
Daily: 8-8

You only have to step into the fragrant and crowded Simpson store to realize that these folks have the quality and selection necessary for any floral need. The place is overflowing with unusual flowers, plants, and arrangements for use at home, at parties, or at weddings. Unlike many of the Upper East Side operations, this one has reasonable prices and saleshelp you can talk to without being hassled. It is easy to understand why they are so busy, but they still take a personal interest in even the smallest order. I would especially recommend Simpson if you have your mind set on some very uncommon flower or plant. They're also open every day until 8 p.m., even on Sundays.

STAMENS & PISTILS
875 Third Ave (at 53rd St)
593-1888
Mon-Fri: 9-7; Sat: 11-6

Stamens & Pistils' owner Asa Ige is Hawaiian born, and he's very familiar with the plants that most people would think of as exotic. In addition to being able to identify these blooms, Ige teaches tropical design at the Parsons School of Design. His style is to show off exotic flowers in the best possible way. His customers are usually savvy, knowledgeable people, who ask for flowers by name. Ige handles special events for major corporations, commercial shows, and office affairs.

SURROUNDINGS
224 W 79th St
580-8982
Mon-Sat: 10-7

This replica of an English parlor garden is as noteworthy for its exotic flower and fauna as it is for its famous clientele. Carly

Simon, Estelle Parsons, and Diane Keaton are regulars, and what draws them to the shop are imported flowers from all over the world, crafts that include collector's items from the United States, and exotic plants that are ready to be taken home. The plants are definitely unusual. (If your house is going to be featured in a magazine, how can you have ordinary ivy growing beneath your window?) Surroundings also offers landscape architecture, plant maintenance, and buying services, as well as all the horticultural supplies and paraphernalia necessary for an exotic plant's long, healthy life. The flowers come from Europe and Africa, with lilacs, lilies, tulips, and roses available year-round, and mimosa, heliconia, and anthirium representing the exotic end. A special event reminder service is available.

SURA KAYLA
484 Broome St
941-8757
Daily: 11-7

The minute you walk into this colorful establishment you will see things that will look just right in every room of your apartment or home. Dried and fresh flower arrangements are beautifully executed, and their topiary tree selection is as good as any in the city.

Furniture, Mattresses

AMERICANA WEST
120 Wooster St
966-WEST
Daily: 12-6

Paralleling the current interest in foods from the Southwest, Americana West shows New York's best selection of furniture and accessories from that part of the country. Color and style are the name of the game here; the merchandise will light up any dreary corner. Nearly everything is made in Santa Fe, New Mexico. There are tables, chairs, beds, cabinets, and just about everything a cowboy likes to use on his time off the saddle!

APARTMENT LIVING
12 W 21st St
260-5050
Mon-Wed, Fri, Sat: 10-6; Thurs: 10-8; Sun: 12-5

Now, in what other city would there be a mammoth business with a name like Apartment Living? And where else would such a store, in addition to touting its specialization in multi-use furniture specifically designed for city apartments, have to offer substantial discounts to be noteworthy? Probably nowhere else, but for New York it's perfect. Apartment Living does specialize in furnishings for apartments. Most, if not all, is the kind New Yorkers love: lots of drawers, shelves, and storage space in functional form. Periodically, this specialty store also picks up pleasing accessories so that apartment furnishing can become an almost one-stop job when done here. But the real drawing card is the 40 percent discount offered on almost all bedding. New York-style sofa and hide-a-beds, as well as more universal mattresses and boxspring sets, are available. Rumor has it that Apartment Living's prices are the best in town. If not, they're close.

ARISE FUTON MATTRESS COMPANY

652 Broadway	57 Greene St
475-7722	925-0310
1296 Third Ave (at 74th St)	265 W 72nd St
988-7274	496-8410

Mon-Sat: 11-7; Sun: 1-5

Futons are thick sleeping mats popular in Japan. They look much like upholstered cushions with cotton batting and unbleached muslin casings. Arise claims to have introduced them in 1970, and success has been such that in a few years, no one will need a further introduction to them. There are four different styles currently available, ranging from the standard futon to the "Living Health Imperial" models. So, while the classic futon has all-cotton batting, Arise's other models incorporate cores of various fibers for greater resiliency. In addition, the adaptation to New York has been made with the introduction of folding futon beds and even convertible sofas. These don't pull out; they simply drape the furniture. Frames are also available.

AU CHAT BOTTE DECORATION

903 Madison Ave (bet 72nd and 73rd St)
772-3381, 772-7402
Mon-Sat: 10-6

Au Chat Botte is known for the finest imported clothing for babies and children. Now, the perfectly dressed child can hang his overalls on the perfectly executed bedpost in a room that's color coordinated and designed by Au Chat Botte Decoration. This store is a source for wardrobes, cribs, toy chests, tea tables, bookcases, changing tables, high chairs, and various other baby furnishings. Bibs, changing pads, bassinet linings, towels, linens, quilts, and even doll accessories can be ordered and color-coordinated. When

Au Chat Botte is finished with a baby and its room, it is apparent that they have dealt with an heir apparent—and his parents.

BAR MART
123 Bowery (at Grant St)
226-7148
Mon-Fri: 8:30-5; Sat: 10-3:30

If you are looking for a home bar, bar stools, or counter stools, no place has a better selection than Bar Mart. Custom-made bars for home or commercial use are a specialty. You can even pick up accessory items like ice buckets and glassware at sensible prices.

BED BEDDER
37 W 20th St (bet Fifth and Sixth Ave)
243-6315
Mon-Fri: 9-6; Sat: 9-4; closed Sat in July, Aug

If space is a problem in your living arrangements, then a visit here is worthwhile. Bed Bedder was one of the pioneers in the classic contemporary furniture business, and they know all the tricks in making sure every square inch of your furniture is usable. They feature trundle beds with and without headboards, one of the best selections of bunk beds around, platform beds, wall units, dressers and desks, computer furniture, chairs and sofas, and even loft and canopy beds. Special custom work and designs are a specialty, and they work in all the quality hardwoods: maple, birch, oak, walnut, cherry, ash, teak, and mahogany. For young people starting in a less-than-spacious apartment, I'd recommend a trip here for quality goods and fair prices.

BRASS BED FACTORY
3 W 35th St (at Fifth Ave)
594-8777
Mon-Wed, Fri: 10-6; Thurs: 10-8; Sat, Sun: 12-5

This store is only two and a half blocks from Macy's, but the prices are not in the same neighborhood. Samples are available in the showroom, or you can order a standard-sized bed, custom-made. The Brass Bed Factory has been doing this for years, and it has an excellent reputation. It manufactures and sells directly to the consumer more than 20 different styles of brass beds, available in all sizes. If this is not enough, they are open to custom orders as well. Most of the styles are replicas of original antiques, and to their credit they work with heavy solid brass exclusively. I particularly appreciated the magnificent four-poster and canopied styles. They show off brass to its best advantage.

BRASS BY BEN KARPEN
212 E 51st St
755-3450
Mon-Fri: 9:15-5:30; Sat: 10-4; closed Sat in summer

If it's made of brass, Ben Karpen has it, and at a good discount, too. The specialty is furniture: headboards, tea carts, tables, and the like, but there is also a fair amount of accessories, serving pieces, and giftware to complement the furniture. All of his current stock, even that which is custom-manufactured, is totally lacking the "early farmhouse" look. If it does look familiar, you probably spotted it in scenes for advertisements or television and films. Karpen does a good business in rentals to photographers and the like. If that is impressive, do not overlook the knickknack department. It is one of the best around, with incredibly reasonable prices. Check the big-name catalog prices, then check the same thing here. They now carry a good selection of reproduction antique, art deco, and art nouveau brass furniture and accessories, as well as modern styles—all handmade at low prices.

CHURCHILL FURNITURE
44 E 32nd St (bet Park and Madison Ave)
686-0444
Mon-Thurs: 9-7; Fri: 9-4:30; Sun: 11-5

In your digs for just a short time? Want to furnish your kid's room at college? The answer is to rent, and Churchill is the place to go. They offer short and long term rental, with a large variety of styles in almost every price range. Free interior-design service is available, and they offer option-to-purchase plans for your rental pieces.

DECORATORS WAREHOUSE
616 W 46th St (bet 11th and 12th Ave)
489-7575
Mon-Fri: 10-6; Sat, Sun: 11-5; closed Sat and Sun in
  July, Aug

Decorators Warehouse tells New Yorkers that it aims to be "the Loehmann's of the furniture business," and city residents need no further introduction. Those who have never heard of Loehmann's will learn from a visit to either establishment that the name is synonymous with merchants who obtain the very latest, most fashionably high-quality items as jobbers and then sell them to the public at prices commanded elsewhere for just average merchandise. Loehmann's is unequaled in the clothing field, and Decorators Warehouse is working on a similar reputation for furniture.

It's not unusual to see complete model rooms reassembled on one floor and completely accessorized. All of it is sold at an excellent discount price, reflecting its origins from over 75 different decorator and designer sources. There are those who say that Decorators Warehouse has the best prices for furniture in town. And anyone who has seen the selection will agree that it is awesome. Just get there fast. The stock is constantly changing.

DEUTSCH
31 E 32nd St
683-8746
Mon-Fri: 9-5; Sat: 10-4; closed Sat in summer

Wicker and rattan began to become popular in the mid-1970s, but Deutsch had been in the business for 20 years by that time. They originally sold mainly to interior designers, furniture stores, and large businesses, but now the public can benefit from this high quality merchandise. All of it is imported, and there are no cheap weaves here. Roger Deutsch himself is rightfully proud of their position in the field, and he is the one you should seek out for advice when you shop.

FLEUR DE LIS ANTIQUES
489 Broome St
925-3000, 1-800-622-7377
Fri-Sun: 12-5

In a 12,000 square foot warehouse gallery, these folks show the largest selection of popularly priced European art deco furniture in the city. They specialize in armoires, dining room and bedroom sets, and cocktail bars from the 1925-1938 period. This was the time when bars were first used in homes, and some of the models are outstanding conversation pieces. English and Scotch country pine furniture and Victorian and art nouveau pieces are also specialties. Refinishing and rental services are available.

FRANK EASTERN COMPANY
599 Broadway (at Houston St)
219-0007
Mon-Fri: 9-5; Sat: 10-2; closed Sat in summer

First things first. No, I'm not related to this particular Frank, and I'm resisting the use of all the puns on the name that I've accumulated over the years! For business supplies and furniture, however, Frank Eastern Company should be a first choice. They are capable of completely furnishing a business office or corporate headquarters with tables, desks, chairs, files, bookcases, partitions, and a full line of computer work stations for home or office. Frank Eastern Company specializes in advanced ergonomic seating chairs that prevent backache and premature fatigue. The company president has personally conducted 20 years of extensive research in this field and has actually tested over 1,700 different chairs (from all over the world) in an ongoing attempt to find the ultimate chair for the person who works at a desk or a computer. And all of it is always sold at a discount. Smart people, these Franks!

HOWARD KAPLAN—FRENCH COUNTRY STORE

35 E 10th St	827 Broadway (at 12th St)
529-1200	674-1000

Mon-Fri: 10-6

For years, Howard Kaplan was a purveyor of quality French-country antiques for a business that operated on a wholesale-retail basis, with corresponding prices for different customers. The dichotomy in prices and the inability to furnish complete settings eventually got to Kaplan, and he decided to do something about it. His solution was to open his own shop, which is totally dedicated to French-country styles at reasonable prices. The shop carries everything from napkin rings and toothpick holders to massive chests and dining tables in the French-country motif. Some are antiques, some are newly manufactured, but all the items fit Kaplan's two criteria: fair prices (although not necessarily inexpensive, they are the least expensive around for that particular item), and a wide selection that covers every room in the house.

JAMES ROY

15 E 32nd St (bet Fifth and Madison Ave)
679-2565
Mon-Sat: 9:30-5:15

James Roy advertises that his prices are a guaranteed one-third less than those of the regular manufacturer's list price, and they have the documentation to prove it. For that alone, they should be a first choice for furniture buyers, but there is more! James Roy manages to maintain that discount by maintaining minimal stock and having most of his sales specially ordered. That way customers don't have to pay for overhead or large showrooms of furniture.

Rather, they are invited to sift through the catalogs of major manufacturers and/or come to James Roy with specific manufacturer's and model numbers. They will then order the furniture and/or give a quote that is at least that guaranteed one-third off. They will not quote prices on the phone, but are most gracious, with no hard sell, in person.

JENSEN-LEWIS
89 Seventh Ave (at 15th St)
929-4880
Mon-Wed, Fri, Sat: 10-7; Thurs: 10-8

Jensen-Lewis had its origins in the late 19th-century sail-making business of Charles Jensen and the canvas-awning business of Edward Lewis. In 1932, the two businesses united to become the premier canvas-awning dealer in the country. In 1964, the business expanded to include the making and retailing of canvas furniture. In very short order, the canvas furniture took off, and the business now concentrates on canvas products and accessory pieces. Nowadays at Jensen-Lewis, there are bunk beds and bedroom sets, wardrobes in two heights and four sizes, home and office furniture, dining-room tables, lamps, and kitchen accessories. There's loads more too, and we haven't even touched on the basic items such as canvas chairs, bags, pillows, and futons. Not all of this is in canvas, but it does all fit the "Jensen-Lewis look." You'll recognize it when you see it. It's relaxed, practical, and very comfortable.

KENTSHIRE GALLERIES
37 E 12th St (bet University Pl and Broadway)
673-6644
Mon-Fri: 9-5; Sat: 10-2 (Oct-Apr)

Kentshire presents eight floors of English furniture and accessories, circa 1690-1870, with particular emphasis on the Georgian and Regency periods. This gallery has an excellent international reputation, and the displays are a delight to see even if the price tags are a bit high. There is also a collection of 18th and 19th century English jewelry.

KLEINSLEEP/CLEARANCE
176 Sixth Ave (bet Spring and Vandam St)
226-0900
Mon-Sat: 10-7; Sun: 11-6

Kleinsleep is a chain of stores in the New York area specializing in bedding needs. At each store, the byword is *discount,* and at this downtown location, everything is reduced even further. This is the final resting place of Klein's floor samples, closeouts, weird no-sells, mismatches, and just plain mistakes. Since almost all of these pieces are going to be covered with linens, almost none of the mistakes matter in the least, and a trip down here is a must for anyone in need of a bed. They boast that all sizes and types of sleeping furniture are available, including brass headboards. In particular, they claim New York City's largest showing of inner-spring and platform box springs. At the very least, this is a company that is experienced and knows what it's doing. The customer gets advice, expertise, and exceptional bargains. Shipping is additional, but considering the neighborhood, it is usually well worth it. It is against the New York City health code to sell a used bed. Therefore, the leftovers sold here are just that; they're not used.

NEW YORK FURNITURE CENTER
41 E 31st St (bet Park Ave S and Madison Ave)
679-8866
Mon-Wed, Fri, Sat: 9:30-5; Thurs: 9:30-8

The New York Furniture Center is situated in a five-floor building, less than a block from the impossible-to-get-into New York Furniture Exchange, and it takes full advantage of its location. The New York Furniture Exchange is only "to the trade," and no retail consumer can gain access. But nearby are dozens of businesses dealing in all kinds of home furnishings, and the New York Furniture Center is one of the best. Here customers can come closest to the wholesale market and still receive retail amenities. There are bedrooms, dining rooms, living rooms, sofa beds, leather pieces, wall pieces, and occasional furniture in nearly every design and period. Because of the large area, many sample settings are on display. With their immense inventory, N.Y.F.C. can usually deliver more rapidly than other stores. If the piece selected is stocked in one of their three warehouses, delivery can be arranged within a few days. There is a free decorating service by professional staff designers, and full trade discounts given only to accredited designers and dealers are offered. All merchandise can be specially ordered with many options that are usually available only on custom-made furniture. N.Y.F.C. is a factory-authorized showroom display building for some of America's finest furniture makers, and it should be your first stop for furniture shopping.

THE OAKSMITH
1321 Second Ave (bet 69th and 70th St)
535-1451
Daily: 10-8

When you must assemble literally thousands of pieces of paper, an old-fashioned roll-top desk is extremely handy. I should know, as that is exactly what happens each time a new edition of this book is prepared. Stuart Sackin runs a shop that is dedicated to these fine old pieces, as well as all kinds of antique pine furniture, brass and iron beds, and leaded glass lamps. He also offers a decorating service to help with special problems, and he customizes interiors with furniture. Now if I could just get him to help me "customize" all those little notes I've collected from my fact-finding tours of the city! How about it, Stuart?

OOPS (ORIGINALS ON PERMANENT SALE)
528 LaGuardia Pl (bet Bleecker and Third St)
982-0586
Tues, Wed, Fri, Sat: 12-6; Thurs: 12-9

OOPS is no accident for the clever furniture shopper. It deals with the class of furniture normally only available to designers and architects but sold to the public due to some mishap that occurred on its way to wholesalers. It may be damaged, but it is just as likely to be overstock, a cancellation, discontinued stock, or a showroom sample. So the chances of getting a bedroom suite or living-room conversation pit with matching end tables are small, but OOPS is a top-notch source for distinctive individual pieces and vastly reduced prices. Since they deal in designer pieces (they claim the majority of their furniture can be seen in the Museum of Modern Art permanent collection), it is possible to collect specific names or styles, if not specific suites. The stock is not limited to current manufacturers; in fact, a store specialty is finding originals or creating approved reproductions of recent trends, such as Eero Saarinen's art deco. They are also quite frank about the item's origin and how it got to be at OOPS in the first place.

OSBORNE & OSBORNE
508 Canal St
431-7075
Daily: by appointment

Primarily noted for their functional, no-nonsense approach to life, the Shakers made their own furniture in line with their religious philosophy. Kipp and Margot Osborne's store is devoted to Shaker-style furniture. Each piece is custom-made, which lets the Osbornes select woods and colors (they primarily work in oak and walnut). They can add un-Shakerlike drawers and hidden compartments to their pieces, because each piece is made to customer specification. The Osbornes make furniture in all sizes and dimensions, though they like to stick to Shakerlike proportions. They will create almost any type of furniture within those guidelines, and prices are less than those of genuine Shaker relics. The only disadvantage is that the Osbornes have become very popular, and a commissioned work can take between six and nine months for completion. The move to their own 1836 Federal row house in 1982 gave them greater space for work and display purposes. As a result, the Osbornes find themselves creating more and more of their own pieces, although many are still Shaker inspired.

T & K FRENCH ANTIQUES
120 Wooster St
219-2472
Mon-Fri: 11-6; Sat: 12-6

If you have the craving to accent your home with interesting French antiques, then T & K should be one of your first stops. They import directly from France and display an unusually interesting collection of antiques, including turn-of-the-century coffee dispensers, oak ice cream boxes, chicken coops, baskets, doctor's cabinets, and a fine collection of iron items. For unusual chairs and bird cages, look no further. I even saw a magnificent antique walnut doctor's table.

WICKER GARDEN
1318 Madison Ave (at 93rd St)
410-7000
Mon-Sat: 10-5:30; closed Sat in July, Aug

Pamela Scurry may be the quintessential yuppie New Yorker. She owns a successful business, has a son and a daughter, a Chemical Bank executive for a husband, and a penthouse apartment on Fifth Avenue that has been featured in *The New York Times*. Her business, the Wicker Garden, has garnered similar attention and spawned additions that paralleled Scurry's own life. The Wicker Garden was established as a prime source for wicker furniture and accessories displayed in a Victorian garden setting, but when Scurry needed furniture for her children, Wicker Garden's Baby, upstairs in the Wicker Garden, was created. And when her children needed clothing to match their stunning antique bedroom suites, the Wicker Garden's Children was set up to outfit them and other such lucky children. Upstairs, there is an infant furnishings department, with museum-quality wicker furniture and accessories, including antique quilts, linens, and lace infant furnishings as well as a line of hand-painted furniture.

WICKERY
342 Third Ave (at 25th St)
889-3669
Mon-Fri: 10:30-6:30; Sat: 10:30-6

The Wickery handles wicker, rattan furniture, and accessories in tortoise shell, rolled bamboo, burned bamboo, or rattan core. Sizes range from basket to hamper size, and prices range from pennies to hundreds of dollars.

WIM AND KAREN'S SCANDINAVIAN FURNITURE
319 E 53rd St
758-4207
Mon-Wed, Fri: 10-6; Thurs: 10-7:30; Sat: 10-5

Wim Sanson's collection of Scandinavian furniture is light, airy, and functional. Unlike most Scandinavian and modern imports, they look and feel solid, which make them a good investment. Wim and Karen import oak, teak, and rosewood furniture for every room in the house. All of it is made in factories abroad. If you think that all Scandinavian furniture is blond Danish modern, Wim and Karen deserve your visit. Most noteworthy is the encouragement they have given native Scandinavian designers. Many of the styles sold here are unique and suited for life on both sides of the Atlantic. It is possible that the mobile New York lifestyle finds its most sympathetic counterpart in Scandinavia. The convenient wall units in particular seem to bear this out, but there are also bedroom suites and super leather furniture for living-room seating.

ZONA
97 Greene St
925-6750
Mon-Wed, Fri, Sat: 10:30-6; Thurs: 11:30-7;
Sun: 12-5:30

While we witness the arrival of Tex Mex on the city's restaurant menus, Zona has arrived in SoHo with echoes of the Southwest in housewares and furniture. The store revolves around the furniture, but it is set off by the fine Soleri bells, gardening tools, decorative terra cotta and "found objects." All are "imported" from the

Southwest and display good taste and a melding of images. I wonder if there's a store in Texas that sells New York hide-a-beds and egg creams!

Games—Adult

COMPLEAT STRATEGIST
11 E 33rd St (at Fifth Ave)
685-3880
Mon-Wed, Fri, Sat: 10:30-6; Thurs: 10:30-9

320 W 57th St (bet Eighth and Ninth Ave)
582-1272
Mon-Sat: 11-8; Sun: 12-5

603 Fifth Ave (Rockefeller Center)
265-7449
Mon-Fri: 10:30-5:30

Several years ago, the Compleat Strategist was established as a fortress for military games and equipment. As the only such sanctuary in the city (possibly the country), it was an overwhelming success and was soon overrun with military strategists. As time went on, they branched out into science fiction, fantasy, murder mystery games, and adventure games and books. And when this, too, seemed to capture the imagination of the public, the Compleat Strategist opened two more outposts on 57th Street. So today, people who are refighting the Civil War can browse alongside Dragon Masters at three locations in the city. The stock is more than ample for any military or Dungeons and Dragons addict, and the personnel are knowledgeable and friendly. For the less feisty, they have chess and backgammon sets, and even Monopoly. This is adult games with no sneering or innuendo—unless you're playing the villain.

DOUBLING CUBE
37 W 20th St (bet Fifth and Sixth Ave, room 304-5)
243-6240
Mon, Wed-Fri: 10:30-7; Tues: 10:30-5:30

Only in New York! This outfit is the only business in the country that supplies backgammon sets, monogrammed poker chips (10 kinds), chess equipment, and all kinds of gaming devices for home use. No need to go to Atlantic City; just head to Doubling Cube and pick up your blackjack, crap and roulette layouts, wheels, dice, and other game parts. They will even tell you where you can play all these games right here in Manhattan.

GAME SHOW
474 Sixth Ave (bet 11th and 12th St)
633-6328
Mon-Sat: 12-8; Sun: 12-5

If you can't find the kids or adult game you have heard about at the Game Show, it probably doesn't exist. This store is crammed with the best of the lot, and the folks here love to talk to the customers about their stock. I wonder if they were able to finance their inventory with some winnings from Monopoly?

MARION & COMPANY
315 W 39th St (16th floor)
868-9155, 594-1848
Mon-Fri: 8-5:15

After 80 years, this shop is still a homey, family-run business, despite the fact that they have a virtual monopoly on the adult-games supply business in New York. The majority of that business is on the wholesale level. Fun is what is marketed here. The main drawing card is cards, which come in every imaginable size, shape, and color. A purchase can evoke a lecture on the subtle distinctions between playing cards used in foreign countries. (Aside from the somewhat commonly known differences in face card appearances, which go to curly-haired, straight-haired, and all-male characters—including the queen, who is, obviously, not called that—European cards are marked on all four corners, while the American are only marked on two. "Much harder on left-handed players," says Eddie.) Marion & Company also distributes backgammon, dominoes, casino chips, crap tables, and all sorts of dice. They purchased their own dice factory in Manhattan, but even with that, they are hard-pressed to keep up with the demand. Eddie feels that legalized gambling in New York is inevitable, but it won't have any effect on his business. They are already selling all that they possibly can, because their quality is high and their prices are incredibly low.

VILLAGE CHESS SHOP
230 Thompson St (bet Bleecker and Third St)
475-9580
Daily: noon-midnight

People who play chess in the Village can walk to the Village Chess Shop to play a game for about $1.50 an hour. And those who are searching for really unique chess pieces would be wise to patronize this shop. Chess sets are available at the Village Chess Shop in everything from nuts and bolts to ebony or onyx, with all kinds in between. Many of those boards can be flipped over for backgammon, and, in fact, Village Chess—its name notwithstanding—has many outstanding sets for that game as well. In short, the Village should be a first stop for the moving of chess pieces, whether its from one square to the other or from their store to your home.

Gifts and Accessories

ACCENTS & IMAGES
1020 Second Ave (at 54th St)
838-3431
Mon-Fri: 11-7; Sat: 10-5

The merchandise is almost incidental to the display, which has come to be known throughout the city as being innovative, fascinating, and brilliant. In fact, a visit to Accents & Images is now almost *de rigueur* for many New York itineraries, even though most of those who see it haven't the vaguest idea what it is they sell. Well, they sell decorating accents and accessories, and the prices are moderate. But what is really sold here is savvy and atmosphere. The two owners, Ron Prybycien and Christopher McCall, are young men with designer credentials who opted for a retail store whose design they could personally supervise. The result broke both new ground and decorating dogma. Nothing is permanent. Walls slide, floors platform, panels pop in and out, and almost every month, there is a different featured exhibit. Most of all, this is a store that teaches as it sells. Exhibits featured here are frequently reflected in department-store model rooms several months later.

ADELE LEWIS
227 W 29th St
594-5075
Mon-Fri: 8-5

This operation may be called a pottery specialty shop. Everything is neat, clean, and well organized, and each item appears to be something special. In addition to baskets and pots, there is a fine collection of one-of-a-kind decorative pieces for the home. Prices are high, but the service and selection more than make up for it. You can find one-of-a-kind wicker log holders, Mexican jugs in descending order, and decorative accessories. There are also display pieces for stores; imported baskets from China, Spain, the Philippines, and Indonesia; and stone and pottery pieces from Mexico. And this is just a start. Partly because of its location and its name, this is one of the city's biggest secrets.

AMETHYST
32 E Seventh St
979-9458
Tues-Fri, Sun: 12-7; Sat: 12-9

Be forewarned that East Seventh Street is not a through street as you would expect; Cooper Square is a good place to get oriented for finding this hidden street. Jeryme English, a friend in Salem, Oregon, likes anything and everything purple—clothes, table-cloths, toilet paper, you name it. She would be in color heaven in Amethyst. Guy de Ville and Mario Cavallini have assembled a marvelous collection of lavender and purple antique and designer jewelry pieces, collectibles, and kimonos. Only in the Big Apple could you find such a store specializing in goods of just one color.

BERTABRASIL BUTIK
151 W 46th St (bet Sixth and Seventh Ave,
   seventh floor)
354-9616
Mon-Fri: 9-5:30; Sat: 9-2

This is a loft discount boutique featuring a number of well-known names in watches, sunglasses, electronics, cosmetics, and some clothing items. Don't expect to find depth in any classifications, but you can find some good bargains if you don't mind disinterested salespeople and zero ambiance. A good place to get the birthday gift for Aunt Gertrude who sends you three handkerchiefs each year for Christmas!

BRASS LOFT
20 Greene St (off Canal St)
226-5467
Tues-Sun: 11-5:30; Summer: Mon-Fri: 11-5:30

Michele Rosenthal and Ruth and Gayle Hoffman run the Brass Loft. After a visit here, any other metal pales in comparison, and that isn't just due to the brightness of polished brass. Nearly everything in the shop is made of brass or copper, and many of the configurations are most unusual, if not unique. Brass fireplace equipment, screens, sconces, candlesticks, hurricane lamps, chandeliers, and planters (large and small) are just a few of the Hoffmans' items. In addition, Brass Loft will repair and polish almost any brass and copper item, and they even electrify vases for lamps. Completed, many of them are unusually striking. Bar rails, handrails, and carpet rods are custom-made for homes and restaurants. This factory outlet is the best source in the city for brass gifts at any price, and the 40 percent discount doesn't hurt.

CAROLE STUPELL
29 E 22nd St
260-3100
Mon-Sat: 10-6

Imagine the fun of being able to set a table with the most beautiful accessories available anywhere! If anyone were able to do this, the first place they should visit is Carole Stupell. In my opinion, this is the finest home accessory store in the country. The taste and thought that has gone into the selection of the merchandise is simply unmatched. Keith Stupell, second generation chip-off-the-old-block, has assembled a fabulous array of china, glassware, silver and gift treasures and displays them in spectacular settings. In addition, the store offers a large range of special china and glassware replacement patterns which date back over 30 years. The prices are not in the bargain range, but the quality is unequalled. Film companies often use Stupell merchandise to decorate their productions.

CAT STORE
562 Amsterdam Ave (at 87th St)
595-8728
Mon-Sat: 12-8; Sun: 12-5

Meow. I have to admit I'm not a cat lover, but this place is a find for those who are. The largest selection of cat-related merchandise in the city is available here, including cat-motif jewelry, accessories, and houseware. They point out that the items relate to both domestic and wild cats; read that to mean that there are some highly unusual catty things for sale in this emporium!

CERAMICA GIFT GALLERY
1009 Sixth Ave (bet 37th and 38th St)
354-9216
Mon-Fri: 9:30-6:15; Sat: 11-5

We've been looking a long time for a place that has good bridal-registry giftware at discount prices. It's one of the biggest requests from readers. Well, finally, we've found just the place, and the convenient midtown location is an extra bonus. At Ceramica Gift Gallery, you'll find most, if not all, major brands of china, crystal, tableware, and collectibles, including Waterford, Royal Doulton, Gorham, Minton, Wedgwood, and Lenox. In addition, they ship anywhere in the country and will accept mail and phone orders. (To ameliorate the expense of long-distance calls, they will refund $2 on out-of-state orders. That's particularly nice because it means their overhead doesn't include an "800" number, which is eventually paid for by the consumer.) Discounts can go as high as 50 percent, and they will quote prices over the phone.

CHERCHEZ
862 Lexington Ave (at 65th St)
737-8215
Mon-Fri: 11-6; Sat: 11-5:30

Cherchez' world is timeless, or at least not of our time. The store is jammed with the sweet and exotic scents of dried flowers and herbs. There are scented drawer-lined papers, flower-bouquet room sprays, scented hangers, shoe stuffers, and hundreds of sachets for closet, bed, or bath. Don't overlook the antique clothing (with some magnificent Victorian lace items), the Liberty of London garments, the Colefax and Fowler accessories, the hand-loomed-in-Vermont mufflers, and the handmade lap robes from Wales. That such a small shop carries so much is amazing.

CRYPTOGRAPHICS
40 E 32nd St
685-3377
Mon-Fri: 8:30-5

Whether it's a bowling trophy or the Man of the Year award, Cryptographics can design a piece that will be exactly right. Their basic line is anything that has to do with awards, and that includes plaques, nameplates, badges, signs, executive gifts, trophies, premiums, lamination, and signs. Any of these can be personalized quickly on the premises, but given ample time, Cryptographics can design outstanding pieces. The personalized gift items make really unique presents.

FLIGHTS OF FANCY
450 E 78th St (bet First and York Ave)
772-1302
Tues-Fri: 12-7; Sat: 10-6; Sun: 1-6

Flights of Fancy's shop exudes charm, with its 1850 clapboard facade, soft music gently beckoning passers-by, and the Americana "treasures" Don Detrick has arranged in a Victorian parlor setting. Many of the gifts are handmade and exclusive to the shop, and the window display, which changes weekly, often showcases only one item in a line. That item is often so unusual and special that orders pour in from customers around the country. Prices range from $2 to $2,000, so there is something for every kind of gift giving. Some suggestions? It's hard to be specific since the stock is always changing. But there is a handmade American theme that runs through the selection, and the best sellers include Pet Portrait Dolls, jewelry, and home-accessory designs. (The Pet Portrait Dolls incorporate a photo of any pet on a doll resembling it, which is then dressed in historical or literary costume.) There are other dolls, toys, soft sculptures, and miniatures available on the premises or by customer order and the largest selection of one-of-a-kind gifts in the city.

HUBERT DES FORGES
1193 Lexington Ave (at 81st St)
744-1857
Mon-Fri: 10-6:30; Sat: 10-5

R. Oscar Moore has provided New Yorkers with a great gift shop that's overflowing with antique and new items. There are old English and French accessories, like bird cages, umbrella stands, prints, designer wrapping paper, and pillows. He is especially proud of his showing of antique (1880) French majolica. What a place this is to pick up a gift for your favorite hostess or to give your family (and your home) a special lift with a really unusual treasure.

JENNY B. GOODE
1194 Lexington Ave (bet 81st and 82nd St)
794-2492
Mon-Fri: 10-6:30; Sat: 10-6

Jenny B. Goode appears on everybody's list as *the* place for special household gifts. It is a super source for really unusual gift items; in fact, it's the type of place where you're tempted to buy something for yourself! Jenny keeps the store stocked with contemporary and antique jewelry and pottery, tapestry pillows, lace shams, majolica pottery, all kinds of scarves, silver and silver-plated items, plush toys for the kids, handmade tapestry-and-lace photo albums, and imported frames. There's something for everyone. Jenny B. Goode could charm Scrooge.

JOHNNY JUPITER
1185 Lexington Ave (bet 80th and 81st St)
744-0818
Mon-Sat: 10-6

This is a very special gift store that specializes in one thing: fun. It's fun to shop in a place where the saleshelp match the spirit of the merchandise. Here you can find all kinds of always-popular toys and novelties, collectibles, party supplies, gift wrappings, greeting cards, party favors, baskets, and everything in-between. If you're having a party, this is the place to come first; they'll help you with all sorts of ideas and help coordinate events. Custom gift wrapping is available. When Junior turns six and you want to do something special that he won't forget, Johnny Jupiter can be your best friend.

JOMPOLE COMPANY
330 Seventh Ave (at 29th St, third floor)
594-0440
Mon-Wed, Fri: 10-5; Thurs: 10-7; Sat: 10-3;
    closed Sat in summer

When the local bank offers an electric blanket to anyone depositing $500, or the boss gives every employee a clock radio for Christmas, or the academy gives every graduate a silver pin, odds are that it was bought here. Jompole is a dynamite company. They offer great service at super prices, and Irving Jompole and Shirley Smith are two of the friendliest, funniest people around. They bill themselves as suppliers of business gifts, sales incentives, premiums, and awards, and they claim to have supplied everything from lollipops and imprinted toothpicks to diamonds, color televisions, and Cadillacs. Their stock in trade is crystal, sterling silver, and china. There is no name they don't carry or can't get, and, of course, it is sold at a substantial discount (30 to 50 percent). "Very nice," you say. "But I'm not a bank, employer, or school." No problem, Jompole provides the service to individuals at the same discount price. Jompole warns that everything is not always in stock (this is mostly a brokerage operation), but anything can be ordered. Customers are invited to call or come in to peruse the catalogs and place orders. Shipping is reasonable (sometimes free), and the prices may be the lowest in town.

L S COLLECTION
765 Madison Ave (at 65th St)
472-3355
Mon-Sat: 10-6

Even if you have no intention of buying a thing, you'll get a thrill out of seeing this superb collection. Seldom have I seen home and office accessory items done in such superb taste. This store is Japanese owned, and obviously the proprietors have enough financial backing to send their buyers into the market to find the very best available. Each piece is almost museum quality. You'll find any number of dishes, vases, glassware, tea and coffee sets, nifty-gifties, desk pieces, and leather goods that would be "just the thing" for your "dream pad." Prices are not low, but for the quality represented, they are not out of line.

MABEL'S
849 Madison Ave (bet 70th and 71st St)
734-3263
Mon-Sat: 10-6

Mabel, owner Peaches Gore's black-and-white cat and business trademark, has gone to cat heaven, but her namesake store continues to delight hordes of Madison Avenue shoppers. The store is jam-packed with handmade accessories for decorating body and home, and virtually everything is made around an animal or fantasy theme. They have elegant to whimsical hand-painted furniture, hooked rugs, old-fashioned lamps, chic wearables, and all are inspired by animals! Mabel must be looking down on this scene with "cataleptic" glee!

NATURE COMPANY
Seaport Marketplace, 8 Fulton St
422-8510
Mon-Sat: 10-9; Sun: 12-8

One of the most fascinating of the newer trends in merchandising is the appeal to the naturalist, and no one does it better than the Nature Company. The store is a treasure chest for the browser or the buyer; you don't have to be a nature lover to appreciate the unusual selection. There are beautiful marble desktop boxes, attractive jewelry, nature posters, books for the outdoors lover, inflatable toys, telescopes and watches, birdfeeders and birdbaths, and all sorts of items that a stargazer would find irresistable. My favorite is a set of sound recordings on tape or CD that reproduce the music of the environment. Imagine being lulled to sleep by the rippling charm of a mountain stream!

ONLY HEARTS
386 Columbus Ave (at 79th St)
724-5608
Mon-Sat: 11-8; Sun: 12-7

This has to be one of the most fun shops in New York. Helena Stuart offers the romantic in the family a fascinating array of intimate apparel and lingerie, heart-shaped or heart-printed jewelry, balloons, boudoir pillows, soaps, tissues, and even plungers decorated with heart-shaped tops. You might run into Cher or Dustin Hoffman or Bruce Springsteen in the shop; then you can say you have had one of New York's most unusual romantic experiences!

PLANET EARTH
23 Lexington Ave (at 23rd St)
677-7005
Mon-Wed: 11-9; Thurs-Sat: 11-10; Sun: 12-7

If you can't get on one of the space shuttles, going to Planet Earth is just about the best alternative. They are a theme gift shop: "Gifts from the earth and beyond." Here you will discover meteorites, natural stone jewelry, nature and science toys and artifacts, and new age music. Lorraine Simone is a former science teacher who wanted to bring city folk closer to nature and scientific applications; opening this unique shop was the answer. She welcomes class trips, hands out tourist information, and gives classes on the use of crystals and other human-potential concerns.

REINWAHL AND LEONARD
New York Hilton (downstairs)
1335 Sixth Ave
582-4184
Daily: 7:30 a.m.-11:15 p.m.

It's not often that you find a really good specialty shop in a hotel, but the New York Hilton has an exception. Reinwahl and Leonard is one of the most complete gift, novelty, and food shops in the midtown area. Quality items for that special occasion, snacks for the hotel room, and unusual souvenirs of the Big Apple are attractively displayed *and* attractively priced. Unlike most hotel gift shops, this one does not inflate the price tag for the captive hotel customer.

SAMUEL SCHECHTER WORLD OF GIFTS
29 Park Row (bet Ann and Beekman St)
227-9044
Mon-Fri: 9-5:30

The cast of players here reads like a "Who's Who in the Gift World." Gorham, Georg Jensen, Lunt, Reed and Barton, and Wallace in silver; 1847 Rogers, Towle, and Christofle in silverplate; Bulova, Seiko, and Atmos in clocks; Baccarat, Lenox, Lalique, and Val St. Lambert in crystal; Bulova, Longines, Wittnauer, Patek-Phillippe, Piaget, and Rolex in watches; Cross pens; Dunhill lighters; Franciscan, Haviland, Lenox, Noritake, Minton, Royal Doulton, Spode, and Wedgwood in china and giftware; Hummel, Bing and Grondahl, Lladro, and Rosenthal and Boehm in figures. This is only a partial listing, but I am sure you get the picture. Plain Jane surroundings, but very competitive prices with special orders, gift wrapping, and shipping available. A great place to shop for Christmas, graduation, and family occasion gifts.

SEASHELL BOUTIQUE
208A Columbus Ave (bet 69th and 70th St)
595-3024
Mon-Fri: 6-9; Sat: 12-9; Sun: 1-9

Seashell Boutique shares its very precious space with designer jewelry (semiprecious stone, porcelain, and sterling), small gifts, and other items in addition to shell objects. What they all have in common is their natural origins and their size.

TROPICA ISLAND TRADERS
170 Fifth Ave (at 22nd St)
627-0808
Mon-Fri: 8:30-7; Sat: 10-6; Sun: 11-5

All that is missing here are the hula-dancers in their native outfits! If your travel wishes take in Hawaii, but the budget won't allow it, then head to the Flatiron district and feast your eyes and your tummy on attractive and tasty island specialties. There are musical items, tropical clothing and accessories, handmade jewelry, carvings, baskets, and a delicious variety of Hawaiian food items, including those great Maui potato chips. There is always some flavorful coffee brewing, and you can get some goodies to go along with your drink.

WOLFMAN-GOLD & GOOD COMPANY
116 Greene St (bet Prince and Spring St)
431-1888
Mon-Sat: 11-6; Sun: 12-5

This SoHo shop is described as a "marriage of contemporary and antique table settings," and that probably says it best. There are linens available by special order that would look classy in a Park Avenue penthouse, and a series of white-on-white tableware that would blend with the starkest loft in SoHo. Some of the tableware is imported from France and England; some is domestic. But all of it is elegant. The store also stocks baskets, cutlery, glasses, linens, doilies, home accessories, furniture, and one of the best collections of cloth napkins in the city. The linens can be specially ordered, and Holophane light fixtures can be similarly ordered for the ultimate table setting. This is a first-choice source for an exquisite house gift.

Greeting Cards

GREETINGS
45 Christopher St (bet Sixth and Seventh Ave)
242-0424
Daily: 11-11

This store, part of a small nationwide chain, claims to have the largest collection of contemporary greeting cards and gifts in the country, and one would be hard-pressed to prove them wrong. The sheer number of cards is mind-boggling, and the types and titles cover topics that Hallmark never thought of. "Congratulations on your divorce" is one wry example. Don't overlook the stationery department; it's really unique and well stocked with a collection of

New York City memorabilia. It makes the "I love New York" campaign look malnourished. For any type of stationery, Greetings deserves a "hello."

UNTITLED
159 Prince St (at W Broadway)
982-2088
Mon-Sat: 10-9; Sun: 12-8

The Metropolitan Museum and the Louvre each have approximately 1,500 art cards. Untitled, whose reputation is not nearly as well known, has 4,000-plus cards in stock at any given moment. Those cards include modern-art postcards, greeting cards, and note cards, many of which are unused or old cards. The postcards are filed as either pre- or post-1945 and within those classifications by artists' names. There are also postcards of famous photos and depictions of every possible type of art known. Some of these items are good for gags, and some are suitable for framing. And it's all neatly cataloged.

Hearing Aids

EMPIRE STATE HEARING AID BUREAU
25 W 43rd St
921-1666
Mon-Wed, Fri: 9-5:30; Thurs: 9-6; Sat: 9-1;
    closed Sat in summer

If President Reagan left no other legacy, he did set a shining example of not being ashamed to wear a hearing aid. The new aids are so small that most people are not even aware of their use. Empire State has been in the business for over 30 years, and carries the top names in the field: Seimens, Bosch, and Danabox. They have mature and skilled personnel who will do the proper testing and fitting in a quiet, unhurried atmosphere.

Hobbies

AMERICA'S HOBBY CENTER
146 W 22nd St
675-8922
Mon-Wed, Fri: 8:45-5:30; Thurs: 8:45-6:30; Sat: 8:30-3:30

Hobbies and models are a serious business here, but there's a lighthearted touch to remind everyone that hobbies are *fun*. It is evident everywhere in the shop, but nowhere more so than when Marshall Winston introduces himself as the "known authority on vehicular hobbies.'' Winston's vehicular hobbies include model airplanes, boats, ships, trains, cars, radio-controlled materials, model books, helicopters, tools, and "everything for model builders." They also sell wholesale to dealers and by mail order to retail customers. In fact, they fill more orders by mail than at the store. Ask for the catalog for a good indication of what they have for your specific interests.

JAN'S HOBBY SHOP
1431A York Ave (at 76th St)
861-5075
Mon-Sat: 9-7; Sun: 11-5

When Fred Hutchins was young (he's now in his thirties), he was obsessed with building models and dioramas, particularly those on historical themes. Eventually, it became economically viable for his parents to buy his favorite source of supply. Now, he runs the shop. So, while the front of the shop is still your run-of-the-mill hobby shop, the star of the show is clearly the grown-up Fred and his childhood hobby, and you can bet on Fred's ability to keep Jan's stocked with everything a serious model builder could possibly want. Jan's has a superb stock of plastic scale models, model war games, paints, books, brushes (and other paraphernalia), toys, trains, planes, ships, and tank models. But in the meantime, Fred has gone professional. He creates models and dioramas to order for television, advertising, and private customers. In addition to his craft skills, he is also noted for his accurate historical detail. And there is yet a third business: showcase building. Because any hobbyist likes to show his wares, Fred builds custom-made wood and plexiglass showcases for that purpose. Incredibly, he even offers two-day service. He also has remote-controlled cars, ships, and tanks. The shop has become a full service center for electrical remote-controlled cars. Did I mention that Jan's is one of my favorite examples of New York retailing?

Housewares and Hardware

AMERICAN STEEL WINDOW SERVICE
111 W 17th St (bet Sixth and Seventh Ave)
242-8131
Mon-Fri: 7:30-4:30

Peter Weinberger has one of the most esoteric businesses in the city, a business that his family has been in for over 75 years. What he does (just down the block from Barney's men's store) is sell window hardware. If you need a lock, latch, handle, or bracket, American undoubtedly has it. The "store" itself is a tiny office, but the warehouse is right next door. It resembles nothing so much as someone's garage crammed full of window hardware. How he stays in business (and for 75 years at that) is beyond comprehension.

BARSON HARDWARE
35 W 44th St (bet Fifth and Sixth Ave)
944-8181
Mon-Fri: 8:30-6; Sat: 10-5

A hardware store in the middle of Manhattan that is well-organized and competitively priced? Impossible? No, sir. Founder Barney Rubin's daughter, Anita, and Dave Schneiderman operate a store that has everything from first-aid kits to drill bits to 29 sizes of scissors to hair curlers to fire extinguishers. They specialize in travel needs, unique kitchen and houseware items, and tools and plumbing needs. The best part is that the personnel know their stock and will be able to come up with the answer to fix that "whatjamagig" in the bathroom. And if you have a language problem, the staff includes people who are fluent in six languages, including Hebrew and Yiddish.

BLACK AND DECKER
50 W 23rd St (bet Fifth and Sixth Ave)
929-6450
Mon-Fri: 8:30-5:30; Sat: 9-4

Black and Decker is a name well-known for power tools. At this location, the company sells, services, and reconditions Black and Decker tools and small appliances. If you already own such power tools, this is the place to bring them when they don't work, since the company knows its product better than anyone else. If you wish to purchase tools, this is also a good source. New tools are sold at a discount, while reconditioned items go for even better prices. And everything is sold with a two-year guarantee. This is a real find. Imagine buying a power saw on your trip to ultra-urban New York!

BRIDGE KITCHENWARE
214 E 52nd St
688-4220
Mon-Fri: 9-5:30; Sat: 10-4:30

Bridge Kitchenware is a unique-to-New York store that supplies almost every restaurant and institution within 500 miles. Bridge carries bar equipment, cutlery, pastry equipment, molds, glassware, copperware, cast ironware, woodenware, flatware, stoneware, and kitchen gadgets. All goods are professional quality and excellent for the home gourmet. Be sure to see the line of imported copperware from France, as well as the professional knives and baking pans. After trying them, people use no other. The pepper-mill collection, while not abundant in choice, has several top-quality items designed for function rather than funkiness. Bridge takes its name from owner Fred Bridge, not from the nearby 59th Street Bridge.

BROADWAY PANHANDLER
520 Broadway (bet Spring and Broome St)
966-3434
Mon-Fri: 10:30-6; Sat: 11-5:30; closed Sat in summer
Over 8,000 different items of cutlery bakeware and cookware are available at this SoHo store. Broadway Panhandler made its reputation supplying restaurants and hotels, and it sells everything at low prices.

CATHAY HARDWARE CORPORATION
49 Mott St (at Canal St)
962-6648
Thurs-Tues: 10-8
In the heart of Chinatown, this gem of a shop has been dispensing Chinese cooking items, utensils, hardware, and restaurant equipment since 1928. There's no more authentic place to get your wok, chopsticks, or egg-roll roller, and prices and quality are geared for the professional. This is also a great place to find an unusual house-warming or shower gift.

CK & L SURPLUS
307 Canal St (at Broadway)
966-1745
Mon-Fri: 9-6; Sun: 10-5:30
In New York, a shopping trip for hardware wouldn't mean a thing without a trip to Canal Street. And on Canal Street, CK & L is the oldest and best. Years ago, these very same Canal Street stores dealt in industrial and war surplus. With the passing demand for military supplies and an influx of electronics, the Canal Street surplus stores turned to areas best described as "hardware whatever." All of the stores do business the same way. Sawed-off cardboard boxes, containing an assortment of homogeneous but totally implausible merchandise are "displayed" in front. There could be a box full of round washers, mouse traps, electric sockets, telephone coils without terminals, or things that are totally unidentifiable. The junk in the front is there to draw the customer inside the store, where the *real* merchandise is sold. There are power tools, accessories, simple tools, plumbing and electrical goods, and sup-

plies. The only connection that the inside of the store has with the outside is that everything sold comes from surplus stock. Thus, prices, even for the complete line of hardware, are much lower than retail ones uptown. When you see the place, you'll understand immediately why the overhead is so low.

CLOSET KING
113 W 10th St (bet Sixth and Greenwich Ave)
741-0027

185 Amsterdam Ave (bet 68th and 69th St)
496-0199

880 Lexington Ave (bet 65th and 66th St)
288-7871

Mon-Sat: 10-6

Spend any time in New York, and you'll know that rarer than a parking space is a place to park yourself or your belongings. Living quarters in the city have always been notoriously tight, but with the current economy, people are staying put, and small apartments are being measured for every inch of usable space. Frequently, closets —if they exist at all—are the first things to go. They are reincarnated as nurseries, bars, bathrooms, eating areas, and even at-home offices. So, it was inevitable that there would be experts who would specialize in organizing closet space, and Don Constable and his Closet King staff do just that. The overall aim is to provide a maximum amount of storage space customized to the customer's needs. The real boon here is that since the three stores exist to sell components, they encourage "do it yourselfers." So, a customized system can be planned out and purchased here, but self-installed at a fraction of the cost a professional closet organizer would charge. Yes, such people exist. And they're not mothers!

CONRAN'S
2-8 Astor Pl (at Broadway)
505-1515
Mon-Sat: 10-9; Sun: 12-7

160 E 53rd St (at Third Ave, Citicorp Center)
371-2225, 800-431-2718
Mon-Sat: 10-9; Sun: 11-7

Terence Conran's enterprise is not new to the home-furnishings and housewares business. His Habitat stores exist across Europe, and the same operating style has been brought to the New York store. The look is young. The furniture is sleek, modern, clean of encumbering frills and decorative accents, comparatively inexpensive, and, most important, portable. A good percentage of Conran's line can be carried out of the store at the time of purchase, and that is one of its canons. Some of the furniture items are blatant copies of more expensive lines. They were originally created for the store and are simply assembled under one roof for the first time. Conran's also has linens, lighting, bath accessories, and toys. The entire store can be billed as a housewares store, but there is a specific housewares section on the second floor. There are china, glass, cookbook, and cookery sections as well. Everything is displayed on long open shelves, warehouse style, and all is neat and sleekly done. Many of the items are unique to the store. Simply pick what you want, load it into a shopping cart, and wheel it to the checkout counter; it's almost entirely self-service.

D. F. SANDERS
386 W Broadway (bet Spring and Broome St)
925-9040
Mon-Sat: 11-7; Sun: 12-5:30

952 Madison Ave (at 75th St)
879-6161
Mon-Sat: 10-6; Sun: 12-5

127 E 57th St (bet Lexington and Park Ave)
753-2121
Mon-Sat: 10-6; Sun: 12-5

In addition to the usual (which in any other city would seem highly unusual) assortment of kitchenware, Sanders specializes in commercial and industrial products for home use. Sanders delights in offering the best industrial products for individuals. The formula has paid off; the store has expanded into three locations. Industrial shelving, butcher-block tables (meant for a butcher, not a suburban buffet), and shelving are solid, substantial pieces and worthy additions to any home. The store's emphasis is on the best the industrial world has to offer a homemaker, period. And many of the comfortable yuppie generation love it. The new 57th Street store features upscale glass, linen, and jewelry items.

GARRETT WADE
161 Sixth Ave (at Spring St)
807-1155
Mon-Fri: 9-5:30; Sat: 10-3

The Garrett Wade customer is a person who uses and appreciates fine woodworking tools, for the store prides itself on offering only the best-made tools from all over the world. The main business is the mail-order selling of the finest tools available. The catalog is almost more than all-encompassing. It doesn't just list every imaginable woodworking aid, it makes a point of explaining each piece's function and advantage over its peers. It reads like a "how to" guide. While some of the pieces are incomprehensible to a layman, Garrett Wade never accepts that supposition. They assume that anyone could put together their rocker, or, at the very least, appreciate the function of their lightweight spokeshave. And after a visit here, you may become a believer, too.

HOFFRITZ
331 Madison Ave (at 43rd St)
697-7344
Mon-Sat: 9-6

Other locations include:
Penn Station (main terminal), Grand Central Station,
    203 W 57th St, World Trade Center (shopping
    concourse), Rockefeller Center (street level)

Hoffritz is another New York institution. Its mainstay is cutlery, but its image is built upon an enormous selection of gifts, housewares, optics, clocks, radios, games, and gadgets. The selection of knives is unrivaled anywhere. A customer who walks into a Hoffritz store to ask for a cheese knife is offered a dozen different varieties, and this is true even in the small stores. But New Yorkers love Hoffritz most of all for its unusual gadgets. Cherry pitters, self-supported magnifying glasses, folding glasses, and portable barometers are just a small portion of what's available. Some are frivolous and some vital, but all Hoffritz things make great gifts and conversation pieces. People know that a gift from Hoffritz (superstitions about knives aside) will be valued and appreciated. No matter how strange, Hoffritz products are well-made and serve a definite use. One of the handiest items is folding scissors for pocket or handbag. And Hoffritz stores are handy, too; they are in just about every neighborhood.

LUDLOW HARDWARE AND VARIETY
246 Broome St (at Ludlow St)
673-1642
Mon-Fri, Sun: 9:30-5; closed Fri in July, Aug

This is one of the last "Mom and Pop" hardware stores in the city, and the ambiance and prices reflect its advantages. Ludlow has just about the lowest price tags around on hardware, housewares, paint, and tools. They also make keys. Another advantage is the fact that "Pop" speaks Russian, Polish, Yiddish, and even a good bit of English.

M. WOLCHONOK & SON

155 E 52nd St (bet Third and Lexington Ave)
755-2168, 755-0895
Mon-Fri: 8:45-5:45; Sat: 9-4; closed Sat in July, Aug

Wolchonok has been a family wholesale-retail business in the midtown area for over 60 years. In those years, the neighborhood has influenced their business and vice versa. So, while they could have been a general hardware store elsewhere, in Manhattan Wolchonok is the prime source in furniture hardware, particularly legs and replacement pieces. Their business card says, "legs, legs, legs." (I wonder if they get calls from people expecting the Rockettes.) If a given limb, as the Victorians would call it, is not in stock, Wolchonok can make it to order. They do the same thing with towel bars, cafe curtain rods, brass switch plates, and decorator hardware. Speaking of the Victorians, the line of porcelain plumbing fixtures is authentically reproduced, while the other end of the bathroom spectrum features futuristic metal and lucite fixtures. And while "legs, legs, legs" are the business specialty, they can stand on an equally extensive line of casters, sockets, and glides. This may be one of the city's most esoteric shops (a furniture-leg replacement center!), but they are some of the nicest people, and they offer help and advice as if everyone were replacing their legs, legs, legs daily.

P.E. GUERIN

23 Jane St (bet Greenwich St and Eighth Ave)
243-5270
Daily: 9-4:30 by appointment only; closed first two
        weeks of July

Andrew F. Ward, P.E. Guerin's current president, is the fourth generation of the oldest decorative hardware firm in the country and the only foundry in the city. What's more, they've been on Jane Street for the more than 125 years of the firm's existence. In that time, though, the firm has grown into a worldwide operation. The main foundry is now in Valencia, Spain (although work is still done at the Village location), and there are branches and showrooms across the country and in Puerto Rico. The Jane Street home is still the headquarters for the manufacturing and importing of decorative hardware and bath accessories. Much of it is done in brass or bronze, and Ward boasts that the foundry can make virtually anything in those materials, including copies and reproductions. The Gueridon table has garnered design and production awards and also has a worldwide reputation. Their fixtures enjoy a similar reputation, and yet no job is too small for this firm. It operates like the hometown industry it thinks it is. So they offer free estimates (for blueprints, etc.) and help with such hardware problems as locks that don't seem feasible. Their work is impressive.

PRO KITCHEN WARE
4 Bleecker St (at Bowery)
529-7711
Mon-Fri: 9-4:45

After the initial shock of high rents in Manhattan, many folks break into a cold sweat thinking about the additional financial outlay for equipping that new abode. Kitchenware can run into big dough in some of the uptown housewares stores, so I would suggest a visit to Pro, where there are vast quantities of the basic necessities at a considerable discount. Restaurant operators also find this a good spot to stock up on items in quantity.

SIMON'S HARDWARE
421 Third Ave (bet 29th and 30th St)
532-9220
Mon-Fri: 8-5:30; Sat: 10-4:30

This is really a hardware supermarket. Customers take numbers just as they would at a bakery counter. No one minds waiting because Simon offers one of the city's finest selection of quality hardware items, including custom-made decorative fixtures. The personnel are extremely patient, even if you just need a thing ("You know, it fits like this.") for fixing the handle on the chest of drawers Grandmother left you.

VAN WYCK DRAPERY HARDWARE SUPPLY
39 Eldridge St (near Canal St)
925-1300
Mon-Thurs: 8-5; Fri: 8-4; Sun: 9-4;
    closed Sun in summer

New York has four pages of listings in the yellow pages devoted solely to *retail* hardware stores, so to be singled out, a particular store has to be special. Van Wyck merits this distinction by virtue of its specialty in drapery hardware. Harold Lamm stocks all manner of drapery hardware, as well as supplies, urethane foam, and drapery trimmings. This is a particular boon to the new do-it-yourself drapery makers, since they can buy the materials in the neighboring fabric shops, pick up the hardware here, and set it all up with one shopping trip. Should the draperies be ready-made (and these, too, can be purchased at a discount from the neighboring stores on Grand Street), the same holds true. Even if the draperies were purchased elsewhere, the discount here makes a trip to the Lower East Side for hardware worthwhile.

W. G. LEMMON
755 Madison Ave (bet 65th and 66th St)
734-4400
Mon-Fri: 9-6; Sat: 9-5:30

W. G. Lemmon is a neighborhood housewares and hardware store that is totally aware of its location. Considering that the neighborhood is the Upper East Side in general and Madison Avenue in particular, W. G. Lemmon has to be just a bit special, and it is. While there is run-of-the-mill hardware and housewares here, and while there is nothing glamorous about a nail, W. G. Lemmon manages to make this home-supply store look like a housewares boutique and gift center.

WILLIAMS-SONOMA
20 E 60th St (bet Madison and Park Ave)
980-5155
Mon-Fri: 10-7; Sat: 10-6; Sun: 12-5

From humble beginnings in the wine country of Sonoma, California, this store has expanded over the nation and is now referred to as the "Tiffany of cookware stores." The serious lady or gentleman of the kitchen will find a vast display of quality cookware, bakeware, cutlery, kitchen linens, specialty foods, cookbooks, small electricals, kitchen furniture, glassware, and tableware. The store also offers a gift and bridal registry service, cooking demonstrations, free recipes, gift baskets, and assistance for corporations or individuals with their shopping needs. Ask for their very attractive catalog, whch includes a number of excellent meal ideas.

Icons

MANIC
125 E 57th St
755-0640
Mon-Sat: 11-6

Authentic icons of good quality are becoming increasingly difficult to find. And those that are available have risen considerably in price. It used to be that a visitor to Beirut could obtain some fine Russian pieces, but no more. Manic, in the new antiques center, has a fine selection from its sister store in Paris. It is a good idea to read up on icons before dropping by; you'll be able to better appreciate the historical significance of these beautiful pieces.

Imports

Afghan

NUSRATY AFGHAN IMPORTS
215 W 10th St (at Bleecker St)
691-1012
Mon-Thurs: 12-9; Fri, Sat: 12-11; Sun: 12-8

Abdul Nasraty has transformed a corner of the Village into a corner of Afghanistan that is fascinating and free of politics. There are magnificently embroidered native dresses and shirts displayed alongside semiprecious stones mounted in jewelry or shown individually. Another part of the store features carpets and rugs, while yet another displays antique silver and jewelry. Nusraty has an unerring eye; all of this is of the very best quality, and often it is unique as well. The business also operates on both a wholesale and retail level. Short of a trip to Afghanistan (something few are currently wont to do), Nusraty is probably the best source for Afghan goods on this continent.

African

FOLKLORICA
89 Fifth Ave (bet 16th and 17th St)
255-2525
Mon-Fri: 10-7; Sat: 11-6; Sun: 12-6

Originally a small shop specializing in African imports, Folklorica has been expanded by Pamela Levy and Jack Bregman to include an international selection of quality crafts and art, with a new emphasis on South American handiwork, in addition to the original African products. There are such traditional crafts as baskets, rugs, dolls, tapestries, jewelry, musical instruments, and artwork. The colors and tones of everything seem to blend perfectly, as if they scoured the world for those items that would look best in their shop. They have an art gallery in the back of the shop.

British

KURLAND-ZABAR
19 E 71st St (at Madison Ave, suite 1A)
517-8576
By appointment "or chance"; closed Aug

This store is worth the browsing time, if nothing else. It's the only gallery specializing in British arts and crafts in this country, and what a show it is! There are outstanding pieces of British and American furniture, silver and decorative art pieces from the 1840-1940 period, including Gothic revival, aesthetic movement, Renaissance revival, and modernist styles. Special services include locating particular pieces, bidding at auction in New York or London for a customer (for a fee, of course), or helping develop a collection. Take along your goldest credit card.

Canadian

ALASKA GALLERY
31 E 74th St (near Madison Ave)
879-1782
Tues-Sat: 11-6

They don't exactly consider what they sell here to be Alaskan. Owners Nicholas Di Gianni and Jack Bryan devote this New York gallery to Eskimo art, and "Alaska" is just a title. Much of the work comes from Canada as well as Alaska, and the shop is also called the Gallery of Eskimo Art, which is a more apt description. Connoisseurs of contemporary Eskimo art are not what you'd call legion, but there are enough to support the shops and their exhibits. Each show highlights a different aspect of Northern carving. Many of the artists are totally unknown, because most still reside in their original villages. Other artists have large followings, and *their* pieces can go for thousands of dollars. What is most surprising, at least to me, is that the style isn't primitive at all. These artists are members of the 20th century; their crafts may be rooted in centuries-old traditions, but they have been adapted to modern times.

Chinese

CHINESE PORCELAIN SHOP
822 Madison Ave (bet 68th and 69th St)
628-4101
Mon-Fri: 10-5:30; Sat: 11-5; closed Sat in summer

Rebecca Rice Jones and her partners began this company in 1985 as a source for Chinese decorative arts, with a particular emphasis on porcelain and furniture. Soon she had outgrown her quarters. The quaint aspect of having to climb up half a flight of stairs sets the mood for one to become enthralled with the porcelain, period hardwood and lacquer furniture, Chinese rugs and carpets, cloisonné, woodcarvings, prints, and watercolors which make up the colorful stock. And that half-flight climb helps keep the overhead down!

SEOUL HANDICRAFT TRADING
284 Fifth Ave (at 30th St)
564-5740
Mon-Sat: 9-6; closed first week in July

Last time I looked, Seoul was in South Korea, but that doesn't stop these folks from importing the most unique and exquisite embroidered bedding and linens from China. For those of you who are familiar with Chinese embroidered tablecloths, the fine detailing of these sheets and comforters will come as no surprise. As direct importers, the price is right.

WING-ON TRADING
145 Essex St
477-1450
Daily: 10-6

No need to go to Hong Kong to get your set of Chinese porcelain or earthen ware. Wing-On, even though located in the other than well organized Lower East Side, has a clean and complete stock of all kinds of household goods, Chinese and Oriental groceries, vases and the like. One of their specialties is Chinese tea, and they have just about any kind at prices considerably lower than your local grocery store.

General

BACK FROM GUATEMALA
306 E Sixth St
260-7010
Mon-Sat: 12-11; Sun: 2-10

CHRYSALIS
340 E Sixth St (bet First and Second Ave)
533-8252
Tues-Sun: 2-10

Even if these weren't two of the most intriguing import stores, I'd patronize them just for their names. Joe Grunberg and Susan Kaufman are the owners and buyers, and their devotion to Guatemalan artifacts is obvious. Their merchandise includes ethnic clothing, wall hangings, and jewelry from Central and South America and from Asia as well. There are both exotic and classic styles of ethnic clothing. (Ms. Kaufman is a specialist in antique Tibetan jewelry.) Back From Guatemala also has the city's best collection of cloisonné earrings from mainland China. And there's more: preshrunk cotton clothing, masks, handmade sweaters, and artifacts from 30 different countries. A new hot item is the beautiful handmade chiffon scarf with glass beads from the Middle East. Back From Guatemala has contacts with 35 countries and hundreds of world travelers, so it offers the best. Grunberg and Kaufman are among the most charming of New York's store owners. Their other store, Chrysalis, offers beautiful crystals, contemporary and ethnic jewelry, puppets, stationery, body scents, and accessories.

JACQUES CARCANAGUES
114 Spring St (bet Greene and Mercer St)
925-8110
Tues-Sun: 11:30-7

After a stint in the diplomatic service, Frenchman Jacques Carcanagues decided to assemble and sell the best of the world's artifacts that he had run across in his travels. So, while the store has no particular ethnic or historical persuasion, it is, in his own words, "a complete ethnic department store, not a museum." Afghan textiles and Near Eastern rugs are everywhere, as are more jewelry and pieces of pottery than can be counted. What it all has in common is that it is (despite protestations to the contrary) all of museum quality. It is also very appealing to SoHo shoppers. The business is divided between the retail operation in the front and the import-distribution business in the back. The overall effect is nothing so much as an Eastern marketplace; all that is lacking are the water pipes and music. Actually, truth to tell, the water pipes are probably floating around the store somewhere as well. All in all, Jacques Carcanagues is an artifact specialist. Fortunately, he can pick out what will look great in a home as well as a museum.

Himalayan

HIMALAYAN CRAFTS AND TOURS
1228 Lexington Ave (at 83rd St)
744-8892
Mon-Sat: 11-7

There's more to the Himalayas than Mt. Everest and the Abominable Snowman, and that which is marketable is for sale here. Shozo and Yoko Miyahara preside over an emporium of imports from Nepal, Tibet, and Northern India—in short, any country that even remotely can claim contact with the Himalayan mountains.

Despite the exotic tundra image this description evokes, many of the items are easily adaptable for city life. The hand-detailed boots are desired as much for their warmth as for their show-stopping fashion quality. The Tibetan rugs are similar conversation pieces. And, of course, the shop houses much more—batik paintings, art, statues, antiques, carpet bags from Afghanistan, African beads, and incredibly attractive sweaters. True to its name, the shop also arranges tours of the home country; there is probably no one more knowledgeable on the subject anywhere outside the mountains. But the real attraction here are the boots and sweaters. If you run into the Abominable Snowman on your trip, at least you'll be properly dressed.

TIBET STORE
21 Cleveland Pl (bet Spring and Kenmare St)
925-6145
Daily: 12:30-6:30

One of the best contenders for "I dare you to find this address," the Tibet Store has other geographical displacement problems as well. They are two blocks from Chinatown and a similar distance from Little Italy, while being in the heart of the SoHo art scene. For another, why is the store called *Tibet* when the boundaries for the merchandise are the Himalayas? And finally, virtually all of the items in the Tibet Store are handmade by Tibetan refugees living in Nepal. Maybe "The Refugees in Nepal Store" didn't fit the SoHo image. And not surprisingly, virtually everything in the store fits the New York image very well. There is beautifully designed and appliquéd clothing, and most of it is handcrafted. In addition, there are Himalayan arts and crafts that depict local life and lore — Tibetan, not SoHo.

Indian

HANDBLOCK
487 Columbus Ave (bet 83rd and 84th St)
799-4342
Mon-Wed, Sat: 10-7; Thurs, Fri: 10-8; Sun: 11-7

Handblocking, an ancient art of India, is what gives this store both its name and wares. The four partners divide their time between overseeing production in India and merchandising at this store and their other ones in Canada. There are linens, place mats, napkins, tablecloths, bed covers, and dish towels, all created in India of cotton tinted in brilliant colors and handblocked in designs that range from traditional to contemporary. One can also find rugs, dishes, jewelry, and pottery. The merchandise is distinctive and fashionable.

HIND INDIA COTTAGE EMPORIUM
1150 Broadway (at 27th St)
685-6943, 685-2460
Mon-Fri: 9:30-6:30; Sat: 11-5

Hind India Cottage Emporium features clothing, jewelry, handicrafts, and gifts imported directly from India. Moti R. Chani has a sharp eye for the finest details, and the saris and other Indian clothing he sells reflect that. The clothing is prized by both Indian nationals as well as neighborhood residents for its sheer beauty. The garments, made completely of cotton and featuring many unique madras patterns, come in sizes small, medium, and large. Pay particular attention to the leather bags and jewelry.

Irish

IRISH BOOKS AND GRAPHICS
90 W Broadway (at Chambers St)
962-4237
Mon-Fri: 11-5; Sat: 12-5

These days it might be a lot safer to shop here than in the home country! Angela Carter has changed the name of her shop from Keshcarrigan (that was a mouthful), but has not changed the great selection of new and used Irish books, posters, old maps, and engravings. Books are offered in both Irish Gaelic and in English.

MATTIE HASKINS SHAMROCK IMPORTS
205 E 75th St (at Third Ave)
BU8-3918
Mon-Sat: 11-6

The folks at Shamrock Imports (especially Kathleen) did not like the slight jab in the last edition about the housekeeping at Mattie Haskins. Now this delightful bit of old Ireland has been cleaned up and is downright easy to shop in. Haskins dispenses anything and everything Irish, from tapes to candy to newspapers to tweed hats and caps. Along with the merchandise, you get a bit of Irish lore from Cathy and Tom and Kathleen. The store has been a New York institution since the year I was born (I won't tell you when that was), so you know it has been around for quite a while. It's the best source for Irish fun other than St. Pat himself.

Italian

CAROSELLO MUSICALE COMPANY
119 Mulberry St (near Canal St)
925-7253
Mon-Fri: 10-11; Sat, Sun: 9 a.m.-1 a.m.

Every section of New York with a concentrated ethnic population has a group of stores that serve the specific needs of that nationality. Usually, the group will include a bakery and coffee shop, a bookstore, and an import shop featuring various items of the homeland, and there is often one shop devoted to a distinctive characteristic of that nationality as well. What, therefore, could be more natural than a shop in Little Italy dedicated to recordings and music? Carosello is primarily an Italian music shop specializing in Italian recordings, operas, and sheet music. But Carosello is also a bookstore, import store, and gift shop. So you can find perfumes, Italian newspapers, magazines, and gifts as well as Caruso recordings. The atmosphere is informal—but proud—and frequently the customers can be heard humming an aria while checking record labels. But even if you don't buy anything here, check out the espresso and breads at any of the neighboring cafes.

Japanese

O-ZORA
238 E Sixth St (at Second Ave)
228-1325
Mon-Sat: 11-7

Jiro Tsuji was a woodworker and cabinetmaker in his native Japan. The latter skill was much more in demand than the former when he made the move to New York, but he never outgrew his healthy respect for Japanese woodworking and hand tools. When finding them became difficult, he and his wife, Eileen, opened their own shop in the East Village. They called the store O-Zora, which is Japanese for limitless (as in "the sky's the limit"), so while hand tools are the basis of the business, virtually anything Japanese can be uncovered in this tiny store. Tsuji had the right idea. The Japanese tools, which range from antique to power saws and drills, are prized for their design and quality and are often exclusive to the shop. Artisans seek out O-Zora, and amateurs are carefully instructed in the use of the tools, much as they are in the use of sushi and sashimi knives and traditional Japanese clothing. The Tsujis make periodic buying trips to Japan, and whatever strikes their fancy ends up on O-Zora's shelves.

THINGS JAPANESE
1109 Lexington Ave (bet 77th and 78th St, second floor)
249-3591
Tues-Sat: 11-5

Things Japanese believes that the things Japanese most in demand are prints. So while there are all sorts of Japanese art and crafts, the prints highlight the selection. They know the field well and believe that the market for prints, while almost exhausted on the high-priced, established end, is only just beginning for newer or unknown artists. The store will help would-be collectors establish a grouping or assist decorators in finding just the right pieces to round out the décor. And to round out the print image, there are also original 18th- to 20th-century Japanese woodblock prints. Okay, you say, that's *still* prints, so be assured that there are porcelains, baskets, chests, lacquers, and books as well. Prices range from 10 dollars to several thousand dollars, and everything is accompanied by a certificate of authenticity. Things Japanese claims that you need to appreciate both the subject matter as well as the artistry in its things, and that's not a difficult task at all.

Mediterranean

MEDITERRANEAN SHOP
876 Madison Ave (at 72nd St)
879-3120
Mon-Fri: 10-5:30; Sat: 10-5; closed Sat in summer

This Madison Avenue shop specializes in imported dinnerware and tableware. Tableware here is a category broad enough to include desk tables, and it's a toss-up whether the hand-embroidered linens or the exclusive Florentine desk accessories are the bigger drawing card. A good rule of thumb is that if it rests on a table top and is imported from a Mediterranean country, the Mediterranean Shop will have it. And all of it seems to shimmer like the waters of its namesake. Pay particular attention to the imported hand-painted dinnerware and exquisite hand-embroidered pillows.

Mexico

AMIGO COUNTRY
19 Greenwich Ave (bet 10th and Christopher St)
620-5796
Mon-Sat: 11-8; Sun: 12-6

Hola! Mexico lives in Greenwich Village. This little bit of Mexico is about as evocative of south of the border as one can get. The store specializes in imported crafts and home furnishings, and nearly all are handmade. Lest you think that means only baskets and sombreros, there are mirrors, pine furnishings, hand-blown glass, ceramics, rugs, stunning crafts, and the work of Gorky Gonzales. If a customer requests a specific item, they will try to find it in Mexico. They boast that they are "New York's Mexican marketplace," but that doesn't really do them justice. This is one charming place to shop, whether it's for an entire décor or a single item. They're mighty simpatico here.

Middle Eastern

PERSIAN SHOP
534 Madison Ave (bet 54th and 55th St)
355-4643
Mon-Sat: 10-7

Persia, of course, no longer exists; today, that area is, more or less, Iran. But the Middle Eastern mystique is strong enough at this shop to encompass the ancient kingdom. Merchandise includes a representative sample of past and present Oriental jewelry, magnificent brocades—the kind that used to hang behind a sheik in his palace—gifts, and *objets d'art*. What seems to be a pattern in import shops—native dress that can be adapted to chic urbanites—is available, too. In the Persian Shop, it takes the form of caftans and Bedouin dresses (in small, medium, and large sizes) that can be worn by either sex (the natives wear them that way). The selection is marvelous. The Persian Shop has water pipes, of course, and authentic espresso makers, too. Men, check out the sensational ties.

Russian

VICTOR KAMKIN
149 Fifth Ave (at 21st St)
673-0776
Mon-Fri: 9:30-5:30; Sat: 10-5

With the lessening of tension between the superpowers, more and more interest is being shown in all things Russian. Fluency in the Russian language is more and more prized in business and government, and Victor Kamkin can be of great help in this area. His store features books in Russian, translations from Russian, guidebooks, art albums and reproductions, textbooks, and dictionaries. There is also an excellent stock of Russian music items (records and CDs), souvenirs (like lacquer boxes and dolls), and videocassettes. An added feature is a subscription service for Soviet magazines and newspapers.

Scottish

SCOTTISH PRODUCTS
133 E 55th St
755-9656
Mon-Fri: 10:45-6; Sat: 10:45-4; closed Sat in summer

Mrs. K. Graeme Ramsay brags, "We are an old-fashioned Scottish shop, full-service style," and this Scottish oasis in the city dispenses the best of the old country. For natives, there are more hometown touches than could be enumerated here ("But *no* liquor," says Ramsay firmly), and for non-natives, it's all of Scotland's best. Imports include bagpipes, kilts, skirts, jewelry, and tartan tams. These are the genuine articles. In addition, there are ties, souvenirs, travel rugs, and more tartan and clan goods than were probably ever assembled in Glasgow. Of course, this makes good Ramsay's boast that Scottish Products has the biggest and best selection of its kind in this country. And everything is dispensed with a smile. She's right! This is the finest that Scotland has to offer.

South American

PUTUMAYO
857 Lexington Ave (bet 64th and 65th St)
734-3111
Mon-Sat: 11-7; Sun: 12-5

339 Columbus Ave (at 76th St)
595-3441
Mon-Sat: 11-8; Sun: 12-6

147 Spring St
966-4458
Mon-Sat: 11-7; Sun: 12-6

Store hours extended an hour in summer (except Sun)

The majority of the merchandise at Putumayo comes from South America, but there is a touch of Asia as well. The emphasis is on fashion from around the world, and there is a strong line of folk art, artifacts, and antiques. Putumayo displays an extensive collection of South American outerwear. For summer, there are cotton sundresses and wrap skirts: cool, comfortable, and practical.

Ukrainian

ARKA
26 First Ave (bet First and Second St)
473-3550
Daily: 10-6

There's a little bit of everything here, but all of it has a Ukrainian accent, which explains why Arka bills itself as the Ukrainian department store. Most of the locals, particularly the Ukrainian natives, stop in for conversation, newspapers, and atmosphere. Those from farther locales overlook the décor to gaze at the native crafts and artwork (decidedly *not* arts and crafts!), literature, music, records, and musical instruments. In the heart of the Ukrainian neighborhood, Arka is distinctive in its selection of Ukrainian instruments, particularly the bandura. It looks like a large mandolin, sounds like a small harp, and is usually played by a Ukrainian in an embroidered shirt. These, too, are available here (the shirts, not the Ukrainian).

SURMA "THE UKRAINIAN SHOP"
11 E Seventh St (near Third Ave)
477-0729
Mon-Sat: 11-6

Since 1918, Surma has conducted business as the "general store of the Slavic community in New York City." My only quarrel with that description is why it should be limited to the city, since it seems capable of serving the entire hemisphere. More than a store, Surma is a bastion of Ukrainianism, and once inside, it is difficult to believe that you're in New York. Another quote sums it up: "Visit Surma and spend time in the old country." Fortunately, language is not much of a problem. The clothing here is ethnic opulence. There are dresses, vests, shirts, hand-tooled and soft-soled leather dancing shoes, hundreds of blouses, dresses, vests, and accessories. All are hand-embroidered with authentic detailing. For the home, there are accent pieces (including an entire section devoted to Ukrainian Easter egg decorating), imported brocaded linens, and Surma's own Ukrainian-style honey (very different and very good). Above all, Surma is known for its records, stationery, and books; not surprisingly, the business is also known as the Surma Book and Music Company. Particularly note the collection of paintings and the stationery, which features modern-day depictions of ancient Ukrainian glass painting. Surma has even published *A Guide to the Ukraine,* a listing of Ukrainian-related spots in New York.

Jewelry

BELLE EPOCH
211 E 60th St (bet Second and Third Ave)
319-7870
Mon-Sat: 11-7; Sat in summer: 11-5:30; open every
day in Dec

The owner of this unique shop started out with a store that specialized in antique and one-of-a-kind jewelry pieces some years ago, and then quickly branched out into reproductions, perfume bottles, and marcasite Austrian crystals. Nowadays, Belle Epoch carries an enormous selection of earrings as well as modern jewelry, and maintains both a wholesale and retail business. Retail customers benefit from the lack of middlemen. Belle Epoch has a reputation for predicting what the latest in jewelry is going to be, sometimes months before the fashion arbiters do.

BILL SCHIFRIN
4 W 47th St (National Jewelers Exchange, booth 86)
245-4269
Mon-Fri: 10-5

From a booth in the National Jewelers Exchange—better known for its diamond engagement rings than its plain wedding bands—Bill Schifrin presides over a collection of 1,873 unusual wedding bands. Prices range from a few dollars to several thousand dollars, depending upon the complexity of the work and the stones used. If you have the time, Bill Schifrin will tell you a story about each ring. If it's not about where it came from or how he got it, then it's a story about someone who bought a similar one recently. He's been doing this for over 40 years, and after all this time, you'd think he'd be cynical. He's not; he's "just cautious," and his stories and prices draw customers from all over the world. The selection isn't bad, either.

CIRCLE GALLERY
725 Fifth Ave (Trump Tower, level 4)
980-5455
Mon-Sat: 10-6

This particular store features one of the most extensive collections of "Art to Wear" jewelry in the world, with prices to match the uniqueness of the fabulous pieces. There are over 100 originals signed by such well-known artisans as Cocteau, Agam, Braque, Erté, and Vasarely. This boutique is more like a museum, and is a must for anyone who has a keen eye for what will be the upcoming trends in more moderate-priced jewelry.

FORTUNOFF
681 Fifth Ave (at 54th St)
758-6660
Mon-Wed, Fri, Sat: 10-6; Thurs: 10-8

This is one of the best stores in Manhattan devoted to quality merchandise. Prices on all items are very competitive, and the store has a reputation for meeting or beating any legitimately quoted price in town. Although there are extensive and well-stocked houseware and gift departments, it is in the jewelry area that the store really shines. There is a jeweler in residence at all times. Fortunoff shows one of the largest and finest collections of 14-, 18-, and 24-karat gold jewelry in the city, as well as a fine selection of precious and semiprecious stones and name-brand watches from the top watchmakers around the world.

FRAGMENTS II
107 Greene St
226-8878
Mon-Fri: 9-5 (by appointment, preferably)

This is an unusual operation. You'll find a jewelry operation that sells wholesale on the first level and retail on the second floor. There is a vast selection of very attractive designer necklaces, pins, earrings, and other accessories at good prices. If you can use a larger quantity (some great gift possibilities), they will take care of you in the first-floor showroom.

JAN SKALA
1 W 47th St
246-2942, 246-2814
Mon-Sat: 9:30-5

Jan Skala is located in the diamond district, that mysterious one-block area of Manhattan which purportedly handles every diamond imported into this country. The retail customer's place here is nebulous at best. Jan Skala, a reliable, non-"tourist trap" diamond dealer, is not adverse to retail customers. Jan Skala is ostensibly wholesale only, but its ground-floor storefront is the first spot off Fifth Avenue to welcome retail customers. In addition to diamonds, there is a large selection of pocket watches, antique watches, and jewelry. The latter includes a good selection of Russian enamels, Fabergé eggs, and the like. Quite a sight to see, even if you don't buy.

MAX NASS

118 E 28th St (bet Park Ave S and Lexington Ave)
679-8154
Mon-Fri: 9:30-6; Sat: 9:30-4

The Shah family are jewelry artisans; Arati is the designer, and Parimal ("Perry") is the company president. Together, they make and sell handmade jewelry, as well as service, repair, and restore antique jewelry. As Max Nass, they deal in virtually any type of jewelry—antique (or merely old), silver, gold, and semiprecious. Two special sales every year bring their low prices down even lower. One lasts for the last three weeks in January (33 percent discount); the other is for two weeks in July (25 percent discount). In between, Arati will design pieces on whim or on commission. The necklaces are particularly impressive; his work is often one-of-a-kind. The store also restrings and redesigns necklaces. I can only assume Max Nass is the name of a previous owner. He sure isn't Parimal S. Shah.

MYRON TOBACK

25 W 47th St (bet Fifth and Sixth Ave)
398-8300
Mon-Fri: 8:30-4; closed first two weeks in July and
  Dec 25-Jan 1

You must meet Myron Toback. Ostensibly, he is a refiner of precious metals with a specialty in findings, plate, and wire. Not very exciting or helpful to the average customer, you might think. But that's where you'd be wrong. Note the address. Toback is not only in the heart of the diamond district, he is a bona fide landlord of a new arcade that is crammed full of wholesale artisans of the jewelry trade, and taking their cue from Toback, they are open and friendly to individual retail customers. So note Toback as a source of gold, gold-filled, or silver chains sold by the foot at a wholesale price. And don't overlook the gold and silver earrings, beads, and other jewelry items at prices laughably less than those at establishments around the corner on Fifth Avenue. Even though most of the customers are professional jewelers or wholesale organizations, Toback is still simply charming to do-it-yourselfers, schools, and hobbyists. Toback delights in showing people how to bypass jewelry middlemen in putting together their own custom-made items.

OCINO
66 John St (bet Nassau and William St)
269-3636
Mon-Fri: 8:30-6

Ocino is a fantastic find, right in the middle of the financial district. At Ocino, there are diamonds, custom-made jewelry (both to individual customer specifications and corporate advertising or logo inscriptions), handmade jewelry, resetting and redesigning, top brand-name watches, and gold chains sold by weight for those who want to make their own jewelry. For the latter, Ocino claims the lowest prices in the city. Ocino calls itself the "quality store downtown" and offers tableware by Lenox, Royal Copenhagen, Waterford, Kosja Boda—you get the idea. Despite having a virtual monopoly on those brands in the area, everything is sold at enough of a discount to be among the best priced anywhere in the city.

PEDRO BOREGAARD
48 W 48th St (suite 904)
819-1060
Mon-Fri: 10-5:30 by appointment

Pedro Boregaard's credentials as a master jeweler are impressive, to say the least. He apprenticed under masters in Germany and England, then came to this country in 1974 to work at Tiffany's. He ended up co-supervising a large crew there, and did some designing for top names in the field. Few have the native talent he possesses, and his unusual pieces are sure to attract attention for any occasion. Magnificent necklaces, earrings, and bracelets are all one-of-a-kind.

RENNIE ELLEN
15 W 47th St (room 401)
869-5525
Mon-Fri: 10-4:30 by appointment only

A trip to New York without meeting Rennie Ellen is a trip without experiencing what New York shopping is all about. For openers, she is a wholesaler offering the discounts that New York's wholesale businesses are famous for. Second, she deals in diamonds—the real thing—which are certainly knockout souvenirs to bring back from the city. Third, she is a woman who has made it. Not only was she the first woman diamond dealer in the male-dominated diamond district, but feminism has made her a world-renowned consumer advocate. Rennie Ellen personally spent so much time and effort to keep the diamond district straight and honest that she earned the title "Mayor of 47th Street." Finally, only a fool would negotiate a purchase in any wholesale area without knowing the merchant. This is particularly true when one is dealing with diamonds, since thousands of dollars depend upon quirks visible only to a jeweler's eye. In such a field, Rennie Ellen's reputation is impeccable. Rennie Ellen deals exclusively in diamond jewelry. There are pendants, wedding bands, engagement rings, and diamonds which, Rennie says, fit all sizes, shapes, and budgets. All sales are strictly confidential and are made under Rennie Ellen's personal supervision.

ROBERT LEE MORRIS
409 W Broadway (bet Spring and Prince St)
431-9405
Mon-Fri: 11-6; Sat: 12-7

ARTWEAR
456 W Broadway
673-2000
Mon-Fri: 11-6; Sat, Sun: 12-7

ARTWEAR
AT&T Bldg
550 Madison Ave (at 56th St)
593-3388
Mon-Sat: 11-6

Robert Lee Morris ran Artwear as a jewelry gallery, slightly off Madison Avenue. Nobody noticed. So, he moved the entire show (and show it is) to SoHo, and suddenly Artwear was everywhere. The Robert Lee Morris gallery offers his artwork solely, while the original Artwear and the AT&T branch still showcases jewelry to be worn. The shop at West Broadway features more innovative pieces, while the Madison Avenue gallery displays more of the precious jewelry. Uptown department stores run window displays based upon Artwear's wares, newspapers are forever reporting the latest Artwear features, and fashion magazines are either borrowing Artwear artifacts or shooting on the premises. Between periodic exhibitions of the latest in contemporary jewelry, Artwear sells the jewelry of 40 different artists. Jewelry is a very loose way of describing it; the real emphasis is on *art*.

SAITY JEWELRY
725 Fifth Ave (Trump Tower, level 5)
308-6570
Mon-Sat: 10-6

Whether you want to buy or just browse, this is a must for those interested in one-of-a-kind jewelry. Saity has the largest collection of high quality American Indian jewelry in the area; many items are rare collectors' pieces. There are outstanding ivory masterpieces from China, Tibet, India, Nepal, and Africa, along with some beautiful handcrafted sterling-silver jewelry. The prices and the quality are both high, but there is no question about the authenticity of the merchandise.

SAVAGE UNIQUE JEWELRY

59 W Eighth St	267 Columbus Ave
(near Sixth Ave)	(at 72nd St)
473-8171	724-4662
Mon-Sat: 11-7; Sun: 1-5	Mon-Sat: 12-8; Sun: 1-6

Outrageous is the word here! Very unusual and unique watches, flamboyant accessories, and spectacular earrings will dazzle your eye. This is not a place for the conservative matron, but the fashion-conscious will be able to rub shoulders with many soap-opera actors and rock stars. Be sure to check out the large assortment of gold rings. As a special service, they will make appointments after hours for out-of-city visitors.

UNDERGROUND JEWELER

147 E 86th St	175 E 86th St
348-7866	369-0920
Mon-Fri: 10-8; Sat: 10-7	Mon-Sat: 10-8; Sun 12-6

Subway arcades are neglected areas of commerce in New York (unlike in Vienna, for example), and with good reason. There is very little sold deep underground that could withstand the scrutiny of the light of the day. Furthermore, most shops whose sales depend upon bright, open displays that attract casual passers-by do not believe potential clientele exist in a subway. There are two exceptions. The nut concessions are pretty universal, and depend almost entirely upon impulse buying. The Underground Jeweler is the other exception, and it's worth the trip to see why. It carries jewelry from 60 countries. Most is of a whimsical nature and not made of valuable metals or precious stones, but all is very attractive and definitely not of the costume-jewelry class. One of the Underground's specialties is gold with real stones. The stones are mostly birthstones, or of birthstone class (semiprecious), and gold settings are used primarily because they won't make your finger turn green. The African wood carvings—rings, gifts, and statues—are sensational, and some of the genuine folk jewelry is just great. Imagine row upon row of hand-worked silver pendants of international origins. This is not the place to go for an engagement ring, but it's a perfect spot for many other types of jewelry. They now do ear piercing.

Ladders

PUTNAM ROLLING LADDER COMPANY
32 Howard St (bet Lafayette St and Broadway)
226-5147
Mon-Fri: 8-4:30

This is a great esoteric shop on an esoteric street. What, you might ask, would anyone in New York do with those magnificent rolling ladders used in traditional formal libraries? And could there possibly be enough business to keep a place like this running all those years? The answer is that Putnam has been in existence since 1905. Clever New Yorkers turn to Putnam for designing access to their lofts—both in general and for sleeping lofts in particular. Here's a partial list of the different ladders, which come in many different woods: rolling ladders, rolling work platforms, telephone ladders, portable automatic ladders, scaffold ladders, pulpit ladders, folding library ladders, library stools, aerial platforms, library carts with steps, steel warehouse ladders, safety ladders, electric step ladders for industrial use, mechanics' stepladders, Alpine, Crosby, Peerless, Durable, twin and dual-purpose stepladders, extension ladders, window cleaners' ladders, sectional ladders, shelf ladders, extension trestle ladders, custom ladders, and many more. Putnam is a step up.

Leather Goods, Luggage

BETTINGER'S LUGGAGE SHOP
80 Rivington St
674-9411, 475-1690
Sun-Fri: 9-6

This tiny shop can be located by keeping an eye peeled for a mound of luggage heaped all over the sidewalk in front of the store. Inside, it is even more crowded, but, amazingly, the people who run Bettinger's can put their fingers on almost any type of luggage in only a few minutes. Their merchandise includes Samsonite, American Tourister, Ventura, and Mark and Andiano luggage, camp trunks, briefcases, and leather envelopes in both first quality and irregulars. The prices are probably the best in New York. In any event, they're at least 30 percent lower than you'd pay uptown.

HIDES IN SHAPE
555 Madison Ave (bet 55th and 56th St)
371-5998

630 Third Ave (at 41st St)
661-2590

Mon-Fri: 10-6; Sat: 11-6; Third Ave store closed Sat

There is something especially classy about good leather merchandise, and this store excells in the field. There are briefcases, attachés, portfolios, all kinds of handbags and evening bags, wallets, belts, and accessories. Some are made especially for Hides in Shape, others are direct imports from Italy. No one knows how to craft leather better than the Italians, and in this emporium the prices are very reasonable for the quality. Monogramming is available, and so is professional repair service.

JOBSON'S LUGGAGE
666 Lexington Ave (bet 55th and 56th St)
355-6846, 800-221-5238
Mon-Sat: 9-6

Apparently, the key to a luggage store in New York is to offer a vast selection at very good discount prices. With the exception of a store such as T. Anthony, which depends on its quality and service to offset its high prices, most of the stores we've checked out offer good variety and a range of discounts. Naturally, the stores we've listed are the best of the genre. At Jobson's, they claim to have the largest selection of brand-name luggage, attaché cases, and small leather goods in the metropolitan area. I don't know about that, but it *is* enormous. They also claim that their large volume in sales enables them to sell at guaranteed low prices that are close to wholesale. Believe it or not, that is not enough to gain recognition in this book. There must be a dozen other stores with similar claims, but it is Jobson's sales staff and personal attention that sets it apart. The staff guides each customer, pointing out the advantages and disadvantages of each model. You need such guidance, and getting it at the best prices is a bonus.

T. ANTHONY
480 Park Ave (at 58th St)
750-9797, 800-722-2406
Mon-Fri: 9:30-6; Sat: 10-6

T. Anthony handles luxurious luggage of distinction. Anything purchased here will stand out in a crowd as being of really fine quality, and that is a distinction that T. Anthony customers expect and receive. Every person who comes into the store receives courteous attention. Luggage comes in sizes from small overnight bags to massive pieces that just fall short of being steamer trunks. (Actually, were this the day of ocean voyages, they would still carry those as well.) Gifts have a similar range. All are based on the leather-luggage theme, but the wallets, key cases, and billfolds are distinctive gifts, individually or in matched sets. No discount prices here, but the quality and service are well-established New York traditions. Exclusive T. Anthony products are also available through the store's catalog.

Lighting Fixtures and Accessories

JUST BULBS®
938 Broadway (at 22nd St)
228-7820
Mon-Fri: 8-5

From a practical point of view, this is probably the only shop in the world that can supply certain types of bulbs. In addition to the obvious ones, Just Bulbs has a collection for use in old fixtures. The staff boasts that the store houses almost 25,000 different types of bulbs. It's hard to imagine half that many exist. The shop looks like an oversized stage dressing-room mirror, and everywhere you look, there are bulbs connected to switches that customers are invited to flick on and off.

JUST SHADES
21 Spring St
966-2757
Thurs-Tues: 9:30-4

This lighting fixture store specializes in shades. As experts on shades, they are equally expert on the proper shade for the proper lamp and share their expertise with retail customers. Their experience encompasses the entire subject, and they carry only the finest shades. They have lampshades of silk, string, parchment, and just about any other material imaginable. Interestingly, they said their biggest peeve was customers who "neglect" (a polite way of putting it) to take the protective cellophane off their shades. They say that it is bad for the lamp, and the shade actually collects ruinous dust.

LEE'S STUDIO GALLERY
211 W 57th St (near Broadway)
265-5670
Mon-Fri: 10-6:30; Sat: 10-6

Across the street from Lee's Art Shop, and right next door to the Hard Rock Cafe, is Lee's Studio Gallery. This is the premier lighting store in midtown. Designs come from almost every corner of the world. In conjunction with the lighting, Lee's also offers furniture and accessories to complement almost any décor. All items are stocked in Manhattan, so delivery (or pickup) is relatively easy and quick. Ask for Rick for special service.

LIGHTING PLUS
676 Broadway (bet Second and Third St)
979-2000
Daily: 10-7

Maybe you are better than I am when it comes to electrical problems, but I never seem to have the right "whatjamacallit" when it's necessary to do some simple electrical job. These days most stores have a limited selection of electrical supplies, but not Lighting Plus. You'll save a lot of time and some electrical headaches by heading here first for one of New York's best assortments of lighting fixtures and lamps, appliances, audio and video tapes, and just about every other kind of electronic accessory imaginable.

LOUIS MATTIA
980 Second Ave (bet 51st and 52nd St)
753-2176
Mon-Fri: 9-6

Few stores repair or stock parts for lamps. Louis Mattia does. In his crowded shop, he has enough spare parts to fix almost any lamp. Consequently, he is patronized by a wide variety of customers: socialites who need a priceless heirloom repaired; decorators such as Denning-Fourcade; and other merchants who need quick repairs on slightly damaged merchandise for their customers. All of them receive prompt and courteous attention from one of the most knowledgeable staffs in New York.

NEW YORK GAS LIGHTING COMPANY
145 Bowery (bet Grand and Broome St)
226-2840
Mon-Fri: 9-5; Sat, Sun: 10:30-5

The definitive source for gas fixtures and other items of that bygone era, New York Gas Lighting Company is mentioned repeatedly by decorators. Purists and antiques lovers use the store as a source for parts, authentic oil lamps, and chandeliers. Others shop here for artifacts, conversation pieces, and mood-setters. Either way, it's a nostalgic step into the past, which is especially enjoyable since everything is sold at up to 60 percent less than anywhere else. And what a selection! Be sure to go through all the rooms; the place is a smorgasbord of lighting fixtures.

TUDOR—ELECTRICAL SUPPLY

222-26 E 46th St (bet Second and Third Ave)
867-7550
Mon-Thurs: 9-5; Fri: 9-4:30

Although you may feel like you need an engineering degree to enter Tudor Electrical, the staff is geared to explaining everything in stock to even the proverbial novice who doesn't know how to replace a light bulb. Light bulbs are the store's forte. No one has ever counted the varieties available, but they are cataloged by wattage, color, and use by a staff who can almost immediately pull out the best bulb for your needs. If Tudor stocks it, you can believe there's a reason for it. Quartz, tungsten, and halogen bulbs don't distort light, while incandescent and fluorescent lamps offer the best of both kinds of lighting for desk work. Energy-efficient bulbs come with vital instructions, which is a boon to people who feel that you need a degree to separate wattage from lumens from output. And better still, while discounting at least 20 percent off list price, Tudor Electrical Supply will guide a customer to the best bargains.

UNIQUE LAMP SHADES
AND ACCESSORIES

323 Second Ave (bet 18th and 19th St)
260-4670
Mon-Fri: 8-4

Perry presides over a collection of lighting instruments that seems truly unique and gives full credence to their name. As anyone who has ever tried to replace a simple lampshade knows, the choice is not simple. Often, the shade can cost more than the lamp, and a cheap or inappropriate shade can ruin the effect of an expensive lighting fixture. The range of choices can be staggering to the poor soul who has only come to replace a frayed shade. Perry is better than most shopkeepers at helping you make the right choices. Unique's shades are custom-made and measured. Most are also handmade, as are many of the lighting accessories.

UPLIFT

506 Hudson St
929-3632
Daily: 1-8

The big question is what the name Uplift has to do with a store that mainly sells art deco and Victorian lighting fixtures. Perhaps it is because the bases of many of the pieces are figures of nude women in various poses of lifting things. Or maybe the view is uplifting! In any event, Uplift has one of the largest collections of original American art deco chandeliers in the country. They have some less expensive reproductions and a full line of fantasy figures, like wizards and dragons made of pewter. They will rebuild old torchiere lamps so that they are like new, but taller. Uplift also has accessories for lighting fixtures: lamps, wiring, bases, and shades, including glass shades for lamps suspended from the ceiling. I guess that is a form of uplift, too.

Magic

FLOSSO AND HORNMANN MAGIC
45 W 34th St (room 607)
279-6079
Mon-Fri: 10:30-5:30; Sat: 10:30-4

Harry Houdini got his tricks and kicks here, which is not surprising, since he was but one of a score of professional magicians who have owned this shop since its creation in 1856. Flosso and Hornmann is proof that magic is timeless, not only because its clientele spans all ages, but because the store seems unchanged since Houdini's time. In part, that's due to the dim light and dust, but mostly it's because the stock is so complete. It's hard to think of a trick that's *not* stocked here, and it's just as hard to find one that you haven't seen before. The staff, if asked, will show you what's new. You have to visit the store to understand how amazing that is. In addition to magic acts, the shop carries books, manuals, historical treatises, and photographs, and even creates stage sets. For its final act, ladies and gentlemen, it produces a professional magic catalog. For amateurs, the best thing about the catalog is that many of the tricks are explained in detail. Don't tell a living soul!

LOUIS TANNEN
6 W 32nd St (fourth floor)
239-8383
Mon-Wed, Fri: 9-5:30; Thurs: 9-7; Sat: 9-3

Levitate upstairs to this jam-packed magic store, and Tony Spina (or any of the other helpful personnel) will cheerfully demonstrate the latest in magic. Unlike many such shops, this one welcomes amateurs, and there is a large stock of simple, inexpensive acts. In case they *do* leave the customer baffled, the staff will patiently explain them. There is also a series of mail-order catalogs that seem to be produced as rapidly as rabbits. All are annual *Catalogs of Magic* and contain the store's inventory—over 8,000 individual items and

350 books about magic. But unlike the store, the catalogs seem to be for people who know what they are doing. They also publish a magazine, *Magic Manuscript*.

Maps

HAGSTROM MAP AND TRAVEL CENTER
57 W 43rd St (at Sixth Ave)
398-1222
Mon-Fri: 9-5:30

The Hammond Map store was one of the finest in the business for three-quarters of a century. Now, as Hagstrom, under the supervision of Mr. Warner, the map specialist, it is a big name in maps in its own right. As the only complete maps and chart dealer in the city, they highlight the maps of other manufacturers and five branches of the U.S. government, as well as their own. There are also nautical, hiking, global, and travel guides. They have a free quarterly newsletter, and they ship maps virtually all over the map!

Memorabilia

ANNA SOSENKO
25 Central Park W (bet 62nd and 63rd St)
247-4816
Mon-Sat: by appointment

After a quarter of a century in business, Anna Sosenko has moved the operation to her home. She sells and maintains a magnificent collection of autographs and personal memorabilia. Most of the collection is show-business oriented, and the better items are framed. Anna Sosenko loves what she is doing, and it shows. Her advice is to stick to a particular specialty; she has merchandise to start you in your collecting career with hundreds of samples, and most are reasonably priced.

LOST CITY ARTS
275 Lafayette St (bet Prince and Houston St)
941-8025
Mon-Fri: 11-7; Sat, Sun: 12-6

Are you looking for a special old Coca-Cola advertising piece or a souvenir from a New York World's Fair? Lost City specializes in such items, with an emphasis on architectural antiques, old advertising fixtures, and a great collection of old New York souvenirs.

MEMORY SHOP
109 E 12th St (off Fourth Ave)
473-2404
Daily: 11-6

This dirty basement is virtually a Hollywood archive. The Memory Shop claims to have 1 million posters, 500,000 press books, and over 8 million photographs in stock. If it exists, it's buried here somewhere. Customers don't browse; they know exactly what they want, hand in the order, and the counter clerk gets it. This is probably because *only* the clerk could find it. If you have a fetish for *Gone with the Wind* or some other old movie, this is the place for you. The Memory Shop is especially eager to fill requests from libraries and film students.

MOTION PICTURE ARTS GALLERY
133 E 58th St (10th floor)
223-1009
Tues-Fri: 11-5:30; Sat: 12-5; closed Sat from
Memorial Day to Labor Day and all of Aug

Ira Resnick runs the world's only gallery that treats movie posters as works of art. His Motion Picture Art Gallery is just that: a gallery that displays the original posters and lobby cards from motion pictures as artwork and sells them. His customers include film buffs and vintage poster collectors and investors. (A *Casablanca* poster could be had for a couple of dollars in the early Sixties. Today, the same poster fetches upwards of $20,000.) There are over 5,000 items in stock here.

MOUSE 'N AROUND
197 Bleecker St (bet Sixth Ave and MacDougal St)
529-5656
Mon: 11-7; Tues-Sat: 11-10; Sun: 12:30-7:30

Perhaps it was inevitable that a boutique devoted to Mickey and friends would come to life in New York. So don't call the exterminator. At Mouse 'n Around, the mouse is strictly Mickey, and the stock is almost entirely based on Mickey Mouse and other cartoon characters. The big cheese is clothing. There are sizes for the whole family; they claim the largest selection outside of Disneyland. But it doesn't stop there. There are baby layettes, from blankets to booties, in guess what theme? Interior decorating gets a nod with clocks, figurines, ceramics, and even holiday decorations. The adult cartoon clothing is at their boutique (99 MacDougal St).

MOVIE STAR NEWS
134 W 18th St (bet Sixth and Seventh Ave)
620-8160
Mon-Sat: 10-6

In what is becoming the movie memorabilia center of the city, Movie Star News claims to have the world's largest collection of movie photos. If you thought the heyday of movie stars was long gone, don't tell the folks here, because the stars, past and present, still shine brightly in this shop. Movie Star News offers posters, press books, and other cinema publicity materials as well. The selection is arranged like a library, and the Kramers, who run Movie Star News, do a lot of research for magazines, newspapers, and the media. This is the closest thing to Hollywood on the East Coast.

MYTHOLOGY UNLIMITED
370 Columbus Ave (bet 77th and 78th St)
874-0774
Mon-Sat: 11-11; Sun: 11-6

You have to see Mythology Unlimited to understand it. You'll find anything from an autograph party for the author of a book on diners to an exhibit of contemporary art and objects that can be politely described as weird. There's the regular stock of tons of archaic postcards, pins, posters, ray guns, tin toys, personalized rubber stamps, screen prints, masks, toys, knickknacks, earrings, salt and pepper shakers, antique toys, Mexican masks, and Burmese puppets. This eclectic shop is a celebration of whimsy and pop art, right across the street from the castlelike Museum of Natural History.

ONE SHUBERT ALLEY
1 Shubert Alley (bet Broadway and Eighth Ave)
944-4133, 800-223-1320 (mail order only)
Mon: 10:30-8:30; Tues-Sat: 10:30 a.m.-11:30 p.m.;
   Sun: 12-7

Shubert Alley is a narrow alleyway in the Broadway theater district, which is often used as a shortcut between theaters. One Shubert Alley is the only retail establishment on the alley, and it's a fascinating place to browse. You will find T-shirts, posters, recordings, buttons, and other paraphernalia from current shows both on and off Broadway. There is a mail-order catalog and a special number for telephone orders.

PERFORMING ARTS SHOP
Metropolitan Opera House at Lincoln Center
(downstairs)
580-4356
Mon-Fri: 10-8

This little-known shop on the lower level of the Metropolitan Opera House is an aria unto itself. Everything on sale has a tie to the performing arts, no matter how tenuous. (A Harbor Sweets chocolate called Metropolitan Mint, which merits inclusion by virtue of its name, and a Tea for Two teapot are two of the extremes.) But all of it is high quality, and all is done in good taste. (How could you be located beneath Marc Chagall's panels and sell salt-and-pepper shakers?) So, there are topnotch gifts—all with a performing-arts motif, an enviable collection of printed matter that is so encompassing that there are rumors of an underground link to the Library of the Performing Arts one building over, and much more. Records and tapes are balanced by beach towels and Beethoven T-shirts. And if you want to check out that underground rumor, the Performing Arts Shop also arranges tours of Lincoln Center. They should start with better directions to their own shop.

SILVER SCREEN
35 E 28th St (bet Park and Madison Ave)
679-8130
Mon-Fri: 12-7

If the 1950s were the silver years for you, this is your shop. Ken, Carol, and Irma sell posters, autographs, movie magazines, and other theatrical memorabilia. In addition, they rent out old photographs in either black and white or color. The place is jammed with memories of old movie and stage personalities and events, and they evoke tears and thrills of glamorous yesteryears. Clients must write or phone their wants. *No browsing!*

Mirrors

SUNDIAL FABRICATORS
1388 First Ave (at 74th St)
734-0838, 873-8154
Mon-Fri: 8-4:30; Sat: 10-4

The people at Sundial claim they supply "decorative treatments of distinction," and everyone who has ever seen a cramped New York apartment suddenly expand with the use of a few strategic mirrors will understand how they can make that claim. Sundial deals with professional decorators as well as do-it-yourselfers, and both reap the benefit of the staff's years of experience. There are mirrors for home, office, and showrooms (their office is a factory showroom). In addition, Sundial will remodel, resilver, and move mirrors in need of those services. Sundial also custom-designs window treatments, doors, blinds, shades, storm windows, room dividers, and more. The primary service here, however, is the decorating advice.

Music, Musical Instruments and Equipment

BLEECKER BOB'S GOLDEN OLDIES RECORD SHOP
118 W Third St (bet MacDougal St and Sixth Ave)
475-9677
Mon-Fri: noon to 1 a.m.; Sat, Sun: noon to 3 a.m.

Let us sing the praises of Bleecker Bob's, who is nothing if not perverse. (Name another store open till 3 a.m. on Christmas Day!) For one thing, although there is a real Bob (Bob Plotnik, the owner), the store isn't on Bleecker Street. For another, Bleecker Bob is almost an institution to generations of New Yorkers who have sifted through the selection of virtually every rock record ever recorded. Yet what did *The New York Times* finally cite Bleecker Bob's for? "The archetypal punk-plus record store." Come on, folks! With a stock that includes all those old records (including rare jazz), autograph parties for rock stars, and a boast that they can fill any wish list from their stock, Bleecker Bob's is obviously much more than a punk-rock store. It is also *the* gathering place in the wee hours of the morning in the Village (where that *ain't* the wee hours of the morning). But above all, it's one great source for out-of-print, obscure, and imported discs.

COMPACT DISC
1187 Second Ave (bet 62nd and 63rd St)
838-DISC
Mon-Thurs: 11-10; Fri, Sat: 11-11; Sun: 12-9

Compact discs have revolutionized the music business; they're popular not only for homes, but also for cars and personal portables. The Compact Disc has one of the largest and most complete selections of both sizes of discs, with music for just about anyone's interests. The store's stock is well organized, making shopping a pleasure.

DAYTON'S
48 E 11th St (bet Broadway and University Pl)
254-5084
Mon-Fri: 10-6; Sat: 10-5:30; Sun: 12-5

Located across the street from the Strand Book Store, Dayton's is to records what the Strand is to books. They both have the same sources—reviewers' copies and promotional materials—and they both pass on their savings to retail customers. Dayton's reviewers' copies go for a price much less than the list price. I am talking here of best sellers or "hit parade" material; lesser works are relegated to lesser stores. Dayton's own boast is that they specialize in long-playing phonograph records, particularly those that are out-of-print. Again, this applies solely to best-selling records in mint condition, which partly explains the high cost. Customers may also browse through their huge inventory of rare and out-of-print records at 799 Broadway (corner of 11th St).

DETRICH PIANOS
211 W 58th St (near Broadway)
246-1766
Mon-Fri: 10-6; Sat: 10-4

Kalman Detrich fled Hungary for the United States many years ago, bringing his love and knowledge of pianos with him. His shop, within earshot of Carnegie Hall, ministers to any of the myriad needs the piano player might have. Detrich will tune, repair, polish, rent, buy, sell, and even buy back a piano with all the finesse of his Old World training. But his specialty is antique pianos. He lovingly restores them, and the few that he can't restore, he polishes to a gloss and sells as furniture rather than as musical pieces. The small shop is jammed with the cream of whatever is being revitalized at the moment, and passersby cannot help but understand Detrich's attitude when viewing the finished results. Detrich also has a sideline that he calls "gifts for musicians," and for music lovers he stocks music boxes, books, and figurines. The music boxes are good enough to warrant a shop to themselves.

DRUMMERS WORLD
133 W 45th St (bet Sixth and Seventh Ave)
840-3057
Mon-Fri: 10-6; Sat: 10-4

Rap, tap, tap! This is a great place, unless the patron is your teenager or upstairs neighbor. In any case, Barry Greenspon and his staff take great pride in guiding students as well as professionals through one of the most well-rounded percussion stores in the country. Inside this drummer's paradise, you'll find everything from commonplace equipment to one-of-a-kind antiques and imports. All of the instruments are high-quality symphonic percussion items, and the customers receive the same attention whether they are members of an orchestra or kitchen-spoon rappers. For the latter, the store offers instructors, instruction, and how-to books. And there are esoteric and even ethnic instruments for virtuosos who want to experiment. Drummers World has a catalog and will ship anywhere in the country.

FOOTLIGHT RECORDS
113 E 12th St (bet Third and Fourth Ave)
533-1572
Mon-Fri: 11-7; Sat: 10-6; Sun: 12-5

Footlight Records has a passion for rare and odd records, but there's an emphasis on show tunes and jazz rather than a general hodgepodge of discounted current recordings. This is not to say that Ed McGrath and Gene Dingenary's prices aren't good. In fact, for many of the albums, their prices are the best around, but that is really the point—these records just *aren't* around elsewhere. If an original cast album was made of a Broadway show, Footlight has it. Often, its customers are the artists themselves, who haven't copies of their own performances! What is more impressive is the organization that enables the store's personnel to know almost at a glance what is and is not available. Not an easy task when the stock is constantly being sold and much of it is out-of-print or hard-to-find recordings. There are show tunes, whole collections of '40s, '50s, and '60s artists, and probably every Big Band record ever made. Their compact disc selection is impressive

FORD PIANO SUPPLY COMPANY
4898 Broadway (bet 204th and 207th)
569-9200
Mon-Fri: 8:30-5:30

John Ford's father was in the piano-repair business. When John took over, he began collecting odds and ends whenever he found them, and he soon had more piano parts than pianos in his shop. Along with the best collection of supplies for piano repairs, Ford also garnered a reputation as *the* place to go for piano tuners. So, Ford all but abandoned the buying and selling of instruments and concentrated on the rebuilding of pianos (often from scratch) and the supplying of piano parts. The Ford family can refinish, tune, rebuild, or adjust any kind of acoustic piano. They will custom-make covers and benches as well as pedals, and there is an array of piano-tuning tools, lamps, chairs, and coasters. The Fords will happily conduct tours of their piano-rebuilding factory, which is a sight to see. But for the most part, Ford's customers never come to the shop. When you're the only store in town supplying everything for pianos, most customers order by mail or telephone. The Fords also rent and tune pianos. They are truly a family business; they are awaiting the day when little John Ford III is old enough to join the family ranks.

GRYPHON RECORD SHOP
251 W 72nd St (second floor)
874-1588
Daily: 10-8

Gryphon is one of just a handful of stores specializing in rare and out-of-print LPs. They're world-famous for their collection. Raymond Donnell knows his business; he's able to help the customer search out the most elusive LP, be it classical, jazz, Broadway, pop music, or the spoken arts. But the emphasis is on classical recordings.

JAZZ RECORD CENTER
135 W 29th St (12th floor)
594-9880
Tues-Sat: 11-7; June 1-Labor Day: open Mon-Fri,
    closed Sat

This is the only jazz specialty store in the city, and in its jam-packed spaces it features a listening area for "tryouts" of records. The house specialty is out-of-print jazz records, but there are also books, posters, photos, and periodicals on the topic. The Center buys and sells collections, runs a search service, fills mail orders, offers appraisals, and holds an annual jazz rarities auction. All of this is run by an amazing man, Frederick Cohen. Here's a world-famous specialist on jazz history running his shop from the 12th floor of an old office building. Business is so good that he moved to larger quarters several years ago, and now all records are arranged in browser bins. This is a charming guy who really knows his business.

JOSEPH PATELSON MUSIC HOUSE
160 W 56th St
582-5840
Mon-Sat: 9-6; closed Sat in summer

Behind Carnegie Hall, Joseph Patelson is the shop known to every student of music in the area. From little first-graders in need of theory books to artists from Carnegie Hall in need of an extra copy of sheet music, everyone stops here first because of the fabu-

lous selection as well as the excellent prices. The stock includes
music scores, sheet music, music books, and orchestral and opera
scores. All are neatly cataloged and displayed in open cabinets, and
one can pore through the section of interest—whether it be piano
music, chamber music, orchestral scores, opera scores, old popular
songs, concerts, ethnic scores, or instrumental solos. Nelson Sullivan and Daniel Patelson are models of informative saleshelp. They
are there for guidance, but never interfere with a customer combing
the files. Sheet music, incidentally, is filed the way records are elsewhere. You flip through the files to find what you want, and bring
it up to the counter to be checked out. There are some musical
accessories, like metronomes and pitch pipes, as well. Patelson's is
an unofficial meeting house for the city's young artists. Word goes
out that "We're looking for a violinist," and meetings are often
arranged in the store.

LAST WOUND-UP
290 Columbus Ave (bet 73rd and 74th St)
787-3388

889 Broadway (at 19th St)
529-4197

South St Seaport, Pier 17
393-1128

Hours vary

This super store is dedicated to any kind of object that can be
wound up. Within that classification, things are divided into music
boxes and windup toys, with a roughly equal division between the
two, though owner Nathan Cohen harbors a slight prejudice for the
music boxes. He makes many of the boxes in stock, and his avo-
cation is helping customers make their own music boxes out of
almost any suitable container. The Last Wound-Up also sells the
components to do this. The completed boxes for sale range from
valuable antiques to modern models. Many are from abroad, and
several are encrusted with gems. (The Victorian boxes in particular
were endowed with as many different jewels as they could hold.)
There are also fun boxes of no intrinsic value, except for the tunes
they play, as well as boxes of great value made of crystal and gold.
While Cohen believes every home should have several boxes, he is
not unmindful that other items can be wound up as well. So, there
are barking dogs and minstrels, windup toys, plush musical toys,

musical banks, and who-knows-what-else lining the walls. The original Edison phonographs were also operated by crank, so the Last Wound-Up has several of those. Despite the fact that most families threw them out, they are quite valuable now.

LYRIC HIGH FIDELITY
1221 Lexington Ave (bet 82nd and 83rd St)
535-5710, 439-1900
Mon-Sat: 10-6

2005 Broadway (bet 68th and 69th St)
769-4600
Mon-Wed, Fri, Sat: 10-6; Thurs: 10-8

Lyric is the place for sound fanatics who know what they're doing. As Lyric's Michael Kays says, they're not for beginners, but anyone who has the knowledge and necessary cash can indulge his wildest audio fantasies at Lyric. Cash is as important as knowing the merchandise; you can part with between $1,000 and $60,000 in a morning's worth of shopping here. Lyric has been in business for over 20 years, selling equipment to people who want—and get—the best. Kay sniffs at names like Sony, which the average person considers to be top-of-the-line. Lyric carries only the best lines of each component, and the names of its suppliers are unknown to all but the most discriminating audiophiles. If that's you, this is the store for you.

MANNY'S
156 W 48th St (bet Sixth and Seventh Ave)
819-0576
Mon-Sat: 9-6

Manny's is a huge discount department store for musical instruments. "Everything for the musician" is their motto, and it is borne out by a collection of musical equipment so esoteric that different salesmen are experts in different departments. There is an emphasis on modern music, as evidenced by the hundreds of autographed pictures of contemporary musicians and singers on the walls, and the huge collection of electronic instruments. Even the photos tend to be of the musicians who rely on electronic components rather than classical music. This does not, however, preclude classical instruments, and there is a good collection of them as well. The best part is that all of the musical instruments, accessories, electronic equipment, and supplies are sold at very good discount prices. They have full audio facilities. If you're into electronic music, Manny's should be your first choice.

MUSIC MASTERS
25 W 43rd St (bet Fifth and Sixth Ave)
840-1958
Mon-Fri: 10-5:30; Sat: 10-2:30

In the heart of the theater district, Music Masters carries a full stock of records and tapes, with a strong emphasis on Broadway show albums and an even better collection of opera recordings. (The Metropolitan Opera was resident of this neighborhood in its pre-Lincoln Center days.) Music Master claims to stock 98 percent of all classical recordings and boasts the largest collection of opera and theater material on records, tapes, and CDs. The house specialty is hard-to-find LPs and tapes. Of course, few are that hard for them to find. Music Masters also sells audio equipment and music boxes. This is a great place for browsing and listening.

MUSIC STORE AT CARL FISCHER
62 Cooper Sq (at Seventh St and Fourth Ave)
677-0821
Mon-Sat: 10-5:45

Outside the Carnegie Hall area, the Music Store at Carl Fischer offers the best selection of sheet music from all publishers and categories, including pop, jazz, folk, rock, and classical. Everything is reasonably priced, with real bargains to be found in the older music. (That's in terms of publication, not composition.) The store also has extended research facilities and background information for piano, vocal, instrumental, band, orchestral, and choral music. And that pretty much covers it all.

NOSTALGIA . . . AND ALL THAT JAZZ
217 Thompson St (bet Bleecker and Third St)
420-1940
Mon-Thurs: 1-8; Fri: 1-9; Sat: 1-10; Sun: 1-7:30

Guess what they sell here! Time's up: the answer is—envelope please—nostalgia records and LPs, especially jazz records. Most of the recordings are of early radio programs, jazz programs, and soundtracks of old shows. There are a few vocal LPs, too. All are very reasonably priced. The shop has set up a sideline in photography, and Kim Deuel and Mort Alavi do a healthy business in the production, cataloging, and reproduction of photos. Nostalgia will reproduce any photograph, in any size or quantity, up to 30″ × 40″. They also have a good collection of posters, movie and jazz stills, and large (16″ × 20″) show-business photos, in black and white *and* color. Prices are excellent.

ORPHEUS REMARKABLE RECORDINGS
1047 Lexington Ave
737-6043
Daily: 9-6

Remarkable here means "not cheap," but none of Orpheus' remarkable recordings descend to the depths. The emphasis is on culture, and that's as in highbrow and not Culture Club, so look for the classics and performance recordings as opposed to popular tunes. Orpheus also has a good selection that is not bound by time. If the very best recording of *Aïda* was made in 1947, then that's the one they stock. If it was made last month, so much the better. And while Orpheus is small, it is extremely well organized and there's nothing crammed away in the basement. That's too bad; I could think of some great puns to say about that.

RITA FORD
19 E 65th St (at Madison Ave)
535-6717
Mon-Sat: 9-5

Rita Ford collects antique music boxes, and in the process she has become an expert in all aspects of the business. Her stock consists of old valuable music boxes, old not-so-valuable pieces, and pieces in various states of disrepair (Rita Ford also does repairs). The main stock in trade is expertise; Rita Ford trades on her ability to know all there is to know about the music-box business. She is an acknowledged expert on various music-box scores, workings, and outer casings. Some of her pieces are rare, one-of-a-kind, perfect antiques and are priced accordingly. Somewhat more reasonable are the contemporary pieces based upon original antiques.

TOWER RECORDS
See below for addresses and phone numbers
Daily: 9 a.m.-midnight

Tower Records provides a selection of music that can satisfy any New Yorker, young or old. Their stores are busy, crowded, noisy, and fun. There is almost as much amusement in watching the parade of shoppers as there is in enjoying the music. The stores at 692 Broadway at East Fourth Street (505-1500) and 1961 Broadway at 66th Street (799-2500) carry records, tapes, and CDs; the annex at Fourth and Broadway (505-1500) features classical, Western, and used records. Tower Video Stores (discs and equipment) are located at 1977 Broadway at 67th Street (496-2500), 215 East 86th

Street between Second and Third Ave (369-2500), and Fourth and Lafayette (505-1166).

VENUS RECORDS
61 W Eighth St (at Sixth Ave)
598-4459
Mon-Sat: 11-7; Sun: 1-6

If rock and roll is your thing, rock on down to Venus (it's on the second floor; buzz to get in), and you'll find one of New York's finest selections of Fifties and Sixties reissues and original editions, hard-core, punk, and new and used rock records not usually found in the Top Twenty. Venus carries imported and independent releases, many out-of-print items, and a large selection of 45's. A wholesale service is available, as well as special orders for individual customers.

VINYL MANIA RECORDS
Five stores on Carmine St (see below)
924-7223
Mon-Fri: 11-9; Sat, Sun: 11- 7

There is no other record store quite like this one. If you can't find it at one of their five outlets, it probably doesn't exist. The specialties are as follows: 60 Carmine (12″ dance, R&B, funk, rap, hip hop, and house); 30A Carmine (12″ dance, sleaze, and morning music); 41 Carmine (12″ dance, rock, industrial, oldies, 45s, and CD singles); 30B Carmine (jazz); 43 Carmine (CDs, LPs, cassettes, mostly rock, and some R&B.) You can see why they call these places "adventures in recorded music"!

Newspapers, Magazines

A&S BOOK COMPANY
304 W 40th St (bet Eighth and Ninth Ave)
Annex: 274 W 43rd St (at Eighth Ave)
695-4897, 714-2712
Mon-Fri: 10-6; Sat: 10-5

For some reason, the sleazy Times Square area has always had back-dated-periodicals shops, even before the ubiquitous porno dives. A&S, one of the best, is a source of back issues of nearly every possible periodical. The more respectable the magazine, the better the possibility of finding it. Prices for what was originally very cheap but is now hard to find are reasonable, though they often surprise people who once threw out the very issue they now seek. A&S specializes in cinema, sports, and fashion magazines. You can avoid the neighborhood altogether and shop by mail or phone.

HOTALINGS NEWS AGENCY
142 W 42nd St
840-1868
Mon-Fri: 7:30 a.m.-9:15 p.m.; Sat, Sun: 7 a.m.-8 p.m.

As every homesick out-of-towner should know, hometown newspapers can be picked up at Hotalings for the regular price, plus the cost of transportation. Newspapers are sold on the day of issue (or soon thereafter), and many non-natives keep in daily contact with their homes through these papers. However, as many a Hollywood movie will attest, Hotalings also carries back issues (thereby enabling the hero to learn that his adversary has ceased to exist months ago, so he can return home). Back issues are erratic at best, and the days of sending the secretary out for the papers from Peoria for the past six months probably never existed, but there is still a pretty ample selection here.

Occult

GEMSTONED
2 Waverly Pl (bet Mercer St and Broadway)
674-0970
Mon-Sat: 12-8; Sun: 12-6

Fred Rubenfeld, the owner, describes his store as an oasis amid the hustle-bustle of New York. The shelves are filled with unusual mineral and gem specimens from all around the world, flower and crystal essences, and a big selection of metaphysical books. The store provides help to those who want to find out more about metaphysical teachings and even features weekly meditations and monthly classes. It isn't a branch of Tiffany's, for sure!

MAGICKAL CHILDE
35 W 19th St (at Fifth Ave)
242-7182
Mon-Sat: 11-8; Sun: 12-6

I asked the proprietor, Herman Slater, how one could describe this incredible place to readers of a book on New York. He answered that his shop was an "occult emporium," and I guess that is the best formal description. You have to see this place to believe it; there is nothing else quite like it in New York. There are shelves and bins of quartz crystals, gemstones, books, ritual accessories, videos, herbs and oils, powders and incenses, curios and tarot cards, jewelry and just about anything else that fits the occult image. The aisles are filled with readers and lookers, and they are just about as fascinating as the merchandise. Oh, yes, there are skulls, too.

Optical

COHEN'S FASHION OPTICAL
117 Orchard St
674-1986
' Hours vary at locations throughout the city

Cohen's is a chain of optical stores whose drawing card is the ability to have eyeglasses ready in one hour (in most cases). While not the first (or only) store to do this, Cohen's does have one of the best reputations. Furthermore, anyone in Manhattan who is in desperate need of a new pair of glasses (and it happens more frequently than imagined) benefits from the convenient locations. Cohen's also has qualified people to conduct eye examinations and fill prescriptions for glasses and contact lenses. Designer frames and brand-name contact lenses are sold at discount prices.

GRUEN OPTIKA CORPORATION
1225 Lexington Ave (bet 82nd and 83rd St)
628-2493

1076 Third Ave (bet 63rd and 64th St)
751-6177

GRUEN OPTIKA WEST
2382 Broadway (at 88th St)
724-0850

Mon-Fri: 9:30-6:30; Sat: 9:30-4:30; open Sun on
    West Side: 12-5

The trend in optical stores is toward larger and more industrial settings. Gruen bucks the tradition, and except for opening a West Side branch in 1985, it boasts the same faces and personal quality care year after year. Gruen enjoys a reputation for excellent service, be it emergency fittings or one-day turnaround, and there's a super selection of specialty eyewear. Their sunglasses, sport spectacles, and party eyewear are particularly noteworthy. The atmosphere is summed up by the continuous music and availability of Dom Perignon and caviar. It's plain to see that these people care.

LUGENE OPTICIANS
38 E 57th St
486-7500

660 Madison Ave (at 60th St)
486-7525

987 Madison Ave (at 77th St)
486-7520

1221-A Third Ave (at 71st St)
486-7502

Mon-Sat: 9:30-6

Lugene is one of the nation's finest eyewear retailers. Its innovative designs are created and produced exclusively for them. They introduce new collections six times a year. They also offer custom-made frames, 14- and 18-karat gold frames, lorgnettes, genuine tortoise-shell frames, and a full line of opera glasses and mini-binoculars. They are very professional and accommodating people. Everything here is of top quality, but don't expect bargain-store prices.

PILDES
111 Nassau St
227-9893
Mon-Fri: 8-6; Sat: 8:30-3:30

1010 Third Ave (at 60th St)
421-1322
Mon-Wed, Fri: 9-7; Thurs: 9-7:30; Sat: 10-6; Sun: 12-5
    (closed Sun in summer)

Pildes is the only "while-you-wait" eyeglasses chain in New York, and it has an impeccable reputation. Nothing fancy here, just frames, styles, and service, and all are first-class.

Photographic Supplies

ALKIT CAMERA SHOP
866 Third Ave (bet 52nd and 53rd St)
832-2101

222 Park Ave S (at 18th St)
674-1515

Mon-Fri: 8:30-6:30; Sat: 9-5

If you're professional enough to want to go where the photographers of the Elite and Ford modeling agencies go, Alkit is the shop for you. But come here even if you haven't the faintest idea which end of a camera to look into. Most establishments that deal with the real pros have little time for rank amateurs. Not so here. Nothing gives Edward Buchbinder, the store's owner, more pleasure than introducing the world of photography to a neophyte. And few stores are better equipped to do so. Alkit maintains a full line of cameras, film, and equipment, as well as stereos, TVs, VCRs, and electronics. The shop repairs and rents these items, and it also maintains a professional catalog of preferences for and gripes about particular models. The attitude is always briskly professional. Buchbinder hastened to point out that the stereo and TV line is not an extraneous frill: many of his best customers find it essential to work with one or both playing in the background.

BEN NESS CAMERA AND PHOTO STUDIO
114 University Pl (bet 12th and 13th St)
255-4270
Mon-Fri: 8:30-6; Sat: 10:30-5

Those who know what they want in photographic supplies will find them here. The shop bills itself as a "Kodak professional stock-house," and that is but a part of it. The store stocks everything from Matthew Brady's camera to prototypes not yet on the market. And remember *all* of this is discounted. For proof, ask for Ben Ness' price list. Special student discounts are also available.

BIG APPLE CAMERA AND SOUND
99 Chambers St (at Church St)
233-1865
Mon-Sat: 9-6; Sun: 11-5

Big Apple specializes in selling the best cameras and the handiest beepers at the best prices. They are not averse to phone or mail inquiries; they will even quote prices over the phone. Cameras and photographic equipment stocked by Big Apple represent all of the major names, and the staff will instruct customers on the merits of each of them. And now for the best part: tell the folks you read about them in Gerry's *Where To* . . . and you'll get a discount that will probably equal the price of this book!

47th STREET PHOTO
67 W 47th St

115 W 45th St (bet Sixth Ave and Broadway)

116 Nassau St

35 E 18th St (bet Park and Broadway)

260-4410

Mon-Thurs: 9-6; Fri: 9-2; Sun: 10-4

You can't beat the prices on all kinds of cameras and photographic equipment at this bustling emporium. Watch their newspaper ads, and you'll save the price of a ticket to Hong Kong (but you'll miss the fun of haggling). When I complained about the poor phone service here, they took my remarks to heart, and added four more lines and doubled the telephone sales staff. Thanks! The branch on 18th Street offers darkroom services.

NEWMAN PHOTOGRAPHICS
400 Lafayette St (at Fourth St)
505-1840
Mon-Fri: 9-6 (evenings and weekends by appointment)

Whether you are a professional or an amateur, Newman can take care of your photographic needs. They do excellent work producing Cibachrome prints, most of them exhibition quality. The nice part of this operation is that they are patient and understanding with those of us who need counseling and advice. They are not professional retouchers, but they can spot and make minor changes. Lamination and print-mounting service is available off premises.

WILLOUGHBY'S CAMERA STORE
110 W 32nd St (bet Sixth and Seventh Ave)
564-1600
Mon-Wed, Fri: 9-7; Thurs: 9-8; Sat: 9-6:30;
    Sun: 10:30-5:30

This is the largest camera shop in the world, boasting a large stock, extensive clientele, and a good reputation. Willoughby's can handle almost any kind of camera order. For those in doubt, there is always the mail-order division. Write and ask for something really esoteric. It's my bet that Willoughby's can fill it without a problem. In addition to selling all kinds of cameras, Willoughby's also services them, supplies photographic equipment, and recycles used cameras. This is truly a photographic emporium *plus*.

Pictures, Posters, Prints

ARGOSY BOOK STORE
116 E 59th St
753-4455
Mon-Fri: 9-6; Sat: 10-5; closed Sat in summer

The main stock in trade here is ostensibly books (the older and rarer the better), but knowledgeable browsers usually pass the books by in favor of the antique maps and prints. There is an excellent collection of early American paintings and prints (Currier and Ives, among others) and a combination of maps and prints that makes a marvelous background. In fact, if a bookstore could be classified as a decorating accessory store, Argosy would qualify. The books are valued as much for their appearance and bindings as for their age and rarity, and maps and prints are similarly rated. Argosy handles first editions and Americana garnered from estate sales, and will buy books from private sources. The specialties are antique prints, maps, autographs, and, surprisingly, medical books. The personnel seem very impressed with their own knowledge and position, so some customers feel intimidated here. Too bad. Otherwise, it's a great place to browse and shop.

OLD PRINT SHOP
150 Lexington Ave (bet 29th and 30th St)
686-2111, 683-3950
Mon-Sat: 9-4:30; closed Sat in summer

Strolling down Lexington Avenue and glancing at the Old Print Shop, one might think that time was suspended in the 19th century. Established in 1898, the shop exudes an old-fashioned charm that makes it appear timeless, and its stock only reinforces that impression. Kenneth M. Newman specializes in Americana. That includes original prints, paintings, town views, Currier and Ives prints, and original maps that reflect America as it was. Most of the nostalgic bicentennial pictures that adorned calendars and stationery were copies of prints found here. Historians, amateur and professional, have a field day in this shop, and often purchase things that simply strike their fancy and have nothing to do with their original request. Kenneth Newman also does custom framing—"Correct period framing," he hastens to add—and prints in his frames are striking. Everything bought and sold here is original. (Newman also purchases estates and single items.) A great place.

POSTER AMERICA
138 W 18th St (bet Sixth and Seventh Ave)
206-0499
Tues-Fri: 11-7; Sat, Sun: 12-5

You've never seen a poster gallery more interesting than this one! Jack Banning's store features original posters circa 1870 to 1950, nearly all of which are lithographs. But ah, the setting! For 10 years, he ran Poster America, the oldest gallery in the country devoted to vintage poster art. When that gallery on Ninth Avenue proved too small, he found and renovated a former stable and carriage house that used to serve the department stores on Ladies Mile in the 1880s. These new quarters sport a magnificent mahogany-and-glass storefront, a huge, well-appointed gallery, and elegant living quarters for Banning. Poster America is known for the brilliant graphics, sheer size, and magnitude of its pieces. It is also the exclusive agent for California designer David Lance Goines.

TRITON GALLERY
323 W 45th St (bet Eighth and Ninth Ave)
765-2472
Mon-Sat: 10-6

Theater posters are the show here, and Triton presents them like no one else. The complete list of current Broadway posters is but a small part of what's available, and it's balanced by an almost equally complete range of older show posters from here and abroad. Show cards are a standard $14'' \times 22''$ size and seem to be the most readily available items. Posters range in size from $23'' \times 46''$ to $42'' \times 84''$ and are priced according to how rare, how old, and how much in demand they are. None of these criteria, incidentally, have much to do with the actual success of the show. Often, hundreds of posters were printed for shows that lasted less than a week and no one has a use for. At the same time, a hit like *Annie* has produced more posters than anyone could use, so its show cards cost no more than some of the totally obscure ones. The collection is not limited to Broadway or even American plays, and some of the more interesting pieces are of plays from other times. Triton also does custom-framing, and much of the business is done via mail and phone orders. Ask for Triton's catalog.

Plastics

PLASTIC PLACE
309 Canal St (bet Mercer St and Broadway)
226-2010
Mon-Fri: 8:30-5; Sat: 8:30-4

This large loft is dedicated to plastics, both the lucite and soft plastic variety. Primarily wholesalers, they will cut anything from cubes to wall coverings, free of charge. Some of their line includes waterproofing material, lucite cubes, and sheets of plastic. They are particularly accommodating to do-it-yourself customers.

PLEXI-CRAFT QUALITY PRODUCTS
514 W 24th St
924-3244
Mon-Fri: 9:30-5; Sat: 11-4

Plexi-Craft offers anything made of lucite and plexiglass at wholesale prices. If you can't find what you want among the pedestals, tables, chairs, shelves, and cubes, they will make it for you. The personnel are extremely helpful in pointing out the various styles in cocktail tables, shelves, magazine racks, and chairs.

Religious Arts

GRAND STERLING SILVER COMPANY
345 Grand St (bet Essex and Ludlow St)
674-6450
Sun-Thurs: 10:30-5:30

Ring the bell, and you will be admitted to a stunning collection of silver religious art. You'll also find almost anything from silver toothpick holders to baroque candelabras over six feet tall. Grand Sterling will also repair and resilver any silver item, be it religious or secular. They are manufacturers and importers of fine sterling hollowware, and silver is revered with a dedication unmatched elsewhere.

HOLY LAND ART COMPANY
160 Chambers St (bet W Broadway and Greenwich St)
962-2130
Mon-Thurs: 9-4:30; Fri: 9-4; Sat: 9-1 bet Thanksgiving
and Christmas

Across the street from Cheese of All Nations, there's another world at Holy Land Art Company. The store offers all kinds of religious articles to churches and the public. On hand is everything from Bibles to altars, although the latter, along with custom-made statues of wood, bronze, and marble, are usually specially ordered directly for churches rather than individuals. In December, Holy Land is anything but pastoral, as customers snap up creches, nativity scenes, and chalices. There's a tremendous selection, and the prices are reasonable. The company says that its work for churches is evenly divided between new buildings and refurbishing and reconstruction.

MORIAH ART CRAFTS
699 Madison Ave (bet 62nd and 63rd St)
751-7090
Mon-Thurs: 9-5; Fri: 9-4

Peter and Michael Ehrenthal, a father-and-son team, run Moriah with a sense of timelessness. It's only when you become aware of the heavy security measures that you know exactly what city you're in and what era. Otherwise, it could be anywhere at all, from a fine museum to a Middle Eastern farmers' market. The specialty is antique Judaica and ceremonial art, and it is doubtful that anyone in the world knows the business as well. Members of the Appraisers Association of America, the Ehrenthals are acknowledged specialists in the field. They come across a tremendous selection of old items of Jewish interest, and usually have first choice as to what they wish to keep and sell.

Rubber Goods

CANAL RUBBER SUPPLY COMPANY
329 Canal St (at Greene St)
226-7339
Mon-Fri: 9-5; Sat: 9-4:30

"If it's made of rubber, we have it" is this company's motto, and that sums up the supply at this wholesale-retail operation. There are foam mattresses, bolsters, cushions, pads, pillow foam, pads cut to size, hydraulic hoses, rubber tubing, and sponges. And there is much, much more. They are right. If it's made of rubber, Canal Rubber Supply has it.

Screens

TONEE CRAFTS CORPORATION
108 Wooster St
966-4213
Mon-Fri: 9-5; Sat: 10-4

The lovely screens that slide back and forth between rooms and between house and garden in Oriental settings are usually Shoji screens, and the genuine article is seldom available outside Asia. Some years ago, however, the natural connection between light, free-standing space dividers and studios, lofts, and even offices dawned on some Japanese merchants, and this outpost of Japanese construction came to SoHo, an area where it was especially needed. Though this is one of the few Shoji outlets anywhere—and may be the only one manned by authentic native craftsmen—Tonee is not limited solely to Shoji screens. For one thing, the screens are defined by use, size, style, and material. For another, the Fusuma screen is also available, though the only thing it has in common with the Shoji is that they are both screens. If that sounds like so much Japanese jibberish to you, perhaps it explains best why an expert such as Tonee is the perfect person to guide a customer through the maze of screens, tatami mats, and general construction that the company offers.

Security Devices

CCS COUNTER SPY SHOPPE
630 Third Ave (near Fourth St)
557-3040
Mon-Fri: 9-5:30 by appointment

Fascinated by James Bond and all of his gadgets? You'll marvel at this shop, which supplies security items for business and private use. There are covert video systems, night-vision equipment, debugging devices, voice-stress analyzers, and bulletproof cars. They even have bulletproof T-shirts! These people are the best in the business, and advertise themselves as the only antiterrorist boutique in Manhattan. Appointments are a must, and confidential demonstrations and security consultations can be arranged.

EMPIRE SAFE COMPANY
433 Canal St (at Varick St)
226-2255
Mon-Fri: 9-5; Sat: 10-3; closed Sat in July, Aug

Things have been safe around here since 1904! The same family has been in the business for three generations, and now they have the largest showroom of safes in the country. You can find vaults and safes for homes, offices, and restaurants. A great exhibit of antique and art deco safes is well worth seeing. Empire also services all makes of safes, so if some uninvited caller should visit your premises, these folks are the first to call after dialing 911!

Signs

CRYPTOGRAPHICS
40 E 32nd St
685-3377
Mon-Fri: 9-5

This is a handy service place to know about. They offer a complete service for signs, awards, advertising specialties, executive gifts, bulletin boards, and directories. Customized merchandise for businesses, organizations, and individuals is done quickly and accurately with engraving and silkscreening facilities on the premises.

LET THERE BE NEON
38 White St
226-4883
Mon-Sat: 9:30-5:30 by appointment

Though the image of neon is modern, it harks back to Georges Claudes' capture of it (from oxygen) in 1915. And while "the flashing neon sign" is perhaps the ultimate urban cliché, Rudi Stern has turned the neon light into a modern art form. So, Let There Be Neon operates as a gallery. At any given moment, there is an assemblage of sizes, shapes, functions, and designs to entice the browser. Though they all have a common neon base (with transformer in the base), that is all they have in common. Almost all of Let There Be Neon's sales are custom-made, commissioned pieces. Stern claims that even a rough sketch is enough for them to create a figurative (literal or abstract) sculpture within 10 days. Each project is proof that neon is a versatile and easily used art form. There's a glow about the place!

Silver

EASTERN SILVER COMPANY
54 Canal St (second floor)
226-5708
Sun-Thurs: 9:30-5; Fri: 9:30-1 (showroom closed Fri)

Ascend to the second floor, ring the bell, and you enter a wonderland of silver, from floor to ceiling. Not all of it is clean or polished, but it has the potential of becoming as beautiful as only silver can be. The stock includes virtually any product made of silver or pewter, and the amazing thing is that Robert Gelbstein seems to be able to put his hand on any desired item almost immediately. Eastern has a large collection of Jewish ceremonial silver and secular silver items, such as candlesticks and wine decanters. However, most of the collection would be perfect gracing any home. Prices are extremely reasonable, and the quality is A-1. This place is a real find.

ROGERS AND ROSENTHAL
22 W 48th St (room 1102)
827-0115
Mon-Fri: 10-5

Rogers and Rosenthal are two big names in the elegant place-setting business, and while this store claims that it is just a coincidence and that *their* Rogers and Rosenthal are merely the founders' names, the shop's title is an excellent sign of what is inside. Rogers and Rosenthal has to be one of the very best places in the city, if not *the* best, for silver, china, and crystal. A visit to verify this statement isn't even necessary, since nearly all their business is done by mail. ("Very slow delivery," they warn!) This shop features every major brand name, and an immediate 25 percent discount on every piece by mail is an added bonus. They will send price lists upon request, and what isn't in stock will be ordered. They are very accommodating.

TIFFANY AND COMPANY
727 Fifth Ave (at 57th St)
755-8000
Mon-Sat: 10-5:30

What can you say about a store that's such an institution that it has appeared in plays, movies, books, and even slogans? Almost nothing, except that the store really isn't *that* formidable or forbidding, and it can even be an exciting place to shop. For the curious, let's begin by stating that, yes, there really is a Tiffany Diamond, and it can be readily viewed on the first floor. That floor also houses the watches and jewelry departments, and while browsing is welcome, salespeople are quick to approach lingering customers. The second floor houses clocks, silver jewelry, sterling silver, flatware, bar accessories, centerpieces, leather accessories, stationery, scarves, and knickknack gifts. The third floor highlights china and crystal. The real surprise—and a fact not known to many New Yorkers—is that Tiffany has an excellent selection of reasonably priced items. Many items come emblazoned with the Tiffany name, wrapped in the famed Tiffany blue box, and at prices less than those of some neighborhood variety stores.

Sporting Goods

Art

CROSSROADS OF SPORT
36 W 44th St (bet Fifth and Sixth Ave)
764-8877
Mon-Fri: 10-5

Crossroads here seems to refer to intersecting country lanes, and the store personnel are quick to tell you that sports to them is decidedly not team sports. So, it's not surprising that the atmosphere at the oldest sporting art gallery and gift shop in North America is reminiscent of a hunting club library. In addition to an admirable collection of books, artwork, prints, and paintings relating to the store's definition of sports, there is also a variety of tankards, serving pieces, and tableware decorated with sporting motifs. Many of the books are collector's items, as is the artwork (note particularly the 18th-century prints). Crossroads is a primary source for appraisals and purchase of sporting art, and they are accomplished enough to trace and find any item that they don't have in stock. If there's a bit of country gentleman in you, stop by. It's the closest thing to the hunt club you'll find in the city.

Bicycles and Accessories

BICYCLE RENAISSANCE
491 Amsterdam Ave (at 84th St)
724-2350
Mon-Sat: 10-7; Sun: 10-5; summer: 10-7 daily

Biking here is a way of life, just as health foods are to most of the staff. Among the services are the custom building of bikes and winter storage. Their mechanics aim for same-day service on all makes and models. As for brands—well, they are all here, with an accent on racing and mountain bikes. In stock are Peugeot, Motobecane, and custom frames for Stronglight, Campagnolo, Ideale, and many others. I appreciate the fact that this was the only bike shop that did not pretend to have discount rates. And, in fact, its prices were exactly on par with the so-called discount stores.

BICYCLES PLUS
1400 Third Ave (bet 79th and 80th St)
794-2929
Daily: 10-7

Bicycles Plus rents bikes for use in Central Park and elsewhere, but they don't need rental clients to draw in business. The store is owned by bicycle mechanics Jeff Loewi and Larry Duffus, who know cycling upside-down and inside-out. Their bikes, which include B.M.X., mountain, triathalon, and racing bikes, are sold with a five-year guarantee. The salespeople are absolutely into their sport.

14th STREET BICYCLES
332 E 14th St (near First Ave)
228-4344
Daily: 9:30-6:30

For some reason, Stuyvesant Town is bicycle country, and there are a half-dozen bicycle stores within a three-block area. To be patronized by the locals, a bike shop here has to be special, and this one is. This bicycle house has an excellent reputation, but with so many other shops in the area, a little comparison shopping can't hurt. All bikes (Trek, Panasonic, Metro, Riley, and Ross) are discounted.

GENE'S DISCOUNTED BICYCLES
242 E 79th St (at Second Ave)
288-0739
Mon-Fri: 9:30-8; Sat, Sun: 9-7

This is *the* bike shop in New York. Gene's features children's bikes, racing bikes, tour bikes, fat tire bikes, and BMX bikes—all made by the leading manufacturers from around the world. Names like Nishiki, Ross, and Peugeot are represented in quantity, and all kinds of accessories are available. Gene will repair or rent any kind of bike, and now he offers a big selection of exercise equipment, including aerobic bikes, tread mills, and home gyms. He also guarantees that he'll meet or beat any competitor's price. The service is good, the personnel knowledgeable, and the selection tremendous.

STUYVESANT BIKE SHOP
349 W 14th St
254-5200
Mon-Fri: 9:30-6:30; Sat: 10-6; Sun: 12-5

Salvatore Corso, the owner of Stuyvesant Bike Shop, lives and breathes cycling, and will proselytize to anyone willing to listen. Backing him up is a four-floor establishment dedicated to the world of cycling and brimming with bicycles, accessories, burglar alarms, scooters, tricycles, and the like. With all that space, Salvatore Corso is also willing to store bikes over the winter months. This shop, too, has an incalculable storehouse of spare parts, which enables it to attempt most repairs within 24 hours. Other items offered include tandems, triplets, adult tricycles, exercisers, 3-, 5-, 10-, and 15-speed bikes, children's bikes, and racing equipment.

Billiard Equipment

BLATT BILLIARD
809 Broadway (bet 11th and 12th St)
674-8855
Mon-Fri: 9-6; Sat: 9:30-4; closed Sat in summer

Blatt is home for a store outfitted from top to bottom with everything for billiards. You also get friendly pointers from a staff that seems at first glance to be all business.

Darts

DARTS UNLIMITED
30 E 20th St (bet Park Ave S and Broadway)
533-8684
Tues-Fri: 12-5:30; Sat: 11-4

Most towns have sporting goods shops, but few have even a department (or display) for darts. In New York, things are different. There's Darts Unlimited, an emporium dedicated solely to darts and darting equipment. The collection of darts, dartboards, accessories, and English darting equipment (England's pubs are where it all started, you know) makes you wonder why they are not more prominent in other sports stores. Indeed, it seems that playing darts is a neglected game in America. Which is a shame, since it's good not only for exercise but for channeling aggression!

Diving

RICHARDS
233 W 42nd St (bet Seventh and Eighth Ave)
947-5018
Mon-Sat: 9-7:30

Aside from being near the Port Authority bus terminal, there's nothing positive that can be said about the neighborhood, but much can be said about Richards' stock. The store calls itself an aqua-lung and skin-diving center, but there's also all kinds of sporting goods, clothing, and cameras. The clothes are of the army-navy-surplus variety. And in keeping with the low rent (and lowlife) of the area, everything in the store is discounted. They claim to be the largest diving shop in the country.

Fishing Equipment

CAPITOL FISHING TACKLE COMPANY
218 W 23rd St (Chelsea Hotel, near Seventh Ave)
929-6132
Mon-Fri: 8-5:30; Sat: 9-4

Historical records show that over 100 years ago, the 42nd Street Library and the adjacent Bryant Park were once a cemetery and later a reservoir, so distinct and countrified was their location in relationship to the rest of the city. Thus, it is somewhat possible that in 1897, when Capitol Fishing Tackle Company was established, its present location might have justified a store dedicated to fishing. Today, in the hustle and bustle of Chelsea, the store is totally incongruous and yet it is typical of New York. Where else would one find a fishing store so totally landlocked that a subway roars beneath it, and yet it offers bargains unmatched at seaport stores? Capitol features a complete range of fishing tackle with such brand names as Penn, Shimano, Tycoon Finnor, Garcia, and Daiwa at the lowest possible prices. There is a constantly changing selection of specials and closeouts that can only be described as fantastic. All of it is achieved by Capitol's buying up surplus inventories, bankrupt dealers, and liquidations. Almost nothing in the store was purchased at full wholesale, and those savings are passed on to the customer.

Game Tables

V. LORIA AND SONS
178 Bowery (bet Delancey and Kenmore St)
925-0300
Mon-Fri: 10:30-6; Sat: 10-4; closed Sat in summer

This family business, established in 1912, is a mecca for indoor sports enthusiasts. One can find a complete line of equipment. There are bowling and billiard items, pool tables and such pool supplies as cues and chalk, plaques, and awards—not to mention ping-pong, shuffleboard, and poker tables. When the family champion is triumphant, the winner's trophy can be ordered from Loria as well. It is impossible *not* to try out some of the equipment right on the premises, and Vernon and Roger Loria don't seem to mind.

General

EASTERN MOUNTAIN SPORTS (EMS)
20 W 61st St (at Broadway)
397-4860

611 Broadway (at Houston St)
505-9860

Mon-Fri: 10-8; Sat: 10-6; Sun: 12-6

Eastern Mountain Sports started in Wellesley, Massachusetts, at the height of the backpacking craze. Despite its geographic origins, there's a natural connection with New York, which is cold (weatherwise, of course), and the residents are fanatics for anything that is compact and functional. What could be more functional than thermal clothing that fits in a pocket? So, EMS' camping grounds in New York were an immediate success. In fact, it was so successful that it spawned a branch in SoHo as well as in several suburban malls and became the flagship store for a European conglomerate. It's the place to go for authentic outdoor clothing and gear (service, too), although prices can be bettered elsewhere. Still, for one-stop shopping, it's an excellent source for authentic equipment, and the authentic stuff is of better quality and price than that of the department stores. Incidentally, EMS covers virtually *all* outdoor sports. That includes mountain climbing, backpacking, skiing, hiking, tenting, kayaking, and camping. And there's much more.

G&S SPORTING GOODS
43 Essex St (at Delancey St)
777-7590
Mon-Fri, Sun: 9:30-6

If you have a sports buff in the family and are looking for a place to buy him (or her) a birthday or Christmas gift, I'd recommend G&S. They have a large selection of sneakers, balls, gloves, toys and games, sports clothing, and the accessory items that any jock would like to receive. That isn't all the good news; the prices reflect a 20 to 25 percent discount. Brand names include Adidas, Puma, Converse, Nike, Reebok, Spaulding, New Balance, Wilson, Prince, Head and Avia.

HERMAN'S

110 Nassau St	135 W 42nd St
233-0733	730-7400
Mon-Fri: 9-6; Sat: 9-5	Mon-Fri: 9:30-7; Sat: 9:30-6
39 W 34th St	845 Third Ave (at 51st St)
279-8900	688-4603
Mon-Fri: 9:30-7; Sat: 9:30-6:30; Sun: 12-5	Mon-Fri: 9:30-7; Sat: 9:30-6

1185 Avenue of the Americas
944-6689
Mon-Fri: 10-7; Sat: 10-6

With only a moderate selection of women's and children's gear, Herman's is almost no *her* and almost all *man*. Long before the running and physical-fitness craze, this chain of sporting goods shops was set up to equip men for the enjoyment of sports, and the more macho, outdoorsy, or competitive the sport, the better. There are woodsmen's vests, plaid flannel shirts, and camping equipment, but there is more emphasis on clothing than equipment. As for price—in general, you can do better. But there is a sale every week on something, and those prices can be good. Add the convenience of a vast selection of equipment for all types of sports, and you know why the Herman's chain is growing.

MODELL'S

280 Broadway	243 W 42nd St
267-2882	575-8111
200 Broadway	109 E 42nd St
964-4007	661-5956

Hours vary (closed Sun)

Modell's is an old New York family chain. Founded in 1889, it is still a family-run operation with a personal touch. The store specializes in men's wear (with a nod to the ladies when the look is fashionable), sporting goods, footwear, luggage, and sundries. The guiding philosophy is to sell these items as cheaply as possible. Prices are never high, and the quality is usually excellent. Modell's, for example, carries most brand-name sneakers at rock-bottom prices.

PARAGON SPORTING GOODS
871 Broadway (at 18th St)
255-8036
Mon-Fri: 10-8; Sat: 10-7; Sun: 11-6

This is truly a sporting-goods department store, with over 80,000 square feet of specialty shops devoted to all kinds of sports equipment and apparel. There are separate departments for skis, team equipment, athletic footwear, skateboards, ice skates, racquet sports, aerobics, swimming, golf, hiking, camping, diving, biking, sailing, and whatever else you want to do in the great outdoors. There are also a number of gift items, and the stock is arranged for easy shopping. Paragon has cleaned up their act since its early days; it is now a pleasure to shop in this vast wonderland of fun.

SPIEGEL'S
105 Nassau St (at Ann St)
227-8400
Mon-Fri: 9-6; Sat: 10-5; closed Sat in summer

You wouldn't expect to find a good, competent place to buy sporting goods in this neighborhood, but Spiegel's is here, and they would be top-notch in any location. The most advantageous point (aside from the lack of competition) is their discount prices, which are as good as those anywhere in the city. In addition, the selection is ample, the saleshelp excellent, and the supply amazing for a store of its size. Call first, and they will tell you if they have what you want. They run advertisements in the *Times* for special items, and then their prices can't be beat.

Guns

JOHN JOVINO COMPANY
5 Centre Market Pl (at Grand St)
925-4881
Mon-Fri: 9-6; Sat: 8-1

When you have been in the same business for nearly 80 years, you should know nearly everything there is to know in that line. So it is with this company. In the gun business since 1911, John Jovino has the largest selection of guns in New York, and Juan Cabrera is an expert in the field. Brands featured include Colt and Smith and Wesson, and they have handguns, rifles, shotguns, and ammunition. At the moment they are installing a firing range, and they should be in the gun-instruction business in the near future.

Horseback-Riding Equipment

H. KAUFFMAN AND SONS
139 E 24th St
684-6060
Mon-Sat: 9:30-6:30; Sun: 11-5

If you're into horses and horseback riding, Kauffman's is the place to seek out. Kauffman's handles the subject so well that no one ever thinks that one of the world's finest equestrian supply shops is not only located in the midst of one of the world's largest cities, but it is miles from the borough's only bridal paths. It is taken for granted that for the very best in riding equipment, Kauffman's is the place to go. This specialty store has literally everything for the horse and its rider. (It even manages to sell a good amount of hay!) In addition to the saddles, bridles, and riding equipment, there is a good line of gifts for horse lovers. Ladies' side saddles, Kauffman told me, are about the only thing he doesn't stock. A catalog is published for $3. Being a horse fancier, I found this place a fascinating spot, and it's very well stocked.

MILLER'S
117 E 24th St
673-1400
Mon-Sat: 9-5:30; summer: Sat: 9-4

Typically, New York just couldn't make do with only one world-famous equestrian equipment source, so Miller's offers the city its second on the same block. But this flagship is only a very small part of a large business. The Miller symbol (two boots) is displayed in hundreds of shops across North America that carry all or part of the exclusive Miller line, and that line is so distinctive that it covers a rider and his horse from head to hoof. Sizes suit men, women, children, stallions, mares, and colts. The haberdashery offers proper riding gear and saddles. (The Hermes saddles are registry numbered and go for a mere $2,300 and up!) There are boots, helmets, riding shirts, plaques, and riding potpourri. That makes Miller's a good bet for those who have never ridden, as well as for the U.S. equestrian team. For horse lovers, this is a super place to find gifts for both horses and their owners.

Marine

GOLDBERGS' MARINE
12 W 37th St (at Fifth Ave)
594-6065
Mon-Wed, Fri: 9:30-5:45; Thurs: 9:30-7:45;
    Sat: 9:30-3:45

Goldbergs' sells marine supplies as if it were situated in the middle of a New England seaport rather than in the heart of Manhattan. The staff looks like a ship's crew on leave in Manhattan, and they are as knowledgeable as they would be if that were the case. Some of the things they carry include marine electronics, sailboat fittings, big-game fishing tackle, life-saving gear, ropes, anchors, compasses, clothing, clocks, barometers, and books. Many of those items—the ropes and compasses, for example—are of professional quality, and Goldbergs' is an excellent source for purchasing such items for dry-land purposes. Foul weather suits are a star attraction, but there is also a line of clothes suitable for yacht owners. Landlubbers are treated kindly, since Goldbergs' realizes that some of the gear is purchased for other purposes. (The fishing line is used in many crafts; artists buy it by the yard.) They are even kinder to genuine marine people and weekend sailors.

HANS KLEPPER CORPORATION
35 Union Sq W (near Broadway and 17th St)
243-3428
Mon-Fri: 9:30-5:30; Sat (April-Aug): 10-4

Hurry down to Union Square to get your own portable boat. That means folding kayaks, rigid kayaks, and even sailboats. In fact, Hans Klepper considers itself New York's portable boat center, and as compact as its products may be, this is not a small business. Klepper has expedition equipment, boating accessories, and more information than even the most avid enthusiast could absorb. Most remarkable, however, is that nearly all of the equipment is easily transported.

Outdoor Equipment

AMERICAN YOUTH HOSTEL
EQUIPMENT STORE
75 Spring St (at Crosby St)
431-7100
Mon-Wed, Fri: 10-7; Thurs 10-9; Sat: 10-5

One of the best-kept secrets in New York is the American Youth Hostel Equipment Store. Even calls to the American Youth Hostel organization fail to elicit any recognition that there might be a store. This is particularly true in the winter. So, if you are making a trip down to Spring and Crosby Street just to see the store, it is best to call first to see if it is open. Why, then, should anyone bother? Because the American Youth Hostel people are to bicycle travel what the AAA is to cars. They even have an emergency road service that ships parts to stranded cyclers. In short, they know the field cold. The store sells a wide variety of A.Y.H.-approved camping outerwear and biking and backpacking equipment. There is a 64-page catalog offering everything from oiled wool mittens to down parkas to flashlights, not to mention all kinds of biking gear. If they've got it, it's the best. No matter what the season, though, their forte is planning tours for biking or skiing. The first official hostel in the city is located at 891 Amsterdam Avenue at 103rd Street.

HUDSONS NEW YORK
97 Third Ave (bet 12th and 13th St)
473-7320
Mon-Thurs: 10-8; Fri, Sat: 10-7; Sun: 12-6

This family-owned emporium has been in the same location for over 70 years. They offer a huge selection of classic American clothing and accessories for town and country living. The lower level features camping and outdoor gear. Someone described the store as "a sort of new age roughwear emporium." A store catalog features 100 pages describing what is available by mail order.

TENTS AND TRAILS
21 Park Pl (bet Broadway and Church St)
227-1760
Mon-Wed, Fri: 9:30-6; Thurs: 9:30-7; Sat: 9:30-6

If Hizzoner the Mayor ever wants to get away from it all and go camping, he will not have to go far to get the necessary equipment. Right in the heart of the canyons near City Hall is one of the best camping outfitters anywhere. Tents and Trails is exclusively devoted to camping, and the folks here are experienced and helpful. They carry top names in every classification. There are boots from Asolo, Hitech, Nik, and Vasque. The camping stock features such brands as Northface, Lowe, Madden, Camp Trails, and Marmot. And there are backpacks, sleeping bags, tents, down clothing, and much more. Tents and Trails rents camping equipment on a first-come, first-served basis. It is a great way for you to see if camping is your thing without making a big investment.

Running

ATHLETIC STYLE
118 E 59th St (bet Park and Lexington Ave)
838-2564
Mon-Thurs: 10-6:30; Fri, Sat: 10-6

This was originally a running-shoe shop, because the owners were and are avid joggers. But the store has prospered and grown, and it is now one of the top outlets for sports clothing in terms of quality and attitude. One of the reasons for this is that owners Vic and Dave are always on the job. There is an expanded variety in footwear, including Tiger, Nike, Topsider, and Avia. In clothing, you can find Russell Athletic, Naturalife, Speedo, Hind, and Dance France. Adults and children will find a well-selected stock of clothing and accessories and an atmosphere that is conducive to fun shopping.

SUPER RUNNERS SHOP

1337 Lexington Ave   360 Amsterdam Ave
  (at 89th St)   (at 77th St)
369-6010   787-7665

1170 Third Ave (at 68th St) Herald Center (fifth floor)
249-2133   564-9190

Mon-Wed, Fri: 10-7; Thurs: 10-9; Sat: 10-5:30; Sun: 1-6
(Lexington store: 12-5); Herald Center: Mon-Sat: 10-7

Gary and Jane Muhrcke are runners, as is every member of their staff. And when they are *not* running, they are advising other runners at Super Runners Shop. The original store was located in Huntington, Long Island, and Gary or Jane would grab a handful of shoes whenever they ventured into Manhattan and would peddle them on the street to whoever ran by. Their reputation grew so fast that the handful became a van-full, the street a permanent spot, and then a legitimate store, and ultimately branches of that store. Although their prices have risen with the move, they are still probably the most knowledgeable and reasonable athletic shoe store around. Unlike many such stores, they do not stock one brand exclusively. The staff of Super Runners Shop really believes that each person has to be fitted individually, both in terms of sizing and need. What's more, if a mistake in sizing is made, they will cheerfully correct it, although they claim such mistakes are few and far between. Super Runners Shop stocks men's and women's sizes (a few children's, too) and a full range of paraphernalia for devotees. In fact, they consider themselves a running-equipment source.

Skating

PECK AND GOODIE
919 Eighth Ave (bet 54th and 55th St)
246-6123
Mon-Sat: 10:30-6

Roller skating is a popular means of summer transportation in Manhattan, so there are plenty of skate shops. But Peck and Goodie seems to have been in business forever, offering equipment and apparel to skaters who need the best with minimum fuss. Now, they are doing the same for the scores of people who have suddenly rediscovered skating. The store offers a complete stock of roller and ice skates and accessories. Boots, blades, brackets, and braces are available, along with expert advice. And with faddish skates costing a hundred dollars a pair or more, it's wise to go to an expert.

Skiing

SCANDINAVIAN SKI SHOP
40 W 57th St (near Sixth Ave)
757-8524
Mon-Wed, Fri, Sat: 9-6; Thurs: 9-7

Despite its name, this shop is really an all-around sporting goods store with an emphasis on skiing and other winter sports. They have a full range of goods, from skis and skiwear to a complete department that offers repairs and ski advice as well as outfitting. The shop has also developed a good reputation for serving other, decidedly non-Scandinavian sports as well. It is capable of outfitting its customers in tennis and hiking gear as well as in skis, and its selection of competition swimwear rivals the namesake specialty. The store also carries exercise equipment.

Soccer

SOCCER SPORT SUPPLY COMPANY
1745 First Ave (bet 90th and 91st St)
427-6050, 800-223-1010
Mon-Fri: 10-6; Sat: 10-3

Max and Hermann Doss, the proprietors of this 50-year-old soccer and rugby supply company, operate as if they were located in merry old England instead of New York. And, indeed, they are international; half the business is involved in importing and exporting equipment around the world. Soccer Sport garners the finest rugby and soccer equipment available and ships it to its customers. Visitors to the store have the advantage of choosing from the entire selection, as well as having guidance from a staff that knows the field perfectly.

Tennis

MASON'S TENNIS MART
911 Seventh Ave (bet 57th and 58th St)
757-5374
Mon-Sat: 9-7; Sun: 11-4

This is a loyal family shop. It was supplying tennis paraphernalia long before the tennis craze hit and will probably continue to do so long after it has peaked. They outfit for tennis, stock for it, play it, etc. In fact, as owner Mark Mason puts it: "We have everything but the courts, and if real estate wasn't so high, we'd have that, too." They carry the clothing lines of tennis designers: Ellesse, Fila, Maser, Nike, and Tacchini, a selection Mason claims is unrivaled anywhere. And once you're looking good on the court, Mason can supply rackets, ball machines, bags, and any other tennis paraphernalia you could possibly think of. They even offer a same-day stringing service for the unfortunates who didn't bring three or four rackets to the U.S. Open. Prices are not cheap, except for the annual sale in January and February. If you want the best at reasonable prices, that's the time to get it.

Stationery

DEMPSEY AND CARROLL
STATIONERS AND FINE ENGRAVERS
38 E 57th St (at Park Ave)
486-7509
Mon-Wed, Fri: 9:30-6; Thurs: 9:30-7; Sat: 10-5:30

Your stationery is your calling card to the world, your statement of who you are and what you stand for. Fine, you say: you'll get your formal stuff from Tiffany's and the more casual paper at Ffolio or one of the classy but personal establishments. Of course, the trendy are into pads of paper from Bloomies, but none of this will really do much for your *image*. Dempsey and Carroll are formal stationers who have been in business in New York for over 100 years. For many years, they have been in residence at the 57th Street flagship store of Lugene, the opticians, with whom they are affiliated. (Perhaps they feel that after you give your vision a new look, you should work on the correspondence you are now able to see.) The less knowledgeable will continue to go to Tiffany's; the more secure, to the more liberal establishments. But the secure and totally correct correspondents name Dempsey and Carroll as their stationers, and visit frequently to see what the latest traditional trends are. You can be assured that any purchase here will be totally correct, and many families have had the assurance for so many years that they never visit the store. They just pick up the phone to reorder.

FFOLIO 72
33 E 68th St (at Madison Ave)
879-0675
Mon-Fri: 10-6; Sat: 11-5:30

One of the true pleasures of New York are the small shops that are absolutely the best in their own particular specialty. Ffolio 72 is one of them. Muriel Glaser, the owner, ran the stationery section at Bendel's in its golden years, and no one knows the business better than she. She can bind books in the finest leather or suede, or create stationery so distinctive that your mother-in-law will actually look forward to receiving your letters. There are wonderful gift items throughout this attractive store, and the selection of cards, stationery, imprinted papers, invitations, and the like are of the very highest quality. Muriel has trained her associates to be extremely helpful, and I can say from personal experience that this is *the* place to get distinguished writing accessories. I am always happy to report that my correspondence cards came from Ffolio 72.

KATE'S PAPERIE
8 W 13th St (at Fifth Ave)
633-0570
Mon-Fri: 10-7; Sat: 10-6

Here you will find one of the largest selections of decorative and exotic papers in the country. Kate has papers of all kinds and descriptions, including papyrus, hand-marbled French paper, Japanese lace papers, handmade paste papers, and just about anything else you can think of in the paper classification. But that isn't all at this unique store. There are leatherbound albums and journals, classic and exotic stationery, and paper-related items, like jewelry, crafts, boxes, and desk accessories. They will do custom printing and engraving, and personal or business embossing.

RITE STATIONERY
113 Ludlow St (at Delancey St)
477-0280, 477-1724
Daily: 8-5

Considering the company this shop is keeping, there should be a fence, hedge, or at the very least a warning separating Rite Stationery from its fellows in this category. While all these stores deal in paper and the accessories necessary for correspondence, a visit here is more inclined to make you put pen to paper for an angry letter of complaint than to invite friends for cocktails at eight. This is just about as far from Tiffany's and Fifth Avenue as you can get. This Lower East Side store's claim to fame is its proximity not to the Plaza Hotel, but to the Ludlow Street entrance to the Municipal Garage. So why, you ask, do we mention it? Because of its great prices and because it takes all kinds to create mail, and there are many times when you really don't need formal engraved calling cards. They specialize in school stationery.

U&I STATIONERS
200 W 55th St
265-0965
Mon-Fri: 8-7:30; Sat: 12-4 (call first)

In a crowded store in the heart of midtown Manhattan, one can find any kind of stationery item, from ballpoint pens to chairs and wooden files at a discount. No fancy fixtures here, just good service and a large selection of office and information-systems supplies. U & I also does printing, at the same reasonable prices marked on their in-store goods.

Telephones, Fax Machines

FONE BOOTH
12 E 53rd St (bet Fifth and Madison Ave)
751-8310
Mon-Wed, Fri, Sat: 10-6; Thurs: 10-8

Until fairly recently, New Yorkers had no choice but to rent their equipment from the phone company. What few outlets there were for procuring additional equipment were usually disguised as "communications experts" selling shortwave radios, dictation equipment, and answering machines, and only parenthetically marketing extension phones, jacks, and plugs. When private equipment became legal, Harvey Stuart's store was one of the first to come out of the closet and into the phone booth. His Fone Booth carries anything an average phone user could want and then some.

All of it, of course, at great prices. Besides jacks, extensions, answering machines, and cords, the Fone Booth has automatic dialers, cordless phones, Fax machines, and a set of push-button phones capable of connecting with any telephone network in the world. Harvey Stuart himself is an authorized dealer of Sony and Panasonic.

PHONE CITY
126 E 57th St (bet Lexington and Park Ave)
644-6300
Mon-Fri: 9:30-7; Sat: 10-6; Sun: 12:30-5:45

Long gone are the days when all the phones in the house or in the office look alike. Today we can fit the telephone into the decorative scheme of any room or office, or even match it to the character of the user. In my office, I have a great red-and-black phone shaped like a woman's shoe! Phone city has the largest selection of telephones in New York, including cordless phones, answering machines, cellular units, beepers, Fax machines, telephone accessories, and business telephone systems. They install telephone jacks almost anywhere, and they install and service multiline business telephone systems. These people know most of the answers to your questions about this fast-changing technology.

Tobacco and Accessories

BARCLAY-REX

7 Maiden Lane	70 E 42nd St (bet Madison
(near Broadway)	and Park Ave)
962-3355	692-9680
Mon-Fri: 8-6	Mon-Fri: 8-6:30; Sat: 10-5:30

This is a tobacco connoisseur's shop, and a specialty tobacco shop at that. The specialty is pipes (cigars are an anathema and cigarettes more so), and third-generation owner Vincent Nastri knows the field inside out. His shop is prepared to create a pipe from scratch, fill it with any imaginable type of tobacco (including a good house brand), repair it if it should break, and offer all sorts of advice on proper pipe care and the blending of pipe tobacco. Nastri has a good reputation for prompt quality repairs and easonable prices. If you have no sentimental attachment to the pipe, it might pay to buy a new irregular pipe that can be had for u surprisingly low price. As with most specialties, there are esoteric models available at astronomical prices. If you have upwards of $1,000 to send up in smoke, Nastri can come up with something really extraordinary.

BARNEY'S 42nd STREET
25 W 42nd St (near Fifth Ave)
354-1366
Mon-Fri: 8-6:30; Sat: 9-5

Barney's looks like just another drugstore from the street, but its forte is a tremendous line of discounted cigars, cigarettes, and tobacco. The discerning shopper can see evidence of the collection both from the street (the tobacco is sold in the back of the store) and from the unusual number of customers who patronize a store that ostensibly sells sundries. Barney's prices on tobacco are supposed to be the best in town; they certainly are the best in midtown.

CONNOISSEUR PIPE SHOP
51 W 46th St (bet Fifth and Sixth Ave)
247-6054
Mon-Fri: 10-6; Sat: 10-5

Edward Burak is essentially an artist. A pipe artist, that is. At his shop he has assembled a collection of hand-carved beauties that range in price from $20 to over $3,500. His store features natural unvarnished pipes, custom-made pipes, custom-blended tobacco, and expert repair of all kinds of pipes. Burak will also do appraisals for insurance purposes. Although you have to be careful these days *where* you smoke a pipe, if it comes from Connoisseur you'll probably get admiring glances from anyone who really knows quality.

INTERNATIONAL SMOKE SHOP
153 E 53rd St (Citicorp Center)
755-8339
Mon-Sat: 7-7

The Citicorp Center is one of the city's best tourist haunts, in part because its trilevel lobby is full of restaurants and other interesting shops that keep "tourist hours." Despite this (and despite an intense campaign to make the shopping area a mecca for browsing), the area can seem cold and impersonal. So even if it had no other virtues, Citicorp's International Smoke Shop would be noteworthy as a friendly oasis in a frigid zone. The International Smoke Shop's Richard Barnett is one of the truly great people in the city. He is courteous, helpful, insightful, and genuinely down-to-earth in a place that prides itself on sleekness and sophistication. I would recommend a visit here just to meet him. True to its name, the store stocks all kinds of tobacco and tobacco paraphernalia. But it also carries books, magazines (including foreign publications), gifts, Lotto tickets, New York souvenirs, and imported chocolate. In short, his stock would enable the visitor to spend a whole day in the Citicorp and keep himself amused, well-read, well-fed, and in reach of plenty of tobacco. What's amazing is that the shop stocks it all in a very limited space, which is kept as neat as a pin. Barnett values the imported cigars and cigarettes, and you'll value his friendship.

J R TOBACCO
11 E 45th St (at Madison Ave)
983-4160
Mon-Fri: 7:45-6; Sat: 9-4

For years, Lew Rothman has claimed that he offers the world's largest selection of cigars at the world's lowest prices. Now that cigar smoking isn't quite as popular as it used to be, he has diversified into the fragrance business, offering the same kind of discount prices on most major fragrance lines. The cigars come in over 3,000 different brands, and the fragrances in over 50 top names. Prices are 20 to 50 percent off marked retail.

PIPEWORKS & WILKE
16 W 55th St
956-4820
Mon-Fri: 9-5:45; Sat: 9:30-5

Elliott Nachwalter started creating briar pipes in Stowe, Vermont, more than a decade ago. He then moved to New York and established Pipeworks as the outlet for his exclusive handmade, custom-designed pipes. Nachwalter can create a pipe from a customer's design as well as his own. Only Grecian Plateux briar is used for each pipe, and each goes through a 130-step process between design and the finished product. Once a pipe is in hand, customers can return to Pipeworks for custom tobacco blends, antique pipes, or repairs. Chances are that it won't be a Pipeworks pipe that needs repair. Each is guaranteed for five years for most parts, and Nachwalter says they are created to last a lifetime. There is also a great assortment of antique pipes.

Toys, Model Trains

Good news for toy shoppers: Toys "R" Us has signed a letter of intent to open their first Manhattan store at Herald Center. The store will be situated on the ground floor and three additional levels, and it will occupy 70,000 square feet of space. New Yorkers are in for a treat; Toys "R" Us is the leading mass merchandiser of toys in the country. It is a superbly operated store, with a selection of merchandise and a price policy presently unequalled in the city.

BIG CITY KITE COMPANY
1201 Lexington Ave (at 82nd St)
472-2623
Mon-Wed, Fri, Sat: 10-6; Thurs: 10-7;
  Sun (seasonally): 12-6

Of course you would expect New York to have a store dedicated totally to kites, and of course it is a great one. David Klein sells kites for people's houses: mobiles and wall hangings. He sells custom-made specialty kites and brilliantly colored fighter kites made of tissue paper. He also has a kite-repair service. Prices begin at about $2 and go as high as $300. The lack of fanatacism and the presence of genuine devotion is most evident in the community programs that Big City sponsors. There are kite festivals, kite exhibitions, even "kite-ins."

B. SHACKMAN AND COMPANY
85 Fifth Ave (at 16th St)
989-5162
Mon-Fri: 9-5; Sat: 10-4

In the midst of the wholesale toy district, B. Shackman has been playing house since 1898. But their play is a very serious business devoted to the manufacturing, importing, and sale of toys, novelties, and miniatures. Though a large portion of their business is still on the wholesale level, this is obviously a business run by people who enjoy what they are doing. They are willing to take time to share their vocation with amateurs and single retail customers. This is one of the few such firms in the area to do so. Shackman carries a full line of aforementioned specialties. However, the items of interest to retail customers are their miniatures and a striking collection of Victoriana. Again, this is not at all in keeping with its neighbors, but Shackman's excels in Victorian postcards, Christmas tree decorations, old-fashioned greeting cards, and children's books. There are also antique dolls, contemporary stuffed toys, and paper dolls.

BURLINGTON ANTIQUE TOYS
1082 Madison Ave (at 82nd St)
861-9708
Tues-Sat: 12-6 and by appointment; closed Sat in summer

Anyone who has been to the Forbes Gallery knows that toy soldiers are not just for children. Anyone who has been to Burlington Antique Toys has undoubtedly discovered that this is definitely not kid stuff. The toy soldiers are antiques, as is virtually everything else in the store. That roll call includes toy cars, airplanes, boats, and other tin toys. Best of all, Burlington proves that not only fabulously rich men can play with toy soldiers or float their own armadas. This is a place for everyman. And the folks here couldn't be nicer.

DOLLHOUSE ANTICS
1308 Madison Ave (bet 92nd and 93rd St)
876-2288
Mon-Fri: 11-5:30; Sat: 11-5

Dollhouse Antics is straight out of childhood dreams. Their official claim is that they are a shop dedicated to miniatures, but the shop is run more like a playroom, and any of the three owners always seems to be ready to join in the games. But dollhouse-making is serious business here. Ever heard of custom-made dollhouses? Or mouse houses? The most popular orders are for replicas of ancestral homes, and you can bet your made-to-order miniature needlepoint rug that these dollhouses aren't made for eager little children. Dollhouses come in kit form, but when money is no object (or if the fun of assembling it yourself wanes), the store will put it together for you. But be wary: like real houses, these models need to be furnished. If you can afford the scaled-down Oriental rugs, custom upholstery, special wallpaper, lumber, electrical supplies, and made-to-order furniture, you'll eventually want to redecorate the whole house.

ENCHANTED FOREST
85 Mercer St (bet Spring and Broome St)
925-6677
Daily: 11-7

The Enchanted Forest is one of the very few shops that physically and philosophically matches its name. The husband-and-wife team of owners, David Wallace and Peggy Sloane, hired theatrical set designer Matthew Jacobs to create an enchanted-forest backdrop for a collection of toys, whimsies, and artwork. The announced intention of the shop was that it would be a "gallery of beasts, books, and handmade toys celebrating the spirit of the animals, the old stories, and the child within" with an emphasis on *gallery*. One can go into a crystal cave that transforms into an old wooden wardrobe, through which one passes into a small Victorian room. Other featured items include a fine selection of fairy tales, mythology, children's stories, and various eclectic gems. It is truly an enchanted place.

F.A.O. SCHWARZ
767 Fifth Ave (bet 58th and 59th St)
644-9400
Mon-Wed, Fri, Sat: 10-6; Thurs: 10-8; Sun: 12-5

Longtime readers of this book will remember that I was not very gentle with F.A.O. Schwarz in previous editions. I was unhappy with the service and lack of sales supervision. Well, this prestigious, world-famous toy store has since moved to new and larger quarters in the General Motors building, across the street from the old store. The result is a distinct improvement in appearance and services. Schwarz is the "cutting edge" of the toy business, and toy manufacturers are just as eager to get their new items in this store as ready-to-wear manufacturers are to see their goods at Bloomies. The new store has two floors, arranged into small shops that specialize in stuffed animals, bears, games, electronics, dolls, and all the other gadgets you'd expect to find in a first-rate toy emporium. Thank goodness there seems to be a new regime of saleshelp; they attentively follow you around the store as you pick out gifts for the kids (and for yourself). If you're in a hurry but want to get Susie and Sam a little something, you can stop at a special counter right at the door and pick up an already wrapped present. Now if they would just get some supermarket carts to help you shop, well, I might take back all those nasty things I once said. Anyway, I have to confess that I have always been a rather loyal Schwarz customer; after all, their catalog was one of the first things I was able to read. Hmmm, that goes back a few years!

KIDDIE CITY TOYS
35 W 34th St
629-3070
Mon, Thurs, Fri: 9:30-9; Tues, Wed: 9:30-7; Sat: 9:30-6; Sun: 11-5

Midtown's answer to Toys "R" Us! Discount prices on over 18,000 items makes this store an attractive place for shopping for kids. Most of the merchandise is on the second floor, but a handy pickup station is available by the street-floor entrance. Check-out facilities are a bit cramped, but careful shoppers can make up for the unattractive surroundings by picking up all kinds of toys, games, sports items, trains, dolls, building sets, and video software at considerable savings.

MANHATTAN DOLL HOUSE
176 Ninth Ave (at 21st St)
989-5220
Wed, Fri: 10-6; Thurs: 12-7:30; Sat: 10-5

Time marches on, and sadly some of New York's most talented folks are no longer with us. Jenny Grunewald, who did the doll hospital part of this operation, has passed away, so now her son-in-law Edwin Jacobowitz operates the Doll House. He boasts the city's largest collection of dolls (including Madame Alexander), doll houses, and doll paraphernalia. Jenny's husband, Herman, still comes in the shop from time to time, so you could have the pleasure of visiting with him and seeing how he can create a castle-like home for the new princess you might purchase for your grandchild!

MONDE MAGIQUE
125 E 57th St (at Lexington Ave)
755-4120
Mon-Sat: 11-6

This is one of those places in which you look but don't touch. You can buy, of course, but be sure to check the number of zeros on the price tag. Monde has a fabulous collection of 19th-century French automata, wind-up figures, which perform movement to the accompaniment of music. Christian Bailly, the owner, recently moved his Paris shop to New York, so now we can enjoy what is probably the finest group of museum-quality antique toys in the country. Just to give you an idea, prices start in the $7,000 range!

RED CABOOSE
16 W 45th St (bet Fifth and Sixth Ave, fourth floor)
575-0155
Mon-Fri: 10-7; Sat: 10-5:30

At the Red Caboose, owner-operator Allan T. Spitz will tell you that 99 percent of his customers are not wide-eyed children, but sharp-eyed adults who are dead serious about model railroads. Since these are the people Spitz serves, it is difficult for a Christmas-morning engineer to adequately describe his stock, but I'll try. The Red Caboose claims to have 100,000 items in stock. That includes a line of 300 hand-finished, imported brass locomotives *alone*. That doesn't begin to cover the tracks or track gauges available. (Spitz claims that the five basic sizes—1:22, 1:48, 1:87, 1:161, and 1:220, in a ratio of scale to life size—will allow a model railroader to build layouts sized to fit into a desk drawer or a basement.) The store also carries the city's largest model-ship selection, and HO and N gauge equipment. If there is a model-train district, it is probably located on the upper floors of the buildings on this block. For that reason, Spitz offers a 20 percent discount on purchases over $10 (on most lines).

SECOND CHILDHOOD®
283 Bleecker St
989-6140
Mon-Sat: 11-6

Enchantment is the only word to describe this store, which deals in antique toys and childhood paraphernalia. The customer not only seems to go back in time to his childhood interests, but childhood in general seems to be a time suspended. The stock changes constantly, but all of it is authentic and in excellent condition. I saw wicker doll carriages, hoops (from both the Gay '90s and the 1950s), china dolls, dollhouse furniture and miniatures, and toys that stirred forgotten memories. No matter what the age, customers love this place. Prices range from 50 cents to over $1,000, so there is usually something for everyone. Wisely, browsing is encouraged, since the charm of these toys is that they really grow on you. The longer you stay, the more impossible it will be to leave without a reminder of your childhood.

TOY BALLOON
204 E 38th St
682-3803
Mon-Fri: 9-5

I wandered in here by accident, but you'll want to wander in on purpose. This is a serious adult business. Balloons are dealt with here in exactly the same manner that any business would deal with its product, but how *can* one be serious when the product is balloons? The Toy Balloon tries. Balloons are sold individually or in multitudes of up to 50,000. Types are so varied that there are graduations in diameter, thickness, style, and type (including Mylar balloons). Sizes range from peewees to blimps, while shapes include dolls, rabbit heads, hearts, dachshunds (a personal favorite; they're often used to advertise hot dogs), and extra-elongated shapes. Most of the business is done for advertising campaigns, and the Toy Balloon will make up and sell personalized logos, styles, or two-colored messages. This specialty store also sells complete kits and everything the balloons require.

TRAIN SHOP
23 W 45th St (basement)
730-0409
Mon-Fri: 10-6; Sat: 10-5

The second major resident of model-train row, this shop differs from its fellow traveler only by its basement location and its insistence that it has *no* specialty. It merely stocks everything. The Train Shop's manager (engineer?) is Paul Schulhaus, who is about as knowledgeable as they come, and his assistant, Russ, sums up the stock by saying, "Look around. If you need help, just give us a holler." Now isn't that just the way they'd do it at the local station? To name *some* specifics, the shop claims to have at least 30,000 different model pieces in stock. What is not in stock can be ordered, but they do not maintain their own catalog. (They accept phone and mail orders.) Walther's Catalog includes the Train Shop and lists the unique items they have. (One favorite is a train engine, complete with its own realistic sound system.) But the stock can in no way be described. It is simply incredible and an awful lot of fun! Prices are competitive with the store's neighbors, and where else would you find two such shops within hollering distance?

Typewriters

TYTELL TYPEWRITER COMPANY
116 Fulton St (bet William and Nassau St, second floor)
233-5333
Daily: 10:30-4 by appointment

Detective story readers know that a typewriter's keys are as individual as fingerprints, and in New York Martin and Pearl Tytell have made a name for themselves by identifying typeface for over 50 years. Today, the so-called "questioned document" service has become a major operation that requires the full-time expertise of Pearl and the Tytell's son, Peter, while Martin devotes his time to running the typewriter sales and repair business, with rentals on the side. They have also become a rehabilitation center for old and antique typewriters. With a 57-year-old collection of typewriters and typewriter parts, they can restore virtually any machine. Tytell's is also the United Nations, the Smithsonian, and the Elaine's of the typewriter business. The typefaces you can choose from are as varied as the types on a printer's chart. If English isn't the language you want, that's no problem. Martin Tytell will craft, by hand, a set of keys in any one of 145 languages. If you're in a hurry, he's been farsighted enough to have made up foreign-language typewriters for such emergencies. In addition to typewriters for every language, he can make up keys of corporate logos, six-pitch double-case type (good for teleprompter reading), phonetic alphabets, stencil cutting, and jumbo type. There are over 2 million pieces of type in stock, as well as typewriters so old they're rented by movie studios for props. Tytell's list of clients reads like a who's who of typewriter users.

Variety, Novelty

BARGAIN SPOT
64 Third Ave (at 11th St)
674-1188
Mon-Sat: 8:30-5

In one of Cynthia Freeman's books, the heroine makes her money by starting out in a pawnshop. The Bargain Spot also started in a pawnshop, but in this case, it's the consumer who makes the money. Established in 1909, the Bargain Spot is also known worldwide as the Unredeemed Pledge Sales Company, and that name says it all. If something has been pledged and left, the Bargain Spot will purchase it and resell it. But the heyday of pawnshops in New York is long gone, so no one could rely on that alone for business. Today, the company uses its base of pawnshop spoils to buy, rent, sell, and exchange a tremendous variety of items. The clientele is hard to believe (my office didn't believe it included me!), but all of them are obviously smart shoppers who know great bargains when they see them. At this aptly named shop, it's possible to buy everything from diamonds to typewriters to antiques, and if you call first, they will happily tell you what is in stock. Cynthia Freeman's protagonist isn't the only one to know a fortune can be made in pawnshop redemptions.

COME AGAIN
246 E 51st St (at Second Ave)
308-9394
Mon, Tues: 10:30-7:30; Wed-Fri: 10:30-8:30;
    Sat: 10:30-7:30

Come Again? Yes, you have it right. This book contains something for everyone's taste! Come Again is a one-stop shopping center for all your sexual needs. There are vibrators, bondage equipment, exotic lingerie for men and women, adult books, oils and lotions, party gifts and favors. Now they boast the first of its kind: an X-rated shop-at-home adult toy and lingerie video catalog. They claim it "combines an hour's hot entertainment with the convenience of shopping at home." Now if the entertainment gets too hot, you can always turn it off and return to reading this book. It doesn't have quite the same sizzle!

EVE'S GARDEN
119 W 57th St (14th floor)
757-8651
Tues-Sat: 12-6:30

One of the real pleasures of the "New York Is Book Country" fairs each September on Fifth Avenue is the opportunity to meet and exchange views with readers and business folk who are, or who would like to be, featured in this book. During one of these fairs, Dell Williams, who runs Eve's Garden, suggested I visit her unusual emporium. The descriptive line in her literature is "We grow pleasurable things for women." Well, you get the picture. It may not be a must-see place on your shopping list, but after all, this is a book designed for every type of reader, and some will find a unique selection of merchandise at this liberated garden.

GORDON NOVELTY COMPANY
933 Broadway (at 22nd St)
254-8616
Mon-Fri: 8:30-4:30

Paper parasols (and for that matter, lace, rayon, and Chinese parasols), animal masks, half- and full-face masks, rubber masks, wigs, mustaches, sideburns, beards, Groucho Marx glasses, clicking teeth, noses, eye patches, tails, and various costumes all reside at Gordon Novelty. The store celebrates Halloween year-round, though it must be an absolute zoo on that holiday. (And I'm not referring to the two-dozen animal masks.) The practical joker could have a field day here with such fun items as breakaway bottles, buzzers, an invisible-dog leash, clown hats, and squirting boutonnieres. There are more balloons than one could count, and did I mention hats and disguises, puzzles, decorations, and party favors cataloged along thematic lines? Well, those are here as well. One can go really wild at Gordon's, and as might be expected, the personnel are helpful and enjoy a good joke—on you!

JOB LOT TRADING COMPANY—
THE PUSHCART

140 Church St	80 Nassau St
962-4142	619-6868
Mon-Sat: 8-6	Mon-Fri: 7:45-6:15

After only a day in New York, even the most casual visitor becomes aware of black-and-white paper bags (depicting jam-packed pushcarts) being carried around in all sizes by all sorts of New

Yorkers. Close examination would reveal that these bags all emanate from Job Lot Trading. Job Lot and the Pushcart were originally two separate stores that were dislocated by the World Trade Center. Of those original residents, only a few survived, and none survived as spectacularly as these two stores, which merged (on different floors of the same store), took over a building, and, week after week, offer some of the best bargains in the city. Job Lot carries an odd number of consignments that are unsalable through normal retail channels for one reason or another. Absolutely everything is sold below wholesale. The stock changes constantly, so some people make weekly shopping trips. There is no telling what can turn up here.

ODD JOB TRADING
7 E 40th St (bet Fifth and Madison Ave)
686-6825

66 W 48th St (bet Fifth and Sixth Ave)
575-0477

149 W 32nd St (bet Sixth and Seventh Ave)
564-7370

Mon-Thurs: 8-5:30; Fri: 8-4:30; Sun: 10-5

Another of the jobbers in the wake of Job Lot-The Pushcart, Odd Job has been around for a while and seems to consistently come up with good buys on quality merchandise. What differentiates Odd Job from the other half-dozen stores of its type is that its quality merchandise is more *au courant*. You never know what is going to turn up here; it can be anything from book racks to perfume, but it's always interesting. It's also the perfect place for gifts for the folks back home, where they'll never know how little they cost, unless you tell. Odd Job is perhaps the most aggressive of the closeout stores. They are expanding rapidly, and now have the reputation of being the best of its kind. Whether they can continue to provide the same remarkable bargains to a fleet of stores remains to be seen.

ROMANO
628 W 45th St (entrance on 12th Ave)
581-4248
Mon-Fri: 8-5:30; Sat: 8-4:30

Nomenclature is a problem here. Romano goes under at least two other names, Paris-Rome and Rome Outlet. Not terribly well-known to New Yorkers, it is as patronized by visitors (especially foreign visitors) as the airports. Perhaps the various names come about from the confusion of customers seeking it out in dozens of languages. What do they know that natives don't? Simply that this part of town—best known for redeeming impounded cars and boarding the Circle Line tour boat—operates like a miniature Hong Kong. The only ships to speak of are the aforementioned Circle Line and cruise ships, but the neighborhood seems to think that crewmen and ship stevedores are docking every day with money to spend for gifts back home. So, the stock is a hodgepodge of American—distinctly American—culture. Luggage, watches, Rayban sunglasses, bath towels, pens, cordless phones, electronic games, designer scarves and umbrellas, tennis rackets, china, and small electric appliances are all in stock at excellent discount prices. There has to be a good reason for landlubbers to come all the way over here, and Samsonite at 50 percent off will do it. Nothing is sold at list price, and many of the items (watches in particular) are sold at the best prices in town.

SOHO EMPORIUM
375 W Broadway (bet Spring and Broome St)
966-7895
Tues-Fri: 12-8; Sat, Sun: 11-8

Shopping here is more of a fun experience than a serious venture. The Emporium is a consortium of small individual shops selling an eclectic mixture of new and used clothing for the entire family, as well as accessories, artifacts, and gifts. A visit here will indeed brighten your spirits and give you hope that innovation is still part of the American dream.

STAR MAGIC

743 Broadway   275 Amsterdam Ave
   (bet Eighth St and Astor Pl)   (at 73rd St)
228-7770   769-2020

Mon-Sat: 10-10; Sun: 11-8

Step through Star Magic's door, and you step through a time warp into the future. For Star Magic—from its midnight-black ceiling with suspended galactic spheres to its spacecraft-like walls—is designed to make a visitor forget contemporary New York and enter into a timeless universe. The setting is inducement enough to pay a visit. Star Magic's theme is "Yesterday's magic is today's science," and that perhaps is the only way to describe the eclectic selection that owners Shlomo Ayal and Justin Moreau call space-age gifts. There are toys (in this case, literally for children of all ages) with a scientific bent and scientific items strictly for fun. There are books specifically chosen for their ability to make a reader "ponder the cosmos." Star Magic offers minerals and prisms, scientific instruments to explore the universe, high-tech toys, and new age music that is positively futuristic. Over and out.

Videotapes

Good Bet: Blockbuster Video, 85th and Lexington (439-0960)

PALMER VIDEO STORE
470 Hudson St
463-9377
Daily: 10 a.m.-midnight

The nice thing about this store is that you are able to see all the titles easily; they are displayed in a neat and orderly way. This store carries the popular and hot titles, as well as the unusual ones. There is a membership plan, a discount for frequent users, reservation privileges, many titles for sale, and no deposit required for members.

VIDEO ACCESS
592 Columbus (at 89th St)
769-4444

2617 Broadway (at 99th St)
316-6666

2821 Broadway (at 109th St)
749-3900

Open seven days a week, hours vary by store
(open late weekends)

Video Access offers over 7,000 titles of the latest movies for sale or rent, and you can visit them every day of the year. They will transfer foreign tape formats to the standard one used in this country. They rent camcorders, VCRs, and TVs, and sell a full range of accessories and prerecorded movies at reasonable prices.

THE VIDEO STORE

276 Third Ave	44 Greenwich Ave
475-7400	675-6600
90 University Pl	224 W 72nd St
243-0400	679-3400
949 First Ave (at 52nd St)	
888-4545	

Daily: 10 a.m.-midnight

Billed as *the* video store in the Village, the Video Store boasts a large selection of cult and foreign films and obscure tapes, and operates much as a good bookstore would. The Video Store even does title searches, back lists, special orders, and out-of-print orders for videotapes and films. It is, indeed, the latest trend in media communication. *The New Video Times,* which resembles an early *Village Voice,* is a chronicle of the store's activities. Issues boast of the latest acquisitions and services ("Rent a VCR machine for only $12.95 a day"), while the various movies in stock are high-lighted and reviewed. For any other industry, it would be odd to see a full-scale tabloid newspaper issuing from a store, but at the Video Store the media is definitely the message, and they want everyone to get it. This is also one of the few video sources in the city that discounts as well. Ask for the copy of their *Times.* It gives the best view of what the Video Store is all about.

Wall Coverings

JANOVIC PLAZA
67th St and Third Ave
772-1400

159 W 72nd St
595-2500

771 Ninth Ave
245-3241

215 Seventh Ave
645-5454

161 Sixth Ave (at Sprint)
627-1100

Mon-Fri: 7:30-6:30; Sat: 9-5:45; Sun: 11-5

Once upon a time, the Janovics ran a neighborhood paint store. But when the neighborhood is in Manhattan, even a paint store isn't likely to be mundane. When the image was brushed up and fashion and fads influenced their wall coverings, the business expanded across town. Today, the Janovics cover the Upper East and Upper West Sides, and those who shop for paint as they do for croissants, shop at Janovic. It's not really just the trendiness that makes Janovic such a success. The updated image is still based on the old store's years of experience with New York wall problems.

PINTCHIK
278 Third Ave (at 22nd St)
982-6600, 777-3030
Mon-Fri: 8:30-7; Sat: 9-6; Sun: 11-5

Discount wallpaper shops are few and far between in Manhattan, despite its reputation as the discount center of the world. But Pintchik is one such source. They discount paint and wall coverings, as well as the supplies that go with them. Two of the better wall coverings they carry are Laura Ashley and Marimeko patterns—by coincidence, two manufacturers that have large stores in Manhattan. Nonetheless, Pintchik can always beat even the manufacturer's prices, except during the rare clearance sales at the previously named stores. An advantage (besides price) is that unlike the fabric stores (and basically that is Laura Ashley's and Marimeko's trading card), Pintchik's staff is well-versed in the city's painting and wall-covering needs. They are very good at coming up with solutions to problem walls (and there probably isn't an apartment in the city without a problem wall), as well as making accommodations to city living. (Needless to say, white backgrounds don't go over very well with city soot.)

SHELIA'S WALLSTYLES DECORATING CENTER

274 Grand St (bet Eldridge and Forsyth St)
966-1663
Sun-Thurs: 9:30-5; Fri: 9:30-2

Grand Street is a strange place for a wallpaper store, since those locals who are into wall decorating almost universally use the paint-pattern-on-paint school of design. But Shelia opened her shop about a decade ago and proved so successful that she now has imitators. And why not? She took her cue from the retail motif of the Lower East Side and sells everything at a good discount. And then she located her store on a block that is quickly becoming the mecca for fashion-and-budget-conscious home decorators. The result is the very best in wall coverings, drapes, bedspreads, vertical and horizontal blinds, shades, and coordinated accessories. Those who want a tissue box to match the boudoir can find it at Shelia's—and at a discount, to boot.

VII. "Where To" Extras

Auctions

There are two totally different auction scenes in New York. For want of better terms, we'll call them the highbrow and lowbrow. The highbrow scene is on the Upper East Side, the traditional home of the exclusive art galleries. A few decades ago these galleries were the only place in the city to purchase decorative arts. When Sotheby Parke Bernet and Christie's arrived on the scene, all that changed. The majority of that caliber of merchandise in New York is now sold via auction. A word of warning: Both types of auctions are attended by professional buyers. You won't beat them. The best you can expect is to top their wholesale price, which will still be less than retail. Check *The New York Times* antiques pages on Fridays and Saturdays for announcements of upcoming auctions.

CHRISTIE'S
502 Park Ave (at 59th St)
546-1000

Christie's, a British import, vies with Sotheby Parke Bernet as the biggest in the industry. They differ only in that Christie's has tried to transplant the European experience here and, at the same time, added almost weekly auctions in Americana. Aside from that, look for strong showings in antiques, art, books, coins and numismatics, clocks and timepieces, furniture, photographs, porcelain, and sculpture.

CHRISTIE'S EAST
219 E 67th St
606-0400

Christie's East is the junior branch of Christie's and sells anything of value that would not "pass the clientele at the big Christie's," says the lady at the reception desk. Don't take that to mean Aunt Minnie's favorite painting. We're still talking big names and big bucks, but the prices, styles, and collections are somewhat more whimsical. Look for pop art and collections of dolls, toys, stamps, paintings, and folk ar .

PHILLIPS
406 E 79th St
570-4830

Phillips is another auction house with European origins and a sterling reputation, but the name isn't as well-known as Christie's or Sotheby. With their worldwide connections, they have access to some of the finest sources and collections in the world. They also specialize in old-line service; the genteel can bid on Phillips' European actions without leaving the office. You may not have heard of them, but the pros have. Try to strike up a friendship with the staff if you want equal footing!

SOTHEBY PARKE BERNET
1334 York Ave (at 72nd St)
606-7000

Sotheby holds the really grand sales and makes headlines with record-setting bids. They deserve the attention, because they are well-organized, attentive, professional, and knowledgeable. If you only have time for one auction, come here and watch a master deal with the old masters. If it is very, very valuable, then Sotheby handles it. The Sotheby Arcade, in the same building, holds a couple of auctions each week for more affordable antiques and artwork. Sotheby is open for viewing even when there is no immediate auction. Go! It's an experience you shouldn't miss.

WILLIAM DOYLE GALLERIES
175 E 87th St (bet Lexington and Third Ave)
427-2730
Mon-Fri: 9-6; Tag sale: Mon-Fri: 8:30-4:30; Sat: 10-5

This is the biggest American-owned auction house, and their sales reflect that. The merchandise is often from estate collections of books, jewelry, artwork (including sculpture), and furniture, and the prices are high. Some of the auctions are worth attending for the sheer entertainment value.

Now for the lowbrow. As the seat of regional government headquarters, New York City is the site of many auctions held for the purpose of clearing government warehouses. Some are funky, some fun, and a few are fabulous. At all of them you will be required to purchase a paddle to bid. It costs about $25, which will be put toward the price of your purchases or refunded if you don't use it. None of these auctions accept personal checks; it is either cash or certified check. You are required to settle your account before the auction is over, unless you establish a large reserve before the auction starts. Professional buyers also show up at lowbrow auctions and rush up the bids. But keep an eye out for small lot sizes; the pros aren't usually too interested in them.

NEW YORK CITY DEPARTMENT OF GENERAL SERVICES
566-7552, 566-6234

The Department of General Services is responsible for supplying and maintaining the city's vehicles and plants. They run general auctions for the vehicles every two weeks at the Brooklyn Navy Yard. (Call 669-8546 for information.) Commercial real estate (obtained mostly through tax foreclosures) is auctioned off at One Police Plaza about once every two months. Most are commercially zoned vacant lots located throughout the city.

NEW YORK CITY DEPARTMENT OF HOUSING PRESERVATION AND DEVELOPMENT
General Services: 806-8001

Property in all five boroughs of New York City is auctioned off at One Police Plaza five times a year. There is usually ample notification in the newspapers; the city will notify you personally as well. Most of the stock comes from abandoned property and tax liens. But remember, if people abandon property in this city of sky-high real estate, there is usually a reason. Sometimes, however, a real live one comes up. Also, there's always a couple of literal "odd lots" that the city owns, and they can often be had for a song. You, too, could own real estate in New York! Donald Trump, watch out!

NEW YORK CITY DEPARTMENT OF SANITATION
Encumbrance Unit
566-5208, 566-5533

Sotheby it isn't, but neither is it what you may think! You see, in addition to taking garbage off the streets, the Sanitation Department is responsible for carrying out eviction proceedings and auctioning off the confiscated property. You are required to bid on an entire lot at these auctions, which are held at least once a week at different locations at 1 p.m. Inspection is usually a day in advance.

NEW YORK CITY PARKING VIOLATIONS BUREAU
791-1450

New York's labyrinthe of parking regulations yield up to 10,000 violators who get their vehicles towed away each year. Those who do not redeem their cars lose them forever in a surprisingly short period of time. The Parking Violations Bureau holds auctions three days a week. At all locations, viewing begins an hour before the 11 a.m. auction. Tuesday and Thursday sales are conducted at Pier 60 (at 20th St). Wednesday sales are held at both Pier 26 and the 203rd Street Pound. Of course, you should realize that the owner of a car of value usually pays off the fine, so most of the cars that make it to auction are older and well-worn. Also, you will not get to make a detailed inspection under the hood before purchase; and all cars are sold "as is."

NEW YORK CITY
POLICE DEPARTMENT AUCTION
Property Clerk Division
One Police Plaza (bet Chambers and Centre St)
406-1369 (recording), 374-5905 (property clerk's office)

Several times a year the Police Department holds auctions that, depending on your point of view, are either exhilarating or depressing. Everything auctioned off is recovered contraband that couldn't be returned to its rightful owners. Giving "New York's finest" credit, assume that 50 percent of all the stolen goods are returned. Thus, what one inspects at the auction is a fraction of what is annually stolen. The selection of items will boggle the mind. Hundreds of motorcycles and mopeds, wheelchairs, car seats, radios, stereos, toilet seats, furniture, and bicycles are but a small part of the "general merchandise." The Sunday before the auction the department publishes ads in the *Daily News* and *The Times*. You will get more information from the phone recording than the Property Clerk's Office. The viewing is at one of two sites in Queens. It is a necessity, since the bidding is conducted in Manhattan.

NEW YORK STATE DEPARTMENT OF
GENERAL SERVICES
Surplus, Albany, NY
518-457-6335

Don't be put off by the long-distance phone number and address. The State Department of General Services unloads surplus vehicles, furniture, and other items at locations around the state on the average of once every two weeks. In Manhattan, the site is usually the Adam Clayton Powell Jr. State Office Building at 163 West 125th Street. Call or write to the above office for specific information about each auction. The vehicles were usually driven by state officials and have high mileage. Occasionally there is a truck or fire engine.

POST OFFICE AUCTION
33rd St and Eighth Ave (basement)
330-2931

You must attend this at least once in your life! The Post Office auction is so huge it takes two days. Viewing takes place on the same day as the auction, starting at 8 a.m. The auction begins at 10:30 a.m., and merchandise can be picked up the next day. A call to the above number will give you the dates of the next auction and any other pertinent information. You may also write for information. Everything auctioned here has been lost, damaged, or unclaimed in the mail. You'll be amazed by what shows up . . . even Tiffany watches!

Churches and Synagogues of Note

Abyssinian Baptist Church (132 W 138th St, near Lenox Ave) The oldest black church in the city and the largest place of worship for blacks in the country.

Central Synagogue (E 55th St and Lexington Ave) The city's oldest Jewish (Reform) synagogue still in use.

Grace Church (E 10th St and Broadway) A Renwick masterpiece, especially worthwhile seeing for its Gothic revival architecture.

Holy Trinity Greek Orthodox Cathedral (319 E 74th St, bet First and Second Ave) You might think you're in ancient Greece when you visit this architectural masterpiece.

Marble Collegiate Church (W 29th St and Fifth Ave) Dr. Norman Vincent Peale made this one famous.

New York Islamic Center Mosque (E 96th St and Third Ave) A new and lavish addition to the city's religious landscape.

Riverside Church (W 122nd St and Riverside Dr) John D. Rockefeller was responsible for this huge 22-story edifice, which is a must for all to visit.

St. Bartholemew's Church (E 50th St and Park Ave) A midtown Episcopal Church, which has been in the midst of a controversy over the use of its air space, a valuable commodity in New York real estate.

St. John the Divine Cathedral (W 112th St and Amsterdam Ave) One of the largest cathedrals in the world.

St. Nicholas Russian Orthodox Cathedral (15 E 97th St, bet Fifth and Madison Ave) Here you can see what Russian churches used to be like.

St. Patrick's Cathedral (E 50th St and Fifth Ave) Probably the best-known and most important church in the city, another work of architect James Renwick.

St. Peter's Lutheran (E 54th St and Lexington Ave) Cozily housed inside the towering Citicorp Center, it is a modern beauty.

Temple Emanu-El (E 65th St and Fifth Ave) A large, magnificent Jewish house of worship.

Trinity Church (Broadway and Wall St) A treasure trove for history buffs; the churchyard is not to be missed.

Flea Markets

Annex Antiques Fair & Flea Market, Sixth Ave from 24th to 26th St, 243-5343, Sat, Sun: 9-5

Antique Flea & Farmers Market, P.S. 183, E 67th St bet First and York Ave, 737-8888, Sat: 6-6

Canal West Flea Market, 370 Canal St, 718-693-8142, Sat, Sun: 7-6

Greenwich Village Flea Market, P.S. 41, Greenwich Ave at Charles St, 752-8475, Sat: noon-7

I.S. 44 Flea Market, Columbus Ave bet 76th and 77th St, 316-1088, Sun: 10-6

Walter's World Famous Union Square Shoppes, 873 Broadway at 18th St, 255-0175, Tues-Sat: 10-6

Yorkville Flea Market, 351 E 74th St, 535-5235, Sat: 9-4 (closed in summer)

Museums

ABIGAIL ADAMS SMITH MUSEUM
421 E 61st St
838-6878
Mon-Fri: 10-4; Sun: 1-5 (Sept to May); Tues: 5:30-8 p.m.
(June, July)

Constructed in 1799, the Abigail Adams Smith Museum is an historic building, which originally served as a carriage house for a 23-acre East River estate planned by Colonel William Stephens Smith and his wife, Abigail Adams Smith, daughter of President John Adams. In 1826, the carriage house was converted into the Mount Vernon Hotel, a popular day resort. Today, this New York City landmark features Federal and Empire decorative arts in Greek Revival interiors.

AMERICAN CRAFT MUSEUM
40 W 53rd St (opposite the Museum of Modern Art)
956-3535, 956-6047
Tues: 10-8; Wed-Sun: 10-5

Sponsored by the American Craft Council, this museum is situated in striking new quarters, which were custom-made to its specifications in a condominium building owned by CBS. A spiral staircase sports a canoe floating through it, and many of the showcases and exhibits are *objets d'art* themselves. Several shows are mounted at the same time to display various aspects of American crafts. Admission is free on Tuesday evenings, from 5 to 8 p.m., courtesy of a grant from Mobil Oil.

AMERICAN MUSEUM OF NATURAL HISTORY
Central Park W at 79th St
769-5100
Sun-Tues, Thurs: 10-5:45; Wed, Fri, Sat: 10-9

This is the granddaddy of all the city's museums; it has something for everyone. To see everything—from the dinosaurs and enormous suspended whale (perennial children's favorites) to the gems and minerals—could take several days. The Hall of Asian Peoples, the Christmas exhibits, and the special shows and collections inspire visitors to return again and again. Adjacent to the museum is the Hayden Planetarium (769-5900), which features changing sky shows on astronomy and space science. Both the American Museum of Natural History and the Planetarium should be avoided during school hours, unless you want your experience in natural history to be limited to "Child Behavior Outside the Classroom."

ASIA SOCIETY GALLERY
725 Park Ave (at 70th St)
288-6400
Tues-Sat: 11-6; Sun: 12-5

The mainstay of this collection is John D. Rockefeller's Asian art collection. But there are changing exhibits and an excellent gift gallery downstairs.

AUNT LEN'S DOLL AND TOY MUSEUM
6 Hamilton Terrace (at W 141st St)
926-4172
Daily: by appointment

This one is a charmer. Aunt Len is Mrs. Leon Holder Hoyte, an octogenarian and former schoolteacher who shares her doll collection with the public, at her townhouse on Hamilton Terrace. *Shares* isn't exactly the right word—Aunt Len makes a visitor feel like a member of the family when she shows off her collection of more than 5,000 dolls, from the Queen Anne era to the present. And her

Harlem house is as charming as the dolls. There is a $2 admission fee, and Aunt Len doesn't receive visitors unless they have an appointment.

BLACK MUSEUM OF FASHION
155 W 126th St (bet Lenox and Seventh Ave)
666-1320
Mon-Fri: 12-8 by appointment only

Located in a renovated brownstone, this museum was founded in 1979 by Lois Alexander, who wrote her master's thesis on fashions designed and created by black people. The museum's display guides visitors through 3,000 garments, from the 1800s to the 1980s. A stitch-for-stitch duplicate of the gown worn by Mrs. Abraham Lincoln at her husband's inaugural ball is here. It's the creation of Barbara Ann Black, a teacher at the Harlem Institute for Fashion, which is next door to the museum. The original gown, now on display at the Smithsonian in Washington, D.C., was designed by a slave named Elizabeth Keckley, who literally sewed her way to freedom (she also clothed Mrs. Stephen Douglas and Mrs. Jefferson Davis). The collection also includes an authentic slave dress from Staunton, Virginia; the yellow dress which Rosa Parks was making for her mother when she was arrested for refusing to give up her bus seat; and costumes created for *Grind, The Wiz,* and other musicals.

CENTER FOR AFRICAN ART
54 E 68th St (bet Fifth and Madison Ave)
861-1200
Tues-Fri: 10-5; Sat: 11-5; Sun: 12-5

Housed in two adjoining townhouses, the Center for African Art covers traditional art from Africa with three changing exhibits, which are augmented by films, slide shows, and lectures.

CHILDREN'S MUSEUM OF MANHATTAN
212 W 83rd St
765-5904
Tues-Fri: 1-5; Sat, Sun: 11-5

The Children's Museum of Manhattan was the brainchild of Bette Korman, a kindergarten teacher who felt that children needed "laboratories" to explore the world during nonschool hours. She was right. The museum is immensely popular. It has moved several times, each location providing additional space for hands-on exhibits for kids.

CHINA HOUSE GALLERY/CHINA INSTITUTE IN AMERICA
125 E 65th St
744-8181
Mon-Sat: 10-5

The museum has arts, crafts, and exhibits from China—of course.

CITY GALLERY
2 Columbus Circle
974-1150
Mon-Fri: 9-5

This white elephant of a building was originally the Huntington Hartford Museum. When it fell upon hard times, it was taken over by the city for the Department of Cultural Affairs and the Visitors and Convention Bureau. The space also serves as an exhibit area for the two groups, where you might see the unveiling of a new map or subway renovation. The exhibits change constantly (once in a while there is a sensational one), and admission is free.

CLOISTERS
Fort Tryon Park
923-3700
Tues-Sun: 9:30-5:15 (March-Oct)
Tues-Sun: 9:30-4:45 (Nov-Feb)

The Cloisters in northern Manhattan is a branch of the Metropolitan Museum of Art devoted exclusively to medieval art. The grounds are magnificent (try to catch the sunset over the Hudson), as are the displays. There are free public tours every Tuesday, Wednesday, and Thursday at 3 p.m. in spring, summer, and fall. During the winter, they are held on Wednesday only, and concerts are held on various Sundays, fall through spring.

COOPER-HEWITT MUSEUM
Fifth Ave at 91st St
860-6868
Tues: 10-9; Wed-Sat: 10-5; Sun: 12-5

Housed in Andrew Carnegie's Fifth Avenue mansion in the heart of Museum Mile, the Cooper-Hewitt is the Smithsonian's National Museum of Design. There are permanent collections of pottery, textiles, and wallpaper. Exhibitions change regularly, each one focusing on contemporary or historical design. Although no part of the permanent collection is on long-term view, objects from the museum's vast collection are often used in the rotating exhibits.

EL MUSEO DEL BARRIO
1230 Fifth Ave
831-7272
Tues-Fri: 10:30-4:30; Sat, Sun: 11-4

El Barrio is the local name for Spanish Harlem, the area above the Upper East Side and below Harlem. The only museum of its kind in the country, it highlights the culture and art of Latin America, with a special emphasis on that of Puerto Rico.

FORBES GALLERIES
62 Fifth Ave (at 12th St)
206-5548
Tues, Wed, Fri, Sat: 10-4; Thurs: group tours

Malcolm Forbes, the publisher extraordinaire, has amassed several collections in his lifetime. (His penchant for hot-air ballooning is one of the few that couldn't be cataloged.) In 1985 he finally put it all together in galleries specifically constructed on the ground floor of the Forbes building. The large exhibition space is highlighted by the works of the czar's jeweler, Peter Carl Fabergé. Included in the latter is the world's largest collection of Fabergé Imperial Eggs, each of which is valued at over $1 million. The rest of the collection should pale in comparison, but it doesn't. Forbes' collection is that of a man who could afford to fulfill his whims and share them with others. There are 500 toy boats (some are so incredible in detail that they look seaworthy), 12,000 lead soldiers, and a room of 200 inscribed trophies commemorating the sublime and the ridiculous. Changing exhibits of paintings, photographs, and American historical documents and related memorabilia fill two additional galleries. This is the best museum collection in town *outside* of a museum. And Mr. Forbes deserves a hearty round of applause for sharing it.

THE FRICK COLLECTION
1 E 70th St
288-0700
Tues-Sat: 10-6; Sun: 1-6
Children under 10 not admitted

The Frick collection is housed in the former home of Henry Clay Frick, whose interest was in 14th-century through 19th-century art. Though absolutely unreceptive to children, the Frick offers help to any serious student of painting, sculpture, European antique furniture, enamel images, or European and Asian porcelain. This is a quiet, serious place off the tourist trail. Free concerts and lectures are available.

HISPANIC SOCIETY OF AMERICA
Broadway at 155th St
926-2234
Tues-Sat: 10-4:30; Sun: 1-4

This is one of the showcases of the Washington Heights Museum Group. Located in the center of Audubon Terrace, it boasts a very impressive collection of decorative and fine arts of the Iberian peninsula, from ancient to modern times. Goya, El Greco, Veláz-quez, Sorolla, and Ribera are just a few of the painters represented.

IBM GALLERY OF SCIENCE AND ART
Madison Ave at 56th St (downstairs in IBM Building)
745-6100
Tues-Fri: 11-6; Sat: 10-5

The changing exhibits in this free gallery are mostly devoted to art and science. Some of them are the hottest things in town. Call first, since there are stretches between exhibits when nothing is scheduled. Kids love this one.

JAPAN SOCIETY GALLERY
333 E 47th St
752-0824
Tues-Sun: 11-5

The headquarters of the Japan Society (across the street from the United Nations) boasts a stunning gallery, library, outdoor Japa-nese garden, and a building that is an example of the best of Japanese architecture. There are rotating exhibits of Japanese art, weekday concerts, and a film series on weekends. Call for the ex-hibit schedule.

JEWISH MUSEUM
1109 Fifth Avenue (at 92nd St)
860-1888
Mon, Wed, Thurs: 12-5; Tues: 12-8; Sun: 11-6

Housed in an old Fifth Avenue mansion, the Jewish Museum has left most of the original house intact and added a museum wing. The permanent collection concentrates on paintings, graphics, and sculpture inspired by the Jewish experience, and an unparalleled showing of Judaica. The Jewish Museum's gift shop is one of the best in the city. It should be considered a first choice for Jewish ceremonial art, artifacts, books, and ritual objects.

METROPOLITAN MUSEUM OF ART
Fifth Ave at 82nd St
Wed-Sun: 9:30-5:15; Tues: 9:30-8:45

No visit to New York is complete without spending at least part of a day at the Met. The collections are fabulous and extensive, including ancient Egyptian, Greek, Roman, ancient Near East, Medieval, Renaissance, Asian, Oceanic, Precolombian, and contemporary American art. The American wing houses the finest collection of American paintings, sculpture, and decorative arts in the country. The Lila Acheson Wallace wing houses contemporary art. The Astor Court is a replica of a famous Chinese scholar's garden. The Lehman wing exhibits furniture and paintings as they were in the Lehman house. Upstairs there are countless masterpieces—so many that even the greatest philistine should have seen at least a dozen of them as reproductions at some time in his life. European sculpture and decorative arts galleries include porcelain, ceramics, silver, clocks, and pottery. Added attraction: the steps outside are a favorite lounging and meeting place for residents and visitors alike.

MUSEUM OF AMERICAN FOLK ART
2 Lincoln Sq
595-9533
Daily: 9-9

This is the only urban museum devoted to folk art made between 1776 and 1914. You'll want to visit the two gift shops, one at the museum and the other at 62 West 50th Street (247-5611). You'll be fascinated by the old pieces in the museum and impressed with the works in the shops, which are done by contemporary artisans in the folk-art tradition.

MUSEUM OF AMERICAN ILLUSTRATION
128 E 63rd St (bet Park and Lexington Ave)
838-2560
Mon, Wed-Fri: 10-5; Tues: 10-8

Housed in what was once J. P. Morgan's carriage house, this museum highlights the very best illustrations from the past and present. Admission is free, and the exhibits are very well organized. You can see exhibits on paperback-book covers, historic illustrations, etc.

MUSEUM OF BROADCASTING
1 E 53rd St
752-7684
Tues: 12-8; Wed-Sat: 12-5

This museum is literally for children of all ages; the older the child the more enjoyable the visit. It is a repository of television and radio's finest hours. Everything in the archives is entertaining. Children are warmly welcomed here, and the staff will recommend selections. There is no admission, but donations are suggested. And while there's not a reservation policy per se, it helps to call ahead or arrive early in the afternoon.

MUSEUM OF HOLOGRAPHY
11 Mercer St
925-0526
Tues-Sun: 12-6

The black-and-white banner outside this building heralds the world center for information on holography. The museum has the world's largest collection of holograms and hosts over 60,000 visitors a year. When it started, it was necessary to provide very basic information on holography, but over the years holograms and three-dimensional images created with laser light have become an accepted part of modern life. Today the museum exhibits holograms and images and mounts exhibitions explaining the artistic, scientific, and commercial uses of the medium. There's a permanent exhibit titled *In Perspective,* which features the history of holography and a continuous video called *Holography: Memories in Light.* There is a gallery downstairs and a gift shop with some really unique items.

MUSEUM OF MODERN ART
11 W 53rd St
708-9400
Fri-Tues: 11-6; Thurs: 11-9

A popular place, even among non-museum lovers, the Museum of Modern Art is much appreciated in New York for its efforts to be modern in attitude as well as acquisition. This is best exemplified by the sculpture garden, which is not only open to those who wish to sit and muse in peace, but is frequently the scene of free or inexpensive summer-evening concerts. MOMA also sponsors film festivals and revivals that are unsurpassed by commercial theaters, and stocks its gift shop with magnificent items. The latter offers games for both children and adults, copies of various home furnishings on exhibit in the museum itself, and the best selection of posters in the city. For those who do not care to take the inexpensive decorating route with MOMA posters, the museum offers paintings for rent. Rates are very reasonable (albeit with substantial deposits). Among those who use this service are diplomats on short visits; art connoisseurs who would rather have limited access to great art than a lifetime with mass-produced prints; people who need experts to prescribe the limits of good art from which they can select; and people whose tastes constantly change. This last category includes roommates who have divergent tastes; they rent paintings alternate months as a compromise.

MUSEUM OF THE AMERICAN INDIAN
Broadway at 155th St
283-2420
Tues-Sat: 10-5; Sun: 1-5

The Museum of the American Indian was originally a part of the Washington Heights Museum Group. They all occupied a block in Harlem. The Museum of the American Indian became the largest in the world devoted to the Indians of the Western Hemisphere and outgrew its exhibition space. The collection includes personal belongings from Sitting Bull, Crazy Horse, and Red Cloud, along with 1,000 books on the subject. There are also untold numbers of baskets, artifacts, costumes, wood carvings, bead and quill work, and weapons. For years the staff has worked in very inadequate quarters, but there will soon be a new building sponsored by the Smithsonian Institute in Washington.

MUSEUM OF THE AMERICAN PIANO
211 W 58th St
246-4646
Tues-Sat: 12-4

This may be the only museum in the country devoted to restored American pianos. Visitors with a specific interest in period instruments are invited to play pianos built as early as the turn of the 19th century. There is a collection of about 30 pianos, dating from the late 1700s to the 1940s. In addition, there is a "rogue's gallery," featuring such oddities as the remains of a concrete grand piano and a portable piano intended for use on long trips by train or ship.

MUSEUM OF THE CITY OF NEW YORK
Fifth Avenue at 103rd St
534-1672
Tues-Sat: 10-5; Sun and holidays: 1-5

This is an incredible place dedicated to the history and artifacts of the world's most incredible city. Located at the top end of

Museum Row, it departs from its sisters in having both a more informal style and a free-admission policy (they don't turn away donations, but they are not mandatory). The permanent exhibitions include the Dutch, marine, fire, doll's house, silver, furniture, print, map, and painting galleries, period alcoves, the John D. Rockefeller Sr. rooms, and exhibitions on costumes, theater, photography, and toys. One of the perennial favorites is the exhibit of fire engines. The museum sponsors several programs that celebrate the city. There are Sunday walking tours in the spring and fall.

NATIONAL ACADEMY OF DESIGN
1083 Fifth Ave (at 89th St)
369-4880
Tues-Sun: 12-5

This museum's setting is part of the exhibit, since it's housed in the handsome beaux arts mansion that was the former home of Archer M. Huntington and his sculptress wife, Anna Hyatt. The school of fine arts sponsors an annual exhibition, a permanent collection on American art, and rotating exhibitions on American and European art. That this is an academy of design is seen in the selection of architectural drawings and exhibits, along with paintings and artwork.

NEW MUSEUM OF CONTEMPORARY ART
583 Broadway (bet Houston and Prince St)
219-1222
Wed, Thurs, Sun: 12-6; Fri, Sat: 12-8

The Museum of Modern Art is pure establishment compared to this storefront show in the historic Astor building in SoHo. Exhibits change on a regular basis, and they walk a fine line between what is "museum quality" and what is being exhibited in the galleries in the neighborhood. It's a good source for a fast lesson on the contemporary art scene.

NEW YORK CITY FIRE MUSEUM
278 Spring St (bet Hudson and Varrick St)
691-1303
Tues-Sat: 10-4

A great place for fire-engine buffs. This museum displays hand-pulled and horse-pulled apparatuses going back as far as 1735. Kids will love to see some of the old fire trucks, and parents will be intrigued to learn more about the practical side of fighting fires.

THE NEW YORK HISTORICAL SOCIETY
170 Central Park W (at 77th St)
873-3400
Tues-Sun: 10-5

This is the oldest museum in New York (founded in 1804), and it specializes in American and New York historical materials. The permanent collection includes 433 of John James Audubon's 435 original *Birds of America* watercolors, colonial silver, early American toys and arts and crafts, and a permanent exhibit of Tiffany glass and lamps. For scholars, there is a first-rate research library.

NEW YORK TRANSIT MUSEUM
(Boerum Pl and Schermerhorn St, Brooklyn)
(718) 330-3060
Mon-Fri: 10-4; Sat: 11-4

One of the most fascinating places in the city is the subway system. Strap hangers may not agree, but even the most jaded underground commuters would be fascinated by the New York Transit Museum. I say "would be" because most have never heard of this super exhibit, which is set up in an unused subway station in Brooklyn. The exhibit is housed in the old Court Street Station; exit at the Hoyt-Schermerhorn station and follow the signs.

PIERPONT MORGAN LIBRARY
29 E 36th St (at Madison Ave)
685-0610
Tues-Sat: 10:30-5; Sun: 1-5

Pierpont Morgan started collecting books and manuscripts while still a boy. His collection of books, etchings, manuscripts, and sketches ultimately grew to be one of the most extensive in the city. The Renaissance-style palazzo offers changing exhibits based upon the house collections and includes autographs, letters, music manuscripts, original texts and first editions, medieval manuscripts, master drawings, and rare books.

POLICE MUSEUM
235 E 20th St (bet Second and Third Ave, second floor)
477-9753
Mon-Fri: 9-3

This one-room museum on the second floor of the Police Academy is undergoing renovations to increase its exhibition area. That's good news not only for the cadets downstairs but for the kids and fans of police work, who frequent the displays of weapons, police technology, equipment, and various paraphernalia.

They always seem to want to see more than can be displayed. And indeed, this is fascinating stuff: an Al Capone style "persuader," handcuffs that adorned the wrists of a Lincoln conspirator, fingerprints of such infamous people as "The Son of Sam," more nightsticks and day sticks than you would want to shake a fist at, a 1901 police locker, a slot machine circa Mayor LaGuardia, and photographs that are tributes to the history of the police department. The staff here couldn't be more helpful. There are also several educational programs and "hands on" lectures.

SCHOMBURG CENTER FOR RESEARCH IN BLACK CULTURE
515 Malcolm X Blvd (at 135th St)
862-4000
Mon-Wed: 12-8; Thurs-Sat: 10-6

The Schomburg Center is the premier place for research and for artifacts in black culture. In addition to an extensive collection of literature, photography, and archives on the black experience, there is African art and ongoing programs in black culture.

SOLOMON R. GUGGENHEIM MUSEUM
1071 Fifth Ave (at 89th St)
360-3500
Tues: 11-8; Wed-Sun: 11-5

The Guggenheim, a Frank Lloyd Wright building, is as sleekly modern as its collection of paintings. It was designed around a continuous ramp that looks like an inverted snail, according to some critics. Admirers maintain that the structure makes it easier to see and appreciate paintings without the stifling, formal atmosphere of most museums. Because of its radical design and its fine collection of modern paintings and rotating exhibits, the Guggenheim is a must on every museum-goer's list. The Guggenheim's efforts to expand are as much the talk of the art world as its current collection. How do you improve a Frank Lloyd Wright classic? There are many who say you can't.

STEINWAY HALL
109 W 57th St (near Sixth Ave)
246-1100
Mon-Wed, Fri: 9-6; Thurs: 9-9; Sat: 9-5

Steinway Hall is the showroom and showcase for the Steinway Piano company, and the setting is magnificent enough to be classified as a museum and to have been used as the backdrop of several dozen movies. The newest Steinway pianos are displayed in a room with a ceiling often compared to the Sistine Chapel, dramatic marble columns, and an art collection that rivals those of some museums in the city. With a patron's hand, Steinway invites all to view the artwork and, yes, even to try out the pianos. The only proviso is that professional artists selecting instruments for use in concerts come first. But then again, who would want to sit down and play in front of the Philharmonic's guest soloist? Tours of the entire premises—which point out salient features that could be overlooked amid the abundance of art on display—can be arranged by merely asking the receptionist to show you the hall. One fellow Oregonian termed it the best thing he saw in New York, and I can only add a "bravo" to Steinway for their taste and willingness to share these riches with us.

THEODORE ROOSEVELT BIRTHPLACE
28 E 20th St (bet Broadway and Park Ave)
260-1616
Wed-Sun: 9-5

T.R. was a born-and-bred New Yorker, although the site more commonly associated with him is his family's homestead, Sagamore Hill, in Oyster Bay, Long Island. This building, on the site of the brownstone that was demolished in 1916, was reconstructed in 1923 to simulate his boyhood home. Approximately 40 percent of the furniture is original to the house, and another 20 percent was gathered from family members. The adjoining lot originally held the companion brownstone that had been purchased by T.R.'s grandfather for his son Robert at the same time that he purchased number 28 for Theodore Sr. During the reconstruction of 1923, it was purchased and turned into museum galleries and other facilities. Today, it is operated by the National Park Service, which makes this a national park on East 20th Street! That's one bit of trivia, and here's some more. Ask any New Yorker where this place is, and I bet they won't know. As for the "other" presidential Roosevelts, the close kinship was between Theodore and Eleanor. Eleanor Roosevelt, whose maiden and married names were the same, was T.R.'s niece. He gave her away at her wedding. F.D.R. was a seventh cousin.

UKRAINIAN MUSEUM
203 Second Ave (at 12th St)
228-0110
Wed-Sun: 1-5

Located in the heart of the Ukrainian community in New York, this museum has a fine collection of Ukrainian fine art and folk art in both permanent and changing exhibitions. Interesting hand crafted objects are available in the gift shop.

WHITNEY MUSEUM OF AMERICAN ART
945 Madison Ave (at 75th St)
570-3676
Tues: 1-6; Wed-Sat: 11-5; Sun: 12-6

Federal Reserve Plaza
33 Maiden Lane
943-5655
Mon-Fri: 11-6

Equitable Center
Seventh Ave (bet 51st and 52nd St)
554-1113
Mon-Wed, Fri: 11-6; Thurs: 11-7:30; Sat: 12-5

Philip Morris
Park Ave at 42nd St
878-2550
Mon-Wed, Fri, Sat: 11-6; Thurs: 11-7:30

The epitome of a contemporary urban art museum, the Whitney was founded by Gertrude Vanderbilt Whitney to house her collection of American contemporary art and sculpture. (Whitney was a sculptress herself.) The exhibit eventually grew to include over 6,000 pieces, and the management decided to make it more accessible to all the people of New York. The Whitney was one of the first museums to establish branches in office buildings in the city.

YESHIVA UNIVERSITY MUSEUM
2520 Amsterdam Ave (bet 184th and 185th St)
960-5390
Tues-Thurs: 10:30-5; Sun: 12-6

Located on the main campus of Yeshiva University, this museum has outstanding exhibits of contemporary arts, decorative arts and crafts, and Jewish culture. There are programs for children and adults, and tours are available.

New York On the Water

Central Park: Dine at the Boathouse, then take your date for a rowboat ride. Located on the lake, off East Drive at 72nd Street. Prices are reasonable, and boats are available seven days a week in nice weather (call 517-2232).

Circle Line: A number of sailings, from 9:45 a.m. until midafternoon, give you a great view of the great island. The tour lasts three hours, and starts at Pier 83 at West 42nd Street (563-3200).

Highlander V: If Malcolm Forbes invites you to take a cruise with him on this 151-foot ocean liner, be sure to accept. Accommodations include a master suite with steamroom and whirlpool, a movie theater, and a dining room for a dozen guests. A 13-man crew takes care of every desire, and in case there is an emergency at The office, a chopper will take you back to land. Then, one of Malcolm's motorcycles can be used to speed you to your destination. Sorry, I can't give out the phone number.

Pan Am Ferry Boat to LaGuardia Airport: High-speed ferry boats whisk you from Wall Street to the plane in 30 minutes, at a cost of around $20.

Petrel: A number of cruises of varied lengths are available on this 70-foot yawl, which operates from Battery Park. The Petrel is in service seven days a week, and the 45-minute "Executive lunch hour" trips are particularly popular (825-1976).

Pioneer: You can take your choice of a number of sailings in the summer months on this 103-year-old sailboat. Call and find out which one will fit your schedule (669-9400).

Seaport Line: The DeWitt Clinton and the Andrew Fletcher sail from Pier 16 (South St Seaport) with a variety of excursions. There are luncheon sailings, jazz brunches on weekends, and 90-minute sightseeing trips. The young folk in the family will enjoy the evening music cruises (406-3434).

Spirit of New York: A red, white, and blue experience for the patriots and romanticists, with stops at the Statue of Liberty. The address is Pier 11, East River, near Wall Street. Meals are available, and it is a good idea to call for reservations for moonlight fun on weekends (279-1890).

Staten Island Ferry: The Hong Kong Star Ferry and the Staten Island Ferry are the last two bargains on water in the world. The Staten Island Ferry's 20-minute ride costs 25 cents for the round trip, and the view of Manhattan is sensational.

World Yacht Cruises: Feel like the V.I.P. you are, while the crew does all the work during noon buffets, dinner and dancing, or Sunday brunch. Prices are in keeping with the luxury class. The address is Pier 62 at West 23rd Street and 12th Avenue. It is a good idea to call to make sure that what you want is available (929-7090).

Parks and Recreation

Through New York City's Department of Parks and Recreation, you can find facilities for almost any interest you might have. In Manhattan there are 2,598 acres of parkland—17 percent of the borough!

Astronomy: Call 860-1815 (Dr. Gregory Matloff) for information.
Badminton: Call 718-699-4231 for information.
Baseball: For permits to use diamonds, call 408-0209.

Basketball Courts: Central Park, the Great Lawn near 85th St, midpark; Riverside Park, W 101st to W 111th St.

Bicycling: Central Park drives are closed to motor vehicles on holidays, on summer weekdays (10-3, 7-10), and on weekends from 7 p.m. Fri to 6 a.m. Mon. Bicycle rentals at Loeb Boathouse.

Bird Watching: Central Park, the Ramble (73rd to 79th St), and the Hallett Nature Sanctuary (near E 59th St and Fifth Ave); Fort Tryon Park, Heather Garden, north of Fort Washington Ave; Riverside bird sanctuary, W 114th to W 120th St.

Boating Area: Central Park, Loeb Boathouse, the Lake, off East Dr at 74th St (April-Oct).

Boccie Courts: 34 courts at the Cuvillier, East River, Harlem River Dr, Highbridge, Thomas Jefferson, Roosevelt, and Walker parks; playgrounds at 96th St and First Ave, and East River Dr and 42nd St; Thompson St playground; and Randall's and Wards islands.

Bowling Lawn: Central Park, near Sheeps Meadow, 67th St near West Dr (May-Nov). For permits, call 360-8133.

Bridle Paths and Stables: Central Park, Claremont Riding Academy (724-5100).

Carousels: Central Park, 65th St midpark (879-0244).

Carriage Rentals: Central Park S, $17 for first half hour, $5 each additional quarter hour (246-0520).

Chess and Checkers: Central Park, Chess and Checkers House, 64th St, midpark (indoor play, weekends only, 11:30 a.m.-4:30 p.m.; outdoor play, weekdays, terrace of Chess and Checkers House), pieces available at the Dairy, 64th St; Washington Sq Park, southwest corner; Manhattan Chess Club, 154 W 57th St, 10th floor (admission charge).

Croquet Lawns: Central Park, near Sheeps Meadow, 67th St near West Dr (May-Nov). For permits, call 360-8133.

Day Camps: Central Park, N Meadow Center, off 97th St Transverse, midpark; Columbia Playground, 143 Baxter St; Morningside Park, 410 Morningside Ave; Jackie Robinson Play Center, W 146th St and Bradhurst Ave; Payson Playground, Dyckman St and Payson Ave.

Fishing: Riverside Park, Hudson River, along the Esplanade, W 72nd to W 84th St, and W 91st to W 100th St.

Folk Dancing: Central Park, east shore of Turtle Pond, 81st St, midpark, Sun 2-6 p.m. (call 673-3930 after noon on Sun).

Golf Courses: None in Manhattan.

Handball Courts: Central Park, North Meadow Center, off 97th St transverse, midpark; Riverside Park, W 72nd St and Hudson River, W 101st to W 111th St, and W 147th to W 152nd St.

Ice Skating: Sky Rink, 450 W 33rd St, 16th floor (695-6555); Wollman Rink, Central Park, East Dr and 63rd St (517-4800); Lasker Rink, Central Park, near 110th St and Lenox Ave (397-3106); Rivergate Ice Rink, E 34th St and First Ave; Rockefeller Center (757-5730).

Kite Flying: Central Park, Sheeps Meadow.

Marinas: Riverside Park, 79th St Boat Basin, Hudson River (362-0909).

Model-Boat Ponds: Central Park, Conservatory Water, 74th and Fifth Ave.

Picnic Areas: Central Park, Sheeps Meadow, East Meadow, pool shores; Riverside Park, W 93rd to W 98th St, W 147th to W 152nd St.

Recreation Centers: Carmine St (Clarkson St and Seventh Ave, 397-3107); Mount Morris/Marcus Garvey (Mount Morris Park W and 122nd St, 397-3118); Alfred E Smith (80 Catherine St, 397-3108); E 54th St (348 E 54th St, 397-3155); W 59th St (533 W 59th St, 397-3166); Hansborough (35 W 135th St, 397-3136).

Rodeo: Randall's Island, Black World Championship Rodeo (675-0085).

Roller Skating: Central Park rental, Mineral Springs Pavilion, Sheeps Meadow, enter at W 69th St.

Running Tracks: Central Park Reservoir; Downing Stadium (Olympic), Randall's Island; Riverside Park at 74th St; Hansborough Recreation Center (indoor); Carmine St Recreation Center (indoor); E 54th St Recreation Center (indoor); Thomas Jefferson Park.

Soccer Field: Central Park, Great Lawn, 81st to 85th St, midpark; North Meadow, 97th to 103rd St, midpark.

Swimming Pools (indoor): E 54th St (397-3154); Hansborough (35 W 134th St, 397-3134); W 59th St (533 W 59th St, 397-3159); Carmine St (Seventh Ave and Clarkson St, 397-3107).

Swimming Pools (outdoor): E 23rd St (Asser Levy Pl near FDR Dr, 397-3123); Hamilton Fish (128 Pitt St, 397-3171); Carmine St (Clarkson St and Seventh Ave, 397-3107); John Jay (E of York Ave on 77th St, 397-3177); Thomas Jefferson (111th St and First Ave, 397-3112); Lasker (110th St and Lenox Ave, 397-3106); Highbridge (Amsterdam Ave and W 173rd St, 397-3173); Marcus Garvey (124th St and Fifth Ave, 397-3124); Jackie Robinson (Bradhurst Ave and W 146th St, 397-3146); Sheltering Arms (Amsterdam Ave and W 129th St, 397-3128); Szold Place (E 10th St bet Ave C and D, 397-3110); Wagner Houses (E 124th St bet First and Second Ave, 397-3125); W 59th St (533 W 59th St, 397-3159).

Tennis Courts: (92 courts) Central Park, East River Park, Inwood Hill Park, Frederick Johnson Playground, Randall's Island, Riverside Park, and Fort Washington Park.

Zoos: Central Park Zoo (439-6500); Children's Zoo, Central Park (408-0271).

Billiards have taken off again! At one time there were more than 100 billiard parlors in New York, but that number diminished over the years. Now there is a revival. Here are a few of them.

Billiard Club: 220 W 19th St (206-7665)
Cafe Society: 915 Broadway (529-8282)
Chelsea Billiards: 54 W 21st St (989-0096)
Julian's Billiard Academy: 138 E 14th St (475-9338)
Tekk: 75 Christopher St (463-9282)

Seasonal New York

January: The *New Year* starts with the famous dropping of the ball (at one time, an apple) in teeming Times Square. There are New Year's celebrations all over town.

February: *Chinese New Year* in Chinatown is not to be missed.

The Dog Show comes to Madison Square Garden. "The Best in Show" champion often makes the front page of the daily newspapers.

March: *St. Patrick's Day Parade* goes up Fifth Avenue. Don't even attempt to do anything in the vicinity that day!

Greek Independence Day Parade also marches up Fifth Avenue.

April: The *Easter Parade* seems to have gotten bigger over the years. It's a street festival more or less centered around St. Patrick's Cathedral on Fifth Avenue. But folks strut their finery all over the city, and you have to see it to believe it.

Macy's Annual Flower Show coincides with the flower season; it's breathtaking.

Opening Day of Baseball Season—The date varies. The Yankees and the Mets usually try to schedule it for different days and weeks, but it doesn't matter. New York goes stark-raving baseball mad, and everything (mostly traffic) seems to grind to a halt.

May: Festival month. There are street fairs every weekend. The most gastronomic and gigantic is the *Ninth Avenue International Festival.* Ninth Avenue is wholesale food country, particularly for the various ethnic groups in Hell's Kitchen (as the local neighborhood has often been called). The festival includes nearly 20 blocks of delicacies. For one weekend in May, Ninth Avenue becomes an epicurean United Nations. Don't miss it.

June: June is the beginning of summer festivities in the city. This is when the arts take to the streets, and the *Philharmonic*, the *Metropolitan Opera*, and the *Theatermobiles* (sponsored by the Parks Department) perform free in various parks throughout the city. In Central Park, *The Shakespeare Festival* is in residence at the Delacorte Theater, and there is a concert series at the Band Shell in midpark. Many of the corporate office buildings as well as the National Parks Services' sites have concerts and programs that are open to the public. Check the newspapers for exact details. Some of the sites for concerts throughout the summer are Federal Hall, Rockefeller Center (lunchtime concerts), the World Trade Center Plaza, the Citicorp Center Atrium, I.B.M. Plaza, and the Jazz Festival on the West Side docks near the Financial Center. Battery Park City also has functions. In addition, the *American Crafts Festival* is at Lincoln Center.

July: There are the *Summerpier* concerts at the South Street Seaport, the *Summergarden* concerts in the sculpture garden of MOMA, the *Golden Memorial Band Concerts* at Lincoln Center, and the *Washington Square Music Festival*. All of these are free. Ever since the Tall Ships extravaganza for the bicentennial, New York has celebrated Independence Day with displays of fireworks, and the *Harbor Festival* centers around the sailing ships.

August: All of the aforementioned summer-long projects continue, and there is more.

The *Greenwich Village Jazz Festival* is held at some of the country's greatest jazz clubs.

Washington Square Art Show: Enterprising artists exhibit in Washington Square all year round. This, however, is the officially sanctioned show. At the same time, there's the *Washington Square Music Festival*.

Harlem Week is celebrated in Harlem.

September: Parades include the *Labor Day Parade*, the *Steuben Day Parade*, and the *African-American Day Parade*. The *U.S. Open Tennis Championships* are held in Queens, and *the Mayor's Cup Schooner* race takes place at the South Street Seaport. But the big story is festival time:

New York Is Book Country: Held on a Sunday in mid-September on Fifth Avenue between 47th and 59th streets. I haven't missed it since its inception, and it gets better every year. Come say hello!

The Feast of San Gennaro: Little Italy is transformed. People crowd the streets of this Italian section of the Village to revel in the food, the aromas, and the music of Italian Americans.

Columbus Avenue Festival: This is for all the yuppies who were in the Hamptons during the Ninth Avenue Festival.

Third Avenue Fair: This is a celebration of the people and shops along Third Avenue.

October: Parades include the *Hispanic Day Parade,* the *Columbus Day Parade,* and the *Pulaski Day Parade,* all on Fifth Avenue. There is an *Oktoberfest* in Yorkville and the *Second Avenue Autumnal Jubilee. Halloween* is celebrated with an annual, riotous parade in the Village.

November: There are two major events in November, both of which are synonymous with New York.

The New York City Marathon: The biggest and the best of its kind. It runs through all five boroughs and captures the spirit of the city like nothing else.

The Macy's Thanksgiving Day Parade: Locally this is known as "Macy's Day Parade," as if it is Macy's that owns the day. But of course it belongs to everybody. The parade is such a tradition that there probably isn't a child in the city who hasn't been to it at least once, and most Americans get to see it on TV.

In addition, November heralds the start of the *Christmas show at Radio City,* the *"Star of Christmas"* show at the Hayden Planetarium, the *Big Apple Circus* at Damrosch Park (Lincoln Center), and the unveiling of the seasonal windows in the stores on Fifth Avenue.

December: The lighting of the Rockefeller Center Christmas tree kicks off the Christmas season for the city. Performances of *The Nutcracker by the New York City Ballet* at Lincoln Center are a tradition for the city's children, and on weekends the *Fifth Avenue Mall* is set up from 34th Street to 57th Street.

Sights

BATTERY PARK
Southern tip of Manhattan

This is basically the southernmost point of Manhattan Island (excluding the islands in the harbor), so it was the site of the city's early fortifications. Castle Clinton (344-7220) was an 1812 fort that later served as Castle Garden and the home of the New York Aquarium. I qualified my opening sentence with *basically* because much of this end of Manhattan is built on landfill. The most recent extension is Battery Park City, which, as its name implies, is almost a city in itself.

CARNEGIE HALL
57th St and Seventh Ave
247-7800 (box office), 903-9600 (information)

Don't ask anyone for directions to Carnegie (pronounced Car-n-Gee) Hall. It's one of the oldest jokes in the city: "How do you get to Carnegie Hall?" "Practice, practice, practice." The recently renovated hall is the historic home of concerts, performances, and recitals for a variety of groups. There are apartments upstairs that have housed the world's great musicians, and the Russian Tea Room, another landmark, is "slightly to the left" of Carnegie Hall.

CENTRAL PARK
59th St to 110th St (bet Fifth Ave and Central Park W)

There is enough to see and do in Central Park to take several days. The most romantic way to see the park is by horse and carriage. They are very strictly regulated. A 30-minute ride has a standard rate posted right on the side of the carriage. No matter what the driver tells you, that's all you have to pay, unless you strike a deal for a longer ride.

Central Park consists of 840 acres smack-dab in the center of the city. Landscaped pathways, two rowing lakes, countless meadows, two ice-skating rinks, and grounds dedicated to recreation—this magnificent park is Fredrick Law Olmsted's legacy to the city. And what a legacy it is! There's Belvedere Castle (772-0210), near the West 79th Street entrance, which often serves as the backdrop for the plays in the open-air Delacorte Theater. Originally, the castle served as a weather center. Nowadays it serves as a learning center for science-and-nature programs. Call for a list of programs and hours.

Central Park is best known for its playgrounds. All are modern, child-safe, and outfitted with some of the most imaginative equipment in the country. Two of the best are on the East Side: the Sand Playground at 85th Street across from the Metropolitan Museum, and the Estee Lauder Adventure Playground next to the zoo entrance at 71st Street. On the West Side there's more celebrity status, but the playgrounds themselves aren't as special.

The newly renovated Central Park Zoo (64th St, 861-6030) is run by the New York Zoological Society, the same folks who run the Bronx Zoo. There are three "biomes," or climate zones, which feature arctic pools, tropical rain forests, and man-made "natural" habitats. Visitors nostalgic for the Victorian cages and inhabitants of the old zoo are apt to be disappointed. Penguins, red pandas, sea lions, harbor seals, otters, and snow monkeys are on view, but the larger animals (elephants, zebras, rhinoceroses, etc.) can now be seen only at the Bronx Zoo. The Children's Zoo (408-0271) remains unchanged. It's a marvelous place, featuring better fairy-tale attractions and animals than many tourist parks. Don't miss the huge Delacorte Clock at the entrance to the Children's Zoo. There is a modest admission charge for both zoos.

The merry-go-round nearby is another recent restoration. Located in almost the exact center of the park (62nd St entrance), it is almost as wonderful to look at as it is to ride.

The Dairy (near 64th St, west of the zoo, 397-3156), another restored building, really was a dairy, where children could stop for a glass of milk. (There are differing opinions as to whether cows were ever actually in residence.) Today it is the park information office and a center for free family activities throughout the year. It also has a semipermanent display of pictures and artifacts relating to the park. It is so picturesque that one of the most popular "family activities" at the Dairy is getting married.

Next to the beautifully restored Bethesda Fountain are two boating lakes (Loeb Boathouse, E 72nd St, 288-7281) and a pond devoted to toy sailboats.

In the summer the park resounds with activity. Softball games are played throughout the park. There are leagues for Broadway plays, TV soap operas, magazine staffs, Wall Street tycoons, and all kinds of companies and organizations. Joseph Papp's New York Shakespeare Festival presents full, star-studded productions of Shakespeare's plays at the Delacorte Theater throughout the summer, and the admission is free.

When the temperature drops, it is ice-skating season. The rehabilitation of the Wollman Memorial Skating Rink (off E 64th St, 517-4800) was a *cause célèbre* for years until Donald Trump glided to the rescue and rebuilt in six months what it took the city to bungle in as many years. Trump runs the rink, and it stands as a symbol of what the tycoon can accomplish. It is beautifully maintained. The Louise Lasker Skating Rink (397-3142), also run by Trump, at the very northern end of the park (107th St and Central Park North), is an unknown gem patronized mostly by the locals and hockey professionals. In the summer, it is a pool.

The next big project in Central Park is the creation of an 11-acre lake complete with an eighth of an acre island in what was once Hatlem Meer, about 150 feet from the Lasker rink. It's to be a bit of unspoiled nature at the north end of the park.

CHINATOWN, LITTLE ITALY,
THE LOWER EAST SIDE

The lines between these neighborhoods blur as the years pass by. For local color and some of the best Chinese meals this side of the Great Wall, visit Chinatown. For equally good Italian food, go to Little Italy, where cheeses, breads, and pastries are knockouts. If it's festival time, you're in luck: the streets will be overflowing with good things to eat. Hurry through the Bowery (travel on Grand Street, and you can avoid it altogether), and you're on the Lower

East Side. *That,* folks, is an experience. If I had time for only one place in the city, the Lower East Side would be it. It resembles nothing so much as a crowded Old World bazaar, especially on Sundays, and the bargains are sensational. However, if shopping, pushing, and shoving, and hordes of rude people bother you, stick to the city's more refined neighborhoods.

CITY HALL AND MUNICIPAL BUILDING
Broadway at Murray St

City Hall proper is the building where the mayor works, but most of the activity here is ceremonial. The real action takes place in the Municipal Building, just across the park. The four-year, $60 million renovation project required 40 miles of scaffolding, and the mayor says it is the largest such project in history.

EMPIRE STATE BUILDING
Fifth Avenue at 34th St
736-3100
Daily: 9:30 a.m.-midnight

Built on the site of the original Waldorf-Astoria hotel (which was built on the site of two Astor homes), this 102-story building has come to represent the epitome of New York. Some New Yorkers still swear that this is the tallest building in the world, even though they probably have never even been to its famous observation deck. Some trivia: The point atop the building was supposedly built as an anchor for dirigibles. The top glows different colors for different occasions. A plane crashed into the building in the 1940s. You can get married on the observation deck. And downstairs next to the observatory office is the Guinness World Record Exhibit Hall (947-2335).

GENERAL GRANT NATIONAL MEMORIAL
Riverside Dr at 122nd St
666-1640

Here lies the answer to "Who is buried in Grant's tomb?" It is open from 9 to 5, Wednesday through Sunday.

HAYDEN PLANETARIUM
Central Park at 81st St
873-8828

Attached to the Museum of Natural History, the Hayden Planetarium features sky shows on astronomy and space science as well as special presentations for children. The Planetarium also features two floors of astronomical displays, including the black-light gallery of the planets, the hall of the sun, and an exhibit that gives you your weight on other planets.

INTREPID SEA-AIR SPACE MUSEUM
Pier 86, 46th St and Hudson River
245-2533

The *Intrepid* has had political and financial problems, but it's hard to sink an aircraft carrier cum museum in the Hudson River. There are four different sections, each devoted to the navy, the history of the *Intrepid,* and Pioneers in Space or Space Technology. The best part is examining firsthand the actual planes and the technology on board.

JACOB JAVITS CONVENTION CENTER
(from 35th to 39th St, bet 11th and 12th Ave)
216-2000

It's hard to come up with words that will do this building complex justice. Until it was built, New York never really had a viable convention center. The I. M. Pei lattice-work structure has a 15-story atrium and glass walls, which reflect the New York skyline. It spans 28 acres and boasts 640,000 feet of prime exhibit space.

LINCOLN CENTER
Broadway at 64th St
877-1800

The complex includes the Juilliard School; Avery Fisher Hall, the home of the New York Philharmonic; Alice Tully Hall, which features plays and the Chamber Music Society of Lincoln Center; and the New York State Theater, which is the home of the New York City Opera (as well as the performing arts branch of the New York Public Library). In season, there are also crafts fairs and the Big Apple Circus on the plaza.

NEW YORK PUBLIC LIBRARY
Fifth Ave at 42nd St
221-7676
Mon-Sat: 10-5:45

For years the library was in a very sorry state. Of course, even in its saddest days, the library was the finest facility of its kind in the world. During the city's financial crisis in the 1970s, library hours were drastically cut, and the ensuing protests were loud enough to reach the powers that be in politics and society. Vartan Gregorian was brought in to head the library, and fund-raising socialites took the library as their cause. Under Gregorian (he has since left) halls were restored and exhibit spaces were reopened. There are now changing exhibits, and some of them are the hottest tickets in town. Don't miss the free tours offered daily at 12:30 and 2:00. And here's the real New York acid test: What are the names of the two lions on the front steps? Answer: Patience and Fortitude. They were named by Mayor Fiorello LaGuardia.

NEW YORK STOCK EXCHANGE
20 Broad St
623-5167

Note that the Stock Exchange is *not* on Wall Street (another bit of trivia). The visitor's gallery is informative and entertaining. Kids love it.

RADIO CITY MUSIC HALL
Ave of the Americas at 50th St
757-3100

The home of the world-famous Rockettes, Radio City Music Hall has become a landmarked attraction. Every trip to New York should include Radio City. Nowadays movie premières have been replaced with concerts and special shows. Don't forget to check out the art deco bathrooms. The rest of this fabulous theater, including the labyrinthine backstage and the mammoth stage, can be seen via a daily tour (246-4600). The spectacular Christmas show is a must-see.

ROCKEFELLER CENTER
From 47th to 52nd St, bet Fifth and Sixth Ave
489-2947

This is one of the must-see spots in the Big Apple. Situated in the heart of the city, this complex includes Radio City Music Hall, a skating rink, some great restaurants, the NBC studios (664-4000), and miles of an underground concourse full of interesting shops.

SOUTH STREET SEAPORT
East River at Fulton St

There are dozens of different aspects to the South Street Seaport, which is a restoration of the port of New York. Wall Street workers use it as an informal base for lunch and after-work meetings. Tourists take in the Seaport Museum (732-7678), the movie "The Seaport Experience" (210 Front St, 608-7888), and the ships (there are always at least three "tall ships" in residence). Shoppers shouldn't miss Pier 17 and the Fulton Market, a restored 1822 building which once housed the Fulton Fish Market. A special treat: the South Street Seaport Museum's book and nautical-chart store (209 Water St, 406-0380).

STATUE OF LIBERTY
NATIONAL MONUMENT
Liberty Island
Ferry Information: 269-5755, (201) 435-9479
Statue Information: 363-3200

The lady was spiffed up for her centennial, and she is now said to be the top tourist attraction in the country. While New York and New Jersey have been disputing each other's claims for jurisdiction over Liberty Island, for years the National Parks service has operated the monument with access from both states. Because of the dispute, the Circle Line, which operates the ferries to the Statue, serves both states. The statue itself has two public viewing areas. One is at the top of the pedestal, and the other is at the top of the crown. A third area in the torch is not accessible.

TIMES SQUARE
42nd St and Broadway

This famous square takes its name from the tower at the intersection of the lower part of a double x formed by the merging and crossing of Broadway and Seventh Avenue. It was originally the home of *The New York Times,* which is still just down the block on West 43rd Street, and the around-the-building electronic news tape still remains, as does the tradition of dropping a ball from the tower on New Year's Eve. On the side streets in the midforties and along Broadway are the legitimate Broadway theaters. Avoid Fantasia and any of the establishments that seem less than legitimate; they probably are. And if you want to avoid the hectic Times Square subway stations, take a cab or the M106 bus.

UNITED NATIONS
First Ave, 43rd to 49th St
Tour information: 754-7713

The United Nations offers an opportunity to visit international territory in New York. The land, donated by the Rockefellers, is considered international, and the UN boasts its own postage system, dining facilities, and gift shop, none of which are subject to New York taxes and regulations. Open meetings of the Security Council, General Assembly, and various committees are free to the public, and tickets can be obtained at the visitors' desk. The *Times* prints a notice of meetings on the day they occur. There are also guided tours in the languages of the United Nations. Be warned that security measures are such that strollers and baby carriages are not admitted on UN grounds, and touring with children is uncomfortable at best. Children under five are not admitted on the tours.

WORLD TRADE CENTER
West, Church, Vesey, and Liberty St
466-4170

The twin towers had their year as the world's tallest buildings. They are still New York's tallest buildings, and they offer breathtaking views of the city, the harbor, and New Jersey. (It's not true that you can see as far as Pennsylvania.) The observation deck (466-7397) on the 107th floor of 2 World Trade Center is the world's highest exposed deck. For safety's sake, it is glass enclosed. The entire complex is larger than some cities; it includes seven buildings and many attractions as well as business offices.

HINT: *Not to be missed is a nighttime tour of the city, so you can enjoy the magnificent lighting of some of Manhattan's outstanding buildings. Start at 57th Street and Fifth Avenue with the Crown Building and Trump Tower, then continue on to Citicorp Center, the Waldorf-Astoria Hotel, Rockefeller Center, 230 Park Avenue, the Chrysler Building, the Empire State Building, Grace Church, the Foley Square courthouses, the Municipal Building, City Hall, the Woolworth Building, and the new World Financial Center at Battery Park.*

Special Days

1990

New Year's Day	Monday—January 1
Martin Luther King's Birthday	Monday—January 15
Lincoln's Birthday	Monday—February 12
St. Valentine's Day	Wednesday—February 14
Washington's Birthday	Monday—February 19
St. Patrick's Day	Saturday—March 17
Passover (1st Day)	Tuesday—April 10
Good Friday	Friday—April 13
Easter	Sunday—April 15
Mother's Day	Sunday—May 13
Memorial Day	Monday—May 28
Father's Day	Sunday—June 17
Independence Day	Wednesday—July 4
Labor Day	Monday—September 3

Rosh Hashana ....Thursday—September 20
Yom Kippur ....Saturday—September 29
Columbus Day ....Monday—October 8
Halloween ....Wednesday—October 31
Election Day ....Tuesday—November 6
Veteran's Day ....Sunday—November 11
Thanksgiving Day ....Thursday—November 22
Hanukkah ....Wednesday—December 12
Christmas ....Tuesday—December 25

1991

New Year's Day ....Tuesday—January 1
Martin Luther King's Birthday ....Monday—January 21
Lincoln's Birthday ....Tuesday—February 12
St. Valentine's Day ....Thursday—February 14
Washington's Birthday ....Monday—February 18
St. Patrick's Day ....Sunday—March 17
Good Friday ....Friday—March 29
Passover (1st Day) ....Saturday—March 30
Easter ....Sunday—March 31
Mother's Day ....Sunday—May 12
Memorial Day ....Monday—May 27
Father's Day ....Sunday—June 16
Independence Day ....Thursday—July 4
Labor Day ....Monday—September 1
Rosh Hashana ....Monday—September 9
Yom Kippur ....Wednesday—September 18
Columbus Day ....Monday—October 14
Halloween ....Thursday—October 31
Election Day ....Tuesday—November 5
Veteran's Day ....Monday—November 11
Thanksgiving Day ....Thursday—November 28
Hanukkah ....Monday—December 2
Christmas ....Wednesday—December 25

Special Telephone Numbers

Emergency Services

AAA Highway Conditions 757-2000
AAA Road Service 757-3356
Alcoholics Anonymous 473-6200
Ambulance 911
Arson Hotline 718-403-1300
Babysitters Guild 682-0227
Better Business Bureau 533-6200

Child Abuse 1-800-342-3720
Child Care (part-time) 757-7900
Crime Victims Hotline 577-7777
Day Care Council of New York 398-0380
Day Care (NYC Health Dept) 334-7813
Doctor Line referral (free) 876-5432
Emergency Dental Service .... 679-3966 or 677-2510
Emergency Medical Service .... 420-4000 or 718-326-0800
FBI 553-2700
Fire 911
Gas, Electric, and Steam Emergency (Con Edison) 683-8830
Immunizations 349-2664
New York Women Against Rape 777-4000
Parents League of New York 737-7385
Passport Office 541-7700
Poisoning .... 340-4494 or 764-7667
Police 911
Police Precinct Locations 374-4303
Rape Hotline 267-RAPE
Sanitation, Garbage, and Snow Removal 334-8590
Sewers 966-7500
Suicide Prevention 532-2400
Telephone Repair Service 611
Tips Concerning Violent Crimes 577-TIPS
Water 285-9503

Complaints

Consumer (stores, services, etc) 577-0111
Corruption 825-5900
Housing 960-4800
Mail Fraud 330-3844
Noise 966-7500
Pets 285-9503
Rats 285-9503
Sidewalks 323-8501
Smells 966-7500
Taxes 718-935-6000
Trash 334-8590

Entertainment

Free daily events (recording) .... 360-133.
Madison Square Garden (sports events) 563-8300
Manhattan Dial and Dine (restaurants) 226-3388
New York Convention and Visitors Bureau 397-8222

New York Public Library 340-0849
Sportsphone 976-1313

Information

Airports 1-800-AIR-RIDE
Bureau of Labor Consumer Price Index 337-2405
City Phone (general) 567-9930
Customs Services 466-5550
Federal Information Center 264-4464
Health Department 285-9503
Hospitals 566-8650
Plant Hotline 220-8681
Postal 967-8585
Public Library 340-0849
Sky Reporter 769-5917
Social Security 1-800-234-5772
Stock Market 976-4141
Tel-Med (health topics) 439-3200
Time of Day 976-1616
Vaccinations (travel) 349-2664
Veteran's Benefits 620-6901
Weather 355-1212
Weather Trak (access code needed) 540-3000
Welfare 553-5185
Zip Code Hotline 967-8585

Transportation

TRAINS
Amtrak 1-800-872-7245
JFK Express 718-858-7272
Long Island Railroad 718-454-5477
Lost Property (bus, subway) 718-625-6200
Metro North 532-4900
Metroliner 582-6387
New Jersey Transit 201-460-8444
PATH Train 732-8920
PATH Train (Newark Airport) 466-7649
Staten Island Rapid Transit 718-447-8601
Subway Information 718-330-1234

BUSES
Carey Transportation (airports) 718-632-0500
Continental Trailways 730-7460
George Washington Bus Terminal 564-1114

Greyhound Bus 971-6363
NYC Bus Information 718-330-1234
Port Authority Bus Terminal 564-8484

TAXIS
NYC Taxi and Limo Commission (lost property, complaints)
.... 869-4513

AIR TRAVEL
Manhattan Air Lines Terminal (tickets, information) .. 986-0888
JFK Airport 718-656-4520
LaGuardia Airport 718-476-5000
Newark Airport 201-961-2015

One final number: If you don't trust your alarm clock, try 540-WAKE. Dial-a-Wakeup will get you out of the sack for $2.

INDEX

NOTES

NOTES

NOTES

NOTES

NOTES